ARCO'S

NEW COMPLETE WOODWORKING HANDBOOK

REVISED

by Jeannette T. Adams

**Arco Publishing Company, Inc.
New York**

Revised Edition
Third Printing, 1978

Published by Arco Publishing Company, Inc.
219 Park Avenue South, New York, N.Y. 10003

Copyright © 1960, 1975 by Arco Publishing Company, Inc.

Library of Congress Catalog Card Number 74-25024

ISBN 0-668-03822-5

Printed in the United States of America

Preface

THIS BOOK has been produced to satisfy a demand for a complete handbook on woodworking, and covers every phase of this important subject.

Emphasis has been placed on providing complete directions for using and maintaining every hand- and power-driven woodworking tool used in the workshop.

Instructions for making new woodworking projects or for making repairs, and finishing and polishing furniture are fully illustrated with detailed and dimensional drawings, diagrams, and photographs. Lists of required tools and materials are also given.

Every effort has been made by the author to give the worker authoritative information on all up-to-date materials; as well as information that will enable him to select the requisite tools wisely, keep them in good condition, and choose the correct material for any object he may desire to construct. This information can be of inestimable value to the worker.

All projects and procedures described are well within the abilities of the average worker who has the inclination to use tools intelligently. Practicability has been the main consideration.

This book comprises descriptions of different kinds of wood and wood products. A complete chapter on glues and gluing methods; a chapter on painting tools and equipment; and a chapter on paints, painting, and finishing procedures. To facilitate quick reference several tables have been included.

The COMPLETE WOODWORKING HANDBOOK has been planned with the conviction that it will be a welcome and valued aid to those who have long desired a complete handbook on the subject.

J. T. A.

Acknowledgments

THE AUTHOR desires to acknowledge with thanks the assistance of the following national organizations and branches of the government that have co-operated in the production of this book:

American Steel & Wire Co., American Brush Co., Armstrong Cork Co., Atlas Press Co., Black & Decker Mfg. Co., California Redwood Association, Carborundum Co., Cleveland Twist Drill Co., Delta Power Tool Division – Rockwell Manufacturing Co., DeVilbiss Co., Devoe & Raynolds Co., DeWalt Division – American Machine & Foundry Co., Douglas Fir Plywood Association, E. I. duPont de Nemours & Co., Franklin Glue Co., Henry Disston & Sons, National Lumber Manufacturers Association, National Paint, Varnish and Lacquer Association, National Retail Lumber Dealers Association, Nicholson File Co., Northern Hemlock & Hardwood Manufacturers Association, Northern Pine Manufacturers Association, Pittsburgh Plate Glass Co. – Brush Division, S. C. Johnson & Son, Sherwin-Williams Co., South Bend Lathe Works, Southern Pine Association, Stanley Works, U. S. Department of Agriculture, U. S. Forest Service – Forest Products Laboratory, United States Plywood Corp., United States Steel Corp., Western Pine Association, and Yale & Towne Manufacturing Co., American Institute of Timber Construction, American Plywood Association, Insulation Board Institute, Mall, National Bureau of Standards, Porter-Cable, United States Department of Agriculture, United States Department of Commerce, University of Wisconsin.

Preface to the Revised Edition

A HOME should have the fundamental requirements that will make it appealing for many years after it is built. Many wood houses are in existence today that were built more than two hundred years ago. The modern wood-frame house, with wood and wood-product covering materials, is economical and long lasting.

Bring your dream house down to earth. Install the latest in equipment and the most modern in treatment, but remember that good taste, good planning, and good construction are necessary if you want to obtain the ultimate in satisfaction from your home. To help you acquire a better understanding of what is meant by good construction the author has added a number of chapters to the new COMPLETE WOODWORKING HANDBOOK covering suitable materials and building fundamental principles. Because the things that make for good construction are largely hidden from view and, therefore, may not appear to have much to do with the complete house, most people are inclined to pay little attention to this feature. This handbook is also meant as a guide for those without this type of construction experience. It is not too technical an undertaking for the average homeowner to see that the fundamental requirements for good construction are provided for in planning and improving a home. You will be in a better position to evaluate bids, and you can also protect your interests, if you know something about lumber as well as the principles of construction.

Attractive design and sturdy construction need not be luxuries enjoyed only by those who can afford more expensive homes. They are qualities which should be included in even the humblest homes.

In the new COMPLETE WOODWORKING HANDBOOK you will find information on various phases of construction, covered in such a way to give you confidence that you are building, remodeling, or adding fundamental requirements that will be sturdy and that will not require costly repairs at a later date.

In addition to the chapters on hand- and power-driven woodworking tools and machines, painting tools and equipment, woodworking projects, glues and gluing methods, and working with plywood, you will find new chapters on wood and wood products; on paints, painting, and finishing procedures; added information on working with wood; and additional portable electric power tools. Many new reference tables have been included throughout the handbook.

The final chapters add information and illustrations on construction of stairs; floor framing; basement rooms; exterior wood coverings; floor coverings; interior doors, frames, trim, cabinets, and other millwork; exterior frames, windows, and doors; thermal insulation, vapor barriers, and sound insulation; porches and garages; roof coverings; and ventilation.

The author aims to prove that the new COMPLETE WOODWORKING HANDBOOK will be invaluable to the homeowner, builder, and others.

J. T. A.

Table of Contents

:

METRIC EQUIVALENTS OF FRACTIONS, INCHES, AND FEET

Measurement in Inches	Millimeters	Centimeters	Measurement in Inches	Millimeters	Centimeters
1/64	.39688	.039688	5/8	15.87500	1.587500
1/32	.79375	.079375	41/64	16.27188	1.627188
3/64	1.19063	.119063	21/32	16.66875	1.666875
1/16	1.58750	.158750	43/64	17.06563	1.706563
5/64	1.98438	.198438	11/16	17.46250	1.746250
3/32	2.38125	.238125	45/64	17.85938	1.785938
7/64	2.77813	.277813	23/32	18.25625	1.825625
1/8	3.17500	.317500	47/64	18.65313	1.865313
9/64	3.57188	.356188	3/4	19.05000	1.905000
5/32	3.96870	.396870	49/64	19.44688	1.944688
11/64	4.36563	.436563	25/32	19.84375	1.984375
3/16	4.76250	.476250	51/64	20.24063	2.024063
13/64	5.15938	.515938	13/16	20.63750	2.063750
7/32	5.55625	.555625	53/64	21.03438	2.103438
15/64	5.95313	.595313	27/32	21.43125	2.143125
1/4	6.35000	.635000	55/64	21.82810	2.182810
17/64	6.74688	.674688	7/8	22.22500	2.222500
9/32	7.14375	.714375	57/64	22.62188	2.262188
19/64	7.54063	.754063	29/32	23.01875	2.301875
5/16	7.93750	.793750	59/64	23.41563	2.341563
21/64	8.33438	.833438	15/16	23.81250	2.381250
11/32	8.73125	.873125	61/64	24.20930	2.420930
23/64	9.12813	.912813	31/32	24.60625	2.460625
3/8	9.52500	.952500	63/64	25.00313	2.500313
25/64	9.92188	.992188	1	25.40000	2.540000
13/32	10.31875	1.031875	2	50.80000	5.080000
27/64	10.71563	1.071563	3	76.20000	7.620000
7/16	11.11250	1.111250	4	101.60000	10.160000
29/64	11.50938	1.150938	5	127.00000	12.700000
15/32	11.90625	1.190625	6	152.40000	15.240000
31/64	12.30313	1.230313	7	177.80000	17.780000
1/2	12.70000	1.270000	8	203.20000	20.320000
33/64	13.09688	1.309688	9	228.60000	22.860000
17/32	13.49375	1.349375	10	254.00000	25.400000
35/64	13.89063	1.389063	11	279.40000	27.940000
9/16	14.28750	1.428750	12 (1 ft.)	304.80000	30.480000
37/64	14.68438	1.468438	24 (2 ft.)	609.60000	60.960000
19/32	15.08125	1.508125	36 (3 ft. or 1 yd.)	914.40000	91.440000
39/64	15.47813	1.547.813			

METRIC EQUIVALENTS

Linear Measure

1 centimeter		0.3937 inches
1 inch		2.54 centimeters
1 decimeter	3.937 inches	0.328 foot
1 foot		3.048 decimeters
1 meter	39.37 inches	1.0936 yards
1 yard		0.9144 meter
1 dekameter		1.9884 rods
1 rod		0.5029 dekameter
1 kilometer		0.62137 mile
1 mile		1.6093 kilometers

Approximate Metric Equivalents

1 decimeter	4 inches
1 liter	1.06 quarts liquid, 0.9 quart dry
1 meter	1.1 yards
1 kilometer	5/8 of a mile
1 hektoliter	2–5/8 bushels
1 hectare	2–1/2 acres
1 kilogram	2–1/5 pounds
1 stere or cubic meter	1/4 of a cord
1 metric ton	2,204.6 pounds

APPROXIMATE CONVERSION FACTORS FOR CHANGING

FROM CUSTOMARY UNITS TO METRIC UNITS.

Symbol	When You Know	Multiply by	To Find	Symbol
LENGTH				
in	inches	2.54	centimeters	cm
ft	feet	30	centimeters	cm
yd	yards	0.9	meters	m
mi	miles	1.6	kilometers	km
AREA				
in^2	square inches	6.5	square centimeters	cm^2
ft^2	square feet	0.09	square meters	m^2
yd^2	square yards	0.8	square meters	m^2
mi^2	square miles	2.6	square kilometers	km^2
	acres	0.4	hectares	ha
MASS (weight)				
oz	ounces	28	grams	g
lb	pounds	0.45	kilograms	kg
	short tons (2000 lb)	0.9	tonnes	t
VOLUME				
tsp	teaspoons	5	milliliters	ml
Tbsp	tablespoons	15	milliliters	ml
fl oz	fluid ounces	30	milliliters	ml
c	cups	0.24	liters	l
pt	pints	0.47	liters	l
qt	quarts	0.95	liters	l
gal	gallons	3.8	liters	l
ft^3	cubic feet	0.03	cubic meters	m^3
yd^3	cubic yards	0.76	cubic meters	m^3
TEMPERATURE (exact)				
°F	Fahrenheit temperature	5/9 (after subtracting 32)	Celsius temperature	°C

°F
-40 0 32 40 80 98.6 120 160 200 212 °F

°C
-40 -20 0 20 37 40 60 80 100 °C

APPROXIMATE CONVERSION FACTORS FOR CHANGING FROM

COMMONLY-USED METRIC UNITS TO CUSTOMARY UNITS.

Symbol	When You Know	Multiply by	To Find	Symbol
		LENGTH		
mm	millimeters	0.04	inches	in
cm	centimeters	0.4	inches	in
m	meters	3.3	feet	ft
m	meters	1.1	yards	yd
km	kilometers	0.6	miles	mi
		AREA		
cm^2	square centimeters	0.16	square inches	in^2
m^2	square meters	1.2	square yards	yd^2
km^2	square kilometers	0.4	square miles	mi^2
ha	hectares(10,000 m^2)	2.5	acres	
		MASS (weight)		
g	grams	0.035	ounces	oz
kg	kilograms	2.2	pounds	lb
t	tonnes (1000 kg)	1.1	short tons	
		VOLUME		
ml	milliliters	0.03	fluid ounces	fl oz
l	liters	2.1	pints	pt
l	liters	1.06	quarts	qt
l	liters	0.26	gallons	gal
m^3	cubic meters	35	cubic feet	ft^3
m^3	cubic meters	1.3	cubic yards	yd^3
		TEMPERATURE (exact)		
°C	Celsius temperature	9/5(then add 32)	Fahrenheit temperature	°F

CHAPTER 1

Wood and Wood Products

⋮

About 25 billion board feet of wood products are used each year by the construction industry in the United States. Much of this is used for homes and farm buildings. In addition, more than 6 billion board feet of lumber are used annually to maintain, repair, and remodel structures.

Today it is more important than ever to select the most appropriate wood product for each use in residential and farm construction. *Wood products* are now being made in more forms and from a greater variety of species than ever before. What was most suitable for a particular use a few years ago may not be so today.

The *wood-based panel products* (wood, particle board, hardboard, and structural insulating board) industry produces another 28 billion square feet of material in various thicknesses. Most of this material is used in remodeling or in new construction.

This chapter presents in brief the essential requirements for the usual wood-frame building purposes and shows how various woods and wood-based products meet these specific requirements. It also emphasizes some basic principles (often overlooked) that should be followed in good construction. (*See* Chap. 3, Working with Wood.)

While lumber is widely used in frame construction, sheet materials are also important. Wood-based panel materials are now broadly of three types: plywood, building fiberboard, and particle board.

Plywood is a glued panel made up of layers of veneer (thin

1

sheets of wood) with the grain of adjacent layers at right angles to each other. The kind of glue used determines whether it is interior or exterior type. Plywoods are classified by kinds and by qualities of faces (Fig. 1). Those with hardwood faces are usually classed as *decorative,* and those with softwood faces, as *construction.* Exceptions for softwood plywood include, *for example,* face veneers of knotty pine or clear, cabinet grades, which are decorative. Plywood is graded on both front and back faces, in that sequence. (*For example,* A-C, B-B, C-D.) (*See* Chap. 3, section on Plywood.)

Building fiberboards are produced with fibers interfelted so the board has some natural bonding. Additives improve the bond and impart strength. Boards of this type are generally classified by density into *structural insulating* boards (with a density of between 10 and about 31 pounds per cubic foot), *medium hardboards* (with a density of between about 31 and 50 pounds per cubic foot), and *high-density* or *regular hardboard* (with a density of over 50 pounds per cubic foot).

Particle boards are produced by gluing small particles of wood together into a panel. Hotsetting resins produce the bond necessary to give the panels form, stiffness, and strength. They are generally classified as low-density when the board has a density of less than 37 pounds per cubic foot, medium-density when the density is between 37 and 50 pounds per cubic foot, and high-density when the board weighs more than 50 pounds per cubic foot.

CLASSIFICATION OF WOODS FOR PRINCIPAL HOME USES

To select lumber and other wood-based material wisely, one must first single out the key requirements of the job. Then it is relatively easy to check the properties (distinguishing characteristics, qualities, or marks common to a species or group, usually classified as physical, mechanical, or chemical properties) of the different woods to see which ones meet these requirements.

A builder or a property owner may believe that he needs a strong wood for the siding of his house or barn when he really requires a wood that takes paint well, is resistant to weathering, and develops little or no warping. Or he may think he needs a

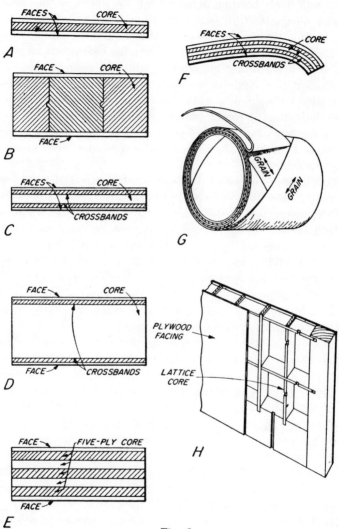

Fig. 1.

Types of plywood and crossbanded construction: *A*, 3-ply (all veneer); *B*, 3-ply (lumber core); *C*, 5-ply (all veneer); *D*, 5-ply (lumber core); *E*, 7-ply (all veneer); *F*, 5-ply bent work (all veneer); *G*, 5-ply, spirally wrapped (all veneer); *H*, section of hollow-core door.

wood with high bending strength for the joists of his house, whereas adequate stiffness is more important. Other considerations include the moisture content of the wood, its ability to resist distortion (warping), and its shrinkage characteristics.

In *buying* sheathing material, one should consider not only the original cost but also the cost of application. Such factors as relative nailholding qualities, insulation values, and the possible elimination of corner bracing should also be considered. It is not necessary to purchase only the best quality lumber or wood-based products. Lower and cheaper grades serve satisfactorily for many uses.

The number of uses and the service requirements of wood vary so greatly that it is practically impossible to classify woods precisely according to their suitability for different uses solely on factual data. Such data, however, can be supplemented by the mature judgment of technical workers who have been impartially studying and testing the various woods for years and have observed the performance of many woods under widely varying conditions. The opinion of such workers has been included, therefore, in classifying common United States wood species for principal home and farm uses.

Wood species are divided into two classes: *hardwoods,* which have broad leaves, and *softwoods* or conifers, which have scale-like leaves or needles. The terms hardwood and softwood do not denote hardness or softness of the wood. In fact, some hardwoods like cottonwood and aspen are less dense (or hard) than some softwoods like southern pine and Douglas fir.

The native species listed here are in general use and are classed conservatively for each specific purpose. Occasionally a species may be underrated for a particular use, or its range of suitability may be underestimated. But, from the general public's standpoint, the ratings are on the side of safety.

The following classification is simple and applies to average, typical conditions under which wood serves in a particular use. No attempt has been made to draw fine distinctions between woods. Neither is it to be implied that all species of woods in the same class are equally suitable.

Grades vary considerably by species. Therefore, a sequence of first-, second-, third-, fourth-, and fifth-grade material is given for specific uses. In general, the first grade is for a high or special use; the second, for better than average use; the third, for average; and fourth and fifth, for more economical, but still acceptable, construction. (*See* Chap. 3, section on Lumber Grades.)

SUITABILITY OF WOODS AND WOOD-BASED PRODUCTS FOR VARIOUS HOUSE USES

Foundations—Sills and Beams

Usual requirements: High stiffness and strength when used as a beam, good decay resistance, good resistance to withdrawal and lateral movement of nails. Good strength in compression perpendicular to grain (sills). Most woods are satisfactory as sills where dry conditions prevail, but for predominantly wet conditions, preservative-treated wood should be used. (*See* Chap. 21, section on Wood Sill Construction.)

Woods combining usual requirements in a *high degree:* White oak. (Fine for sills and beams in crawl spaces. Heartwood has high decay resistance, but wood that is all heartwood usually costs more.) Douglas fir, western larch, southern yellow pine, and rock elm. High in strength and nail-holding qualities. (Sills and beams in basement or dry areas. Under moist conditions they require preservative treatment.)

Woods combining usual requirements in a *good degree:* Cedar and redwood. (Sills only, as these species do not have the high bending strength desirable for beams. Heartwood has high decay resistance.) Poplar, eastern and west coast hemlock, and red oak. (These woods require good preservative treatment if exposed to moist conditions or long periods of high humidity.)

Woods combining usual requirements in a *fair degree:* Ash, beech, birch, soft elm, maple, and sycamore. (Good as beams and fair as sills, but they require good preservative treatment if exposed to moist conditions.) Northern white pine (eastern) and Idaho white pine (western), ponderosa pine, sugar pine, spruce, and white fir. (Satisfactory for sills, but they require good preservative treatment if exposed to moist conditions or high humidity.)

Grades used: Softwood sills that might be used in houses with crawl spaces are generally of second- or third-grade softwood dimension material. For less exacting standards, but nonetheless satisfactory for secondary buildings, fourth-grade material may be used. If lumber is not treated, all heartwood pieces should be selected for sills near ground level and in moist areas where condensed moisture may be absorbed by sills. Hardwood sills are usually first-grade dimension in the best construction and second-grade in ordinary construction.

Foundations—Plates and Sleepers

Usual requirements: Good natural decay resistance (or treated with preservative) under moist conditions, good nail-holding qualities and medium density. (Used as plates on concrete slab walls where top of wall is near finish grade, as sleepers on concrete slabs for fastening of finish flooring, and similar uses.)

Woods combining usual requirements in a *high degree:* White oak. (Heartwood has high decay resistance, but it costs more.)

Woods combining usual requirements to a *good degree:* Redwood, Douglas fir, western larch, southern yellow pine, rock elm, and other medium-density species for normal conditions.

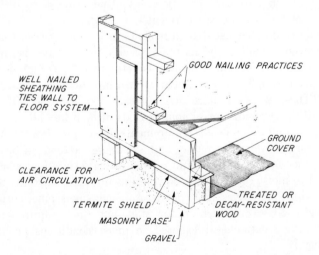

Fig. 2. Foundations of temporary or portable buildings.

Pressure-treated southern yellow pine, red oak, hemlock, and Douglas fir for damp conditions.

Woods combining usual requirements to a *fair degree:* Northern and Idaho white pine, ponderosa pine, sugar pine, spruce, white fir, ash, beech, birch, maple, and sycamore for normal conditions.

Grades used: Third-grade dimension lumber of most softwood species under normal conditions.

Framing—Joists, Rafters, and Headers

Usual requirements: High stiffness, good bending strength, good nail-holding qualities, and freedom from pronounced warp. For this use dryness and size are more important factors than inherent properties of the different woods. Allowable spans vary by species.

Woods combining usual requirements in a *high degree:* Douglas fir, western larch, and southern yellow pine. (They are ex-

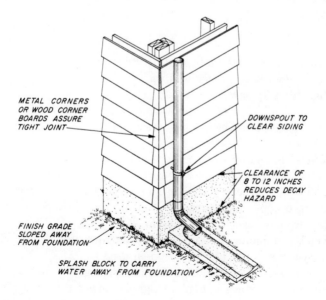

Fig. 3. Siding joints and downspout.

tensively used.)   Ash, beech, birch, maple, and oak. (Seldom used since they are more difficult to obtain in straight pieces and harder to nail and saw than the preceding group.)

Woods combining usual requirements in a *good degree:* Eastern and west coast hemlock, eastern and Sitka spruce, lodgepole pine, and white fir. Northern and Idaho white pine, ponderosa pine, sugar pine, and redwood. (Seldom used because of adaptability to more exacting uses such as millwork, siding, and finish. Lower strength may be compensated for by using larger joists and rafters.) Poplar. (Seldom used.)

Woods combining usual requirements in a *fair degree:* Elm, gum, sycamore, magnolia, and tupelo. (Seldom used.)

Grades used: Second-grade dimension of most softwood species is used in first-class construction. Third-grade is used in a large percentage of lower-cost dwellings. The fourth grade is satisfactory for small buildings but contains more crooked pieces than higher grades. Lumber used in trusses is often first grade and second grade, depending on the type of truss, span, species, and the type of member. (*See* Chap. **21**, sections on Floor Joists.)

Framing—Studs and Plates

Usual requirements: Moderate stiffness and nail-holding qualities, freedom from pronounced warp, and moderately easy workability (easy to saw and nail).

Woods combining usual requirements in a *high degree:* Douglas fir, western larch, and southern yellow pine. (Extensively used.)

Woods combining usual requirements in a *good degree:* Eastern and west coast hemlock, spruce, white fir, balsam fir, lodgepole pine, and aspen. Northern and Idaho white pine, ponderosa pine, sugar pine, and redwood. (Seldom used because of adaptability to more exacting uses as finish.)

Woods combining usual requirements to a *fair degree:* Elm, gum, sycamore, and tupelo. (Seldom used.)

Grades used: Because high bending strength is of secondary importance for studs and plates, grades lower than those commonly used for joists and rafters are satisfactory. Third-grade softwood dimension lumber is satisfactory for most dwellings built to good construction standards. Hardwoods in first- and second-grade dimension are used in all types of construction.

Subfloors

Usual requirements:

Lumber. Requirements are not exacting, but moderate stiffness, medium shrinkage and warp, and ease of working are desired.

Plywood. Moderate stiffness when finish is strip flooring; high stiffness for wood block or resilient finish flooring. Good nailholding qualities.

Softwood plywoods for use as subfloors with or without underlayment are classified by density, hence stiffness and strength, into groups. For each grouping a limit for span and loading is established. This is shown on each piece of plywood by a number such as 32/16. The first number indicates maximum span when used as roof sheathing, and the second number indicates maximum span when used as subfloor. The 16 here indicates that the maximum span for living area space is framing 16″ on centers.

Woods combining usual requirements in a *high degree:*

Lumber. Douglas fir, western larch, and southern yellow pine. (Commonly used.) Ash and oak. (Seldom used because of adaptability to more exacting uses.)

Plywood. Group 1 and 2 softwoods: Douglas fir, southern yellow pine, and western larch.

Woods combining usual requirements in a *good* degree:

Lumber. Hemlock, ponderosa pine, spruce, lodgepole pine, aspen, balsam fir, and white fir. (Commonly used.) Northern and Idaho white pine, sugar pine, and poplar. (Seldom used because of adaptability to more exacting uses.) Beech, birch, elm, hackberry, maple, oak, and tupelo. (Not used extensively, harder to work. Maple, elm, and oak often available locally.)

Plywood. Group 3 and 4 softwoods: Cedar, redwood, Sitka and Englemann spruce, west coast hemlock, noble fir, and white fir.

Grades and types used (minimum recommended):

Lumber. Third-grade softwood boards are used extensively in better quality houses. In lower-cost houses, both third and fourth grades are used. The fourth grade is serviceable and does not entail much waste, but it is not as tight as the higher grades. When hardwoods are used, second-grade boards are commonly used in more expensive houses and third grade in lower-cost houses.

Plywood. Standard interior grade (C-D) plywood under ordinary conditions. In baths, kitchens, or when exposed to weather, use standard grade with exterior glue. (*See* Chap. 21, section on Subfloor.)

Wall Sheathing

Usual requirements:

Lumber. Easy working, easy nailing, and moderate shrinkage.

Plywood. Good nail-holding qualities, workability, and resistance to racking.

Structural insulating board and hardboard. Good resistance to water, to nailhead pull-through, and to racking if properly attached.

Materials combining usual requirements in a *high degree:*

Lumber. Cedar, hemlock, northern and Idaho white pine, ponderosa pine, sugar pine, redwood, aspen, spruce, balsam and white fir, basswood, lodgepole pine, and poplar. (Good racking resistance when applied at 45° but not adequate when applied horizontally without bracing.)

Plywood. Douglas fir, southern pine, and western larch.

Structural insulating board and hardboards. When applied vertically in 4′ by 8′ or longer sheets with perimeter nailing.

Materials combining usual requirements in a *good degree:*

Lumber. Douglas fir, western larch, and southern yellow pine. (Not as workable as previous lumber group.)

Plywood. Cedar, redwood, Sitka and Englemann spruce, west coast hemlock, noble fir, and white fir.

Structural insulating board. Regular density structural insulating board (about 18 pounds per cubic foot in density) is furnished in 2′ or 4′ widths and, when applied with long edges horizontal, do not provide necessary resistance to racking forces of wind or earthquake. Other bracing must then be provided.

The more prevalent way to install insulating board sheathing is in 4' widths with long edges vertical. With proper fastening around the perimeter and along interior framing, adequate resistance to racking is provided. Manufacturers' recommendations should be followed for fastening.

Hardboards. Hardboards are not generally used as wall sheathing but may be used as combined siding sheathing.

Lumber. Most woods are satisfactory for sheathing, though some woods are less time consuming to work than others. The third grade of Common softwood boards makes a serviceable sheathing when covered with a good building paper. First and second grades provide a tighter coverage but still require coverage with building paper. Fourth and fifth grades may be used as sheathing in lower-cost houses, but they are not generally available. Both entail some loss in cutting. When a hardwood is used for sheathing, second-grade boards are adaptable to more expensive houses and third-grade to lower-cost houses.

Plywood. Most species of plywood can be used with satisfactory results. For exterior finish such as shingles or shakes, thickness of softer plywoods should be increased to obtain greater nail penetration. Use standard interior (C-D) under ordinary conditions; or, use standard interior with exterior glue if house is in an unusually damp location.

Structural insulating board. Structural insulating board is furnished in three grades: regular density, intermediate density, and nail base. Regular density is manufactured in both the $\frac{1}{2}''$ and $\frac{25}{32}''$ thicknesses; the other two grades are only made $\frac{1}{2}''$ thick.

Intermediate density sheathing is somewhat more dense, hence stronger and stiffer, than regular density. Furnished only in 4' by 9' sizes. When properly applied with long edges vertical, it satisfies racking requirements while the $\frac{1}{2}''$ thick regular density board usually does not. Nail base sheathing is more dense than intermediate density and in addition to providing racking resistance has sufficient nail-holding strength to hold some kinds of siding on the wall when special nails are used. Insulating board sheathing must be attached to framing with large-headed (roofing) nails or special staples. These fasteners should have a corrosion-resistant coating.

Roof Sheathing

Usual requirements:

Lumber. Moderate stiffness, good nail holding, little tendency to warp, and ease of working.

Plywood. Adequate stiffness for span and roof loading. Sheathing-grade plywoods are classified into groups by density, therefore strength and stiffness. Each grouping sets the distance between supports for proper application and performance. Each sheet is marked with a number such as 32/16.

Woods combining usual requirements in a *high degree:*

Lumber. Douglas fir, western larch, and southern yellow pine. (Commonly used.) Ash, beech, birch, elm, hackberry, maple, oak, and tupelo. (Not extensively used; harder to work.)

Plywood. Group 1 and 2 softwoods: Douglas fir, southern yellow pine, and western larch.

Woods combining usual requirements in a *good degree:*

Lumber. Hemlock, ponderosa pine, spruce, lodgepole pine, aspen, and white and balsam fir. (Commonly used.) Northern and Idaho white pine, sugar pine, redwood, and poplar. (Seldom used because of adaptability to more exacting uses.)

Plywood. Group 3 and 4 softwoods: Cedar, redwood, Sitka and Englemann spruce, west coast hemlock, noble fir, and white fir.

Grades and types used:

Lumber. Third-grade Common softwood boards are used extensively in better-quality houses. In lower-cost houses, both third and fourth grades are used. Fourth-grade is serviceable but not as tight as third-grade. When hardwoods are used, second-grade boards can be used in high-quality houses and third-grade in low-cost houses.

Plywood. Use standard interior grade (C-D) under ordinary conditions. For unusually damp conditions use standard interior grade with exterior glue.

Plank Roof Decking

Usual requirements: Moderate stiffness and strength, moderate stability, and moderate insulating value. (For short to moderate spans of 2′ to approximately 16′ in length, flat and low pitch roofs.)

Materials combining usual requirements in a *high degree:* Solid or laminated wood decking (edge matched) of southern yellow pine, Douglas fir, or other softwood (1⅝" to 3⅝" thick).

Materials combining usual requirements in a *good degree:* Structural insulating roof deck.

Grades and types used:

Wood decking. With solid wood for high-quality houses, first grade; slightly lower class, second grade; standard use (houses and garages), third grade. With laminated wood for high-quality houses, first grade (select or decorative one face); lower-cost houses and other buildings, second grade (service type).

Structural insulating roof deck. Specially fabricated products. Types vary by (a) thicknesses (1½", 2", and 3" depending on span and insulation requirements), (b) surface treatment, and (c) vapor barrier needs.

Shingles and Shakes

Usual requirements: High decay resistance, little tendency to curl or check, and freedom from splitting in nailing. (Roof and sidewalls.)

Woods combining usual requirements in a *high degree:* Cedar, cypress, and redwood. (Principal shingle woods; heartwood only, edge grain.)

Woods combining usual requirements to a *good degree:* Northern and Idaho white pine, ponderosa pine, and sugar pine. (Handmade shingles or shakes from locally grown timber; for best utility require good preservative treatment.) White oak. (Handmade shingles or shakes from locally grown timber. They require care in nailing.)

Grades used:

Roofs. In western red cedar, cypress, and redwood, first-grade shingles (all-heart, edge-grained clear stock) should be used for the longest life and greatest ultimate economy. Other all-heart but not edge-grained grades, such as second grade in redwood, western red cedar, and cypress, are frequently used to reduce initial cost and for low-cost houses and secondary buildings. (*See* Chaps. 24 and 30, sections on Wood Shingles and Shakes.)

Sidewalls. Same species as used for roofs. For best construction on single-course sidewalls use first grade (all-heart, edge-grained clear). For double-course sidewalls use third grade for undercourse and first grade for outer course for best construction. Use second-grade outer course to reduce costs.

Exterior Trim

Usual requirements: Medium decay resistance, good painting and weathering characteristics, easy working qualities, and maximum freedom from warp.

Woods combining usual requirements in a *high degree:* Cedar, cypress, and redwood. (Heartwood has natural decay resistance, edge grain preferable for best paint-holding qualities. Most adaptable to natural finishes and stains.) Northern and Idaho white pine, ponderosa pine, and sugar pine. (Adaptable to ordinary trim.)

Woods combining usual requirements in *good degree:* West coast hemlock, ponderosa pine, spruce, poplar, Douglas fir, western larch, and southern yellow pine. (Edge-grained boards and special priming treatment advisable to improve paint-holding qualities.)

Grades used: First grades (A, B, or B and Better Finish) are used in the best construction. Second grades (C and D Finish) are used in more economical construction and first- or second-grade Common boards where appearance is not important. Clear finger joint boards are often used when trim is to be painted.

Frames and Sash

Usual requirements: Good to high decay resistance, good paint holding, moderate shrinkage, freedom from warping, good nail holding, and ease of working.

Woods combining usual requirements in a *high degree:* Cypress, cedar, and redwood. Northern and Idaho white pine, ponderosa pine, and sugar pine. (Principal woods used for sash and window and outside doorframes. Usual preservative treatment consists of a three-minute dip in water-repellent preservative.)

Woods combining usual requirements in a *good degree:* Douglas fir, western larch, and southern yellow pine. (Require dip treatment.) White oak. (Harder to work and higher shrinkage than softwoods. Usually used for outside doorsills and thresholds.) (*See* Chap. **27**, Exterior Frames, Windows, and Doors.)

Grades used: Grades of lumber for sash and frames are shop grades and are of primary interest to manufacturers rather than users. The majority of door and window frames and sash are treated with water-repellent preservative at time of manufacture. Decay-resistant species should be considered for basement frames and sash where resistance to moisture and decay is more important. Under severe moisture conditions, pressure-treated material is desirable.

Siding

Usual requirements: Good painting characteristics, medium decay resistance, easy working qualities, and freedom from warp. (For lap siding, drop siding, matched vertical boards, vertical boards and battens, and others, *see* Chap. **24**, sections on Sidings.)

Lumber siding. Woods combining usual requirements in a *high degree:* Western red cedar, cypress, and redwood. (Extensively used. Heartwood preferable; edge-grained siding has best

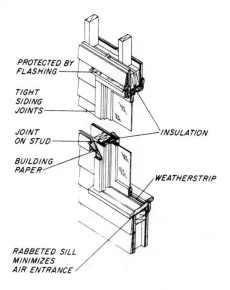

Fig. 4. Frames.

paint-holding qualities. Most adaptable of species to natural finishes and stains.)

Woods combining usual requirements in a *good degree:* Northern and Idaho white pine, sugar pine, and white cedar. (Heartwood has medium decay resistance.) West coast hemlock, ponderosa pine, spruce, and poplar. (Edge grain for best paint retention in such species as hemlock.)

Woods combining usual requirements in a *fair degree:* Douglas fir, western larch, and southern yellow pine. (Edge grain only.)

Grades used: Redwood and cypress first siding grades (Clear Heart) and western red cedar in a first-grade (Clear) for best quality construction. In other softwoods the first grade (B and Better) siding is used in best-quality houses. Siding in more economical types of construction is usually of second grade (C or D), but third grade (No. 1 and No. 2) is available in a number of species. Rough-sawn siding patterns in the lower grades are suitable for stain finishes.

Other siding materials. Paper-overlaid plywood or lumber (resin impregnated in the paper overlay) in sheet form or in manufactured forms for board and batten effect, and in patterns for horizontal siding. Rough-textured plywoods in various patterns and exterior grades are suitable for stain finishes.

Medium hardboard in densities of 32 to 50 pounds per cubic foot. In sheet form or in manufactured widths for horizontal siding. May be plastic-coated or factory-primed ready for finish paint coats.

High-density or regular hardboards in densities of 50 to 70 pounds per cubic foot. In panel form only. Four by 8 foot or longer applied with long edges vertical. Such hardboards are not usually recommended for use as lapped (clapboard) siding.

Combined sheathing siding. Wood-base panel products can provide both the function of sheathing and siding when applied in large sheets to provide racking resistance and reduction of air infiltration. Special plywoods like rough-sawn western red cedar and "Texture 111" with exterior gluelines are manufactured for this use.

Medium-density hardboards and to a limited extent high-density hardboards are also manufactured for this use. They may have a plain or embossed surface. Plywood and hardboard may be grooved to create reversed board and batten effects or may have a plain surface and be applied with battens to create the board and batten effect.

Plywood is usually stained. Hardboard may be painted or stained.

Decking and Outdoor Stepping

Usual requirements: High decay resistance, nonsplintering, good stiffness, strength, wear resistance, and freedom from warping. (If painted, should have good paint retention.)

Woods combining usual requirements in a *high degree:* White oak. (Edge grain.) Locust and walnut. (Usually unavailable except when cut from locally grown timber.)

Woods combining usual requirements in a *good degree:* Douglas fir, western larch, redwood, cedar, and southern yellow pine. (Edge grain only, heartwood preferred.) For moderate life, Douglas fir and southern yellow pine require preservative treatment. (Softer woods not as wear resistant.)

Grades used: Second (C Finish) or a higher grade in softwoods and first and second Finish grades in hardwoods are used in high-quality construction. In lower-cost construction, first-grade Dimension in hardwoods and as low as second-grade Di-

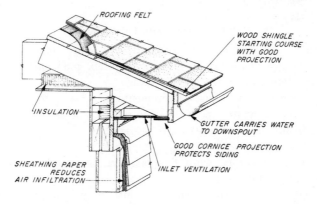

Fig. 5. Cornice and gutter details.

mension in softwoods are used. First and second grades in softwoods are serviceable but wear unevenly around knots.

Interior Trim with Natural Finish

Usual requirements: Hardness, freedom from warp, pleasing texture and grain.

Woods combining usual requirements in a *high degree:* Oak, birch, maple, cherry, beech, sycamore, and walnut. Cypress (pecky) and maple (curly or bird's eye).

Knotty surface. Cedar, ponderosa pine, spruce, sugar pine, gum, and lodgepole pine.

Woods combining usual requirements in a *good degree:* Douglas fir, west coast hemlock, western larch, southern yellow pine, redwood, aspen, and magnolia. (With conventional architectural treatment.)

Grades used: High-class hardwood interior trim is usually first-grade Finish (A grade). The softwood Finish Grade A or B and Better is commonly used in high-quality construction. In the more economical types of construction, C grade is serviceable. D grade requires special selection or some cutting to obtain clear material. Special grades of knotty pine, pecky cypress, and others are available to meet special architectural requirements in some types of high-quality construction.

(*See* Chap. 21, Interior Doors, Frames, Trim, Cabinets, and Other Millwork.)

Interior Trim with Paint Finish

Usual requirements: Fine and uniform texture, moderate hardness, absence of knots and discoloring pitch, good paint holding, and freedom from warp and shrinkage.

Woods combining usual requirements in a *high degree:* Northern and Idaho white pine, ponderosa pine, sugar pine, and poplar. (Where likelihood of marring is negligible.)

Woods combining usual requirements in a *good degree:* Hemlock, redwood, spruce, white fir, magnolia, basswood, beech, gum, maple, and tupelo.

Douglas fir, western larch, and southern yellow pine. (Edge grain most satisfactory.)

Grades used: C Finish is the lowest softwood grade commonly

used for high-quality paint and enamel finish. D Finish can be used but requires some selection or cutting. First-grade Common is used for ordinary or rough paint finishes. In more economical homes second-grade Common may be used for ordinary or rough-paint finishes. Smooth-paint finishes are difficult to obtain and maintain over knots in first-, second-, and third-grade Common softwoods.

First-grade Finish in the hardwoods is used for exacting requirements of high-quality paint and enamel finish in more expensive homes. The second-grade Finish in hardwoods is also used but requires some selection or cutting. Second-grade boards in hardwoods may be used for interior trim in the low-cost home, but for interior trim that is to be painted, softwoods are generally used.

(*See* Chap. 16, Paints, Painting, and Finishing Procedures.)

Underlayment for Finish Floors

Ordinarily all finish flooring except standard strip flooring and ½″ or ¾″ wood-block floor are laid with an underlayment between the subfloor and the finish flooring. This is especially necessary for resilient floor surfacing (rubber, vinyl, vinyl asbestos, or asphalt in tile or sheet form) because of its thinness, flexibility, and tendency to *show through* the pattern of the surface beneath it. (*See* Chap. 21, section on Subfloor.)

Floor underlayment serves the following functions:

1. Provides uniform support for finish flooring.
2. Bridges small irregularities in the subsurface.
3. Because joints in floor underlayment do not coincide with those in subfloor, there is less chance for working of joints to loosen or break finish flooring.
4. Provides a smooth, uncontaminated surface for gluing to the base those kinds of finish flooring requiring it.
5. Permits vertical adjustment in floor levels so all rooms are at the same elevation even when different floorings are used. The subfloor usually serves as the working platform. During the period between initial laying of subfloor and installation of finish flooring the surface may be roughened from wetting, dented from impacts, or contaminated with plaster,

dirt, grease, and paint; in fact anything that is tracked or brought into the house.

Some use of combined subfloor underlayment is developing, particularly in factory-built or tract-built housing where subfloors are given special protection during construction or where pad and carpet are installed.

Floor underlayments are plywood, hardboard, or particle board.

Plywood underlayment. Plywood underlayment is a special grade produced for this purpose from Group 1 woods (for indentation resistance). It is produced in ¼″, ⅜″, ½″, ⅝″, and ¾″ thicknesses, and the face ply is C plugged grade (no voids) with a special C or better veneer underlying the face ply to prevent penetration from such concentrated loads as high heels.

Particle board underlayment. Produced in the same thicknesses as plywood, particle board underlayment is often preferred because its uniform surface and somewhat higher density make it more resistant to indentation than plywood when thin resilient flooring is applied over it. Because it tends to change more in length and width with changes in moisture content than plywood, manufacturers' directions for installation and specifications for adhesives should be followed for good performance.

Hardboard underlayment. Produced in 4′ squares, 0.220″ thick and planed to uniform thickness, hardboard underlayment should be installed to manufacturers' specifications for proper performance. It is mainly used on remodeling or in new construction where minimum thickness buildup is desired.

Flooring—Strip and Wood Block

Usual requirements: High resistance to wear, attractive figure or color, minimum warp and shrinkage. (Material should be used at a moisture content near the level it will average in service.)

Woods combining usual requirements in a *high degree:* Maple, red and white oak, beech, and birch. (Most commonly used hardwoods.) White ash and. walnut. (Not commonly used.) Hickory and pecan. (Not commonly available.) Harder to work and nail. More suitable to woodblock flooring.)

Woods combining usual requirements in a *good degree:* Cherry, gum, and sycamore (edge grain). (Not commonly available. Highly decorative and suitable where wear is not severe.) Cypress, Douglas fir, west coast hemlock, western larch, and southern yellow pine (edge grain). (More suitable in low-cost houses in bedrooms where traffic is light.)

Grades used: In beech, birch, and maple flooring the grade of Firsts is ordinarily used for better-quality homes, and Seconds and sometimes Thirds in economy houses. In oak, the grade of Clear (either flat grain or edge grain) is used in better construction, and Selects and sometimes No. 1 Common are used in lower-cost work or where small tight knots provide the desired effect. Other hardwoods are ordinarily used in the same grades as oak.

When *softwood flooring* is used (without covering) in better-quality homes, Grade A or B and Better edge grain is used. Grade D or C (edge grain) is used in low-cost homes.

The three general types of material used for finish floors are wood-strip, wood-block, and resilient flooring such as rubber, vinyl, asphalt tile, or linoleum.

Strip flooring. Strip flooring is usually laid over boards nominally 1″ thick because the boards must be thick enough to hold the nail. (*See* Chap. 25, section on Wood-Strip Flooring.) For best results, the boards for subfloors are laid diagonally and in nominal widths no greater than 6″ or 8″. Plywood $\frac{5}{8}$″ or $\frac{3}{4}$″ thick is also satisfactory. One-half-inch plywood is satisfactory for subfloor when strip flooring is nailed to floor joists.

Wood-block flooring. Because wood-block flooring requires an even and uniform base for best results, plywood subfloor is frequently used. (*See* Chap. 25, section on Wood-Block Flooring.) A $\frac{5}{8}$″ or $\frac{3}{4}$″ thickness should be used if block flooring is installed by nailing. Laminated block flooring $\frac{1}{2}$″ thick or less may be used over a $\frac{1}{4}$″ or $\frac{3}{8}$″ plywood or particle board underlayment that has been nailed to a wood subfloor.

Resilient flooring. Because resilient floors are usually quite thin and are installed with adhesives, it is necessary to provide a smooth base. (*See* Chap. 25, section on Base for Resilient Floors.) Plywood, particle board, or hardboard (all of a special underlayment grade) are most frequently used over various types of subfloors. Underlayment screws are commonly used to fasten the underlayment and minimize *popups* that can occur with other fastenings.

Miscellaneous Millwork

Interior millwork usually varies a great deal between houses, both in the type and amount used. Uses in the average home include doors, cabinet doors, shelving, and stairways. Other homes may add the use of such millwork items as fireplace mantels, wall paneling, ceiling beams, china closets, bookcases, and wardrobes.

DOORS

Usual requirements: Freedom from warp (especially for outside doors), good finishing qualities, resistance to denting (hardness), pleasing figure or grain for natural finish or good base for paint.

Other attributes and sometimes requirements of doors include resistance to fire and sound transmission, ability to hold special hardware, means to accept cutouts or openings for windows, and durability. An interior- or exterior-quality glue is used for assembly of doors, depending on where they are to be used. (*See* Chaps. **26** and **27**.)

There are two types of doors manufactured: the panel door with insert panel and solid or veneered stiles and rails, and the flush door with skins bonded to frames. The flush door is manufactured in hollow-core construction (for interior doors) and solid-core (for exterior doors in cold and moderate climates).

Woods combining usual requirements in a *high degree:* Oak and birch. (Natural finish.)

Woods combining usual requirements in a *good degree:* Ponderosa pine, Douglas fir, southern yellow pine, and spruce. Gum for natural finish or painting.

CABINET DOORS

Usual requirements: Pleasing grain, freedom from warp, and moderate hardness.

Woods combining usual requirements in a *high degree:* Maple, oak, birch, and cherry. (Suitable for natural finishes and for plywood flush doors.)

Woods combining usual requirements in a *good degree:* Douglas fir, southern yellow pine, gum, ponderosa pine, magnolia, and poplar for paint finish. (*See* Chap. 26, section on Cabinets and Other Millwork.)

SHELVING

Usual requirements: Stiffness and freedom from warp.

Woods combining usual requirements in a *high degree:* Ash, birch, maple, oak, and walnut. (Suitable for natural finishes.)

Woods combining usual requirements in a *good degree:*

Lumber. Hemlock, spruce, and western larch.

Plywood. Natural finish: Oak and birch. (Most available species.) Painted finish: Douglas fir, southern yellow pine, and other softwoods.

Particle board. Though only one-fourth to one-eighth as stiff as wood or plywood, particle board is being used increasingly where loading is light, extra support is provided, or where spans are short. Frequently veneered or overlaid with higher stiffness materials to provide additional stiffness.

STAIRWAYS

Usual requirements for treads, risers, and stair parts: Hardness and wear resistance (treads, railings), freedom from warp, and pleasing grain. (*See* Chap. 20, Construction of Stairs.)

Woods combining usual requirements in a *high degree:* Oak, birch, maple, walnut, beech, ash, and cherry (exposed treads and risers).

Woods combining usual requirements in a *good degree:* Douglas fir, southern yellow pine, gum, and sycamore (basement or secondary stairs or when stairs are to be carpeted).

WALL PANELING

Usual requirements for natural finish or light staining: Pleasing grain, figure or surface treatment, freedom from warp and shrinkage, and some resistance to abrasion.

Woods combining usual requirements in a *high degree:*

Lumber. Oak, redwood, cypress (pecky), walnut, cedar (knotty), ash, birch, pine (knotty), and cherry.

Plywood. Oak, birch, maple, pecan-hickory, and walnut.

Woods combining usual requirements in a *good degree:*

Lumber. Gum, western larch, Douglas fir, beech, southern yellow pine, hemlock, and ponderosa pine.

Plywood. Cedar, pine, Douglas fir, southern yellow pine, and some imported species. (Some are specially treated to create a variation in the grain for unique surface effects.)

Grades and types used:

Lumber. The best grade in hardwood for high-quality houses is first grade. Softwood first or second grades are commonly used in the better house. Third grade is more economical. Special grades of knotty pine, pecky cypress, and sound wormy oak are sometimes available for special paneling treatment.

Plywood. Unfinished: Good or special surface one side, interior or exterior types. Prefinished: V-grooved and others (good one side or equal).

Other materials. Hardboards with special-grain printing, embossing, or other surface treatments or decorative laminate overlays. Structural insulating board in sheet or plank form for walls and in tile form or lay-in panel for ceiling. (Factory-treated, finished, or special acoustical effect.) Particle boards with veneered plastic or other overlay face.

Barns

Wood and wood-based materials for barns and similar buildings are generally the same as those described for houses. Grades are usually lower, but in some uses strength is the most important factor. The need for the additional strength is often reflected in the recommended grades and species. Lower grades can be used for siding, flooring, and trim than are ordinarily used for houses.

Fence Posts

Usual requirements: High decay resistance and little or no sapwood for untreated posts. Good bending strength, straightness, and high staple holding. Permanent installation requires a good preservative treatment. High sapwood content is desirable for fence posts to be preservative treated.

Woods combining usual requirements in a *high degree:* Black locust and osage orange. (Meet most requirements but not readily available in all parts of the United States.) White oak. (Heartwood only. Generally available in the eastern states, but life is shorter than preceding group if not treated.) Cedar, cypress, and redwood. (Heartwood only. Readily available but do not hold smooth shank staples and nails as well as preceding groups.)

Woods combining usual requirements in a *good degree:* Douglas fir, western larch, and southern yellow pine (preservative treatment required).

Woods combining usual requirements in a *fair degree:* Beech, birch, maple, red oak, and elm. (Equal the best woods when given a good preservative treatment.) Hemlock, spruce, white fir, basswood, cottonwood, gum, tupelo, poplar, and lodgepole pine.

Grades used: Fence posts have no standard grades but are specified by top diameters and by lengths. Treated posts should be branded or stamped to identify the treatment and source.

Gates and Fences

Usual requirements: Good bending strength, good decay and weather resistance, high nail holding, freedom from warp. Treatment desirable for severe conditions. (Should also be lightweight for gates.)

Woods combining usual requirements in a *high degree:* Douglas fir, western larch, southern yellow pine, redwood, and white oak.

Woods combining usual requirements in a *good degree:* Cedar, northern and Idaho white pine, ponderosa pine, sugar pine, and poplar. (Small tendency to warp, weather well, but are low in strength and nail holding. All except cedar have moderately low resistance to decay.) Beech, birch, gum, maple, red oak, and tupelo. (Strong, high in nail holding, but have greater tendency to warp, do not weather so well as preceding group, and are too heavy for gates. All except gum and maple have moderately low resistance to decay.) Eastern and west coast hemlock, white fir, and spruce. (Intermediate qualities except for decay resistance, which is moderately low.)

Grades used: Second- and third-grade softwood Common boards and second hardwood board grades are used in better and more substantial gates and fences. Third-grade hardwood boards are used in smaller and more economical gates and fences. A softwood grade as low as fourth-grade Common boards may be used, but there is a loss due to cutting out the larger defects.

Scaffolding

Usual requirements: High bending strength, high stiffness, high nail holding, medium weight, and freedom from compression failures and crossgrain.

Woods combining usual requirements in a *high degree:* Douglas fir, western larch, and southern yellow pine.

Woods combining usual requirements in a *good degree:* Redwood, spruce, and west coast hemlock. (Lower bending strength.) Birch, white ash, elm, maple, and oak. (Harder to saw and nail.)

Woods combining usual requirements in a *fair degree:* Sugar pine, ponderosa pine, and Idaho white pine. (Low stiffness and strength.)

Grades used: First-grade softwood dimension is usually required for scaffolding that must support loads under conditions that involve hazards. Light scaffolding may be selected from second-grade softwood dimension; in hardwoods, uprights can be selected from first-grade dimension. Selection should eliminate all pieces with compression failures, large or unsound knots, and crossgrain.

Some state building codes designate the grades to be used for scaffolding. Southern pine and western grading rules include special scaffolding plank grades.

Exposed Porches and Platforms

Usual requirements: High decay resistance, good stiffness and strength for framing, and good wear and splinter resistance for decking. (Where wood is exposed to severe moisture conditions, treated material is recommended.)

Wood combining usual requirements in a *high degree:* Redwood, locust, and white oak. (Heartwood only.)

Woods combining usual requirements in a *good degree:* Cedar, Douglas fir, western larch, southern yellow pine, and rock elm. (Edge grain.)

Grades used: First- or second-grade dimension in softwoods and first-grade dimension in hardwoods are the grades ordinarily used.

Sheathing Papers, Vapor Barriers, and Other Sheet Materials

Sheathing paper and *vapor barriers* have several general uses in the construction of houses and other frame buildings. *For example,* sheathing paper resists moisture and wind infiltration when used over unsheathed walls, over lumber sheathing, over all types of sheathing materials with a stucco exterior finish, and as backing for masonry veneer. The paper for such purposes should be waterproof but of the *breathing* type. This allows any escaped water vapor to move through the paper and minimizes condensation problems. Many types of materials are available for this use, including 15-pound asphalt-saturated felt.

Paper (15- or 30-pound felt) is also used as a roof underlayment for asphalt shingles when roof slopes are less than **7** in **12**. Such protection is usually not needed under wood shingles except as an eave flashing to prevent moisture entry from ice dams.

Roll roofing in 45-pound and heavier weights may be used for roofing small buildings and temporary structures. Built-up roofing, consisting of a number of plies of 15- and 30-pound asphalt-saturated felt, is used on low-pitch or flat roofs. For wood decks, a nailed sheet is placed over the deck before installing alternate layers of felt and asphalt or pitch. This type of roof is usually topped with gravel or crushed stone.

Paper or *deadening felt* is often desirable under finish floor, as it will stop a certain amount of dust and deaden the transfer of sound.

Vapor barriers are used in walls, floors, and ceilings, usually in conjunction with insulation, to minimize the movement of water vapor to cold, exposed surfaces. They consist of plastic films, laminated or coated papers, or aluminum foil. For protection from cold weather condensation, they should be applied as close to the inner warm surface as possible, usually just under the interior coverings. They are also used under concrete slabs to prevent ground moisture from coming through. (*See* Chap. **28**, section on Vapor Barriers.)

Vapor barriers are also used as ground covers in crawl spaces to prevent wood framing and other wood materials from becoming damp from ground moisture. These barrier materials consist of duplex paper with asphalt laminate, plastic films, aluminum foil backed with paper, roll roofing, and various combinations of materials.

DETERMINING MOISTURE CONTENT OF WOOD

It is very difficult to tell how dry a piece of wood is by looking at it or feeling it. How then can a determination be made? Two means of measurement are available: (1) by use of an electric moisture meter or (2) by the ovendrying method. In addition, there is one way of getting an approximation.

The moisture meter is simple and fast to use and permits determination of moisture content without cutting the board. Several models are available. When used on wood with a moisture content below about 30 per cent, these meters can be quite accurate.

The most accurate method of determining moisture content is by ovendrying specimens. This is a standard method by which degree of dryness is expressed for technical and commercial purposes. The procedure involves cutting small sections and weighing them. These sections are dried to constant weight in an oven, reweighed, and the moisture content computed. This method is accurate through the whole range of moisture content. Because of the equipment and time involved, it is used mainly where very exact moisture determinations are necessary.

A rough approximation of moisture content can be made at home by the following procedure.

Select several flat-grained boards from the lumber and cut a sample from each. The sample should measure 1″ along the grain and be cut to include the entire width of the board (at least 6″). It should be cut about 6″ to 8″ from the end of the board. Trim the sample so that it will measure exactly 6″ in width and place it in a warm, dry place such as near the furnace, on a heat duct, on a radiator, or in the oven, and leave it for 48 hours or until it ceases to shrink. Then measure the 6″ dimension to determine how much it has shrunk.

If the wood is classed C in freedom from shrinkage, it should not shrink more than ⅛″ if it is to be used for interior trim or finish, nor over twice that amount (¼″) if it is to be used for framing, coverage, or where it is exposed to the weather.

Woods classed as B in freedom from shrinkage should not shrink over ³⁄₃₂″, and class A woods not over ¹⁄₁₆″ if they are to be used for interior trim, finish, or floors. If they are to be used exposed to the weather, B woods should not shrink more than ³⁄₁₆″, or A woods ⅛″. For lumber under 6″ wide use 3″ samples. The shrinkage should not be over half that shown for flat grain. It is best not to use edge-grained samples or samples shorter than 6″; not only are they more difficult to measure, but they do not give a reliable indication of the adequacy of seasoning.

PROTECTION OF WOOD FROM MOISTURE

Dry wood takes up moisture not only from actual contact with water but also from other sources commonly overlooked. It may collect moisture in the form of vapor from damp air or from damp plaster, concrete, soil, or brickwork. Like many other building materials, wood will absorb moisture that has condensed on it, as well as rain or snow that has entered joints and crevices.

The protection of wood from moisture usually requires that it be kept from contact with soil and water; that free circulation of air be provided in damp areas; and that exposed surfaces be protected with paint, varnish, or other coatings. Protective coatings reduce but do not entirely prevent moisture absorption and, therefore, should not be relied upon to compensate for poor drainage and poor ventilation.

Avoiding contact of wood with moisture is of prime importance in considering construction details. Special care must be used at the grade line of a structure or at any point where moisture might come in. Protection from moisture in the ground should be provided even in temporary or portable buildings.

A little additional care at the start in selection of material and construction details will eliminate the later need for frequent replacement of skids, sills, and framing members (Fig. 2). The use of treated wood sills or placing the structure on masonry blocking for good air circulation is good practice. A ground cover will minimize movement of water vapor from the ground and prevent the wood from retaining high levels of moisture content. Vapor barriers such as polyethylene, roll roofing, or duplex asphalt papers are satisfactory.

Clearance of wood parts above the finish grade and drainage of water away from the building by means of a splash block or tiling are also important factors (Fig. 3). It is difficult to miter siding at corners to prevent moisture entry, especially in the wider patterns. Generally, it is better practice to use corner boards or metal corners. Plant growth against the siding or other wood members should be removed as it encourages moisture retention and possible decay. Downspouts and other attachments should be clear of the siding.

Proper use of vapor barriers in walls and ceilings, in crawl spaces, and under concrete slabs will prevent wood from becoming wet and a possible decay hazard.

Correct construction details at window and door frames to prevent rain leakage and reduce air infiltration are important (Fig. 4). Good carpentry will assure tight joints of the siding at the casing and under the sill. Proper flashing at the drip cap and use of building paper around the framed opening will help as will weatherstripping around the sash. Frames and sash are normally treated with a water-repellent preservative at the factory and paint will provide additional protection.

The cornice and gutter details are important if hazards of poor roof drainage are to be eliminated (Fig. 5). Wide cornices and good drip details eliminate many hazards. A width of roofing paper under the shingles at the cornice and good soffit ventilation, in addition to outlet ventilators, will minimize damage that is often caused by ice dams.

CHAPTER 2

Woodworking Hand Tools and How to Use Them

BASIC TOOLS

Before we describe the various hand tools used in woodworking, the following important facts must be noted by the home craftsman. He should purchase tools of good quality only. The difference in cost between an excellent tool and one of inferior manufacture is negligible when it is realized that the performance of a good tool is far superior to that of a cheap tool. Good tools keep their edges longer, are more easily sharpened, and withstand harder usage.

The following basic tools have, from experience, proved to be adequate for most needs:

Hammer, 16 oz.
Screw drivers, 3″ and 5″
Handsaw
Bit brace, 8″
Auger bits, ¼″ and ¾″
Gimlet bit, ⅜″
Screwdriver bit, ⁵⁄₁₆″
Chisels, ¼″ and ¾″
Pair of pliers

Nail set, ¹⁄₁₆″
Awl
Spokeshave
Vise
Marking gauge
Zigzag rule, 4′
Try and miter square, 7½″
Combination oilstone

Additional tools to be secured as required are:

Hand ripsaw
Compass saw
Coping saw

Jack plane
Gouge chisels, ½″ and 1″
Hand drill

Expansive drill	Glass-cutter
Monkey wrench	Grinding wheel (hand)
Countersink	Handsaw set
Miter box	Files
Steel tape	Carriage makers' clamps
Caliper rule	Hand screws

WOODWORKING HAMMERS

The essential parts of a *claw* hammer, the most commonly used woodworking hammer, are shown in Fig. 1. Other types illustrated are the *ripping, upholsterer's,* and *tack* hammers. Hammer sizes

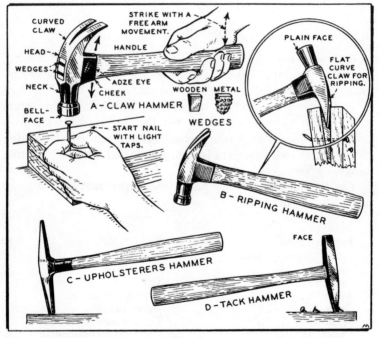

Fig. 1.

are determined by the weight of the head, which ranges from 5 to 28 oz. The heavier hammers are for driving larger nails into soft material or ordinary nails into harder wood. For general use, a 16-oz. hammer is recommended.

Smooth-face hammers are either plain or bell-face. The *bell-face* type is slightly more convex than the *plain*. While the novice cannot drive a nail as straight and as easily with a bell-face hammer, this type is more frequently used because, with a little experience, a nail can be driven flush and sometimes even below the surface of the work without leaving any hammer marks.

Correct method of using a hammer. *Driving nails*—The effectiveness of a hammer is dependent on its weight and the manner in which the blow is struck. To use a hammer correctly, grip it firmly in the right hand, close to the end of handle (Fig. 1). Always strike with a free arm movement. Grasp the nail with the thumb and forefinger of the other hand and place it exactly at the point where it is to be driven. Unless the nail is to be driven at an angle, it should be held perpendicular to the surface of the work. To set the nail, center the face of the hammer on the head of the nail and give it several light taps before removing the fingers. Then drive the nail in as far as desired with a few firm blows, using the center of the hammer face. Nails that do not go in straight or bend shoould be drawn out and thrown away. If, after several attempts, the nail continues to bend or go in crooked, the work should be investigated. If there is a knot or some other obstruction, drill a small hole through the obstruction and then drive the nail through.

Pulling out nails—When nails are pulled out with the claw end of a hammer, the head of the nail should clear the surface of the work sufficiently to permit the claws to grip it. To prevent marring the work and to secure extra and safe leverage, place a small block of wood under the head of the hammer as shown in Fig. 2. Be careful to place the block of wood in the correct position, that is, against the nail, to avoid enlarging the hole from which the nail is pulled.

Clinching nails—For added holding power, nails are sometimes *clinched*. The nails used for clinching must be long enough to penetrate the wood so that at least an inch and a half of the point protrudes from the underside. The protruding point is then bent over in direct line with the grain of the wood and hammered flat. When clinching nails, rest the work on a solid surface and be careful to avoid splitting the wood (Fig. 2).

Toenailing—Driving nails obliquely is called *toenailing*. This type of nailing is employed when the end of one piece of wood is fastened to the side of another, as shown in Fig. 2.

Driving corrugated fasteners—Corrugated fasteners, as shown in Fig. 2, are often called *wiggle nails*. They are used to a large extent in the making of screens and picture frames and for similar purposes. They are procurable with either a plain or saw edge.

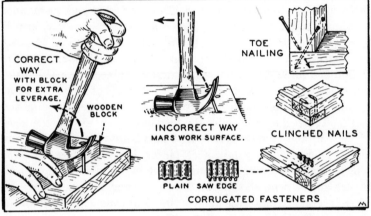

CORRECT WAY WITH BLOCK FOR EXTRA LEVERAGE.

WOODEN BLOCK

INCORRECT WAY MARS WORK SURFACE.

TOE NAILING

CLINCHED NAILS

PLAIN   SAW EDGE

CORRUGATED FASTENERS

Fig. 2.

The *plain-edged* fastener is used for hard wood; the *saw-edged* type for soft wood. When driving corrugated fasteners, use a medium-weight hammer. Strike evenly distributed light blows. It is important that the lumber being fastened together rest on a solid surface while the work is being done.

Ripping—To rip woodwork apart, insert the claw part of a *ripping* hammer into a crack as near to a nail as possible. Use a quick, jolting movement to loosen each nail. Pull out the nails as previously described. Then rip out the boards or woodwork as required (Fig. 1).

Replacing a broken hammer handle—Machine-made hickory handles in various sizes can be secured at most hardware stores. The portion of the broken handle that remains in the hammer head must be removed. The simplest and most effective method of doing this is to drill through it with a twist drill to remove as much wood as possible. It is then easy to split out several small pieces and thus remove the old wedged-in handle.

The end of a new handle is usually larger than required and must be scraped or pared slightly before it will fit into the head of the hammer. However, do not pare it too much, since it must fit very tightly. After the small fitted end of the handle is inserted into the opening in the head of the hammer, tamp the other end of the handle against a solid surface until the head is in place. To prevent the head of the hammer from flying off, the end of the handle must be expanded, after it is in place in the hammer head, by inserting several wooden or metal wedges (Fig. 1). Wooden wedges can be made of either maple or hickory wood. Metal wedges can be secured at any hardware store and are preferable. Do not insert the wedges until the head is on the handle as far as it can go. When using wooden wedges, make a saw cut about as long as the wedge in the end of the handle before inserting it into the head of the hammer. Saw cuts are not necessary when using metal wedges.

HANDSAWS

The essential parts of a handsaw are shown in Fig. 3.

There are many types and sizes of handsaws. The ripsaw and the crosscut saw are most commonly used.

The *ripsaw* is designed specifically for cutting with the grain (Fig. 3). The teeth of the ripsaw are set alternately, that is, one tooth is bent slightly to the left and the next one to the right for the entire length of the saw to give the proper clearance when cutting through the work. A good ripsaw usually has five and one-half points to every inch, with each tooth acting like a vertical chisel, chipping out a small portion of the wood from the *kerf*, or cut.

Crosscut saws are designed to cut against, or across, the grain of the wood. The teeth of a crosscut saw are ground to a *true taper* for the additional clearance required when cutting across the grain. The front faces of the teeth have an angle of 15°, and the backs have an angle of 45°. The upper halves of the teeth are set alternately to the right and to the left to insure proper clearance. The teeth of a crosscut saw have an action similar to that of a chisel (Fig. 3).

The *backsaw* is useful for all types of cabinetwork. Its fine teeth and stiff back make possible the smooth, accurate cutting

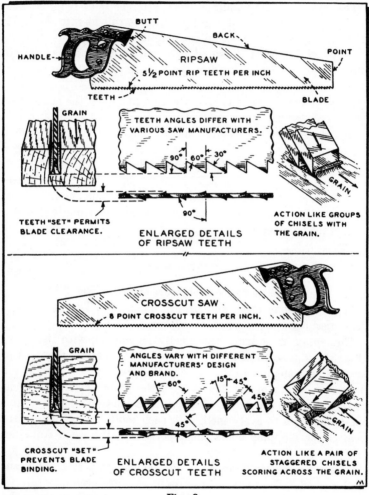

Fig. 3.

necessary for making joints. It is the ideal saw to use for cutting light stock, such as moldings and screen and picture frames. Back-saws are available in 8″, 10″, 12″, 14″, and 16″ lengths, with from 12 to 16 points to the inch. The 12″ length, with 14 points to the inch, is the most popular size (Fig. 4).

There are a great many uses for a *compass saw* in the home

workshop. It may be used for cutting curves and circles and for starting a cut from a hole bored in wood (Fig. 5). It is extremely useful for cutting holes in board and plaster walls and in floor boards to receive gas or water pipes. The compass saw is taper-ground from the tooth edge to a thin back, allowing for clearance. It also tapers to a sharp point and is toothed to the point for easy access to holes and for cutting sharp curves.

An ideal type is an interchangeable compass saw. Different lengths and types of blades are available for it and the handle can be adjusted to any convenient angle. The three blades shown in Fig. 5 can be used for a variety of purposes. The *compass* blade in the center of the illustration is 14″ long, with 8 points to the inch, and can be used for cutting curves and shapes in material up to ⅜″ thick.

Fig. 4. Backsaw.

Fig. 5. Compass saw.

The top blade, known as a *pruning* blade, is 16″ long and, in addition to being used for pruning trees, can also be employed as a general-purpose saw. The other blade in the set is a *keyhole* blade, 10″ long, 10 points to the inch. It can be used for cutting keyholes, sharp curves, and similar small work.

The *keyhole saw* is a special-purpose saw for cutting keyholes and for doing all kinds of cutout pattern, or fretwork, and similar light work. (Fig. 6).

The *coping* saw is designed for cutting curves (Fig. 7). It is

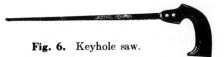

Fig. 6. Keyhole saw.

also used for shaping the ends of molding, for scrollwork, and similar light work on thin wood or plastic. It has very narrow blades, only ⅛″ wide, fitted at each end with a pin that is inserted in a stretcher at each end of the frame. A square nut forced into the handle engages the threaded end of the stretcher. By turning the handle, the blade is tautened. The blade, when stretched tight in the frame, may be turned as required for cutting sharp angles. The frame of a coping saw should be made of good steel. It is usually ⅜″ wide, 3/16″ thick, and 4½″ deep from the tooth edge to the inside of the back. The blades of a coping saw should be made of good spring steel ⅛″ wide, 17 points to the inch, and 67/16″ in length from pin to pin.

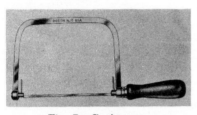

Fig. 7. Coping saw.

Using a handsaw. Each type of saw is designed for a specific purpose and should be used for that purpose only. If you value your tools and the material on which you are working, never use a crosscut saw for work that requires a ripsaw, or vice versa. Ripsaws are specifically designed to cut with the grain of the wood. This is called *ripping*. Crosscut saws are designed for *crosscutting* (sawing against the grain).

To hold a saw properly, grasp the handle firmly with the right hand, with the thumb and index finger touching the sides of the handle (Fig. 8). This grip makes it easy to guide the direction of the saw cut. Always start a saw cut with an upward stroke, using the thumb of the left hand to guide the saw. Never under any circumstances start a saw cut with a downstroke. Draw the saw slowly upward several times at the point where the cut is to be made (Fig. 8). Do this very slowly or your saw will jump; instead of a well-cut piece of lumber you will have a badly cut thumb. When the line of cut has been started properly, proceed to cut on the downstroke.

For ripping, use a ripsaw to permit long, easy strokes. Cutting with just a few inches of blade in the middle of the saw usually makes it difficult to keep the line of cut straight. When ripping lumber, support the work on sawhorses, and start the cut by using the finer teeth at the end of the blade. If the work cannot be supported on sawhorses, place it in a vise. A cutting angle of 60° between the edge of the saw and the face of the work gives best results (Fig. 8).

To begin a crosscut, rest the blade on the waste side of the line of cut, support the side of the blade with the thumb, and draw the saw upward a few times until a slight groove appears (Fig. 8).

When either crosscutting or ripping, it is good practice to cut on the outer, or waste, side of a line; do not attempt to saw directly on the line.

In crosscutting, 45° is the proper angle to maintain between the saw and the face of the work. Extending the forefinger along the side of the handle aids considerably in guiding the blade (Fig. 8). Take long, easy strokes to utilize a maximum of the saw's cutting edge. Always keep saw square with surface of wood (Fig. 9).

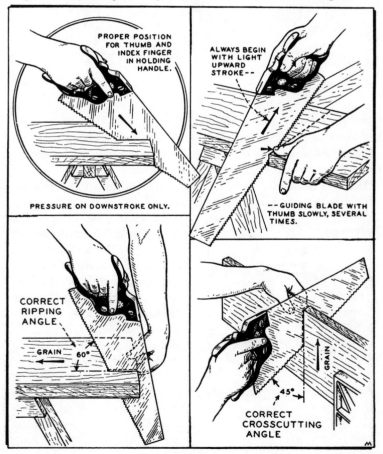

Fig. 8.

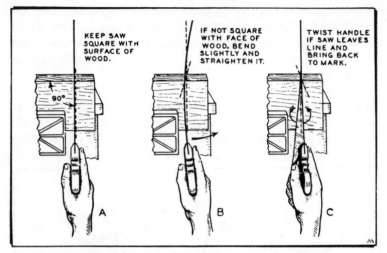

KEEP SAW SQUARE WITH SURFACE OF WOOD.

IF NOT SQUARE WITH FACE OF WOOD, BEND SLIGHTLY AND STRAIGHTEN IT.

TWIST HANDLE IF SAW LEAVES LINE AND BRING BACK TO MARK.

90°

A   B   C

Fig. 9.

When the cut is nearly completed, support the piece to prevent the wood from splintering on the underside. Never twist the piece off with the saw blade or in any other way; cut right through to the end, using light final strokes to avoid splitting.

Using a backsaw. When using a backsaw in a miter box, be sure that the work lines up with the slots in the box. Hold the

work against the back of the box (Fig. 10). Start the cut carefully with a backstroke, holding the handle of the saw slightly upward. As the cutting proceeds, level the saw gradually and continue cutting with the blade horizontal. Hold the saw firmly for clean, straight, accurate cutting.

If a miter box is not used, it is advisable to support the work with a bench hook. For long material, two bench hooks are necessary. A bench hook

Fig. 10. Using a backsaw in a miter box.

and its use is shown in Figs. 11 and 12.

Using a coping saw. A *coping* saw is used to cut curves and intricate patterns in thin wood or plastic. The correct position for use is shown in Fig. 13. A coping saw is generally used with a saddle to support the work. The *saddle* consists of a board cut

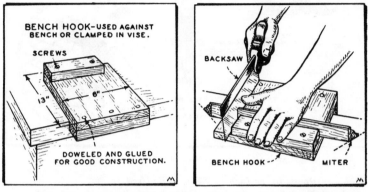

BENCH HOOK–USED AGAINST BENCH OR CLAMPED IN VISE.

SCREWS

13"

6"

DOWELED AND GLUED FOR GOOD CONSTRUCTION.

BACKSAW

BENCH HOOK

MITER

Fig. 11. Bench hook.   **Fig. 12.** Using bench hook.

with a V-notch, about 3″ wide and 3½″ deep, attached to a support. Hold the blade so that it moves vertically. Cutting strokes should be as long as possible to avoid overheating the blade. In cutting scrollwork, furniture overlay, and similar articles, the piece marked with the design to be cut out is held on the saddle and shifted so that the saw can cut along the curves as it progresses. To avoid breakage of blades, change the angle of the blade in the frame when making sharp turns.

Fig. 13. Coping saw.

Setting and sharpening a handsaw. A good saw is a fine tool and will give a lifetime of service if properly handled. The saw teeth will require setting and sharpening from time to time. This may seem to be an involved operation, but if directions are followed carefully, it is not difficult.

A special *saw clamp* (Fig. 14) and several files are all the equipment needed. The following table indicates the file to be used.

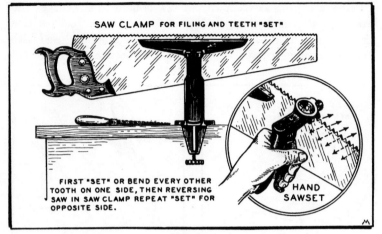

SAW CLAMP FOR FILING AND TEETH "SET"

FIRST "SET" OR BEND EVERY OTHER TOOTH ON ONE SIDE, THEN REVERSING SAW IN SAW CLAMP REPEAT "SET" FOR OPPOSITE SIDE.

HAND SAWSET

Fig. 14.

Points to the Inch	File to Be Used
4½, 5, 6	7" slim taper
7, 8	6" slim taper
9, 10	5" to 5½" slim taper
11, 12, 13, 14, 15	4½" slim taper
16 or more	4½" or 5" superfine, No. 2 cut
For jointing teeth	8" or 10" mill bastard

Examine the teeth of the saw to see if they are uniform in size and shape and are properly set. A good saw will not need resetting of the teeth every time it is sharpened. If the teeth are touched up occasionally with a file of the proper size, they will cut longer and better and retain sufficient set to enable the saw to clear itself. The proper amount of set is shown in Fig. 15.

Before proceeding to set and sharpen a handsaw, study the shape of the teeth. The teeth of saws for crosscutting and for ripping should be similar to those shown at *A* and *B* in Fig. 15. A saw cannot do a good cutting job unless the teeth are even and properly shaped. If the teeth are found to be uneven, it is necessary to joint and file them, using the following procedure.

Jointing handsaw teeth. *Jointing*, or filing, the teeth to the same shape and height is necessary when they are uneven or incorrectly shaped or when the tooth edges are not straight, or slightly breasted. Unless the teeth are regular in size and shape it is wasted effort to set and file a saw.

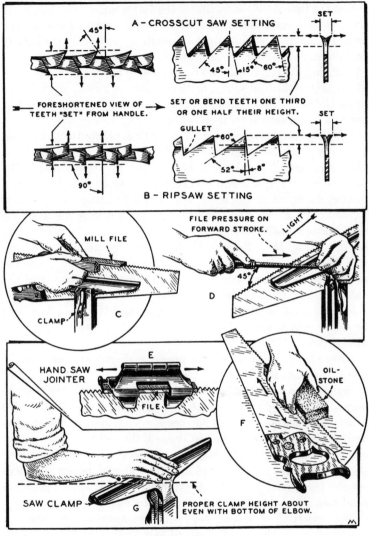

Fig. 15.

To joint a saw, place it in a saw clamp, with the handle of the saw to the right (*C* and *G*, Fig. 15). Lay a mill file, of the proper size, flat lengthwise on the teeth. Pass it lightly back and forth across the tips of all the teeth, for the full length of the blade. If the teeth are very uneven, it is better not to make all of them the same height the first time they are jointed. Joint only the highest teeth first, then shape the teeth that have been jointed. Proceed by jointing the teeth a second time, passing the file along the tops of all the teeth until every tooth is touched by the file. Never allow the file to tip to one side or the other—always file flat. The use of a handsaw jointer is shown at *E*, Fig. 15.

Shaping handsaw teeth. After jointing, proceed with *shaping* the teeth. All the teeth must be filed to the correct shape, with all the gullets of equal depth (Fig. 15). The fronts and backs must have the proper shape and angle. The teeth must be uniform in size, disregarding the bevel, which will be taken care of later. To bring the gullets down to equal depth, place the file well into each gullet and file straight across the saw at right angles to the blade (*D*, Fig. 15). Never hold the file at any other angle during this operation. If the teeth are of unequal size, file in turn the ones with the largest tops until the file reaches the center of the flat top made by jointing; then move the file to the next gullet. File until the rest of the top disappears and the tooth has been brought up to a point. Do not attempt to bevel any of the teeth at this time.

After all the teeth have been properly shaped and are even in height, the next step is setting the teeth.

Setting handsaw teeth. As mentioned previously, the teeth of a good handsaw do not need to be reset every time they require a little sharpening. If it is not necessary to joint and shape the teeth, carefully examine the saw to see if the teeth have the proper amount of *set* (*A* and *B*, Fig. 15). If they have the proper set, the saw is ready for filing; if not, they should be set. Always set the teeth after they have been jointed and shaped but before final filing, to avoid injury to the cutting edges.

The operation of setting saw teeth has a distinct purpose. *A* and *B*, Fig. 15, show end views of saw teeth; the teeth of both crosscut saws and ripsaws are sprung alternately left and right (not more than half the length of each tooth) for the entire length of the tooth edge of the saw. This arrangement enables the saw to cut a kerf, or path, slightly wider than the thickness of the blade itself, giving the necessary clearance and preventing any friction that would cause the saw to bind in the cut. The depth of the set should never exceed half the tooth, whether the saw is fine or coarse. A taper-ground saw requires very little set, because its blade tapers thinner both toward the back and along the back toward the point, thus providing sufficient clearance for easy running.

The simplest method of setting a saw is by the use of a special tool known as a *saw set* (Fig. 16). Fasten the saw in the saw clamp, as shown in Fig. 14. Start at one end of the saw and place the saw set over the first tooth bent away from you. The plunger in the saw set should strike the tooth firmly and squarely. Holding the saw set firmly in place, compress the handle: the tooth will then bend against the saw clamp. Work across the entire length of the saw and set alternate teeth. Reverse the saw in the clamp and set the remaining teeth in the same manner. With the saw still in the clamp, joint the teeth by

Fig. 16. Saw set.

lightly rubbing a file lengthwise over them until they all have flat tops, which will provide a proper guide for filing.

Extreme care must be taken to see that the set is even and regular. It must be the same width from end to end of the blade and the same width on both sides of the blade, otherwise the saw will run out of line and cuts made with it will not be true. After the saw has been properly set, the next step is to file the teeth.

Filing handsaw teeth. The type of file to use for filing the teeth is determined by the number of tooth points to the inch. For a crosscut saw, measure one inch from the point of any tooth. For a ripsaw having 5½ or fewer points to the inch, the teeth near the point of the blade are finer than the rest; therefore measure the regular-size teeth at the butt of the blade. For the best working position, align the top of the clamp with the elbow. Place the saw in the clamp with its handle at the right. Allow the bottom gullets to protrude $\frac{1}{8}''$ above the jaws of the clamp, otherwise the file will chatter or screech.

Filing a crosscut saw. To file a crosscut saw, stand at the first position shown in Fig. 17. Start at the point and pick out the first tooth that is set toward you. Hold the file in the position shown in the illustration. Place the file in the gullet to the left of the tooth, holding it directly across the blade. Swing the file handle left to the correct angle, as shown in Fig. 17. Hold

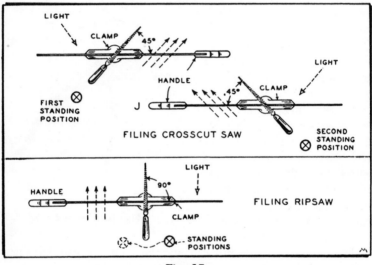

Fig. 17.

the file level and maintain this angle; never allow it to tip either upward or downward. Be certain at all times that the file is set well down into the gullet. Let it find its own bearing against the teeth it touches. For guidance in filing, study and duplicate the shape and bevel of some of the least-used teeth, those near the handle end.

File on the push stroke only: the back of the left tooth and the front of the right tooth are thus filed simultaneously. File the teeth until half of the flat tops previously made on them are cut away; then lift the file from the gullet. Skip the next gullet to the right and place the file in the second gullet toward the handle. Repeat the filing operation as previously described, filing at the same angle as for the first set of two teeth. Proceed by placing the file in every second gullet until the handle end of the saw has been reached.

For the second position, turn the saw around in the clamp with the handle to the left. Take the position shown in Fig. 17 and place the file in the gullet to the right of the first tooth set toward you. This is the first of the gullets skipped when the reverse side of the saw was filed. Now turn the file handle to the desired angle toward the right. Proceed to file until the other half of the flat top made on each tooth as a guide has been cut away and the tooth is sharpened to a point. Continue by placing the file in every second gullet until the handle of the saw is reached.

Be sure that in the final sharpening all the teeth are of the same size and height, otherwise the saw will not cut satisfactorily. When teeth are of uneven sizes, stress is placed on the larger or higher teeth, thus causing the saw to jump or bind in the kerf.

Filing a ripsaw. The procedure for filing ripsaws is similar to that for crosscut saws, with a single exception (Fig. 17). Ripsaws are filed with the file held straight across the saw at a right angle to the blade. Place the file in the gullet so as to give the front of each tooth an angle of 8° and the back an angle of 52°. Place the saw in the clamp with the handle toward the right. Place the file in the gullet to the left of the first tooth set toward you. Continue by placing the file in every second gullet and filing straight across. When the handle of the saw is reached, turn the saw around in the clamp. Start at the point again, placing the file in the first gullet that was previously skipped when filing from the other side. Continue to file in every second gullet to the handle end of the saw.

One final precaution: never try to avoid reversing the saw in the clamp or attempt to file all the teeth from the same side of the blade. This procedure is certain to make the saw run to one side.

Angle and bevel of teeth. The angle of the teeth in crosscut saws is of great importance. Imagine that Fig. 18 is a board, across which a deep mark with the point of a knife is to be made. If the knife is held nearly perpendicular, as at *B*, it will pull harder and will not cut so smoothly as when it is inclined forward, as at *A*. It follows, then, that the cutting edge of the crosscut saw should be at an acute angle, as at *C*, rather than perpendicular, as at *D*.

The angles of 15° front and 15° back for crosscut saws, and

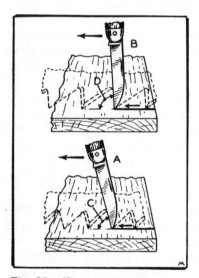

8° front and 52° back for ripsaws, as set at the factory, prove most satisfactory for general use. When a saw has less angle at the front of the teeth than specified above, it is said to have more *hook* or *pitch*. If too much hook is given to the teeth, the saw often takes hold too keenly, causing it to "hand up" or stick suddenly in the cut, thus kinking the blade. When there is too much set, the teeth may be broken, as the resulting strain is out of proportion to the strength of the blade.

Fig. 18. Shapes and angles of saw teeth.

In filing saws for crosscutting, the file is held at an angle; therefore the teeth are given an angle. This angle on the front and back of the teeth is called *bevel*.

How to bevel teeth. The proper amount of bevel to give the teeth is important. If there is too much bevel, the points of the teeth will score so deeply that the wood fibers severed from the stock will not clear and will have to be removed with a file or rasp. In Fig. 19, *B* shows a tooth (enlarged) of a crosscut saw with the same amount of bevel front and back; suitable for softwoods where rapid work is required.

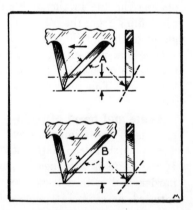

Fig. 19. Bevel of teeth.

A, in Fig. 19, shows a tooth (enlarged) of a saw suitable for medium hardwoods. It has less bevel on the back, which gives a shorter bevel to the point, as at *B*.

These illustrations show that the bevel on the front of the teeth is about the same, but the bevel of the point (looking lengthwise along the blade) is quite different, depending on the difference in the angles of the backs of the teeth. Experience will indicate what bevel is best.

For the beginner, the instructions given under Filing the Teeth should be followed carefully.

Side-dressing saws. After jointing, setting, and filing the saw, side-dress it by laying it on a flat surface and lightly rubbing the sides of the teeth with an oilstone as shown in *F*, Fig. 15.

SCREWDRIVERS

Types of screwdrivers. There are many sizes and several types of screwdrivers. The size is always given by the length of the blade: a 6″ screwdriver has a 6″ blade, and so on. Narrow-tipped blades are designed for small screws, and blades with larger tips for heavier screws. The following types are in general use: common screwdriver, ratchet, spiral ratchet, offset, Phillips.

Common screwdriver—The common screwdriver is available in many sizes, each for a specific size of screw. The various parts of a common screwdriver are shown in Fig. 20.

Ratchet and spiral ratchet screwdrivers—Two variations of the common screwdriver are shown in Fig. 21. They are the ratchet and the spiral ratchet types. Similar in operation to the common screwdriver, the ratchet type drives screws in much faster and works semiautomatically. Blades of various sizes can be secured for both types of ratchet screwdriver, and both types can be set for driving screws in or extracting them. The handle of the ratchet screwdriver turns back and forth in the direction set.

The spiral ratchet screwdriver operates even faster than the ratchet. It can be set for either in or out. To drive the screw, set the blade in the screw slot and push on the handle, steadying the blade with the other hand. The blade makes several turns for each push.

Offset screwdriver—Offset screwdrivers are designed for driving screws located where there is insufficient space to use the conventional type of screwdriver (Fig. 22). The offset screwdriver is made from a piece of either round or octagonal steel with two

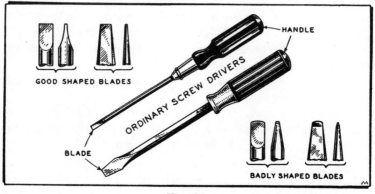

Fig. 20.

blades at right angles to one another and to the shaft at opposite ends. When screws have to be driven in or extracted in inaccessible places, it is sometimes necessary to use both ends of the

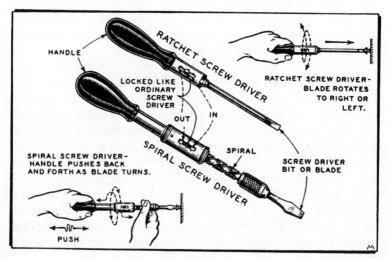

Fig. 21.

offset screwdriver, turning the screw a short distance with one end and then with the other.

Phillips screwdriver—The Phillips screwdriver is used only for driving the Phillips screw (Fig. 22). Phillips screws have a head with two V-slots which cross at the center. The tip of the Phillips screwdriver blade is shaped like a pointed or beveled cross to fit into these slots. To keep the blade in the cross slots of the

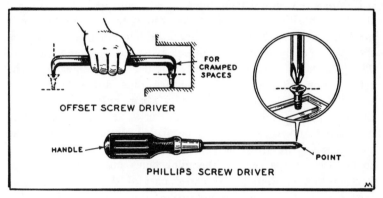

FOR CRAMPED SPACES

OFFSET SCREW DRIVER

HANDLE

POINT

PHILLIPS SCREW DRIVER

Fig. 22.

screw more downward pressure is used. Phillips screws are used to a great extent in radio sets, on moldings, the trim of automobiles, and furniture and cabinetwork. This type of screwdriver cannot slip out of the slot or otherwise damage expensive finishes.

Correct method of using a screwdriver. Choose the right size of screw and screwdriver, and be sure to use the longest screwdriver that is available and convenient for the particular job. The blade of the screwdriver must fit the screw slots. It must be neither too small nor too large. If it is too small, the blade may break. If it is too large, it may slip out and mar the surface of the wood.

The quickest way to ruin any screwdriver is to use it as a can opener, a putty- or paint-mixer, or as a lever.

The tip of a screwdriver must be square. A round-tipped screwdriver is dangerous: it is apt to slip when driving a screw, causing serious injury.

When driving screws with a common screwdriver, grasp the

handle with the thumb side of the hand toward the blade. Use automatic screwdrivers according to directions given by the manufacturer of each type. Place the screw in the pilot hole, hold it straight with the left hand, set the blade in the slot, and start turning the screwdriver, exerting pressure with the right hand. As soon as the screw has taken hold of the wood, remove the left hand, and continue driving the screw in. Hold the screwdriver steady, with the blade in a direct, straight line with the screw.

Before screws are driven, pilot holes should be bored. Locate the exact positions for the screws, and with a small *brad awl* mark the places. For small screws, the holes can be bored with the awl. For large screws, bits or twist drills should be used. The pilot holes should be slightly smaller in diameter than the screw. For softwoods, such as spruce, pine, and similar types, the pilot holes should be bored only about half as deep as the threaded part of the screw. For hardwoods, such as maple, birch, oak, and mahogany, they must be drilled almost as deep as the screw itself. In hardwood, if the screw is large or if you happen to be using brass screws, the pilot holes must first be bored slightly smaller than the threaded part of the screw, then enlarged at the top with a second drill of the same diameter as the unthreaded portion of the screw.

When two pieces of wood are to be fastened together with screws, two sets of holes must be drilled. The top piece is clamped to the lower piece only by the pressure of the screw head, and for this reason the holes are drilled so that the threaded portion of the screw takes hold of only the under piece of the wood. Locate the positions for the screws and mark each with a brad awl. Bore the pilot hole of smaller diameter than the threaded portion of the screw. This pilot hole must be bored all the way through the upper piece of the wood and for about half the length of the threaded part of the screw into the lower piece. Enlarge the pilot hole in the upper piece of wood to the same diameter as the unthreaded portion of the screw. Countersink the clearance hole in the upper piece of wood. Drive all of the screws firmly into place; then tighten each consecutively.

Where flathead or oval-head screws are used, the upper end of the pilot hole should be bored out or countersunk to match in size the diameter of the heads of the screws that are used. Coun-

tersinking is a simple operation, and the tool used is called a
countersink (Fig. 23), its size depending on the size of the screw.
It fits into a brace (Fig. 23).

Driving screws into hardware, hinges, and handles. While
steel screws are used generally in woodworking, brass screws also
are used to some extent for fastening small hinges and hardware
on cabinets and furniture. General directions for the use of
brass screws are approximately the same as for steel screws.

Directions for fastening hinges and other types of hardware, where a recess must be made before the fixtures can be mounted, are described in Chap. 3, devoted to hanging doors and similar work.

When the work does not need to be recessed, place the hardware in the required position and mark the screw holes with a brad awl. Bore the pilot
holes, following the directions given in the previous paragraphs
on the Correct Method of Using a Screwdriver. Where screws
are short, only a pilot hole is needed, but long screws require a
clearance hole of the same diameter and length as the unthreaded
part of the screw.

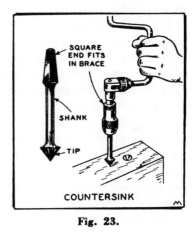

Fig. 23.

Use the largest size of screw that will slip easily through the
holes in the hardware. If the holes in the hardware are countersunk, oval-head or flathead screws to fit the countersink should
be used; if they are not countersunk, use round-head screws. Do
not tighten the screws until all of them have been driven in.

Concealing screws with plugs. It is sometimes necessary to
set screws below the surface of the wood and to conceal them with
a plug of the same type of wood. For instance, the planking on
boats is usually fastened to the frames in this manner. Wooden
plugs of various diameters, made from mahogany, oak, pine,
cedar, and cypress, can be bought from dealers in boat supplies
for this purpose.

To conceal screws with wooden plugs, bore a hole with the bit and brace to fit the plug, then bore the pilot and clearance holes for the screws, and drive the screws into place. To insure a tight fit, put glue or wood filler in the plug hole and drive in the plug with a hammer. When the glue or filler is set, pare off the top of the plugs with a chisel, and sandpaper it even with the surface of the work.

Removing tight screws. To remove a tight screw, use a screwdriver that has a blade with parallel sides, and fits the screw slot perfectly. If the right size and shape of screwdriver is not used, the screw becomes "chewed," making the job more difficult. A tight screw sometimes can be started by giving it a slight twist in a clockwise direction, that is, the same direction which drives it in. If this does not help, twist the screw both ways, backing it out as far as it will go easily, and then turning it part way back in again. Each time this is repeated, the screw usually will back out a little farther until it is all the way out. In some cases, a screw with a damaged slot can be backed partly out, and then turned the rest of the way with a pair of pliers.

Dressing screwdriver blades. A screwdriver is not a cutting tool and for that reason does not have to be sharpened, but it must be dressed or kept in condition. This is done by occasionally grinding it on an emery wheel or by filing the blade with a flat file. Correct and incorrect shapes for a screwdriver are shown in Fig. 20.

When dressing a screwdriver with a file, hold the screwdriver in a vise and file the tip absolutely straight across both ends, at right angles to the shank and the sides, with the faces near the tip as parallel as possible to each other (Fig. 24). Never bevel or round the tip of a screwdriver.

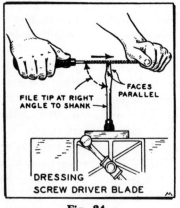

FILE TIP AT RIGHT ANGLE TO SHANK

FACES PARALLEL

DRESSING SCREW DRIVER BLADE

Fig. 24.

When using an emery wheel for dressing a screwdriver, do not hold the blade against the wheel too long, or the friction wheel will heat the steel and draw the temper or soften the blade. When dressing a screwdriver, dip the blade in water at frequent intervals.

PLANES

Planes are used for roughing down the surface of lumber and as finishing tools. They are classified as either *bench* or *block*. The bench plane is always used with the grain of the wood; the block plane for cutting across the grain. Bench planes are made in several types, each of which has outstanding features.

The bench planes in common use are the *smoothing, jack, fore,* and *jointer types* (Fig. 25). The smoothing plane, the shortest of these, is used for finishing or leveling flat surfaces after the rough surface and unevenness has been removed with a jack plane. It is handy to use where only small areas are to be leveled off, as its short length makes it simple to locate and remedy these uneven spots.

The smoothing plane is smaller than a jack plane, but considerably larger than the block plane. It does not cut the end grain of lumber as well as a block plane. It ranges in size from 5½" to 10" in length and is made like a jack plane, but has a shorter sole or bottom. A plane-iron cap to coil and break the shavings is attached to the plane iron. The cutting edge on the blade of a smoothing plane must be set rather close to make a fairly fine shaving.

A fore plane is merely a shorter type of jointer plane, and is sometimes preferable because of its light weight. When it is necessary to true up edges of boards preparatory to fitting them closely or jointing them, the jointer plane is used. These four types of planes are shown in Fig. 25.

Roughing or scrub plane. When more than ¼" of waste is to be removed from a board, a *roughing* or *scrub* plane is used. This plane is available in two sizes, 9½" and 10½" long. A roughing or scrub plane is equipped with heavy rounded blades. It is used to clean up rough, dirty timber and to true up large pieces of wood to approximate size, preliminary to doing a finish job with either the smoothing or jack plane.

Circular plane. This special-type plane has a flexible steel bottom which is adjustable to form a curve for planing either

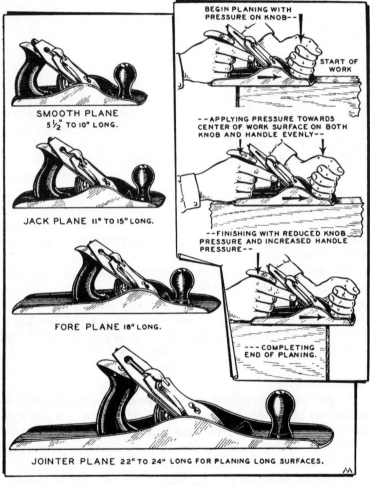

SMOOTH PLANE
5½" TO 10" LONG.

JACK PLANE 11" TO 15" LONG.

FORE PLANE 18" LONG.

JOINTER PLANE 22" TO 24" LONG FOR PLANING LONG SURFACES.

BEGIN PLANING WITH PRESSURE ON KNOB--

START OF WORK

--APPLYING PRESSURE TOWARDS CENTER OF WORK SURFACE ON BOTH KNOB AND HANDLE EVENLY--

--FINISHING WITH REDUCED KNOB PRESSURE AND INCREASED HANDLE PRESSURE--

---COMPLETING END OF PLANING.

Fig. 25.

concave or convex surfaces down to a minimum radius of 20″.

Rabbet plane. Rabbet planes are used to cut out *rabbets,* which are rectangular recesses at the ends or edges of a plank to form what is known as a *rabbet joint.* Rabbet joints are described more fully in Chap. 3 (page 125). The sole, or bottom, of this plane is cut away so that the edge of the cutting iron is in line with the side of the plane. When fitted with a special iron called a *spur*, the rabbet plane can be used also for planing across the grain (Fig. 26).

Modelmaker's plane. The *modelmaker's* plane, also called a *violin* plane, is only 3″ to 4″ in length. The sole is curved in both directions and the blade is rounded, conforming to the same

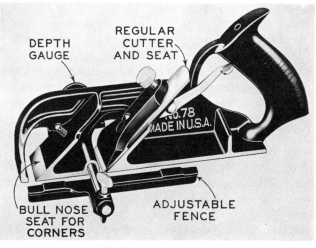

DEPTH GAUGE

REGULAR CUTTER AND SEAT

NO.78 MADE IN U.S.A.

BULL NOSE SEAT FOR CORNERS

ADJUSTABLE FENCE

Fig. 26. Parts of a rabbet plane.

curvature. It can be used to remove excess wood from a flat, convex, or concave surface of any radius down to a minimum of 12″. It is used by patternmakers, violin- and other instrument-makers, and professional modelbuilders. It can be bought only on special order.

Spokeshave. While a spokeshave is not strictly a plane, it sometimes is used for the same purpose and in the same manner. It is an excellent tool for shaping curved pieces.

Adjustment of plane irons. A plane is a cutting tool set in a block of metal or wood which serves to act as a guide to regulate the depth of the cut. The plane iron, a chisel-like tool, does the actual cutting. Like all cutting tools, it must have a keen, sharp edge and be adjusted correctly.

Bench planes, that is, the smoothing, fore, jointer, and jack planes, have a plane-iron cap clamped to the cutting blade to stiffen the iron and break and curve the shavings as they come up through the throat of the tool. The position of the cap in relation to the plane iron is adjustable by loosening the clamping screw. In general, the edge of the cap should be about $\frac{1}{16}''$ back of the cutting edge of the iron. To regulate the thickness of shavings, turn the plane upside down, holding the knob in the left hand and the handle in the right. Look along the bottom of the plane, and with the right hand begin turning the adjusting screw until the blade projects about the thickness of a hair. Then turn the adjusting lever left or right to straighten the blade: the blade should never be at an angle.

In block planes, the blade is locked in position by a lever cap or by a cam lever, which differ slightly in planes produced by different companies. Moving the lever-cap screw, or the lever, in one direction locks the plane iron; moving it in the opposite direction unlocks the iron when it is necessary to remove it from the plane. By means of an adjusting screw, the sharpened lower edge of the plane iron can be moved in and out of the mouth of the plane. A block-plane iron is beveled on only one side of the sharpened edge, and it is set in the frame of the plane with the bevel up.

To adjust a block plane, hold it up with the toe, or front, of the plane facing forward, and the bottom level with the eye. To regulate the thickness of shavings, turn the adjusting screw until the sharp edge of the iron projects slightly through the sole. This is called a vertical adjustment. To produce even shavings, a lateral adjustment is made by loosening slightly the lever-cap screw or the lever cam. Sight along the bottom of the plane. Press the upper end of the blade near the adjustment screw either to the right or left to bring the cutting edge of the blade parallel to the bottom of the plane. Never set one corner of the blade farther out of the throat of the plane than the other. Do not set the blade too far out of the throat; it should project just enough for the edge to be visible and to be felt with the fingertips (Figs. 27 and 28).

Correct method of using a plane. Grasp the handle of the plane with the right hand, holding the knob firmly between the thumb and forefinger of the left hand, with the finger joints of the left hand protruding slightly over the edge of the plane. At

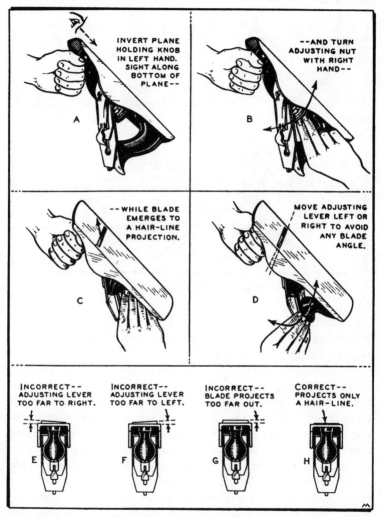

Fig. 27. Adjusting a plane.

the beginning of each stroke, the pressure and driving force is exerted by the left hand. As the stroke progresses, the pressure of the left hand is gradually lessened, and that of the right hand correspondingly increased until the pressure from both of the hands is approximately equal. Continue increasing the pressure

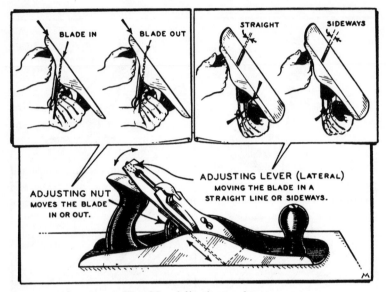

Fig. 28. Adjusting a plane.

from the right hand. At the end of the cut, the right hand will be exerting the power and driving the plane, while the left hand will be guiding the tool (Fig. 26).

When planing, always hold the plane level. If the plane is tilted, it will produce uneven, thick shavings and ruin the trueness of the work. To avoid dulling the cutter unnecessarily, lift the plane above the work on all return strokes. When working on long surfaces, begin at the right-hand side of the board, taking a few strokes; then step forward and take the same number of strokes, repeating until the entire surface of the board has been planed, always *with* the grain. As the work progresses, use a try square and level to determine the accuracy. For the first cuts on any wide surface, a jack plane should be used. Its long face rides over the low spots and dresses down the higher ones. The cutter on a jack plane is ground in a slightly convex form, which facilitates the removal of thick shavings, and at the same time avoids a rectangular shaving that would tend to choke up the throat of the plane. Thus all parts of the blade coming in contact with the work cut smooth, even shavings. This important fact is also true of the cutter on a fore plane, except convexity is slightly less. The convex cutters of both planes will leave a series of slight grooves, but these are easily removed with either a smoothing or a jointer plane.

For cutting against the grain, the block plane is used. Only one hand is employed; grasp the sides of the tool between the thumb and the second and third fingers, with the forefinger resting in the hollow of the finger rest at the front of the tool, and with the lever cap under the palm of the hand. Pressing down and forward at the beginning of each stroke and maintaining an even pressure throughout the forward motion is the secret of properly using a block plane. To avoid splitting, plane the end grain halfway, alternately from each edge. If the plane is pushed all the way across an end grain, the corners and the edge of the work are apt to split off.

Sharpening a plane iron. Sharpening a plane iron involves two operations: *grinding* and *whetting*. As a rule, the cutting edge can be whetted several times before grinding is necessary. A plane iron requires grinding only when its bevel has become short or when the edges have been nicked. Because whetting is done after grinding, the process of grinding is described here first.

While the grinding of a plane iron is similar to grinding a chisel or gouge, two important points must be considered: avoiding burning the cutting edge and maintaining the correct bevel. If a motor-driven grinder is not available, use a small hand-driven grinder equipped with a carborundum wheel of the right type for chisels and plane irons. Either type of grinding wheel must be provided with an adjustable tool rest, which is set to a grinding angle of 25°-30° to produce the desired bevel (Fig. 29).

Grinding a plane iron on a dry emery or carborundum wheel requires considerable care and some experience. Burring can be avoided by grinding

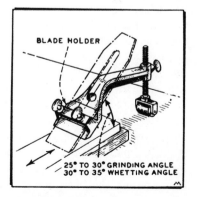

Fig. 29. Grinding a plane iron.

very lightly and by dripping either kerosene or water onto the wheel to keep it from getting too dry, and by frequently dipping the plane iron in water. If these precautions are not taken the edge will overheat or burn, turning a blue-black color, and will lose its temper. Steel that has lost its temper is softened and can never be resharpened.

The edge of a grinding wheel must always be dressed smooth. If it becomes grooved or out of true, dress it with a carborundum stick especially made for the purpose. Hold the carborundum stick against the revolving wheel until the wheel has been smoothed out.

Preparatory to grinding, the plane iron must be removed from the plane. If it is a double plane-iron type, the iron must be separated from the cap by loosening the screw and sliding it along to the end of the slot, where its head will pass through the hole.

The right bevel or grinding angle for plane irons is 25° to 30°. Maintaining it throughout is a simple matter if the adjustable tool rest is used. Turn the wheel toward the tool, at the same time moving the tool from side to side against the wheel. Exert only a slight pressure against the wheel, as too much will cause overheating, thus spoiling the tool. Grind the plane iron until a fine bevel or wire edge appears.

Whetting a plane iron. A plane iron must be whetted after grinding to remove the burr or wire edge and to produce a clean cutting edge. When a plane iron has become only slightly dull, whetting it without prior grinding will usually restore a keen cutting edge. A common oilstone with a fine surface on one side and a rough surface on the other is used, with a light oil, such as kerosene or kerosene mixed with a light motor oil, to float the particles of steel and prevent them from filling up the pores of the stone. The whetting bevel is usually 30° to 35°, slightly greater than the grinding bevel. The bevel must at all times be kept straight. With a steady motion, move the tool parallel to the stone and with a figure-eight movement make certain that all parts of the cutting edge come in contact with the stone (Fig. 30). To maintain the correct bend, use the toolholder shown in the same illustration. After this bevel is cut, or if the blade has been ground, the back of the blade will have a wire edge. Remove this edge by reversing the plane iron and taking several strokes with the blade flat on the stone (Fig. 30). Then complete the whetting by drawing the edge over a small wooden block or a leather strap. Hold the blade up to the light to determine its sharpness. A sharp edge does not reflect light. A dull edge will show as a fine white line; if this occurs, repeat both operations.

Reassembling a plane iron. Reassemble a newly sharpened plane iron with extreme care to avoid nicking its keen edge. Lay the plane-iron cap across the flat side of the iron with the screw in the slot. Pull it down and away from the cutting edge, and turn the cap parallel to the iron when it is almost at the end of the slot. Hold the cap and iron together and slide the cap forward until its edge is about $\frac{1}{16}''$ back of the cutting edge of the iron. To avoid nicking or dulling the blade, do not move the cap or drag it across the cutting edge. When the cap is in proper position, hold the cap and iron firmly together and tighten the screw that will hold the two parts of the double plane iron together. When not in use, lay the plane down on its side to protect the blade, and set the blade far in so that it cannot be damaged by other tools falling against it (Figs. 31 and 32).

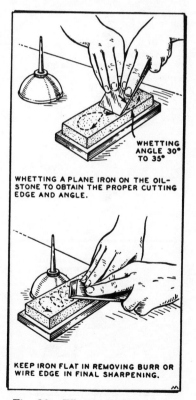

WHETTING ANGLE 30° TO 35°

WHETTING A PLANE IRON ON THE OILSTONE TO OBTAIN THE PROPER CUTTING EDGE AND ANGLE.

KEEP IRON FLAT IN REMOVING BURR OR WIRE EDGE IN FINAL SHARPENING.

Fig. 30. Whetting a plane iron.

CHISELS AND GOUGES

There are many kinds of woodworking chisels and gouges: paring, firmer, framing, packet, sikh, corner, gouge, butt, and mill chisels (Fig. 33). Those most generally used in the home workshop are the framing, butt, and packet types, each of which is available with either a straight or a bevel edge, according to its intended use. All chisels and gouges come in two types known as the tang and the socket (Fig. 34). For general use the socket type is preferable because it is more durable. One end of the steel blade of the socket chisel is formed into a funnel-shaped socket that fits over the tapered end of either a wood or plastic handle. The

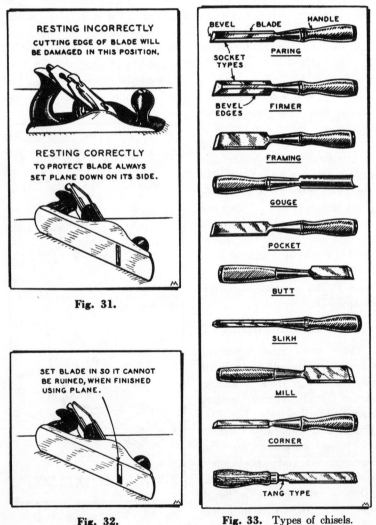

Fig. 31.

Fig. 32.

Fig. 33. Types of chisels.

lighter chisels range from ⅛″ to 1″ in width in gradations of ⅛″. The heavier type range from 1″ to 2″ in width in gradations of ¼″.

While each type of chisel is designed for a specific job, a set of nine or ten, which includes four or five of each of the firmer and framing type, is considered sufficient for general work. The firmer chisel is sturdier than the paring chisel, is capable of doing fairly heavy work, and is used for paring and light mortising work. The framing chisel is a heavy-duty tool that cuts deeply, and it will stand considerable hard handling.

The keen cutting edge of a chisel demands constant care. A chisel never should be used as a can opener, wedge, putty knife, nail remover or screwdriver. When a chisel is not in use, protect its cutting edge

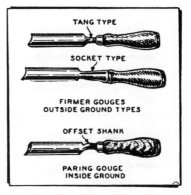

Fig. 34. Types of gouge.

from rust with a coat of oil and hang it up to prevent damage.

Gouges are chisels with rounded edges. There are two main classes of gouges: firmer and paring. The firmer gouge is either outside- or inside-ground. The paring gouge is ground on the inside only. Firmer gouges are used for cutting hollows or grooves. Paring gouges are used to cut surfaces or ends in irregular forms, and are used by patternmakers almost exclusively for the shaping of core boxes and patterns. Both types are available with either socket or tang handles, and the sizes range from ⅛″ to 2″ in gradations of ⅛″.

Wood-carving chisels and gouges. Wood-carving chisels and gouges differ considerably from the ordinary types. The sides, instead of being parallel, taper toward the shoulder, and they are beveled. For general wood-carving, gouges are available in eleven different curves, graduating from almost flat to a deep U-curve. They are classified according to their shape (Figs. 35 and 36).

The small, deep U-shaped gouges are called veiners. Fluters are the larger ones that have quick turns. Flats are those that have a slight curve and are almost flat. In addition to these, there are three V-shaped gouges also known as parting tools,

further classified as being acute, medium, and obtuse.

Wood-carving chisels are classified as firmers and skew firmers, and are either square or oblique on the ends (Fig. 37). Skew firmers with bent

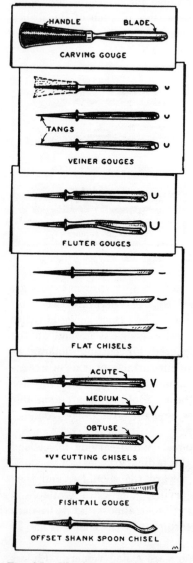

Fig. 35. Wood-carving chisels and gouges.

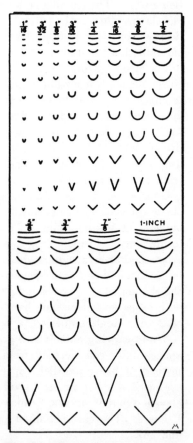

Fig. 36. Chart of sizes and cutting edges of wood-carving chisels and gouges.

shanks are also available for either right- or left-hand use.
Wood-carving chisels are available in eighteen different sizes,
from $\frac{1}{32}''$ to $1''$ in $\frac{1}{16}''$ gradations. They are fitted with either
straight or bent shanks. The firmers range from $\frac{1}{64}''$ to $1''$ in
$\frac{1}{16}''$ gradations. The other wood-carving chisels are available in
six sizes from $1''$ to $2''$ in $\frac{1}{4}''$ gradations. All the smaller sizes
are available with either spade- or fishtail-shaped blades. These
specially shaped blades afford greater clearance back of the cutting edge and are used only
when carving intricate designs
(Fig. 35).

Using a chisel. To preserve
the fine cutting edge of a chisel
or a gouge, use another tool,
such as a saw, auger, or plane,
to remove as much of the waste
part of the wood as possible. A
chisel should be used only for
the finishing cuts.

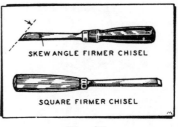

Fig. 37.

Grasp the handle of the chisel firmly with the right hand,
which supplies the driving power. Hold the blade with the left
hand to control the direction of the cut. Secure the work in a
vise, and keep hands away from the cutting edge of tool to avoid
injury. Do not start to cut directly on the guideline, but slightly
away from it, so that any accidental splitting will occur in the
waste portion rather than in the finished work. Shavings made
with a chisel should always be thin, especially when making the
finishing cut. Always cut with the grain as much as possible,
for cutting against the grain splits the fibers of the wood, leaving
it rough. Cutting with the grain leaves the wood fairly smooth.
Make chiseling cuts either horizontally or vertically. Vertical
chiseling cuts are usually made across the grain.

When using a chisel, hold it at a slight angle to the cut instead
of straight. This produces a clean shearing cut that is smooth
when made with the grain and on end grains (Fig. 38). On cross-
grained wood, work from both directions (Fig. 39).

To cut curves on corners or edges, first remove as much waste
as possible with the saw. To cut a concave curve, hold the chisel
with the bevel on the work, and make the cut by pushing down

and then pulling back on the handle (Fig. 40). For a convex cut, hold the chisel with the flat side of the tool on the work and the beveled side up, with the left hand holding the tool and applying the necessary pressure, while the right hand guides it and acts as a brake at the same time. To secure a clean shearing cut, hold the chisel tangent to the curve and move from side to side.

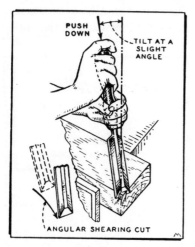

Fig. 38.

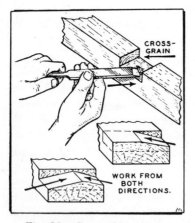

Fig. 39.   Cross-grain paring.

When paring on corners and ends, observe the direction of the grain and begin the cut at the edge of the work (*A*, Fig. 41). This prevents the work from splitting. Round corners are pared in the same manner (*B*, Fig. 41). When making a shearing cut, bring the chisel from a straight to a slanting position, sliding it from side to side as you press it down on the work, as shown at *C* and *D*, Fig. 41.

When paring a shoulder of a joint or cleaning out a corner, first hold the chisel vertically, then tipped to get a shearing cut when you draw it toward you, as shown at *A* in Fig. 42. The position of the chisel for flat or horizontal paring is shown at *B*. When making a shearing cut in a recess or other close place, take half the cut, as in *C*. When it is necessary to work across the grain, the position of the tool for vertical paring is shown at *D*.

Using a gouge. Gouges are used for cutting hollows and grooves, and are handled in the same manner as chisels, with the following exceptions. Gouge cuts are always started at the edge of a cut and driven toward the center. When gouging out a large hollow, cut across grain. Gouges with inside bevels are used in the same manner as chisels with the bevel up, those with outside bevels as chisels with the bevel down.

Using a wood-carving gouge or chisel. Wood-carving chisels and gouges are used in carving designs in low relief. Sketch or trace an outline of the required design on the wood (*A*, Fig. 43). Use a small-sized gouge, or what is known as a pattern tool, to go over the entire outline of the design, cutting on the background side of the outline (*B*, Fig. 43). When doing this, be careful to note the direction of the grain in the raised part of the design. Observe the curves of the design and cut out the outline with the proper curved chisel or gouge, tapping the tool with a mallet (*C*, Fig. 43). Use a gouge to cut out the background. The final step in carving is to model the face of the design by putting in the details with the veiners. Then

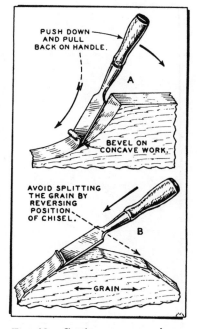

Fig. 40. Cutting concave and convex curves.

clean out the edges and background of the work and even it off (*D*, Fig. 43). To have a really effective piece of wood carving, be careful to avoid cutting under the outline of the design, making the edges too sharp, or even giving too smooth a finish to the carved-out background.

Many beautiful designs can be executed by merely outlining with one of the small gouges or veiners. Work can be improved further by cutting or stamping down the background and by slightly modeling the raised part of the design. The skew chisel is used for chip carving, which is very simple and, when not overdone, very effective (Fig. 44). Trace or draw the design on the work. Make the necessary vertical first cuts with the carving tool to the required depth (*A*, Fig. 44). Then make the second or tapering cut toward the bottom of the first cut. If properly

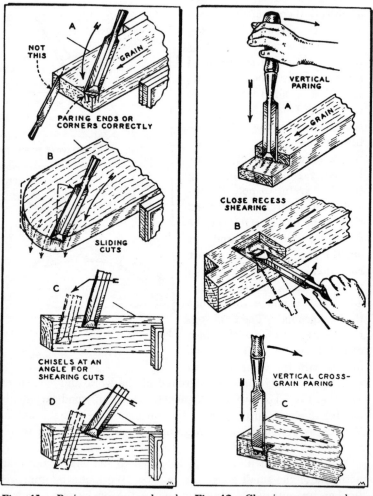

Fig. 41. Paring corners and end sections.

Fig. 42. Cleaning corners and paring shoulders of joints.

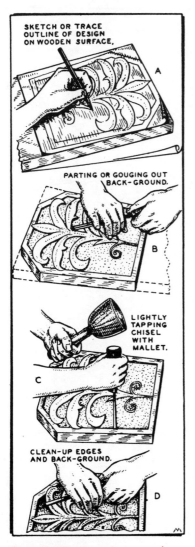

SKETCH OR TRACE
OUTLINE OF DESIGN
ON WOODEN SURFACE.

A

PARTING OR GOUGING OUT
BACK-GROUND.

B

LIGHTLY
TAPPING
CHISEL
WITH
MALLET.

C

CLEAN-UP EDGES
AND BACK-GROUND.

D

Fig. 43. Wood-carving procedures.

cut, the portion to be removed will come out in one chip (*B*, Fig. 44). Another method used for chip carving is shown at *C*, Fig. 44.

Sharpening a chisel or gouge. When the cutting edge of a chisel or gouge becomes dull, whetting will restore its keenness. While the procedure for whetting and grinding a chisel is the same as for a plane iron, the following must be considered. The large bevel of 25° to 30° must be whetted on the coarse side of the oilstone and the small bevel on the fine side. Remove the burr or wire edge on the fine side of the stone. When the cutting edge has become badly nicked or when the tool has lost its original bevel, grinding is necessary. To sharpen a chisel by either whetting or grinding, see the directions for Sharpening a Plane Iron, just a few paragraphs back (Fig. 45).

Whetting and grinding a gouge. Directions for sharpening a gouge are to a large extent the same as for a plane iron or a chisel, with the exception that a gouge is curved and must be sharpened by being turned from side to side as it is pushed forward on the oilstone (*D*, Fig. 46). A slipstone must be used for removing the burr wire edge of a gouge with an outside bevel and for whetting a gouge with an inside bevel (*A*, *B*, and *C*,

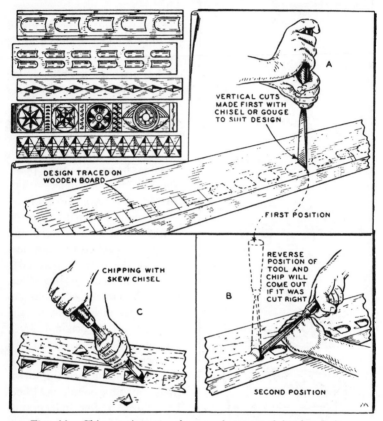

Fig. 44. Chip carving procedures and suggested border designs.

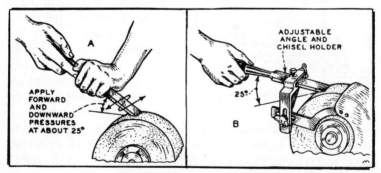

Fig. 45. Sharpening a chisel.

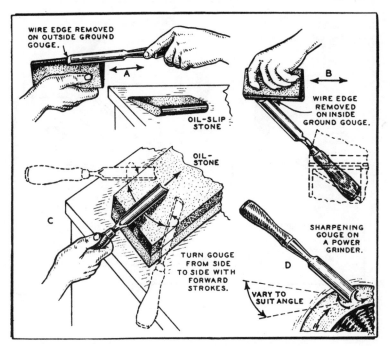

Fig. 46. Whetting and sharpening a gouge.

Fig. 46). When holding the slipstone in the hand, be careful to keep the cutting edge of the gouge true. The wire edge of the gouge with an inside bevel is removed by holding the unbeveled side flat to the stone (Fig. 46).

BRACES AND BITS

The three types of braces are the plain, the ratchet, and the corner brace (Fig. 47). The brace and bit are used for boring holes in wood. The bit bores the holes, while the brace holds the bit in the chuck and turns it. The chuck is adjustable and can hold any type or size of auger bit. A brace can also be utilized as a screwdriver by inserting a screwdriver bit in the chuck.

The most practical type of brace for general use is the one with the ratchet control. This has a ball-bearing handle which

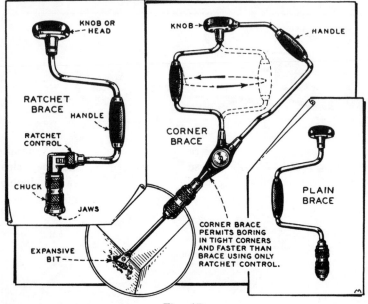

Fig. 47.

makes it easy to turn, and the ratchet can be locked or made to operate in either direction. This brace can be used in places where it is impossible to make a full turn of 360°. In corners or other inaccessible places, the corner brace is used.

Types and sizes of auger bits. Auger bits are available in sizes from ¼″ to 1″ in diameter, graduated by ⅟₁₆″. For boring holes smaller than ¼″ in diameter, drills, gimlet bits, and even awls are used. For boring holes larger than 1″, expansive or Forstner bits are used. Sizes of auger bits are indicated by a number stamped on the shank of the bit which gives the diameter

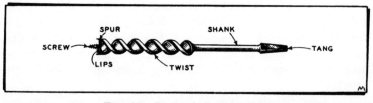

Fig. 48. Parts of the auger bit.

of the hole it will bore, in sixteenths of an inch. A No. 8 auger bit bores a hole ½″ in diameter and a ⁵⁄₁₆″ auger is marked No. 5, and so on.

An auger bit is essentially a cutting tool. The working parts of the bit are the screw, the spurs or nibs, and the lips (Fig. 48). The spurs or nibs score the circumference of the hole, the lips cut the shavings, and the twist or thread of the bit pulls the shavings out of the hole. The three types of auger bits are the single-twist, double-twist, and straight-core or solid-center.

The single-twist and the straight-core types are more generally used in woodworking. These are fast borers, and they clear themselves of chips more readily and quickly than the double-twist type. They are generally used for hard and gummy woods. While the double-twist type works slower than the single-twist, it makes a more accurate and smoother hole. It is generally used for working with softwoods.

Dowel bits. The dowel bit is a shorter bit, averaging about one half the length of the auger bit. As the name indicates, it is used principally for drilling holes for the insertion of dowels (Fig. 49).

Gimlet bits. Considerably longer than any of the other bits, gimlet bits are from 18″ to 24″ in length (Fig. 49). They are used to bore holes through very thick timbers and planks in

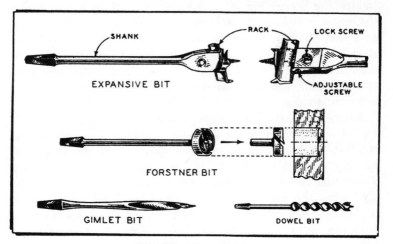

Fig. 49. Types of bits.

heavy construction work. Some gimlet bits have neither screw nor spur.

Forstner bits. The Forstner bit has neither screw, spurs, nor twist (Fig. 49). The lack of a guiding screw makes this bit more difficult to center than the conventional type. Cutting is accomplished by the two lips and a circular steel rim, with the rim centering the bit and scoring the circumference of the hole. These are very accurate bits and are made in sizes up to 2″ in diameter, with the size indicated in sixteenths of an inch on the tang of the tool.

Centering a Forstner bit is a little tricky, but it can be simplified by drawing a circle on the work equal in diameter to the size of the hole that is to be bored. Then start the bit so that the rim cuts into the circumference of the circle. Although more difficult to use than the ordinary type, the Forstner bit has certain advantages. It is used in end wood, where an auger bit does not bore so well, and to bore holes near an end in very thin wood, where the screw on an auger bit would split the stock. A Forstner bit is used to bore holes straight through cross-grained and knotty wood, and to bore a larger hole where a smaller hole has previously been bored. The latter cannot be done with an ordinary auger bit without plugging up the smaller hole.

Using a brace and bit. Insert the bit in the chuck and tighten the brace (Fig. 47). Secure the work in a vise, locate the center of the hole to be bored, and mark it with either a nail or a brad awl. Place the lead screw of the bit on the mark and start boring. To bore a straight hole, check the perpendicular or horizontal position of the bit by sighting the auger or drill from two points 90° apart. Make one of these sights when the boring is begun, and two more after the hole is fairly well started.

Another method of testing the perpendicular or horizontal position of the auger bit is with a small try square. Continue boring, rotating the handle in a clockwise direction, at the same time exerting pressure on the head of the brace with the other hand. The harder the wood, the more pressure has to be applied. Avoid splintering the wood by stopping when the bottom of the lead screw appears on the underside of the work. Remove the work from the vise, reverse it, replace it in the vise, and complete the boring from the reverse side (Fig. 50).

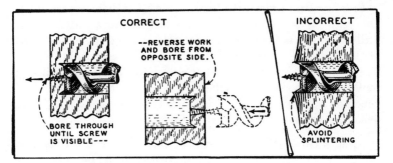

Fig. 50. Correct method of boring.

Boring a hole at an angle is just as simple as boring a perpendicular hole. The only difference is in the sighting. A simple method is to lay out the required angle on a piece of cardboard or thin wood and use this angle in sighting the direction of the auger bit. If the bit is kept parallel to this template, it will bore the hole at the desired angle.

Depth Gauge. A depth gauge is used to bore a hole to a desired depth (Fig. 51). While ready-made gauges are available, a wooden gauge can be made from a small block of wood. Bore a hole in a block, slightly larger in diameter than the bit. The height of the block will vary inversely according to the depth of the hole that is to be bored. The depth gauge is slipped over the bit prior to boring.

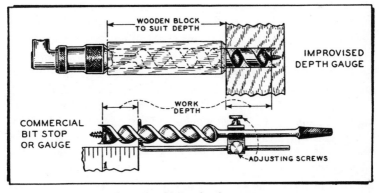

Fig. 51. Using depth gauges.

Twist drills. Twist drills from $\frac{1}{16}''$ to $\frac{3}{4}''$ in diameter are available with tapered shanks to fit in a ratchet brace. Morse twist drills (Fig. 52) are made with a straight shank to fit in the chuck of either a hand, automatic push, electric, or breast drill (Fig. 53). The three-jaw chuck in a hand or electric drill will take drills up to $\frac{1}{4}''$ in diameter. For a larger size, use a breast drill. The chuck on a breast drill takes drills up to $\frac{1}{2}''$ in diameter. Twist drills are available in over fifty sizes.

Using a twist drill. A twist drill must be held steady and be driven at moderate speed in a straight direction. The shank of a twist drill is made of soft steel and will bend if too much pressure is exerted on it. The body of the drill is of tempered steel and if strained or twisted it will snap off. When driven at excessive speed, a twist drill bites rapidly into the wood and the chips do not clear out of the flutes of the drill. The drill then becomes hot, at times hot enough to char the wood and spoil the temper of the drill, ruining its keen cutting edge.

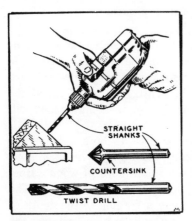

Fig. 52. Morse twist drill and countersink bit.

When the flutes of a twist drill become jammed with chips, the drill squeaks as it revolves. To clear the chips from the flutes, the drill should be withdrawn several times from the hole during the drilling.

Expansion or extension bits. *Expansion* or *extension* bits are used to bore holes larger than $1''$ in diameter (Fig. 49). These bits fit into the chuck of a brace. Two sizes are available: one for boring holes from $\frac{1}{2}''$ to $1\frac{1}{2}''$ in diameter, the other for boring holes from $\frac{7}{8}''$ to $3''$ in diameter. They have adjustable cutting blades which can be set to bore holes of any diameter within their range. Loosening the screw that fastens the spur and the cutting lip to the shank makes it possible to move the spur and adjust the bit to the required diameter. Before using, tighten

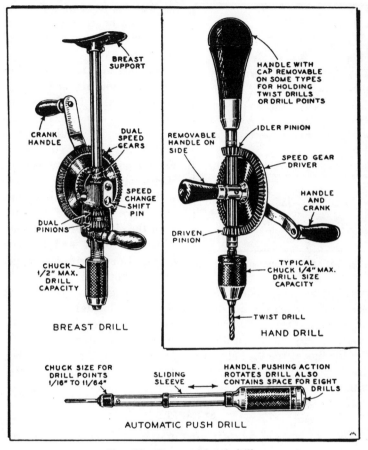

Fig. 53. Types of hand drills.

this screw so that the spur will not slip. The accuracy of the adjustment that has been made should be tested by boring a sample hole through a piece of waste wood. Expansion bits are secured in the chuck of the brace and used in the same manner as other types of bits.

Countersink bits. *Countersink* bits are available in two types: one with a tapered shank fitting into the chuck of a brace, the other with a straight round shank fitting into the chuck of a drill. Countersinks are used to shape the upper portion of a hole

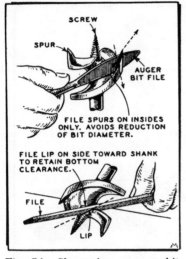

Fig. 54.   Sharpening an auger bit.

so that the head of a flathead screw can be driven flush with or slightly below the surface of the work.

Sharpening an auger bit. An auger-bit file and a slip-stone are used to sharpen an auger bit. The specially designed file is small, double-ended, and tapered so that the narrow portion can be used on small-diameter bits and the wider portion on larger bits (Fig. 54). One end is made with the sides "safe" or uncut, while the other end has cut edges. In sharpening an auger bit, file both the lips and the nibs of the spurs. The safe section of an auger-bit file makes it easy to file either the lips or the nibs without damaging any of the adjacent surfaces. To keep the original diameter of the bit, file the nibs only on the inside. To maintain the proper clearance, file the lips of the bit only on the top surface of the cutting edge. Hold the bit in a vise and maintain its original bevel. After filing, use a slipstone.

SCRAPERS

The two types of scrapers used in woodworking are the *cabinet* scraper (Fig. 55)) and the *hand* scraper. The three styles of hand scrapers generally used are shown in Fig. 56. All are available with either bevel or straight edges.

Cabinet scraper. The cabinet scraper is used as a finishing tool. It takes a finer cut than a plane and is used only on flat surfaces to remove marks left by a plane or to prepare the surface for painting or finishing. It produces a smooth cut on cross-grained wood. The beveled blade, which is set in a two-handled metal frame (Fig. 55), can be removed by loosening the adjusting screw and the clamp thumbscrew. Insert the new blade with the beveled side toward the thumbscrew.

Using a cabinet scraper. Before using a cabinet scraper, place it on a flat wooden surface and adjust the blade so that it is even with the bottom of the scraper by pressing it down lightly against the wood. Tighten both the clamp screw and the adjusting screw and make a test cut on some waste wood. Continue to tighten the adjusting screw between test cuts until the blade projects far enough to produce a thin shaving.

The work should be secured in a vise. Hold the tool in both hands and either push or pull it over the surface of the work. As a rule, it is pushed rather than pulled (Fig. 55).

Hand scrapers. The two types of one-hand scrapers generally used are the hand scraper, which is rectangular, and the molding

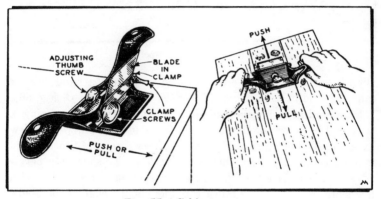

Fig. 55. Cabinet scraper.

scraper, which is curved (Fig. 56). They are made of high-tempered steel in various sizes and can be used on both flat and curved surfaces. They are available with both square and beveled edges. The square-edge type produces a smoother and flatter surface, but is not so fast as the bevel-edge type, and becomes dull sooner. Square-edge scrapers are used for furniture, moldings, and cabinetwork. Bevel-edge scrapers are used for scraping floors and other large areas.

Using a hand scraper. A hand scraper produces finer shavings than a cabinet scraper. While it may be either pushed or pulled, better work results when it is pulled. Hold the blade with the thumb and fingers of both hands; it cuts best when

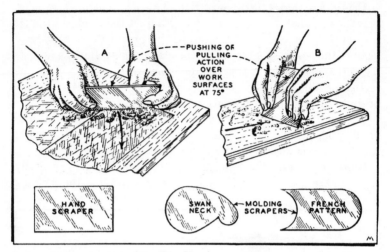

Fig. 56. Hand scrapers.

slightly curved. When either pushed or pulled, a hand scraper must be held at an angle of 75° to the work (*A* and *B*, Fig. 56).

Sharpening a scraper blade. Directions for sharpening a scraper blade are similar to those for a plane iron, with a few exceptions. The cutting edge can be dressed several times before it requires grinding and whetting (Fig. 57). To sharpen a bevel-edge scraper, place the blade, cutting edge up, in a vise. With a smooth mill file held against the side, not the edge of the blade, remove the old burr. The worn-down bevel is restored by filing

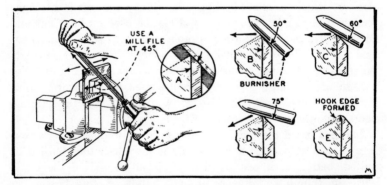

Fig. 57. Sharpening bevel-edge hand scraper and drawing edge.

or grinding the blade to a 45° angle. Maintaining this angle, whet the bevel on the smooth side of an oilstone. To remove the wire edge, whet the blade face-down on the stone. Lay the blade, bevel side down, on the work, with the edge projecting slightly over the edge of the bench. With the burnisher held perfectly flat against the flat side of the blade, a few firm strokes will be sufficient to draw the edge to the required 50°. Proceed to form the hook edge as shown at *C, D* and *E*, Fig. 57.

The procedure for sharpening a square-edge scraper is as follows: Hold file at 90° angle and file edge square (*A*, Fig. 57). Whet edge on oilstone and turn blade on side to remove wire edges. Draw edge with burnisher as shown at *B;* then proceed with steps *C, D* and *E*, Fig. 58.

MEASURING AND LAYING-OUT TOOLS

Prior to cutting lumber to any required size or shape, guiding lines must be accurately measured and laid out. The measuring and laying-out tools are *rules, straightedges, squares,* and *gauges.*

Rules. Rules are used for measuring material to exact dimensions. Those most generally used in woodworking are made of wood and are called *zigzag* and *boxwood.* Both the zigzag and

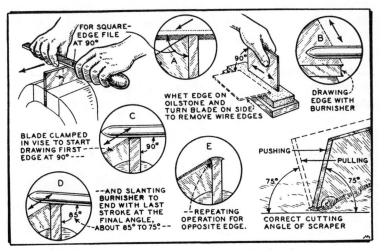

Fig. 58. Methods of sharpening square-edge hand scraper.

boxwood types fold into 6″ lengths. Boxwood is the smaller of the two, can be opened to either 2′ or 3′, and is marked in inches and graduations to ⅛″. The zigzag rule opens to a length of 6′ and is marked in inches and graduations to ¹⁄₁₆″ (Fig. 59).

Steel tape rules are used to measure the diameter of dowels and drills, the thickness of boards and for inside direct measurements.

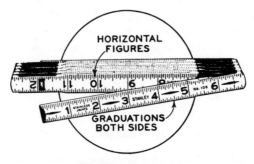

Fig. 59. Zigzag rule.

They are more accurate than other rules for these specific purposes (Fig. 60). They are available in several sizes, ranging from 2′ to 8′ in length, and are graduated in feet, inches, and fractions of inches on both sides.

Where absolute accuracy to ¹⁄₃₂″ is necessary, the caliper rule shown in Fig. 61 is used for both inside and outside measurements. The boxwood caliper rule is used to measure outside diameters or thicknesses (Fig. 62).

Steel straightedges. Steel straightedges are strips of hardened tempered steel that have been accurately ground. They are available in lengths ranging from 1′ to 6′. Unlike rules, they are not

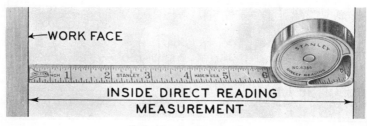

Fig. 60. Steel tape rule.

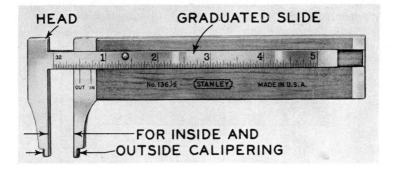

Fig. 61. Inside and outside caliper rule.

graduated in inches or fractions of an inch. They are used as guides for scribing working lines with a knife or pencil when extreme accuracy is required. Straightedges are also used for testing flatness of surfaces.

Squares. The several types of squares used in woodworking are the *carpenter's* or *framing* square, the *try square* with fixed blade, and the adjustable *miter and try square* with sliding blade and spirit level.

Carpenter's or framing squares. The carpenter's or framing square is made of flat steel. It is available in two standard sizes, 24″ by 16″ and 24″ by 18″. The 24″ side is called the body, and the shorter dimension at right angles is called the tongue. Both are marked not only in inches and fractions of an inch, but with several essential tables and scales. They can be used both as rules and as straightedges (Fig. 63).

Try squares. Try squares are constantly used in woodworking for testing the trueness of edges and ends with adjoining edges and with the

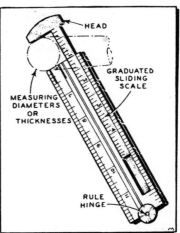

Fig. 62. Boxwood caliper rule.

face of the work after the work has been cut or planed. The common or fixed type is constructed of two parts, a thick wood or iron stock, and a thin steel blade, fixed at 90° to each other;

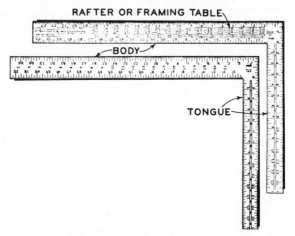

RAFTER OR FRAMING TABLE

BODY

TONGUE

Fig. 63. Carpenter's or framing squares.

the blade is graduated in inches and fractions of an inch. The sizes of the blades vary from 2″ to 12″ (Fig. 64).

The adjustable miter and try square is similar in every respect

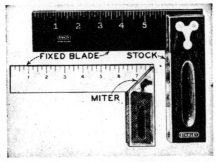

FIXED BLADE   STOCK

MITER

Fig. 64. Try and miter squares with fixed blade.

to the fixed-blade type with the exception that it can be used for both 45° and 90° work (Fig. 65). Its blade can be locked at any point along its length. The stock is fitted with a spirit level.

Using a square. In using a square, a guideline must always be marked across the surface of the work. When it is necessary to cut, plane, or chisel a board square, either a try square or a carpenter's square is used to lay out the work or to mark the necessary guideline. A pencil is quite satisfactory for marking guide-

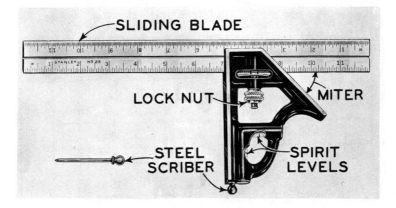

Fig. 65. Adjustable try and miter square.

lines for roughing out woodwork, but where accuracy is necessary, guidelines should preferably be laid out with the blade of a pocket-knife or a bench knife. The tip of the blade should be used to get a clean, accurate line. A guideline must be exactly located and must always be square with the edges of the work. If a board is wide, that is, if it averages wider than the blade of a try square, a carpenter's square must be used. To square a line with a try square, press the stock of the try square firmly against the edge of the board, and mark the guideline along the blade with the point of the pencil or the knife blade (*A*, Fig. 66).

In squaring a line across a board, one edge and one face of the board should be marked with X's so that they can be distinguished as the working edge and face. Then square a line from the working edge across the working face (*B*, Fig. 66). Be certain that the working edge is perfectly flat so that the square does not rock. Always square lines from the working face across both edges. Then, holding the stock of the square up against the

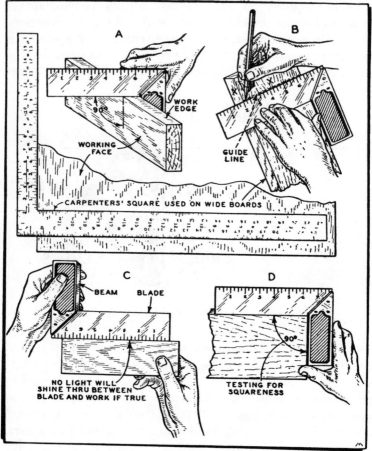

Fig. 66.

working edge, square a line across the face on the side of the board opposite the working edge.

Testing for squareness. To test a board for squareness, place the inside edge of the stock of the square in contact with one surface. Face the light so that it will shine on the work. Slide the square downward and observe where the blade first comes in contact with the surface of the work. If the angle is square and the surface of the work is true, no light will be visible. If the angle does not happen to be square, or if the surface of the work is not absolutely true, light will shine through between the blade and the work (*C* and *D*, Fig. 66).

Gauges. Two types of gauges are used by the woodworker: the *marking* gauge and the *mortise* gauge. The marking gauge is the one more commonly used when absolute accuracy is required. Constructed of either wood or metal, the marking gauge consists of an 8″ bar on which the head of the gauge slides. The head can be secured at any desired point on the bar by means of a thumbscrew (Fig. 67). A sharpened pin or spur affixed near the end of

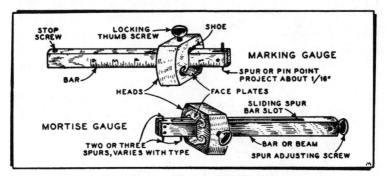

Fig. 67. Two types of woodworking gauges.

the bar scores the gauged line on the work. The bar of the marking gauge is graduated in inches and fractions of an inch.

The mortise gauge is a marking gauge with two spurs instead of one and is used for laying out mortises and tenons. The two spurs, one of which can be set independently, are used to score parallel lines.

Using marking gauges. Set the head of the gauge the required distance from the spur or pin, and secure it in place with the locking screw. Grasp the gauge with the palm and the fingers of the right hand. Press the head firmly against the edge of the work to be marked, and with a motion of the wrist, tip the head forward slightly until the point of the spur just touches the wood. Score the line by pushing the gauge away from you, keeping the head firmly against the edge of the work (Fig. 68). Note that the point of the spur must always be filed sharp and project approximately $\frac{1}{16}$″.

The mortise gauge is used in approximately the same manner as the marking gauge, the only difference being that the two spurs are set the required distance apart by securing the movable one with the thumbscrew in the end of the beam, before the head is adjusted (Fig. 68).

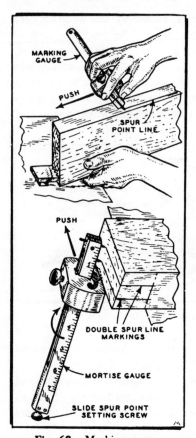

Fig. 68. Marking gauges.

LEVELS

A level is a simple tool that indicates true vertical and true level positions. It may have either an aluminum or a wooden frame in which two or four glass liquid-and-bubble tubes are mounted. Levels made of aluminum are light in weight and do not warp or rust. When there are four tubes, they are mounted in sets of two, each set at right angles to the other.

Using a level. The use of a level on either a flat or a vertical surface is shown in Fig. 69. In either position, when the bubble in one of the tubes is absolutely in the center—that is, between indicated lines on the tube—the work is level or plumb. When the bubble is off center, the work is not level.

CLAMPS

Clamps used in woodworking are the bar clamp, C clamp, hand screws, cabinetmaker's clamp, and cramping clamp. All are used to hold work together under pressure until glue has set firmly. These clamps and their use are shown in Chaps. 3 and 5.

GLASS CUTTER

The procedures for the use of all types and sizes of glass cutters are identical. When cutting glass with this simple tool, a steel ruler or straight edge must be used to guide the tool. Set rule where cut is desired. Exert an even pressure of the wheel of the tool on both the glass and the edge of the ruler or straight edge to score a line at required place on glass. After line has been scored, grip the waste part of the glass in the groove of the cutter and snap gently to break the glass along the scored line.

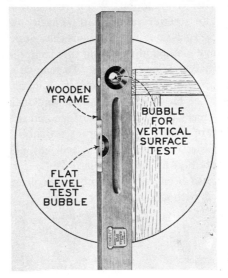

Fig. 69. Vertical plumb test with wood-type level.

TOOL STORAGE AND RUST PREVENTION

Every tool in the workshop should have its proper place. Tools that are most often in use should be kept at hand on a tool rack specially designed for that purpose. Plans and directions for building a tool rack are given in Chap. **18**.

Tools that are not used frequently should be stored in a tool chest or in the individual boxes in which they were originally packed. During the damp spring and summer months, each tool should be coated with a film of oil or grease to prevent rust. When tools are to be stored for any length of time, it is good practice, in addition to coating, to wrap them in paper for protection from moisture and dust.

The cutting edges of tools must be protected at all times. In addition to the tool rack, a well-designed tool chest or a sturdy workbench in which each tool has its own place is desirable. Plans and directions for building a workbench are given in Chap. 18.

Removing rust from tools. When rust forms on hammers, chisels, saws, and screwdrivers, it can be easily removed. While there are several rust-removing solutions that work fairly well, the most satisfactory method of removing rust from these tools is with No. 240 emery paper or emery cloth. To remove a heavy coating of rust from surfaces that must be kept true, like the bottom of a plane, or a surface on which graduations and scales are marked, place this fine emery cloth on a flat surface and rub the tool on it.

This method of removing rust serves a double purpose, for it helps to retain the true surface of the tool and also removes any high or low spots that have been caused by the formation of rust. After the rust has been removed, rub the tool clean with a dry cloth and coat it with a film of oil or grease.

CHAPTER 3

Working with Wood

————— ⋮ —————————————————————

In selecting wood for a given purpose, the ease with which it may be worked is sometimes a factor, especially when hand tools are to be used. (*See* Table 1 showing classification of certain hardwood and softwood species according to ease of working with hand tools.)

Woodworking nowadays is largely done with portable power tools or machines rather than with hand tools. Different woods vary in their machining properties just as they do in other properties. In addition, several machining operations are involved, all of which must be considered in appraising the machinability of any given wood.

BASIC CHARACTERISTICS OF WOODS

The choice of one wood species in preference to another for any of the principal home or farm uses should seldom be based on a single vital property. Usually a favorable combination of two or more basic qualities or characteristics should determine the selection. Distinguishing characteristics, qualities, or marks common to a species or group are usually classified as physical, mechanical, or chemical properties.

Today it is more important than ever to select the most appropriate wood product for each use in the home. Wood products are now being made in more forms and from a greater variety of species than ever before. What was most suitable for a particular use a few years ago may not be so today.

Standard sizes for boards and dimension are larger for lumber surfaced green than lumber surfaced dry. When lumber surfaced green dries to the standard dry moisture content, it will shrink to approximately the standard dry surfaced size.

Most hardwoods differ substantially from softwoods in their properties (basic characteristics) and in their uses. As a class, hardwoods are heavier, harder, shrink more, and are tougher. Hardwoods and softwoods are similar in stiffness, so on a weight basis the softwoods are actually much stiffer. In strength as a post and in bending strength the two groups are more directly comparable than they are in weight, toughness, and hardness. Nevertheless, more commercial hardwoods than softwoods can be rated high in bending strength.

The softwoods are used principally in construction work, whereas hardwoods furnish most of the wood for interior finish and flooring as well as for furniture, implements, and other industrial uses. In addition to normal construction uses, 2" and thicker lumber is also sold stress-graded for more carefully engineered components such as trusses.

Hardness

Hardness is the property that makes a surface difficult to dent, scratch, or cut. Generally, the harder the wood, the better it resists wear, the less it crushes or mashes under loads, and the better it can be polished. On the other hand, the harder wood is more difficult to cut with tools, harder to nail, and more likely to split in nailing.

Hardness is of particular concern in flooring, furniture, and tool handles. Hardness is also important in selecting interior trim such as door casings, base, and base shoe, as well as door jambs, sills, and thresholds. These portions usually receive the hardest wear in a house.

There is a decided difference in hardness between the springwood and the summerwood of woods such as southern yellow pine and Douglas fir. In these woods the summerwood is the denser, darker colored portion of the annual growth ring. Differences in surface hardness thus occur at close intervals on a piece of such wood depending on whether springwood or summerwood is encountered. In woods like maple, which do not have pronounced springwood and summerwood, the hardness of the surface is quite uniform.

The classification of a species as a hardwood or softwood is not based on actual hardness of wood. Technically, softwoods are those cut from coniferous or evergreen trees, whereas hardwoods are those cut from broad-leaved and deciduous trees. Actually, some of the softwoods are harder than some of the hardwoods.

As a group, the *hardwoods* can be divided into (a) dense and (b) less dense. The *softwoods* can be divided into (a) medium density and (b) low density.

A number of woods are strong favorites for building purposes largely because of their softness and uniformity rather than their hardness. Northern white pine (eastern) and Idaho white pine (western), poplar, white fir, and basswood are traditional examples. Others are ponderosa pine, sugar pine, and cedar. The ease with which these woods can be cut, sawed, and nailed has put them in a high position for general use. This is less important in present-day construction because portable power tools make it easier to handle such dense species as Douglas fir and southern yellow pine. In fact, the use of these denser species allows greater spans for joists and rafters than can be used for equal-sized members of the softer woods.

Differences in hardness are great enough to affect the choice of woods for such uses as flooring and furniture on one hand, and for siding, millwork, and cabinets on the other.

Weight

Weight, in addition to being important in itself, is generally a reliable index of strength. A heavy piece of wood is generally stronger than a lighter piece of the same moisture content and size, whether it is of the same or of a different species.

Wood weights, as commonly expressed, are either in the green or in the air-dry condition. Green weight of wood is the weight before any drying takes place. Air-dry weight of wood refers to the weight after drying by exposure to atmospheric conditions for a time, either outdoors or in unheated sheds.

Shrinkage or Swelling of Wood

Most materials change in dimension with changes in temperature or moisture. Wood, like many other fibrous materials, *shrinks* as it dries and *swells* as it absorbs moisture. As a rule, much shrinking and swelling of wood in houses can be avoided by using wood that has been dried to a suitable moisture content.

For most species, the shrinkage or swelling in width of a flat-grained or plain-sawed board is often approximately twice that of an edge-grained or quarter-sawed board of the same width (Fig. 1). Lumber that is cut tangent (roughly parallel) to the annual growth rings of the tree produces plain-sawed boards in hardwoods and flat-grained or slash-grained boards in softwoods. Lumber that is cut at right angles to the annual rings, or parallel to the radius of the log, produces quarter-sawed boards in hardwoods and edge-grained or vertical-grained boards in softwoods. Edge-grained boards or other items cut from a species with high shrinkage characteristics will, therefore, prove as satisfactory as flat-grained boards or items cut from species with lower shrinkage characteristics. The normal wood of all species shrinks or swells very slightly along the grain (lengthwise).

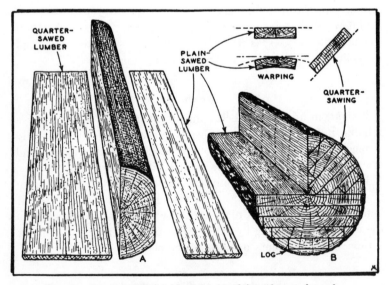

Fig. 1. Quarter-sawed and plain-sawed boards cut from log.

Shrinkage of wood begins when moisture in the wood is removed by drying below the fiber saturation point (approximately 30 per cent moisture content). When wood reaches a moisture content of 15 per cent, about one-half of the total shrinkage has occurred. The moisture content of wood in service constantly changes since it adjusts to corresponding changes in surrounding atmospheric conditions.

The moisture content of woodwork installed within heated buildings reaches a low point during the heating season and a high point during the summer. The moisture content at the time of installation should be near the midpoint of this range. If this rule is followed, slight shrinkage will occur during some seasons and a slight swelling during others.

Plywood is relatively free from shrinkage and swelling as compared to solid wood because its construction generally consists of alternate laminations of veneers laid with grain at 90° to each other. From soaked to ovendry condition, the shrinkage of plywood in length and width is generally quite uniform and ranges from only about 0.2 to about 1.2 per cent. After manufacture, plywood has a low moisture content and normally does not require drying out before use.

Warping

The *warping* of wood is closely allied with shrinkage. Lumber that is cross-grained, or is from near the pith (core) of the tree, tends to warp when it shrinks. Warping can be reduced to a minimum by the use of edge-grained dry material.

Preventing defects due to shrinkage. Although wood will shrink under certain conditions, it will give satisfactory service when the shrinkage factor is recognized and properly controlled. Problems due to shrinkage can be greatly reduced by: (1) using seasoned woods as required by conditions of use; (2) protecting by paint, water repellents, or other protective coatings all exposed surfaces of dry wood in place so that rapid moisture changes will not occur; (3) selecting woods with low inherent shrinkage; or (4) using edge-grained material in preference to flat grain for critical uses.

Following the first two rules will insure wood that meets the ordinary requirements of construction. More exacting requirements, such as those of doors, window sash, and frames, require in addition either the selection of woods from the low- or moderate-shrinkage groups or the use of edge-grained material. Special conditions often prevent the application of all four rules. One or more of the rules can always be applied in order to enable wood to meet the requirements satisfactorily in most cases.

Ease of Working with Wood

Wood is generally easy to cut, shape, and fasten with ordinary tools directly on homesite. (*See* Table 1.) For some purposes the difference between woods in ease of working is negligible, but for others it may decidedly affect the quality and cost of the finished job. In general, ease of working is of first importance to the worker and/or indirectly to the one who pays the bill. Fabrication and assembly at the factory of cabinets, windows, frames, doors, and other units have greatly reduced the time required for the worker at the house.

TABLE 1

Classification of certain hardwood and softwood species according to ease of working with hand tools

HARDWOODS

Group 1—Easy to work	Group 2—Relatively easy to work	Group 3—Least easy to work
Alder, red	Birch, paper	Ash, commercial white
Basswood	Cottonwood	Beech
Butternut	Magnolia	Birch
Chestnut	Sweetgum	Cherry
Yellow-poplar	Sycamore	Elm
	Tupelo:	Hackberry
	Black	Hickory, true and pecan
	Water	Honeylocust
	Walnut, black	Locust, black
		Maple
		Oak:
		Commercial red
		Commercial white

SOFTWOODS

Cedar:	Baldcypress	Douglas-fir
Atlantic white-	Fir:	Larch, western
Incense-	Balsam	Pine, southern yellow
Northern white-	White	
Port-Orford-	Hemlock:	
Western redcedar	Eastern	

Pine:	Western
Eastern white	Pine, lodgepole
Ponderosa	Redcedar, eastern
Sugar	Redwood
Western white	Spruce:
	Eastern
	Sitka

Harder and denser woods with high load carrying capacity and wear resistance should not be passed over just because softer woods are easier to work. A reasonable balance must be drawn in selecting wood for a specific use.

A skilled worker working with lumber that is well seasoned and manufactured can get good results from even the more difficult to work woods. An unskilled worker is more likely to get good results only from the softer woods. However, with portable power tools, jigs for installation of hinges and door locks, and other modern labor-saving methods, skill is no longer the major factor it was when hand tools were the only means of cutting and fitting on the job.

The classification of the more common woods according to their working qualities is based on a combination of the hardness, texture, and character of the surfaces obtainable.

Paint Holding

Good paint performance or ability of a wood surface to hold paint depends on three factors: (1) the kind of paint, (2) surface conditions and application factors, and (3) the kind of wood.

Different woods vary considerably in painting characteristics, particularly for outdoor exposure. The best species for exterior painting are such common woods as the cedars, redwood, ponderosa pine, or white pine.

Paint is more durable on edge-grained surfaces than on flat-grained surfaces.

Knots, especially resinous ones, do not hold paint well and contribute to abnormally early paint failure. High content of pitch is set adequately by proper high-temperature seasoning of the wood.

Class B and class C woods and plywood are best finished with pigmented stains that penetrate the wood surface and do not form a continuous film on the surface. Such stain finishes do not fail by cracking and peeling of the coating from the wood as does paint. The stains are also recommended for use on shingle and shake sidewalls and rough-sawn lumber and siding.

Nail Holding

As a rule, fastenings are the weakest link in all forms of construction and in all materials. Therefore, the resistance offered by the wood to the withdrawal of nails is important. Usually the denser and harder the wood, the greater is the inherent nail-holding ability, assuming the wood does not split.

The size, type, and number of nails have a marked effect on the strength of a joint. Figure 2 illustrates good nailing practice at the foundation wall. Correct placement of the nails is as important as the size and number.

The resistance of nails to withdrawal increases almost directly with their diameter. If the diameter of the nail is doubled, the

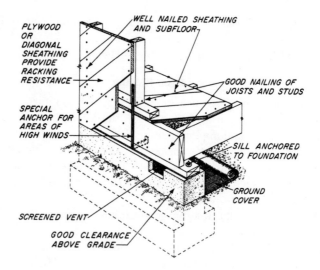

Fig. 2. Nailing at foundation wall.

holding strength is doubled, providing the nail does not split the wood when it is driven. The lateral resistance of nails increases as the 1½ power of the diameter.

The nail most generally used in wood frame construction is the common nail. However, galvanized and aluminum nails are used extensively in applying siding and exterior trim because these nails resist rusting. The galvanized nail is slightly better than the common bright nail in retaining its withdrawal resistance.

Superior withdrawal resistance has been shown by the deformed shank nail, which is produced in two general forms, the annular groove and the spiral groove shanks. The annular groove nail is outstanding in its resistance to static withdrawal loads but not as good as the spiral groove nail when subjected to racking loads. The spiral groove nail is superior to the plain shank nail in its resistance to withdrawal loads.

Interior carpentry uses the small-headed finish nail, which can be set and puttied over.

The moisture content of the wood at the time of nailing is extremely important for good nail holding. If plain shank nails are driven into wet wood, they will lose about three-fourths of their full holding ability when the wood becomes dry. This loss of holding power is so great that siding, barn boards, or fence pickets are likely to become loose when plain shank nails are driven into green wood that subsequently dries. Thus the most important rule in obtaining good joints and high nail-holding ability is to use well-seasoned wood.

Prevention of splitting. The splitting of woods by nails greatly reduces their holding ability. Even if the wood is split only slightly around the nail, considerable holding strength is lost. Because of hardness and texture characteristics some woods split more in nailing than do others. The heavy, dense woods, such as maple, oak, and hickory, split more in nailing than do the lightweight woods such as basswood, spruce, and balsam and white fir.

Predrilling is good practice in dense woods, especially when large-diameter nails are used. The drilled hole should be about 75 per cent of the nail diameter.

Woods without a uniform texture, like southern yellow pine and Douglas fir, split more than do such uniform textured woods as northern and Idaho white pine, sugar pine, or ponderosa pine.

In addition to predrilling, the most common means taken to reduce splitting is the use of small-diameter nails. The number of small nails must be increased to maintain the same gross holding strength as with larger nails. Slightly blunt-pointed nails have less tendency to split wood than do sharp-pointed nails. Too much blunting, however, results in a loss of holding ability.

Decay Resistance

Every material has its distinctive way of deteriorating under adverse conditions. With wood it is *decay*. Wood will never decay if kept continuously dry or continuously under water. Fortunately, most wood in ordinary houses is in dry situations and, therefore, not in danger of decay. It is only in certain parts of the house that decay resistance is important, such as areas where wood may become damp or where it touches or is embedded in the ground.

To protect wood from decay, there are three things which can be done, either singly or in combination: (1) make sure it is dry when installed and kept dry in service; (2) use the heartwood of a decay-resistant species where occasional wetting and drying can be expected; or (3) use wood that has been given a good preservative treatment for places where moisture is certain to get in, as from contact with the soil or because of poor drainage or ventilation.

Heartwood Content

When selecting untreated wood for use where the decay hazard is high, one must consider the *heartwood content*, because only the heartwood is decay resistant. When the sapwood of the species of tree is normally narrow, as it is in the woods rated as class A, the lumber runs high in heartwood content even without special selection. When the sapwood is normally wide, as in woods rated as class C and even in class B, the commercial run of lumber contains considerable sapwood.

To obtain decay-resistant lumber, even in the species classed as A in decay resistance, it is necessary to eliminate the sapwood by special selection. Specially selected lumber, sold in *all heart* grades, is procurable in cypress, redwood, western red

FIGURE **103**

cedar, and Douglas fir. However, all-heart grades in southern yellow pine are special and are not easily obtainable.

Figure

Figure is due to various causes in different woods. In woods like southern yellow pine and Douglas fir, it results from the contrast between springwood and summerwood in growth rings; in oak, beech, or sycamore, it results from the flakes or rays in addition to the growth rings; in maple, walnut, and birch it results from wavy or curly grain; and in gum it results from infiltrated coloring matter.

Except where the figure in wood results from flakes or rays, it is more pronounced in flat-grained lumber than in edge-grained. Figure resulting from wavy or curly grain or from infiltrated color does not occur in all lumber of a given species, but only in lumber from occasional legs. To be certain of getting figured lumber in maple, walnut, or gum, special selection is necessary.

Woods with outstanding knots, such as pine and cedar, or with other characteristics such as those of pecky cypress, or *white speck* Douglas fir, are often selected because of their novel patterns. The finish selected for these types of wood tends to accentuate rather than obscure the knots or other features. The advantage of figure or color may appear in the interior trim, in the floor, or in a wood-paneled wall.

The color of the wood has a decided influence on the figure. However, stains are so commonly and easily applied to most woods that natural color is usually not the first consideration, except where a very light color is decided. Woods classed as A are highly figured, and an ordinary commercial run will have a pronounced figure. Class B woods have more modulated figures and sometimes require special selection to obtain the desired figure. Class C woods are seldom satisfactory where figure is desired.

Odor and Taste of Wood when Dry

None of the common woods has sufficient odor to prevent satisfactory use in building construction. It is only when the wood is used for food containers that *odor* and *taste* are critical. When green, all woods have some odor and will impart a woody taste

to very susceptible foods. After the woods are dried, many have
practically no odor or taste. The principal objection to odor and
taste in wood is that they contaminate the food they touch, especially butter and cheese. On the desirable side, the aromatic
odor of the cedars is prized for such uses as clothes closets and
chests. The woods in class A are suitable for use in contact with
foods that absorb odors. The woods in class C have a strong
resinous or aromatic odor and are unsuited for use in direct contact with foods that absorb odors. Woods in class B cannot be
used in contact with very susceptible foods, like butter, but they
do not have the strong odor and taste of the aromatic and
resinous woods.

Bending Strength

Bending strength is a measure of the load-carrying capacity
of members that are ordinarily used in a horizontal or moderate
slope position and rest on two or more supports. Examples of
members in which bending strength is important are rafters,
ceiling and floor joists, beams or girders, purlins, bridge stringers,
and scaffold platforms.

Even though a species is low in bending strength, it may still
be selected for uses where this property is essential. However,
larger sizes are then required to obtain the same load-carrying
capacity.

A small increase in the depth of a beam produces a much
greater percentage increase in bending strength than it does in
volume. An increase of 1″ in the depth of a 10″ beam (from
10″ to 11″) will increase its volume 10 per cent, whereas the
bending strength of the beam is increased 21 per cent. An increase
in the width of a beam, increases the bending strength by the
same percentage as the volume. An increase of 1″ in a beam
10″ deep will increase both bending strength and volume by 10
per cent.

No simple rule can be given to determine the size of girder,
joist, or plank required to carry a given load. Tables of safe
load for given spans, sizes, species, and spacings may be obtained
from various lumber associations.

The *softwoods* in class A, such as Douglas fir, southern yellow
pine, and western larch, dominate the structural field. They are
used both for heavy construction (barns and bridges) and light

construction (dwellings and small farm structures). In heavy
construction, softwoods in class B are used only occasionally.
In light construction, softwoods in class B, such as white fir,
hemlock, and Idaho white pine, are used extensively. Their light
weight and ease of working enable them to compete with the
stronger woods.

The *hardwoods* in classes A and B have largely dropped out
of the construction field, not because they are unsuited to the
use, but because of their value for uses with more exact requirements for furniture, flooring, and veneers in plywood.

Stiffness

Stiffness is a measure of the resistance to bending or deflection
under a load. In the floor and ceiling joists of a house, stiffness
is more important than actual breaking strength because it is
deflection or sag that must be reduced to a minimum to avoid
plaster cracks in ceilings and vibration in floors. (*Breaking
strength* refers to the load required to break a material; *stiffness*
refers to its ability to sustain loads with a minimum of deflection
or sag.) Stiffness is important also in shelving, ladder rails,
beams, and long slender columns.

Whereas stiffness is of great importance in floor joists, the
advantages of using a relatively stiff species will be lost if the
members are not fully dry at time of installation, so the fastenings and bracing hold well. Straight, well-seasoned joists of a
species that is relatively low in stiffness may give better results
than an inherently stiff wood that is green or carelessly installed.
If the wood is sufficiently dry and the installation is good, however, species differences with respect to stiffness are important.

Differences in stiffness between species may be compensated
for by changing the size of members. Depth and length of members have a greater effect on their stiffness than on other strength
properties. *For example*, a change of $\frac{1}{32}''$ in the thickness of a
$\frac{25}{32}''$ board produces a change of 12 per cent in the stiffness of
the board laid flat in a floor. A $10''$ joist has about one-fourth
more wood in it than an $8''$ joist, but set on edge in a building
it is more than twice as stiff. Softwoods in class A and class B
dominate the uses where stiffness is the most important requirement. Woods in class C are relatively unimportant, since they

are seldom used in heavy construction and only occasionally in light construction. When woods in class C are used where stiffness is desired, it is because other properties are more important. The woods in class A have the highest stiffness, but they are heavier and harder than those in class B.

Light weight is quite commonly desired in combination with stiffness. The softwoods meet this requirement much better than the hardwoods, and softwoods in class B are often chosen in preference to those in class A since the weight of the latter excludes them.

Posts

Posts or *compression members* are generally square or circular in cross section, usually upright, and support loads that act in the direction of the length. *Strength in compression* is an essential requirement for posts supporting beams in a basement or crawl space, for supports of root cellars, for storage bins, and for posts in similar heavy construction where the length is less than eleven times the smallest dimension. It is not important in fence posts, which carry no loads.

In small houses the size requirements of posts, with the smallest dimensions less than one-eleventh of the length, are determined by bearing area, stiffness, and stability, rather than by actual compressive strength. Therefore, it is necessary to use posts large enough to carry much greater compressive loads than are ever placed upon them. No great consideration need, therefore, be given to compressive strength endwise in selecting wood for small houses.

Where exceptionally heavy loads are involved, as in supports for underground cellars, consideration should be given to the compressive strength of different woods. Even where compressive strength is an important requirement, the woods in any class may be safely used, provided the lower strength of class B and C woods is compensated for by using timber of larger cross-sectional area.

When the length of the post or column is greater than eleven times the smallest dimension, stiffness becomes an important factor in determining the load-carrying ability. Unbraced supports, such as squared posts in machine sheds or barns and poles in pole-type structures, are generally so slender that they should be judged by their stiffness rather than their compressive strength.

Toughness

Toughness is a measure of the capacity to withstand suddenly applied loads. Therefore, woods high in shock resistance are adapted to withstand repeated shocks, jars, jolts, and blows, such as are given ax handles and other tool handles. The heavier hardwoods—hickory, birch, oak, maple, and ash—are much higher in shock resistance than the toughest of the softwoods. These hardwoods are used almost exclusively where an exceptionally tough wood is required. The woods in class A completely dominate the uses where toughness is the outstanding requirement, and hickory dominates class A.

Toughness is a desirable property in uses other than those in which it is required. Tough woods give more warning of failure than do brash woods. It is, therefore, a factor in beams and girders where heavy loads are applied. The selection of class C woods should normally be avoided for these two uses.

SURFACE CHARACTERISTICS OF COMMON GRADES OF LUMBER

Lumber is purchased by home owners because of its appearance as well as its working characteristics and strength properties. The appearance is dependent largely on the grade, and there is some degree of uniformity in the appearance of the same grade in different woods. Different woods are more uniform in appearance in the select grades than in common or dimension grades because most knots, pitch pockets, and the like are eliminated from the select grades.

In the common grades, where knots and similar surface features are allowable, there are differences in the same grade of different woods. These differences affect the appearance of the wood and at times its suitability for a use. *For example,* the number of knots and like features in a board averages, in different species, from about 5 to 20 per 8 board feet regardless of grade. Second- and third-grade common boards are selected for greatest utility. Fourth and lower grades permit moderate utility. (Grades for the various species for board and dimension lumber are described in a following section.)

Distinctive and Principal Uses

The *distinctive* and *principal uses* to which a wood is put are indicative of its properties. Distinctive and principal uses are those to which a wood is most generally fitted. The fact that a wood's distinctive use is for ax handles, for woodenware, or for fence posts tells one who is familiar with these uses much more about the wood than does a verbal description or a table of properties, unless he has been trained to combine and evaluate the properties. A knowledge of the requirements for ax handles obtained from actual experience gives a good idea of the combination of toughness, breaking strength, stiffness, and texture to be found in a wood used for that purpose.

LUMBER GRADES

Ordinary building lumber is graded by lumber manufacturers, by associations, or by official grading and inspection bureaus.

Softwood Lumber

Finish or select grades. Finish or select grades of lumber generally are named by the letters A, B, C, and D. The A and B grades are nearly always combined as B and Better, so that only three grades are in practical use.

Therefore, in lumber for interior and exterior finishing or other similar uses, only B and Better (first grade), C (second grade), and D (third grade) in softwoods need to be considered. However, considerable knotty pine and cedar in third grade are selected for use as paneling.

Common boards. Grade names for common boards are not uniform for all softwood species. *For example,* in redwood boards Select is the first grade, Construction the second grade, Merchantable the third grade, and Economy the fourth grade. With such woods as Douglas fir, west coast hemlock, Sitka spruce, and western red cedar, the grade designations are Select, Merchantable, Construction, Standard, Utility, and Economy. A different set of board grades described by the Western Wood Products Association bears the names 1 Common, 2 Common, 3 Common, 4 Common, and 5 Common. The same set of grade names and descriptions is used in the northeast and lake states for species such as eastern spruce, balsam fir, red and jack pine, eastern hemlock, and northern white cedar. For the southern pines, the board designations are No. 1, No. 2, No. 3, and No. 4.

Dimension lumber. Light framing (2″ to 4″ thick, 2″ to 4″ wide), and joists and planks (2″ to 4″ thick, 6″ and wider) are graded for strength to a common set of grade names and descriptions under all six softwood grading rules published in the United States and under the National Lumber Grades Authority in Canada. The light framing grades are Construction, Standard, and Utility, and the joist and plank grades are Select Structural, No. 1, No. 2, and No. 3. There is also a Structural Light Framing category for roof truss and similar applications that has the same grade names as for joists and planks. Load-carrying design values vary by species and use category. Therefore, it is important to note that common grade names do not imply equal strength or stiffness.

Trade practices. It has been the practice for the lumber retailer to quote prices and make deliveries on the basis of local grade classification or on his own judgment of what the user needs or will accept. However, there is a growing practice to put *indelible marks* on all building lumber at the sawmill, stating the grade, species, size, degree of seasoning, and identity of the supplier. The Federal Housing Administration (FHA) and most code authorities require that framing lumber used in the construction of FHA-insured units be so grade-marked.

The *softwoods* are graded to meet fairly definite building requirements. Select grades of softwoods are based on suitability for natural and paint finishes: A Select and B Select or B and Better are primarily for natural finishes, and C Select and D Select are for paint finishes. The Utility Board and Dimension grades are based primarily on their suitability for general construction and general utility purposes as influenced by the size, tightness, and soundness of knots.

Hardwood Lumber

The wood of the hardwood trees is graded on the basis of factory grades more than for building requirements. Factory grades take into account the yield and size of cuttings with one clear face that can be sawed from the lumber. The two highest factory grades are known as Firsts and Seconds and are usually sold combined.

Hardwoods for construction are grouped into three general classes: Finish, Construction and Utility Boards, and Dimension. A Finish has one face practically clear, while B Finish allows small surface checks, mineral streaks, and other minor variations.

Construction Boards and Utility Boards have No. 1, No. 2, and No. 3 grades and are based on the amount of wane, checks, knots, and other defects present in each board.

Dimension grades (2″ thick) are classed as No. 1 and No. 2 depending on the number of defects.

Strength Factor

The ordinary grades of building or so-called yard lumber are based on the size, number, and location of the knots, slope of grain, and the like more than on the strength of the clear wood. Common softwood boards used in conventionally constructed houses and other light-frame structures are not related directly to the strength of the unit itself. Rather, sheathing, subflooring, and roof boards supplement the framing system and may also add to the rigidity of the structure.

The main purpose of boards used in the construction of a building is as a covering material. They also facilitate nailing for siding, flooring, and roofing materials. For these purposes they must have some nail-holding properties as well as moderate strength in bending to carry loads between the frame members. Ordinarily, third- and fourth-grade boards are adequate for this purpose.

Finish and Select grade softwood boards are selected for their appearance rather than strength. They are used mainly for trim and finish purposes, and, consequently, the grade is chosen based on the type of finish used—natural, stained, or painted.

Softwood Dimension lumber is selected because of its strength and its stiffness. Therefore, the size, number, and location of knots are important and related directly to the intended use. *For example,* in house floors and walls, where construction is designed to minimize vibration and deflection so far as possible, stiffness rather than breaking strength is most important. Generally, grade affects strength more than stiffness—the lower the grade, the lower the strength.

Finishing and Appearance Factor

The *finishing* and *appearance* of *wood* is normally associated with the various Board grades rather than Dimension grades. With varnish and natural finishes, A and B Select in softwoods (commonly sold as B and Better) and A Finish in hardwoods assure the best appearance. Some pieces in .the B and Better grade are practically clear, although the average board contains one or two small surface features that preclude calling it Clear.

Where the very smoothest appearance is not required, second Finish grade in softwoods and hardwoods gives good satisfaction. The number of knots, pitch pockets, and other nonclear features per board in C Select averages about twice that of B and Better. The proportion of these features that are small knots is greater in C Select than in B and Better. Because of its decorative effects, knotty lumber selected from the first and second Common board grades is frequently in demand for paneling.

For painting where wood is not exposed to the weather, the surface features permitted in the second Finish grade are such that they can be well covered by paint if the priming is properly done. The third Finish grade, with some cutting out of defects, gives almost as good quality as the second grade, but the number and size of the knots are considerably greater, and often the back of the pieces is of lower quality. Where smoothest appearance at close inspection is required under exposure to the weather, first Finish grade gives the best results.

For painted surfaces that do not receive close inspection (summer cottages, barns, and the like) and where protection against the weather is as important as appearance, the first and second Board grades are satisfactory. The larger knots and pitch pockets in the second-grade Common softwood boards do not give as smooth and lasting a painted surface as do the smaller ones in the first grade, but the general utility is good.

Tightness Factor

First-grade Common softwood and Utility hardwood boards are suitable for protection against rain or other free water beating or seeping through walls or similar construction. These and the Finish grades are usually kept drier at the lumber yards than are the lower grades and will, therefore, shrink and open less at the joints if used without further drying. Where only tightness against leakage of small grain is required in a granary or grain bin, second-grade boards may be used with a small amount of cutting to eliminate knotholes. When used as sheathing with good building paper, second-grade boards are satisfactory even though knotholes and other similar openings do occur.

Wear-Resistance Factor

Edge-grained material wears better than flat grain, narrow-ringed wears better than wide-ringed, and clear wood wears more evenly than wood containing knots. The first Finish grades in softwoods and hardwoods ordinarily contain very few defects and withstand wear excellently. The second grade in softwoods and in hardwoods sufficiently limits knots and surface character-istics to assure good wearing qualities. Third-Finish grade and first-grade boards limit the size and character of knots, although not the number, and are satisfactory where maximum uniformity of wear is not required.

Decay-Resistance Factor

Any natural resistance to decay that a wood may have is in the heartwood. The decay resistance of the species so far as af-fected by grade therefore depends upon the proportion of heart-wood in the grade. While this is true of all species, it is of practical importance only in woods with medium or highly decay-resistant heartwood.

The lower grades usually contain more heartwood than do the Select grades. If decay resistance is really needed for the pur-pose at hand, the first and second board grades are more decay resistant than are the Finish grades, except in the case of the special Finish grades known as All Heart.

The full decay resistance of grades below the second grade is reduced by the presence of decay that may have existed in the tree or log before it was sawn into lumber. Under conditions conducive to decay, such original decay may spread, although some types of decay, notably peck in cypress, red heart in pine, and white pocket in Douglas fir, are definitely known to cease functioning once the lumber is properly seasoned.

Price Factor

The spread in price between Select Finish and Utility Board grades varies considerably from time to time, depending upon supply and demand. The cost of the lower Select grades is substantially greater than the upper Board grades of softwoods. With such a difference in price it is obviously important not to buy a better grade than is needed. *Any tendency to buy the best the market offers for all uses is wasteful of both lumber and money,* for in uses such as sheathing, the lower and cheaper grades will render as long and satisfactory service as the higher-priced grades.

The price spread between the combined grade of first- and second-Finish grades and the Common grades of hardwoods is also large. This is of minor importance to builders because most of the hardwood purchased by them has already been manufactured into some form of finished product, such as flooring or interior trim.

Roughly, the combined grade of first and second Finish may have a market value from 50 to 100 per cent greater than that of the highest Common grade and contain from 25 to 50 per cent greater than that of the best Common grade, and contain from 25 to 50 per cent more clear face cuttings of the sizes specified in the grading rules. If large clear face pieces are required, they can best and possibly only be obtained from the first and second grades. But if only medium-sized or small clear face pieces are required, they can be obtained from the Common grades.

STANDARD LUMBER ITEMS AND WOOD-BASED PRODUCTS SOLD IN RETAIL LUMBERYARDS

Lumber is sold as a number of standard general-purpose items and also as certain special-purpose items. Retail lumberyards carry all the general-purpose items and the more important of the special-purpose items. A brief description of framing and dimension, boards and sheathing, flooring and siding, and other lumber and related items commonly carried by most retail lumberyards is given in this section.

Many lumberyards carry stock items in wood species besides those common to the United States. Larger lumber companies may also have their own sash and door plants and will make to order any wood unit listed in the plans or specifications of frame buildings. The popularity of the wood truss has also brought about the fabrications of these items at many lumberyards.

Dressed Thicknesses and Widths of Lumber

Lumber as ordinarily stocked in retail yards is surfaced (dressed) on two sides and two edges. This is to make the lumber ready to use and uniform in size without further reworking and also to avoid paying transportation costs on material that would have to be cut off on the job. The amount that is reasonable and desirable to dress off has varied considerably in the past and has been the subject of some controversy and misunderstanding among producing and consuming groups. American lumber standards have been set up by the lumber trade with the assistance of government agencies in such a way as to largely take care of the situation.

American lumber standards and common trade practices now provide dressed sizes. Table 2 shows nominal- and minimum-dressed sizes of boards, dimension, and timbers. (The thicknesses apply to all widths and all widths to all thicknesses.) Table 3 shows nominal- and minimum-dressed dry sizes of finish, flooring, ceiling, partition, and stepping at 19 per cent maximum moisture content. (The thicknesses apply to all widths and to all thicknesses *except* as modified.) The column designated nominal size shows the dimensions according to which lumber is usually described. The last column shows the actual dimensions of lumber when it is sold surfaced.

When the dimensions of dressed lumber are less than those shown in the table for the actual sizes enumerated, the lumber is known as substandard. Items of some woods are commonly sold in substandard sizes. It is well to check the dimensions before selecting a wood so that allowance can be made in both price and utility for substandard sizes or proper credit given for oversizes.

TABLE 2

Nominal- and minimum-dressed sizes of boards, dimension, and timbers
(The thicknesses apply to all widths and all widths to all thicknesses)

ITEM	THICKNESSES			FACE WIDTHS		
	NOMINAL	Minimum Dressed		NOMINAL	Minimum Dressed	
		Dry	Green		Dry	Green
		Inches	*Inches*		*Inches*	*Inches*
Boards				2	1½	1$\frac{9}{16}$
				3	2½	2$\frac{9}{16}$
				4	3½	3$\frac{9}{16}$
				5	4½	4⅝
	1	¾	$\frac{25}{32}$	6	5½	5⅝
				7	6½	6⅝
	1¼	1	1$\frac{1}{32}$	8	7¼	7½
				9	8¼	8½
	1½	1¼	1$\frac{9}{32}$	10	9¼	9½
				11	10¼	10½
				12	11¼	11½
				14	13¼	13½
				16	15¼	15½
Dimension				2	1½	1$\frac{9}{16}$
				3	2½	2$\frac{9}{16}$
				4	3½	3$\frac{9}{16}$
	2	1½	1$\frac{9}{16}$	5	4½	4⅝
	2½	2	2$\frac{1}{16}$	6	5½	5⅝
	3	2½	2$\frac{9}{16}$	8	7¼	7½
	3½	3	3$\frac{1}{16}$	10	9¼	9½
				12	11¼	11½
				14	13¼	13½
				16	15¼	15½
Dimension				2	1½	1$\frac{9}{16}$
				3	2½	2$\frac{9}{16}$
				4	3½	3$\frac{9}{16}$
				5	4½	4⅝
	4	3½	3$\frac{9}{16}$	6	5½	5⅝
	4½	4	4$\frac{1}{16}$	8	7¼	7½
				10	9¼	9½
				12	11¼	11½
				14		13½
				16		15½
Timbers	5 & Thicker		½ Off	5 & Wider		½ Off

TABLE 3

*Nominal- and minimum-dressed dry sizes of finish, flooring, ceiling, partition,
and stepping at 19 per cent maximum moisture content
(The thicknesses apply to all widths and all widths
to all thicknesses except as modified)*

ITEM	THICKNESSES		FACE WIDTHS	
	NOMINAL	Minimum Dressed	NOMINAL	Minimum Dressed
		Inches		*Inches*
Finish	3/8	5/16	2	1½
	½	7/16	3	2½
	5/8	9/16	4	3½
	¾	5/8	5	4½
	1	¾	6	5½
	1¼	1	7	6½
	1½	1¼	8	7¼
	1¾	1⅜	9	8¼
	2	1½	10	9¼
	2½	2	11	10¼
	3	2½	12	11¼
	3½	3	14	13¼
	4	3½	16	15¼
Flooring	3/8	5/16	2	1⅛
	½	7/16	3	2⅛
	5/8	9/16	4	3⅛
	1	¾	5	4⅛
	1¼	1	6	5⅛
	1½	1¼		
Ceiling	3/8	5/16	3	2⅛
	½	7/16	4	3⅛
	5/8	9/16	5	4⅛
	¾	11/16	6	5⅛
Partition	1	23/32	3	2⅛
			4	3⅛
			5	4⅛
			6	5⅛
Stepping	1	¾	8	7¼
	1¼	1	10	9¼
	1½	1¼	12	11¼
	2	1½		

Framing and Dimension

Dimension is primarily framing lumber, such as joists, rafters, and wall studs. It also comprises the planking used for heavy barn floors. Strength, stiffness, and uniformity of size are essential requirements. *Framing* or *dimension* lumber is stocked in all lumberyards but often in only one or two of the general-purpose construction woods such as Douglas fir, southern yellow pine, white fir, hemlock, or spruce. It is usually a nominal 2″ thick, dressed one or two sides to 1½″ dry. (*See* Table 2.) It is nominally 4″, 6″, 8″, 10″, or 12″ in width, and 8′ to 20′ long in multiples of 2′. Dimension thicker than 2″ (up to 5″) and longer than 20′ is manufactured only in comparatively small quantities.

Perhaps the one most suitable grade for permanent construction wall framing, based on economy and performance, is the third grade in the various species. The grade most generally suitable for joists and rafters for permanent and first-class construction is the second grade of the various species. Satisfactory construction is possible with lower grades, but pieces must be selected and there is considerably more cutting loss. Many species have structural grade classifications that may be used for trusses and other structural components. These structural grades allow greater loads than do equal spans of the lower grades.

Boards or Sheathing

Boards are general-purpose items used most often to cover framing members as flooring, roofing, and wall sheathing. They are available at all lumberyards in one or more kinds of wood most frequently used in building construction. Boards are usually of nominal 1″ thickness, dressed on two sides to ¾″ dry thickness, and are usually manufactured in all grades from first to fifth. (*See* Table 3.) However, as sheathing material, the third and fourth grades are most often used.

Boards or sheathing are manufactured in a number of patterns. They may be square-edged (surfaced on four sides), generally supplied in nominal 4″, 6″, and 8″ widths. They are also available in dressed and matched pattern (tongued-and-grooved) and in shiplap (Fig. 2a). Dressed and matched material is most commonly sold in 6″ widths; shiplap, in 8″, 10″, and 12″ widths. In addition to sheathing and subflooring, boards are used for rough siding, barn boards, and concrete forms. The advent of the pole-type construction has developed the need for center matched sheathing in 2″ by 6″ nominal size. Many lumber companies stock this item preservative-treated.

Siding

Siding, as the name implies, is made and generally used for exterior coverage. It is produced in several general patterns: bevel siding, drop siding, and V-edge siding or paneling (Fig. 2a). Bevel siding is ordinarily stocked in Clear, A grades and B

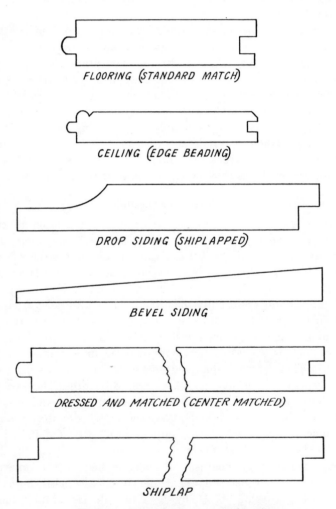

FLOORING (STANDARD MATCH)

CEILING (EDGE BEADING)

DROP SIDING (SHIPLAPPED)

BEVEL SIDING

DRESSED AND MATCHED (CENTER MATCHED)

SHIPLAP

Fig. 2a. Six typical patterns of lumber.

grades of redwood, western red cedar, hemlock, white and ponderosa pine, and spruce. Drop siding is stocked in C and Better
and No. 2 Common grades, and V-edge siding are Douglas fir and
southern pine.

Other exterior lumber coverings include *boards* and *battens*
and other combinations for vertical application. These are commonly rough-sawn boards in Finish grades that are given a
stain finish.

Bevel siding (Fig. 2a) is commonly supplied in ½″, ⅝″, and
¾″ thicknesses in nominal 6″, 8″, and 10″ widths. Special patterns are available in 12″ widths. Drop siding is normally ¾″
in thickness and 5¼″ in face width. (*Face width* is the coverage
width when material is in place.) V-edge siding is ¾″ thick and
6″, 8″, and 10″ nominal width (Fig. 2a). Bevel siding ordinarily
is not used for garages, barns, and similar buildings because of
cost. Also it is normally laid horizontally over lumber, plywood,
or other wood-base sheathing. Some of the thicker grades are
occasionally used without sheathing on small garages when the
studs are spaced no more than 16″ on center. Bevel siding is
lapped from 1″ to 1½″ depending on spacing required between
window heights.

Drop siding (Fig. 2a), because of its uniform thickness, is
most often used without sheathing and is applied horizontally.
Drop siding has a ⅜″ to ½″ lap. *Matched* pattern drop siding
is also available. V-edge dressed and matched siding may be
applied horizontally or vertically. When it is applied vertically,
blocking is required between the studs or vertical members to
provide for nailing, if sheathing is not of plywood or lumber.
Board and batten combinations require the same type of backing.

The lap of the bevel siding, combined with the actual width,
makes it necessary to use from 120 to 150 surface feet for every
100 square feet of surface to be covered. Drop siding requires
somewhat less than 115 board feet of 1″ by 6″ drop siding to
cover 100 square feet of surface, discounting cutting loss.

Other siding materials that are available in many lumberyards include paper-overlaid plywood siding and medium- and
high-density hardboard. These materials can usually be obtained in 4-foot-wide sheets or prepackaged in narrow sections
ready for installation. Medium- or high-density overlaid ply-

wood sheets in ½" and greater thicknesses can be applied vertically directed on framing members with proper spacing, serving both as sheathing and siding, for barns and other buildings. Batten strips are normally used over the vertical joints.

Flooring

Flooring (Fig. 2a) is made chiefly of hardwood such as maple, oak, birch, and beech, and of the harder softwood species such as Douglas fir and southern pine. At least one of the softwoods and two of the hardwoods are stocked in most lumberyards. Flooring is usually of nominal 1" by 3" and 1" by 4" sizes. Dressed thickness is $^{25}/_{32}$", and face widths are 2¼" and 3¼". Thicker flooring, in Douglas fir and southern pine, is available and is used for porch flooring without need for a subfloor. Edge grain proves the most satisfactory. Thinner hardwood flooring, usually square-edged, is another form sometimes used as a finish floor.

Block or parquet flooring is 3- or 5-ply plywood or laminated form is available in ½" and $^{25}/_{32}$" thicknesses and is also made in particle board form. Block flooring is usually installed with a mastic adhesive. When placed on concrete floors, a sealer is used under the block floor and a vapor barrier under the concrete slab to prevent moisture problems.

Edge-grained flooring shrinks less in width than flat-grained flooring. It is more uniform in texture, wears more uniformly, and joints do not open up as much. *Flat-grained flooring* costs less and is commonly used where appearance is not important. Both edge- and flat-grained flooring are carried in stock by many dealers.

Most *softwood flooring* is either southern yellow pine or Douglas fir. The higher grades are commonly finished with varnish or sealer. The lower grades are perhaps most suited for dark stained or painted finishes. Southern pine has five grades: A, B, C, D, and No. 2 flooring. A and B grades are often combined and are classed as B and Better. Douglas fir has edge- and flat-grained classifications—edge grain in B and Better, C, and D grades, and flat grain in C and Better, D, and E grades.

Hardwood unfinished flooring has many grade classifications depending on the species. Oak flooring has edge-grained grades classed as Clear and Select. Flat-grained oak flooring can be obtained in grades of Clear, Select, No. 1 Common, and No. 2 Common. Maple, birch, and other species have classifications of First, Second, and Third grades.

Exterior Molding and Finish

Exterior moldings and finish are used on cornices, at gable ends, and other finish areas of buildings. Houses may ordinarily be designed with a closed cornice for a desired architectural appearance, but sheds, barns, and other buildings are usually constructed with an open cornice or rafter overhang. *Exterior moldings* are usually furnished in clear ponderosa pine, southern yellow pine, and Douglas fir. Many types and sizes are available including crown molding, brick molding, and bed molding as well as moldings used for door and window trim.

Exterior finish material is furnished in the Select grades in nominal sizes from 1″ by 2″ to 1″ by 12″ and also in 1¼″ by 6″ and 1¼″ by 8″, all surfaced four sides (S4S). The nominal 1″ finish is used for cornice construction and the 1¼″ at gable ends or other areas where siding terminates. Woods used include ponderosa pine, western red cedar, redwood, and west coast hemlock.

Shingles

Most *wood shingles* available in retail lumberyards are of western red cedar, although redwood, white cedar, and cypress are also sometimes stocked. Three grades of shingles are classed under Red Cedar Shingle Bureau rules in three lengths:

No. 1 Blue Label shingles are all clear, all heart, and all edge grain, and are used for the best work since they are less likely to warp. *No. 2 Red Label shingles* have clear butts about two-thirds to three-quarters of their length and may contain some flat grain and a little sapwood. This grade is often used for roofs of secondary buildings or to cover sidewalls. *No. 3 Black Label shingles* have knots and other defects that are undesirable for surface exposure but have a 6″ to 10″ clear butt depending on their length. This grade is sometimes used as the undercourse in double-course application of sidewalls. An *undercours-*

ing shingle is produced expressly for use on double-course side-walls.

Shingles are produced in three lengths—16″, 18″, and 24″. The 16″ shingle, the one most likely to be stocked by retail lumberyards, has a standard thickness designated as 5/2-16 (five shingles measure 2″ thick at the butt when green). The 16″ shingles are based on a 5″ exposure when used on roofs, and four bundles will cover 100 square feet (one square). When used in single-course sidewall application, three bundles of 16″ shingles will cover 100 square feet laid with a 7″ exposure. Bundled shingles come in random widths of 3″ and up. Five 18″ shingles measure 2¼″ at the butt, and four 24″ shingles measure 2″ at the butt when green.

Door and Window Frames

Wood door and window frames, sash, and other similar mill-work items are sometimes available in retail lumberyards in standard sizes. Sash and door manufacturers produce ready-hung window units, and the frame, weather-stripped sash, and trim are prefitted, assembled, and ready to be placed in the rough wall opening. However, in smaller retail yards it is usu-ally necessary to order before actual use because many window and door sizes and styles are not stock items.

Ponderosa pine is a species used by most manufacturers for frames and window sash, but southern pine and Douglas fir are sometimes used for frame parts. Frames for outside doors are usually provided with oak sills to increase their resistance to wear. However, some sills of the softer woods are supplied with metal edgings located at the wearing surfaces.

Most present-day millwork such as door and window frames, sash, and exterior doors are treated at the factory with a water-repellent preservative. This treatment not only aids in resisting moisture but also in minimizing decay hazards.

Plywood

Plywood is a term generally used to designate glued wood panels that are made up of layers, or plies, with the grain of one or more layers at an angle, usually 90°, with the grain of the others. The outside plies are called faces or face and back, the center ply or plies are called the core, and the plies immediately below the face and back, laid at right angles to them, are called the crossbands. (*See* Chap. 1, Fig. 1.)

Because plywood is widely available, relatively low in cost, and easy to apply, it can be used to advantage in the construction of homes and farm buildings. It is principally used as a covering material such as subfloor, wall sheathing, and roof sheathing. It is often used for walls and roofs without additional covering for secondary farm buildings. Plywood may also be used for cabinetwork and as an interior-finish wall-panel material fabricated in many forms from a variety of species.

The two common types of plywood are *interior* and *exterior*. The names designate their recommended uses. Sheathing grades are also available. One form of plywood has a resin-impregnated paper overlay on two sides; in this form it is sometimes used as an exterior siding or finish without the benefit of sheathing. This type of plywood is made with waterproof glue and consequently is suitable for exterior use.

Both exterior and interior types are available with a variety of sizes and grades of face veneers, ranging from A-A and paper-overlaid faces to C-D sheathing grade. The following are general thicknesses and grades commonly used in frame construction:

Plywood in the *Standard interior grade* commonly used for wall sheathing should be ⅜″ or ½″ thick if a siding is applied over the plywood. *Rough-textured or patterned exterior* plywood (stained finish) used as exterior finish without sheathing is usually ½″ or more thick depending on the spacing of the studs and the species of plywood. *Plywood roof sheathing* (Standard interior, C-D) should be at least ⅜″ thick if Douglas fir or southern pine plywood is used and rafters are spaced 16″ on center. When rafters are spaced 24″ on center, plywood sheathing should be at least ½″ thick if Douglas fir or southern pine is used and ⅝″ thick if other western softwoods are used.

Douglas fir or southern pine plywood used as *subflooring* should be at least ½″ thick and other softwood plywood ⅝″ thick when *strip flooring* is employed. When *wood-block finish floor* is specified for houses, plywood should be ⅝″ thick. For a *resilient finish floor*, the plywood should be ¾″ thick. Side- and end-matched Douglas fir plywood in 1⅛″ thickness is available for use when supports are spaced as much as 48″ on center. Plywood used for subfloor and for wall and roof sheathing may be interior or exterior. For exterior use, plywood should always be exterior type.

Hardwood plywood is available in a number of species, and its main use is as a finish covering. The three types available are: Type 1, fully waterproof bond; type 2, water-resistant bond; and type 3, moisture-resistant bond. *Grades* consist of Premium; Good, suitable for natural finish; Sound, suitable for a smooth painted surface; Utility, used as sheathing or similar coverages; and Backing. Knots, splits, and other defects are allowed in the Utility and Backing grades.

Much hardwood plywood is used as veneers for flush-solid and hollow-core doors. Because of its variety of uses, standard hardwood plywood is available in widths of 24″ to 48″ and lengths from 48″ to 96″.

Other Sheet Materials

Many types of sheet materials in addition to plywood are being used for sheathing walls because they are easily applied and resist racking.

Structural Insulating Board

Structural insulating board sheathing in ½″ and $25\frac{}{32}$″ thicknesses is available in 2′ by 8′ and 4′ by 8′ sheets. The 2′ by 8′ sheets are applied horizontally and usually have shallow V or tongued-and-grooved edges. The 4′ by 8′ sheets are square-edged and applied vertically with perimeter nailing. These building boards are made water resistant by means of an asphalt coating or by impregnation.

When insulating board sheathing is applied with the 2′ by 8′ sheets horizontally, the construction normally is not rigid enough. Auxiliary bracing, such as 1″ by 4″ let in bracing, is necessary.

A wall with enough rigidity to withstand wind forces can be built with 4′ by 8′ panels of three types: regular-density sheathing $25\frac{}{32}$″ thick, intermediate-density material ½″ thick, or nail-base grades. Panels must be installed vertically and properly nailed. Each manufacturer of insulating board has recommended nailing schedules to satisfy this requirement.

Interior structural insulating board ½" thick and laminated paperboard in ½" and ⅜" thickness may be obtained in 4' by 8' sheets painted on one side, or in paneled form for use as an interior covering material. These materials are also produced in a tongued-and-grooved ceiling tile in sizes from 12" by 12" to 16" by 32"; thicknesses vary between ½" and 1". They may be designed to serve as a prefinished decorative insulating tile or to provide acoustical qualities. The present practice of manufacturers is to furnish interior board either plain or acoustical with a flamespread-retardant paint finish.

Medium Hardboard

Medium hardboards are generally available in nominal ⁷⁄₁₆" and ½" thicknesses in 4' wide sheets or in the form of siding. This material provides good service when used as exterior coverage in sheet form or as lap siding. The 4' by 8' sheets are applied vertically, with batten strips placed over the joints and between for decorative effect.

High-Density Hardboard

High-density hardboard in standard or tempered form is commonly supplied in ⅛" and ¼" thick sheets of 4' by 8' size. It may be used for both interior and exterior covering material. As with plywood or medium hardboard, the high-density hardboard in the thicker types can be applied vertically with batten strips or horizontally as a lap siding.

In perforated form, both types of hardboard are used as soffit material under cornice overhangs to ventilate attic spaces. In untreated form, high-density hardboard of special grade is also used as an underlayment for resilient flooring materials. Hardboards can be obtained with decorative laminated surfaces that provide a pleasing appearance as interior paneling.

Particle Board

Particle board, a sheet material made up of resin-bonded wood particles, is most often used as an underlayment for resilient flooring. It is also adaptable as covering material for interior walls or other uses where they are not exposed to moisture. Particle board is usually supplied in 4' by 8' sheets and in

⅜″ thickness for paneling, in ⅝″ thickness for underlayment, and in block form for flooring. It is also used for cabinet and closet doors and as core stock for table tops and other furniture.

Interior Finish and Millwork

Interior finish and millwork include doorjambs and doors; casing, base, base shoe, stool, apron, and other trim and moldings; stair parts; and various cabinets, fireplace mantels, and other manufactured units. Such interior trim as casing and base is stocked in most retail lumberyards in several patterns and at least one species of wood.

Ponderosa pine, Douglas fir, and southern yellow pine are the softwoods usually available. Oak and birch are hardwoods most likely to be stocked by lumberyards. Species not carried in stock may be obtained and manufactured on special order. Interior trim, moldings, and other interior finish are ordinarily furnished in a clear grade. Paneling in pine, cedar, and similar woods usually contains knots and other grain variations for a decorative effect.

Inside doorjambs are ¾″ thick and vary in width from 4½″ to 5⅜″, depending on the type of interior wall finish—drywall or plaster. *Base* may vary in size from ⁷⁄₁₆″ by 2¼″ to ⁹⁄₁₆″ by 3¼″ and wider. The modern trend is toward a narrow base, except in strictly traditional interiors. Base shoe is ½″ by ¾″ in size, although quarterround, ¾″ by ¾″, is sometimes used as a molding between the base and the finish floor.

Casing and other trim around door and window frames may be obtained in several patterns and sizes. Two common patterns are the *Colonial* type with a molded face and the *Ranch* or *Bevel* trim with a simple beveled face and rounded corners. These types of casing are usually ⅝″ or ¾″ thick and 2¼″ to 2¾″ wide.

Cabinets, fireplace mantels, and *stair parts* are usually *special-order items* that the lumber dealer must order from the manufacturer. *Interior doors* in flush or panel type are often stocked in standard sizes by many of the larger retail yards. Interior doors are normally 1⅜″ thick and vary in width from 2′ for small closets, to 2′ 6″ and wider for other doors. Standard height is 6′ 8″ for doors used on the first floor and 6′ 6″ for doors used on the second floor. There is a trend in some interior designs of houses to use full wall-height doors. This eliminates the need for headers, head casing and trim, and other construction details associated with lower doors.

Standard exterior doors are 1¾" thick and 6' 8" high. Panel doors with solid wood rail and stiles and solid-core flush doors are the types most often stocked in retail lumberyards for exterior use.

PREPARING PIECES FOR USE

Cutting lumber out in rough. All lumber must be squared, to find any deviation from a right angle, straight line, or plane surface, and trued to the required size before proceeding with the actual work. The tools required for squaring, truing, and preliminary cutting are: a jack or smoothing plane, block plane, straightedge, rule, marking gauge, saw, knife, and pencil.

Cut the lumber out in rough, and wherever possible discard the parts that have large knots, knotholes, bad rips, or similar imperfections. Make an additional allowance of ¼" to ⅜" in width and ½" to 1" in length for material to be removed during the squaring and the truing-up operations. This allowance from time to time will vary slightly from the given amount.

Preparing a working face. The first step in preparing a working face on rough lumber is to test for straightness. When two diagonally opposite corners of a board are higher than the other two corners, a board is said to be "in wind." It is then necessary to plane with the jack or smoothing plane across the high corners until the board is straight. To find out whether a board is in wind, place a straightedge on each end of the surface across the grain (*A*, Fig. 3). Sight under the straightedges in the direction of the grain of the wood. If the straightedges are parallel, the surface of the stock is not in wind. If they are not parallel, then the pieces in wind must be trued up.

To test for general straightness lengthwise, sight or use a straightedge along the grain of the board.

To test for straightness across the grain, place the blade of an inverted try square on the surface of the stock, hold the board

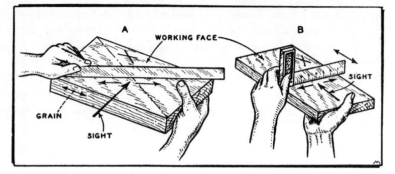

Fig. 3.   Testing with straightedge for flatness of lumber.

Preparing a working edge.   When the trueness of the face of the lumber has been checked by making the three tests just specified, mark the tested working face with a cross to show that it has been squared and trued (*A*, Fig. 4).   This marked face is now the side from which all other tests for squareness and trueness should be made (*A*, Fig. 4).

To prepare a working edge, use either a jack or smoothing plane.   Secure the work, which we will now term the stock, in a vise and take several light, even shavings on the edge of the stock (*B*, Fig. 4).   Between each of the shavings, test the edge by pressing the handle of the try square against the marked working face and the blade on the edge of the stock.   Slide the at eye level, and sight toward the light (*B*, Fig. 3).   If there is light between the blade and the stock, the surface is not level.

The next step is planing for smoothness.   Use either the smoothing or the jack plane, pressing down firmly on the top of the plane at the beginning of the stroke, and gradually releasing the tension at the end of the stroke.   If a board is slightly warped, the working face can be trued up easily by planing across the grain until full-length shavings are obtained.

blade along the edge of the stock.   When no light can be seen between the blade and the edge of the stock, the working edge is square and true.   Mark the edge with a cross to show that it is the working edge.

Preparing a working end.   To prepare a working end, mark the required width on the working face of the stock with the

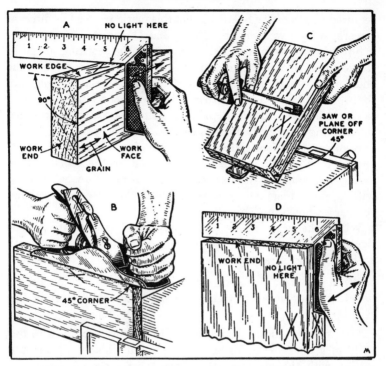

Fig. 4. Preparing, squaring, and testing working surfaces.

marking gauge. This is a guideline to show how much of the corner can be cut off by the saw prior to planing the ends. Cut off the corner outside the gauged line with the saw at about a 45° angle to prevent the stock from chipping or splitting while planing against the grain to that corner (*C*, Fig. 4).

Now square a line around the entire piece, holding the handle of the try square first against the working edge and then against the working face (*D*, Fig. 4). Plane to the marked line with the block plane, and test for squareness with both the face and working edge, and mark with a cross to denote the working end (*B* and *D*, Fig. 4).

Squaring to required length. To square the stock to the required length, measure from the working end and mark off the required length of the board. From this mark, proceed as directed for preparing a working end (*B*, *C*, and *D*, Fig. 4).

Squaring to required thickness. Set the marking gauge to the required thickness and mark a line around the edges and the ends of the stock, with the head of the gauge held tight against the working face. Using either a jack or smoothing plane, and taking thin, even shavings, plane the stock down to the marked line, testing frequently for squareness and trueness.

Removing surface defects. Lumber often has surface defects caused by the mill planers or shapers or by the tools used in truing and squaring the lumber. These usually can be removed with a cabinet scraper and sandpaper. The use of a cabinet scraper is shown in Chap. 2.

Where the grain of the wood has been torn slightly, plane lightly with a smoothing plane and scrape the surface smooth with a cabinet scraper.

When the grain has been torn badly, use either a commercial wood filler, or a sawdust-and-glue filler, described later in this chapter.

First remove all loose splinters from the torn section with the point of a brad awl or knife. With the knife blade, fill the torn section with the filler slightly above the surface of the board. Allow approximately 24 hours for it to set and harden and then sand it down to the surface of the board.

Solid or firm knots can be smoothed down to the surface of the lumber with a scraper and sandpaper, but loose knots must be removed and the hole filled.

Lumber that has been handled roughly may have a number of dents, which often can be eliminated by dropping a few drops of water on the dented surface and by picking at the spot with the point of a knife or brad awl. This causes the fibers of the wood to swell and thus fill the dent. After the moisture has dried out, sand down the spot even with the surface of the board.

Small splits sometimes can be removed by the use of a filler. A bad split in the end of a board can be repaired by cutting out a wedge-shaped section of the board where the split occurs, and by gluing in a piece cut exactly to fit the opening.

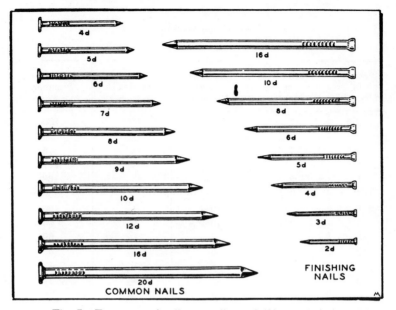

Fig. 5. Two types of nails generally used (⅔ actual size).

NAILS, SCREWS, OTHER FASTENERS, AND HARDWARE

Common and finishing nails. Although there are many varieties of nails, the two kinds most generally used are common and finishing nails. Common nails are used for the framework of buildings, and for subfloors and general rough woodworking. They have flat heads and pyramid-shaped points and are available in various sizes and gauges (Fig. 5).

Finishing nails are used to secure trim and all finishing woodwork into place. They have pyramidal points and small heads, called brad-heads. Finishing nails are usually countersunk (Fig. 5).

Sizes of both common and finishing nails are designated by the old English penny system. When and how this system origi-

TABLE 4

Common and finishing nails

COMMON NAILS*

Size in Penny	Length in Inches	Diameter Gauge Number	Diameter of Head in Inches	Approximate Number to a Pound
2 d	1	15	$\frac{11}{64}$	830
3	$1\frac{1}{4}$	14	$\frac{13}{64}$	528
4	$1\frac{1}{2}$	$12\frac{1}{2}$	$\frac{1}{4}$	316
5	$1\frac{3}{4}$	$12\frac{1}{2}$	$\frac{1}{4}$	271
6	2	$11\frac{1}{2}$	$\frac{17}{64}$	168
7	$2\frac{1}{4}$	$11\frac{1}{2}$	$\frac{17}{64}$	150
8	$2\frac{1}{2}$	$10\frac{1}{4}$	$\frac{9}{32}$	106
9	$2\frac{3}{4}$	$10\frac{1}{4}$	$\frac{9}{32}$	96
10	3	9	$\frac{5}{16}$	69
12	$3\frac{1}{4}$	9	$\frac{5}{16}$	63
16	$3\frac{1}{2}$	8	$\frac{11}{32}$	49
20	4	6	$\frac{13}{32}$	31
30	$4\frac{1}{2}$	5	$\frac{7}{16}$	24
40	5	4	$\frac{15}{32}$	18
50	$5\frac{1}{2}$	3	$\frac{1}{2}$	14
60	6	2	$\frac{17}{32}$	11

FINISHING NAILS*

Size in Penny	Length in Inches	Diameter Gauge Number	Diameter of Head Gauge Number	Approximate Number to a Pound
2 d	1	$16\frac{1}{2}$	$13\frac{1}{2}$	1351
3	$1\frac{1}{4}$	$15\frac{1}{2}$	$12\frac{1}{2}$	807
4	$1\frac{1}{2}$	15	12	584
5	$1\frac{3}{4}$	15	12	500
6	2	13	10	309
8	$2\frac{1}{2}$	$12\frac{1}{2}$	$9\frac{1}{2}$	189
10	3	$11\frac{1}{2}$	$8\frac{1}{2}$	121
16	$3\frac{1}{2}$	11	8	90
20	4	10	7	62

* The above tables are reprinted from the *Catalog of U.S.S. American Nails* by courtesy of the American Steel and Wire Company.

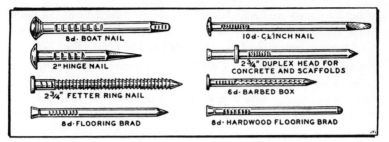

Fig. 6. Special-application nails (⅔ actual size).

nated is rather vague, but it is still in use. The standard abbreviation for the English penny is *d*, and this abbreviation is used in specifying common or finishing nails.

Special-purpose nails. Special-purpose nails are nails that have been modified to meet special requirements. There are over a hundred varieties of such nails in use today. They are made for plasterboard, concrete forms, shingles, crates, boats, flooring, and many other specific purposes (Fig. 6). Some special-purpose nails are graded in sizes according to their length in inches, others are designated and graded by the penny system.

Brads and wire nails. Brads are pyramid-pointed brad-headed nails of small diameter. The heads are considerably smaller than the heads of finishing nails. Brads are used in cabinetwork and other types of fine work where it is necessary to countersink nailheads.

Wire nails are flat-headed and pyramid-pointed, and are smaller in diameter than common nails. Wire nails are used in working with light, thin wood which a common nail invariably would split.

Brads and wire nails are available in sizes from ³⁄₁₆″ to 3″ in length. Their diameter is measured by the American Steel and Wire Gauge Standards and ranges from No. 24 to No. 10 gauge.

Wood screws. The two most commonly used wood screws are the flat-head and round-head. Two variations of the round-head screw are the oval-head and fillister-head types (Fig. 7).

Wood screws are sized according to their diameter and length. Diameters range from No. 0, which is .060″, to No. 24, .372″. The length of a flat-head screw is the over-all length; the lengths of both fillister- and round-head screws are taken from the point to the underside of the head of the screw; while that of the oval-head type is computed from the point to the head (Fig. 7).

Corrugated screws. Corrugated fasteners are sometimes called wiggle nails. They are available in various sizes, with either a plain edge or a saw edge, and are used for fastening the miter joints in window screens and frames and in screen doors, and also for tightening loose joints in furniture and woodwork. .

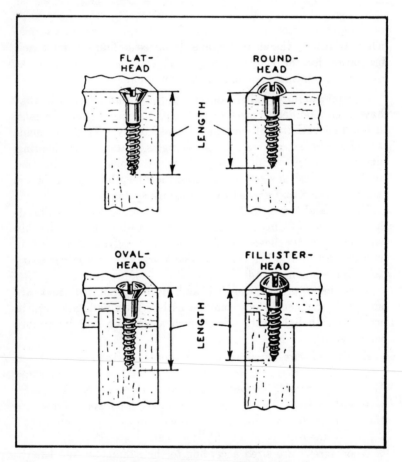

Fig. 7. Wood screws and types of heads.

The one with a saw edge is used for softwoods, the plain edge type for hardwoods. When fastening work with a wiggle nail, it is necessary to rest the work on a solid surface. Drive in the fastener with a medium-weight hammer, using evenly distributed light blows.

Dowels. Dowels are round wooden sticks ranging in size from 1/8″ to 1½″ in diameter and to 3′ in length. They are used for strengthening edge-to-edge joints, for plugging screw holes, and for many other special purposes in woodworking.

Screw fasteners. Screw fasteners are made from either plain or galvanized steel, and are available in various sizes and forms. They are easily installed wherever required and are widely used as hooks (Fig. 8).

Hooks and eyes. Hooks and eyes are available in many shapes and sizes, and are made either of brass or of plain or galvanized steel. They are used as fasteners on screen and cellar doors, on storm windows, and for many other purposes (Fig. 9).

Bolts and nuts. Various types and sizes of bolts and nuts are used on the standard equipment found in modern houses. The carriage bolt and the machine bolt are the two types in general use.

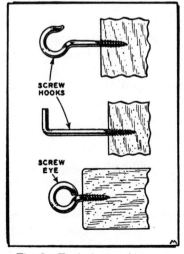

Fig. 8. Typical screw fasteners.

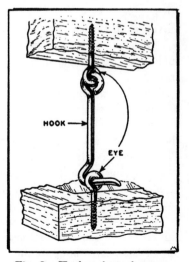

Fig. 9. Hook-and-eye fastener.

The carriage bolt has an oval head and is square for a short distance below the head. This square portion of the shank keeps the bolt from turning when it is screwed into place. The machine bolt has no square section on its shank, but it has a square head which is held with a wrench or pliers while the nut is tightened.

Other types are wing bolts, wing nuts, cap screws, cap nuts, and lock nuts. Wing nuts and bolts are useful as fasteners when a nut has to be taken off at frequent intervals.

Washers. Washers are disks of steel, cast iron, or brass with a hole in the center. They are available in various sizes. A washer is inserted over the end of a bolt before the nut is screwed on to prevent the nut from digging into the wood. Washers give added strength to assembled parts and separate moving parts that are held together by a bolt.

Hinges. The types of hinges most often used are the butt, strap, tee, spring, and rule-joint.

The butt hinge has a removable pin, making it possible to remove a door from its frame without removing the hinges (Figs. 10 and 12). Butt joints are available in iron, brass, bronze, and other ornamental metals, in various sizes and in a wide range of prices.

The strap hinge is used primarily on gates and on cellar and storm doors (Figs. 10 and 13). It has two long triangular-shaped leaves, each tapering from the pin to the end. One of the leaves is screwed to the flat surface of the door, and the other to the surface of the frame, instead of to the edges of both door and frame.

The T-hinge has one rectangular-shaped leaf similar to an ordinary hinge, and the other leaf is triangular-shaped, similar to a strap hinge (Figs. 10 and 13). The T-hinge is used when there is not enough room on the doorframe for a strap hinge. This type is available in sizes ranging from 2″ to 8″.

The spring hinge is a special type fitted with an inner spring. It is used only on screen doors and is available in sizes from 1½″ to 3″ (Fig. 11).

The rule-joint hinge is designed for use on table leaves. It is similar to the conventional type of hinge, with the exception that one of the leaves is approximately twice the length of the other. It is available in sizes ranging from ¾″ to 2″.

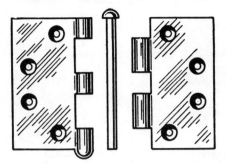

BUTT HINGE

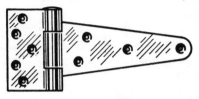

T - HINGE

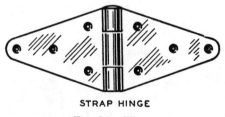

STRAP HINGE

Fig. 10. Hinges.

Locks. There are hundreds of varieties of locks available for use on house doors and on furniture drawers, but there are only two classifications of locks: the mortise and the rim lock. The mortise lock is installed in a slot or mortise in the door or drawer, while the rim lock is secured to the inside surface. Mortise locks are used extensively in better modern construction; rim locks in older houses and those of cheap construction.

Both the mortise and the rim lock may be either a cylinder or tumbler type of lock, and there are a great many styles and

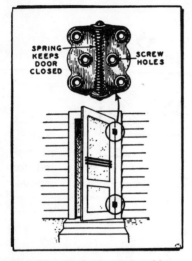

Fig. 11. Fast pin spring hinge used on screen doors.

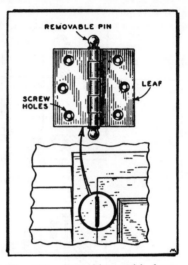

Fig. 12. Butt hinge with loose pin.

varieties of each type (Fig. 14). The cylinder lock is opened with a small, flat, grooved key, notched along one edge. Doors equipped with cylinder locks can be double-locked, and this type is used extensively on outside doors. The tumbler lock is opened and closed with a large key that has a notched blade at the end. Tumbler locks are found in older types of houses, and in modern construction are used on bedroom, bathroom, and other inner doors.

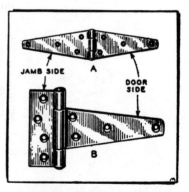

Fig. 13. A, strap hinge; B, T-hinge.

Latches. Latches are used if closet and cupboard doors are to be kept shut but not locked (*A*, Fig. 15). They consist of a beveled bolt that fits into a slot and is held in place by a spring. To open the latch, the bolt is withdrawn by turning a handle to the right.

Another type of latch generally used on screen doors is shown at *B*, Fig. 15.

Hasps. Hasps are generally used on cellar doors, barns, outhouses, and places where other fixtures to prevent entrance are not required. They are available in a variety of sizes, and are usually of galvanized steel (*C*, Fig. 15).

Mending plates. Mending plates are used to strengthen weak joints, to reinforce corners, to mend splits, and for general reinforcement purposes.

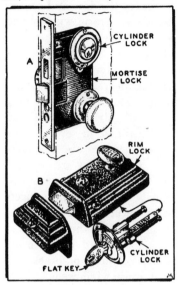

Fig. 14. Mortise and rim locks with pin tumbler cylinders.

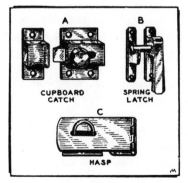

Fig. 15.

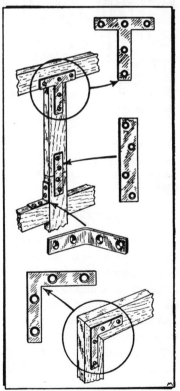

Fig. 16. Types of mending plates and how they are used.

Fig. 17. Types of window and screen hangers and where they are used.

They are made of flat steel in a variety of shapes and sizes, with countersunk holes drilled for the flat-head screws used to secure them (Fig. 16).

Storm window and screen hangers. Storm window and screen hangers are fixtures installed on the top edges of storm windows and screens to enable them to swing outward (Fig. 17). They are usually made of galvanized steel and are available in several sizes. These hangers are demountable, that is, they are designed so that the windows or screens can be lifted off the hangers when swung to a horizontal position. Together with these hangers it is advisable to use a type of hook or bracket to hold storm windows in any desired open position (Fig. 17).

HOW TO MAKE WOODWORKING JOINTS

In woodworking, the making of well-fitted and properly constructed joints is of utmost importance. Although nails, screws, bolts, and other types of fasteners are used extensively in the construction and maintenance of a house, the home craftsman also should be familiar with the common joints used in woodworking and with the proper methods of making them before he attempts to construct, alter, or repair furniture or cabinets.

The common joints in woodworking are the lap, butt, rabbet, dado, mortise-and-tenon, dovetail, miter, and tongue-and-groove joints. All of the joints used are shown in Figs. 18 to 21.

Lap joints. The types of lap joints are the half lap, halved cross lap, end or corner lap, and middle half-lap. They are used

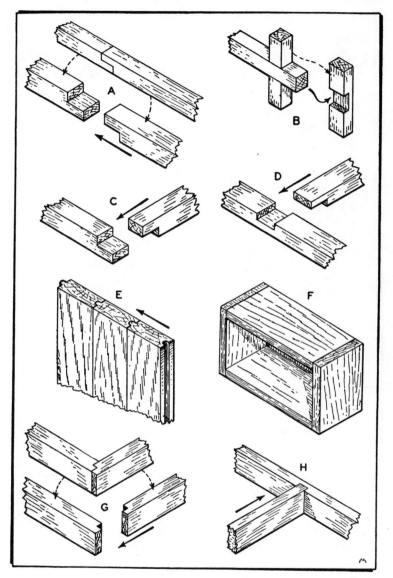

Fig. 18. Common joints.

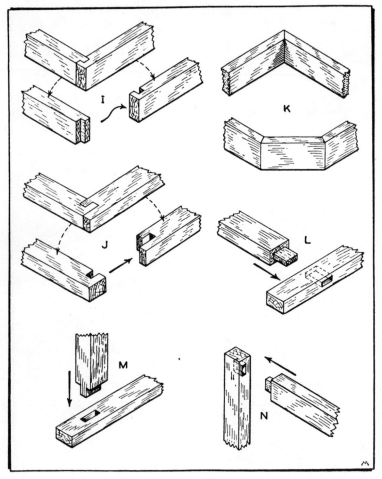

Fig. 19. Common joints.

in the construction of book shelves, stretchers on chairs, easels, kitchen cabinets, and in similar projects (Figs. 22, 23, and 24). The middle half-lap joint is the most commonly used. This joint is laid out by superimposing one piece of the wood upon the other to mark accurately the width of each cut (*A*, Fig. 25). Then clamp the two pieces together in a vise, and with the try square draw the lines for the width of this cut accurately square across both work edges. Remove the work from the vise, and again using the try square, square the shoulder lines of both the face and the edge of the work (*B*, Fig. 25). Gauge and mark the depth of the required notches with the marking gauge (*C*, Fig. 25).

Again secure the work in the vise, and saw down to the required depth with the backsaw. Be sure to make the saw cuts on the waste part of the stock (*D*, Fig. 25). If the notches are more than ¾″ in width, make several cuts to facilitate the removal of the waste material. Chisel down to the gauge line on each side of the notch. To prevent breaking the grain of the wood and to produce a clean, smooth cut, the chisel should be slanted outward very slightly (*E*, Fig. 25). The final step in the making of the middle lap joint is to finish the cut to a uniform depth (*F*, Fig. 25).

The end half-lap joint is made in the same manner as the middle

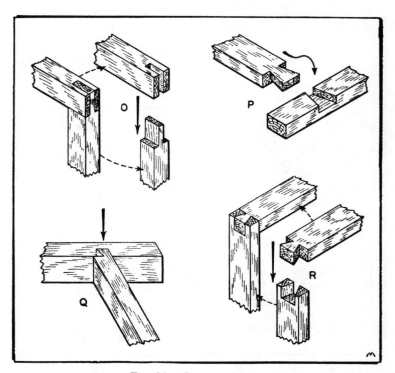

Fig. 20. Common joints.

lap joint, with the exception that only one shoulder is to be cut and the line of the bottom of the joint is gauged across the end

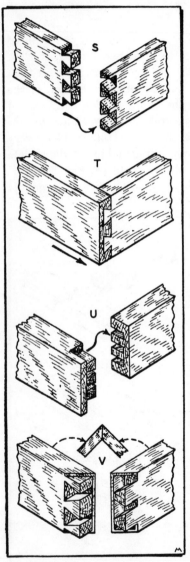

of the stock. As the bottom of this joint is accessible from the end of the stock, it can be sawed out and trimmed to the line with the chisel.

The other types of lap joints are merely variations of the two just described, and directions for making them are similar.

Butt joints. The butt joint is the simplest joint and is the only one in which nails or screws must be used. It is used only for rough construction (*F*, Fig. 18). Though it is extremely simple to make, test the edges to be joined for absolute squareness with the try square before the pieces are fitted together.

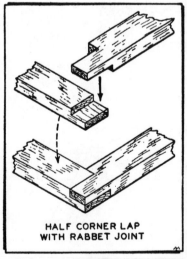

HALF CORNER LAP
WITH RABBET JOINT

Fig. 21. Common joints.

Fig. 22.

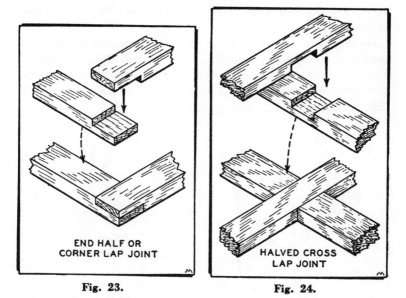

Fig. 23.

Fig. 24.

Rabbet joints. Rabbet joints are formed by recesses, or rabbets, cut out on the edges of the work so that they may be fitted into each other or secured further with a spline fitting into them. Rabbet joints are used in the construction of cabinets, table-tops, and similar projects. The rabbet joints commonly used are the rabbet on end and the rabbet on edge (*A* and *B*, Fig. 26). The shiplap (*C*, Fig. 26) and the rabbet and fillet (*D*, Fig. 26) are two variations of the lap joint.

To make a rabbet on end, lay out the joint by squaring a line for the side or shoulder of the joint across the face of the board and down the edges. This line should be as far from the end of the board as the thickness of the joining piece (*A* and *E*, Fig. 26). Then gauge the required depth of the rabbet, and mark the lines on the two edges and on the end with the marking gauge (*F*, Fig. 26). Cut out the material to be removed with a backsaw (*G* and *H*, Fig. 26).

A handy tool for cutting rabbets is the rabbet plane (Chap. 2). The depth gauge and fence on the rabbet plane regulate the width and depth of the recess to be cut.

The rabbet on edge is cut in the same manner as the rabbet on

end, except that the recess is cut on the edge instead of on the end
of the board.

Dado joints. Dado joints are grooves cut across the grain of
the board, into which a second piece of wood is fitted accurately.
They are used in the construction of end tables, cabinets, bookcases, and similar projects. A housed dado joint is one in which

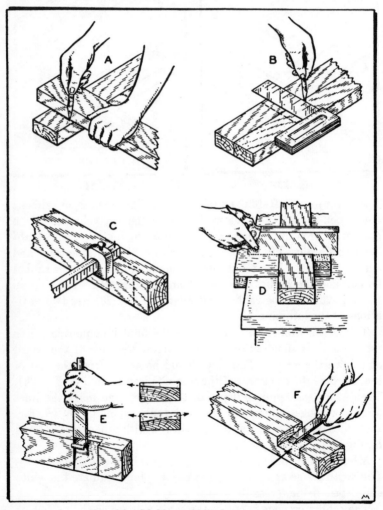

Fig. 25. Making middle half-lap joints.

the entire end of the second piece fits into the dado, or groove (*G*, Fig. 28). In a stopped or gained dado joint, the dado does not extend entirely across the face of the work (*E*, Fig. 27). Other types are the dovetail and shoulder-housed dado (*I*, Fig. 28), (*F*, Fig. 27).

Fig. 26. Rabbet joints and how to make them.

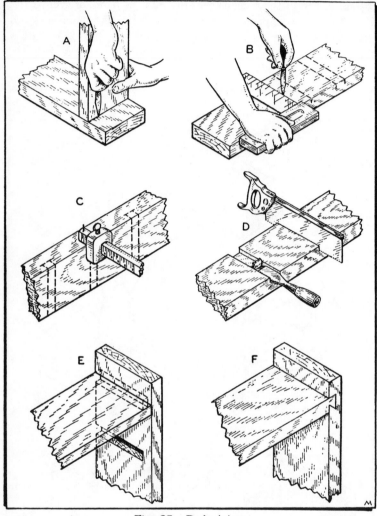

Fig. 27. Dado joints.

To lay out a plain dado, set the board to be housed on end on the face of the board in which the dado is to be cut, and mark the width of the dado accurately on the face of the board (*A*, Fig. 27). Square lines with a try square across the face of the board through the marks and down both edges (*B*, Fig. 27). Then mark

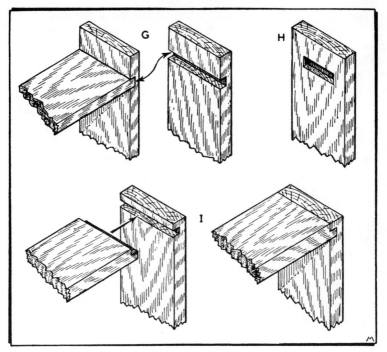

Fig. 28. Dado joints and stopped dado.

the required depth with a gauge, connecting the two marked lines (C, Fig. 27). Using a backsaw, make the necessary cuts; remove the waste wood with a chisel (D, Fig. 27) as previously described in the paragraphs on Lap Joints.

A stopped dado is laid out in the same manner as a plain dado, with the exception that it does not extend across the full width of the board (E, Fig. 27). The depth is marked on the work edge only. To fit the housed piece into a stopped dado, lay out the shoulder of the housed piece, mark, and cut in one corner to a length equal to the depth of the dado. When making a stopped dado, cut a small section of the inner end of the dado with a chisel to regulate the depth and to assist in sawing the sides. Cut the sides with a backsaw, and remove the bottom of the cut with a chisel. Sawing and chiseling should be done alternately, a little at a time, to avoid cutting the inner part of the joint too deep.

The dovetail (F, Fig. 27), housed (G, Fig. 28), and grooved

types (*H*, Fig. 28) are three other variations of the dado joint. A combined dado-and-rabbet joint is laid out and made in the same manner as a plain dado, except that a rabbet, or a recess, is cut on the end of the housed piece (*I*, Fig. 28).

Mortise-and-tenon joints. The mortise-and-tenon joint is used extensively by skilled woodworkers. When properly laid out and accurately made, it is strong and dependable. To assure maximum strength and rigidity, it must be fitted very accurately. Mortise-and-tenon joints are used in the construction of desks, tables, chairs, and cabinet furniture that will be subject to hard usage. While there are several kinds of these joints, the directions given here are for the type known as the blind mortise-and-tenon joint. The description and drawings of the procedure in making this joint will help the woodworker to lay out and make any of the other types (Figs. 19 and 20).

The tenon section should be made first. Cut and square both pieces of the work to the desired dimension and plainly mark both faces of each piece for easy identification. From the end of the piece in which the tenon is to be cut, measure back a distance equal to the length of the tenon, then square the shoulder line and mark it around this piece (*A*, Fig. 29).

For general purposes, the tenon in this type of joint should be one-quarter to one-half as thick as the entire board. To lay out the thickness of the tenon correctly, locate the exact center of one edge, accurately measure with a rule one-half the thickness of the tenon each way from the center, and mark these places with the point of a knifeblade or a brad awl (*B*, Fig. 29). Set a marking gauge to these points, and mark both lines across the end and down both edges to the shoulder line previously marked around the board. All gauging must be done from the face side of the work (*C*, Fig. 29).

The width of the tenon also must be laid out very carefully, and the lines gauged through these points across the end and down both sides to the shoulder line (*D*, Fig. 29). With the try square as a guide and using the point of a sharp knife, score the shoulder line repeatedly, to a depth of about $\frac{1}{16}''$ (*E*, Fig. 29).

Fasten the work securely in the vise, and using a very sharp chisel, cut a narrow triangular groove along the outside of the scored line on the waste material (*F*, Fig. 29). Fasten the work

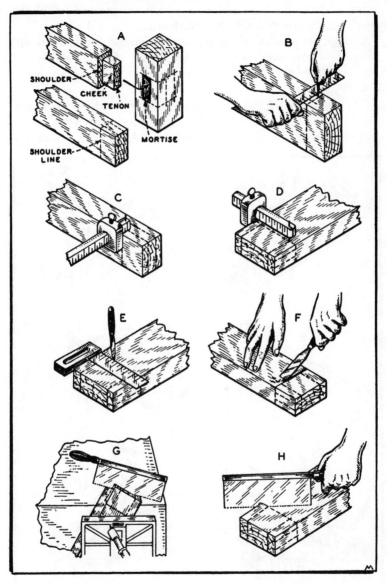

Fig. 29. Making mortise-and-tenon joints.

at an angle in the vise, and with a backsaw proceed to cut the cheeks of the tenon to the shoulder line (*G*, Fig. 29).

Change the position of the piece in the vise so the next cut will be made square with the face of the work. Now proceed to cut the shoulder of the tenon to the required dimension with the backsaw (*H*, Fig. 29).

The length of the mortise must equal the width of the tenon. To determine the position of the mortise, square lines with the try square across the work at points shown at *I*, Fig. 30. Locate the

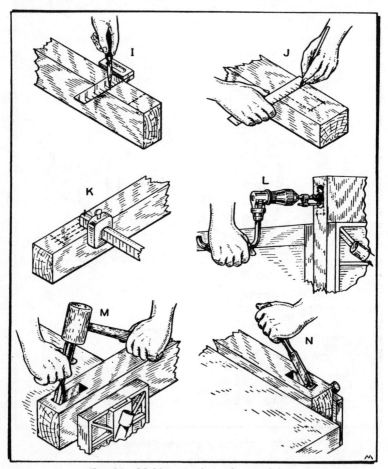

Fig. 30. Making mortise-and-tenon joints.

exact center of the piece, and measure each way from the center exactly one-half the thickness of the tenon to lay out the correct width of the mortise on the other board. Mark these points (*J*, Fig. 30). Now, carefully check the width of the mortise to make sure that it is equal to the thickness of the tenon. Gauging from the working face, mark through these points, stopping at the end of the mortise. A center line should also be gauged lengthwise of the mortise, as shown at *K*, Fig. 30.

Secure the work firmly in a vise. Select an auger bit $\frac{1}{16}''$ smaller than the width of the mortise, and adjust the bit gauge to bore holes $\frac{1}{8}''$ deeper than the length of the tenon. Place the spur of the bit on the center line, keeping the bit exactly perpendicular to the face of the work. Begin boring a series of overlapping holes, with the first hole just touching the end of the mortise and the last hole touching the opposite end (*L*, Fig. 30).

With the work held securely in the vise, as shown at *M*, Fig. 30, and using a small, sharp chisel, clean out the waste material by cutting out both sides of the mortise as the depth increases. Pare the walls of the mortise to the gauge line, keeping them perpendicular to the face of the work (*N*, Fig. 30). The final step is to square the ends and remove waste material from the bottom by using a chisel a little narrower than the width of the mortise.

Dovetail joints. Dovetail joints are used by skilled woodworkers in the construction of fine furniture, drawers for tables or desks, and projects where good appearance and strength are desired. A dovetail joint has considerable strength, due to the flare of the projections, called pins, on the ends of the boards, which fit exactly into similarly shaped dovetails. The spaces between the pins and between the dovetails are called sockets, or mortises. The pins are visible on the ends of the work, and the dovetails are visible on the face of the work.

The angle of the dovetail must not be made too acute; this would defeat the purpose of additional strength because an acute angle is weakened by the short grain at the corners of the angle.

The first step in determining the angle of the dovetail is to square a line from the edge of the board, measuring 5″, 6″, 7″, 8″, or 9″ along the board from the edge. Measure 1″ from the line along the edge, and connect the points with a line (Fig. 31). To mark the other angles make a template, that is, a pattern of cardboard or thin wood, of the angle selected (Fig. 32), and use it as a guide.

While the strongest joints are those in which the pins and the dovetails are the same size, for the sake of appearance the dovetails are usually made larger than the pins, though not more than

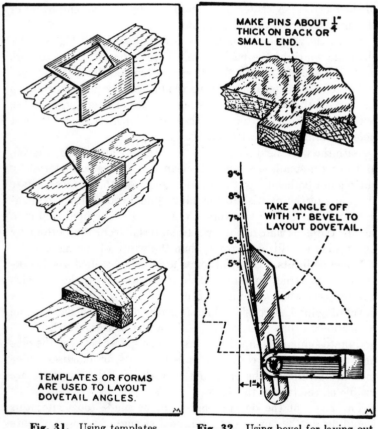

Fig. 31. Using templates.　　**Fig. 32.** Using bevel for laying out dovetails.

four times the width of the pins. The thickness of the pin and the width of the dovetails will vary in a great many instances, but it is considered good practice to make the pin or its corresponding socket about $\frac{1}{4}''$ on the narrow side.

The three most widely used types of dovetail joints are the half-lap dovetail, the single dovetail, and the multiple dovetail. Dovetail joints are not easy to make, and the beginner is strongly advised to practice on waste material before attempting an actual project.

The single dovetail joint shown in *A*, Fig. 33, is the most commonly used.

To make it with two half tongues and a whole dovetail (Fig. 33), first locate the shoulder lines of the joint by measuring the thickness of each piece of wood. Mark the position of the shoulder line and square this line. On one piece, lay out the tongue with a template and cut to required size (*A*, Fig. 33). Saw the sides of this piece with the backsaw (*B*, Fig. 33) and then remove the waste material to the shoulder line with a chisel (*C*, Fig. 33). Hold this piece on the other board to mark the shape of the dovetail (*D*, Fig. 33). Cut out with saw and chisel (*E* and *F*, Fig. 34).

To make the joint with a whole pin fitting into a socket between two half dovetails, square these marks across the end and reproduce the angle on the other side, reversing

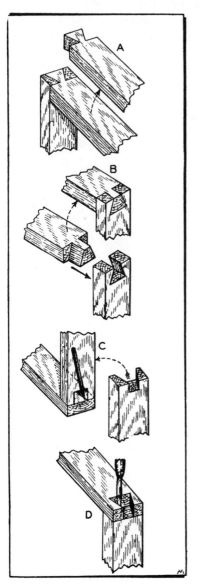

Fig. 33. Making a single dovetail with two half-pins.

the procedure outlined for the first type. That is, the sockets between the two half dovetails are first laid out, marked, and cut; then the pin is laid out from the sockets and cut to fit.

A through multiple dovetail joint is merely a series of single dovetails extending along the entire length of the end of the board (Fig. 34). The first step is to mark and square a shoulder line (*A*, Fig. 34). Divide and mark this width into as many divisions

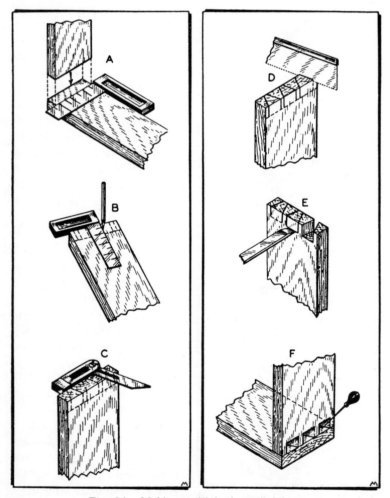

Fig. 34. Making multiple dovetail joints.

as required for dovetails, and measure half the thickness of the pins from each edge and from each side of the divisions (*B*, Fig. 34). Square the divisions to the end, and using a template or bevel, mark the slant on the other side (*C*, Fig. 34). Saw the sides of the pins with the backsaw (*D*, Fig. 34). Finish by chiseling the bottoms of the sockets and cleaning them out with a smaller chisel (*E*, Fig. 34). Now mark the dovetails from the pins with either the point of a knife or a brad awl, and cut out the pins in the manner described for the sockets (*F*, Fig. 34).

Miter joints. Miter joints are used almost exclusively in making picture frames and screens. They are merely butt joints with the angle at the corner halved between the two pieces that are to be joined (Fig. 35). Miter joints are usually cut at an angle of 45°.

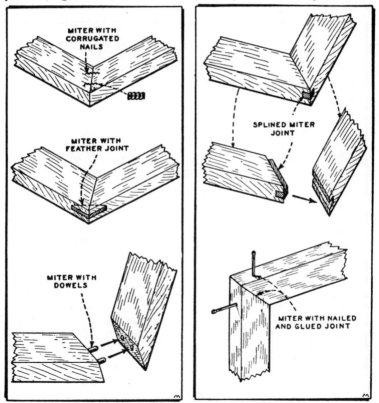

Fig. 35. Miter joints.

While it is a simple matter to mark out an angle of 45°, miter joints are usually sawed in a miter box (Chap. 2).

A miter box is an accurate tool for reproducing an angle of cut, from 30° to 90°, in pieces that are to be fitted together. The material is set in the miter box at the required angle and is cut with the backsaw. When a large number of miter joints are to be nailed or glued together, a special clamp or picture-frame vise is used (Figs. 36 and 37).

Dowels, tongues, or slip feathers are sometimes used instead of nails to strengthen the joint further. When tongued miter joints are made, each of the pieces is grooved, and a wooden tongue of required size is glued into the groove. This strengthens the miter joints, and also prevents the pieces joined in this way from warping.

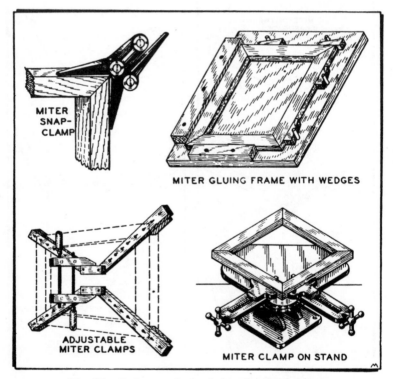

Fig. 36. Various methods of clamping glued miters.

In making a slip-feather miter joint, a groove is cut only part way through with a backsaw. A thin piece or sliver of wood is glued into the groove, and the protruding excess wood is trimmed flush with the work with a chisel (Fig. 35).

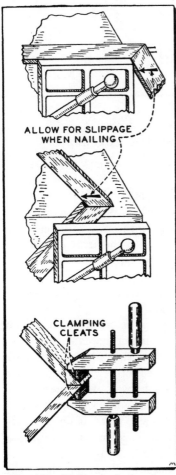

Fig. 37. Nailing and clamping miters.

When dowels are used to reinforce a miter joint, the holes for them are drilled at an angle to a depth of from 1″ to 2″. Use a drill slightly larger than the diameter of the dowels. Before insertion of the dowels, file or sand off the square corners. Insert some glue in the holes and coat the dowel with the glue. Fit together and clamp (Fig. 35).

Other methods used for reinforcing miters are shown in Fig. 35.

Tongue-and-groove joints. It is impractical to make tongue-and-groove joints in the home workshop, as finished tongued-and-grooved lumber, when specified, is supplied by the dealer. This type of joint is made by cutting a groove longitudinally with the grain of the wood on one side of a board and a tongue on the other side to fit the groove of an adjoining piece. The tongue-and-groove joint is used principally in flooring.

CHAPTER 4

Working with Plywood

⋮

LAYING OUT PLYWOOD FOR CUTTING

The large size panels in which plywood is manufactured simplifies every step of construction. With panels at hand, the only step that has to precede actual construction is laying out the work for cutting. It is worth while to do this with care and to avoid waste and simplify your work. When many pieces are to be cut from one panel, you will find it easiest to sketch the arrangement on a piece of paper before marking the plywood for cutting. Be sure to allow for a saw kerf between adjacent pieces.

Try to work it out so that your first cuts reduce the panel to pieces small enough for easy handling.

One of the most important points to watch in planning your sequence of operations is to cut all mating or matching parts with the same saw setting. Watch the direction of the face grain when cutting. Except where indicated otherwise in the plan, you will usually want this to run the long way of the piece. Mark on the better face of the plywood unless you are going to cut it with a portable power saw; in that case, mark it on the back.

Hand-sawing. When hand-sawing, place plywood with good face up (Fig. 1). Use a saw having 10 to 15 points to the inch. Support the panel firmly so it will not sag. You can reduce splitting out of the underside by putting a piece of scrap lumber under it and sawing it along with the plywood. It also helps to hold the saw at a low angle as shown in illustration. Be sure to use a sharp saw.

Power sawing. Power sawing on a radial or table saw should be done with good face of plywood up. Use a sharp combination

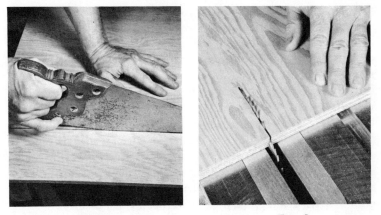

Fig. 1.   **Fig. 2.**

blade or a fine-tooth one without much set. Let the blade protrude above the plywood just the height of the teeth (Fig. 2).

You will find handling large panels an easier one-man job if you
build an extension support with a roller. It can have a base of its
own or may be clamped to a saw horse.

Portable power saw. A portable power saw should be used
with the good face of the plywood down, as shown in Fig. 3.
Tack a strip of scrap lumber to the top of each saw horse and

Fig. 3.   **Fig. 4.**

you can saw right through it without damaging the horse. Be
sure to keep your saw blade sharp.

Planing plywood edges. Planing plywood edges with a plane
or jointer will not be necessary if you make your cuts with a
sharp saw blade. If you do any planing, work from both ends
of the edge toward the center to avoid tearing out plies at the
end of the cut (Fig. 4). Use a plane with a sharp blade and
take very shallow cuts.

Sanding. Sanding before sealer or prime coat is applied
should be confined to edges (Fig. 5). Fir plywood is sanded
smooth in manufacture—one of the big timesavers in its use—
and further sanding of the surfaces will merely remove soft
grain. After sealing, sand in direction of grain only.

PLYWOOD CONSTRUCTION JOINTS

Butt joints. Butt joints, like those shown in Fig. 6, are
simplest to make, suitable for ¾″ plywood. For thinner panels,
use a reinforcing block or nailing strip to make a stronger joint
as shown in Fig. 6. In both cases, glue will make the joint many
times stronger than if it were made with nails or screws alone.

Fig. 5.   **Fig. 6.**

Fig. 7.   Fig. 8.

Frame construction. Frame construction shown in Fig. 7 makes it possible to reduce weight by using thinner plywood, since it has amazing strength. Glue as recommended in Chapter 5.

Dado joints. Dado joints (Fig. 8) quickly made with a power saw, produce neat shelves. Use a dado blade (shimmed out) to produce these grooves in a single cut.

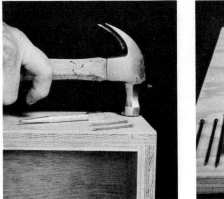

Fig. 9.   Fig. 10.

Rabbet joints. Rabbet joints like this one shown in Fig. **9** are neat and strong, and easy to make with power tools. You will find this an ideal joint for drawers, buffets, chests, or cupboards.

PLYWOOD FASTENERS

Nails. Nail size is determined primarily by the thickness of the plywood you are using. Used with glue, all nails will produce strong joints. For ¾″ plywood, 6d casing nails or 6d finish nails. For ⅝″, 6d or 8d finish nails. For ½″, 4d or 6d. For ⅜″, 3d or 4d. For ¼″, use ¾″ or 1″ brads, 3d finish nails, or (for backs where there is no objection to heads showing) 1″ blue lath nails. Substitute casing for finish nails wherever you want a heavier nail (Fig. 10).

Pre-drilling is occasionally called for in careful work where nails must be very close to an edge. As shown in Fig. 11, drill bit should be slightly smaller diameter than the nail to be used.

Space the nails about 6″ apart for most work (Fig. 12). Closer spacing is necessary only with thin plywood where there may be slight buckling between nails. Nail and glue work together to produce a strong, durable joint.

Fig. 11.   **Fig. 12.**

Fig. 13.   Fig. 14.

Flat-head wood screws. Flat-head wood screws are useful where nails will not provide adequate holding power. Glue should also be used if possible. Sizes shown here are minimums; use longer screws when work permits. This list gives plywood thickness, diameter and length of smallest screws recommended, and size of hole to drill: ¾″ plywood, No. 8, 1½″, ⁵⁄₃₂″ hole; ⅝″ plywood, No. 8, 1¼″, ⁵⁄₃₂″ hole; ½″ plywood, No. 6, 1¼″, ⅛″ hole; ⅜″ plywood, No. 6, 1″, ⅛″ hole; ¼″ plywood, No. 4, ¾″, ⁷⁄₆₄″ hole (Fig. 13).

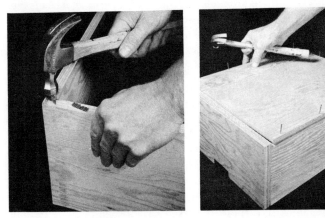

Fig. 15.   Fig. 16.

Screws and nails should be countersunk and the holes filled with wood dough or surfacing putty as shown in Fig. 14. Apply filler so it is slightly higher than the plywood, then sanded level when dry. Lubricate screws with soap if hard to drive. Avoid damage to plywood surface by using Phillips head screws.

Corrugated fasteners. Corrugated fasteners can reinforce miter joints in ¾" plywood and hold joints together while glue sets as shown in Fig. 15. For some kinds of plywood jobs, sheet-metal screws are valuable. These screws have more holding power than wood screws, but come only in short lengths and do not have flat heads. Bolts and washers are good for fastening sectional units together and for installing legs, hinges or other hardware when great strength is required.

DRAWER CONSTRUCTION

Drawers made with hand tools. This drawer, shown upside down in Fig. 16, is easily made with saw and hammer. Butt joints are glued and nailed. The bottom should be ⅜" or ½" fir plywood for rigidity. The drawer front extends down to cover the front edge of the bottom.

Additional strip of wood, glued and nailed to front panel, as shown in Fig. 17, reinforces the bottom of this second type of drawer made with hand tools. Reinforcing permits use of economical ¼" fir plywood for drawer bottoms.

Drawers made with power tools. Power tools make sturdy drawers easy to build. Figure 18 shows one side (dadoed on outer face for drawer guide) being put into place. Rabbet drawer front (at right) to take sides; dado sides to fit drawer back. All four parts are grooved to take ¼" plywood bottom.

Two types of guides, both calling for the use of power tools, are shown in Figs. 19 and 20. The drawer side has been plowed before assembly to fit over a strip glued to the side of the cabinet (Fig. 19). Procedure is reversed for the version in Fig. 20. Here the cabinet side has been dadoed before assembly. A matching strip is glued to the side of the drawer. Even heavy drawers slide easily on guides like these if waxed or lubricated with paraffin after finishing.

Fig. 17.   Fig. 18.

Drawer bottom forms guide. Hand tools only are required to make the drawer shown in Fig. 21. The secret is its bottom, made of ⅜″ or ½″ plywood. This bottom extends ⅜″ beyond the sides of the drawer to form a lip. Ease edges and apply paraffin for easy operation. Power tools will permit making a stronger and lighter version of the same drawer. Bottom is ¼″ plywood cut ⅜″ wider than the drawer on each side. See details of construction shown in Fig. 22.

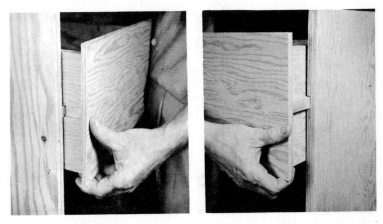

Fig. 19.   Fig. 20.

Extended bottom of drawer described and shown in Fig. 23 fits into slots formed by gluing pieces of ⅜″ plywood to the inner surface of each side of the cabinet. Gap just wide enough to take the lip is left between the pieces. The drawer shown in Fig. 24 slides in slots dadoed into the ¾″ plywood sides of the cabinet. When power tools are used, this is one of the simplest of all methods of drawer-and-guide construction.

Fig. 21.

Fig. 22.

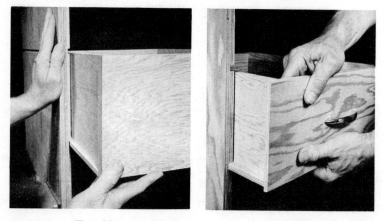

Fig. 23.

Fig. 24.

SHELF HANGING

The neatest and strongest way to hang a shelf is by making a dado joint or using metal shelf supports. A dado shown in Fig. 8 requires power tools and does not permit changing shelf height.

Figure 25 shows inexpensive shelf supports that plug into blind holes ⅝″ deep drilled in the plywood sides of the cabinet. Drill additional holes to permit moving shelves when desired. Another device is the use of slotted metal shelf strips into which shelf supports may be plugged at any height. For a better fit, set shelf strips flush in a dado cut, or cut out shelves around shelf strips.

SLIDING DOORS

Close-fitting plywood sliding doors are made by rabbeting top and bottom edges of each door (Fig. 26). Rabbet back of front door, and front of back door. This will let doors almost touch, leaving little gap for dust and increases the effective depth of the cabinet. For ⅜″ plywood doors rabbeted half their thickness, plow two grooves in top and bottom of cabinet ½″ apart. With all plywood doors. seal all edges and give backs same paint treatment as front to maintain plywood's balanced construction.

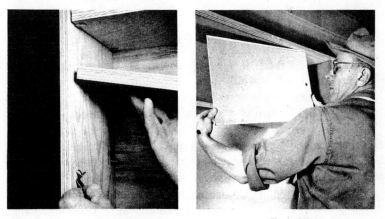

Fig. 25.   **Fig. 26.**

For removable doors, plow bottom grooves ¾₆″ deep, top grooves ⅜″ deep (Fig. 27). After finishing, (see previous paragraph) insert door by pushing up into excess space in top groove, then dropping into bottom. Plowing can be simplified by the use of a fiber track made for sliding doors of this type.

Only hand tools are required when this version of the sliding-door is used. Front and back strips are stock ¼″ quarter-round molding. The strip between is ¼″ square, as shown in Fig. 28. Use glue and brads or finish nails to fasten strips securely.

Fig. 27.   Fig. 28.

CABINET BACKS

Standard method of applying backs to cabinets and other storage units calls for rabbeting sides. Cabinet at left in Fig. 29 has rabbet just deep enough to take plywood back. For large units that must fit against walls that may not be perfectly smooth or plumb, the version at right in this illustration is better. This rabbet is made ½″ or even ¾″ deep. The lip that remains after back has been inserted may be easily trimmed wherever necessary to get a good fit between plywood unit and house wall.

When hand tools are used, attach strips of ¼″ quarter-round molding for the back to rest against (Fig. 30). Glue and nail back to molding.

Fig. 29.

Fig. 30.

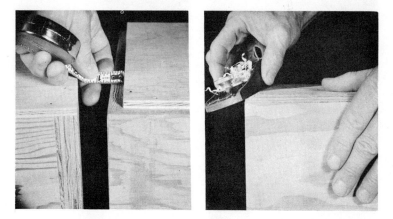

Fig. 31.

Fig. 32.

Two methods of applying cabinet backs without rabbets or moldings are shown in Fig. 31. One by nailing the back flush with outside edge. Second by setting the back ½″ to ⅞″ away from edges. The back becomes inconspicuous when cabinet is against the wall.

Bevel cabinet backs that must be applied without a rabbet to make them less conspicuous are made as shown in Fig. 32. Install ⅜″ plywood back flush with the edges of the cabinet, then bevel with light strokes of a block plane.

Nail the cabinet back into rabbet by driving nails at a slight angle as shown in Fig. 33. Use 1″ brads or 4d finish nails. Where back will not be seen, the 1″ blue lath nails shown in illustration may be used.

Two-hand staplers are excellent for nailing cabinet backs (Fig. 34). They drive long staples, setting them below the surface if desired, and greatly speed up the work. They are sometimes available on loan or rental.

Fig. 33.

Fig. 34.

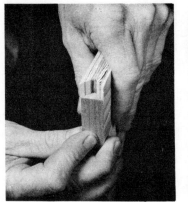

Fig. 35.

Fig. 36.

EDGE TREATMENT

Figures 35, 36, and 37 show three ways to finish plywood edges. You can achieve handsome, solid results by cutting a V groove and inserting a matching wood strip, but this method is comparatively difficult.

Thin strips of real wood edge-banding (Fig. 36) now are available in rolls ranging in various widths. They are coated with

Fig. 37.

Fig. 38.

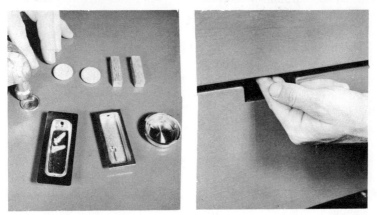

Fig. 39.

Fig. 40.

pressure sensitive adhesive. Simply peel off backing paper and apply to plywood edges according to the manufacturer's recommendations. Figure 37 shows one edge already covered with strip of Douglas fir to match plywood.

Laminated plastic surfacing materials may be applied to edges of tables with same contact cement used in applying to table tops. As shown in Fig. 37, apply to edges first, then to counter or table top. A thicker, more massive effect can be secured by nailing a 1″ or 1¼″ strip all around underneath edge.

To fill end grain on plywood edges that are to be painted, several varieties of wood putty are available; either powdered, to be mixed with water, or prepared, ready for use. Plaster spackling also works well. Sand smooth when thoroughly dry and then finish the job.

PULLS, HANDLES, AND CATCHES

Drawer pulls and door handles. Drawer pulls and door handles of the types shown in Fig. 38 are widely available. Use them in metal or wood to style your job. They come in a variety of traditional and ranch styles as well as in many modern designs.

Sliding and rolling doors are most easily equipped with finger cups that you simply force into round holes. For large doors, use the rectangular cups or large round ones that are fastened in with screws. Round pulls at top are suitable where clearance is adequate, or you can make simple rectangular grips from wood (Fig. 39).

The simplest drawer pull of all is a notch cut into the top of the drawer front. It may be rectangular, V shaped, or half-round. You can omit the notch from every other drawer, opening it by means of the notch in the drawer below, as shown in Fig. 40. By sloping drawer fronts, the drawer may be pulled out by grasping the projecting bottom edge.

Catches come in many varieties besides the conventional friction type shown in Fig. 41. The touch type shown in illustration and being installed, permits the door to open at a touch. Magnetic catch has no moving parts to break. Roller catches and the new ones made of polyethelyne are smoother and more durable than the plain steel friction catches.

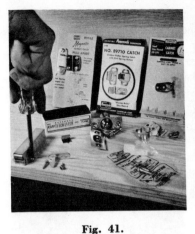

Fig. 41.

Fig. 42.

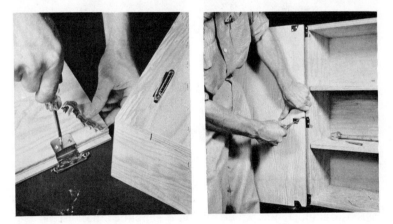

Fig. 43.

Fig. 44.

DOOR HARDWARE

Surface hinges. Surface hinges are quickly mounted. They require no mortising, add an ornamental touch, and are available in many styles. A pair of H or H-L hinges will do for most doors; for larger doors or to add rigidity to smaller ones, use a pair of H-L plus one H (Fig. 42), or use three of the H type. Tee or strap hinges help prevent sag in large doors. On tall doors, one or two added hinges between those at top and bottom help to minimize warping.

Overlapping (lipped) doors are neatly hung with semi-concealed hinges (Fig. 43). They are excellent for plywood since screws go into flat grain. These have ½″ inset, are made for doors of ¾″ plywood rabbeted to leave ¼″ lip. Such hinges are made in many styles and finishes, semi-concealed or full-surface.

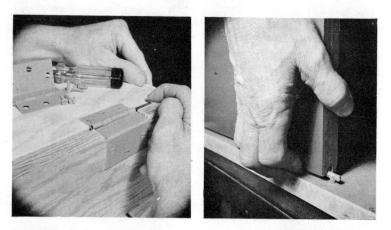

Fig. 45.　　　　　　　　　　**Fig. 46.**

Concealed pin hinges. Concealed pin hinges give a neat modern appearance to flush doors (Fig. 44). They mount directly onto the cabinet side. Construction is simplified, because no face frame is necessary. Only the pivot is visible from the front when the door is closed. Use a pair of these hinges for small doors, three (called *a pair and one-half*) for larger doors.

Semi-concealed loose-pin hinges. Semi-concealed loose-pin hinges like these offer the same appearance when door is closed as ordinary butt hinges, since only the barrel shows (Fig. 45). They are much better, though, for flush plywood doors because screws go into flat plywood grain. A variation called a chest hinge may be used in the same way.

T guides. Door bottom is kept in line by a simple T guide for each door as shown in Fig. 46. Two strips of ¼″ quarter-round molding, with ¼″ space between, will form slot if power tools are not available for making the slot.

Metal brackets. Two metal brackets should be fastened to the top of each door with a pair of screws. Nylon wheels with ball bearings roll in a double-lipped track that is fastened to the door frame with screws (Fig. 47). (Single-lipped track is also made for single doors.) Installation is very simple, with no mortising

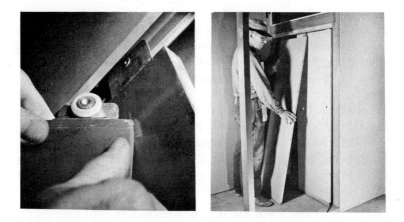

Fig. 47.   **Fig. 48.**

required.

Rollers. Rolling doors for closets and large storage units may have rollers mounted at either top or bottom (Fig. 48). Top-mount hardware shown in Figs. 46, 47, and 48, usually is smoother in operation, particularly when the door is tall and narrow.

CHAPTER **5**

Glues and Gluing Methods

‚Äî‚Äî‚Äî‚Äî‚Äî‚Äî‚Ä¢‚Ä¢‚Äî‚Äî‚Äî‚Äî‚Äî‚Äî‚Äî‚Äî‚Äî

Gluing is done extensively in woodworking, and in the production of various types of wood products. Modern glues, processes, and techniques vary as widely as the products made, and developments have been many in recent years. In general, however, it remains true that the quality of a glued joint depends upon the kind of wood and its preparation for use, the kind and quality of the glue and its preparation for use, the details of the gluing process, the types of joints, and the conditioning of the joints. Depending on the glue used, service conditions also affect the performance of the joint to a greater or lesser extent.

GLUING PROPERTIES OF DIFFERENT WOODS

Table 5 gives the gluing properties of the woods widely used for glued products. The classifications are based on the average quality of side-grain joints of wood that is approximately average in density for the species, when glued with animal, casein, starch, urea resin, and resorcinol resin glues. A species is considered to be glued satisfactorily when the strength of the joint is approximately equal to the strength of the wood.

Whether it will be easy or difficult to obtain a satisfactory joint depends upon the density of the wood, the structure of the wood, the presence of extractives or infiltrated materials in the wood, and the kind of glue. In general, heavy woods are more difficult to glue than lightweight woods, hardwoods are more difficult to glue than softwoods, and heartwood is more difficult than sapwood. Several species vary considerably in their gluing characteristics with different glues (Table 5).

TABLE 5

Classification of various hardwood and softwood species according to gluing properties

HARDWOODS

Group 1	Group 2
(Glue very easily with different glues under wide range of gluing conditions)	(Glue well with different glues under a moderately wide range of gluing conditions)
Aspen. Chestnut, American. Cottonwood. Willow, black. Yellow-poplar.	Alder, red. Basswood. Butternut. Elm: American. Rock. Hackberry. Magnolia. Mahogany. Sweetgum.
Group 3	**Group 4**
(Glue satisfactorily under well-controlled gluing conditions)	(Require very close control of gluing conditions, or special treatment to obtain best results)
Ash, white. Cherry, black. Dogwood. Maple, soft. Oak: Red. White Pecan. Sycamore. Tupelo: Black. Water. Walnut, black.	Beech, American. Birch, sweet and yellow. Hickory. Maple, hard. Osage-orange. Persimmon.

SOFTWOODS

Group 1	Group 2	Group 3
Baldcypress. Cedar, western red- Fir, white. Larch, western. Redwood. Spruce, Sitka.	Cedar, eastern red-. Douglas-fir. Hemlock, western. Pine: Eastern white. Southern yellow. Ponderosa.	Cedar, Alaska-.

GLUES USED FOR VARIOUS JOBS

Animal glues have long been used extensively in woodworking; *starch glues* came into general use, especially for veneering, early in this century; *casein glue* and *vegetable protein glues*, of which *soybean* is the most important, gained commercial importance during and immediately following World War I for gluing lumber and veneer into products that required moderate water resistance. *Synthetic resin glues* were developed more recently but now surpass many of the older glues in importance as woodworking glues. *Phenol resin glues* are widely used to produce plywood for severe service conditions. *Urea resin glues* are used extensively in producing plywood for furniture and interior paneling. *Resorcinol* and *phenol-resorcinol resin glues* are useful for gluing lumber into products that will withstand exposure to the weather. *Polyvinyl resin emulsion glues* are used in assembly joints of furniture.

Broadly, synthetic resin glues are of two types—*thermosetting* and *thermoplastic*. Thermosetting resins, once cured, are not softened by heat. Thermoplastic resins will soften when reheated.

Many brands of glues made from fish, animal, or vegetable derivatives are sold in liquid form, ready for application. Their principal use in woodworking is for small jobs and repair work. They are variable in quality and low in water resistance and durability under damp conditions. The better brands are moderate in dry strength and set fairly quickly. They are applied cold, usually by brush, and are pressed cold. They stain wood only slightly, if at all.

CHOOSING THE RIGHT TYPE OF GLUE

No one glue is ideal for every project. Choose the best type of glue suitable for the job at hand from the following descriptions.

Liquid hide glue. Liquid hide glue has several advantages. It is very strong because it is raw-hide-tough and does not become brittle. This glue is easy to use, light in color, resists heat and mold. It has good filling qualities and gives strength even in poorly fitted joints Liquid hide glue is excellent for furniture work, and wherever a tough, lasting wood-to-wood bond is needed. It is a favorite glue for cabinetwork and general wood gluing. Because it is not waterproof, do not use it for outdoor furniture or for boat building.

Liquid resin glue. Non-staining, clean and white liquid resin glue can be used at any temperature, and is recommended for quick-setting work where good clamping is not possible. It is a fine all-around household glue for mending and furniture making and repair, and is excellent for model work, paper, leather, and small assemblies. Liquid resin glue is not sufficiently moisture-resistant for anything to be exposed to weather, and is not so strong and lasting, as liquid hide glue for fine furniture work.

Resorcinol. Resorcinol is a very strong and waterproof glue. It works better with poor joints than many other glues do. This type of glue should be used for work that may be exposed to soaking: outdoor furniture, boats, and wooden sinks. *Do not* use it for work that must be done at temperatures below 70°. Because of its dark color and mixing, it *should not* be used unless waterproof quality is needed.

Powdered resin. This light-colored almost waterproof powdered resin is very strong, but brittle if the point fits poorly. It should be used for woodworking and general gluing whenever considerable moisture resistance is needed. *Do not* use powdered resin with oily woods or with joints that are not closely fitted and tightly clamped. When using this resin, be sure to mix it for each use.

Powdered casein. Powdered casein is strong, fairly water-resistant, works in cool locations, and fills poor joints well. It can be used for most woodworking jobs and is especially desirable with oily woods, such as teak, lemon, and yew. Powdered casein will stain acid woods such as redwood, and is not moisture re-sistant enough for outdoor furniture. It must be mixed for each use.

Flake animal. Flake animal glue has the same advantages as liquid hide glue, but it must be mixed, heated, kept hot, and used at high temperatures. It is good for quantity woodworking projects that justify the time and trouble of mixing and heating the glue. This glue is not waterproof, and is too much trouble to use for small jobs or most home shop work.

GLUING METHODS

Successful wood gluing ordinarily means a joint that lasts almost forever and is stronger than the wood itself. Liquid hide glue is ideal for furniture building and repair. It has the rawhide toughness that has made hide glue the craftsman's choice for generations. It can be purchased in ready-to-use liquid form, that eliminates tedious preparation and the necessity for speed and critical temperature control.

Select a fine glue and then follow the six simple steps shown in Figs. 1 to 6.

Scrape or sandpaper the old wood until it is bare and clean, making sure that all the old glue is removed (Fig. 1). Most glues work by penetrating the porous wood grain.

Test the fit of the joint before applying the glue (Fig. 2). With the poor fit often unavoidable in repair work, be sure to use a glue with good gap-filling qualities.

A brush is the best applicator, particularly if your glue comes in a wide-mouth can as shown in Fig. 3. Be sure to apply glue to both of the surfaces to be jointed.

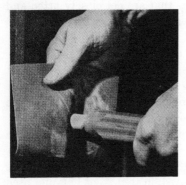

Fig. 1.

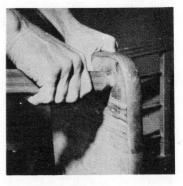

Fig. 2.

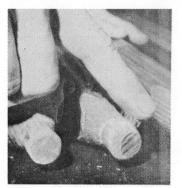

Fig. 3.   Fig. 4.

You will get a strong joint more quickly if you let the glue become tacky (Fig. 4) before joining the parts.

The joint should be pulled tightly together and held in that position (Fig. 5). (See section on clamps in this chapter.)

Most glues set better and faster in a dry, warm (not hot) room. It is safest not to disturb the joint until the glue is set, following the time given in Table B. An ordinary heat lamp (Fig. 6) will speed up the drying of the joint.

Fig. 5.   Fig. 6.

TABLE 6

GLUE TYPE	ROOM TEMPERATURE	HOW TO PREPARE	70° Clamping Time Hardwood	Softwood
Liquid Hide	Sets best above 70°. Can be used in colder room if glue is warmer.	Ready to use.	2 hours	3 hours
White Liquid Resin	Any temperature above 60°. But the warmer the better.	Ready to use.	1 hour	1½ hours
Resorcinol	Must be 70° or warmer. Will set faster at 90°.	Mix 3 parts powder to 4 parts liquid catalyst.	16 hours	16 hours
Powdered Resin	Must be 70° or warmer. Will set faster at 90°.	Mix 2 parts powder with ½ to 1 part water.	16 hours	16 hours
Powdered Casein	Any temperature above freezing. But the warmer the better.	Stir together equal parts by volume glue and water. Wait 10 minutes and stir again.	2 hours	3 hours
Flake or Powdered Animal	Must be 70° or warmer. Keep work warm.	For each ounce glue add 1½ ounces water (softwood) or 2 ounces water (hardwood).	1 hour	1½ hours

HINTS ON APPLYING GLUE

Work at proper temperature. Temperature is important, and you will get better results if the work, the glue, and the room are all 70° or warmer. Flake animal glue should be used hot. Liquid hide glue must be warm to spread it properly (Fig. 7). Resorcinal and powdered-resin glues will not set properly at less than 70°. If you must work at a lower temperature, liquid resin glue, which can be used at any temperature above 60°, should be used.

Size end grain. The end grain of any wood is highly absorbent, and if it is permitted to soak up the moisture of the glue a weak joint may result. This can be avoided by giving the end grain a thin preliminary coat of the glue you are using (Fig. 8), applying it a few minutes ahead of time. When you spread the glue over the rest of the joint, be sure to give the end grain a second coat of the glue.

Fig. 7.

Fig. 8.

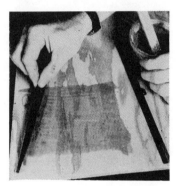

Fig. 9.

Fig. 10.

Use suitable applicator. Old saw blades with fine teeth, such as hacksaw or utility saw blades, make good spreaders for covering a large area. Figure 9 shows a plywood cupboard door panel being prepared for covering with burlap. Discarded windshield wipers are good spreaders too.

Oil can. Chair rungs and similar joints can be reglued even when it is not feasible to pull them apart. Drill a small hole into the joint and inject the glue with an oil can (Fig. 10).

Glue tube. Glue tube is a handy applicator for gluing small objects (Fig. 11). It is useful too for running a line of glue around the edge of an article, or for applying glue to a long strip of molding.

Cover all surfaces evenly. A *roller* of the type sold in camera shops permits putting a thin, uniform coat of glue on a big surface. Large *paint brushes* can also be used. The small brush shown in Fig. 12 is a whisk broom cut off short for stiffness. With this type of brush you can get a thinner coat than with an ordinary soft brush.

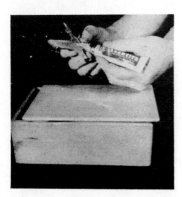

Fig. 11.

Fig. 12.

CLAMPING

Common gluing clamps. Good woodworking depends on good gluing. Good gluing depends on adequate clamping. Therefore, building a clamp collection is an important step toward better work. A good place to begin is with an assortment of C-clamps. They are the least expensive and most versatile of clamps. Next, you will want long clamps for gluing up stock and large frames— two or preferably three of them. Wooden-jaw hand screws do so many jobs that they are like a third hand. As need for them arises you will want to add many special clamps such as press screws, edge-clamp fixtures, miter clamps, spring clamps, surface clamps, and a band clamp.

Hand screw. The hand screw is the woodworker's favorite, because its jaws are wood and it may often be applied directly to the work without danger of marring it. The adjustable type hand screw works on odd shapes like the ironing board shown in Fig. 13.

The right and wrong use of the hand screw are shown in Fig. 14. The clamp at the left is properly adjusted so that its jaws are parallel. The clamp at the right is not properly adjusted. These clamps can be quickly adjusted by gripping both handles and twisting them at the same time.

Fig. 13.

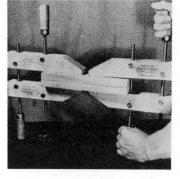

Fig. 14.

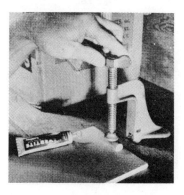

Fig. 15.

Fig. 16.

Surface clamp. The surface clamp or the bench clamp can be fastened to any table or bench top. Its special bolt drops below the surface when the clamp is slipped off, leaving the top clear for other work. This kind of clamp is very handy when gluing small objects since it requires only one hand (Fig. 15), leaving the other free to hold the work.

Spring clamps. Many delicate jobs can be done with spring clamps like the one shown in Fig. 16 that no other kind of clamp will do as well. These overgrown clothespins come in assorted sizes, and are handy for light assemblies. Some of these clamps have rubber-covered jaws to protect the work.

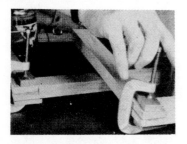

Fig. 17.   Fig. 18.

Fig. 19.   Fig. 20.

C-Clamps. C-clamps will do a wide assortment of jobs and substitute reasonably well for many other types of clamps. Protect the work by inserting small blocks of wood under the jaws of the clamps (Fig. 17).

Deep-throat C-clamps. As shown in Fig. 18, deep-throat C-clamps can do many jobs that ordinary clamps cannot. They can reach to the center of small work and put on the pressure where it is needed most. As with other C-clamps their metal jaws call for scraps of wood to avoid marring the work.

Quick clamp. The quick clamp does the work of a heavy C-clamp. In construction it is actually a short bar clamp. Its special virtue is that it can be adjusted in an instant by sliding the head along the bar (Fig. 19). The screw is needed only for putting on pressure

Edge-clamp fixture. This fixture works with a quick clamp to solve a common and difficult gluing problem. It is used most often to glue strips to the edges of boards, or as shown in Fig. 20 to join work in the shape of a T. The quick clamp grasps the work and the edge clamp puts on the pressure.

Pipe type or long clamps. These clamps can be purchased complete as shown in Fig. 21, or you can buy just the fixtures and put them on ordinary water pipe. With these fittings you can make your own long clamps at a small cost, and have any length you want.

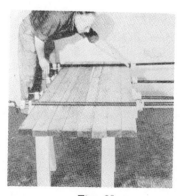

Fig. 21.

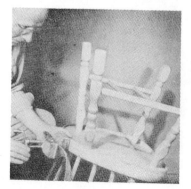

Fig. 22.

Fig. 23.

Band clamp. The band clamp wraps itself around curved or irregular shapes and squeezes from all directions. The bands are either made of steel or heavy canvas. Steel is best for round objects, and canvas for odd shapes. For general home-shop use with varying shapes, it is best to use canvas (Fig. 22).

Miter clamp. This clamp is a clever extra pair of hands. You can put it on a miter joint or something like the joint in the back of a chair, open the joint by twisting the handles, apply glue, then close the joint tightly (Fig. 23).

TYPES OF GLUED JOINTS

Side-grain surfaces. With most species of wood, straight, plain joints between side-grain surface (Fig. 24, A) can be made substantially as strong as the wood itself in shear parallel to the grain, tension across the grain, and cleavage. The tongued-and-grooved joint (Fig. 24, B) and other shaped joints have the theoretical advantage of larger gluing surfaces than the straight joints, but in practice they do not give higher strength with most woods. Furthermore, the theoretical advantage is often lost, wholly or partly, because the shaped joints are more difficult to machine than straight, plain joints so as to obtain a perfect fit of the parts. Because of poor contact, the effective holding area and strength may actually be less on a shaped joint than on a flat surface. The principal advantage of the tongued-and-grooved and

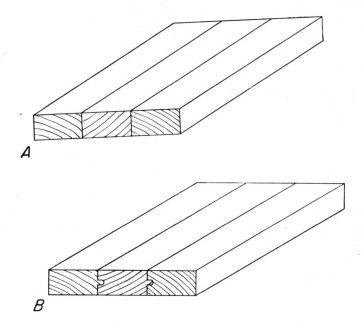

Side-to-side-grain joints: *A*, Plain; *B*, tongued-and-grooved.

Fig. 24.

other shaped joints is that the parts can be more quickly aligned in the clamps or press. A shallow tongue-and-groove is usually as useful in this respect as a deeper cut and is less wasteful of wood.

End-grain surfaces. It is practically impossible to make end-butt joints (Fig. 25, A) sufficiently strong or permanent to meet the requirements of ordinary service. With the most careful gluing possible, not more than about 25 percent of the tensile strength of the wood parallel with the grain can be obtained in butt joints. In order to approximate the tensile strength of various species, a scarf, serrated, or other form of joint that approaches a side-grain surface must be used (Fig. 25). The plain scarf is perhaps the easiest to glue and entails fewer machining difficulties than the many-angle forms.

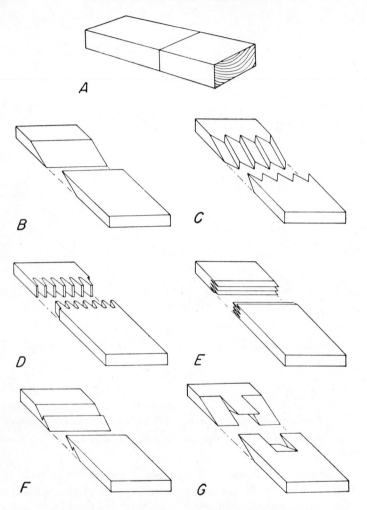

End-to-end-grain joints: *A*, End butt; *B*, plain scarf:
C, serrated scarf; *D*, finger; *E*, Onsrud; *F*, hooked scarf:
G, double-slope scarf.

Fig. 25.

End-to-side-grain surfaces. End-to-side-grain joints (Fig. 26) are also difficult to glue properly and, further, are subjected in service to unusually severe stresses as a result of unequal dimensional changes in the two members of the joint as their moisture content changes. It is therefore necessary to use irregular shapes of joints, dowels, tenons, or other devices to reinforce such a joint in order to bring side grain into contact with side grain or to secure larger gluing surfaces (Fig. 26). All end-to-side-grain joints should be carefully protected from changes in moisture content.

Conditioning glued joints. When boards are glued edge to edge, the wood at the joint absorbs water from the glue and swells. If the glued assembly is surfaced before this excess moisture is dried out or distributed, more wood is removed along the swollen joints than elsewhere. Later, when the joints dry and shrink, permanent depressions are formed that may be very conspicuous in a finished panel.

When pieces of lumber are glued edge to edge or face to face, the glue moisture need not be dried out but simply allowed to distribute itself uniformly throughout the wood. Approximately uniform distribution of glue moisture can usually be obtained by conditioning the stock after gluing for 24 hours at 160° F., 4 days at 120° F., or at least 7 days at room temperature with the relative humidity, in each case, adjusted to prevent significant drying.

In plywood, veneered panels, and other constructions made by gluing together thin layers of wood, it is advisable to condition the panels to average service moisture content. In cold-gluing operations, it is frequently necessary to dry out at least a part of the moisture added in gluing. The drying is most advantageously done under controlled conditions and time schedules.

Drying such glued products to excessively low moisture content materially increases warping, opening of joints, and checking. Following hot-press operations, the panels will often be very dry, and it may be desirable to recondition them under circumstances that will cause them to regain moisture.

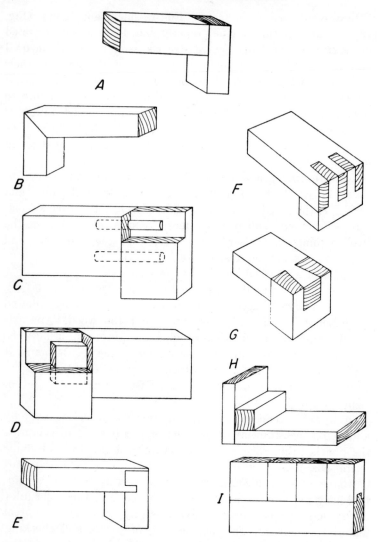

End-to-side-grain joints: *A*, Plain; *B*, miter; *C*, dowel; *D*, mortise and tenon; *E*, dado tongue and rabbet; *F*, slip or lock corner; *G*, dovetail; *H*, blocked; *I*, tongued-and-grooved.

Fig. 26.

CHAPTER 6

Hand Power Tools

PORTABLE ELECTRIC SAWS

Portable electric saws are available in various sizes, ranging from 6½″ for the amateur builder, up to 9¼″ for the more advanced or professional worker.

Motor. These saws are equipped with a "Universal" type motor and will operate either on D.C. or A.C. current at 25, 40, 50, or 60 cycles, of the specified voltage. Standard voltages are 115 or 220, with 125 or 240 volts available.

Inspect carbon brushes in the motor at regular intervals, and if worn away replace immediately to prevent damage to the motor armature. The manufacturer's service department will be glad to instruct you in brush inspection and furnish the correct brushes.

Current. Be sure to specify the voltage when purchasing a portable electric saw. *Always* check the voltage specifications on the nameplate of your equipment with the voltage of your supply line.

Cable. Three-conductor cable is used on all saws. The third wire is for "grounding." Do not permit the cable to lie in grease or oil which ruins the rubber. Wipe it off occasionally and avoid rough handling. When not in use coil it loosely without sharp bends or kinks and keep it off the floor. Extension cables are described in this chapter.

Grounding. Every electric tool *should be* grounded while in use to protect the operator against shock. Proper grounding is a good habit to develop under all circumstances, but is especially important where dampness is present. The unit is equipped with

approved 3-conductor cord and 3-blade grounding type attachment plug cap to be used with the proper grounding type receptacle, in accordance with the National Electrical Code. The green
colored conductor in the cord is the grounding wire which is connected to the metal frame of the unit inside the housing and to the
longest blade of the attachment plug cap. *Never* connect the
green wire to a "live" terminal.

If your unit has a *plug* that looks like the one shown in Fig.
1, A, it will fit directly into the latest type of 3-wire grounding
receptacles. The unit is then grounded automatically each time
it is plugged in. A special grounding adaptor (Fig. 1, B) is supplied to permit using 2-wire receptacles until the correct receptacle is properly installed. The green grounding wire extending
from the side of the adaptor must be connected to a permanent
ground, such as a properly grounded outlet box, conduit or water
pipe before plugging in the tool.

If the unit has a *plug* like the one shown in Fig. 1, C, no adaptor
is furnished and it should be used in the proper standard matching
3-wire grounding receptacle. The unit is then grounded automatically each time it is plugged in.

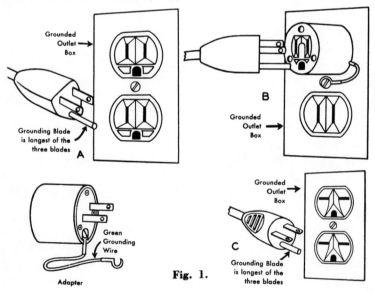

Fig. 1.

OPERATION

Connect the grounding-wire first, as described previously in this chapter, and then plug into power supply. Before pressing trigger switch to start motor, rest front of saw "shoe or base on the work and line up blade with cutting line. Be sure that blade teeth are not yet in contact with work and that lower blade guard is free. Pull trigger and guide saw through its cut with firm pressure, but without forcing. Undue force actually slows down the cutting and produces a rougher cut.

Keep blades sharp. Dull or incorrectly set teeth may cause the saw to swerve or stall under pressure. If the saw stalls *do not* release trigger switch, but *back* the saw until the blade momentum is regained. Then either shut off motor or start to cut again. This procedure will greatly increase the life of your saw switch.

To make a *pocket cut*, first set the saw shoe at the desired cutting depth. Then rest the toe or heel of shoe against the work (heel, when using 6½″ saw). Carefully draw back the lower blade guard by lifting the provided lever *before starting the motor*. Next, lower the saw until the blade teeth lightly contact the cutting line. This will allow you to release the lower blade guard as contact with the work will keep it in position to open freely as the cut is started. *Now*, start the motor and gradually lower the saw until its shoe rests flat on the work. Advance along the cutting line as in normal sawing. For starting each new cut, proceed as above for your own protection. *Do not* tie back the lower blade guard.

Caution! To insure against accidents *always* disconnect the cable plug before making adjustments or inspection. *Always* disconnect the saw cable when not in active use.

ADJUSTMENTS

Cutting depth adjustments. In cutting any material with steel blades the most efficient depth adjustment is one that permits the tooth depth only of the blade to project below the material (except when using carbide tipped blades, when just ½ of the tooth tip should project below the material). This keeps blade friction at a minimum, removes sawdust from the cut and results in cooler, faster sawing (Fig. 2).

For 6½", 7¼", 8" saws. Correct cutting depth is obtained by adjusting the quick clamping lever on the side at the rear of the saw. Adjustment of the clamping lever on the 6½", 7¼" and 8" saws is made by loosening the set screw, removing and indexing the lever to its proper clamping location, replacing it and tightening the set screw.

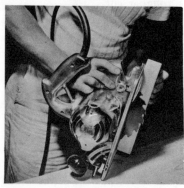

Fig. 2.

Fig. 3.

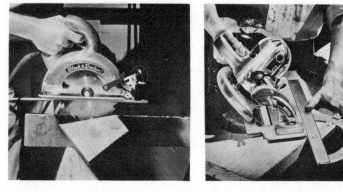

Fig. 4.

Fig. 5.

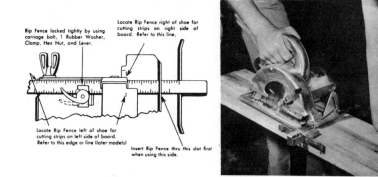

Rip Fence locked tightly by using carriage bolt, 1 Rubber Washer, Clamp, Hex Nut, and Lever.

Locate Rip Fence right of shoe for cutting strips on right side of board. Refer to this line.

Locate Rip Fence left of shoe for cutting strips on left side of board. Refer to this edge or line (later models)

Insert Rip Fence thru this slot first when using this side.

Fig. 6. **Fig. 7.**

For 8¼″, 9¼″ saws. Correct cutting depth for these saws is obtained by adjusting either or both of the built-in front and rear cutting depth adjustments. By using both adjustments, the handle remains in the most comfortable cutting position. *Always* be sure to retighten wing nuts securely after making adjustments.

Bevel Angle Adjustments. The 6½″, 7¼″, 8″, 8¼″ and 9¼″ saws have an adjustable shoe which permits bevel cutting at any angle between 45° and 90°. The quadrant on the front of these saws is calibrated for accurate adjustment. Loosen the wing nut and tilt the shoe to angle desired. Retighten wing nut securely. See Figs. 3 and 4.

ACCESSORIES

Protractor. This is a surprisingly simple and practical device that is calibrated in degrees and can be set to cut any angle by moving the holding arm to correct degree. Use the bevel adjustment on the saw in conjunction with the protractor for compound mitres. To operate, the saw shoe (either side) is lined up with the protractor's straightedge and is advanced along this edge (Fig. 5).

A protractor is also useful for laying out any carpentry work involving angles.

Rip fence. The rip fence saves time in rip sawing (Fig. 6), eliminating the need to scribe guide lines. It greatly improves ripping accuracy. Fence is calibrated to ⅛ of an inch. It may be used on either right or left hand side of the saw. To attach, slide fence through proper openings provided in the shoe as shown in Fig. 7. Clamp firmly at desired position with quick acting lever.

BLADES

Changing blades. To change a saw blade, first disconnect the cable plug to prevent injury or damage resulting from accidental pressure on the trigger switch. Then insert nail through hole in blade so that it rests against bottom of saw shoe and prevents blade from turning. With a wrench, turn holding screw counterclockwise to loosen and remove screw and washer. Retract lower guard and lift off blade. Remove inner clamp washer and clean both faces of each clamp washer, blade, and blade screw threads —this prevents uneven seating of the blade. Replace inner clamp washer, new blade—trade-mark side out (with teeth pointing toward front of saw), outer clamp washer, and blade holding screw and tighten holding screw clockwise with wrench until secure.

Combination blades. This is the latest type, precision engineered, fast-cutting blade for general service ripping and crosscutting (Fig. 8, A). Each blade carries the correct number of teeth to cut chips rather than scrape sawdust. Blade teeth receive less wear and stay sharp longer, and give definitely smoother cuts. Cutting efficiency has been increased by using redesigned sturdier teeth, reduces any tendency of the blade to "flutter" or vibrate.

Extensive tests have shown that a greater number of teeth reduces cutting efficiency, because of an increased scraping action. On the other hand, a lesser number increases the toothload to a point where the cutting edges rapidly become dull and burnt.

Crosscut blades. Crosscut blades were designed specifically for fast, smooth crosscutting (Fig. 8, B). They make a smoother cut than the combination blades.

Planer blades. This blade makes very smooth cuts, both rip and crosscut (Fig. 8, C). It is ideal for interior wood working, and is hollow-ground to produce the finest possible saw-cut finish.

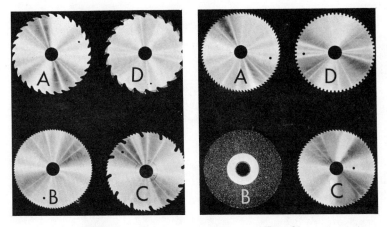

Fig. 8. **Fig. 9.**

Carbide-tipped blades. The carbide-tipped blade is the keenest and most durable blade yet developed for cutting building materials (Fig. 8, D). This blade stays sharp thirty times longer than normal steel blade when cutting lumber. The carbide tips are brazed into a special alloy steel blade. It has been established that the diamond-like hardness of these tips will retain their edges up to 50 times longer than steel.

Flooring blades. Flooring blades should be used on jobs where occasional nails may be encountered (Fig. 9, A). They are especially useful in cutting through flooring, sawing reclaimed lumber and in opening boxes and crates.

Abrasive discs. These blades are all of the top-quality resinoid-bonded, abrasive cut-off type (Fig. 9, B). They are used for cutting and slotting in ceramics, slate, marble, tile, transite, etc. Also for cutting thin gauge, non-ferrous metals.

Non-ferrous metal-cutting blades. These blades have teeth shaped and set for cutting soft, non-ferrous metals, including lead (Fig. 9, C).

Friction blades. Friction blades are ideal for cutting corrugated galvanized sheets. They cut faster, with less dirt, than abrasive discs. Blade is taper-ground for clearance (Fig. 9, D).

COMBINATION ELECTRIC SCREW-DRILL

A completely new combination tool, the electric screw-drill, is an efficient tool for craftsmen, builders, and hobbyists. It is equipped with a positive-clutch electric screw-driving mechanism. The screw-drill has a locking collar that permits operator to quickly convert to direct drive for general-purpose drilling. The unit is amply powered by a "Universal" motor for 115 volts, A.C. or D.C., and includes a 3-jaw geared chuck and key, and screw-driving bit and finder assembly.

Fig. 10.   Fig. 11.

Used as a drill, the unit is capable of drilling holes up to $\frac{3}{8}''$ diameter in steel. It can also be used to drive hole saws, masonry bits and wood augers (Fig. 10).

In its screw-driving position, the screw-drill drives wood screws up to #10 x $1\frac{1}{2}''$ size, or self-tapping metal screws up to size #12 (Fig. 11).

OPERATION

Chuck. When operating, first, always bottom the bit in the chuck. This permits the chuck jaws to grip the shank fully and prevents cocking the jaws. Second, use *all three holes* in the chuck body to tighten as much as possible. Only one hole is needed to release the bit. Third, use *only* a chuck key to tighten or loosen the chuck jaws. If you lose the chuck key, obtain a new one at once.

To obtain maximum life from the jaw assembly, lock your chuck firmly with the key to prevent drill slippage, and when the chuck is not in use, leave it with the jaws open.

Removing the chuck. To remove the chuck, place the chuck key in the chuck and strike key a sharp blow using a hammer or other object in the same direction that tool normally runs. This will loosen the chuck so that it can be easily unscrewed by hand. *Disconnect* tool before making any changes or adjustments.

Switch. Grasp the tool firmly before pressing trigger switch "ON". The tool will remain "ON" as long as pressure is maintained on the trigger. Releasing trigger automatically turns the motor "OFF".

To lock the switch "ON" pull trigger and hold it "ON"; press in locking button and hold it in; then release trigger. Motor will now stay "ON" until trigger is again squeezed and released— the trigger will snap out and the motor will turn "OFF". Practice this a few times.

Drilling. To adjust the unit for drilling, viewing the unit from the chuck end, rotate the adjustment collar counterclockwise until the word "drill" is at the top of the unit. If the collar stops before reaching this point, turn the chuck slightly; the adjustment collar can then be rotated to the proper position (Fig. 12).

For screw-driving rotate the adjustment collar in a clockwise direction until the word "screw" is at the top of the unit. This will disengage the clutch teeth which will automatically be engaged when pressure is applied in driving screws.

The two Allen set screws located in the front part of the gear case are properly adjusted by the factory and should not be readjusted unless the adjusting collar is loose.

Mark exact center of hole with a center punch or nail to guide the drill bit. Clamp or anchor the work securely to insure accuracy and prevent damage or injury. Thin metal should be backed up with a wooden block to prevent bending or distortion

Fig. 12.

Fig. 13.

of the work. Keep bits sharp and use a lubricant when drilling ferrous metals other than cast iron. Relieve pressure on the tool when bit is about to break through to avoid "stalling" the motor. Be sure that the chuck jaws are tightened securely and do not constantly overload the tool. In general, high speed and light feed are recommended.

When drilling wood, particularly deep holes, partially remove the bit from the hole several times while in motion. This will clear the chips, speed up drilling and prevent overheating (Fig. 13).

In drilling brick, cement, cinder block or similar materials, use carbide tipped masonry drill bits. Ordinary steel bits would be dulled rapidly in this type of work.

Driving screws. Adjust the collar to the screw driving position, then insert the correct screw driving bit into the chuck. (See Fig. 11). Make sure that the chuck jaw rests squarely on the "flats" of the bit. Tighten chuck jaws securely so that there is no chance of slippage. Turn on the unit and the chuck and bit will idle until the bit is engaged in the screw head and pressure is applied. The unit should be grasped firmly with both hands and a steady forward pressure applied—the screw will be driven down tight. At this point the clutch comes into operation and will ratchet or slip until the unit is removed from the screw.

It is suggested that you practice by driving a few screws into a scrap piece of lumber until you get the "feel" of this procedure (Fig. 11).

MAINTENANCE

Brushes. Inspect carbon brushes frequently and replace them when badly worn. Cartridge-type brush holders are used to make this operation easy for you. Merely remove the end cover on the switch handle by taking out screws which hold cover in place. Then remove brush caps with a screwdriver and take out the brush and spring assemblies. Springs should have enough tension to hold the brush firmly against the commutator. Be sure to replace badly worn brush assemblies.

Always keep brushes clean and sliding freely in their guides. After several brush replacements, the commutator should be inspected for excess wear. If a groove has been cut by the brushes, the tool should be sent to the manufacturer for repair.

Cable. The cable is the "life line" of your tool, therefore keep it clean by wiping it off occasionally. Be sure to keep it out of oils and greases which ruin the rubber. Coil it neatly when not in use and avoid dragging it across sharp surfaces or using it as a handle to lift the tool.

When using the tool at a considerable distance from power source, an extension cable of adequate size must be used to prevent loss of power. Use the table below for 115 volt current.

Extension Cable Length in Feet	*Gauge of Cable Wire Required*
25, 50, 75, 100, 200	18, 18, 18, 18, 16

Lubrication. The gears should be re-lubricated regularly in from sixty days to six months, depending on use. Remove gear housing, flush out all old grease with kerosene and, with gears in place, refill the housing only half full. The commutator and armature bearing may be lubricated by one or two drops of oil on the armature shaft through the hole provided in the handle cover.

ELECTRIC HAND FINISHING SANDER

This new dustless finishing sander for use in the home and shop has been designed for simple, quick attachment to any vacuum cleaner, and the unit gives the cleanest sanding jobs possible. Dust is instantly removed from the work surface to provide more healthful working conditions and keeps the abrasive paper sharp for more efficient sanding.

It operates on an orbital-action principle, powered by a special sander motor to deliver 4300 orbits per minute, producing a satin-smooth finish upon any surface. Speed and power of the unit permit sanding *with, against,* or *across* the grain of wood surfaces without danger of swirl marks or scratches. Light, compact, and easy to handle, this sander permits even a novice to get professional results effortlessly, on all sanding or refinishing jobs (Fig. 14).

Fig. 14.

Abrasive Paper. "Electro coated," aluminum oxide abrasive paper is the best to use with your finishing sander; 150 or 4/0 fine grit, open grain paper will give you the smoothest finish; and 60 or 1/2/0 coarse grit, open grain will give you the greatest material removal consistent with the proper wood finishing practice.

Do not use ordinary sand paper as its coating qualities are inferior. However, in certain metal sanding applications, emory cloth of various grits will prove to be more durable.

Attaching abrasive paper. The dustless finishing sander is supplied with a dust collecting skirt, snap-in hose connector, hose and coupling. To attach the abrasive paper to this unit the dust collecting skirt should be removed. Two studs on either side of the skirt clamp around the bottom of the sander housing. With thumb pressure on both sides of skirt and two index fingers on inner edge of skirt, pull out and up. This will release studs and allow skirt to be removed (Fig. 15, A). The sandpaper tightening sprockets are now completely exposed.

After selecting the correct grade of grit apply the abrasive paper between the sprocket and the platen and tighten the sprocket by using the T-shaped key provided, or a screwdriver. (Key may be attached to cable, using the slot provided in the key.) This sprocket should be tightened until the abrasive paper is about ¼" underneath the sprocket (Fig. 15, B).

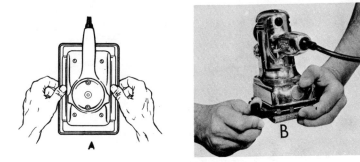

Fig. 15.

Fasten the other edge of the abrasive paper in the same manner.
You will find this new type clamping mechanism holds the abrasive paper taut. If it should become loose during operation, tighten the sprockets immediately. This will preserve the life of your abrasive paper.

ASSEMBLY

The finishing sander, after the abrasive paper has been mounted in place, can be converted to a dustless unit by assembling the dustless equipment as follows:

Remove round plug (Fig 16, A) in the rear of the finishing sander by prying under the edge with a screwdriver or knife. Snap on the dust collecting skirts so that the two studs (Fig. 16, I) fit firmly over the lower edge of the sander housing. Insert the metal coupling (Fig. 16, B) with the detent pin inserted in the rear end of the sander. It may be necessary to manually depress the detent pin. Now attach the hose to the coupling using the smaller hose end (Fig 16, C). To the other end of the hose attach a vacuum cleaner (any type). In connecting the hose to the vacuum cleaner use either the adapter supplied, or hose end itself (which may be attached over or into the inlet). See Fig. 16, depending upon the type of vacuum cleaner connection.

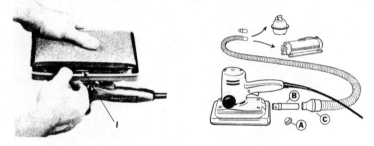

Fig. 16.

OPERATION

Before using the finishing sander, examine the trigger switch. Squeezing this trigger turns the tool "ON"; releasing it turns the tool "OFF". However, on most sanding applications it is more convenient to lock the switch "ON", with the locking pin, which projects from the side of the switch handle, just above the trigger. To do this, first squeeze the trigger and hold it "ON", and press in the locking pin. Then release the trigger. The switch will remain "ON". To turn the motor "OFF", merely pull the trigger and release it. The black molded knob may be screwed into any of three positions to suit the operator. The knob can be threaded into either side or in front of the motor housing.

After turning on the vacuum cleaner, which is attached to your finishing sander, grasp both control handles of the sander firmly, and use the tool freely without forced effort or unnecessary downward pressure. Excessive pressure will slow cutting action and reduce abrasive life. The weight of the tool itself, in most cases, will prove to be sufficient (Fig. 17).

It is not necessary to sand only with the grain of the wood. Move the sander in any direction over the work area to effect rapid and convenient coverage. Sand only long enough to obtain a smooth surface, as the cutting action of the tool is rapid and too much material may be removed with prolonged sanding (Fig. 18).

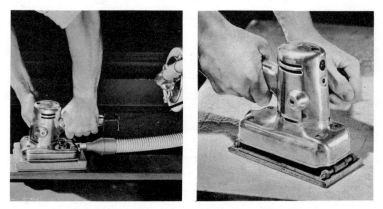

Fig. 17.   **Fig. 18.**

For best results sand progressively with coarse paper first; then, medium; then, fine paper. To obtain what might be called a "superfinish", wet the surface with a sponge or rag and let it dry. The grain of the wood will rise slightly and the surface feel rough. Now, re-sand with 150 or 4/0 grit paper for extra-smooth results.

Of course, the more effective your vacuum cleaner, the more dust removal; therefore, the bag of the vacuum cleaner should be emptied periodically to assure maximum suction.

Note: To remove metal coupling (Fig. 16), rotate coupling so that arrow is on top and then remove.

MAINTENANCE

Motors. This finishing sander is equipped with a "Universal" motor which can be used, at the voltage specified on the nameplate, with either alternating current at 25, 40, 50 or 60 cycles, or with direct current. Voltage should not vary more than 5 per cent, over or under the voltage shown on the nameplate, or serious overheating and loss of power can result. All motors are tested by the manufacturer, and if the tool fails to operate, proceed as follows: (1) Check supply line for blown fuses; (2) see that plug and receptacle are making good contact; and (3) inspect carbon brushes and replace them if they are worn away.

Brushes. Inspect carbon brushes frequently and replace when badly worn. Cartridge-type brush holders are used to make this operation easy. After disconnecting tool, merely remove both brush caps with a screwdriver and take out the brush and spring assemblies. Springs should have enough tension to hold the brush firmly against the commutator. Be sure to replace badly worn brush assemblies.

Be sure to keep brushes clean and sliding freely in their guides. After several brush replacements, the commutator should be inspected for excess wear. If a groove has been cut by the brushes, the tool should be sent to the manufacturer for repair.

Cable. Be sure to keep the cable clean by wiping it off occasionally as it is the "life line" of your tool. Keep it out of oils and greases which ruin the rubber. Coil it neatly when not in use and avoid dragging it across sharp surfaces or using it as a handle to lift the tool.

When using the tool at a considerable distance from power source, an extension cable of adequate size must be used to prevent loss of power. Use the table below for 115 volt current.

Extension Cable Length in Feet	*Gauge of Cable Wire Required*
25, 50, 75, 100, 200	18, 18, 17, 14, 12

Lubrication. The gears should be re-lubricated regularly from sixty days to six months, depending on use. Remove gear housing, flush out all old grease with kerosene and, with gears in place, refill the housing only half full. The commutator and armature bearing may be lubricated by one or two drops of oil on the armature shaft through the hole provided in the top of the tool.

ELECTRIC HAND POWER PLANE

This hand power plane is designed for a comfortable operating balance. Handles and thumb-rest are so placed as to provide an accurate planing "feel" and afford the correct "inward and downward" pressure for each planing operation.

Motors. The power plane shown in Fig. 19 is equipped with a "Universal" motor which can be used, at the voltage specified on the nameplate, with either alternating current at 25, 40, 50 or 60 cycles, or with direct current. Voltage should not vary more than 10 per cent, over or under, the voltage shown on the nameplate or serious overheating and loss of power can result. All motors are tested by the manufacturer, and if the tool fails to operate take the following action: (1) Check your supply line for blown fuses; (2) see that the plug and receptacle are making good contact; and (3) inspect carbon brushes and replace them if they are worn away.

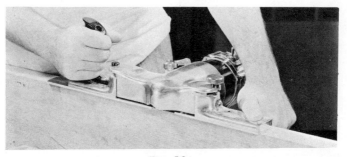

Fig. 19.

Brushes. Inspect carbon brushes frequently and replace them when badly worn. Cartridge-type brush holders are used to make this operation easy for you. Merely remove both brush caps with a screwdriver and take out the brush and spring assemblies. Springs should have enough tension to hold the brush firmly against the commutator. Be sure to replace badly worn brush assemblies.

Keep brushes clean and sliding freely in their guides. After several brush replacements, the commutator should be inspected for excess wear. If a groove has been cut by the brushes, the tool should be sent to the manufacturer for repair.

Cable. When using a power plane at a considerable distance from power source, an extension cable of adequate size must be used to prevent loss of power. Use the table below for 115 volt current.

Extension Cable Length in Feet	*Gauge of Cable Wire Required*
25, 50, 75, 100, 200	18, 16, 16, 12, 10

Grounding. As previously described.

Adjustments. Place a straightedge or scale along the rear shoe of the plane and with a screwdriver, turn adjusting screw (Fig. 20), until the highest cutting edge of the cutter touches the scale of straightedge. This adjustment must be accurate, or poor results would be obtained and, when once adjusted properly, the adjustment should not be changed unless the cutter is replaced or resharpened.

To adjust the depth of cut, place a straightedge or a piece of wood along the rear shoe of the plane and turn the knurled knob (Fig. 21) for the depth of cut desired. This is determined by the space between the front shoe and the straightedge or piece of wood (Fig. 21). The depth of cut is adjustable from zero to $\frac{3}{32}''$. A depth of cut of $\frac{1}{32}''$ is recommended.

The adjustments referred to above are necessary each time a cutter is replaced or sharpened.

To adjust the vertical guide at right angles to the shoe of the plane, slightly loosen wing nuts (Fig. 22, A) and using a square, move the vertical guide so that it is at 90° to the shoe.

The vertical guide is adjustable outward to a 120° obtuse angle and inward to a 45° angle for bevel planing. To adjust the vertical guide for bevel planing, loosen wing nuts (Fig. 22, A) and adjust it to the degree of bevel required. The quadrants at the wing nuts are graduated, however, for very accurate work, a protractor or similar device should be used when adjusting the vertical guide,

Fig. 20.   **Fig. 21.**

Fig. 22.

after which wing nuts (Fig. 22, A) should be tightened securely.

Lock screws (Fig. 22, B) are used to apply tension on both the front and rear shoes of the plane. These screws are properly tensioned at the factory, but after a long period of use it may be necessary to slightly tighten them with a screwdriver.

OPERATION

When using the power plane, grasp both handles firmly and place the thumb of the left hand on the recess of the top of the shoe (Fig. 19). Place the plane on the board using downward pressure with the left hand until the cutter engages, after which downward pressure is applied by both hands, and the vertical guide should be engaged against the side of the board using side pressure. At the completion of the cut, pressure is relieved from the left hand and exerted to the right hand at the rear of the tool, and the forward feed should be reduced so as to minimize chipping at the end of the cut.

The forward movement of the plane in operation depends upon the type of wood being planed. Softwood such as pine planes very rapidly; however, when planing hardwood and particularly plywood, the forward feed of the plane should be slowed down so that the cutter will cut freely.

If the plane is moved forward too slowly the cutter will have a tendency to burn certain kinds of lumber, and if moved too fast, the speed of the motor would be reduced, causing it to be overloaded and result in premature wear on the cutter. The fact that wood has different densities and occasional knots will be encountered, it is impossible to predetermine the forward movement of the plane. The user will soon learn by the sound of the motor when the forward movement of the plane is correct.

It is suggested that a piece of scrap lumber be used to familiarize the user with the tool. There are instances where the wood being planed would have high spots, and these spots should be removed before making a complete cut the length of the board. This is best done by drawing an accurate line on the side of the board, so that the high spots can be easily located.

To get the most out of your plane keep it clean, blow dust and chips from it when necessary, and always keep both the vertical guide and shoes free of resin or any other foreign matter so that smooth surfaces will always be applied to the board being planed. For the best results keep the cutter sharp at all times. When not in use, store the plane in a dry place. A thin coat of oil or paste wax will retard rust.

Safety procedures. Always disconnect the plane from the power supply when making any adjustments. Be sure to disconnect the plane from the power supply when not in use. Handle sharp cutters carefully to avoid injury.

Lubrication. The power plane is completely lubricated at the factory. All ball bearings are of the closed-type and lubricant lasts the life of the bearings.

ELECTRIC HEAVY DUTY HAND ROUTER

The hand operated router shown in Fig. 23 is the latest development in electric woodworking tools. It is efficiently designed for speed and accuracy in performing the finest joinery, and most beautiful cabinet work such as beading, grooving, routing, fluting, cove-cutting, dovetailing, dadoing, rabbeting, making joints, and similar operations. Its use enables the home woodworker to rapidly accomplish inlay work, decorative edges, and many types of bas-relief carving and wood-finishing. (See Parts shown in Fig. 23)

This router is powered by a special router motor, and operates on a direct-drive principle, no gears are necessary, and the motor speeds up to 21,000 r.p.m. Feeding properly into the work it leaves an extremely smooth finish that requires little or no sanding.

GENERAL OPERATING PROCEDURES

The router consists of two major parts—the *motor* and the *base* (Fig. 24). The motor housing is designed in such a way that it forms a firm support for the router in an inverted position. This extra convenience feature leaves both of the operator's hands free to insert or remove bits and cutters. The base is equipped with a smooth surface sub-base, held in place by three countersunk screws. This sub-base protects the working surface from mars or scratches while doing fine cabinet work. It may be

HAND POWER TOOLS

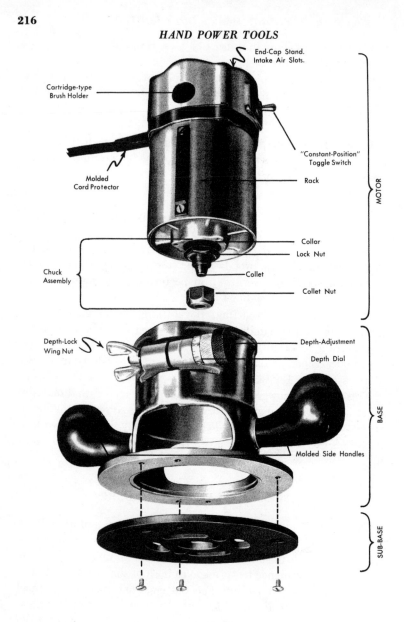

End-Cap Stand.
Intake Air Slots.

Cartridge-type
Brush Holder

"Constant-Position"
Toggle Switch

Molded
Cord Protector

Rack

Collar

Lock Nut

Chuck
Assembly

Collet

Collet Nut

MOTOR

Depth-Lock
Wing Nut

Depth-Adjustment

Depth Dial

Molded Side Handles

BASE

SUB-BASE

Fig. 23.

easily removed to facilitate use of large bits and cutters, or to add depth-of-cut when a longer bit or arbor is not available.

ASSEMBLY

Figure 25 shows the assembled motor and base. To *assemble,* loosen the wing nut (A) on the base, and insert the motor into the base until the rack and pinion (B) which regulates the depth-of-cut, engages. Tighten wing nut and set router up in inverted position. The unit is now ready for inserting a bit or an arbor to hold cutters.

Fig. 24.   Fig. 25.

MAINTENANCE AND CARE

Motor and current. The router is powered by a "Universal" router motor. It operates at nameplate voltage on alternating current (25 to 60 cycles), or on direct current. Voltage variation of more than ten per cent will cause loss of power and overheating. Be sure to check the voltage specifications on the nameplate of your equipment with the voltage of your supply line. Inspect the carbon brushes in the motor at regular intervals, and if worn away replace them immediately to prevent damage to the motor armature as instructed by the manufacturer.

Cable. Every router is equipped with a *three-conductor cable*. The third wire is for "grounding." (See Grounding in section on Portable Electric Saws, Chap. 6.) *Do not* permit cable to lie in grease or oil which ruins the rubber. Wipe it off occasionally and avoid rough handling. When not in use coil the cable loosely without sharp bends or kinks, and keep it off the floor.

If an extension cable is necessary to reach a power outlet, be sure that the cable is made of a wire size large enough to carry current to the router without too great a drop in voltage. A long extension cable of inadequate size will cause a voltage drop, loss of power and damage to the motor through overheating. When using an extension make sure that it is a 3-conductor cable. Connect the third wire of the cable on the tool to the third wire of the extension. Then ground the other end of the extension with the third wire, as described under Grounding. If more than one extension cable is used, connect the various third wires, grounding the one nearest the electrical receptacle.

Use the following table for 115 volt current.

Extension Cable Length In Feet	*Gauge of Cable Wire Required*
25, 50, 75, 100, 200	18, 16, 14, 12, 10

OPERATION SAFETY

Make sure that the tool is *properly grounded* before operating. To operate, grasp the tool firmly, not gingerly in your hand. *Do not* turn the power "ON" until you are in working position. Then place the tool in working position and press the toggle switch.

Always pull the plug before you change bits or cutters.

Every tool is thoroughly tested before leaving the factory and should be in perfect operating condition when it reaches the user. If, at any time, your unit fails to operate, it will save you time and expense to check the following possible causes of failure:

1. Is your supply line dead? Check for blown fuses.
2. Are the receptacle and plug making good contact? Check for bent prongs and loose wires.
3. Are both brushes touching commutator? Check for good

brush contact. Carbon brushes should be inspected at regular intervals and if worn away should be replaced immediately to avoid motor damage.

4. Check voltage specifications on the nameplate with the voltage of your supply line. See Motor and Current previously described in this chapter.

Lubrication. All *routers* are completely lubricated at the factory and are ready for use. All *ball bearings* are of the closed type and are grease sealed with sufficient lubricant packed in them to last the life of the bearing.

ATTACHING BITS AND CUTTERS

Figure 26 illustrates how a straight bit is inserted into the collet-type chuck. The shank of the bit or cutter arbor should be inserted to a depth of at least ½″. *Make sure electric current is disconnected when performing this operation.*

Fig. 26.   **Fig. 27.**

After the bit is inserted, the two open-end wrenches are employed to tighten the chuck, as shown in Fig. 27. One of the two wrenches is fitted to the upper, or collet nut, and the other is attached to the collar at the bottom. Hold the lower wrench stationary and turn the upper wrench from right to left to tighten bit or arbor in chuck securely. Reverse the procedure to loosen and to remove the bit when necessary.

Located between the collet nut and the collar is a *lock nut,* which neither wrench will fit, and which is tightened before the unit leaves the factory. This lock nut needs no further attention from the operator.

REGULATING CUTTING DEPTH

Place the router on flat surface, on its base, loosen wing nut (A), and turn knurled knob (C) until the bit very lightly touches the surface on which it is resting (Fig. 28). Tighten the wing nut and set router up on end.

With router inverted, the built-in micrometer-type depth adjustment (D) is set on the zero calibration. Each graduation on the depth dial represents $\frac{1}{64}$ of an inch. To set bit to desired cutting depth, loosen wing nut, turn outer knob (C), reading depth on dial (D); then tighten the wing nut. The graduated scale provides direct depth-reading in 64ths of an inch, without measuring, up to 1 inch.

OPERATING THE ROUTER

There are a number of fixtures and attachments used to control and guide the router—the straight and circular guide, slot and circle cutting attachment, template guides, dovetail joint fixture, and the hinge mortising template. These, as well as other fixtures such as a home-made T-square are illustrated and described in this chapter.

In using the router, the base should be held firmly and flat on the surface, and the tool should be moved from left to right in straight cutting at a rate sufficient to maintain a high motor speed. In irregular or circular cutting move the router counter-clockwise. Feeding the router too slowly may cause the bit or cutter to burn the wood, whereas excessive speed in feeding will cause undue wear on the bits and cutters and at the same time result in an inferior cut.

Various wood densities make it impossible to set down just how fast this feeding should be done. After short practice in using the router, you will soon acquire the *feel* of the tool for the correct feeding speed.

In some instances, such as extremely hard wood, it is necessary to make several passes at varying depths until the desired depth-of-cut is obtained.

Bits and cutters should be kept sharp at all times.

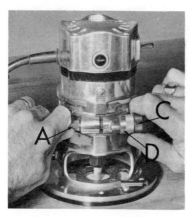

Fig. 28.

Free-hand routing. Although the router is more widely used with some form of guiding device for greater cutting accuracy, there are many applications to which it is put *free-hand*, that is, routing that is guided only by the operator's skill. Raised letter work. A variation of this is routing the letters themselves out of a flat surface. Surface stock removal may be accomplished free-hand, carefully following a pencilled layout. Skilled wood carvers often use a router to gouge out background and prepare work for final carving. The results and beauty of work that can be done in this fashion are limited only by the artistic ability and skill of the operator.

T-square guide. A simple device for guiding the router when making straight cuts on flat surfaces is the home-made T-square (Fig. 29). This T-square can be easily made out of scrap lumber, but make sure its edges are perfectly smooth and straight. It is

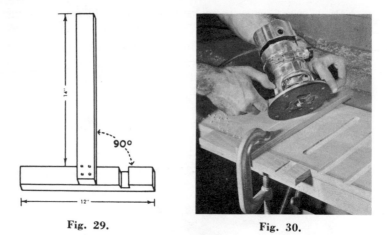

Fig. 29.   Fig. 30.

placed on the surface being routed and held in position by means of a clamp, as shown in Fig. 30. The base of the router is guided firmly along the edge of the T-square to make a straight cut. Measurements shown in the illustration are ideal for most applications with the router. They may, however, be altered to suit your specific needs. Other home-made guiding devices are discussed later in this chapter.

STRAIGHT AND CIRCULAR GUIDE

The straight and circular guide (Fig. 31) is the most popular device used with the router. It enables the operator to make straight, curved, or angular cuts with ease and accuracy.

Attaching and adjusting. Figure 32 shows how the straight and circular guide is attached with four screws through the metal brackets, and firmly tightened to the router base. The two wing nuts (A) are loosened and the guide is adjusted along the length of the round metal rods and positioned in relation to the bit or cutter where the cut is to be made, after which wing nuts (A) are tightened.

The guide has a built-in vernier-type adjustment device that is used to adjust the guide accurately. In making fine adjustments, tighten the wing nut (B), loosen two wing nuts (A), and turn the knurled knob (C) to either right or left until the guide is accurately positioned, then tighten wing nuts (A) securely. Figure 33 shows operating position.

There are times when the length of the guide is insufficient to give the router ample support. When such is the case, a piece of wood may be attached to the front end of the guide using two wood screws and a piece of smooth lumber about 8″ or 10″ long and 2″ to 3″ wide (Fig. 34). Two holes are provided in the straight edge for this purpose.

Fig. 31.

Fig. 32.

Fig. 33.

Fig. 34.

Straight cuts. When routing along the edge of straight pieces, the straight edge (Fig. 31) is attached to the guide and held against the straight edge of the work as the router is fed along cutting line as shown in Fig. 33.

Curved and angular cuts. Routing is accurately accomplished along curved or angular edges by removing the straight edge, (AA), from the straight and circular guide. This leaves two points of contact to guide the router along irregularly shaped edges. Figure 35 illustrates this operating position, using the router to put a decorative edge around circular table top.

Fig. 35.

Fig. 36.

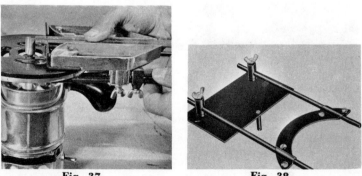

Fig. 37.

Fig. 38.

Inside cuts. When cutting inside edges such as rabbeting for screens, the straight and circular guide is attached in the reverse position as illustrated in Fig. 36.

Measuring feature. For added accuracy, the straight and circular guide features a slotted recess along the bottom which permits the insertion of a rule or scale for use in adjusting the edge of the guide in relation to the cutting edge of the bit. Figure 37 shows how this measurement is made, assuring precision results on any routing project.

SLOT AND CIRCLE CUTTING ATTACHMENT

The slot and circle cutting attachment is used with the router for cutting evenly spaced slots and grooves, discs, circular holes and concentric designs. In circle cutting, or slot cutting, the attachment can be adjusted for diameters or lengths from 1″ to 22″ (Fig. 38).

Figure 39 shows the router in operating position when cutting a medium sized circle. Move the router always in a counterclockwise direction. Figure 40 illustrates the completed operation. *Note* that a ¼″ hole was first drilled in the center of the circle to hold the attachment guide pin. A straight bit of sufficient depth to pass through the wood was used—with a scrap piece of lumber being placed underneath the work to prevent cutting into the workbench.

Fig. 39.   **Fig. 40.**

Interesting circular designs can be made using this attachment such as the one shown in Fig. 41. *Note* that two different bits were used to obtain an artistic result. *Note* how a circular opening can be improved by routing an attractive molding as shown in Fig. 42.

With the circle cutting pin removed and a guide bar assembled in its place, this attachment serves as a guide for cutting slots and grooves. In the example shown in Fig. 43, the first slot was made by using the end of the lumber as a guide, and the second slot was cut in the same manner as illustrated. This operation can be repeated, or the distance between slots varied by adjusting the two wing nuts on the attachment.

IT IS EASY TO MAKE CUTS AND JOINTS

MAKING DADO CUTS

Dado cuts, frequently used in the construction of shelving, bookcases, furniture, etc., can readily be made with a router and the correct-size straight bit.

Figure 44 illustrates three types of dado cuts commonly used —the *through dado* (A), the *half-blind dado* (B), and the *blind dado* (C).

When making a *through dado*, it is well to use a piece of scrap lumber on each edge of the board so as to prevent chipout. A *half-blind dado* is accomplished by stopping the machine before it reaches the entire width of the board. *Blind dado* cuts are made by first positioning the router at a given point, then lowering it into the lumber slowly and feeding it forward the required distance.

When making dado cuts, select a bit, if possible, that will be the diameter of the thickness of the board that is to be used in the groove. A strip of wood should be clamped to the board receiving the dado cut to serve as a guide on which the base of the router is supported.

Guiding the router on dado cuts is best accomplished with the straight and circular guide, as previously discussed. The T-square may also be used as shown in Fig. 30.

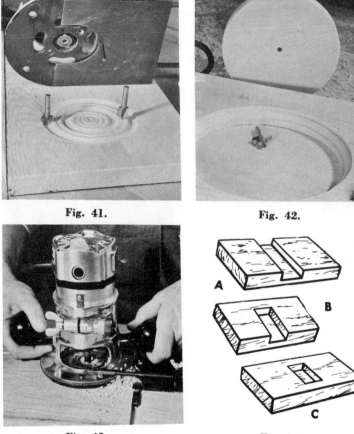

Fig. 41.

Fig. 42.

Fig. 43.

Fig. 44.

THE DOVETAIL DADO

One of the strongest joints possible in fine cabinet work is the *dovetail dado*. It prevents twisting or warping, and is unsurpassed where tightness of finished joint is an important factor, such as in making doors and frameworks of various types. The router, fitted with a dovetail bit is capable of turning out dovetail dadoes with speed and accuracy.

Figure 45 illustrates the routing of a dovetail groove. *Note* that an improvised fixture is clamped to the work for use in controlling the movement of the router. The groove shown is a *half-blind* groove, since it will not extend completely across the board.

Fig. 45.   **Fig. 46.**

After the groove is cut, the same bit is used to rout out the male section. *Note* in Fig. 46 that the piece being routed is held in a fixture, with the straight and circular guide being used, first along one edge, and then along the other edge of the fixture to control the router. When one side is finished, the router is reversed and the opposite side is cut.

The width of the dovetail dado need not be confined to the size of the bit, since several adjacent cuts may be made to provide any desired width-of-joint. This also applies when cutting the male section.

MAKING RABBET CUTS

Rabbet cuts are used for making rabbeted drawer fronts, cabinet doors, and many other types of joints. Figure 47 shows how this operation is performed, using a rabbeting bit.

In Fig. 48, a straight bit is used, which should be placed in the chuck and adjusted to the required depth of cut. The router may be controlled by means of the straight and circular guide, which is adjusted to the desired width of the rabbet cut. It is best to select a bit that is larger in diameter than the width of the finished cut so that a less critical adjustment is necessary in the guide. A simple home-made fixture (Fig. 49) can be used to hold small pieces in routing position as shown in Fig. 48.

When making rabbet cuts, it is usually better to make them across the end grain of the lumber first, and then along the grain. This procedure tends to eliminate chipping at the edges.

Fig. 47.

Fig. 48.

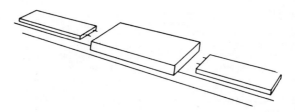

Fig. 49.

TONGUE-AND-GROOVE JOINTS

Tongue-and-groove joints enable two or more boards to be firmly and uniformly joined together to provide a large, flat surface, such as a table or dresser top. They are frequently used in fine cabinet work and interior designing. For maximum accuracy and strength, boards being joined by the tongue-and-groove method should first be made smooth and true.

All grooves are cut first. On the edge of one board, the location and the width of the groove should be outlined with a sharp pencil or knife. The router is fitted with a straight bit, slightly smaller in diameter than the groove, and adjusted to the zero depth setting. The straight and circular guide is attached to the router and adjusted, so that one edge of the bit is positioned against one side of the drawn outline. The built-in vernier adjustment on the guide provides maximum accuracy in making this adjustment. The bit is next adjusted to the desired cutting depth and the cut is made, guiding the router against one side of the board (Fig. 50). The second cut is made by guiding the router on the opposite side of the board. This method assures the groove to be in the exact center of the board. Without changing any adjustments on the router, proceed to cut all grooves in all boards that are to receive them.

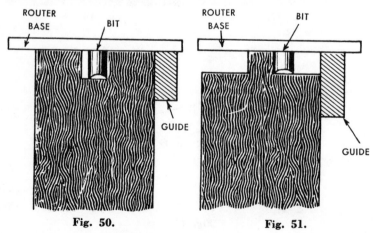

Fig. 50. Fig. 51.

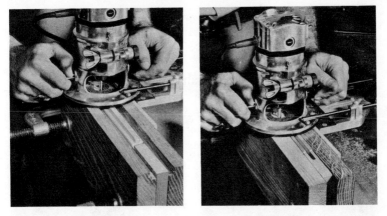

Fig. 52.   **Fig. 53.**

When cutting the tongues, the depth adjustment should be about $\frac{1}{64}''$ more shallow than the groove, to allow space for glue. The straight and circular guide is adjusted and each side of the board is routed until a tongue of the correct width is made (Fig. 51). Without changing any adjustments, proceed to cut all pieces that are to have tongues.

When routing tongue-and-groove joints on short pieces of lumber, it is advisable to use a fixture for holding the pieces while they are being machined (Figs. 52 and 53).

MORTISE-AND-TENON JOINTS

Mortise-and-tenon joints are frequently used in the construction of furniture, doors, windows, screens, and in many other projects needing firm, strong joints.

Cutting the mortise. To make a joint of this type, first outline on the piece of wood that is to be mortised, the length and width of the mortise. This can be done with a sharp pencil or a knife. When the mortise is to be in the exact center of the board, it is best to use a straight bit, smaller in diameter than the width of the mortise (Fig. 54).

Place the piece to be mortised in a fixture that is suitable to hold it securely. Place the straight bit in the router chuck to at least a $\frac{1}{2}''$ depth, and adjust the bit to zero setting. Attach straight and circular guide to the router and adjust it to ride along the edge of the fixture at a distance to place the edge of the bit exactly on one side of marked rectangle where the cut is to be made.

Loosen wing nut and turn knurled knob on the router until the bit is adjusted to the necessary depth of cut. In hard lumber it may be necessary to make several passes with the router to obtain the necessary depth of mortise.

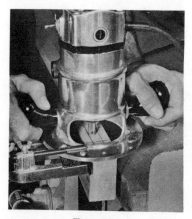

Fig. 54.

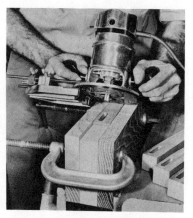

Fig. 55.

Fig. 56.

Fig. 57.

Tighten all adjustments securely, start router and lower the revolving bit slowly into the wood that is to receive the mortise, until the base of the router rests flat on top of the fixture. The router is then moved forward to cut the desired length of the mortise.

After this first cut is completed, the router guide is placed against the opposite side of the fixture and the second cut is made to provide the correct width of the mortise. It will be in the exact center of the board. Without disturbing the adjustments on the router, proceed to cut all pieces that are to be mortised.

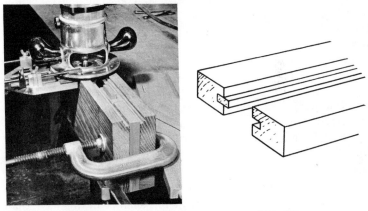

Fig. 58.   **Fig. 59.**

There are times when a mortise is to be located to one side of the center of the board, such as in making table legs (Fig. 55). To do this, select a bit of the proper size, adjust it to the proper depth and proceed to cut the mortise as described, guiding the router along only one side of the fixture.

When a large number of mortises are to be made, an improvised stop can be attached to the fixture so as to limit the movement of the router in its lengthwise motion, thereby making all mortises the same length.

Cutting the tenon. The board to receive the tenon is held in the fixture (Fig. 56). A straight bit is placed in the router and the depth of cut adjusted about $\frac{1}{64}''$ less than the depth of the mortise. This provides space for glue when the object is being assembled. The straight and circular guide is attached to the base of the router and adjusted, so that when it is passed along both sides of the fixture, a tenon of the proper width is made. The vernier adjustment on the guide is very helpful in making this adjustment. After the length of the tenon has been cut, it is then cut to width. This is done by guiding the router along the end of the fixture. After one side is cut, the piece is reversed and the other side is cut. Do not change the router adjustments until all tenons have been made.

Note that all mortises will have round ends and the tenons will have square ends as shown in Figs. 57 and 58. The mortise can be made square with a chisel, or the tenon can be made round to fit the mortise with a file. In either case, a satisfactory joint will result.

SPLINE JOINTS

Spline joints are used in joining two or more pieces of lumber together to build up a large surface (Fig. 59). Generally speaking, in ¾″ lumber a spline of ¼″ thickness and a depth of ¼″ to ⅜″ is usually sufficient. The edges of the boards that are to be joined together should be made smooth and true.

The edge of the groove to be cut is outlined on the board with a sharp pencil or knife. A straight bit, smaller in diameter than the width of the groove, should be placed in the router, and then the router should be adjusted to the zero setting. Place the straight and circular guide on the router, and adjust it so that one edge of the bit is along one edge of the drawn outline. Use the vernier adjustment for making these measurements.

The depth of cut is then adjusted, and the cut is made along one side of the board after which the router is used on the opposite side of the board. The result will be a perfect groove in the exact center of the board. When short pieces of lumber are to be joined, it is best to hold the wood in a fixture (Fig. 60). Without changing any of the router adjustments, proceed to cut all grooves.

Plywood is frequently used in making the splines. The same kind of wood being joined can also be used. If it is, the grain in the spline should run in opposite directions to the boards being joined together. Blind spline joints are made where the edge of the glued up pieces is to be uniform in appearance. This is done by starting the groove a short distance in from the end of the board and the cut is stopped a short distance in from the other end of the board. Figure 61 shows how a blind spline joint should be made to join together a heavy frame.

Fig. 60.   Fig. 61.

DOVETAIL JOINTS

Due to their strength and neat appearance, dovetail joints are frequently used in the construction of drawers and boxes. To make them by hand, using a chisel and mallet, requires considerable skill and patience. The dovetail kit shown in Fig. 62 permits this type of joinery to be accomplished with speed and accuracy.

Two sizes of finger templates are available for use with the dovetail fixture (Fig. 63). One is for use with lumber $\frac{7}{16}''$ to $1''$ thick, and the other with lumber from $\frac{5}{16}''$ to $\frac{5}{8}''$ thick. The edges of the two boards that are to be joined are cut at the same time, insuring a perfect fit.

Figure 64 illustrates how the lumber is held in the fixture, and Fig. 65 shows how the cut is made. Figs. 66 and 67 show the

Fig. 62.

Fig. 63.

Fig. 64.

Fig. 65.

cuts completed, and Fig. 68 illustrates how the drawer pieces are grooved to accommodate the drawer bottom.

The router can also be used to enhance the appearance of drawer fronts as shown in Fig. 69.

TEMPLATES

The best method of duplicating shapes, especially those of intricate design, is by *template routing*. This consists of transferring the desired design to a pattern, or template, and cutting it out. This template is clamped to the material being routed and the router, fitted with a bit and a template guide is directed along its pattern for perfect duplication. Once the template is cut, it may be reused again and again for production-line uniformity.

Figure 70 shows several types of template guides available for use with the router. These serve to guide and restrict the movement of the router within the desired area being cut. Figure 71 represents the template guide and bit in cutting position. *Note* that the pattern, or template, should be made slightly larger than the opening wanted, to compensate for the size of the template guide used.

Fig. 66.

Fig. 67.

Fig. 68.

Fig. 69.

Fig. 70.

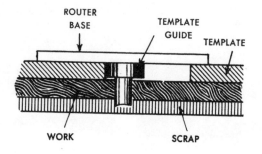

Fig. 71.

Fig. 72.   Fig. 73.

Routing the template. The design is usually first drawn on paper and then transferred to the template material, which may be hardwood, plywood, or composition board (Fig. 72). This design may be cut out with a jig or band saw or the router may be used as follows:

Remove sub-base from the router to provide maximum visibility. Place the drawn template on a piece of smooth scrap material and clamp both to the workbench. Fit the router with a straight bit and adjust the cutting depth to about $\frac{1}{16}''$ deeper than the thickness of the template material. The design is then routed out freehand, with careful guiding, and keeping the bit slightly away from the drawn line. After all first cuts are made, go over them again and slowly rout to the drawn line.

After the template is cut, all edges should be made smooth with a file or sandpaper, for any irregularities in the template will be automatically transferred to the finished piece.

TEMPLATE ROUTING

The template is used as follows:

Tack the template to the piece that is to be routed using small brads and locating them in section that will be scrapped. Place a piece of scrap lumber under the work to protect the bench top, as shown in Fig. 73. With the sub-base and template guide attached to the router, a straight bit is placed in the chuck and adjusted to the desired depth of cut. This depth adjustment will depend on the hardness and the thickness of the wood being routed. Usually several passes of the router at varying depths are necessary to produce a smoother surface than a single heavy cut. Turn the current on and lower the revolving bit into the wood until the base of the router is flat on the template. With the template guide in contact with the template, the router is then guided within the design until the area is completely cut as shown in Fig. 74.

After each section is cut out, turn off the current and allow the bit to stop revolving before moving to the next opening. Continue until all openings have been cut.

Should a bas-relief effect be desired instead of a through cut, the same procedure is followed except that the depth of cut is adjusted so as not to pass completely through the material being routed.

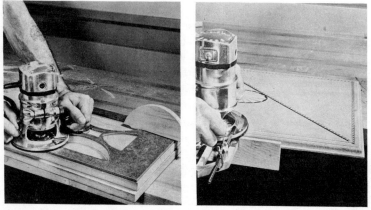

Fig. 74.   **Fig. 75.**

INLAY WORK

Because of the accuracy and smooth, high-quality cuts possible with the router, it is an excellent tool for inserting inlays. Inlay strips, which greatly enhance the beauty of finished woodwork, and add to its value, can be conveniently purchased in a wide variety of shapes and designs.

In applying an inlay strip around a table top proceed as follows:

1. Draw an outline completely around the entire surface to indicate the exact position of the finished inlay.

2. Fit router with a straight bit of the exact same width as that of the inlay and adjust cutting depth to slightly less than the thickness of the inlay. (The set inlay will protrude slightly above the surface for sanding to a perfectly smooth, flush finish.)

3. With the straight and circular guide attached to the router and set at the correct, outlined position of the inlay, the table top is routed around the entire inlay area, as shown in Fig. 75. When finished, the corners will be round—cut them square with

a thin blade chisel or knife.

4. Place inlay in the routed groove, fit correctly, and miter at each corner.

5. Place glue in the groove, insert fitted inlay, and clamp, using a strip of paper and a long board for protection and uniform pressure along inlay.

6. After the glue sets, remove clamps and thoroughly and carefully sand surface.

7. Follow the same procedure for inlaying in each of the tapered legs. Fit legs and clamp as shown in Fig. 76, while this work is being done.

8. Locate center design (Fig. 77) in the exact center of the table top, and outline by tracing around the inlay piece with a sharp, thin knife blade. Care must be taken not to cut any deeper than the thickness of the inlay, itself.

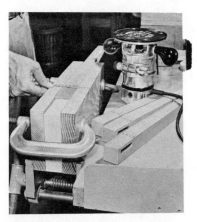

Fig. 76.

Fig. 77.

9. Fit the router with a straight bit and, with the sub-base removed, adjust depth of cut to slightly less than the thickness of the inlay.

10. With the correct depth established, rout out center section free-hand, carefully restricting cut to about $\frac{1}{32}''$ from knife-cut outline. (This $\frac{1}{32}''$ is hand-trimmed with knife blade.)

11. Apply glue to the recess, insert inlay, and clamp securely. Most inlays are protected on one side by pressure-sensitive paper. *Be sure* to insert this type of inlay with the paper side up.

12. When glue has set, remove all clamps and sand entire surface to a smooth, even finish.

The care and patience required in accomplishing fine inlay work by hand can only be imagined by one who has not actually tried it. However, with the electric router this same type of work becomes only one of many jobs accomplished with the speed and accuracy of the professional craftsman.

MAKING YOUR OWN MOLDING

Many types of novel and decorative wood molding can be easily accomplished with the router, using either bits or cutters. Such molding cuts can be made directly along the edge of the work, such as table and desk tops, bookcase shelves, etc.; or they can be made separately and fastened wherever desired.

Figure 78 illustrates two types of molding made with the router, using the pilot part of the bit to guide the tool along the edge of the work. After the molding is shaped with the router, a saw is used to cut the molding from the lumber, as illustrated.

Moldings of this type are extremely useful in baseboard work, picture-framing, panelling, etc. By using various combinations of bits and cutters, the unique designs possible are limitless.

Figure 79 shows a molded edge being applied directly to the edge of a table top, using a bit with a pilot end to guide the tool.

Fig. 78.

Fig. 79.

The straight and circular guide as shown in Fig. 31 may also be used when the cut desired must be made with a straight bit.

MAKING TAPERED LEGS

Tapered legs, such as are often used in making tables and chairs, can easily be made, using the router and a simple fixture (Fig. 80). The size of the fixture will depend upon the size and length of the leg

Tapering fixture. To make this tapering fixture, proceed as follows:

Secure a board of sufficient size for the base (A). The two upright pieces, (B) and (C) are made from the same stock and shaped as shown in the illustration. They should be about ½″ higher than the thickness of the leg that is to be tapered. Fasten pieces (B) and (C) to base (A), spaced so that the square leg can be placed between them (Fig. 81). A tapered wedge (D) should be made to fit between boards (B) and (C) (Fig. 80). This is used to elevate one end of the leg being tapered.

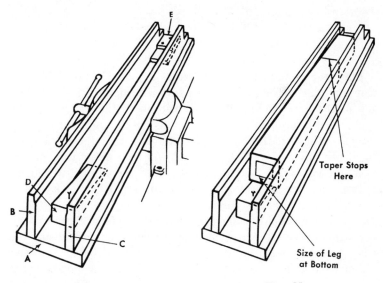

Fig. 80.   Fig. 81.

Tapered leg. Most tapered legs are made square a certain distance down from the top in order to accommodate an apron. Therefore, draw a line across the leg where the taper is to stop. Determine the size that the leg should be at the bottom and draw the outline as shown in Fig. 81. It is only necessary to do this with one leg as, after all adjustments are made, all legs will be alike. The fixture should be held in a vise or fastened by clamps to the work bench.

Fig. 82.   Fig. 83.

Place the straight leg in the fixture against the stop (E) and clamp in place. The router, fitted with a straight bit, is rested on top of the fixture (Fig. 82) and, using both the wedge and the router depth-adjustment, bit is set to cut to the depth of the drawn outline on the leg bottom. Be sure that the adjustment for depth of cut is such that the cut will stop where the line has been drawn on the leg to accommodate the apron. When all adjustments are accurately made, a nail is partially driven into wedge (D) to hold it securely.

The router is guided along the outer edge of the fixture, using the straight and circular guide and the cuts are made, using the tool on each side of the fixture and readjusting the straight and circular guide until the entire side of the leg is machined. Taper all legs on one side, then, with the same setting, cut the adjacent sides. A small wedge is used at the tapered end to prevent end-play while leg is being machined (Fig. 83).

Without changing the cutting-depth on the router, cut the remaining two sides of the leg. To set this cutting depth, remove nail holding wedge (D) and move wedge inward until bit meets the drawn outline of the leg bottom. Insert small wedges (Fig. 84) to prevent end-play while routing. Figure 85 illustrates final cut being made.

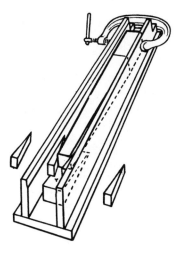

Fig. 84.

Fig. 85.

Legs for fine furniture are often made from hardwood, in which case it may be necessary, depending upon the taper, to make several passes at different depths of cut until the desired depth is obtained. The speed with which the router operates is such that the tapered legs will require only a minimum amount of sanding.

ADDITIONAL PORTABLE ELECTRIC POWER TOOLS

Portable power tools are tools that can be moved from place to place. Some of the most common portable power tools that you will use in woodworking are electrically powered and include drills, sanders, saws, and wrenches.

Drills

The *portable electric drill* shown in Fig. 86 is probably the most frequently used power tool. Although it is especially designed for drilling holes, by adding various accessories you can adapt it for different jobs. Sanding, sawing, buffing, polishing, screwdriving, wire brushing, and paint mixing are examples of possible uses. The sizes of portable electric drills are classified by the maximum-size straight-shank drill it will hold. That is, a $\frac{1}{4}''$ electric drill will hold a straight-shank drill up to and including $\frac{1}{4}''$.

The revolutions per minute (rpm) and power the drill will deliver are most important when choosing a drill for a job. You will find that the speed of the drill motor decreases with an increase in size, primarily because the larger units are designed to turn larger cutting tools or to drill in heavy materials, and both these factors require slower speed.

If you are going to do heavy work, such as drilling in masonry or steel, then you would probably need to use a drill with a $\frac{3}{8}''$ or $\frac{1}{2}''$ capacity. If most of your drilling will be forming holes in wood or small holes in sheet metal, then a $\frac{1}{4}''$ drill will probably be adequate.

The *chuck* is the clamping device into which the drill is inserted. Nearly all electric drills are equipped with a three-jaw chuck. Some of the drill motors have a hand-type chuck that you tighten or loosen by hand, but most of the drills used have gear-type, three-jaw chucks which are tightened and loosened by means of a chuck key (Fig. 87). *Do not* apply further pressure with pliers or wrenches after you hand-tighten the chuck with the chuck key.

Always remove the key *immediately* after you use it. Otherwise the key will fly loose when the drill motor is started and may cause serious injury to you or others. The chuck key is generally taped on the cord of the drill; but if it is not, be sure you put it in a safe place where it will not get lost.

Most portable electric drills have controls similar to the ones shown on the $\frac{1}{4}''$ drill in Fig. 86. This drill has a momentary

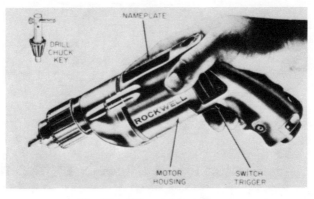

Fig. 86. ¼″ portable drill.

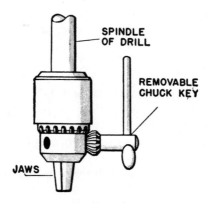

Fig. 87. Three-jaw chuck and chuck key.

contact trigger switch located in the handle. The switch is squeezed to start the electric drill and released to stop it.

The trigger latch is a button in the bottom of the drill handle. It is pushed in, while the switch trigger is held down, to lock the trigger switch in the "ON" position. The trigger latch is released by squeezing and then releasing the switch trigger.

Fig. 88. Portable electric sander.

Sanders

Portable sanders are tools designed to hold and operate abrasives for sanding wood, plastics, and metals. The most common types are the disc, belt, and reciprocating orbital sanders.

Disc Sander

Electric disc sanders (Fig. 88) are especially useful on work where a large amount of material is to be removed quickly such as scaling surfaces in preparation for painting. This machine *should not* be used where a mirror smooth finish is required.

The disc should be moved smoothly and lightly over the surface. *Never* allow the disc to stay in one place too long because it will cut into the material and leave a large depression.

Belt Sander

The *portable belt sander* (Fig. 89) is commonly used for surfacing lumber used for interior trim, furniture, or cabinets. Wood floors are almost always made ready for final finishing by using a belt sander. Whereas these types of sanding operations were once laborious and time-consuming, it is now possible to perform the operations quickly and accurately with less effort.

The belt sanders use endless sanding belts that can be obtained in many different grades (grits). The belts are usually 2″, 3″,

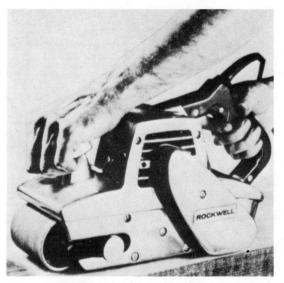

Fig. 89.   Portable belt sander.

or 4″ wide and can be easily changed when they become worn or when you want to use a different grade of sanding paper.

When preparing to use the sander, *be sure* that the object to be sanded is firmly secured. Then, after the motor has been started verify that the belt is tracking on center. Any adjustment to make it track centrally is usually made by aligning screws. The moving belt is then placed on the surface of the object to be sanded with the rear part of the belt touching first. The machine is then leveled as it is moved forward. When you use the sander, *do not* press down or *ride* it, because the weight of the machine exerts enough pressure for proper cutting. (Excessive pressure also causes the abrasive belt to clog and the motor to overheat.) Adjust the machine over the surface with overlapping strokes, always in a direction parallel to the grain.

By working over a fairly wide area and avoiding any machine tilting or pausing in any one spot, an even surface will result. Upon completion of the sanding process, lift the machine off the work and then stop the motor.

Some types of sanders are provided with a bag that takes up the dust that is produced. Be sure to use it if it is available.

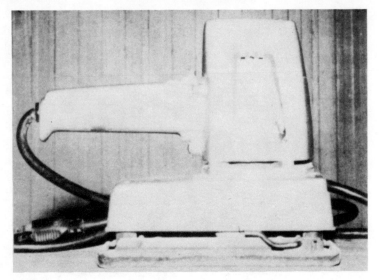

Fig. 90. Orbital sander.

Orbital Sander

The *orbital sander* (Fig. 90) is so named because of the action of the sanding pad. The pad moves in a tiny orbit, with a motion that is hardly discernible, so that it actually sands in all directions. This motion is so small and so fast that, with fine paper mounted on the pad, it is nearly impossible to see any scratches on the finished surface.

The pad, around which the abrasive sheet is wrapped, usually extends beyond the frame of the machine so it is possible to work in tight corners and against vertical surfaces.

Some models of the orbital sanders have a bag attached to catch all dust that is made from the sanding operation. Orbital sanders (pad sanders) do not remove as much material as fast as the belt sander or disc sander but do a better job on smoothing a surface for finishing. If both a belt or disc sander and an orbital sander are available, you should use the belt or disc sander for rough, preliminary work and the orbital sander for finishing. The sandpaper used on the sander may be cut to size from a bulk sheet of paper or may be available in the correct size for the sander you are using. The paper is wrapped around a pad on the sander and is fastened to the pad by means of levers on the front and rear of the sander. The lever action fasteners make changing the paper easy and quick.

Portable Circular Saw

The *portable circular saw* is becoming more and more popular as a woodworking tool because of the time and labor it saves, the precision with which it works, and its ease of handling and maneuverability.

Because of the many changes being made in the design of these saws, only general information will be given in this section. Information concerning a particular saw can be found by checking with the manufacturer.

The sizes of portable electric saws range from one-sixth horsepower with a 4″ blade to one-and-one-half horsepower with a 14″ blade. They are so constructed that they may be used as a carpenter's handsaw, both at the job site or on a bench in the woodworking shop.

The portable electric saw (Fig. 91) is started by pressing a trigger inserted in the handle and stopped by releasing it. The saw will run only when the trigger is held.

Most saws may be adjusted for crosscutting or for ripping. The ripsaw guide shown in Fig. 91 is adjusted by the two small knurled nuts at the base of the saw. When the guide is inserted in the rip guide slot to the desired dimensions, the nuts are then tightened to hold it firmly in place.

In crosscutting a guideline is generally marked across the board to be cut. Place the front of the saw base on the work so that the guide mark on the front plate and the guide line on the work are aligned. *Be sure* the blade is clear of the work. Start the saw and allow the cutting blade to attain full speed. Then advance the saw, keeping the guide mark and guide line aligned. If the saw stalls, back the saw out. *Do not release* the starting trigger. When the saw resumes cutting speed, start cutting again.

Additional adjustments include a depth knob and a bevel thumbscrew. The depth of the cut is regulated by adjusting the depth knob. The bevel-adjusting thumbscrew is used for adjusting the angle of the cut. This permits the base to be tilted in relation to the saw. The graduated scale marked in degrees on the quadrant (Fig. 91) enables the operator to measure his adjustments and angles of cut.

The bottom plate of the saw is wide enough to provide the saw with a firm support on the lumber being cut. The blade of the saw is protected by a spring guard which opens when lumber is being cut but snaps back into place when the cut is finished. Many different sawblades may be placed on the machine for special kinds of sawing. By changing blades, almost any building material from slate and corrugated metal sheets to fiberglass can be cut.

To change saw blades, first disconnect the power. Remove the blade by taking off the saw clamp screw and flange, using the

Fig. 91. Portable electric circular saw.

wrench provided for this purpose. Attach the new saw blade making certain the teeth are in the proper cutting direction (pointing upward toward the front of the saw) and tighten the flange and clamp screw with the wrench.

Caution: Do not put the saw blade on backwards. Most blades have instructions stamped on them with the words *this side out.*

The *portable electric saw* is one of the *most dangerous power tools* in existence when it is not properly used. *Be sure* the board you are sawing is properly secured so it will not slip or turn. After making a cut *be sure* the saw blade has come to a standstill before laying the saw down.

When using an electric saw remember that all the blade you can normally see is covered and that the portion of the blade that projects under the board being cut is not covered. The exposed teeth under the work are dangerous and can cause serious injury if any part of your body should come into contact with them.

The blade of a portable circular saw should be kept sharp at all times. The saw blade will function most efficiently when the rate of feed matches the blade's capacity to cut. You will not have to figure this out: you will be able to feel it. With a little practice you will know when the cut is smooth and you will know when you are forcing it. Let the blade do its own cutting. The tool will last longer and you will work easier because it is less fatiguing.

Saber Saw

The *saber saw* (Fig. 92) is a power-driven jigsaw that will let you cut smooth and decorative curves in wood and light metal. Most saber saws are light-duty machines and are not designed for extremely fast cutting.

There are several different blades designed to operate in the saber saw and they are easily interchangeable. For fast cutting of wood, a blade with coarse teeth may be used. A blade with fine teeth is designed for cutting metal.

The best way to learn how to handle this type of tool is to use it. Before trying to do a finished job with the saber saw, clamp down a piece of scrap plywood and draw some curved as well as straight lines to follow. You will develop your own way of

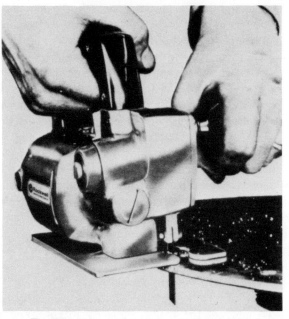

Fig. 92. Saber or bayonet saw operations.

gripping the tool, and this will be affected somewhat by the particular tool you are using. On some tools, *for example,* you will find guiding easier if you apply some downward pressure on the tool as you move it forward. If you are not firm with your grip, the tool will tend to vibrate excessively and this will roughen the cut. Do not force the cutting faster than the design of the blade allows or you will break the blade.

Electric Impact Wrench

The *electric impact wrench* (Fig. 93) is a portable hand-type reversible wrench. The one shown has a ½″ square impact-driving anvil over which ½″ square drive sockets can be fitted. Wrenches also can be obtained that have impact-driving anvils ranging from ⅜″ to 1″. The driving anvils are not interchangeable, however, from one wrench to another.

The electric wrench with its accompanying equipment is primarily intended for applying and removing nuts, bolts, and screws. It may also be used to drill and tap wood, plastics, metal, and other material, and drive and remove socket-head, Phillips-head, or slotted-head wood, machine, or self-tapping screws.

Before you use an electric impact wrench depress the on-and-off trigger switch and allow the electric wrench to operate a few seconds, noting carefully the direction of rotation. Release the trigger switch to stop the wrench. Turn the reversing ring located at the rear of the tool. The ring should move easily in one direction (which is determined by the current direction of rotation). Depress the on-and-off trigger again to start the electric wrench. The direction of rotation should now be reversed. Continue to operate for a few seconds in each direction to be sure that the wrench and its reversible features are functioning correctly. When you are sure the wrench operates properly, place the suitable equipment on the impact-driving anvil and go ahead with the job at hand.

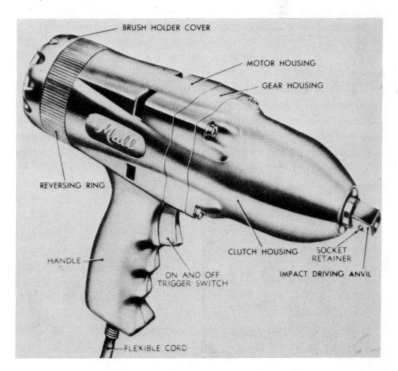

Fig. 93. Reversible electric impact wrench.

CHAPTER 7

Radial-Arm Machine

The radial-arm machine is a complete workshop. It will saw, dado, and shape with complete accuracy. With the proper attachments added, the machine will function as a jointer, drill press, router, lathe, saber saw, sander, grinder, buffer, and polisher.

PRINCIPLE OF OPERATION

The radial-arm type of power tool shown in Fig. 1 is in effect a mechanical arm that features the easy dexterity of a human arm. Flexibility with this tool means that the cutting member can be placed in any position throughout all three dimensions (length, width, and depth). This is possible because of the unique

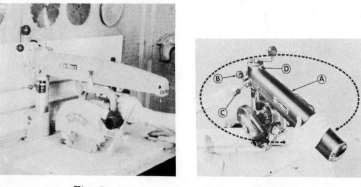

Fig. 1.   Fig. 2.

design allowing full maneuverability through a complete circle in any of the three directions.

The three-dimension flexibility is possible with the motorized mechanical arm, shown in Fig. 2. The radial arm (*A*) rotates 360° for right- or left-miter cuts. Release clamp (*B*) and lift latch (*C*), then easily swing the arm to any angle. The eye-level calibrated miter scale (*D*), shows the angle required. The "built-in" stops at 0° and 45° automatically locate these common angles. Never shift the lumber for miters, as the radial-arm machine puts the saw at the exact angle, and you pull across for perfect cuts. An accurate measuring scale, on the right side of the arm, gives you instant measuring for ripping.

Figure 3 shows the shoulder action of the mechanical arm. As the arm is raised or lowered, it measures for you. Each full turn of the elevating handle (*A*) lifts or lowers the arm (*B*) $\frac{1}{8}''$. One-half turn gives you $\frac{1}{16}''$. This is a precision depth control.

The elbow action of the mechanical arm is illustrated in Fig. 4. The yoke, which holds the motor, is beneath the arm and rides freely on it. Release the yoke clamp (*B*) and lift the locating pin (*C*), then swing the yoke right or left. It automatically stops at all four 90° positions, giving quick, positive adjustment for rip and crosscuts. The clamp (*D*) locks the saw in the desired rip position.

Fig. 3.

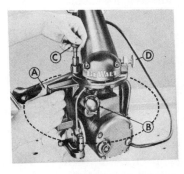

Fig. 4.

Figure 5 shows the wrist movement of the mechanical arm. Pull out the clamp (*A*) and locating pin (*B*). Tilt the motor (*C*) for the angle desired on the bevel scale (*D*). Then, relock *A*. The motor unit automatically locates the popular 0°, 45°, and 90° bevel positions. Your compound angles and bevel cuts are measured for you with unequaled accuracy, and there is no limit to the bevel cuts.

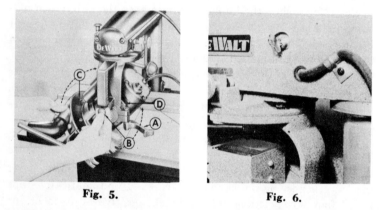

Fig. 5.   **Fig. 6.**

The flexible operation of this machine is based on the following three simple radial adjustments; the arm can be swung horizontally through 360° around its column; the yoke can be revolved horizontally through 360° under its roller carriage; and the motor can be tilted within the yoke to any angle desired. These adjustments enable you to place the cutting tool easily in any position.

Radial-arm machine sizes. Radial-arm machines are available in a range of sizes from ¾ to 10 h.p., the smallest being the most popular one for home workshop use. This size machine cuts 2½″ deep with a 9″ blade, crosscuts 15″ wide on 1″ stock, and rips to the center of 48″ wide panels.

This machine is equipped with a *direct-drive motor*. There are no belts, pulleys, gears, or other devices to maintain. The cutting tool is mounted directly on the motor spindle, an operation done above the worktable so that there are no table inserts to be concerned with. The motor operates at 3,450 r.p.m. and is available in either 115-volt single-phase 60-cycle alternating current or 220-, 440-, or 550-volt three-phase 60-cycle alternating current models.

The direct-drive motor has grease-sealed-for-life bearings at each end of the motor shaft so that you never have to oil it. Motors of this type are protected against overloading by a manual-reset thermostat that kicks out when the motor is overheated and loaded. To reset the motor, allow a few minutes, then "push in" the red button on the motor.

Safety features. One of the outstanding virtues of the radial-arm machine is its safety features. A *safety guard*, as shown in Figs. 15 and 16, is used to cover the cutting tool so as to provide maximum safety to the operator. It is adjustable and is provided with a kickback device for use in ripping operations, as well as with an adjustable dust spout that directs the flow of sawdust wherever desired. This guard is used for sawing, dadoing, shaping, and other operations, providing safety factors hitherto not possible with ordinary table saws.

Another important factor is an *ignition-type motor-starting key* (Fig. 6). Only this key will start the motor, and it fits a tumbler-type mechanism that is recessed in the side of the arm. This key is especially important in the home where there are children and, of course, prevents unauthorized use by others.

The fact that the *blade* is mounted above the worktable, instead of below it, is possibly the major safety feature of this machine. Since you can always see what you are doing, you can very quickly do accurate cutting, because you can easily follow the layout marks on the top of the material, and the mechanical arm guarantees a true cut regardless of the angle. For most operations the hand guides the saw blade through the work; this lessens the chance of having the blade clip you. It, of course, eliminates overcutting and spoiling of the material.

Regardless of the operation, all setups are made above the worktable to simplify all jobs. The calibrated miter, rip, and bevel scales, as well as all control handles are above the worktable, clear of the work and easy to reach.

Floor space required. The radial-arm machine is fundamentally a one-wall shop, and the over-all floor space required is approximately 3 square feet. It can be set up even in the smallest basement, utility room, garage, or attic. For example, in the attic, the radial-arm machine can be placed back under the eaves, using space that would otherwise be wasted. Unlike a table saw, the radial arm does not require accessibility from all sides.

When locating the radial-arm machine, space should be allowed for handling material of the maximum lengths required. About 10' on either side will allow for most ripping and handling of long boards. Two feet of the operating area is all that is required at the front of the machine. Table extensions are preferable to support long work, and should be solid or made of wood on metal rollers to help in conveying stock past the blade. Be sure to provide an ample light source, natural or artificial, to enable easy reading of angle and dimension dials and controls. A typical small workshop layout is shown in Fig. 7.

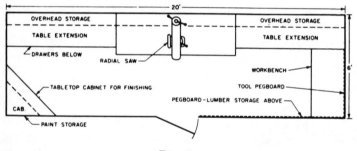

Fig. 7.

The ¾ h.p. machine which takes a 9″ saw blade is practically portable. It may be mounted on saw horses (temporary installation), steel legs, or on a steel cabinet (Fig. 8), or built into a workbench (Fig. 1).

Connecting the machine to the power supply. To obtain the maximum efficiency from your radial-arm motor, the wire from the source of power to the machine should not be less than size 14 (B and S gauge). Be sure that the electric line is fused with a 15-ampere fuse. If an ordinary type of fuse blows during the initial fraction of a second when the machine is turned on, do not put in a new one of higher rating. Replace it with a fuse of the same rating, but of the "slow-blow" or delay type. It contains a special fusible link that withstands a momentary overload without giving way.

Before plugging the cord into the wall or floor outlet, look at the name plate on your machine to see if it is marked 120 volts, because this is the voltage in common use today in homes. If you purchased a radial-arm machine for use on a 240-volt line, be sure the name plate is marked 240 volts. In case the motor runs hot or short of power, call your local power company to check your voltage.

The radial-arm machine, as any other power tool, should *always* be grounded while in use. This precaution will protect the operator against possible electric shock should a short circuit or ground develop while the machine is being connected to the power outlet or during operation. The radial-arm machine offers new and assured grounding protection for your safety. In accordance with a ruling of the National Electric Code, it is equipped with a three-wire cord, one wire being a ground wire. For your complete safety while operating this saw, remember that the three-conductor attachment plug requires a three-prong grounded outlet (5260 series). Just insert the three-prong plug and the machine is instantly grounded (Fig. 9).

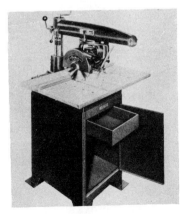

Fig. 8.

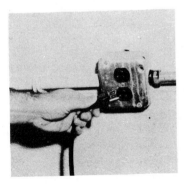

Fig. 9.

To permit use of this tool with a two-prong receptacle, an adapter is available. Match the wider prong of the adapter with the wider hole of the outlet. If you find that the adapter will not fit, file the wider prong to size. When using the adapter, the extending green wire should be connected to the outlet-plate retaining screw (Fig. 10), provided that the outlet itself is grounded, or to any other known permanent ground, such as a water or an electric-conduct pipe.

Caution! If an extension cord is used, be sure it is a three-wire cord and large enough (12 gauge) to prevent excessive voltage loss.

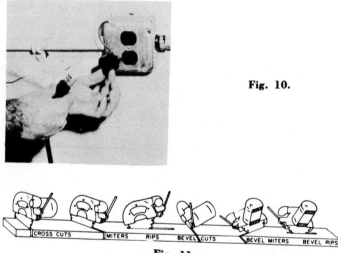

Fig. 10.

Fig. 11.

BASIC OPERATION OF THE SAW

Actually there are only six basic saw cuts in woodworking; *crosscut, bevel crosscut, miter, bevel miter, rip, and bevel rip* (Fig. 11). All other cuts, no matter how intricate, are combinations of these basic cuts.

With a radial-arm saw, the basic cuts are easy and safe. Because the blade is above the table top, you always work on the top side of the material, with your layout marks in clear view. The saw also adjusts to the lumber for all cuts.

CONTROLS

The versatility of the radial-arm saw is due, in part, to its controls. All the controls for depth of cut, miter angles, beveling, etc., are within sight and are easy to reach (Figs. 12, 13 and 14).

Saw-blade kerfs. On the top surface of the table top (*M*, Fig. 13), you will find several saw-blade kerfs $\frac{1}{16}''$ deep which the saw blade (*H*, Fig. 12) will follow or ride in when making most popular cuts. They are a straight crosscut, right 45°, straight 45° bevel, a concave cut in the center of the table for ripping, and a quarter-round circle in the front of the table for the saw blade to follow when swiveling 90° to the in-rip position. The cuts are also made in the guide fence (*N*, Fig. 13).

Elevating handle. The elevating handle (*D*, Fig. 12) raises or lowers the arm, motor, and yoke. Each complete turn of the

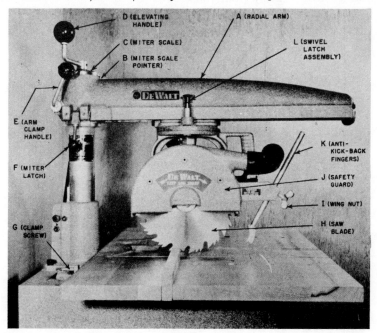

Fig. 12.

crank handle raises or lowers the machine ⅛″. To raise the machine, follow the rotation arrow on top of the column. To lower the machine, turn the elevating handle in reverse of the rotation arrow.

Safety guard. The safety guard (*J*, Fig. 12) is adjustable for cutting any thickness of material up to the capacity of the blade. To make the guard adjustments necessary for ripping, loosen the wing nut (*P*, Fig. 13) which holds the guard to the motor, and rotate the guard down to ⅛″ above the material that is to be ripped (Fig. 15). Retighten the wing nut. Then on the opposite side of the guard, release the thumbscrew (*I*, Fig. 12) which holds the anti-kickback fingers (*K*, Fig. 12), and lower them to ⅛″ below the top of the material being ripped (Fig. 16). Then retighten the thumbscrew. Adjust the dust spout (*O*, Fig. 13) until it is turned toward the back of the machine so as to carry the dust away from you.

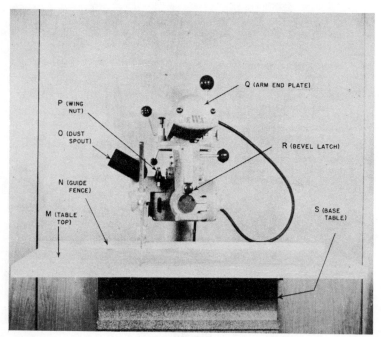

Fig. 13.

Column. The radial arm (A, Fig. 12) revolves a full 360° on the column (EE, Fig. 14). This movement permits you to set the saw for any angle cut desired.

Arm clamp handle. To make this movement, release the arm clamp handle (E, Fig. 12) by pulling it forward and lift the miter latch (F, Fig. 12) from the slot in the column. Swing the arm left or right to the angle desired by following the miter scale (C, Fig. 12) on top of the column, then lock the arm clamp handle.

Miter latch. For quick, positive location for straight cutoff or left and right 45°, seat the miter latch into the proper slot on the column and lock the arm clamp handle.

Yoke and motor. The yoke (X, Fig. 14) and motor (T, Fig. 14) revolve a full 360° on the roller carriage of the radial arm. This movement permits location of the saw in a positive locking position for (1) crosscutting, blade parallel with the arm; (2) in-ripping, swivel yoke and motor left 90° from the crosscut

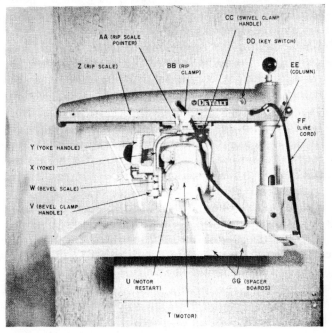

Fig. 14.

Fig. 15.   Fig. 16.

position; and (3) out-ripping, swivel yoke and motor right 90° from the crosscut position. To make these movements, release the clamp handle (*CC*, Fig. 14) by pulling it forward and pulling up on the swivel latch (*L*, Fig. 12). Swivel the yoke to one of the above positions. The swivel latch accurately locates the position. Then tighten the clamp handle by pushing it back.

Rip-lock clamp. The rip-lock clamp (*BB*, Fig. 14) locks the roller carriage to the radial arm for all operations where the material is moved to the cutting tool. When setting the saw for ripping, move the pointer (*AA*, Fig. 14) to the desired width of the rip, by following the ripping scale (*Z*, Fig. 14). Then turn the knurled head of the rip-lock clamp clockwise until tight on the radial arm so that the roller carriage cannot move. The saw may then be set for either in- or out-ripping. Most rip cuts can be made from the in-rip position, whereas wide panel ripping is done in the out-rip position.

The motor mounted in the yoke will tilt to any angle or bevel position desired. To make the bevel adjustment, first elevate the column about twenty turns of the crank to provide clearance above the table. Then grip the safety guard (*J*, Fig. 12) with the left hand and release the bevel clamp handle (*V*, Fig. 14) by pulling it forward. After pulling out the bevel latch (*R*, Fig. 13), move the motor to the desired angle by following the calibrated bevel scale (*W*, Fig. 14). Then lock the bevel-clamp handle by pushing it back. For quick positive location at 0°, 45°, and 90°, the bevel latch will drop into these positions automatically.

TYPES OF BLADES

Combination blade. Power saws usually come equipped with a combination blade which will crosscut, miter, and rip equally well. This blade is adaptable to most home workshop needs to do general-purpose work. The combination blade is divided into segments and provides crosscut teeth and one raker tooth in each segment, with a deep gullet between. This arrangement of the teeth permits the blade to cut freely and smoothly both with and across the grain.

In the *flat-ground blade* (two cutting teeth and one raker), the teeth must be set as shown in *A*, Fig. 17.

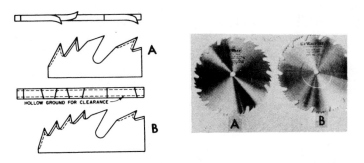

Fig. 17.

Hollow-ground blade. This blade generally has four cutting teeth and one raker, and the teeth have no set (*B*, Fig. 17). The blade is beveled, or hollow-ground, so that it is several gauges thinner near the hub than at the rim. Sometimes called a planer or miter blade, it is generally used by cabinetmakers when cutting stock to finish dimensions, as it cuts very smoothly both with and across the grain.

Carbide-tipped blade. The eight-tooth carbide-tipped saw blade (*A*, Fig. 18) rips and crosscuts like a combination blade, but it remains sharp for long periods of continued operation and outlasts ordinary blades many times over. It is ideal for cutting hardboard, plywood, asbestos board, and other similar materials.

Carbide blades do not, however, produce so smooth a cut in the softer woods as the combination blade.

Ripping blade. The ripping blade (*B*, Fig. 18) is designed to do just one job—cutting with the grain of the wood. The blade will tend to tear the wood on crosscuts, but cuts fast and clean on rip cuts. Since ripping usually puts a heavy load on the motor, this blade is recommended for general ripping jobs.

Cutoff wheels and special blades. Cutoff wheels are flexible abrasive discs which mount on the saw arbor like a blade. The aluminum oxide wheel (*C*, Fig. 18) is used for cutting steel and similar metals, while the silicon carbide wheel (*D*, Fig. 18) works best for ceramics. porcelain, glass, plastics, etc. A special blade (*E*, Fig. 18) is available for cutting non-ferrous metal such as aluminum, copper, etc. It cuts solid, extruded, or tube with the greatest of ease A fine-toothed plywood cutting blade is shown at *F*, Fig. 18. This blade does an excellent job on plywood and gummy, resinous woods.

"Safety" blade. The "safety" blade, shown at *G*, Fig. 18, has only eight teeth, but it is a combination blade, crosscutting and ripping equally well, and it produces a fairly smooth cut. It performs with maximum efficiency at minimum power consumption, and it reduces kickback to a minimum.

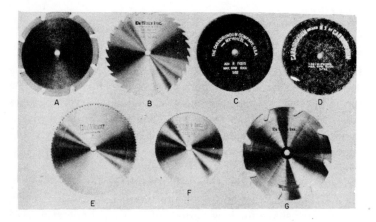

Fig. 18.

MOUNTING A SAW BLADE

When mounting a saw blade, remove the arbor nut and arbor collars. Elevate the radial arm until the blade will slide on the shaft and clear the table top. Then place the ⅜″ arbor collar on the arbor so that the recessed side of the collar will be against the saw blade. Place the saw blade on the arbor. The teeth of the saw blade must point in the direction of rotation when the saw blade is in the proper operating position. (Generally blades are marked "This side out," which means that the side marked should be on the same side as the arbor nut.) Then place the ¼″ arbor collar, recessed side against the saw blade, on the arbor. Now place a wrench on the flat of the arbor shaft to hold it, and tighten the arbor nut with the arbor-nut wrench (Fig. 19). The arbor nut has a left-hand thread, which means that the nut must be turned and tightened counterclockwise.

Fig. 19.

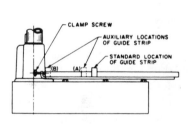

Fig. 20.

Mount the safety guard over the saw blade and adjust it, on the motor stud, to the desired position for the cuts you are going to make and tighten the wing nut.

ALIGNING OPERATIONS

Every radial-arm machine is thoroughly tested, inspected, and accurately aligned before leaving the factory of the manufacturer. Rough handling during transportation may throw the machine out of alignment. Eventually adjustment and realignment are necessary in any machine to maintain accuracy—regardless of the care with which the machine is manufactured.

Checking the guide fence for accuracy. For accurate work, the guide fence must be straight. This wood guide strip is inspected with a master straightedge at the factory before shipment and should arrive in perfect condition. If the machine has been exposed to the weather, it is possible that the wood tabletop parts may be warped so that the guide fence is no longer straight.

It can be made straight by planing and sanding and can be checked with a straightedge or square before proceeding with other adjustments. Be sure that the clamp screws at the rear of the table are tightened. The main table board must be flat. If a straightedge shows this to be warped, it should be planed if necessary when you level the worktable top.

The guide fence, as shown in Fig. 20, is located in the most frequently used position on the worktable. This will take care of the normal cutting jobs. If you want maximum crosscut on 1" material or wider bevel-meter capacity, loosen the clamp screws at the rear of the table top and relocate the guide fence behind the 2" spacer board, location *A*. Be sure to tighten the clamp screws after this is done.

For maximum width in ripping, loosen the clamp screws and relocate the guide fence by placing it at the rear of the table top and against the column base, location *B*. Tighten the clamp screws to hold the guide fence rigidly in position.

If the guide fence should become cut with many kerfs (and it does over a period of time), it can be replaced with a new one. Use a straight piece of pine or similar softwood the same size as the present fence. Plane, sand smooth, and check it with a straightedge or try square for straightness before putting it in place. For several operations, such as *shaping, sanding,* or *jointing,* special guide fences will be required, but these are very easy to make.

Aligning the work top to the arm travel. The table top must align with the arm travel in every horizontal (parallel) position. The table top is mounted on adjustable steel cleats with adjustable jack nuts. To realign the top, *see* Figs. 21 and 22.

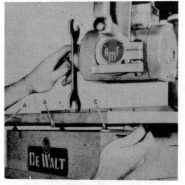

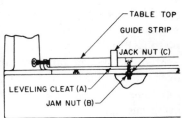

TABLE TOP

GUIDE STRIP

JACK NUT (C)

LEVELING CLEAT (A)

JAM NUT (B)

Fig. 21.   **Fig. 22.**

Insert a steel bar about ½" x ½" x 12") or a wrench between the saw-arbor collars in place of the saw blade.

Bring the motor to the forward position on the arm, swing the bar, and adjust the table top until the tip of the bar when oscillated barely scrapes the table top. Repeat at the back section of the table board, to the right and left, without changing the elevation.

Adjust the table top for the height in various positions until it is perfectly level. Loosen the jam nuts (*B*) under the table channel frame (toy flange), and then you can raise or lower the jack nuts (*C*) as required. Be sure to retighten the jam nuts under the table flange after making the adjustments to hold the table board level.

Squaring the saw blade with the table top. The saw blade can be maintained square with the table top (Fig. 23).

Make sure that the table top is level at all points. Remove the safety guard.

Place a steel square (*C*) against the flat of the saw blade. The square should be placed in the saw gullets and not against the saw teeth. Make sure that the bevel latch is properly seated and the bevel clamp handle is locked.

Remove the etched dial plate (*A*) from the motor yoke by taking out the Phillip's-head screws. You can now get at the two adjusting socket screws (*G*).

Release the two socket screws (*G*) approximately two turns with a socket wrench.

Firmly grasp the motor with both hands and tilt it until the saw blade is parallel to the upright steel square (*C*). After the saw blade is squared with the table top, be sure to tighten the socket screws (*G*) with a socket wrench (*B*). Replace the dial plate (*A*) and safety guard.

Many craftsmen nail a "wear" table of plywood or hardboard over the permanent front table, as shown in Fig. 24. This table top takes the saw cuts, and keeps the permanent table from being cut up.

Fig. 23.

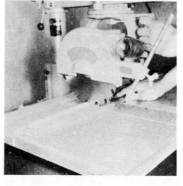

Fig. 24.

A. Nameplate
B. Allen Setscrew Wrench
C. Steel Square
D. Bevel Clamp Handle
E. Bevel Latch Assembly
G. Socket Screws
H. Dial Plate

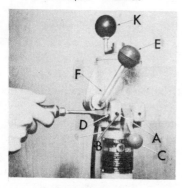

Fig. 25.

A. Allen Setscrew
B. Allen Setscrew Wrench
C. Miter Latch
D. Miter Latch Adjusting Screws
E. Arm Clamp Handle
F. Arm Clamp Handle Stop
K. Elevating Action Handle

Fig. 26.

G. Base Pinch Bolt
H. Hex Jam Nuts
I. Setscrew
J. Allen Setscrew Wrench
L. Column Key Gib

Squaring the crosscut travel with the guide fence. Place a wide board on the table top against the guide fence, and make a cut across with the saw. Check the material for accuracy with a steel square. If the saw blade does not cut square, this means that the arm is out of alignment with the guide fence. To adjust this condition see Fig. 25.

Loosen both the arm clamp handle (*E*) and the miter latch (*C*).

The adjusting screws (*D*) are locked in position by setscrews (*A*). Loosen the screws (*A*) with a ¼″ Allen wrench.

Lay the steel square   against the guide fence.   Move the saw forward along the steel square to determine which way the arm must be moved.

If the blade moves toward the steel square as you come forward, loosen the adjusting screw (*D*) in the rear (left) with a screwdriver and tighten the adjusting screw (*D*) in the front (right) to bring the arm parallel to the steel square. The arm will be parallel when the saw travels evenly with the steel square for its entire length. If the saw blade moves away from the steel square as you come forward, make the opposite adjustments. Loosen the adjusting screw (*D*) in the front (right) with the screwdriver and tighten the adjusting screw (*D*) in the rear (left). When the saw travel is parallel to the square, lock the adjusting screws (*D*) in the front and rear by tightening both Allen setscrews (*A*) with a setscrew wrench (*B*). Engage the miter latch (*C*) and the arm clamp handle (*E*).

Adjusting the base; gripping, tension, and alignment. If at any time there is some motion at the end of the arm after the arm clamp handle is tightened, this indicates that there is play between the column and base or the gib needs tightening. *See* Figs. 25, 26 and 27.

Loosen the base pinch bolt (*G*), all hex jam nuts (*H*), and all setscrews (*I*).

Rotate the elevating crank handle (*K*) to raise or lower the column. Tighten the base pinch bolt (*G*) so that the column still raises or lowers freely and without play.

The adjusting gib (*L*) must be secured against the column key (*2D*) to prevent side motion in the arm. Tighten the top setscrews (*I*) with a 5⁄16″ Allen wrench (*J*) until there is no play (side motion) in the column. Then lock all the hex jam nuts (*H*) securely with an open-end wrench.

Adjusting the arm clamp handle. The arm clamp handle rigidly holds the arm in position for straight or miter cuts. When tightened in position, the arm clamp handle should be upright as shown in Fig. 28. If the arm clamp handle becomes worn so that it goes beyond the vertical position, relocate it.

Remove the clamp-handle stop (*A*) and lift the miter latch (*B*) upward against the side of the arm.

Unwind the arm clamp handle (*C*) by turning it clockwise (to the right). Make about three or four complete turns of this handle.

Push back the arm clamp bolt (*D*) from its hex socket so that the hex head can be turned.

Turn the hex clamp screw (*D*) about one-sixth turn counterclockwise to tighten the arm clamp handle.

Put the hex-screw head (*D*) back in the hex socket, retighten the arm clamp handle (*C*) in the upright position, and insert the arm-clamp-handle stop (*A*).

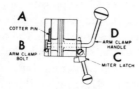

Fig. 27.

Adjusting the roller head bearing to the arm track. The roller carriage is mounted on four ball bearings, two of which are on eccentric shafts whose movement is controlled by $\frac{5}{16}''$ Allen socket screws. To adjust the ball bearings, *see* Fig. 29.

Remove the arm end plate from the arm and bring the saw carriage forward. Swivel the motor into the rip position to get the adjustments.

Loosen the setscrews (*A*) with a $\frac{1}{4}''$ Allen wrench in the front and the rear of the saw carriage since they lock the eccentric shaft (*F*).

Loosen the hex jam nuts (*B*) in the front and rear of the saw carriage so that the eccentric shaft (*F*) can be turned in its socket.

Insert a $\frac{5}{16}''$ Allen wrench (*C*) in the eccentric shaft (*F*) and turn this shaft until the ball bearing it controls just touches the arm track. Do not tighten this bearing too much. Repeat on the ball bearing (*D*) in the rear of the saw carriage. The ball bearing (*D*) in the front and the rear of the saw carriage should now roll smoothly inside the arm. Tighten the hex jam nuts (*B*) and lock the setscrews (*A*) on both ends of the saw carriage.

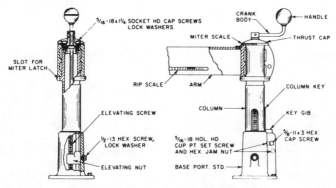

Fig. 28.   Details of the Arm Clamp Handle

Adjusting the crosscut travel parallel to the arm. To make sure the saw blade is cutting exactly parallel to the arm tracks, place a board approximately 6″ wide on the table against the guide fence. Make a cut through the board, and stop just as the board is cut off with the back of the blade still in the board. If there is a slight ridge on the material where the blade is stopped, this will indicate the need of adjustment. Another method of checking is, when making the crosscut, to watch the back of the blade where the teeth come up through the board. If the blade is kicking up the wood fibers on the top surface of the board, this will indicate that the blade is not traveling parallel with the arm tracks. To adjust the crosscut travel, *see* Fig. 30.

If the saw blade is "heeling" on the left side of the cut, loosen the setscrew (*C*) and tighten the screw (*A*), using a $\frac{5}{16}''$ Allen wrench (*F*).

If the saw blade is "heeling" on the right side of the cut, loosen the setscrew (*A*) and tighten the setscrew (*C*) with a $\frac{5}{16}''$ Allen wrench (*F*).

After the above two adjustments are made, the heeling may reappear when you place the saw blade in the bevel cutting position, in which case:

Loosen the setscrews (*A* and *C*), each about one-sixth turn, and tighten the setscrew (*B*) if the heeling is on the material on the bottom side of the saw cut.

Loosen the setscrew (*B*) about one-sixth turn and tighten the setscrews (*A* and *C*) evenly if the heeling appears on the upper side of the cut.

Fig. 29.

A. Allen Setscrew
B. Hex Jam Nut
C. Allen Socket
    Wrench

D. Ball Bearing
    (on eccentric shaft)
E. Ball Bearing
    (on permanent studs)
F. Eccentric Shaft
G. Wrench

Fig. 30.

A. Allen Setscrew
    (saw side)
B. Allen Setscrew
    (bottom yoke trunnion)
C. Allen Setscrew
    (opposite saw side)

D. Rear Trunnion Stud
    Bushing
E. Rear Trunnion Stud
F. Allen Setscrew
    Wrench
G. Saw Arbor Collar
H. Saw Arbor Nut

Adjusting the bevel clamp handle. The purpose of the bevel clamp handle is to hold the motor rigidly in its yoke at any angle even though the bevel latch may be disengaged from the locating holes in the dial plate. The bevel latch locates 90° crosscut, 45° bevel crosscut, and 0° vertical positions only.

To adjust the bevel clamp handle, *see* Fig. 31.

Loosen the bevel clamp handle (*A*) and the hex jam nut (*F*).

Turn the cap screw (*E*) clockwise (to the right) until the bevel clamp handle rigidly clamps the motor in its yoke.

Be sure to tighten the hex jam nut (*F*) after the adjustment is made.

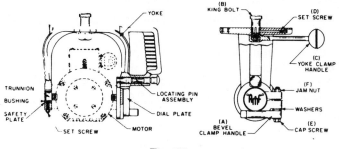

Fig. 31.

Adjusting the yoke clamp handle. There should be no play between the roller carriage and the motor-yoke assembly. The yoke clamp handle in conjunction with the king bolt securely clamp the saw carriage to the yoke. To adjust the yoke clamp handle, *see C*, Fig. 32.

Fig. 32.

A. Screwdriver   C. Yoke Clamp Handle
B. King Bolt   D. Dog Point Setscrew

Remove the saw carriage and the motor yoke completely from the arm.

A dog-point setscrew (*D*) is located in the milled slot on the side of the king bolt (*B*). Its purpose is to keep the king bolt from turning when the yoke clamp handle is loosened or tightened. Remove the setscrew from the slot in the king bolt with a screwdriver (*A*).

Turn the king bolt (*B*) about one-sixth of a turn in a clockwise direction so that the dog setscrew may be located in the next slot in the king bolt. Tighten the dog setscrew in position to hold the king bolt.

This dog setscrew should be drawn up tight and then backed off slightly so that the king bolt can slide freely up and down as the yoke clamp handle is loosened or tightened.

Now that every moving part is in proper alignment, you are ready to start operating the machine. You should, however, observe certain basic rules for maximum safety and efficiency in operation.

BASIC SAW CUTS

The radial-arm saw is a pull-through cutoff type of saw and cuts in a straight line or at any angle. In the crosscutting action, the saw is moved in the same direction as its rotation (*A*, Fig. 33). Ripping must never be done in the same direction as the saw rotation (*B*, Fig. 33). For accurate and smooth cutting, a sharp blade must be used.

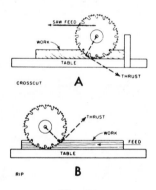

Fig. 33.

Fig. 34.

CROSSCUTTING

When straight crosscutting, the radial arm must be at right angles with the guide fence—indicated as 0° on the miter scale. Locate the miter latch in the column slot at the 0° position, and then securely lock the arm with the arm clamp handle. Now the saw blade should follow the saw kerf in the table top. Use the elevating handle to drop the saw blade until the teeth are approximately $\frac{1}{16}''$ below the top surface of the table in the saw kerf. This clearance is needed to cut through the board. Then return the saw all the way back against the column.

Place the material on the worktable against the guide fence. Adjust the guard parallel to the bottom of the motor, adjust the kickback fingers down to $\frac{1}{8}''$ above the material you will cut off. Turn on the power and give the motor sufficient time to attain top speed. Then pull the saw blade from behind the guide fence in one steady motion completely through the cut (Fig. 34). Never allow it to "walk" too rapidly through the work. Return the saw to the rear of the guide fence before removing the material from the table. Practice to get the "feel" of the cutting action—let the saw blade cut—do not force it.

To cut a board thicker than the capacity of the machine, set the blade just a little over half the thickness of the material. Pull the blade through in the same manner as for straight crosscutting, and then turn it over and complete the cut on the other side.

Right- or left-hand feed. Your first cut will pose the question of whether to use right-hand (Fig. 35), or left-hand feed (Fig. 36). You may have a tendency to use left-hand feed because it puts the holding (right) hand on the side away from the saw. However, right-hand feed generally is more practical and more comfortable, and you will quickly adopt this system.

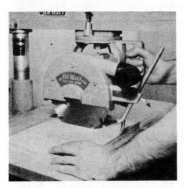

Fig. 35.   **Fig. 36.**

Crosscutting wide boards and panels. To cut a board wider than the capacity of the machine, cut to the limit, then turn it over and complete the cut. Large pieces of plywood can be cut with ease by using the method shown in Fig. 37.

Fig. 37.   **Fig. 38.**

Horizontal crosscutting. This crosscut operation (Fig. 38) is used for cutting across the end of any size of stock. To locate the saw in the horizontal position, raise the radial arm by turning the elevating handle until the blade is approximately 3″ above the table top. With the saw in the crosscut position, pull it to the front end of the arm. Holding the top of the safety guard in your left hand, release the bevel clamp handle by pulling it forward and pull out the bevel latch. Swing the motor and saw into the 90° horizontal position and lock the bevel clamp handle by pushing it back. (The bevel latch automatically locks itself in position.) The blade will now be parallel to the table top, and the motor will be in a vertical position. Then adjust the dust elbow on the guard, parallel to the table top. Push the motor and saw and guard back to the column.

Place the material to be cut against the guide fence and lower the saw blade to the point where the cut is to be made. The depth of the cut will be determined by the location of the material in respect to the saw blade.

Turn on the motor, and with the saw behind the guide fence, pull it through the material in the same manner as when crosscutting. If you wish to form a groove, push the saw back against the column and raise or lower the arm a full turn. Bring the saw forward again and then return it to the column. Repeat this procedure until the desired width of the groove is obtained.

BEVEL CROSSCUTTING

Bevel crosscutting, shown in Fig. 39, is similar to straight crosscutting, but the saw is tilted to the desired bevel angle. With the motor and saw back against the column, elevate the machine so that the blade will clear the table top when swiveling the motor in the yoke. Pull the motor and saw to the front end of the arm. To bevel your motor and saw, place your left hand on top of the safety guard to hold the motor from dropping and release the bevel clamp lock by pulling it forward. Pull out on the bevel locating pin and move the motor to the degree desired by following the bevel scale and pointer. Then lock the bevel clamp by pushing it back. Turn the elevating handle down until the saw-blade teeth touch the bottom of the concave kerf in the center of the table top. Push the motor and saw back to the column. If a common 45° bevel is desired, simply let the locating pin fit the 45° slot. Then lock the bevel clamp.

Place the material on the table top against the guide fence. Adjust the guard and keep back your fingers, the same as in crosscutting. You can make your bevel cutoff on the left side—

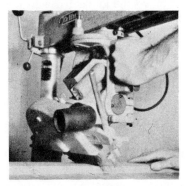

Fig. 39.

Fig. 40.

hold the material with your left hand and pull the motor and saw with your right hand by using the grip handle on the yoke. If cutting on the right side, reverse the hand holds.

MITERING

Mitering is the same as crosscutting except that the radial arm is revolved on a horizontal plane to the angle of the miter.

Right-hand miter. Make sure the motor and saw are back of the guide fence against the column. With your left hand, release the arm clamp handle and lift the swivel latch. With your right hand on the radial arm, swing it to the right to the angle desired by following the miter scales. Then lock the arm clamp handle. The popular 45° miter cut is set quickly with the miter latch seated in the 45° quickset slot in column. Simply lock the arm clamp handle. Now place the material flat on the table top and tight against the guide fence. Adjust the guard parallel to the bottom of the motor; adjust the kickback fingers down to ⅛″ above the material you will cut off. Hold the material with your left hand, and pull the saw through the material with your right hand (Fig. 40). Return the saw to its original position at the rear of the guide fence before removing the material from the table top.

Left-hand miter. Move the radial arm to the left to the desired angle in the manner described for a right-hand miter. To get the full capacity on a left-hand miter, move the guide fence to the rear of the table-top spacer boards.

BEVEL MITERING

A bevel miter (sometimes called a compound or double miter) is a combination of a miter and a bevel (Fig. 41). First set the motor and saw to the angle desired by following the bevel scales and then lock the bevel latch and clamp handle. Then release the arm latch and clamp handle and swing the radial arm into the desired miter position, following the same routine as for miter cuts. To make the cut, follow the normal operating routine described under crosscut beveling.

RIPPING

Straight ripping. Straight ripping is done by having the saw blade parallel with the guide fence and feeding the material into the saw blade. You can rip from either the left or right side of the machine. The feeding of the material to the saw depends on the rotation of the saw blade. When ripping from the right side of the table (in-rip), the motor and saw must be swiveled to the left 90° from the crosscut position. If ripping from the left side of the machine (out-rip), swivel the motor and saw to the right 90° from the crosscut position.

In-ripping. To set your saw to the in-rip position, pull the motor and saw to the front end of the radial arm. Release the yoke-swivel clamp handle by pulling it forward and lift up the location pin. Swivel the yoke clockwise 90° from the crosscut position. (The swivel location pin will snap into position automatically.) Now tighten the swivel clamp handle.

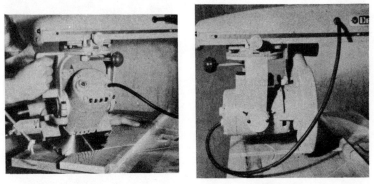

Fig. 41.   Fig. 42.

The rip scale or rule on the right side of the arm is set with the guide fence in its standard position, which is between the stationary top and the spacer boards. With the saw blade against the guide fence, the pointer on the roller head should read zero on the *top* side of the ruler marked "in-rip" (Fig. 42). This rule and pointer can be off as much as $\frac{1}{16}''$ because of difference in the types of saw blades. Some saw blades have set teeth, while others may be hollow ground with no set in the teeth. To adjust the rule, release the two Phillip's-head screws and adjust the scale to the proper setting. Now set your saw to the desired width of the rip by following the pointer and rule. Then tighten the rip-lock clamp screw to hold the saw in position.

With the saw set to in-rip position, you must feed the material into the saw from the right side of the machine. With your left hand approximately 6″ back of the safety guard, hold the material down and back against the guide strip. Now with your right hand, move the material into the saw by standing on the right front side of the machine and let the material slide through your left hand (Fig. 43). When your right hand meets your left hand, continue the balance of the rip by using a pusher board.

Fig. 43.

Fig. 44.

Fig. 45.

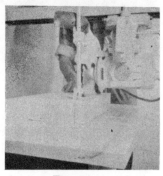

Fig. 46.

Hold the pusher board back against the guide fence and against the end of the board you are ripping and continue on through until the board you are ripping clears the saw blade on the opposite side by 2″ (Fig. 44). Now pull the pusher board straight back.

Out-ripping. When ripping wide materials such as panel boards, you should swivel the saw 90° counterclockwise from the crosscut position to out-rip position. With the saw set to out-rip position, follow the lower edge of the rip rule on the radial arm. This rule can be used to a capacity of 17½″ with the guide fence in its standard position. If ripping wider material, it is necessary to move the guide fence to the rear of the table boards. When the saw is set for out-ripping, the material must be fed into the saw from the left side of the machine (Fig. 45).

Resawing. If extremely thick wood or hardwood is being ripped into thinner boards, it is often necessary to cut part way through the board, invert the board, and complete the cut. This operation is generally called "resawing."

When resawing, the saw should be placed in the in-rip position. The blade should be set just a little over half the width of the board when the board is *less* in width than twice the capacity of the saw. To illustrate this, let us assume that it is necessary to resaw a board 4″ wide by ¾″ thick into two boards 4 by ⅜″. Making an allowance of ⅛″ for the kerf or the wastage material by the blade, and taking into consideration that the capacity of the particular saw blade is 2½″, about 1½″ is left for the second cut (Fig. 46). However, when the width of the board to be resawed is greater than twice the capacity of the machine, make the cuts as deep as possible from each edge. Then finish the ripping by hand. When resawing 4″ stock and larger, use a guide fence approximately 3½″ high.

An important point to bear in mind always when resawing is to keep the same surface of the board against the guide fence for both cuts. Always reverse the board end for end, never side for side. Be sure to follow all the safety rules for straight ripping when resawing.

Horizontal ripping. This operation is similar to horizontal crosscutting except that the cut is made on the side of the stock rather than on the end. To place the saw blade in the horizontal rip position, first set the saw in the in-rip location and then turn it to 90° as indicated on the bevel scale described in horizontal crosscutting.

Place the material to be cut against the guide fence, either standard or auxiliary depending on the thickness, and locate the height and depth of the cut. The rip clamp is tightened and the material is pushed past the blade in the same manner as in straight ripping. If a groove is desired, the arm may be raised or lowered a full turn at a time and the operation repeated until the proper width is obtained.

BEVEL RIPPING

Bevel ripping is simply ripping with the saw motor tilted for angle cuts (Fig. 47). With the saw swiveled to the rip position (either in- or out-rip), elevate the column by rotating the handle and then release the bevel clamp handle and latch. Turn the motor within the yoke to the desired angle. If the popular 45° position is wanted the bevel latch will quickly locate it. If any other angle is desired, set it and securely clamp the motor in place with the bevel clamp handle. Adjust the guard on the infeed end so that it is within ⅛″ of the material, but do not adjust the anti-kickback device. Use a pusher board as previously described to prevent kickback of the material. Push the material through as previously described.

Fig. 47.

Fig. 48.

SPECIAL CUTTING OPERATIONS OF THE SAW

By combining the six basic cuts, previously discussed, you are able to perform such special operations as tapering, chamfering, kerfing, cove cutting, or making saw-cut moldings. While this work may seem more complicated, it is easy and safe to do on a radial-arm saw.

KERFING

It is often necessary to bend wood. When the problem of curved surfaces arises, you have a choice of three methods; (1) bending the wood by steaming it (this calls for special equipment), (2) building the curve up by sawing thick segments of the circle on a saber saw (which means that a great deal of expensive wood would be wasted), or (3) cutting a series of saw kerfs to within ⅛″ of the outside surface to make the material more flexible for bending. The latter is the most practical method (Fig. 48).

The distance between these saw kerfs determines the flexibility of the stock and the radius to which it can be bent. In order to form a more rigid curve, the saw kerfs should be as close together as possible. To determine the proper spacing, the first step is to decide on the radius of the curve or circle to be formed. After the radius has been determined, measure this same distance (the radius) from the end of the stock as shown in Fig. 49, and make a saw kerf at this point. The kerf can be made in the crosscut position, with the blade lowered to ⅛″ of the bottom of the stock.

Now clamp the stock to the table top with a C clamp. Raise the end of the stock until the saw kerf is closed, as shown at *A*. The distance the stock is raised to close the kerf determines the distance between saw kerfs in order to form the curve.

Since most bending operations require many saw kerfs, mark this distance with a pencil on the guide fence. The first kerf is made in the standard crosscut position, with the end of the work butted against the mark. The remaining cuts are located by placing each new kerf over the guide-fence mark and making the new cut.

When the kerfing is complete, the stock is slowly bent until it matches the required curve (Fig. 50). Wetting the wood with warm water will help the bending process, while a tie strip tacked in place will hold the shape until the part is attached to the assembly. Even compound curves may be formed in this manner by kerfing both sides of the work. When kerfing is exposed, veneers may be glued in place to hide the cuts.

When bending wood for exterior work, the kerfs should be coated with glue before the bend is made. After making the bend, wood plastic and putty may be used to fill the crevices. When finished properly, only a close examination will show the method used to make the bend.

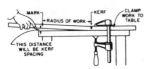

Fig. 49.

Fig. 50.

SAWCUT MOLDINGS

Several attractive moldings can be made with cuts similar to those used for kerfing. The zigzag shape shown in Fig. 51 is commonly called a dentil molding, although this term has a broad application and can include many different shapes.

A spacer mark on the guide fence, as for kerf bending, should be used. The distance from the mark of the blade determines the spacing of the saw cuts. The saw is set in the crosscut position, and the blade is lowered to the depth desired. Repeat cuts are made by alternately turning the work face up and face down, as shown in Fig. 52. The molding is then made by ripping narrow

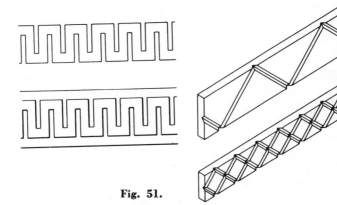

Fig. 51.

strips from the work, as shown in Fig. 53. A ripping operation on work as narrow and delicate as this demands care and accuracy. Use a pusher strip to push the molding past the blade.

Molding should be cut with a hollow-ground or planer blade to assure clean cutting. After the dentil molding is cut, it can be used as an overlay, or the molding can be applied to a heavier backing piece of contrasting color.

TAPER RIPPING

Taper ripping is the process of cutting material to a taper or narrower at one end than at the other. First, make a full-sized drawing or pattern of the taper. Transfer this pattern to a piece of plywood or waste lumber and cut to make the necessary template or jig.

To use the jig, place the flat side against the fence and place the material to be tapered in the stop at the end of the jig. With the saw in the rip position, push the jig past the blade as if it were a normal ripping operation (Fig. 54). Continue the ripping operation on all four sides in the same manner.

Tapering with a radial-arm machine can be done without the use of a specialized jig. This also includes taper ripping long stock which cannot be handled in the jig. Simply by clamping a piece of narrow stock to the lower edge of the material to be ripped, the front edge of the table top becomes a second "guide fence" for this operation. You can taper rip at any predetermined angle with this method. Just decide the degree of taper desired, and then clamp on the lower guide board accordingly.

As shown in Fig. 55, the saw is placed in the out-rip position (that is, swiveled to the right rather than the left) for this tapered-rip operation. This allows the blade to be positioned directly above the front edge of the worktable. Thus, the completed rip cut corresponds exactly to the angle at which the guide board is clamped to the stock.

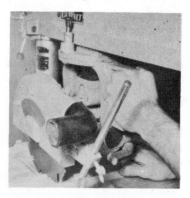

Fig. 52.

Fig. 53.

Fig. 54.

Fig. 55.

Regardless of the method used, a planer blade is the saw to use for taper ripping since it cuts more smoothly.

CHAMFER CUTTING

Chamfer cutting (Fig. 56) is simply making bevel cuts along the top edges of stock. Set the saw in the rip-bevel position at an angle of 20° to 45°. Position the blade so that it overhangs the stock by the desired width of the cut and lock it in place with the rip clamp. Push the stock along the guide fence and through the

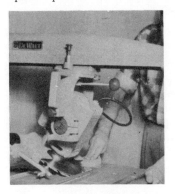

Fig. 56.

Fig. 57.

Fig. 58.

Fig. 59.

blade path. Then reverse the material and cut along the other top edge in the same manner.

Cross-chamfer is achieved by placing the blade in the crosscut-bevel position at the desired angle. Position the blade so that it overhangs the stock by the desired width (as for rip-chamfer). Then pull the motor and saw through in the prescribed crosscut method.

The octagon shape required for spindle lathe work can be cut in the same manner as described for chamfer cutting.

GROOVING

Grooving (Fig. 57) is the same as the horizontal saw cuts previously described. Place the saw in the crosscut or rip position, depending on the type of groove desired, and turn it to the 90° bevel position. Locate the position of the blade (height and depth), place the material against the fence and past the blade, or pull the saw through the material. If the blade strikes the guide fence, the stock should be placed on an auxiliary table. Then raise or lower the blade a full turn at a time and repeat the operation until you obtain the proper groove width.

CONTOUR CUTTING

One of the most novel techniques in radial-arm saw operation is the *contour feed* for cutting coves. On the standard circular saw this is a fairly difficult task, but on the radial-arm saw it is simple. Place the material flat on the table top against the guide fence. Set the saw at a bevel 45° position and swivel the motor 45° to the left. Locate the motor so that the lowest point of the blade is on the center line of the material and tighten the rip clamp. Back the material off from the saw and lower the blade so that it is $\frac{1}{8}''$ below the top surface of the stock. Turn on the machine and push the material past the saw blade as when ripping (Fig. 58). Continue this procedure, lowering the blade one full turn ($\frac{1}{8}''$) at a time, until the desired depth of the cut is obtained. The final cut should be a light one for a smooth finish.

The saw cut can be made in different angle positions for different effects. For instance, you may set the bevel at 45° and the motor swivel at 30°, or the bevel at 30° and the motor swivel at 45°. Experiment with scrap wood until you get the effect you desire.

A half-circle effect, suitable for modern picture frames, is cut by establishing the depth of cut at the edge of the material and pushing the material past the blade in the same manner as just described. (Fig. 59).

Fig. 60.   **Fig. 62.**

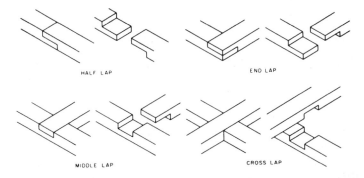

HALF LAP   END LAP

MIDDLE LAP   CROSS LAP

Fig. 61.

SAUCER CUTTING

This cut makes intricate decorative patterns easily. Place the stock flush with the edge of table front and clamp it to the table top. Locate the saw arm so that the lowest portion of the blade is on the center line of the stock, and tighten the rip clamp. Lower the blade until it touches the material, swing the motor to the 90° bevel position, and then lower the motor by turning the elevating handle one full turn. With your left hand on the anti-kickback rod, pull out the bevel latch with your right hand. Then swing the motor in an arc past the stock (Fig. 60). Lower the saw blade one full turn of the elevating handle and continue the cutting process until the desired depth is reached.

LAP-JOINT CUTTING

There are several types of lapped or halved joints (Fig. 61). To make the *end lap*, place the motor in the vertical position (the horizontal crosscut sawing position) and install the auxiliary table in place of the standard guide fence. Both pieces of stock that are to form the joint can be cut at once—laid side by side on the auxiliary table. Make the first cut with the blade passing through the center of the stock, following the technique described for horizontal crosscutting. Then elevate the blade ⅛″ (the width of the blade) by turning the elevating handle one full turn with each successive cut until all excess stock has been removed (Fig. 62).

The other types of lap joints shown in Fig. 61 are combinations of end lap joints and dado cuts.

LOCK-JOINT

The *lock-joint*, when properly made and reinforced with glue or dowels, can be one of the strongest joints available. It is accomplished with the machine positioned exactly as when making the lap joint. Instead of removing half the stock, however, each alternate ⅛″ is left standing (Fig. 63). Use a standard ⅛″ thick blade to make this joint and judge your cuts by remembering that

each complete turn of the elevating handle represents exactly
⅛". The opposite ends are cut opposite so that the two pieces will
mesh together.

TENON AND MORTISE CUTTING

The *tenon* is made in the same manner as the lap joint except
that the stock left standing is in the middle rather than on one
side of the material (Fig. 64). The full tenon, when combined
with a tight-fitting mortise and properly glued or doweled, gives
a very strong joint which is widely used in all phases of cabinetmaking and general woodworking.

The *mortise* is the other half of the joint into which the tenon
fits. Making the mortise consists simply of cutting a groove to
the same width as a previously made tenon (Fig. 65).

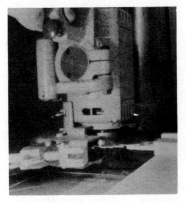

Fig. 63.   **Fig. 64.**

BEVEL-SPLINE JOINT

The *bevel-spline joint* (Fig. 66) is made by bevel crosscutting
the ends of the stock with the motor locked in the 45° bevel position. To make the slot for the spline, reverse the stock on the
table and, with the motor still in the bevel position (but elevated
to the proper height, approximately ⅜", so that the blade will
not completely cut through), pull the saw across the previously

made bevel crosscut, leaving the shallow slot (Fig. 67). Make the spline itself from any ⅛″ rippings you may have. Simply cut to the size desired to fit the spline joint.

Fig. 65.

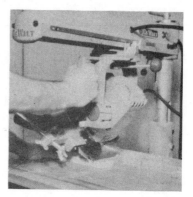

Fig. 66.

DADO-HEAD OPERATIONS

Dado-heads. The first accessory you most likely will choose for your radial-arm machine is a dado head. It contains a series of saw blades (Fig. 68) that can cut grooves, rabbets, mortises, tenons, dadoes, etc., in thicknesses from ⅛″ to $1\frac{3}{16}$″ in a single pass. In other words, the dado head cuts down the time consumed in making most wood joints.

There are basically two types of dado heads; the *flat ground* and the *hollow ground*. While the latter is more expensive, it produces a much smoother cut and should be used in high-quality work. Either type consists of two outside saws, each about ⅛″ thick, whose teeth are not given any set, and inside saws, or "chippers" as they are called—one ¼″, two ⅛″ (some heads include two additional ⅛″ chippers instead of the ¼″ one), and one $\frac{1}{16}$″ thick (thickness at the hub). The cutting portions of the inside cutters or chippers are widened to overlap the adjacent cutter or saw. When assembling a cutter head, arrange the two outside cutters so that the larger raker teeth on one are opposite the small cutting teeth on the other. This produces a smoother cutting and easier running head. Be sure also that the swaged teeth of the inside cutters are placed in the gullets of the outside cutters, not against the teeth, so that the head cuts clean and chips have clearance to come out. And stagger the inside cutters

Fig. 67.

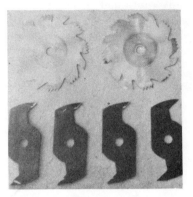

Fig. 68.

so that their teeth do not come together (*A*, Fig. 69). *For example,* if three cutters are used, they should be set 120° apart.

MOUNTING THE DADO HEAD

The dado head is installed on the motor shaft in the same manner as the regular saw cutting blade. In other words, for dado cuts up to ½″, place the ⅜″ arbor collar on the shaft first, with its recessed side against the saw; the dado-head assembly next; then the ¼″ arbor collar, with its recessed side against the dado head; and finally tighten the arbor nut with two wrenches (Fig. 70). For cuts over ½″, omit the ¼″ arbor collar. If using the full dado head, first put on the ¼″ arbor collar, the ¹³⁄₁₆″ dado, and then the arbor nut. Mount the safety guard over the dado head, adjust for the cut on the motor stud, and tighten the wing nut.

In a dado head there is quite a mass of metal revolving at a fairly high speed in the flywheel manner, and if it is not running true it will set up a noticeable vibration. This can be avoided, of course, by staggering the teeth properly and tightening the dado to the full extent.

Never use the chipper blades without the two outside saws. *For example*, to cut a dado ½″ wide, use the two outside saws, each ⅛″ in width, plus a single ¼″ or two ⅛″ chippers. Actually any width dado head can be used (the size being limited only by the length of the motor arbor). However, most dado-head sets have enough blades to make cuts only up to $1\frac{3}{16}$″ wide.

When the width of the finished cut is to be more than $1\frac{3}{16}$″, set up the dado head to a little more than half the required width of the cut and make two successive cuts. Each cut must overlap a bit at the center. If the width of the dado is to be more than

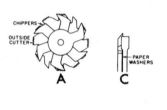

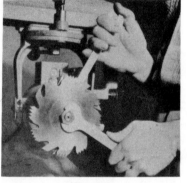

Fig. 69.   Fig. 70.

twice the capacity of the cutter head, set it for a little over one-third of the width and make three overlapping cuts. Figure 69 at *C* shows how the outside saw and the inside chipper overlap, and how a paper washer can be used as needed to control the exact width of the groove. These washers, 3″ to 4″ in diameter, can be cut from paper and are placed between blades and chippers. If you desire to increase the width slightly, cardboard (up to $\frac{1}{16}$″ thick) can be substituted for the paper.

The design of the cutting teeth of the dado head permits cutting with the grain, across the grain, or at an angle.

OPERATING THE DADO HEAD

The dado head is operated in the same manner as the saw. The settings for the various cuts are the same.

Plain dado. A plain or cross dado is a groove cut across the grain. It can be done in the way described for crosscutting. With the motor in the crosscut position, elevate or lower the radial arm until the depth of the groove is obtained. Then pull the motor past the stock, which has been placed tight against the guide fence (Fig. 71).

Angle dado. This cut has many uses in cabinetmaking, construction work, and general woodworking. Among other applications, the angle-dado cut is used to recess treads in stepladders, in joining the sill to the upright members of a window frame, and

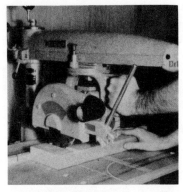

Fig. 71.

Fig. 72.

to recess the narrow strips in shutters, louvers, etc. This cut is made in the same manner as the cross dado, except that the radial arm is moved to the right or left to the desired degree of angle as indicated on the miter scale.

Parallel dadoes. These are a series of dado cuts exactly parallel to one another. With the radial-arm machine, these cuts are easy to make because the material remains stationary, the cutting head doing the moving. As a result, any two cuts made with the radial arm in the same position (whether crosscut or any degree of miter) are always exactly parallel to one another. Mark your guide fence and make successive cuts the exact distance apart.

Parallel dado cuts at right and left miter can be done as shown in Fig. 72.

Blind dado. A blind dado is cut only partly across the board. With the stock against the guide fence, mark off where you wish the dado to stop. Then place a stop clamp on the machine. With the dado head in the crosscut position and the arm set at the proper height, pull the yoke forward until it hits the stop, and then back off the motor. If a square cut at the blind end of the dado is desired it can be made with a wood chisel.

Ploughing. The ploughing operation with a dado head corresponds to the rip cut with a saw blade and is done in the same way. Set the radial arm at 0° (crosscut position); swivel the yoke 90° from crosscut position; move the carriage out on the arm to the desired width and lock; raise or lower the column to the desired depth for the groove. (Remember that each turn of the elevating handle represents exactly $\frac{1}{8}''$.) For a $\frac{1}{4}''$ groove, lower the column two turns from a position where the blades just touch the top surface of the stock. Adjust the safety guard so that the infeed part clears the stock, lock the wing nut, and then lower the anti-kickback fingers $\frac{1}{8}''$ below the surface of the board. Push the material against the guide fence past the blade from right to left in the same manner as when ripping (Fig. 73).

Fig. 73.   Fig. 74.

Rabbeting. Grooving a notch from the side and top of the lumber is simple and effective with the radial-arm machine. Elevate the arm until you have sufficient space beneath the motor to allow the cutting member to swing to a vertical setting. Then release the bevel clamp and the bevel latch to put the dado head in the vertical position (same as the horizontal sawing position).

To set the width of the rabbet, use the rip scale located on the radial arm. Then lower the arm to the desired depth for the groove and pass the material past the cutters from the right side of the table (Fig. 74).

To lay out a rabbet joint, hold one edge of the second member over the end or side of the first and mark the width of the rabbet.

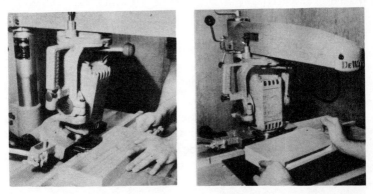

Fig. 75.   **Fig. 76.**

Then draw a line down the sides or end and measure one-half to two-thirds the thickness of the first member as the depth of the rabbet. If the cutter "burns" the stock, it indicates a minor misalignment. Simply release the arm, and swing it approximately 5° to the right-hand interposition. This will relieve the drag and will result in a clean cut.

The bevel rabbet is made in a manner similar to the straight rabbet except that the motor is placed at some angle less than 90° (vertical position), depending upon the degree of the bevel desired (Fig. 75). This cut is widely used throughout construction, cabinetmaking, and general-millwork operations.

Grooving. Although the term "groove" is used to denote many types of dado cuts, it is properly applied to the dado operation made on the side as opposed to the top or end surface of stock. The operation is exactly the same as for rabbeting except that the arm is lowered so that the cutting head is below the top surface of the lumber.

Blind mortising or *blind grooving* is similar to grooving except that the cut is not carried completely through the ends of the stock. In many cases, where the ends of the lumber will be exposed, it is desirable not to show the side groove. In such cases, the stock is "heeled" or pivoted into the cutting head some inches back from the end (Fig. 76).

Mortising and tenoning. For both operations, the motor is placed in the vertical position (as for horizontal crosscutting). A spacing collar is inserted into the dado head at the proper place so that the stock forming the tenon is left standing. On the auxiliary table, place the material against the fence and mark the stock for the tongue or groove depth desired. The dado head should be located at the proper height, and the motor can be brought to the tenon (Fig. 77).

Mortising is actually a reverse cut of the one used for tenons. Making the mortise consists simply of cutting a groove to the same width as a previously made single tenon. Be sure the length of the tenon and mortise is the same.

Fig. 77.

Fig. 78.

Cutting lap joints. The lap joint is found in simple furniture legs, tables, frames, and chairs, as well as in many other pieces. The basic one is the *cross-lap* or *middle-half-lap* joint. Adaptations of this are the edge-lap, and half-lap joints. The cross-lap joint is one in which two pieces cross, with the surfaces flush. They may cross at 90° or any other necessary angle. On modern furniture legs, *for example*, they frequently cross at 45°.

The *edge-lap* joint is identical except that the members cross on edge. The *middle-* or *tee-lap* joint is made with one member exactly like the cross-lap joint and the second member cut as a rabbet. The *end-lap* joint, which is used in frame construction, is made by laying out and cutting both pieces as rabbets. The *half-lap* joint is cut in the same way except that the pieces are joined end to end.

The *end-lap* and *half-lap* joints are actually two tenons with the stock removed from *only* one side.

Cross-lap and *edge-lap* joints are cut similar to a cross dado, except that the lap joints are usually wider. Make the layout and cut in the same manner described for cross dadoes (Fig. 78).

In the *middle-lap* joint, one member is cut like a tenon and the second like a dado. Follow the instructions for making each of these two kinds of cuts (Fig. 79).

Radius cutting. This is a dado operation used to produce a concave cut along the face of a piece of lumber. It is accomplished by elevating the column (the radial arm and yoke remain

Fig. 79. **Fig. 80.**

in the normal crosscut position) and dropping the motor to the 45° bevel position. The motor is moved in or out on the radial arm to the correct position in relation to the stock to be cut and is locked in place. The lumber is then pushed under the cutting head as when ripping or ploughing (Fig. 80). The first cut should be about ⅛″ and the dado head should be lowered one full turn at a time until the desired concave is obtained. This operation is similar to contour cutting with a saw blade, as previously described.

Tongue-and-groove. By cutting a tongue-and-groove, you can make your own flooring, wood panels, etc. The tongue-and-groove is really a combination of tenon and grooving, previously described. With the saw in the horizontal rip position, cut the tongue by using the dado inserts with collars to the exact dimension needed (Fig. 81). Push the stock past the blade to complete the tongue. Cut all the tongues on the panels required first; then turn the stock over and cut the groove (Fig. 82). The groove must match the tongue for a good fit.

Tongue-and-groove cuts can also be made with a molding head on the shaper, as described in the next section of this chapter.

Fig. 81.

Fig. 82.

Fig. 83.

Fig. 84.

Cutting and dadoing. It is possible, by combining a saw blade and the dado head, to get both a cutoff and dadoing operation at the same time. Install the saw blade first on the arbor, followed by the dado head. Then, with the saw in the crosscut position, pull the yoke through the material (Fig. 83). Result—cut-off and dado in the same action. Use a 9″ saw blade and an 8″ diameter dado head, as a rule, for deep cuts.

It is also possible to rip and plough at the same time. Mount the saw blade and dado head on the arbor and put the motor in the rip position. Lower the column to the desired depth and push the stock past the blade and dado head (Fig. 84). Result—both cuts in a single operation.

SHAPER-JOINTER OPERATION

The *shaper attachments* for a radial-arm machine are used for straight and irregular shaping, matched shaping, tongue-and-groove, planing, sizing, and jointing, chamfer cutting, and making drop-hinged leaf joints. It is easy to perform these operations and to turn out the work quickly and accurately. The tilting-arbor shaper of the radial-arm machine offers many advantages over the conventional shaper. For instance, standard makes of shapers are maneuverable in only two directions—the cutting head can be raised and lowered, the guide fence can be moved forward and back. But unlike the radial-arm shaper, there is no provision for tilting the arbor or cutter head. This flexibility adds approximately 50 per cent more shapes to each cutter. Also, you can shape in the center of wide stock, which is impossible with the limited spindle capacity of the ordinary shapers.

Be sure the table is level. It is a good idea to use a ¼″ hardboard top clamped or nailed over the wood table top to minimize friction and to allow the stock to be cut with ease.

SHAPER ACCESSORIES

Nearly all common moldings can be cut on the radial-arm machine with a special cutterhead. Molding heads with a ⅝″ bore come in two- and three-knife styles, either one of which will produce smooth, clean work.

There are also two types of cutters available for shaper work. One is the loose type mounted on a safety head (*A*, Fig. 85) (two styles are illustrated), and the other is the solid cutter (*B*, Fig. 85). The latter is milled from a solid bar of hardened and properly tempered tool steel, ground to the required shape. The loose-type knives are held in the head by means of fillister-head socket screws. Since the spindle moves clockwise and is not reversible, all cutters must point in the same direction.

There are many cutting-knife shapes available. You can start your collection of knives with a few basic types, then add new ones as you need them. There are combination blades that permit different cuts, depending on which part of the contour you

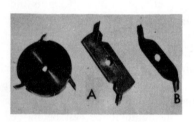

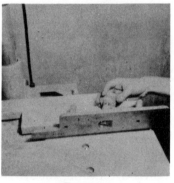

Fig. 85.   **Fig. 87.**

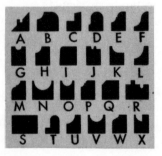

Fig. 86.

	M. Cove and Bead
A. Miter Lock Joint	N. Nosing Cutter
B. Drop-Leaf Table	O. Nosing Cutter
C. Cupboard Door Lip	P. Bead and Cove
D. Fluting Cutter	Q. Surfacing Knives
E. Bead and Cove	R. Tongue and Groove
F. O. G. Molding	S. Straight Jointer
G. Nosing Cutter	T. Fluting Cutter
H. Quarter Round	U. Quarter Round
I. Panel Raising	V. Nosing Cutter
J. Glue Joint	W. Cone and Bead
K. Cupboard Door Lip	X. Cupboard Door
L. Quarter Round	Lip (7° rake)

use. With these, you can shape table edges, make your own moldings, and do many other decorative jobs.

Standard cutters are each designed to do a specific job and usually require use of the full contour of the blade. These can cut shaped edges for glue joints, door lips, tongue-and-groove joints, drop-leaf tables, and quarter-round molding. Figure 86 illustrates profiles of some of the common types of cutters or knives.

The head is mounted on the arbor of the saw in the same way as a saw blade or dado cutter. To mount the molding head, remove the safety guard, arbor nut, cutting device, and arbor collars from the motor shaft. For the solid type of cutter, replace the $\frac{1}{4}''$ arbor collar (recessed portion on the outside), the cutter, and the arbor nut. The safety guard is used when the molding head is in the horizontal and chamfering positions.

To mount the solid-cutter type, place the arbor collars ($\frac{3}{8}''$ and $\frac{1}{4}''$ thick collars first), the molding head, and the arbor nut. The safety guard is used with the molding head in the horizontal and chamfering position. With this type, be sure that the knives are in place and tighten securely.

Right after use, clean the knives of gum and sawdust and coat them with oil to prevent rust. Store them so that the cutting edges will be protected from nicks. The head itself should also be cleaned, especially the slots in which the knives sit. Never leave knives locked in the molding head.

Shaper-jointer fence. A shaper-jointer fence is available for the radial-arm machine and should be used for straight shaping. This fence replaces the standard guide fence (metal portion on the right side) and fits directly into the standard guide slot. As shown in Fig. 87 the infeed side of the fence is adjustable for any capacity up to a full $\frac{1}{2}''$, while the outfeed side remains in a fixed position. This, of course, is of prime importance in the jointing operation when a portion of the surface of the lumber is being removed. Because the infeed side of the fence can be recessed by the exact amount of stock being removed by the jointer, there is always full support of the lumber both before and after contact with the cutting knives. The result is a smooth, clean surface, free from "ripples" and "dimples."

Since the fence is designed for insertion in the guide slot of the radial-arm machine, either the infeed or outfeed side can be independently moved closer to the center of the table or farther out toward the ends. This flexibility of positioning allows the user to place the center ends of the fence right up to within ⅛″ of the cutting diameter of the shaping or jointing head, no matter what that diameter may be.

For certain types of straight shaping, a high fence is desirable because the material being shaped should never be higher than the fence. Figure 88 shows the construction of an easily made jig to replace the standard guide fence and rear table boards. The jig is clamped into place by tightening the thumbscrews at the rear of the table in the usual manner. Note that a square hole has been cut into the horizontal board to allow the motor shaft and arbor nut to project down through the surface of the table.

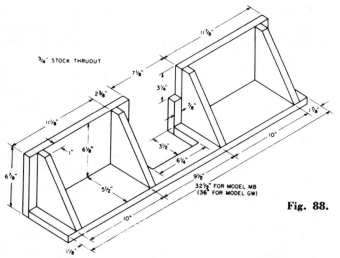

Fig. 88.

Figure 89 shows the action of the molding head extending through the high guide fence and completing the decorative shape on the face of the stock.

Shaper guard. As shown in Fig. 90, the shaper guard totally encloses the cutting knives and the motor spindle. After the shaper guard is fitted into the slotted portion of the motor end bell (Fig. 91), the hole in the guard flange is placed over the stud on the motor in exactly the same manner as when installing the saw guard. To allow the circular wall to be raised to a height permitting the user to check the precision of the cut, two thumbscrews, located on either side of the center wing nut, permit the protecting portion of the guard to be freely raised and lowered on the small circular columns. When raised on the columns, and locked in position by retightening the thumbscrews, the guard permits full access to the cutting knives. Thus you can look and reach beneath the guard (with the motor "off") to position the knives accurately for the desired depth of cut. The easiest way to do this is to place the lumber against the knives. After all adjustments have been made, the guard can be lowered right down to the top surface of the lumber and the shaping operation can begin.

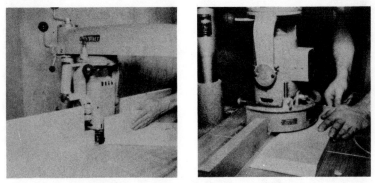

Fig. 89.   **Fig. 90.**

Shaper ring. To allow the shaping head to follow irregular curves, the standard guide fence must be removed from the table top. Then, to maintain the stock in proper relation to the cutting knives, a circular guide ring of the same diameter as the cutting circle of the head must be provided. Although you can buy a steel shaper ring for this purpose, you may find it more convenient and less expensive to make a variety of these rings for your own use.

Figure 92 shows the simple construction of the shaping ring. To determine the diameter, measure the shortest distance between the cutting surfaces of the opposing shaper knives. This will ensure that the stock will enter the knives to an exact and uniform dimension. The inner circle of wood is removed from the ring to allow the motor shaft to project below the surface. The shaper ring is then nailed to a small piece of 1″ scrap lumber which replaces the standard guide when the machine is to be used for this operation (Fig. 93).

SHAPER OPERATIONS

Shaper operations may be divided into four main classifications, according to the methods used in holding or guiding the material against the cutters:

Fig. 91.

Fig. 92.

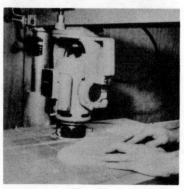

Fig. 93.

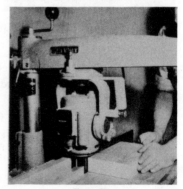

Fig. 94.

Holding the stock against the guide fences. This method is used for cutting stock with straight edges or faces.

Holding and guiding stock against the shaper ring. This method is used principally for cutting stock with curved edges or faces and irregular shapes.

Cutting stock by following patterns. This method is used in production work when many pieces of the same shape have to be made.

Holding stock on special jigs. This method is generally used for stock that cannot readily be held except on special jigs.

General shaper operations are similar to those described in Chapter 13.

JOINTING

Edge jointing. For edge jointing (or face jointing up to two inches) place the four-wing jointer on the arbor shaft and install the jointer fence. To install the jointer, remove everything from the arbor shaft. Then slide on the jointer and tighten the special adaptor nut which comes with the jointer blade. Use the wrenches to tighten. Now place the motor in the vertical position and locate it on the radial arm so that the lead portions of the jointer blades line up with the rear or outfeed fence. Lower the motor to the desired cut by means of the elevating handle.

The 2″ straightedge jointing or surfacing shaper knives can also be used in the same way as the four-wing jointer.

The front or infeed fence must be about $\frac{1}{32}$″ back of the cutter head for light cuts and $\frac{1}{8}$″ back for rough cuts. Turn the handle in back of the infeed fence to bring it in or out. *Always* use the shaper guard whenever possible.

Place the material flat on the table and tight against the infeed fence. Then feed the material past the jointer blade, keeping it against the infeed fence (Fig. 94). When about one-half to two-thirds of the board has passed the cutter head, move your left hand to the board over the outfeed fence. As most of the board passes over the cutter, move your right hand to the board over the outfeed fence to finish the cut. Feed the material slowly past the blade and take two thin cuts rather than one big one.

Face jointing. In face jointing, *always* use a push stick to push the board through. Push the material past the cutter in the same manner as for edge jointing. Always cut with the grain when jointing.

Sizing and jointing. Sizing and jointing in the same operation require an easily made jig (Fig. 95) which has the guide fence located at the front of the table rather than at the rear. The exact width of the finished stock is determined by measuring the distance between the front guide and the cutters. Lock the carriage at the desired position on the arm. Feed the stock into the cutters from the right side of the table (Fig. 96). The result is perfect width and perfect edge with only one cut. To joint the flat surfaces, remove the jig and place the stock against the guide fence. Lower the jointer blade until it hits the top surface and keep lowering it until it takes off the desired amount. Push it past the blade in the rip manner and keep passing it over the surface until the surface is smooth and even.

General jointer operations are similar to those described in Chapter 13.

Fig. 95.

Fig. 96.

Rotary surfacer. This attachment, actually a rotary jointer, will quickly and efficiently cut warped boards down to uniform thickness and convert them into usable stock ready for sanding or finishing.

To install the rotary surfacer, remove all items from the motor shaft. Then screw on the rotary surfacer directly to the motor shaft (Fig. 97). Drop the motor to the vertical position (the surfacer will be in a horizontal position), locate the motor on the arm where the surfacing is to be done, lock the rip clamp, and lower the column until the surfacer knives project slightly below the top surface of the material.

Place the stock flat on the table against the fence and feed the work into the rotary planer from right to left, following the grain.

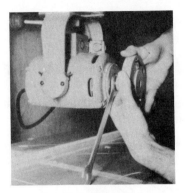 

Fig. 97. **Fig. 98.**

BORING AND DRILLING

The flexibility of the radial-arm machine brings you unlimited boring capacity. Equipped with the boring bit attachments, it overcomes certain limitations of the conventional drill press. *For example*, you are not restricted in the length or width of material you can bore because of the size of the throat opening or the length of the downstroke of the press. The boring action of the radial-arm machine is horizontal rather than vertical. Thus material several feet in length can be end-bored with perfect precision and accuracy. And the depth of the hole to be bored is limited only by the length of the bit itself, not by the stroke of press.

MOUNTING THE BORING BIT

To mount the boring bit, remove the safety guard, the arbor nut, the cutting device, and the arbor collars from the motor shaft. Replace the two arbor collars (the ⅜″ thick collar first) and then screw on and tighten the special motor-shaft adapter (Fig. 98). The desired size of bit can now be placed in the adapter, and the adapter setscrew should be tightened.

Wood-boring bits for the radial-arm machine are available in the following sizes: ¼, ⁵⁄₁₆, ⅜, ½, ⅝, ¾, ⅞, and 1″. Since a left-hand feed and point are required with this machine, conventional bits *cannot* be used.

WOOD-BORING OPERATIONS

For various boring operations, a *simple jig* (Fig. 99) is needed to raise the material above the surface of the table top and to provide a higher guide fence. Place a wedge between the jig and column to add support when boring (Fig. 100).

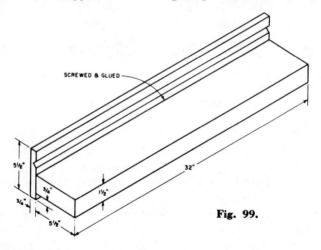

SCREWED & GLUED

5½″

¾″

¾″

5½″

1½″

32″

Fig. 99.

Laying out the work. Accurate layout is a basic requirement of hole boring. The simplest method of marking the location of a hole is to draw lines which intersect at the center of the hole. For such work, a combination square is ideal, since it can be used to draw lines parallel with the edge of the work and as an edge-marking gauge. Dividers are handy when it is necessary to transfer a measurement from one piece to another or to mark off a line in a number of equal spaces. If a pencil is used for marking, select a hard one (3H or harder) and keep it sharp so that the lines will be well defined.

General boring and drilling operations are similar to those described in Chapter 12.

Fig. 100.

Fig. 101.

OPERATION OF THE SABER OR BAND SAW

No tool adds so much to the versatility of the radial-arm machine as a saber or band saw. It will cut all types of intricate scrollwork and irregular curves—either square or beveled—in wood, plastic, or light metal. It can also be used for power filing, sanding, and similar operations.

The *saber saw* shown in Fig 101 will cut material up to 2″ in thickness. The table top of the radial-arm machine allows you to do intricate scrollwork on large panels with full support of the stock, for there is more than 27″ of clearance between the blade and the column.

The *saber-saw unit* mounts directly on the radial-arm motor brackets and takes just about one minute to install (Fig. 102). The Scotch-yoke mechanism encased in the unit converts the rotating motion of the shaft into the reciprocating motion necessary to drive the saber saw. Oil-impregnated bearings eliminate lubrication worries.

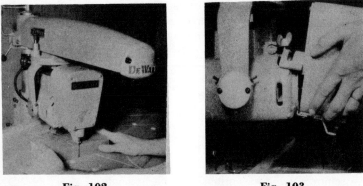

Fig. 102.   Fig. 103.

MOUNTING PROCEDURES

The installation of the saber saw is a simple operation. Before you make the setup for the first time, you must bore a small hole (about ½″ in diameter) through the wood table top to allow the saber-saw blade to project down through the table. This hole can be placed anywhere on the wood top so long as it does not come directly above any of the channel braces in the steel table frame. From experience, a location about three inches to the inside of the second hold-down screw (counting from the rear) is ideal. This position allows maximum use of the table-top working surface.

To mount the saber-saw unit, follow these six steps.

Remove the safety guard and the circular-saw blade (or other cutting tool) from the motor.

Place the pulley, provided with the unit, on the motor shaft (groove toward the motor), then replace and tighten the arbor nut. Check to be sure that the belt is on the pulley in the saber-saw unit. If not, remove the back of the unit by removing the four Phillip's-head screws, slide the belt on the pulley, and replace the back.

Hold the saber saw in your right hand and slightly tilt the bottom in toward the motor. Place the belt in the groove on the motor pulley.

Hook the bottom lip of the saber saw into the groove in the

lower front end of the motor bell (Fig. 103). Then slide the top bracket of the unit into place in the safety-guard stud atop the motor. Replace and tighten the wing nut on the guard stud.

Align the saber-saw blade with the hole in the wood table top by swinging the radial arm to the left and swiveling the motor yoke to the right. Then lock all controls—arm clamp, yoke clamp, and rip lock.

Lower the radial arm by means of the elevating handle until the saber-saw guide barely touches the top surface of the material to be cut.

When saber sawing, the guide fence, in most operations, should be removed from its normal position and placed at the extreme rear of the table.

SABER-SAW BLADES

To operate the saber saw with maximum efficiency, become familiar with the various blades available. For most uses, four blades will do the job. The following table lists various materials and suggests the size of saber-saw blades for cutting them.

Material	Thickness, in Inches	Blade Size, Teeth Per Inch
Softwood	Up to ½	15 or 20
Softwood	Over ½	7 or 10
Hardwood	Up to ½	15 or 20
Hardwood	Over ½	10 or 15
Nonferrous metal	Up to ⅛	20
Nonferrous metal	Over ⅛	15 or 20
Plastic, ivory, bone, etc.		10, 15, or 20

Always use the blade with the coarsest teeth that will cut the material cleanly, and that will cut the sharpest curve in any pattern you are working on. As you progress with your saber sawing, your experience with various materials and blades will help you in choosing a blade for the particular operation on hand.

Mounting the blade. To mount a saber-saw blade, turn the machine on and off until you stop the chuck at the bottom of its stroke. Loosen the Allen-head setscrew on the side of the chuck with a wrench and insert the blade approximately ⅜″ into the chuck against the insert, with the teeth pointing downward (Fig. 104). Then tighten the chuck setscrews and you are ready to start cutting.

Fig. 104.

OPERATING THE SABER SAW

Since the prime purpose of the *saber saw* is to cut curves and patterns, lay out and plan your work before cutting. Except for simple designs that can be sketched directly on the material, it is necessary to make a full-size pattern of work and transfer it to the stock being cut. Be sure you have a clean outline to follow.

For average work, *always* stand directly in front of the blade with both hands resting comfortably on the table. Guide the work with both hands, applying forward pressure with the thumbs (Fig. 105). Make sure the guide finger on the unit always rests lightly on the work.

Where the work is of such length that it will strike the column before the cut is completed, cutting from the side or using an extension table is necessary.

Side cutting requires the motor to be swiveled until the blade of the saber unit is parallel with the guide fence.

General saber or band sawing procedures are similar to those described in Chapter 10.

THE LATHE

The 12″ lathe shown in Fig. 106 is designed as a radial-arm-saw accessory. It is complete and ready to use, taking its driving power from the saw's motor. The lathe also can be operated as a separate unit with any motor ⅓ h.p. or larger.

LATHE PARTS

Wood lathes are designated according to the maximum diameter of the work that can be swung over the bed. A lathe capable of swinging a 12″ diameter disc of wood is called a 12″ lathe. The lathe shown in Fig. 106 will take work 37″ long between centers.

The principal parts of a lathe are the *headstock, tailstock*, and *tool rest.*

Fig. 105.

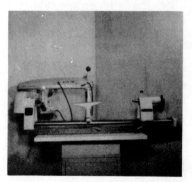
Fig. 106.

Headstock. The headstock contains the driving mechanism, the step pulley for changing speeds, and the spindle. The spindle of the headstock lines up exactly with the tailstock spindle. The two main attachments are the spur center, which fits the headstock spindle and is commonly known as the "live center," and the cup center, which fits the tailstock spindle and is known as the "dead center." The work is mounted between these two centers, the spurs of the live center serving as the driving member. The faceplate is fastened to the headstock spindle in certain types of turnings in place of the spurs.

Tailstock. The tailstock assembly can be clamped to the bed at any position. A hand wheel can be turned to move the tailstock spindle in or out 3¼". This spindle is hollow, with a No. 2 Morse taper. The cup center fits into this end.

Tool rest. The tool rest and holder clamp to the bed and can be adjusted to various diameters of work.

SETTING UP THE LATHE

It is a very simple operation to convert the radial-arm machine into a *wood-turning lathe* by proceeding as follows:

Remove the safety guard and the cutting tool from the motor shaft.

Swivel the motor to the out-rip position and swing the radial arm to the left 90° and lock securely.

Set the lathe on the table top of the radial-arm machine with the base of the lathe tight against the fence. The headstock should be at the left.

Set hold-down clamps with the long part of the L's beneath the machine's table top and the short part resting against the bottom of the lathe base. Locate the two carriage bolts in the holes on the base of the lathe, push them through the clamps, and place the wing nuts on the bolts. Then draw the nuts tight against the bottom of the clamps.

Place the belt pulley on the motor shaft, hub side out, and tighten the setscrew in the hub. Place the arbor nut on the shaft and tighten.

Position the motor directly behind the headstock and align the headstock pulley with the one on the motor shaft. This may require raising or lowering the motor by means of the elevating handle. When aligned, tighten the rip clamp and carriage arm and attach the drive belt.

General lathe turning operations are similar to those described in Chapter 9.

DISC, BELT, AND DRUM-SANDER ATTACHMENTS

With the versatile radial arm, you have a choice of three major types of power sanders—*disc, belt,* and *drum.* Each type has its advantages and uses. But unlike ordinary sanders, the attachments allow you to take full advantage of maneuverability and flexibility of the radial-arm machine. Attached directly to the motor arbor, they can be tilted, swiveled, or elevated, and absolute accuracy is always possible.

ABRASIVES

For power sanding there are four types of abrasive materials to choose from—*flint, garnet, aluminum oxide,* and *silicon carbide.*

Flint. Flint is the oldest of modern abrasives. It is cheap but has little efficiency as compared to other abrasives. Flint paper is good for removing old paint and for other jobs requiring quantity rather than quality.

Garnet. Garnet, a rubylike gemstone, is the hardest of natural abrasives. It is used in most home workshops as the basic paper for finishing wood.

Aluminum oxide. Aluminum oxide is a synthetic abrasive made from bauxite, coke, and iron filings in an electric furnace. Aluminum oxide paper is fast becoming the most widely used all-around paper. It is gray-brown in color.

Silicon carbide. Silicon carbide is another synthetic abrasive made of coke and sand, and is the hardest of all abrasives manufactured today. But it is very brittle and can be used only for glass, ceramics, gemstones, and plastics. Silicon carbide paper appears dark gray to black.

Grit size. This is determined by the number of grains which, end to end, equal 1″. To simplify this situation, many manufacturers label their papers as *fine, medium, coarse,* etc.

Backing. Paper-backed abrasives are generally used for hand sanding. Of the six weights of paper available, the only one suitable for machine sanding is the heaviest weight, *Type E.*

This is satisfactory for disc, spindle, or drum sanders.

There are two weights of cloth backings available to the home craftsman. The heaviest *(Type X)* is drill or twill, a linen or cotton fabric with a diagonal weave.

Type of coating. There are two types of coating—*closed* and *open*. Closed-coat papers have tightly packed abrasive grains that cover the entire surface. The grains on open-coat papers cover 50 to 70 per cent of the surface, leaving open spaces between the grains.

Closed-coat papers are durable and fast cutting, but have the disadvantage of clogging under certain conditions. *Open-coated* abrasives are not so durable, but they are useful for finishing certain surfaces such as soft or gummy woods, paint and other finishes, and soft metals and plastics where the abrasive dust tends to clog the disc or belt.

Forms of abrasives. Abrasive-coated materials can be obtained in *sheets, rolls, discs, drums,* and *belts*.

MOUNTING THE DISC SANDER

Remove the safety guard, saw blade, arbor nut, and two arbor collars from the arbor shaft. Replace the two arbor collars (3⁄8″ one first and recessed sides together), then place the disc plate on the shaft. Place a wrench on the flat of the arbor shaft to hold it, and tighten the disc plate by turning it counterclockwise (Fig. 107).

The abrasive disc must be cemented or glued to the plate. Any good glue may be used. Spread glue on the metal plate, then set the abrasive disc against it. When glue is used, a wood disc of 3⁄4″ stock the same diameter as the plate will have to be placed over the abrasive so that clamps may be applied. The clamps should remain in place until the glue has set.

OPERATING THE DISC SANDER

The *abrasive* used on the disc sander will depend upon the work.

Sanding. Sanding on the disc sander is usually done free-hand, the work being held flat on the auxiliary table and projected into the sanding disc. A smooth, light feed should be practiced. Avoid heavy pressure. The best results on curved work can be obtained by going over the work two or three times with light cuts. Sanding should be done on the "down" side of the disc (Fig. 108). Although it is permissible to sand small pieces on the "up" side, and while it is necessary to use both sides of the disc when sanding end grain on wide work, the surface produced will not be quite so smooth as that sanded only on the side of the disc going down. But with the versatile tilting-arbor disc sander, it is possible to sand large areas with only the down-side portion of the disc.

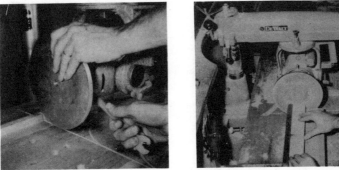

Fig. 107.   Fig. 108.

Surface sanding. To position the machine for general-surface sanding, elevate the radial arm until the motor with disc attached can be tilted to the vertical position. Then move the motor out on the arm until the disc is directly above the path the material will follow along the guide fence, and lock it in position with the rip clamp. Place the stock to be sanded on the table and lower the arm until the disc fits snugly against the top surface of the board. Push the board from right to left along the fence (Fig. 109).

For extra-fine sanding, raise the motor from the 90° bevel position 1° or 2° (indicated as **89** or **88** on the bevel scale). In this position, the sanding will be done on the down-side portion of the disc.

Straightedge sanding. Swing the radial arm 60° to the left and place the motor so that the front of the disc sander is parallel to and along the guide fence (Fig. 110). This is achieved by adjusting the swivel-clamp handle and the swivel-latch assembly. Lock the motor in position with the rip clamp. Lower the radial arm until the disc is within $\frac{1}{16}''$ of the top of the fence.

Butt sanding. Place the motor in the crosscut position and set the auxiliary-table jig in place of the guide fence. With the material tight against the fence of the auxiliary table and making contact with the disc, pull the motor past the material in the same manner as when crosscutting.

Fig. 109.

Fig. 110.

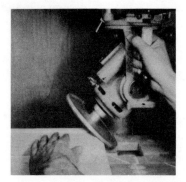

Fig. 111.

Bevel sanding. With the arm in the crosscut position, place the motor at the desired angle of bevel and locate the auxiliary table in place of the guide fence. Position the stock on the jig so that it contacts the sander and pull the disc across the beveled end of the board (Fig. 111). Swinging the motor 1° to 3° to the left will produce a finer job.

Miter sanding. With the motor in the crosscut position, locate the arm at the desired miter angle and replace the guide fence with the auxiliary table. Position the material on the table so that it contacts the abrasive and pulls the motor across the miter end of the board. If finer sanding is required, swivel the motor 1° to 3° to the left.

Rounding corners. Most sanding of corners can be done freehand, sweeping the corner of the work across the face of the sanding disc two or three times until the desired round is obtained. The motor is placed in the crosscut setup and locked into position by the rip lock.

MOUNTING THE BELT SANDER

Before attaching the belt sander to the radial-arm motor, a mounting board must be made. This board is made of ¾″ plywood and the lower projection on it fits into the slot normally occupied by the guide fence. When the spacer-board clamp screws are brought up tight, your 4″ sander will be in place.

Remove the safety guard, arbor nut, saw blade (or other tool), and arbor collars from the motor shaft. Place the pulley on the motor shaft (hub toward the motor) and tighten the setscrew. Replace and tighten the arbor nut.

Now swing the radial arm left until you read approximately 60° on the miter scale. Swivel your motor and extend it out on the radial arm until it is parallel and in line with the pulley on the belt sander. Slip the belt on both pulleys and readjust the motor by extending it farther on the arm or swinging the radial arm right or left a few degrees until the belt is tight. Lock the motor in place by means of the rip clamp. Turn on the machine to check the alignment of the pulleys and the tension on the belt. The belt sander is used mainly for flat work, though with-the-grain edges can be sanded square, beveled, or chamfered.

BELT-SANDER ADJUSTMENTS

The belt sander is provided with two drums over which the abrasive belt travels. The powered drum, the one on which the power pulley is placed, is covered with a rubber sleeve to give traction to the belt. The other drum, which is the idler, is provided with an adjusting device as shown in Fig. 112, which produces the belt tension and keeps the belt tracking. This device consists of four knurled nuts, two at each end of the idler drum.

When placing a belt on the sander, loosen the two inside nuts, releasing all tension, and slip the belt over the pulleys. (Be sure the arrow on the inside of the belt points toward the guide fence.) Tighten both adjustments back to the original position so that there will be sufficient tension for the belt to move when the power pulley is turned over by hand.

Turn the power pulley over several times to determine if the belt is tracking properly. If the belt shifts to the right when doing this, slightly loosen the right outside nut and tighten the right inside nut. This throws the belt to the left. If this does not solve the problem, slightly loosen the left side inside nut and tighten the left outside nut. This will help to throw the belt to the left. Alternate until proper tracking of the belt has been secured. But remember to *loosen lightly* as adjustments are sensitive.

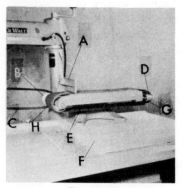

Fig. 112.

A. Work Guide
B. Pulley
C. Motor Belt
D. Tension Adjuster
E. Sanding Belt
F. Mounting Board
G. Idling Drum
H. Driving Drum

Fig. 113.

If the belt is tracking to the left, reverse the procedure given in the previous paragraph. Do not start the machine until you are certain that the belt is tracking on the center of the pulleys.

When the machine is started, it may be necessary to adjust the tension on the belt. To increase the tension, loosen the outside knurled nuts about a quarter turn and tighten the inside nuts until the assembly is forced against the outside nuts. Sometimes it may be necessary to adjust the tension on one side or the other to prevent the belt from shifting to the right or left.

To decrease tension, reverse the instructions given in the preceding paragraph. Too much tension will act as a resistance to your motor and will shorten the life of the abrasive belt.

Occasionally apply a few drops of oil on each end of the drive shaft to lubricate the self-lubricating bronze bearings. Every 4 to 6 months, remove the abrasive belt and screw in the center of the idler pulley. Place a few drops of SAE 30 or 40 oil in the hole. Replace the screw and belt.

OPERATING THE BELT SANDER

Work on a belt sander is generally done freehand, that is, the material to be surfaced is simply placed on the table. Use a light but firm pressure to keep the piece in the proper position. Avoid excessive pressure, since it will scratch the surface being sanded.

MOUNTING THE DRUM SANDER

Small sanding drums come in a range of sizes from 1″ to 3″ in diameter. The most popular is the 3″ size (Fig. 113).

Both the drums and abrasive sleeves are inexpensive and very efficient for edge-sanding curved work.

To mount the 2″ drum, remove the safety guard, saw blade (or other cutting tool), arbor nut, and arbor collars from the arbor shaft. Replace the two arbor collars (⅜″ one first and recessed sides together); then place the drum on the shaft. Place a wrench on the flat of the arbor shaft to hold it, and tighten the drum by hand, turning it counterclockwise. The 3″ drum sander may be used in either the horizontal or vertical position, depending on the operation.

Directions for replacing sleeves are shown in Fig. 114. Cut a 9″ x 11″ sheet of garnet sandpaper of the proper grit into three 3″ x 11″ strips by tearing it against a metal straightedge or hacksaw blade. (Never cut the sandpaper with scissors or a knife, as this will damage the cutting edge of the tool.) Bend the ends of the sleeves by the use of a board as shown at B, Fig. 114. The board must be measured accurately and cut square. Then wrap the sleeve around the drum approximately ¼″ down on it and slip the ends in the slot. Now slip the sleeve on down over the drum. A little talcum powder on the soft-rubber drum will make the sleeve slip on more easily. Squeeze hard to get the slack out of the sleeve and push the ends down into the slot. Then insert the tube that comes with the drum and turn it with a key. The oval tube should fit snugly. Do not force it. If it is too tight, put it in a vise and squeeze the edge; if too loose, squeeze the flat side of the tube.

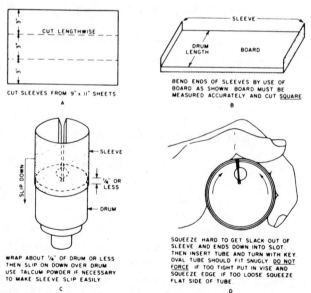

Fig. 114.

To mount the 1″ drum, remove all items from the arbor shaft and replace the two arbor collars (⅜″ one first and the recessed sides together). For this drum operation, use the same adapter as the one used for boring and place it on the shaft. Place a wrench on the flat of the arbor shaft to hold it and tighten the adapter by turning it counterclockwise. The sanding drum is held in place with an Allen-head setscrew in the arbor. The 1″ drum sander can be used in a horizontal position only. One-inch sleeves can be purchased ready made.

VERTICAL OPERATION ON THE DRUM SANDER

When using the 3″ drum sander in the vertical position, locate it over the shaper cutter hole in the table top. The back edge of the guide fence should be notched out for straightedge sanding (Fig. 115). The jointer fence can also be used and be positioned with a $\frac{1}{64}$″ offset between the infeed and outfeed edges (Fig. 116).

With the radial arm raised to its fullest extent, place the drum in the shaper hole and, with the motor in the vertical position, bring the arbor shaft over the drum shaft. Lift the drum and mount it as previously described. Tighten the rip clamp on the arm. With the sander in this position, the lower edge of the drum will be a little below the surface of the auxiliary table so that the entire edge of the stock being finished will come in contact with the abrasive.

When using a drum sander, the material being finished should be kept constantly in motion to prevent overheating and scorching the wood. Wire-brushing the sleeve occasionally will prolong its useful life. Ordinarily, this is most effective if done while the machine is running.

Curved sanding. When sanding curved work, move the work past the drum from right to left.

Straight sanding. Although nearly all drum sanding is done freehand, straight work usually requires a guide fence or the use of the jointer fence. With the motor at the rear, bring the sander forward into the shaper slot on the table. Locate the sander so that its leading edge is in a straight line with the outfeed side of the fence and tighten the rip clamp on the radial arm. Place the material against the infeed side of the fence, start the motor, and push the stock past the drum sander.

In sanding straight work, the work must be kept moving at a uniform rate past the drum. If the work is stopped at any point while in contact with the rotating drum, it may be scored or burned. Uneven feed can produce scoring at intervals along the length of the stock. On long stock it will be necessary to shift the hands alternately. Here the trick is to maintain uniform pressure and rate of feed with one hand while the other is being shifted. In some cases an overhand movement gives satisfactory results.

Fig. 115.

Fig. 116.

HORIZONTAL OPERATION OF THE DRUM SANDER

In the horizontal position, the drum sander will do an effective job of surfacing narrow work when used as shown in Fig. 117. For this operation, use either the auxiliary or stationary table. With the motor raised to its full extent, set the motor shaft in a horizontal position. Place the material tight against the fence, and lower the radial arm until the abrasive hits the start of the stock. Withdraw the stock, turn on the motor, and feed the work against the rotation of the drum. If more smoothness is desired, keep lowering the arm a quarter turn at a time.

Wider boards may be handled in the same manner except that several passes will have to be taken with the sander at the same height. *Always remember* in any surface sanding operation do not attempt too deep a bite in one pass; two or more passes will result in a better job.

Fig. 117.

Sanding rabbets and similar cuts. Sanding the inside corners of rabbets and similar cuts can be easily executed with the drum sander as follows:

The rabbeted stock is set against the auxiliary-table guide fence, and the drum is set to fit in the corner. Then feed the work forward past the drum to make the cut. For operations like this, the sleeve should be mounted so that it projects about $\frac{1}{32}''$ beyond the bottom of the drum, allowing the inside corner to be finished cleanly.

CHAPTER 8

Bench or Circular Saws

A good bench saw, sometimes called a circular saw because of the shape of its blade, is an extremely useful and versatile tool. It can be used for fast and accurate cutting, ripping and resawing lumber, beveling stock to any desired angle, and making all types of tapered cuts. Accessories for making dado, rabbet, and tenon joints and for buffing, polishing, and sanding are available.

Design features. In selecting a bench saw, certain fundamental features of design and construction must be taken into consideration. The essential parts of a medium-priced, well-designed bench saw are shown in Fig. 1.

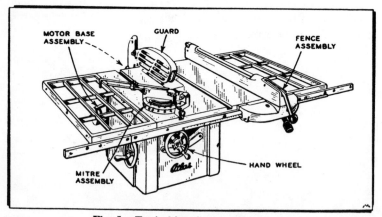

Fig. 1. Typical bench saw and its parts.

A bench saw must have a rigid frame mounted on a firm foundation to insure accurate work.   It must be equipped with a well-machined, perfectly flat, cast-iron table reinforced with strengthening ribs on the underside.   The table must be wide enough to allow the use of the miter gauge from either side of the saw blade.   Where larger working surfaces are required, rigid grille-type extensions that can be attached to the table are available (Fig. 2).   Avoid the type of bench saw that has large openings in the table around the saw blade, with no provision made for insertion or removal of inserts.   This type is extremely dan-

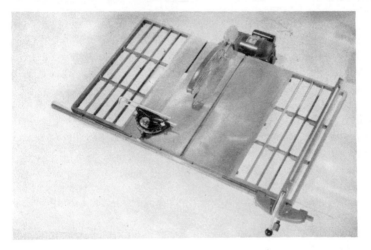

Fig. 2. New grille extensions give large working surface.   Grilles are designed for maximum rigidity.

gerous to operate, and in addition will always tend to chip off the bottom of the material being sawed.   Be sure that metal inserts are flush with the table surface and easily removable.

In some bench saws, saw blade and arbor are fixed and the table can be raised and lowered.   Others have fixed tables with the saw blade and arbor rising and falling.   All good bench saws must have an adjustable table or arbor that regulates the steps of the cut.   All adjustment controls should be readily accessible. All necessary adjustments must be simple and should be accomplished with a minimum of exertion and effort (Figs. 1, 3, 4, 5, and 6).   All good bench saws are equipped with gauges that show the extent of movement made possible by any such adjustments. The better type of bench saw, and this type is especially recommended, in addition to an adjustable table or arbor also has provisions for tilting either the table or the saw. In machines of this type, the tilting should be mechanical and preferably either worm- or screw-controlled (Fig. 3); the latter is positive and is easy to operate. There should also be a gauge to indicate the angle to which the table or the saw is tilted. The indicating scale used in connection with this gauge should be adjustable. Be sure that the manufacturer of the saw has made provision for the adjustment of the alignment of the saw itself with the table, as any unusual strain or accidental bump is apt to put the saw out of alignment. On a well-designed bench saw the arbor should not be threaded for a distance of at least ⅛″

Fig. 3. Wheel at side tilts blade from 0° to 45°. Angle of tilt is shown on a scale. Upper lever locks the tilt mechanism.

from the collar, so as to allow the saw to ride on the arbor and not on the thread.

All efficient bench saws provide for oiling of the bearings, whether they be sleeve or ball bearings. Most of the ball-bearing types are of course dust-sealed, but they will need to be oiled or greased at some future time, and it is inconvenient to have to take an entire machine apart in order to do this. If your bench saw is equipped with oil or grease cups, injection of a little oil from time to time will do no harm.

A circular saw should be provided with a guard that can be adjusted to the various thicknesses of stock, remaining in position over the saw blade even in the tilted position.

When installing power-driven equipment, give serious consideration to the type of motor used. The motor for a bench saw must be of sufficient horsepower to cut wood as thick as the capacity of the saw permits. The saw blade must be at its greatest height at all times when sawing completely through any thickness of wood; in this position less power is required than when the saw is adjusted to just a little higher than the thickness of the wood. To be on the safe side, never use a motor of less than ⅓ h.p. If the saw has a 7″ or 8″ blade and the material that will be used is up to 2″ in thickness, best all-round results will be secured with a ½-h.p. motor. A line shaft providing power for several tools is sometimes used in place of individual motors for each tool. With allowance for power loss in the hanger bearings, plus the number of tools that will be operated at any one time, a considerably more powerful motor will be necessary. However, the ideal home workshop setup has an individual motor for each tool.

The motor in a well-designed bench saw is usually attached to a hinged motor base. The switch box should be mounted on the front of the table for efficiency (Fig. 4).

Checking and adjusting. A standard ½-h.p. motor will pull at one and one-half times its rated power, which means that at capacity load with an 8″ saw this motor will be drawing close to 10 amperes. If the motor is plugged into a circuit that is already overloaded, the line naturally will not supply enough current. As a result the voltage will drop and the motor will overheat struggling to carry the load. Thus perfect motors are frequently condemned for not pulling properly, when the defect really is in the house wiring. It is advisable to have a separate line, made up of at least 10-gauge wire brought in direct from the meter, for the home workshop. If there is a loss of power or motor failure persists, check the line with a voltmeter, checking first with no load and then with a load. Without the load the reading should be approximately that shown on the motor; with a full load the line voltage should not fall more than 5 per cent.

Fig. 4. Box-type switch mounted in handy position at front of table.

Manufacturers of all bench saws provide special instructions for setting them up. Be careful to read these instructions and set up your saw accordingly. Most of the well-constructed machines have been properly aligned before leaving the factory. However, rough handling and unpreventable shocks are likely to change the alignment.

Make the following tests. To check the alignment of the blade with the groove in which the miter gauge is guided, attach a piece of scrap lumber 1¾″ by 1¾″ by 10″ to the miter gauge. Set the miter gauge at 90°. Now, raise the saw to its greatest cutting capacity, using the adjustment control provided for that purpose (Fig. 5). Start the blade running. Move the miter gauge away from you toward the saw in the left-hand groove until the saw cuts halfway through the under edge of the piece of scrap lumber. Now, back the miter gauge away and lift it from the table. Place the miter gauge on the rear end of the saw table and move it toward you until the saw cuts the other end halfway through the underside of the wood. Check both cuts; if they meet exactly the saw is aligned properly. Repeat this same test in the right-hand groove on the table. If the two grooves are equidistant

Fig. 5. Handwheel on front of saw regulates blade height, small knob locks blade when height is set.

from the saw, then you are ready to proceed to the next checking operation. If they are not, make the necessary adjustment of the saw arbor before going ahead with the next test.

Set the miter gauge at exactly 90°. Secure a piece of wood about 8″ wide, hold this tightly against the gauge, and cut one end off. Check the squareness of this cut with an accurate try square. If it is not perfect adjust the miter gauge and make other cuts until the cut is absolutely square. Then file or readjust the indicating point to the correct 90° mark.

Check the alignment of the ripping fence or guide with the

saw (Figs. 6 and 7). Since the saw is correctly aligned with the slots in the table, it is necessary to align the ripping guide with this slot.

If the table is of the tilting type, tilt it to an angle of 90° with the saw blade, then at 45°, and adjust the screws provided for this purpose. The table can then be quickly tilted to either of

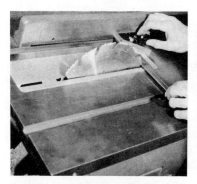

Fig. 6. Checking alignment of miter gauge groove with new blade. The rip fence must first be accurately aligned with the table groove. The fence then makes a convenient surface on which to rest the try square in checking blade alignment.

Fig. 7. Knob permits final accurate adjustment of rip fence. Fence is locked into position with knobbed lever.

these often-used angles, without additional waste of time and labor.

Before attempting to operate the saw make certain that the guard mechanism is properly adjusted and that the guard clears the saw blade. If the saw is equipped with a splitter, check it to be sure that it is directly in line with the saw blade. After all of these preliminary tests, alignments, and adjustments the bench saw is ready for use.

Types of blades. Bench saws are usually equipped with a combination saw, used for ripping, crosscutting, and mitering (Fig. 8). Other types are called planer, fast-cut, and grooving saws.

Planer saws are hollow-ground instead of having the teeth "set." This type of saw requires more power for operation than the combination saw, but makes a smoother cut. However, its use does not by any means entirely eliminate the necessity of planing or jointing the board for final finished edges.

Grooving saws form the two outside parts of a groover or dado

Fig. 8. Saw blades used on the bench saw; left to right: ripping blade, crosscut blade, combination blade, dado blades, dado chippers.

head. The inside members of this type of saw, called "chippers," have two tooth types of different thicknesses, which are used in conjunction with the grooving saws to make different widths of cuts. They cannot be used by themselves. For all general purposes a good ripsaw, a crosscut saw, and a combination saw, together with a dado head that can be built up to $\frac{7}{8}''$, will be adequate (Fig. 9).

Mounting the saw. Before mounting or replacing a new blade on the bench saw clean off any sawdust that may have accumulated on the arbor and the collar. Remove the retaining collar nut. Slide the saw on easily, so as not to damage any of the threads. The teeth of the saw nearest to the operator should point down. Replace the retaining collar nut and screw it up tight so that the saw will not work loose. Before starting the motor rotate the blade by hand, to make sure that the saw clears the groove in the table.

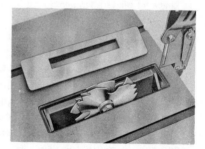

Fig. 9. Dado head in position between the two grooving saws on the bench saw.

Molding cutters and fences. The molding cutter is a benchsaw accessory useful for cutting a large variety of forms or moldings on the edges and ends of boards. It should be perfectly balanced and of solid construction, and the knives should be accurately machined. The knife-holding device must lock the knives firmly in place without their having to be specially adjusted or set. The type of molding cutter shown in Fig. 10 is designed to hold three knives in an automatic-alignment head that saves considerable time and trouble. The knives are made of the best type of high-speed steel, properly hardened and accurately ground to shape. They are available in a number of shapes (Fig. 11).

Fig. 10. Molding cutter.

A molding-cutter fence or gauge is necessary to guide the work while it is being shaped. It is arched in the center to give proper clearance to the head of the cutter when the knives project above the table to the highest point. This type of fence can be set and locked in any required position. It is particularly suitable for the production of several combined shapes (Fig. 11). All of the moldings in this illustration were made with cutters *A, B, C, D, E,* and *F* shown in Fig. 11.

Ripping with the bench saw. Ripping wide boards into narrower pieces is one of the simplest of bench-saw operations, and is one most often used. It relieves the mechanic of one of the most tiresome tasks—that of hand-ripping wide boards. To rip on the bench saw, set the ripping guide by measurement of the distance from the saw blade to the guide, or by setting the ripping guide to the graduated bar on the table. Check the graduated bar frequently, for accuracy in its relation to the saw itself.

The height of the saw above the table is important. To prevent sawdust jamming up the saw, always set it high enough to have several full teeth projecting above the material at the point above the arbor. Unless the teeth project through the wood, the sawdust will not be able to get out and will bind and overheat the saw blade. In ripping without a saw guard on the machine, it will be noted that the higher the saw is adjusted, the more sawdust it will throw up and the more accurately must the ripping guide be aligned with the saw blade.

After making all adjustments place the edge of the board against the guide, start the saw, and proceed to rip the stock.

When the distance between the saw blade and the ripping guide is less than three inches, a pusher stick must always be used. A pusher stick should be specially made for this purpose, preferably of a piece of hardwood, and kept in a handy spot near the saw.

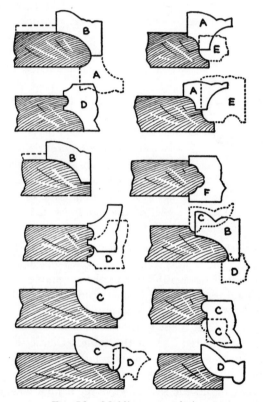

Fig. 11. Molding cutter knives.

To push narrow pieces through without a pusher stick may result in serious injury to the hand.

When ripping warped boards, place the concave side on the table and the convex side up (Fig. 12).

After ripping examine the surface of the cut on both pieces. If one of them appears considerably rougher and shows deeper grooves than the other, it may be because the ripping saw has not been properly aligned or the wood has warped as it passed the blade. The remedy to the former is obvious—realign the saw blade—while the remedy to the latter is to install a splitter. On the better types of bench saws a splitter is incorporated into the saw guard.

Resawing. Another form of ripping is resawing or cutting a board into thinner boards. For resawing, the blade should be set just a little over half the width of the board when the

board is less in width than twice the capacity of the saw (Fig. 13). To illustrate this, let us assume that it is necessary to resaw a board 4″ wide by ¾″ thick into two boards 4″ by ⁵⁄₁₆″. Making an allowance of ⅛″ for the kerf or the wastage of material by the blade, and taking into consideration that the capacity of the particular saw is 2¾″, set the blade to 2¾″. This leaves 1⅞″ for the second cut, which should be sufficient to prevent squeezing and binding of the

Fig. 12. Ripping a board with blade tilted. When sawing warped stock be sure convex side is up.

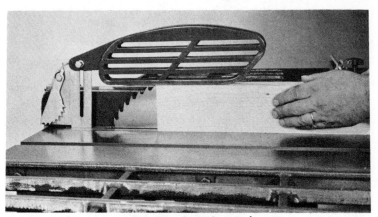

Fig. 13. Resawing stock.

blade. However, when the width of the board to be resawed is greater than twice the capacity of the machine, make the cuts as deep as possible from each edge. Then finish the ripping either by hand or on the band saw. An important point to bear in mind always when resawing is to keep the same surface of the board against the guide for both cuts, then reverse the board end for end, and never side for side. Thus stock twice as wide as the maximum depth of the cut can be resawed. On saw blades of larger capacity, stock can be resawed in one operation. When ripping narrow stock always use a push stick (Fig. 14).

Crosscutting. When crosscutting with a bench saw, particu-

Fig. 14. Always use a push stick when ripping or cutting narrow pieces.

larly where the cut is other than a perfect right angle, accuracy depends on several factors, not the least of which is the operator himself. The miter gauge on most bench saws does not exceed **7″** in length. For this reason extreme care must be exercised in order to hold a board several feet long against such a short length always at the correct angle. One of the first things to do upon acquisition of a bench saw is to attach a straight piece of wood to the miter gauge as a guide for such work. If possible use a piece of laminated plywood, to prevent any warping. This should be at least 17″ by ¾″ by 2″. Near the lower edge, to the left and to the right of the gauge, run a wood screw through to project about ¹⁄₁₆″ and then file the end of the screw to a point. The edge of a board pressed against this point will not slip, and the small indentations that these points will make on the lumber that is being crosscut are not objectionable. The miter gauge must be set and checked to cut a right angle accurately. It will then automatically cut any other angle to which it may be set. The indicated point on the gauge should be filed to offset any slight inaccuracy.

When a board is held against the miter gauge for either cross-cutting or mitering, pressure of the left hand must be directly across the board from the pivot of the gauge and not near one end of the face strip. If the board to be cut off is wider than the distance from the front of the saw to the front of the table, re-verse the miter gauge in its slot. Never hold a wide board against the gauge and let one edge of it come down on the saw, or a couple of badly pinched fingers might be the result (Fig. 15). If the board is too wide to be included in the capacity of the miter gauge of your saw, use the ripping guide.

Miter gauges are usually furnished with metal rods that regu-late the length of the pieces that are being cut off (Fig. 16). When a miter gauge is used in a left-hand table groove no part

of these rods should extend past the miter gauge from the right. When the miter gauge is used in the right-hand table groove the position must be reversed.

Cutting miters. Mitering, or cutting a board across the grain at an angle to its edge, is another form of crosscut-ting, and is performed in ex-actly the same manner. To form a four-sided frame, set

Fig. 15. Crosscutting.

the miter gauge at 45°, the most generally used angle. For a six-sided frame the angle is 30°, and for an eight-sided one, 22½°.

Dadoing and rabbeting. While dadoing and rabbeting can be done on a bench saw, this tool is never intended to produce finished dados and rabbets. Therefore only concealed ones should

Fig. 16. Miter gauge, provided with stop rods for duplicate work, is used in crosscutting. Graduated 60° left and right and indexed every 15°.

be cut on a bench saw; finished dadoing and rabbeting is to be done on a jointer or shaper. Special accessories for this work are called dado heads and groovers.

Dado heads generally include two outside saws, each about ⅛″ thick, whose teeth are not given any set. While they do not make a finished cut, it is reasonably smooth with very few tool markings on the sides. The inside chippers in dado heads consist of one ¼″, two ⅛″, and one 1/16″ (thickness at the hub). The actual cutting portions of these inside cutters or chippers are widened to overlap the adjacent cutter or saw. When assembling one of these cutter heads, place the swaged or widened portion of the inside chipper or cutter so that it fits into the gullet of the adjacent cutter or saw. The chipper teeth should be staggered around the circumference of the outer saws, to distribute the cutting effort more evenly and produce a smoother cut (Fig. 17).

In setting up a dado head on a bench saw be sure to clean off all sawdust and dirt that has lodged on the saw arbor. In a dado head there is quite a mass of metal revolving at a fairly high speed, and if it is not running true it will set up a terrific vibration. Put on the outside dado or groove saw first, then as

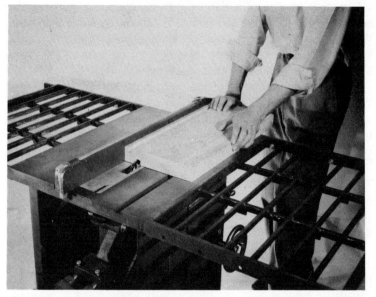

Fig. 17. Cutting a dado. Chippers are used in conjunction with two groover saw blades—never alone.

many chippers as are necessary, then finally the outside saw to make the desired width of cut. Never use the chipper blades without the two outside saws. Dado heads are generally furnished by the manufacturer to make a cut that is variable from $\frac{1}{8}''$ to $\frac{1}{4}''$ and then by sixteenths up to its full capacity of $\frac{13}{16}''$, by combinations of the outside saws and the chippers. For example, to cut a dado $\frac{7}{16}''$ wide, use the two outside saws, each $\frac{1}{8}''$ in width, plus a single 16" chipper in order to make the $\frac{7}{16}''$ cut.

When the total width of the finished cut is over $\frac{13}{16}''$, set up the dado head to a little more than half the required width of the cut and make two successive cuts. Each cut must overlap at the center to make up the required width. If the total width of the dado is more than twice the capacity of the cutter head, set it for a little over one-third of the width and make three overlapping cuts. The design of the cutting teeth of the dado head permits cutting with the grain, across the grain, or at an angle to the grain.

The distance from the dado head to the ripping guide on the bench saw regulates the location of the dado or groove being cut. When the miter gauge is used for dadoing across the grain of the material, mark the location of the dado on the edge of the piece, and locate the groove by that marking.

When one or both ends of the dado stop short of the edges of the material it is called blind-dadoing. This can be done accurately by clamping "stops" to the ripping guide in order to regulate the beginning and the end of the cut. The end of the piece being cut should never come into contact with the ripping guide itself during the operation. Use the guide merely as a means for holding the "stops" in place. Where the grooves being cut are of such a length that the stops are beyond the capacity of the ripping guide, temporarily attach a longer piece of wood to the guide, and mount the "stops" on the longer strip.

Rabbeting is merely cutting a groove along the edge of a board. The procedure is essentially the same as for dadoing and requires the same setups.

Cutting tenons. To cut tenons with a bench saw, first make the shoulder cut. Raise the saw blade to project a distance above the table equal to the depth of the shoulder of the tenon. Tighten the adjusting screw to hold the saw firmly at the required height. Then set the miter gauge as for a square cut, and the stop rods to the required length of the tenons. Cut the shoulders on all the pieces of work requiring this one depth of cut before changing the setting for any other pieces.

The cheek cuts of the tenon are made by clamping or screwing a wide board to the rip fence. Set the rip fence so that the cuts outside the line indicating the cheek cut are nearest the face side of the work. This is necessary in order that the faces of the finished parts will be as flush as possible when they are finally assembled. Make the first cheek cut with the setup shown in Fig. 18. After completing all the pieces required, move the ripping fence and set it for the second cheek cut. For this, hold the face side of the work against the fence as shown in the same illustration.

Taper cutting. Taper cutting is the process of cutting material to a taper, or narrower at one end than at the other (Fig. 19). To cut or rip a board to the desired taper on a bench saw, first

Fig. 18. Cutting a tenon on the bandsaw.

Fig. 19. Adjustable jig is shown cutting a taper on a slender table leg.

make a full-sized drawing or pattern of the taper. Transfer this pattern to a piece of plywood or waste lumber, and cut to make the necessary template or jig. Place the board to be cut against this jig, with the straight edge of the jig against the rip fence of the saw. Then push both the jig and board past the saw blade in the same manner as for straight ripping or cutting (Fig. 12). A right- and a left-hand jig must be made when material has to be tapered on four sides.

Cutting off duplicate work.
In cutting off duplicate work

Fig. 20. Cutting off duplicate work. Note use of stop block instead of stop rods.

stop blocks can be used instead of stop rods as shown in Fig. 20.

Sanding and other operations. The bench saw can be used for cutting composition materials, brake linings, tile, and thin-gauge metals, and for all types of sanding and buffing. Special types of abrasive wheels are available for all of these procedures with center holes the same diameter as the spindle of the bench saw (Fig. 21). Cutting and sanding disks come in various degrees of coarseness, ranging from coarse, which is used for fast cutting or sanding, to fine, for finishing cuts and sanding.

Fig. 21. Sanding disk on bench saw.

Safety rules. It is imperative to stop the bench saw before making any necessary adjustments.

CHAPTER *9*

The Wood-Turning Lathe

A wood-turning lathe is a necessary tool for every motorized home workshop. It is used for making turnings, shaping cylindrical parts of woodworking projects, drilling holes, and a great variety of work of this character. The parts of a standard woodturning lathe are shown in Fig. 1.

While there are a great many kinds of lathes available, it is important that the one purchased be made by a reputable manufacturer who will guarantee his product.

The "swing" or size of a lathe is the maximum diameter of material that can be turned on it. To determine the swing of any particular lathe, measure the height of the centers over the lathe bed and multiply the result by two. If the height of the centers is five inches, then the swing of that particular lathe will

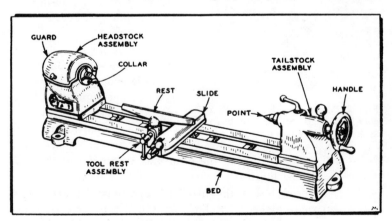

Fig. 1. Typical woodworking lathe and its parts.

be ten inches. For general woodworking purposes secure a lathe that is at least 36″ long between centers, with a swing of 9″ or 10″.

The lathe bed should be constructed of heavy steel. Those constructed of either rods or sections of pipe set up vibrations which make accurate wood-turning an impossibility.

The headstock is one of the most important parts of the lathe, as the power for turning the work is applied at this point. A typical well-designed four-speed lathe headstock is shown in Fig. 2. This type of headstock has the necessary strength at the points supporting the spindle. It is solidly cast to eliminate any danger of its working loose. The choice of speeds on this type of lathe makes it an ideal tool for all general wood-turning. Slow speeds are for turning work of large diameter or for roughing-out. The high speeds are used for finishing, sanding, polishing, drilling, routing, or grinding.

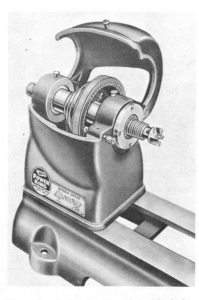

Fig. 2. Lathe headstock with belt guard raised to show spindle bearings assembly and four-step spindle pulley.

The headstock spindle should be made from a solid bar of hard steel, accurately ground and polished, so that it will have a perfect surface for the precision ball bearings on which it spins. It should be large enough to withstand strains placed upon it in turning large pieces of work.

Another important point to consider in the choice of a lathe is the construction of the headstock bearings and the provisions made for lubricating them.

On four-speed lathes the drive pulleys must be accurately made and well-balanced. Pulleys for the V-type belt are especially recommended; this type of belt will not slip.

The tailstock is used to support the other end of the work that is being turned between the centers (Fig. 3). The tailstock, like the headstock, must be of sturdy construction to prevent vibration. It must be accurately machined and fit properly between the rails of the lathe bed (Fig. 4), so that, no matter in what position the tailstock is secured, perfect alignment between the lathe centers is kept. One movement of the lock lever should release the tailstock for repositioning or tightening onto the bed. This eliminates the use of wrenches.

The dead center which fits on the end of the tailstock spindle should be either cone- or cup-shaped with a replaceable pin at its center. The cup-shaped type is preferable for centering the work and keeping it true.

The tool rest must be designed and constructed so that the hand guiding the tool used for turning can be moved easily along the side of the

Fig. 3. View of tailstock showing lever-controlled bedlock built into some of the newer lathes.

tool rest in a parallel line with the work being turned. The base that supports the tool rest must be rigid, and long enough to give proper clearance for the tool rest when turning work of large diameter. To clamp it tightly to the lathe bed the tool rest should have a strong clamping device (Fig. 5).

To do efficient work, the lathe must have a motor of ample power. A good, standard motor of at least $\frac{1}{4}$ h.p. will furnish all the power necessary.

All manufacturers furnish detailed instructions for installing and setting up their lathes. These instructions should be closely followed.

Necessary lathe tools and accessories. The following lathe tools and accessories are necessary for wood-turning (Fig. 6):

Gouges, ½" and ¾"   Spear-point tool, ½"
Skews, 1" and ½"   Round-nose chisel, ½"
Parting tool, ⅛"

In addition to the above, the following measuring tools should be secured:

Ordinary rule, 12"   Outside caliper, 6"
Inside caliper, 6"   Pair of 8" dividers

Fig. 4. Lathe bed and tailstock from rear.

All wood-turning tools are divided into three groups: roughing-off tools, smoothing and cleaning-up tools, and scraping tools. All of the cutting tools listed above fall into one or more of these three groups.

Setting up the lathe. Whenever possible the lathe should be mounted on the left-hand side of the workbench. It should be placed so that the headstock end extends slightly beyond the end of the bench. The motor should be mounted below the lathe. A convenient height to set up the lathe (for a person of average height) is with the center of the headstock about 42″ to 45″ from the floor.

Adjustment of turning speeds for various operations. The

Fig. 5. Lathe tool rest.

ideal wood-turning lathe has four speeds: 700, 1350, 2200, and 4000 r.p.m. As far as speeds are concerned, considerable latitude is permitted in wood-turning. In other words, where a speed of

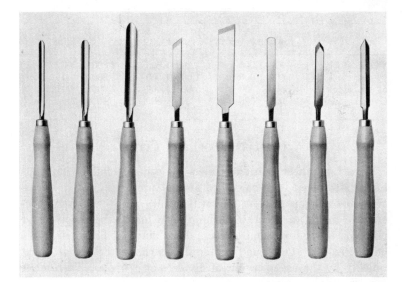

Fig. 6. Adequate set of wood-turning chisels. Left to right, 3 gouges, 2 skews, one round-nose, one spear-point, and one parting chisel.

1350 is specified, any speed ranging from 1100 to 1600 can be used with safety.

The turning speed of the lathe is largely governed by the size of the stock being turned. When turning small diameter stock, use a faster speed than when turning larger diameters.

As a concrete example of the various speeds that are used, let us take a piece of stock approximately 3″ square. The first operation will be to rough-off the corners of the stock. For this job use a speed from 600 to 1200 r.p.m. The lower speed is used for hardwoods, and the faster speed is usually used for any of the softer types of wood. After knocking off the corners of the stock by this preliminary operation, use the second speed of the lathe (from 1200 to 1800 r.p.m) for roughing the material down to preliminary size. For the final finishing cuts turn the work at 2000 to 3000 r.p.m. This same speed can be used for sanding a turning. However, for turning material more than 3″ in diameter an entirely different range of speeds is required. The table of speeds for stock of varying diameters is as follows:

TURNING SPEEDS

	Roughing Off	General Cutting	Finishing
3″ dia. stock	500–1,200	1,200–1,800	2,000–3,000 r.p.m.
4″ dia. stock	600–1,000	1,000–1,500	1,800–2,400 r.p.m.
5″ dia. stock	600– 800	800–1,000	1,000–1,800 r.p.m.
Over 5″ stock	200– 500	200– 500	400– 500 r.p.m.

OPERATION OF THE LATHE

Locating center points. Unless the center points on the ends of the stock that is to be turned are not properly located, a considerable amount of vibration will result, and it will be impossible to make an accurate turning. To locate the exact center point on the end of square stock, draw diagonal lines across the end (Fig. 7). On round material determine the center point quickly by the use of a pair of dividers or calipers. Then make two diagonal saw cuts across the end that is to be at the headstock of the lathe. With a soft-faced mallet drive the spur of the headstock faceplate into the saw-cut at the center point

(Fig. 8). Never under any circumstances drive the piece of wood against the headstock of a lathe by hammering on the far end. This will ruin the bearings on the lathe, and in time will knock the headstock out of correct alignment. To keep the lathe in good working condition never do any hammering on the lathe itself.

Methods used in wood-turning. Two methods are used in wood-turning—the scraping method and the cutting method. The scraping method is slower, but is far simpler to master without an instructor, and has the added advantage of being more accurate than the cutting method. Where speed of operation is not important the scraping method of wood-turning is recommended, especially for the beginner. If you have become skillful in this phase of craftsmanship and desire to speed up the work, then by all means attempt the cutting method. In the basic operations that are described in this chapter, the scraping method will be discussed first.

Mounting the stock. Replace the spur center on the headstock and tighten the

Fig. 7. Locating center of stock by drawing diagonal lines.

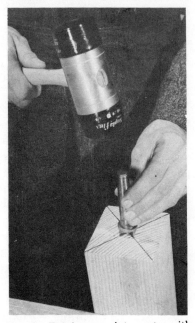

Fig. 8. Driving spur into center with prongs of spur entering saw cuts. Note plastic hammer.

setscrews. Press the work to be turned against the spurs, so that they enter the groove in the end of the material.

Move the tailstock of the lathe so that the point of the dead center of the tailstock is approximately ½″ from the end of the material. Tighten and secure the tailstock firmly to the lathe bed. Proceed by turning the handwheel of the tailstock so that when the head center enters the material it will be set in so firmly that the work cannot be turned by hand. Turn the handwheel in the opposite direction to loosen it just enough so that the work can now be turned by hand. Tighten the dead-center clamp at the top of the tailstock to hold the spindle firmly in position.

Adjusting the tool rest. The proper adjustment of the tool rest is the last preliminary operation before starting the actual turning. The tool rest must always be adjusted so that its top is from ⅛″ to ¼″ above the centers (Fig. 9). The top of the tool rest must never be set below the centers or below the center of the piece that is being turned. The top edge of the tool rest must always be parallel to the stock, and about ⅛″ away from the farthest projecting edge of the stock. Revolve the stock by hand to ascertain that it has the proper amount of clearance. Be sure that all clamps are tight and all necessary adjustments made before turning on the power. Take a position in front of the lathe with the left side turned a little nearer to the lathe than the right. When working on a lathe avoid wearing loose apparel that may be caught by the moving parts of the lathe.

Shaping square stock to a cylinder. The first step in the process of shaping a rectangular piece of material to cylindrical form on a lathe is called roughing. This process consists of cutting off the square corners of the material until the piece is approximately cylindrical.

Use a large gouge for making the roughing cuts. The stock must be properly centered and mounted, and the tool rest adjusted. Assuming that the stock is not over 3″ square, the lathe should be run at a comparatively slow speed and the V-belt should be placed on the second largest pulley.

Hold the gouge in the left hand with the hand against the tool rest and the fingers around the tool. Hold the extreme end of the handle with the right hand and drop the wrist slightly, to permit the side of the left hand to act as a sliding guide along the tool rest (Figs. 10 and 11). The cutting end of the gouge must be held above the material with the handle held lower (Fig. 12). To make the necessary shirring cut, roll the gouge just a trifle toward the right (Fig. 12).

Lift the handle slowly as the work revolves and force the cutting edge of the tool into the wood. For proper disposal of the flying chips, hold the tool at an angle to the axis of the work (Fig. 12). Make the first cut several inches from the dead center. Never start a cut at the end of the stock; the cutting tool is apt to catch and be forcibly thrown from your hand. When rounding off the material do not take long cuts; large chips or slivers of wood are apt to fly off, causing injury to you and to the material. Start the second cut several inches to the left of the first and continue in the direction of the first cut until both meet. When combined, these cuts are called the primary roughing cut. When making this primary roughing cut do not attempt to shape the material to a perfect cylindrical form of the required dimension. During roughing, check dimensions of

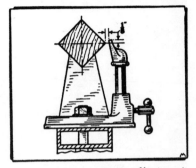

Fig. 9. Proper tool rest adjustment.

Fig. 10. Correct position to start cut.

Fig. 11. Where and how gouge is held.

the cylinder with the calipers. Continue to move the gouge back and forth from right to left on the tool rest until the entire piece of stock is cylindrical in form and approximately ⅛″ larger than the largest diameter of the turning. Then stop the lathe.

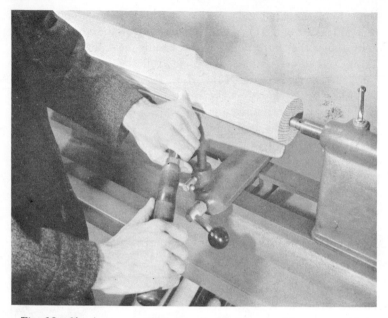

Fig. 12. Shaping square stock to cylindrical form, using a gouge chisel.

The parting tool is used to make the next series of cuts, called sizing cuts. Move the belt to the next smaller pulley to obtain a faster speed.

Readjust the position of the tool rest to $\frac{1}{8}''$ from the cylinder, and tighten in place. For purposes of elementary instruction let us assume that the material is to be turned to a perfect cylinder. Set the calipers to a diameter $\frac{1}{16}''$ greater than that required for the finished work. This allowance has to be made for the finishing cuts and final sanding.

Hold the calipers in the left hand and the parting tool in the right (Fig. 13). Start the lathe running. Using the parting tool, cut a narrow groove in the work several inches from dead center. Take light, thin shavings and do not exert too much pressure on the tool. As the work proceeds check with the calipers the depth of cuts made. Stop cutting when the leg of the calipers passes over the cut without any pressure. Repeat the operation at intervals of about one inch for the entire length of the work. These grooves are called parting or sizing cuts.

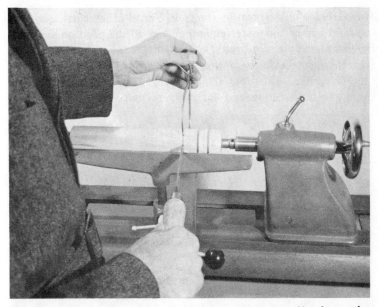

Fig. 13. Sizing stock with parting tool and calipers set ⅟₁₆″ larger than finished diameter. When proper size is reached, calipers will slip over work.

Cutting and smoothing the cylinder to the required dimension is the next and final step. This is called the finishing cut. When making this cut on the lathe by the scraping method, use a square-nose turning chisel or an ordinary woodworking firmer chisel with a long blade. A short-bladed chisel cannot be held properly on the tool rest. Hold the chisel with the beveled side of the blade down and flat against the top of the tool rest (Fig. 14). Use a scraping action and run the tool along the entire length of the material until the cylinder has been smoothed down to the required dimension. Test for squareness with a straightedge laid lengthwise against the work. If it is not perfectly straight give the work another light scraping with the same tool.

A large skew chisel is the tool used for smoothing cylinders by the more difficult but faster cutting or paring method (Fig. 15). It must be laid on the tool rest with its cutting edge above the work and at an angle of approximately 60° to the surface of the work. Draw the chisel back slowly toward you, and raise it until it begins to cut at a point approximately ¼″ above its heel (Fig.

16). Hold it in the position shown in Fig. 17 when cutting **toward** the right end of the material, and change to the position shown in Fig. 18 when cutting toward the left. Start the cut several inches from the right end of the work and work toward the right by sliding the left hand and the tool along the tool rest. Turn the chisel in the opposite direction and cut the remaining portion to the left

Fig. 14. Finish-turning a cylinder with the chisel used as a scraping tool.

end of the work. The use of the skew chisel in cutting cylinders smooth is more difficult than the scraping method. A close study of the illustrations and directions plus continued practice on scrap

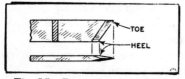

Fig. 15. Parts of a skew chisel.

material are necessary before using the cutting or paring method.

Making sizing cuts. When the material has been turned to a perfect cylindrical form of the required dimension, it is ready for turning or forming to any desired shape or combination of shapes that constitute a finished turning.

Make a full-size dimensioned drawing of the projected turning. Then indicate the points where the sizing cuts are to be made and

Fig. 16.   Finish-turning a cylinder with the skew chisel.

mark them on the drawing (Fig. 19). With a pair of dividers transfer these points from the drawing and mark them on the cylinder. Mount the cylinder in the lathe between the two centers. Place the point of a pencil on each of the marks made by the dividers and revolve the cylinder by hand to mark the entire circumference. Set a pair of outside calipers for a diameter $\frac{1}{16}''$ larger than required, as shown in the full-size drawing or pattern at the point where the first sizing cut is to be made.

The parting tool is used to make the sizing cuts. Place its narrow edge on the tool rest with the point above the line of the centers. Set the point on one of the pencil marks on the turning, start the lathe, raise the handle of the parting tool, and push the point into the material. Check the accuracy of the sizing cut by holding the previously set outside calipers in the groove that has been cut. Continue cutting until the calipers slip easily over the work. Set the calipers for each of the subsequent sizing cuts and proceed in the same manner. Sectional views of completed sizing cuts are shown in Fig. 20. Wood turnings usually consist of several types of cuts, called taper, concave, convex, and bead cuts.

Making the taper cuts.   The round-nose chisel or the gouge is used to make taper cuts by the scraping method. Always cut from the larger to the smaller end of the taper. With the chisel, cut down to within about ⅛″ of the entire depths of the sizing cuts previously made with the sizing or parting tool, using the same procedure as outlined for forming the stock to cylindrical form. Finish with the square-nose chisel. As cutting proceeds, check the work with the calipers set from the full-size drawing.

Fig. 17. Using skew chisel in cutting toward the right.

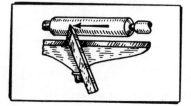

Fig. 18. Position of chisel for left-side cutting.

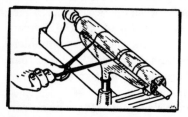

Fig. 19. Cylinder marked with dividers.

The skew chisel is used to make taper cuts by the more difficult cutting method. Place the chisel on the tool rest at an angle of about 60° to the surface of the material and slightly above it. After starting the lathe, draw the chisel back just a trifle, until the heel starts the cut, then draw it a little farther down and back to the original position. Repeat these movements until the actual cutting is being done by the heel of the tool. The entire taper cut can be made with the heel. Avoid the danger of making deeper cuts than required and eventually ruining the turning. The rule of starting the cut from the larger and proceeding to the smaller end of the taper applies also to the cutting method. You should not attempt the cutting method until you have acquired considerable skill in the use of the lathe and lathe cutting tools.

Making concave cuts. The round-nose chisel is used to make concave cuts by the scraping method. After making the parting or sizing cuts and checking dimensions with the calipers, place the round-nose chisel flat on the tool rest with the bevel side down. Hold the tool slightly above the center of the work at right angles to its axis (Fig. 21). Start the lathe and begin the cutting at the top. Complete the concave cut by light cuts with the chisel, working down on each side of the cut previously made by the parting

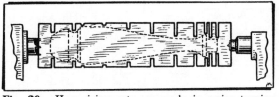

Fig. 20. How sizing cuts are made in series turning.

chisel, to within $\frac{1}{16}''$ of the required depth (Fig. 21). The remaining material can be removed by light smoothing cuts with the chisel or by sanding.

A gouge is used for making concave cuts by the more difficult cutting method. Hold the tool in a horizontal position with the hollow part up (Fig. 22 and B, Fig. 23). Start the cut at the top. Roll and push the tool forward simultaneously to the right and down toward the bottom of the cut, as shown at A, Fig. 23, and in Fig. 24. Note the exact position of the gouge, its necessary rolling motion and the angle of the tool to the work (Figs. 25 and 26). Always start the cut from the high point in the design and work to the lowest point. Then reverse the position of the tool and start the cut at the top of the other left side. The bottom of each side must then be cut alternately, and the cutting tool repeatedly shifted from right to left until the required shape of the concave cut has been produced.

Bead cutting. The diamond-point or the parting chisel is used for bead or convex cutting by the scraper method. Mark the cylinder for the beads as for the other cuts previously described. With either tool make the cut to the desired depth. Hold the diamond-point chisel at a slight angle to the work to round out the corners of the bead (Fig. 27). The parting tool can be used instead of the diamond-point chisel when the beads on the turning are not close together. Round out the right-hand corner of each bead first, then reverse the tool to round out the left corner. Repeat the operation for each bead.

The skew chisel is used for making beads or convex curves by the cutting or paring method. Mark the cylinder where the cuts are to be made. Make the cuts to the required depth with the toe of the skew chisel, as shown at *A*, Fig. 28. Then place the skew chisel flat on the tool rest and at right angles to the axis of the turning, as shown at *B*, Fig. 28. Start cutting at the top of the cylinder, with the heel of the chisel (Fig. 29). Turn the tool gradually and draw it toward you simultaneously as the bottom of the curve is reached, as shown in *C* and *D*, Fig. 28. Then reverse the chisel to cut the other side of the bead.

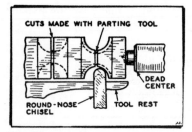

Fig. 21. Scraping method in making concave cuts.

Fig. 22. Cutting method in making concave cuts.

Fig. 23. Right-hand concave cutting direction.

Fig. 24. Concave cutting position.

Faceplate turning. When the work to be turned cannot be held between the live and the dead center on the lathe, a faceplate is used. There are several methods of fastening the work onto the faceplate. The choice of the one to be used is largely dependent upon the shape and size of the turning. "Center screw work" is used for forms that do not require any deep cutting in the center, such as knobs or rosettes, and for other small ornamental turnings. For center screw work a hole is usually provided in the center of the faceplate through which a screw is inserted (Fig. 30).

Where work of a larger nature is to be done, or where the

turning is to be deep, such as a salad bowl, platter, or other large and ornamental piece, a large faceplate is used. This has several holes through which screws are inserted, from the back, into the material that is to be turned (Figs. 31 and 32).

Fig. 25. Gouge position at start of "rolling" cut when making concave cuts by the cutting or paring method.

Before attaching it onto either type of faceplate remove all surplus wood from the material by drawing a circle on it a trifle larger in diameter than desired for the finished work. Cut this circle out with a scroll or band saw. Center the work accurately when screwing it to the faceplate. If the material being used is hardwood, drill small holes in it to start the screws. Use short, heavy flatheaded screws that will enter the work not more than $3/8''$ to $1/2''$. Make certain that the work is securely fastened to the faceplate and that the ends of the screws will not come in contact with the cutting tool when the work is being turned (Fig. 31).

When the shape of the finished work is such that contact with the screws cannot be avoided, the work must be backed up with a disk of the same size. Bore and countersink the holes for the

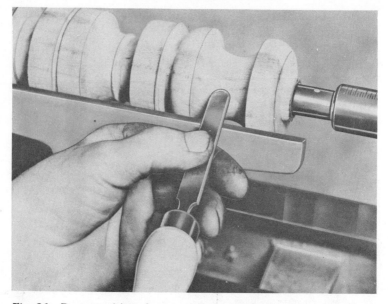

Fig. 26.   Proper position of gouge at the end of "rolling" cut when making concave cuts by the cutting or paring method.

screws at points where they will not come in contact with the tool. Screw this extra disk on work and attach the faceplate to this extra disk, or backing piece as it is called (Fig. 32).

Place the faceplate on the end of the lathe spindle and tighten the setscrews.

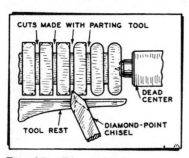

Fig. 27.   Diamond-point tool for rounding beads.

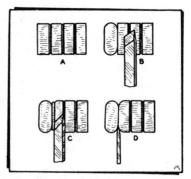

Fig. 28.   Method of cutting beads with a skew.

Fig. 29. Forming a bead with the skew chisel.

Next place the tool rest so that its top edge is about ⅛″ above the center of the revolving turning. Use a large chisel to turn the outside of the work roughly to within ⅛″ of the required diameter.

The various speeds used for faceplate work are dependent on the diameter of the stock, and are essentially the same as for cylindrical turnings. Consult the table of speeds given in this chapter. When the material has been turned to approximately the finished diameter, readjust the tool rest to a position where its T-section is across the face of the turning and at right angles to the center of the lathe bed (Fig. 33).

Use the large gouge first in spacing off the turning if the material is not smooth. Then true up the surface with the flat-nose chisel. If the work is of large diameter, use the straight edge of the chisel; on smaller diameters the side of the chisel can be used.

When making concave cuts, use either the large or the small gouge, or the ¼″ or ½″ round-nose flat chisel. Hold it perfectly flat on the tool post and use a scraping cut. For making rounded-off or beaded members use either the skew-point, the diamond-point, or the flat-nose chisel and employ the same type of cuts.

Sandpapering and finishing turnings. To sandpaper turnings in the lathe, Nos. 0, 000, 0000, and 00000 are usually used. Cut strips of sandpaper about 1" wide. These must be held in both hands with the right hand above, and the left below the turning. To avoid cutting grooves keep the sandpaper in motion while the work is turning in the lathe. Fold the sandpaper and use the edge of the fold to get into the bottom of a V-shaped cut.

Fig. 30. Use of center-screw faceplate for turning.

After sanding the turning smooth, finish and polish it in the lathe. Dilute commercial shellac with an equal quantity of wood alcohol. Make a pad of cheesecloth about 2" square. Dip this into the diluted shellac and then put several drops of a good grade of machine oil on the pad. Hold the pad lightly on the revolving turning, keeping it in contact with all parts of the work and in motion all of the time. The heat generated by friction will harden and glaze the shellac so that it becomes necessary from time to time to redip the pad. Each time the pad is dipped into the shellac additional oil must also be dropped on the pad.

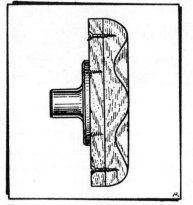

Fig. 31. Faceplate with backing piece.

Fig. 32. Faceplate attached to disk for turning.

Another method of finishing turnings is with beeswax, carnauba, or ordinary paraffin wax. Hold the wax in lump form against the turning as it revolves. The heat generated by friction will melt a portion of the wax and deposit a coating on the turning. After the entire turning has been coated, hold a wad made of soft tissue paper against the turning to give it a good polish. If a higher polish is desired, repeat the entire operation.

Maintenance. All manufacturers of lathes issue specific lubri-

Fig. 33. Faceplate turning.

cation directions. To keep the lathe in good working condition these directions must be followed.

Keep the cutting edges of all lathe tools sharp and free from nicks. The procedure for sharpening the chisels and gouges used for wood-turning are the same as those for grinding and whetting woodworking chisels (Chap. 2).

CHAPTER 10

The Band Saw

The band saw is generally used for cutting outside outlines of work. Contrary to general belief it is not limited to the cutting of thin stock. It can cut either a single thick piece or a combination of pieces, provided the thickness of the stock is less than the clearance between the top guide and the table. It can always be used to advantage to cut single- or multiple-curved parts where cuts are started from the edge of the material. A distinct advantage favoring the use of the band saw is that the saw blade in its cutting action carries all of the sawdust downward, thus leaving the marked guiding lines on the work visible at all times. The important parts of a band saw are: the frame, wheels, bearings, guides, and guards (Fig. 1).

The frame must be sturdy, well-designed, and rigid so as to furnish the required strength without any danger of springing or setting up excessive vibrations.

When choosing a band saw, inspect the rims of both saw wheels and make sure they are covered with rubber. This rubber covering protects the teeth of the blade and furnishes proper adhesion between the narrow blade, which is rotating at high speed, and the rim of the wheel. The upper wheel of a well-designed band saw should be adjustable vertically and tiltable either forward or backward. All good band saws are provided with a blade-tensioning device. This device should be located in a convenient position on the upper wheel.

The wheels revolve at a high speed; therefore all of the bearings in the machine must be of excellent quality and made of bronze. Bearings of inferior quality will wear out quickly, resulting in wobbly wheels, inaccurate work, and, frequently, broken blades.

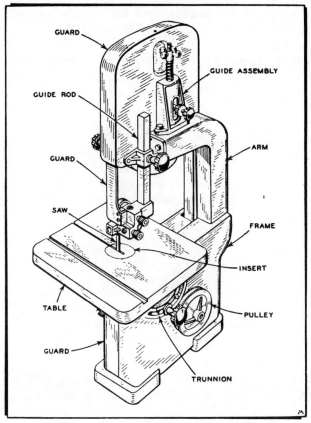

Fig. 1. Typical band saw and its parts.

The bearings must be accessible and fitted with oil cups that will provide sufficient oil to permit running for considerable time without re-oiling.

The drive shaft must be perfectly aligned parallel with the table, or the saw will not run squarely with the table.

Be sure that the table is made of a solid well-ribbed casting that has been machined perfectly smooth and true. The table insert should be made of soft aluminum and must be removable so that it can be replaced quickly and economically whenever necessary. The table must be adjustable and tiltable. An ideal type of table is provided with an accurate scale permitting fast and accurate setting at any desired angle without the use of a protractor. **A** convenient lockscrew should be provided to lock the table wherever it is set (Fig. 2).

Two blade guides above the table and two below should be pro-

Fig. 2. Underside of bandsaw table showing double trunnions, graduated for angle of table tilt. Ribbing of table casting insures permanent accuracy of table surface.

vided to steady and support the blade and direct it for accurate cutting. They should be made of bronze and must be adjustable (Fig. 3.)

The greatest danger in the operation of a band saw occurs when the blade is forced off the wheel, or when it snaps or breaks while the machine is in operation. All well-designed band saws are provided with proper guards covering the blade at all points except the cutting point, and with an additional guard to protect the mechanic from the moving belt (Fig. 4).

Installation. These instructions for installing, adjusting, and operating a band saw will apply to all of the better band saws available. However, various manufacturers have placed some of the controls in slightly different positions from those described. These altered positions may affect to some extent the adjustment of any particular machine. Before proceeding with any adjustments, be sure to check the manufacturer's printed instructions.

Mount the saw on a sturdy, level bench that is high enough so that the top of the saw table will be slightly lower than your elbows. Before bolting it to the bench, be sure that the base of the band saw rests solidly and squarely on all feet. If a level shows it to be not perfectly square, insert shims, which can be made of thin pieces of metal or hardwood, between the base of the tool and the benchtop.

The band saw will require a ⅓ or ½ h.p., 1725 r.p.m. capacitor or repulsion-induction motor. A 2½″ diameter motor pulley (usual size furnished) will deliver a spindle speed of 640 r.p.m. and a cutting speed of 2050 f.p.m., which is just about correct for all types of smooth cutting. The motor can be mounted either behind or below the saw in whatever position is convenient.

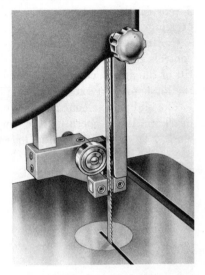

Fig. 3. Two bronze blade guides above the table and two below, and a ball-bearing thrust wheel above and below, support and direct the blade for accuracy.

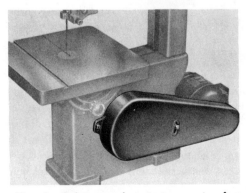

Fig. 4. Safety guard protects operator from moving belt.

You may sometimes experience a slight electric shock when touching the saw. It is possible that this is caused by a static electrical charge set up by the friction of the moving parts and is not necessarily an indication of faulty motor windings or grounds. To correct this condition, ground the saw frame to a water or radiator pipe.

Controls. On most band saws the knob or wheel on the rear controls the blade tension. The double set of knobs controls the tilt of the upper wheel. The outside knob tilts the wheel to track the blade properly and the inside knob locks the tilt setting.

The sliding bar controls the vertical position of the saw guide bracket. When operating the saw place the guide just above the work. To adjust this guide, loosen the lock knob, place guide in proper position, and retighten (Fig. 5).

The table tilt is usually controlled by either a knob or a control

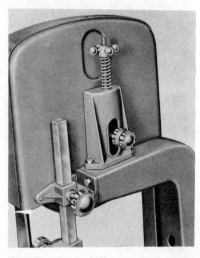

wheel under the table. The table can be tilted and locked securely at any angle between 0° and 45°, with the angle shown on a graduated scale.

The knobs on the saw guide brackets, two above the table and two below, control the thrust wheel and the blade guide blocks. Be sure always to release the setscrews before making any adjustments to the thrust wheel or guide blocks.

Blades used. For all straight and general circular cutting a $\frac{7}{8}''$ blade should be used. This size will cut a circle $2\frac{1}{2}''$ in diameter. A $\frac{1}{4}''$

Fig. 5. Controls for tension, blade support, and upper saw wheel tilt are located at rear of saw.

blade will cut a 2″ circle and a $\frac{3}{16}''$ blade will cut a $1\frac{1}{2}''$ circle. When selecting a blade for any specific job use the widest blade with the coarsest teeth that will cut the sharpest contours of the pattern.

Mounting the blade. To mount a saw blade remove the upper and lower wheel guards. Turn the wheel tension control or knob until the tension is released. Remove the setscrew in the table slot. Pass the blade through the table slot, into the left blade guard, then under the lower wheel between the upper and lower blade guides, and finally over the top wheel. Turn the wheel tension control or knob until a slight tension is felt on the blade. Replace the setscrew in the saw table. The next operation consists in tracking. Rotate the upper wheel by hand in a clockwise direction as viewed from front of saw. If the blade runs off the wheel make the following adjustments: Move both the upper and lower thrust wheels and blade guide blocks away from the blade. Turn the lower wheel by hand and adjust the upper one with the tilt knob or control until the blade runs or tracks in the center of both wheels. Tighten the tilt lock knob firmly and securely.

Checking blade tension. Correct blade tension can be acquired only by experience. Do not put too much tension on the blade. Wide blades can stand more tension than narrow ones. A good general rule is to keep the blade at a tension that is just tight enough to produce a low tone when it is struck (Fig. 6).

Adjusting blade guide blocks and thrust wheels. Two pairs of guide blocks, one above and one below the saw table, align the blade and prevent its twisting. To accommodate the different sizes of blades loosen the setscrews and position the blocks so that they just clear the sides of the blade. Check clearance with a piece of paper. To make sure that the blade passes freely between the blocks rotate the upper wheel by hand. After correct setting is obtained tighten the setscrews securely. Proceed by loosening the upper and lower guide-block slide setscrews and position them so that the front edges of the blocks are even with the bottom of the blade teeth. Retighten the screws.

To adjust the thrust wheels, loosen the setscrews that lock them. Set the thrust wheels into position so that they just touch the saw blade. Retighten the setscrews.

Operating the band saw. Before starting the saw, always lower the blade guide until it is just above the work. Check the blade for proper tension. Be sure that it is mounted properly and the teeth point down on the downward stroke. Examine stock carefully before sawing to make sure that it is free of nails. Feed the work evenly and slowly to avoid twisting the blade or crowding it beyond its cutting capacity.

Never force the material with too hard a pressure against the

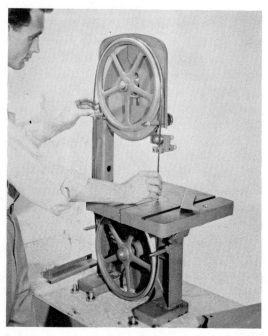

Fig. 6. Correct tension is important in mounting blade.

teeth of the blade. A light contact is sufficient. Move the stock easily and steadily and just fast enough to give.

When the pattern curves, turn the stock so that the blade will follow the line without any danger of twisting. If the pattern has a number of sharp curves, make a series of straight saw cuts in the waste stock opposite each curve before starting. This facilitates removal of waste material and prevents binding.

When it is impossible to continue a cut to the end, cut through the waste stock to the edge of the work and start a new cut at another point. If this is not possible and it is necessary to back out of a cut, draw the work very slowly away from the saw blade. Be sure that the blade follows the saw cut that you are backing out of. Failure to do this carefully may force the blade off the wheels.

Straight sawing. To cut a straight line with a band saw, rest your left hand on the table and use it as a guide while grasping the material and feeding it to the saw with your right hand (Fig. 7).

Cutting curves. In cutting curves either hand can be used as

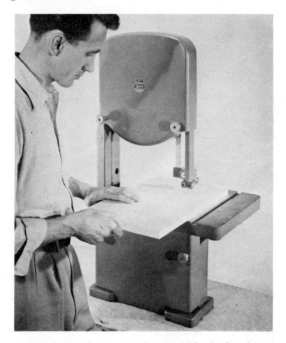

Fig. 7. Making a straight cut with the band saw.

a guide. Cutting curves is quite simple once the knack of properly guiding the saw around them is acquired (Fig. 8). To cut a curve with a sharp, clean edge, exert just a slight pressure of the stock against the side of the blade on the inside of the curve. A ragged instead of a smooth edge will result if you attempt to cut curves freehand, that is, allow the blade to cut without guiding the material. It is important to use a blade of correct width. When cutting small circles use a ⅛″ blade. For larger circles (over 2″ in diameter) a ⅜″ blade must be used. Never attempt to force a wide blade around small curves or circles, and do not use a narrow blade to cut large curves or circles.

Cutting circles. A simple method of cutting circles and true parts of circles is to swing the stock on a pivot (Fig. 9). Cut the board a little wider than the radius of the circle to be cut and clamp it to the saw table. Drive a small nail or brad into this board and file off its head so that it projects about ⅛″ above the

Fig. 8. Cutting curves.

board. This projection will act as the pivot, and should be located at a distance from the blade equal to the radius of the circle to be cut, and on a direct line with the cutting edge of the blade (*C* and *D*, Fig. 9). The radius of the required circle is indicated at *R* in the same illustration. Take care to locate the pivot properly. Then place the center of the stock over the pivot, with one edge against the blade. Be sure that the point of the pivot enters the stock. It is then a simple matter to turn the stock against the blade until a complete circle of the required radius has been cut. If a bevel edge is desired, tilt the table and make the cut in exactly the same manner as for a square edge.

Cutting combination curves. Combination curves, which are cuts combining two or more curves, are cut in series. A typical combination curve is shown in Fig. 10. The first cut is shown at *B*, the second and third cuts are shown at *C*, the fourth and final cut (the fifth cut in this particular case) is shown at *D*.

Cutting circular rails. The method used for making a circular rail out of a narrow piece of stock is shown in Fig. 11. It leaves very little waste and is used principally when cutting top rails out of costly wood or veneer. The dotted line at *A* shows where the first cut is made. After making the cut, glue both pieces together as shown at *B* (the glue joint is indicated by the solid line). The dotted lines at *B* show where the cuts should be made to complete the rail (*C*, Fig. 11).

Multiple cutting. Cutting several pieces of the same pattern or outline at the same time not only saves considerable time but ensures that all of them will be exactly alike. The number of pieces that can be cut simultaneously depends on the thickness of the material and the capacity of the band saw. Multiple sawing can be done very easily if all of the pieces are securely held together with nails at points that will be cut away, that is, in the waste portion of the material, so that the finished work will

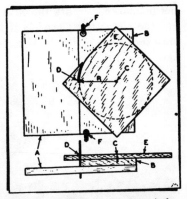

Fig. 9. Jig for bandsawing circles. A, saw table; B, board; C, pivot; D, blade; E, stock; F, clamps.

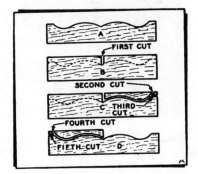

Fig. 10. Steps for cutting combination curves.

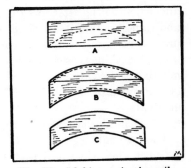

Fig. 11. Making a circular rail.

not be marked. Mark the outline on the top piece and proceed to cut the connected pieces as if they were one solid piece. Make sure that none of the nails come in contact with the teeth of the saw (Fig. 12).

Fig. 12. Multiple cutting. Pieces are nailed together through waste part of stock.

Maintenance and lubrication. Clean sawdust from table trunnions frequently. Make sure that motor and spindle pulleys stay aligned, and keep setscrews tight to prevent scoring of motor shaft and spindle. When saw is not in use, release blade tension. To prevent rust, keep saw table covered with film of oil when not in use. If machine is used frequently, oil bearings or fill oil cups every month with SAE 10 machine oil. Oil the following points at regular intervals of one month (if used infrequently, oil every six months):

Upper and lower wheel bearings;
Table trunnions;
Upper wheel tilt and tension screws;
Blade guide blocks.

CHAPTER 11

The Jig Saw

A jig saw can be utilized for a certain percentage of the work that can be done on the band saw, but it has the added advantage of being able to cut inside curves. Jig saws are used for cutting wood, thin-gauge copper, aluminum, brass, and similar soft metals and plastics. Where delicate scroll work, fretwork, and similar types of ornamental cutting are required, the jig saw is an indispensable tool in the home workshop.

The essential parts of a jig saw are shown in Fig. 1.

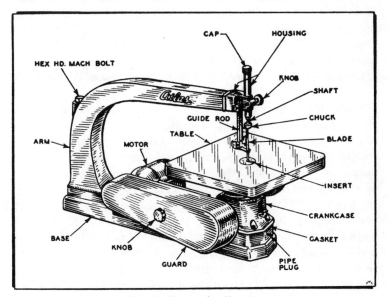

Fig. 1. Parts of a jig saw.

Installation of a jig saw. The instructions in this chapter covering installation, adjustment, and operation are for a standard type of jig saw and apply to all of the better makes. Various manufacturers set some of the controls in slightly different positions which may affect to some extent the adjustment of any particular jig saw. Be sure to check these instructions given with manufacturer's directions before proceeding.

The jig saw must be mounted on a sturdy, level bench or stand. The top of the jigsaw table should be slightly lower than the elbows. Be sure that the base of the saw is level before bolting it in place.

With a ⅓ or ½ h.p., 1725 r.p.m. capacitor or repulsion-induction type motor, the average jig saw has four spindle speeds: 570, 858, 1220, and 1658 r.p.m.

To install the motor, slide the jigsaw pulley onto the motor shaft so that the small step of the spindle pulley is next to the motor; tighten the pulley setscrew. Fasten motor to motor base, but do not tighten bolts securely. Place belt around small step of motor pulley and large step of spindle pulley. Shift motor until pulleys are aligned and belt is absolutely straight. Slide the motor base back until belt is tight, and secure in this position. The motor must rotate counterclockwise facing the pulley end. The belt should be just tight enough to prevent slipping and this tension must be maintained at all times.

Controls on the jig saw. The knob at the rear of the saw table controls the *table-tilt lock*. The table can be tilted 15° to the left, and 45° to the right, with the angle shown on the graduated scale. The trunnion support bracket swivels in a complete circle to permit cutting compound angles. In this type of jig saw, a hose carries air from a pump mounted on the drive shaft to a blower nozzle above the table. This blower hose keeps layout lines free of sawdust and visible at all times (Fig. 2).

The *work hold-down* holds the work against the table, enabling one to concentrate on following the layout lines (Fig. 3). The vertical position is controlled by the adjustable sliding bar. To make any adjustments merely loosen the thumbscrew on the left side of the saw arm, place the hold-down against the work, and retighten the screw. The hold-down may be tilted for angular cutting by loosening the machine screw that holds it in place. The hold-down guide bar must always be placed on the right side of the saw arm when the table is swiveled for the full 90° for cutting long pieces of material.

The *lockscrews* in both the upper and lower chucks lock the blade in the chuck jaws. These lockscrews are usually loosened and tightened by an Allen wrench (Fig. 4).

The *blade guide* and the *blade-support wheel*, located directly

Fig. 2. Heavy ribbed table is mounted on two trunnions, graduated to show angle of tilt. Trunnion support bracket swivels in complete circle to allow cutting of compound angles. Hose carries air from pump mounted on drive shaft to blower nozzle above table.

above the work hold-down, support the blade and keep it running true (Fig. 5). Both can be adjusted vertically and horizontally. For vertical adjustment, loosen the thumbscrew on the left side of the saw arm. For horizontal adjustment, loosen the two screws on top of the guide. To adjust the blade guide to accommodate any width of blade, turn the machine screw on the side of the blade guide. Both guide and wheel should be adjusted so that the teeth of the saw blade rub against them lightly. Position the blade guide so that its front edge is even with the bottom of the blade teeth.

The control knob on the right side of saw arm controls the *blade-tension housing* (Fig.1). Loosen this control to adjust the housing for various lengths of blades.

Selecting and mounting blades. There are two distinct types of blades—the regular jig-saw blade and the Sabre blade. Both come in various sizes. The choice of the type of blade to use depends on the material that is being cut and the circumferences of the curves. A jigsaw blade $\frac{3}{16}''$ wide with eleven teeth to the inch is ideal for general purposes. In addition to this, secure several smaller blades with 12 to 16, and 18 to 20 teeth to the inch. For fine work secure several blades with from 20 to 50 teeth per inch.

Fig. 3. View showing upper operating shaft, blade-support roller and adjustable blade-guide bar, work hold-down, and blower nozzle.

Always use the largest blade with the coarsest teeth that will cut the material cleanly and is able to cut the sharpest curve in any pattern that you are working on. Sabre blades, thicker and wider than ordinary blades, are used for cutting large panels or surfaces. For cutting wood, the thinner and harder it is and the finer the finish desired, the finer the teeth of the blades should be.

The abruptness of the contours to be cut governs the thickness and width of the blade to be used; sharp curves require thin, narrow blades.

Thin-gauge metal can be cut on the jig saw with fine-toothed blades. The width and thickness of metal-cutting blades are governed by the same rules that apply to the selection of wood-cutting blades. To cut plastics, a medium-thin blade with medium teeth is used.

To mount a jigsaw blade insert it approximately $\frac{3}{8}''$ into the

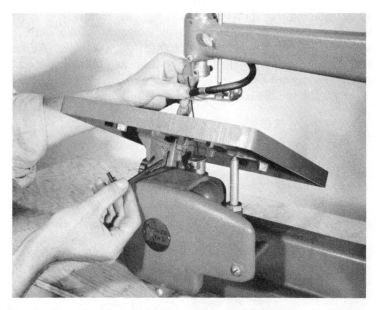

Fig. 4. Inserting blade in jig saw. Blade is first clamped in the lower chuck, then secured in the upper.

Fig. 5. Heavy Sabre blade is held in V jaws of chuck, and guided and braced by a special blade support.

lower chuck with the teeth pointing downward, and tighten the lock screw. Turn the spindle pulley by hand until the blade is **at** the top of the stroke, loosen the blade-tension knob, set the blade about ⅜″ into the upper chuck and tighten the lockscrew. Release the tension-housing lockknob and raise the housing until the desired blade tension is obtained; tighten the lockknob. Be sure that the blade is perpendicular to the table and that the teeth are pointed downward (Fig. 6).

Rotate the spindle pulley by hand. If further blade tension adjustment is necessary, loosen the tension-housing knob, raise or lower housing, whichever is required, and retighten lockknob.

To mount a Sabre blade, remove the table insert plate. Turn the lower chuck 90° clockwise, by removing lockscrew, which holds it to the lower shaft. Replace lockscrew in hole in front of shaft and lock securely. Place blade in the V jaws of the lower chuck so that it is perpendicular to the table (Fig. 5). Tighten the chuck lockscrew. A Sabre-blade guide attachment should be used with this type of blade. This attachment, mounted on the table trunnion bracket beneath the table, is used as an additional support for the blade. Sabre blades are usually used for cutting large panels with the overarm of the jig saw removed (Fig. 7).

Fig. 6. Correct tooth direction.

OPERATING THE JIG SAW

Before attempting to operate the jig saw fill the crankcase with SAE 30 machine oil. Keep the crankcase filled with this oil at all times to keep drive mechanism properly lubricated.

Before starting the motor always turn pulley by hand to make sure proper blade and chuck clearances have been obtained. Apply

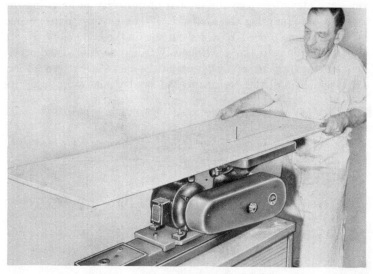

Fig. 7. Sabre blade cutting large panel, with overarm of saw removed.

soap and beeswax to the blade when cutting metal. It assists blade to cut freely and prevents scoring of blade.

Correct speeds. No set rule can be given for speed of operation; the speed used will depend upon the material being cut and the operator's skill. For cutting wood or plastics either of the two medium speeds should be used. For cutting metal the slower speed is employed. Higher speeds result in faster cutting and require more skill. The main objective is to use a speed that will allow easy manipulation and guidance of the work. The faster speeds are usually employed when using Sabre blades. Remembering that a jigsaw blade cuts only on the downward stroke, feed the stock easily and steadily to the saw. After a little practice one can determine quite easily the correct speeds to use.

Cutting to pattern on a jig saw. The jig saw is used principally in the making of small ornamental cutouts such as lawn ornaments, door stops, weather vanes, and similar articles. With this type of work, cutting on the jig saw consists mainly of cutting to a pattern or an outline. Draw the pattern full size on a piece of paper and either trace or paste the paper pattern on the material (Fig. 8). Start the saw at a medium rate of speed, until you have attained a certain amount of dexterity in handling the tool and manipulating the material. When cutting to an outline follow the same procedure as for cutting on the band saw. Never attempt to follow a line continuously from one end to the other. Pick out the most prominent parts of the curve or pattern. First cut these out and then return to the smaller and more intricate

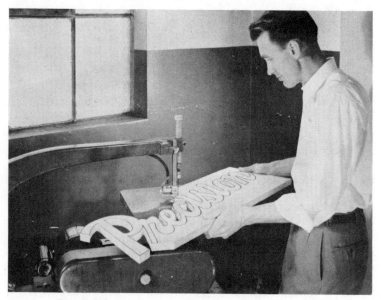

Fig. 8. Cutting along paper pattern pasted on stock.

sections. An inside cut must be started from a hole that has previously been bored by a bit and brace (Fig. 9). Insert the blade in this hole, mount it on the saw, and make the inside cut in the usual manner.

Multiple cutting. Thin material of like size and design can be cut on the jig saw in multiples by fastening the required number of pieces together as described in Chap. 6. When cutting patterns in multiple groups on the jig saw be sure that the saw table is perfectly square with the blade. If the table is not absolutely square the top piece may be perfect, following the outline of the design in every respect, yet the bottom one will be considerably distorted (Fig. 10).

Fig. 9. Sawing a circular ring from 2″ stock. Note hole drilled in stock.

Fig. 10. Multiple cutting on the jig saw.

Lubrication and maintenance. Keep saw crankcase filled with SAE 30 motor oil. Replace oil every month if the saw is used frequently. If it is used infrequently, put new oil in every six months. To drain out old oil, remove drain plug on front of saw base.

The saw table must be covered with a film of oil, when saw is not in use, to keep it from rusting.

Maintain proper belt tension at all times. Keep belt just tight enough to prevent slipping.

Oil the guide-wheel shaft and blade guide occasionally.

Lubricate upper shaft bearing by putting a few drops of SAE 20 machine oil in hole and side, and in top of blade-tension housing at frequent and regular intervals.

CHAPTER 12

The Drill Press

A good drill press can be used for many jobs in the home workshop. In addition to the primary function for which it was originally intended—that of drilling holes in wood and other materials—with inexpensive and efficient accessories now available, a drill press can be used for such intricate procedures as shaping, routing, making mortises and tenons, making dovetail joints, and cutting rabbets and dados. It can also be utilized for making carvings and moldings, and for sanding. The modern drill press can safely be classed with the lathe as being one of the most versatile of the power tools available.

Two types of modern drill presses are shown in Figs. 1 and 2.

Description. A drill press consists of four basic parts, namely, the base, column, table, and head. The head is the term used to designate the entire working mechanism attached to the upper end of the column. The central part of the head is the spindle. The spindle revolves in a vertical position, and is housed in ball bearings at either end of a movable sleeve which is called the quill. The quill and the spindle which it carries, is moved downward by means of a rack-and-pinion gearing, actuated by the feed lever. When the feed lever is released, the quill and spindle is returned to its natural position by means of a coil spring. Adjustments are provided for locking the quill in any desired position by means of the double-acting depth gauge. The same depth gauge allows the operator to preset the depth to which he wishes the quill to travel.

The 14″ drill press is so named, since the diameter of the largest circular piece of work which can be drilled through the center on the drill press table is 14 inches. In other words, the distance from the center of the spindle to the front of the drill press column is 7″. Another indication of the size of a drill press is the distance between the end of the spindle and the table. As can be readily seen this distance is much greater on floor models than on bench model drill presses. In either case, the depth of the hole that can be drilled with one stroke of the feed lever, is approximately 4″.

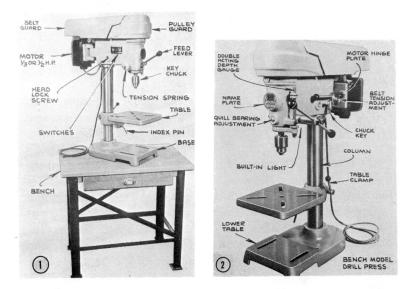

Power and speed. The drill press is usually fitted with cone pulleys so that a variety of selective speeds can be obtained. With a 1725 r.p.m. motor and four step pulleys the speed will range from 710 to 4470 revolutions per minute. Since the shaft stands vertical, only a motor designed for vertical mounting, should be used as a power unit. A one-third horsepower motor is sufficient for average work since this is approximately the power required to drill a one-half inch hole through steel.

Spindles. Interchangeable spindles are supplied for most drill presses, thus adapting the machine for a wide variety of work. The standard spindle has a taper which holds a one-half capacity.

Jacobs key chuck (Fig. 3). Other common types of spindles are also shown in the illustration.

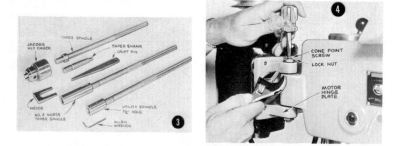

UNPACKING THE DRILL PRESS

A drill press is a precision tool which should be handled with care at all times. It should be carefully unpacked and installed so that all of the fine accuracy built into it by the manufacturer will be retained.

The crate is easily removed from the drill press. Pull out all the nails driven through the sides of the crate into the top and bottom panels. Pull out the nails driven through the side panels into the cross member near the center of the crate. Unhook the looped ends of the binding wires, and lift off the top panel. Unwrap the side panels from the crate. Remove the protective paper, and the bolts which hold the drill press base to the bottom of the crate.

Cleaning the drill press. A cloth soaked in kerosene will remove the heavy grease used to prevent the drill press from rusting in transit. After cleaning, all parts should be wiped thoroughly, and the unpainted surfaces coated with a coat of good machine oil.

INSTALLING THE DRILL PRESS

Mounting the motor. The motor should be unpacked and mounted on the motor hinge plate (Fig. 2) with the cap screws furnished. The hinge plate with motor attached is then mounted on the drill press head between the two cone pivot screws. The screws are then tightened with a screwdriver until play is eliminated, but should be loose enough to allow the bracket to swing freely. The lock nuts on the pivot screws should then be tightened (Fig. 4). Avoid excessive pressure when tightening pivot screws, or the motor base casting may be damaged.

Mount the motor pulley (packed with motor base) on the motor shaft with the small step next to the motor (Fig. 4). Align the motor pulley with the pulley on the drill press spindle, using a good straightedge. Then insert the brass plug and set screw (packed in an envelope with the motor pulley), and tighten set screw to hold the pulley securely.

Next attach the lead wires to the motor. Remove the plate covering the terminals and attach the wires according to the diagram found on the inside of the terminal cover. Replace the cover.

Adjusting belt tension. Place the belt on corresponding steps on both the motor and spindle pulleys. Loosen the belt tightener dock screw (Fig. 5). With the lever in position as shown in Fig. 5; exert enough backward pressure against the motor base until the desired belt tension is obtained. Lock in position by tightening the set screw. The belt should run with a small amount of slack. Adjusting the belt too tight will cause excessive wear on the belt, and also on the motor and spindle bearings. The added friction will absorb power unnecessarily.

Changing spindle speeds. Four direct drive spindle speeds are available, 710 to 4470 r.p.m. being obtained with a 1725 r.p.m. motor. By raising the belt-tightener lever (Fig. 5), the motor is allowed to swing forward, releasing the tension on the belt so that it may be shifted to any one of the four pulley steps. Lowering the lever retightens the belt to exactly the same tension on any of the four pulley steps.

Lubrication. The ball bearings on both quill and spindle are of the sealed type, lubricated for life and will require no further attention. The outer shell of the quill should be lubricated occasionally when in the fully lowered position. The splined end of the spindle shaft should also have a few drops of oil at regular intervals depending on use.

Changing spindles. The first step in removing the drill press spindle is to take off the nameplate on the front of the head (Fig. 2). Lower the quill until the top is exposed through the open-

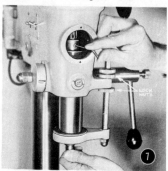

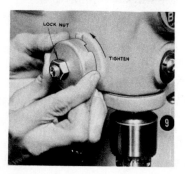

ing as shown in Fig. 6. Tighten the lock nuts on the depth gauge of either side of the head casting lug to hold the quill in this position. With the Allen wrench, remove the small set screw in the spindle lock collar as shown in Fig. 7. Loosen the depth gauge lock nuts and return the quill assembly to its normal position. Gently tap the splined end of the spindle which projects through the upper pulley with a wooden mallet to loosen it from the quill. When the spindle begins to move grasp the lower end (Fig. 8) pulling downward and twisting back and forth until the spindle is completely out of the assembly.

Replacing spindle. To replace a spindle the above process is reversed. Lower and lock the quill in position with the top of the quill exposed through the nameplate opening. Slip the spindle locking collar over the spindle-lock-collar sleeve. Place locking collar and sleeve through the nameplate hole on top of the quill assembly in a vertical position. Insert the spindle in the bottom of the quill and firmly push or lightly tap the spindle in place with "to and fro" twisting motion to aid passage of the spindle through the quill assembly, the locking sleeve and collar, and the splined pulley assembly. With the spindle in place, lower the locking device and firmly seat the spindle locked-collar sleeve against the inner race of the ball bearing in the top of the quill assembly. Make sure the set screw in the spindle collar is 180° from the slot in the spindle lock collar sleeve. With the Allen wrench tighten the set screw (Fig. 7), until firmly seated. Test the spindle with the power "off." There should be no "vertical play," or up and down movement, and the spindle should rotate freely. Unlock the depth gauge lock-nuts and return the spindle assembly to its normal position. Replace the nameplate.

Adjusting spindle return spring. To adjust the return spring, first remove the outer or cap nut entirely and then loosen the second or retaining nut several turns. Grasp the spring housing (Fig. 9) and lift away from the drill press head to disengage the housing notch from the lug on the head casting. Be sure to hold the spring housing firmly to prevent it from unwinding when released from this notch. To increase the tension, turn the housing counterclockwise one-half turn at a time, pushing the housing in at the end of each half turn so that the notch engages the lug. To release the tension, turn the housing by half turns in a clockwise direction, pushing the housing in at the end of each half turn to engage the notch. When proper tension has been obtained, retighten the retaining nut and lock with the cap nut which was removed first.

Adjustments. In average drilling operations, the hole in the center of the table should be directly under the drill so that the drill, after going through the work, will enter the hole in the table. Where it is necessary to drill through the stock on which you are working, the feed lever should always be pressed without the work in place to see that the drill enters the table opening. The drill press table may be tilted and locked at any angle, right or left (Figs. 10 and 11). Holes are drilled in the swivel head for the insertion of the knurled index pin when the table is in the horizontal, vertical, or 45° angle position. When it is necessary to adjust the table to any intermediate angle, the nut on the swivel screw is tightened to lock the table in the desired

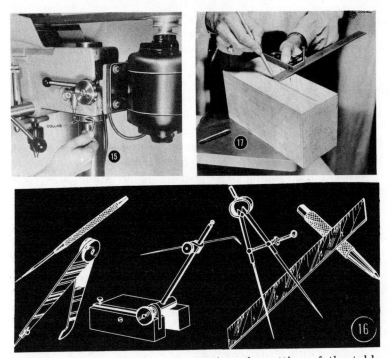

position. When average work requires the setting of the table to a variety of angles, it is advisable to set a scale and adjustable pointer to the under side of the table to locate these positions.

Mounting chuck. Mount the Jacobs key chuck to the taper spindle as shown in Fig. 12. Do not strike the chuck jaws. *Note* that they have been withdrawn into the body of the chuck before it is tapped in place with a wooden mallet or rawhide hammer.

Removing chuck. To remove the chuck from the drill press spindle, insert the slotted steel wedge (Fig. 3), between the shoulder on the spindle, and the top of the chuck, as shown in Fig. 13, and strike the wedge a sharp blow with a hammer. At the same time, hold the chuck with one hand to prevent its falling onto the drill press table when driven off.

Double acting depth gauge. By adjusting and locking the two knurled stop nuts (Fig. 2), depth of the spindle travel can be accurately controlled. By adjusting the lower knurled stop nut, the length of return stroke can be controlled. By tightening both the bottom and top stop nuts, spindle can be securely anchored at any height for routing, shaping, surface grinding or other similar operations which require the vertical movement of the quill to be locked.

Chucking drills. Chucking a drill with a key chuck is easily accomplished as shown in Fig. 14. The drill is usually held in the left hand, while the key is inserted and the jaws tightened with the right. Drills are removed in the same manner, except that the twist on the key is reversed. On no account should the drill be loosened from the chuck unless the hand is in position to prevent it from falling. The insertion of drills and other tools in a spindle which has a hole in the end to receive the shank of the drill is quite simple, the drill being pressed into the hole and the set screws being tightened to hold it. Where taper shank drills are used, the drill is fitted by pressing it into the tapered hole at the end of the spindle, engaging the tang of the drill in the corresponding slot of the spindle. During use the drill becomes tightly wedged in the tapered hole, and must be driven out by the means of a drift key (Fig. 3). One edge of the drift key is flat and the other round. The round edge fits against the upper round part of the slot in the spindle while the flat edge fits against the end of the drill being removed.

OPERATION

The drill press head and work table can be adjusted to various positions on the column. Both are clamped securely in place by double plug binders. The position of the work table, being readjusted more frequently than the head, is provided with a quick acting hand lever which will instantly release or tighten the binder, with a quarter turn of the clamp handle (Fig. 2). The double plug binder in the head is released or tightened by a heavy Allen screw wrench. Great care should be used in adjusting the position of the head on the column. It should be well supported when the binder is released to prevent it from dropping and striking the table, and possibly injuring the chuck, the spindle, or other parts of the head. A column collar (available as an accessory) as shown in Fig. 15, should be mounted below the casting of the drill press head. With this collar in place, the head binder may be released and the drill press head swung from side to side with safety. By placing the collar a few inches below the head it will act as a safety stop when raising, lowering, or changing the position of the head.

Laying out the work. Practically every hole that is drilled requires that first of all, a layout mark be made which will locate either its approximate or exact position. Various tools are used in making the layout ranging from square, hammer, and punch, to expensive instruments essential for very exacting work. A few of the layout tools commonly used are shown in Fig. 16. One of the most useful tools for average work is the combination square. This can be used for center lining, as shown in Fig. 17, in case the work is being done on wood. If the layout work was required

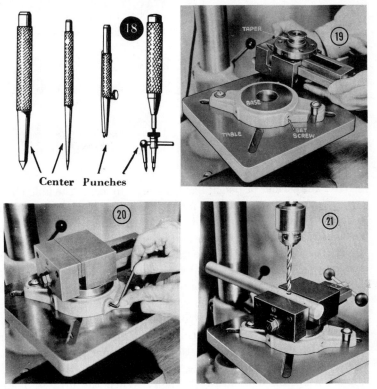

Center Punches

on metal, a scriber or punch would be substituted for the pencil shown in the illustration. Various substances and devices are used to mark on a variety of materials.

After the scriber or pencil has been used to locate the hole position, it is further necessary to indent this point. This is done with a center punch a few of which are shown in Fig. 18. There are various sizes of center punches, and the size selection will depend upon the work, and the accuracy which is required. Center punching should be done carefully so that the punch mark comes at the exact intersection of the layout lines. Despite the care of laying out and clamping, it will sometimes be found that after the drill has cut a few revolutions into the work, the hole is found to be off center. The drill may be led back to the proper position by cutting from one to three or more grooves with a small round nosed chisel, the grooves being on the side toward which it is desired to draw the hole. When the drill is again started, it should drift over to the correct position. This must be done before the drill starts to cut its full diameter.

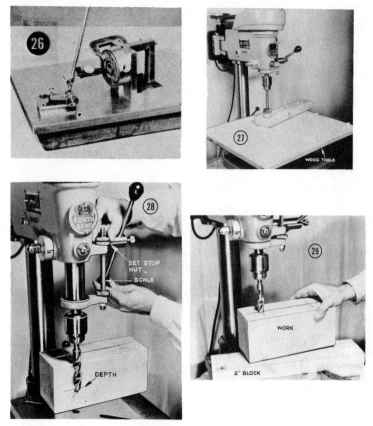

DRILL PRESS VISE

The *drill press vise* offers the most practical method of holding small work while being drilled. The base of the vise (Fig. 19) can be clamped to the slotted work table enabling the vise to hold the work rigidly for drilling or reaming. The center tapered pivot on the upper part of the vise fits into the hole in the base and is clamped in place with the set screws as shown in Fig. 20. These set screws, when turned in part way, allow the upper part of the vise to turn freely. When the set screws are tightened, they securely lock the vise at any desired point in the circle. Figure 21 shows a round metal rod clamped in the drill press vise for drilling The long end of the rod is turned over against the drill press column for added support. In this case it would be unnecessary to tighten the set screw securely. Figure 22 shows an angle plate clamped in the drill press vise. A block of hard wood or metal is placed under the work so that the pressure of the drill will not loosen or force the work out of line. Figure 23 shows a hollow pipe clamped in the drill press vise. For such drilling operations a good center punch mark is essential to keep the drill point from drifting off of the rounded surface. If the hole in this case is to go completely through the pipe it is advisable to drill first through one side, then turn the work over and drill through the other. This will avoid going through the bottom and drilling into your vise.

The various equipment shown in Figs. 24, 25, and 26 show the surface plate, "V" blocks, and angle plate being used in conjunction with surface gauges for layout and checking of final work.

DRILLING PRACTICE IN WOOD

Speeds. Spur bits in sizes up to approximately ¾″ should be worked at speeds between 1800 and 3000 r.p.m.'s. No exact speeds may be given, since this depends to a great extent on the wood, grain, depth of hole, style of bit, etc. Generally speaking, smaller bits can turn faster than larger ones, more speed can be used on soft woods, less speed should be used for deep holes, and more speed can be used for end drilling. Large bits must always be run at a low speed. Multi-spur and expansive bits will burn if worked at greater than 500 r.p.m.

Drilling. The work is properly laid out and the position of the hole marked. The bit is mounted in the chuck. The table should be located so that the bit will pass through the table opening after the hole has been drilled. The drill is forced into the work by pulling on the feed lever. The feed should be slowed down when the operator judges the drill to be almost through the work. The feed should be very slow from this point on to avoid splintering the work as the drill projects through the under side. Most operators prefer to place a scrap block of wood under the work, so that as the drill passes through it meets a solid foundation, and by thus drilling part way into the scrap stock a clean neat hole is left on the under side of the work. In many instances a larger auxiliary wood table is mounted on the regular drill press table to give added support for larger work (Fig. 27).

Drilling to depth. One method of drilling to a specified depth is shown in Fig. 28. The depth of the hole to be drilled is marked on the side of the work. The quill assembly is then lowered with the drill along side the work until it reaches the proper depth, holding it in this position, set the stop nut as shown in the illustration. The quill assembly is then returned to its normal position, the drill is centered on the cross lines of your layout marks and the feed lever is pressed until it is stopped by the lock nuts on the depth gauge. One other method is to bring the point of the drill down against the work and then read the scale on the depth gauge. Then proceed to feed the drill into the work, adding the required depth to the first reading.

Drilling deep holes. One method of increasing the depth over the normal spindle travel is shown in Fig. 29. The first full stroke is made, sinking the drill to a depth of 4″ in the work. The feed handle is then released, and the work lifted with the drill inserted in the hole and a base block is slipped under the work as shown in the illustration. The feed handle can now be pressed again and an additional two inches may be drilled with the same quill travel. In all deep hole drilling, cutting should not continue after the flutes of the bit have passed below the work surface. After this point has been reached, the chips cannot get out, and burning starts immediately. Where it is necessary to go beyond this depth —the bit should be lifted frequently in order to permit clearing the hole of chips.

Drilling large holes. Holes over 1½" diameter can be classified as large holes. The removal of comparatively large amounts of wood causes considerable strain on the work and it is therefore advisable to use clamps. This applies especially to any kind of bit which has but one cutting edge. Other style cutters of the multi-spur or continuous rim pattern can be operated without clamping. Figure 30 shows a multi-spur bit being used.

Drilling in round work. Various methods are in use for drilling a round stock, however, one of the most common is the use of the "V" block. Figure 31 shows a round metal bar being drilled. If the hole is not too large and the feed is relatively slow, clamps will not be found necessary for a drilling operation of this kind. The pressure of the drill securely seats the bar in the "V" block and little pressure will be found necessary to hold it in position.

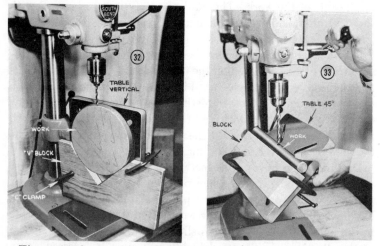

Figure 32 shows a circular disc of wood being drilled around its edge by means of the "V" block method. In this case the table has been locked in a vertical position and a "V" block clamped to the surface and also resting on the lower surface. The wood disc may be held against the surface easily with one hand while the feed lever is operated with the other.

Another method of drilling round work is shown in Fig. 33. In this case, the table is tilted to 45° and a block of wood is clamped to the table as shown in the illustration. The work is laid in the "V" formed by the table surface and the block. The table may be pivoted back and forth in order to center the drill on the surface of the round work.

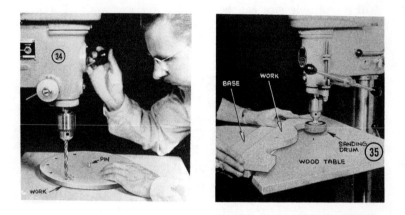

Pivot points. Where the holes are to be drilled around the edge of a circular piece of work as shown in Fig. 34, the work is pivoted on a wood or metal pin which may extend completely through or merely part way from the under side. The use of a pivot pin locates the holes accurately in relation to the center, but does not space them equally around the circle. A jig with a locating pin or indexing head will regulate this part of the work.

MISCELLANEOUS DRILL PRESS OPERATIONS

Grinding. Light surface grinding can be done perfectly on the drill press, using a cup wheel which is mounted on a special spindle. The grit and bond of the wheel should be selected to suit the work, as with any other type of grinding. The speed of the drill press should be about 5000 r.p.m. The work is projected along the drill press table and under the cup wheel, which has been set to take a suitable bite and the quill locked in position. Heavy cuts should be avoided. Good use can be made of a column collar under the drill press head. The work is clamped in place in the vise (Fig. 35), and the drill press head is swung back and forth across the work.

Countersinking. The various types of wood and machine screws are set so that their heads come either flush or below the surface of the work. To make holes for these heads, an ordinary drill of suitable size can be used for average work. For more accurate work, however, regular countersink drills should be used as shown in Fig. 36.

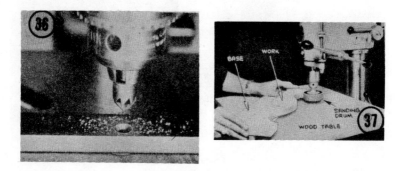

Sanding. Another useful drill press operation is sanding. Sanding drums of various shapes and sizes are available at most machine tool dealers, which will take much of the time consuming work out of hand sanding many of the curved surfaces of your shop projects. A 3″ sanding drum should run at from 1200 to 1500 r.p.m.'s. Smaller sizes should run faster. Drums are used mostly for edge operations, and good use can be made of fences, pivot pins, and other simple jigs to guide the work. Irregular curves are simply fed free hand with a uniform feed and pressure to obtain good work and prevent burning. Figure 37 shows a typical example of free hand edge sanding. The work is supported on the base block in order to center the edge of the sanding drum on the edge of the work.

The main difficulty with free hand edge sanding is that the work must be kept moving at an even pressure against the drum, otherwise a deep cut is made into the work at any place where the operator pauses too long. One way to avoid this fault is to sand with a pattern or against a wood disc exactly the same diameter as the sanding drum, set below the drum and fastened to the table. The pattern is then fastened to the under side of the work and while the pattern rides against the wood disc the work rides against the sanding drum. The same pattern may thus be used to duplicate the first piece as many times as necessary.

CHAPTER 13

Jointers and Shapers

⋮

JOINTERS

A jointer, sometimes called a jointer planer, is essentially a motorized plane. Its principal function is planing the surface of material as it is passed over a revolving cutting head. This power tool is used mostly for surfacing and planing narrow widths and edges of stock prior to the making of glued joints, and for planing and surfacing the faces of lumber. A jointer can also be utilized for rabbeting, chamfering, and similar operations.

The parts of a well-designed jointer are shown in Fig. 1.

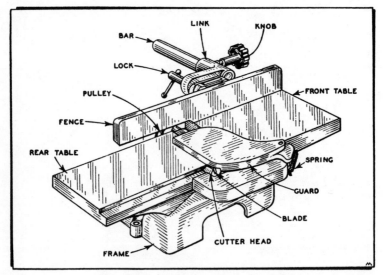

Fig. 1. Typical jointer and its parts.

To do efficient, accurate work the base supporting the tables of the jointer must be sturdy or the cutter heads that rotate at a high speed will not produce an even, smooth surface. The base must be constructed of one piece so that parts cannot work loose or get out of alignment.

A jointer is equipped with two tables: the front or infeed table, and the rear or outfeed table. A control must be provided to raise or lower these tables as required. The tables are accurately machined and are mounted on inclines, so when either raised or lowered they remain level. They should be made of cast iron and preferably ribbed on the underside for additional strength and rigidity. The cutter head of a good jointer is machined out of a solid piece of steel and is the round cutter-head type, sometimes called the safety cutter head. On a round cutter head, the cutting blades or knives project only a slight distance, thus lessening any possibility of injury. These knives should be made of thin, hardened, high-speed steel rather than carbon steel, as the former keep their edges sharp five or six times longer.

The guide or fence should be wide and long, and machined smooth and perfectly straight on the face side. It should be easily adjustable back and forth at any point across the table, and provided with a tilting arrangement combined with a locking device for holding it securely in any desired position.

The jointer shown in Fig. 1 is a standard type and requires a ⅓ h.p., 1725 r.p.m. repulsion-induction or capacitor motor with a $3^{11}/_{16}$″-diameter pulley.

The jointer is usually operated at speeds ranging from 5000 to 8000 r.p.m.

Installation of the jointer. To assemble a new jointer fasten the fence bracket to the right side of the front table with the cap screws provided by the manufacturer. Put the fence on the fence bracket and tighten the lock. To mount the guard in position put the fiber washer on the guard stud. Fasten the guard spring to the cotter pin in the table of the jointer. Push the stud into the hole in the top of the table. Before mounting the jointer cut a hole in the top of the workbench to facilitate chip removal. Mount the jointer on a level bench or table, but check to make sure that the base rests squarely and solidly on all feet before bolting it down. Uneven mounting will eventually throw the tables out of alignment.

Controls and adjustments. The ball crank handle, beneath the front table of the jointer, controls the depth-of-cut adjustment.

The front table lock control on the right side of the jointer locks the front table in position. Before the table can be adjusted, this lock must be released. The knob beneath the rear table controls rear table elevation. Before adjusting the rear table, loosen the hex capscrew found on right side of jointer frame.

The adjusting knob on the fence slide bracket releases and locks fence, when making necessary adjustments for width of cut. The fence tilt lever locks fence in any required position (Fig. 2).

The top of the rear table must be exactly level with the cutting

Fig. 2. Jointer fence adjustments.

arc of the knives. To align the rear table, loosen the table lock screw on right side of jointer and raise or lower the rear table, until it is level with the cutting edge of any one blade at the highest point in its cutting arc. Check accuracy of alignment by placing a straightedge on the rear table with one end projecting over one of the cutter blades. The blade of the cutter should just touch the straightedge.

Each blade in the cutter head must be the same height and parallel with the rear table. To check and make the necessary adjustment proceed as follows: Remove fence and guard. Place a straightedge on the center of the rear table with one end projecting over the cutter blades. Revolve the cutter head by hand. Adjust blades to touch the straightedge. To adjust the blades, loosen the setscrews which hold them in place in the cutter head. If blade is too high, tap it very lightly with a piece of hardwood. If the blade is low, raise it by inserting a small punch under bottom edge of blade. Repeat these operations, placing straightedge along each side of table, and adjusting the blades if necessary. After all of the blades have been checked and adjusted, place paper or metal shims beneath them so they seat firmly. Tighten the blades securely with the setscrews.

To adjust the table depth gauge, proceed as follows: Place a straightedge on the front table so that one end projects over the cutter blades. Adjust table until blades just touch the straightedge. When table is in this position the depth-gauge pointer should be at the zero reading. If not, loosen setscrew that holds pointer and adjust to zero.

To adjust the fence proceed as follows: Loosen the fence tilt lever (Fig. 2). Using a try square, set the fence perpendicular to the table. Tilt gauge pointer, which should now be at the zero reading. If not, loosen setscrew and adjust pointer to zero.

OPERATING THE JOINTER

In jointing or planing boards, the rear table must always be level with the knives at their highest point. This setting must never be changed except, of course, when operations other than planing are performed. To test the accuracy of the alignment of the rear table with the cutting knives, start the machine and run a test piece of material over the knives for several inches. If the tables are correctly aligned, there will be no space showing between the table and the board as the newly planed surface passes over the rear table. If the rear table is too high there will be a slight raising of the board and the cutters will cut more off the first end of the board than off the rear end. If the rear table has been set too low, light will be visible between the board and the rear table (Fig. 3). When the stock is pushed forward, the front end of the board will eventually drop until it rests on the rear table, causing the blades to cut a notch in the material.

Planing. Wood up to 4½" wide may be planed or surfaced

on the jointer without removing the guard or fence (Fig. 4). For wider boards it is necessary to remove both the guard and the fence. Boards exceeding 4½″ in width can readily be surfaced by moving the guard and the fence, and taking several thin cuts of approximately the same width on the inside and outside. When jointing or planing a board on a jointer, always cut with

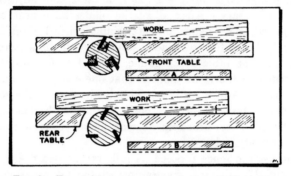

Fig. 3. Top, table set too high; bottom, table set too low.

the grain. If the direction of the grain changes and the jointing is done across or against the grain, feed the stock slowly. Always be sure to examine the material carefully beforehand to make sure that it is free of nails and other obstructions.

Use a wood pusher block when planing boards or strips less than ½″ thick, not only as a safety measure, but to assure accuracy (Fig. 5). It is impossible to hold down thin strips of material with the hand alone and secure a smooth even surface. Material thicker than ½″ can be held down and fed with the hands only. Do not hold the sides or edges of the wood with fingers while the material is passing over the knives.

When it is desired to have the edges square with the surface, set the fence of the jointer to a 90° angle and lay

Fig. 4. Planing boards up to 4½″ wide.

the board on its edge. In feeding the board across the knives, be sure that you hold its entire surface against the fence, exerting as much pressure sideways as down.

Cutting chamfers or bevels. For bevel jointing the same procedure is followed as for planing square edges, except that the fence is adjusted to the correct angle to produce the desired bevel or chamfer. Secure the fence in this position before proceeding to cut the material. Take cuts of medium thickness until the bevel is nearly planed to full shape, then finish with light cuts. Be sure to hold the side of the board in contact with the fence. At the same time hold the board down against the table as you feed it through the machine (Fig. 6).

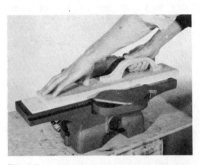

Fig. 5. Always use a pusher when planing thin stock.

Fig. 6. Angular planing with jointer.

Rabbeting. The rabbeting ledge incorporated in the front table of the jointer is merely an extension of the table that helps support the board being rabbeted. To cut a rabbet, remove the guard and slide the fence toward the left side of the table until it is the same distance from the left end of cutter blades as the desired width of the rabbet. Lower the front table to the required depth of rabbet. If the full depth of the rabbet is within the capacity of the machine, make the rabbet in one cut. If the cut is wider or deeper than the capacity of the machine, make it in several cuts, feeding the work slowly (Fig. 7).

Making moldings. A jointer can make only moldings that have a combination of either flat or beveled surfaces. These various cuts and surfaces can be made at different depths and at varying angles. Attractive moldings can be made by combining these cuts. Procedure is exactly the same as for conventional cuts (Fig. 8).

Lubrication. If the machine is used frequently it must be oiled every month. Use SAE 20 machine oil throughout. To oil bearings remove pulley and collar next to bearings. If used

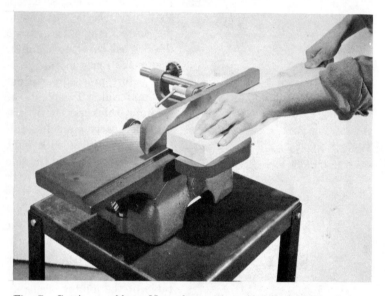

Fig. 7. Cutting a rabbet. Note clearance provided by rabbeting ledge.

infrequently oil every six months. Oil table, frame ways, and all adjusting screws at regular intervals.

Sharpening cutter blades. When the surface of the planed wood begins to have a fuzzy look, or when the stock being jointed begins to chatter, it is necessary to sharpen the cutter blades.

As a general rule, honing the blades with a flat oilstone or medium-grade slipstone is all that is necessary. Before honing, check alignment of blades per directions given in this chapter. Then proceed as follows: Adjust and lock front table ⅛″ below cutting edge of blades. Partly cover sharpening stone with paper to avoid scratching the surface of the table and lay it on the front table. Turn the cutter head so that the stone is resting flat on the bevel of a blade. Hold the cutter head in this position. Rub

Fig. 8. Making moldings. All cuts and surfaces are flat, being made at different depths and angles.

the stone with an even pressure along the length of the blade until the blade is sharp. Treat each blade similarly with exactly the same number of strokes. Readjust the rear table if necessary.

SHAPERS

A shaper is used for straight and irregular shaping, matched shaping, tonguing and grooving, planing, making drop-hinged leaf joints, fluting and reeding, and sanding. It is simple to operate and turns out superior work quickly and accurately. The essential parts of a standard vertical-spindle shaper are shown in Fig. 9. In selecting a shaper be sure that it is sturdy and well constructed. The base should be made of a single casting. All of the controls must be readily accessible. The spindle should preferably be of the stationary type, to insure absolute rigidity at its operating speed of over 10,000 r.p.m. The spindle should be constructed in one piece, of tempered alloy tool steel, and be equipped with a keyed washer and shaft to prevent the cutters from coming loose.

The table must be equipped with a bevel-gear-and-screw mechanism so that it can be moved up and down rapidly. The positioning of the table should be controlled by an easily accessible ball crank and a positive locking device that will clamp the table securely in any desired position (Fig. 10). The bearing

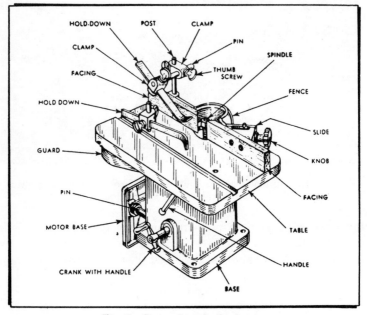

Fig. 9.   Parts of a spindle shaper.

ways of the table should be cast integrally with the base for extreme rigidity. The table top should be accurately ground and well finished to facilitate the sliding of the work. Both the table and the base should be made of heavy iron castings, properly braced to minimize vibration and provide the essential rugged support to accomplish smooth finished work.

A well-designed spindle shaper is equipped with an adjustable fence and hold-downs made of adjustable spring-steel clips. These clips are used to maintain a constant even pressure on the work, holding it securely and firmly against the table and the fence during the entire length of the cut. (Fig. 10).

To hold it in the necessary rigid alignment the shaper should be equipped with two large precision ball bearings. These bearings should be permanently sealed against dust and grit and have an additional cover plate for added protection.

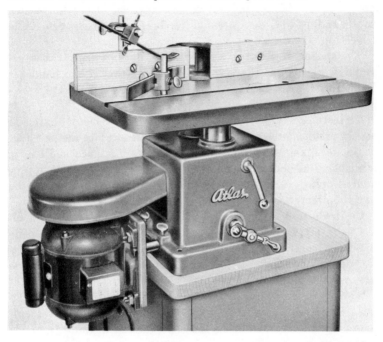

Fig. 10. Spindle shaper, showing motor mounting base and table raising column.

The shaper should be powered with a ⅓ h.p., **3450** r.p.m. capacitor or repulsion-induction type motor and a **3¹¹⁄₁₆″**-diameter motor pulley to obtain a spindle speed of **10,000** r.p.m. This high speed is necessary for the majority of shaper operations.

Assembling. To assemble the shaper remove the fence from the table. Use a cloth soaked with kerosene to remove the usual rust-preventive coating from the surface of the table. Replace the fence and lock in position with the setscrews and washers. Mount the spring hold-down clips. One of these clips is mounted to the fence and the other to the table (Fig. 10). Fasten the two mounting-bracket pins to the motor mounting bracket with the washers and nuts furnished by the manufacturer. Mount the bracket and the belt guard on the rear of the shaper.

Installing. Bolt the shaper to a sturdy level bench that is high enough so that the top of the shaper table is slightly lower than your elbows. Mount the shaper near the rear of the workbench so the adjustable motor mounting bracket extends below the bench top.

The shaper, if possible, should be set up in a central location in the workshop, as the length of the work that it can handle is limited by the distance from the spindle to the walls of the workshop, or to other machines or workbenches.

To install the motor, mount the pulley on the motor shaft and set the motor on the motor mounting bracket. Place the belt over the pulleys, and shift motor until pulleys are aligned and belt is straight. Pull motor back until belt is just tight enough to prevent slipping. Lock motor mounting bracket securely with the two thumbscrews.

Controls and adjustments. The crank handle or wheel on the front of the shaper is used to adjust the table height. The handle or control directly beneath the table locks it securely in the desired position. Before changing the height of the table always release this lock.

Two capscrews are used to lock the fence to the table. To position or set the entire fence for any required depth of cut, loosen these screws, slide the fence the desired distance from the cutting circle, and retighten these two screws.

The knobbed handle of the fence casting controls the positioning of the right fence for depth-of-cut adjustments on operations where the entire edge of the work is to be removed. Always release table fence lockscrew before positioning the right fence.

On a well-designed shaper a machine bolt is used to lock each facing to the fence. To adjust the opening between the faces, loosen the bolts, push the facings to the required position, and retighten. When making these adjustments be sure that the opening is never larger than will just clear the cut.

The only spindle adjustment ever necessary is one to eliminate end play. To make this adjustment loosen the spindle-pulley setscrew. Press spindle downward and push the pulley tightly against the spacer. Lock pulley in this position.

OPERATING THE SPINDLE SHAPER

Types of cutters used. Two types of cutters are available for shaper work. One is the loose type mounted on a safety head, and the other is the solid cutter. The latter is milled from a solid bar of hardened and properly tempered tool steel, and ground to the required shape. It is the safest type of cutter to use and is recommended for the home workshop.

To do creditable work on the spindle shaper, it is not necessary to have many cutters of different shapes and contours. Many different types of moldings can be made with comparatively few cutters (Fig. 11).

Straight shaping. Straight shaping is the process of cutting

Fig. 11. Molding cutters.

a profile or contour on the straight edges of tabletops and benchtops, and cutting moldings on straight lumber.

Select the cutter to be used. Hold spindle firmly with wrench on flat part of the spindle beneath the table. Place the cutter on the spindle and lock it securely in place with the keyed washer and hex nut. At this point check to make sure that the cutter rotates toward the work to be cut. To cut in the desired position on the work, adjust the table to the correct height. Position fence for depth of cut desired and move wood facings of fence just far enough apart to clear the cut. The two fence facings must be aligned for most straight shaping or molding operations. To align the fence facings, place a straightedge against the left one and move the right one up to the straightedge.

Adjust the spring hold-down clips before starting the machine. These clips are used to hold the work firmly against the fence and the table. Do not set clips too tightly against the work—just enough to hold the work down and at the same time permit it to pass the revolving cutters smoothly and evenly. The correct speed to use for straight shaping is about 8000 r.p.m.

Start the machine. Make several trial cuts on pieces of scrap wood to check depth and position of cut before proceeding with the actual work.

Irregular shaping. Irregular shaping is the process of shaping the irregular edges of oval shaped tables, curved legs, chair and table stretchers, and decorative moldings on all types of curved irregular edges (Fig. 12).

For irregular shaping remove the fence and spring hold-down clips and replace with the proper depth collar for the depth of

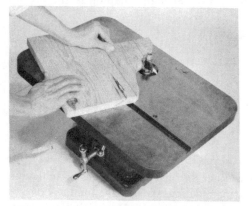

Fig. 12. Irregular shaping on edge of shelf bracket, using shaping depth collar.

the cut to be made. Depth collars are set above or below the cutter or between two cutters, to prevent cutting beyond a certain depth. When the material is cut until its edge strikes the depth collar, the collar naturally prevents the cut from going any farther. The difference in diameter between the cutter and the collar regulates the width of the cut. Lock the collar and cutter on the spindle.

The two methods used for irregular shaping are called irregular shaping to a finished edge and irregular shaping with a template or pattern.

For irregular shaping to a finished edge, finish the edge of the work to the desired shape and sand smooth. Set the cutter on the spindle with the depth collar above it, and adjust it for the required width.

Use the guide pin furnished with the shaper as a fulcrum to support the work until it has been fed into the collar. Place this guide pin in either of the two holes next to the table opening, the right hole if the cutter rotation is clockwise, the left hole if counterclockwise (Fig. 13). The correct speed to use for irregular shaping is 8000 r.p.m. or faster. It is unnecessary to reverse the direction of cut for irregular shaping. Clean cutting can be accomplished both against and with the grain when the cutters are sharp. When cutting against the grain use a slower speed. Make the cut on the bottom, with the work face down and resting on the surface of the shaper table. Make several trial cuts on

Fig. 13. Irregular shaping. Note use of guide pin and shaping depth collar on spindle below cutter.

pieces of scrap wood to check depth and position of cut before proceeding with the actual work.

The template method is usually employed in doing duplicate and matched irregular shaping. The template should be made of plywood, birch, or similar hardwood. Cut it to conform to outline of the work, sand all edges perfectly smooth, and rub a little paraffin wax into them. Place the work face down on the shaper table. Place the template on the work and drive several small wire nails or brads through it, about $\frac{1}{16}''$ into the work to prevent the template from slipping. Adjust the depth collar and cutter for the desired depth of cut. The shaper collar rests against the finished edge of the template and the cutter can cut into the work only as far as the template will permit. Move the template around the entire circumference of the work, keeping its edge in contact with the collar at all times.

Matched shaping, tonguing, and grooving. Matched shaping, sometimes called coped jointing, is used in the construction of cabinets, interior trim, and similar work. A pair of matched cutters is used: one to cut the female portion of the molding forming the joint, and the other to cut the male portion. Matched shaping or coped joints, and tongue-and-groove joints are similar. The procedure for shaping either is exactly the same.

Select a pair of matched cutters of the required size. The female portion of the joint is cut with a single cutter, from $\frac{1}{8}''$ to $\frac{3}{8}''$ or $\frac{1}{2}''$ in width, depending on the thickness of the material. The two methods of making the male portion of this joint are standard procedures. One method is to use a cutter in which a square recess has been ground that will cut a tongue that is a fairly close fit in the female portion of the joint. The other method is to use two cutters of the same outside diameter, with at least a $\frac{1}{2}''$ face on each, with a collar or a spacer washer inserted between them. This separates the cutters so that they will cut a tongue to make a close fit for the female portion of the joint. The latter method is preferable, since the fit of the tongue into the groove can be controlled by varying the thickness of the collar or the spacer washer used.

In making joints of this type the shaper fence is used to guide the work (Fig. 14). Speed and procedure is the same as for straight shaping.

Making dado cuts. Dado cuts are made on a shaper with a male cutter of the required size from a tongue-and-groove cutter set. The procedure is the same as for straight shaping (Fig. 15).

Fig. 14. Matched shaping with the spindle shaper. Cutting tongue for tongue-and-groove joint.

Reeding and fluting. To reed or flute straight or curved irregular work on the shaper, special cutters are required. They are available in a variety of shapes and sizes. The cutting edge

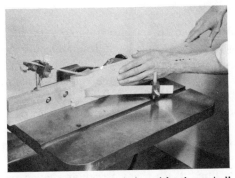

Fig. 15. Cutting a dado with the spindle shaper.

of a reeding cutter consists of two coves coming together in the center of the cutting face. A fluting cutter is the exact opposite and is rounded off on the cutting edge. To save time and to turn out more uniform work when reeding or fluting flat faces, use more than a single cutter. The shaper fence and the hold-down clips are used to guide the work. Procedure is exactly the same as for any other type of straight shaper work.

For curved or irregular work, remove the fence and the spring hold-down clips and replace them with depth collars or a template to gauge the cut. Proceed in the same manner as for irregular shaping. Make a simple jig or template of a piece of wood with a block fastened on each end of the turning. Drive a nail through each of the blocks to act as a center on which to revolve the turning.

Two procedures can be used for gauging the depth of the cut and for guiding the turning against the cutter: one requires the use of depth collars, the other the use of a template. The base board of the jig can be utilized as a template. Where the turning is tapered or curved, it is necessary to taper or curve the edge of the base board to conform.

When the depth collar method is used to determine the depth of the cut, be sure that the collars are of the proper diameter and project beyond the cutter to get a bearing on the turning.

With the template method the cuts may be more accurately gauged and better work accomplished. Cutting is similar to irregular shaping.

Planing. Select a cutter wider than the thickness of the stock. Slide the entire fence to the circumference of the cutting arc. Move the right fence facing back from the left one a distance equal to the depth of cut desired. The left facing acts as a support for the work after it passes the cutter. Move it in and out for planing operations (Fig. 16).

Use the miter gauge attachment to support the work when planing end miter joints.

Drum sanding. Sanding spindles or drums are available for use on the spindle shaper in various types of surfaces graded from rough to fine. With them, irregular shaped pieces of wood are sanded easily and speedily.

To install the sanding drum remove the fence and spring hold-down clips. Set the table slightly above the bottom of the sander, so that all of the wood to be sanded contacts the drum. Install the sanding drum on the spindle (Fig. 17).

For sanding, the spindle speed must be reduced to 1750 r.p.m. A higher speed will burn the wood and glaze the sandpaper.

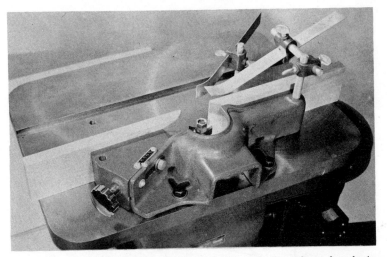

Fig. 16. Left section of spindle shaper fence moves in and out for planing operations. Graduated scale shows depth of cut. Note large opening in fence casting for chip removal.

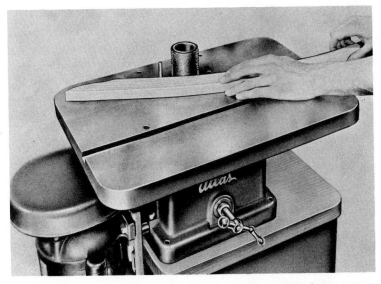

Fig. 17. Using a sanding drum on the vertical shaper.

Lubrication. Keep shaper clean and free from dust at all times. Use SAE 20 machine oil and lubricate regularly at all points shown in Fig. 18. The shaper table should be covered with a film of oil when not in use. If the machine is used frequently, lubricate all points shown at weekly intervals; otherwise inspect and lubricate monthly.

Sharpening cutters. Shaper cutters must be kept as sharp

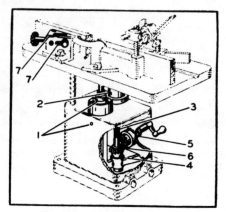

Fig. 18. Lubrication points.

as possible, with special sharpening stones. A flat Arkansas oilstone about 2″ by 6″, and a slipstone made of the same material about 4″ long and tapering from ⅛″ to ⅜″ in thickness, with rounded edges, is required. Also, one about 4″ long and ¼″ square and another 4″ long, 2″ wide, and ½″ thick. An additional oilstone convenient to have on hand is triangular in section with each face 1/16″ wide and 3″ long. With these oilstones it is possible to sharpen almost any cutter used on the shaper.

The action of the cutter when shaping wears the cutting edge. To renew this cutting edge, no great amount of metal need ever be removed at any one time. The cutting angle of the edge must be changed as little as possible.

Select the oilstone that fits the shape or curve of the cutter. Rub the stone lightly, holding it almost flat against the back of the cutting edge. To remove the wire edge that will result from sharpening, lay the cutter flat on the flat oilstone and rub it with a back-and-forth motion.

CHAPTER 14

Sanders

Powered sanders are available in both disc and belt types. Portable belt sanders are used for sanding and finishing work that cannot be done in the home workshop. They come with sanding belts ranging from 1½″ to 3″ or 4″ in width. Their utility is limited to sanding flat surfaces, so they are not especially recommended for use in the home workshop where various-shaped parts have to be done.

A more practical and versatile combination disc-and-belt sander now available is designed to do all types of sanding and finishing (Fig. 1).

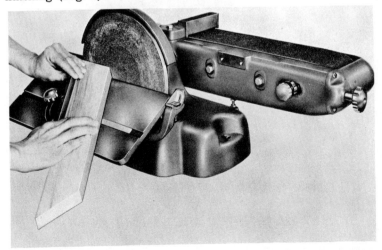

Fig. 1. Disc-and-belt sander for all types of sanding and finishing. Miter gauge on tilted table is used here to finish compound angle with disc sander.

The base and frame of a powered belt-and-disc sander should be constructed of heavy well-braced castings, with the sanding-disc table supported by double trunnions at one end and a single trunnion at the other. To do fine finishing work the belt table must be rigidly braced.

To assure long life and trouble-free performance, both the disc spindle and the belt drums should run on deep-grooved sealed precision ball bearings.

A sanding belt fence should be provided, as it is an essential accessory for all accurate edging operations. The fence should be tiltable 45° both ways from the vertical position with the angle of tilt shown on a graduated scale. To permit duplication of. work without necessity of readjustment, a suitable device should be provided to lock the fence in any desired position (Fig. 2).

The disc table should be tiltable 45° up or down, and be pro-

Fig. 2. A sanding belt fence is essential for accurate edging operations. It tilts 45° both ways from vertical. Angle of tilt is shown on graduated segment.

vided with a lock for securing at any desired angle, with the angle shown on a graduated scale. The table unit should be usable in both belt and disc sanding.

The sander shown in Fig. 1 requires a ¼- or ⅓-h.p., 1725-r.p.m.

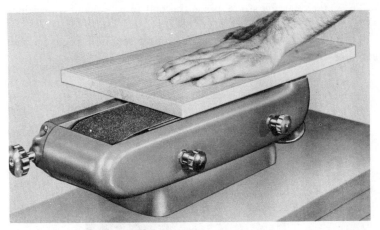

Fig. 3. Using belt sander for finishing the surface of a wide board.

repulsion-induction capacitor motor. This gives it a spindle speed of 1360 r.p.m. and a belt speed of 1150 f.p.m. It is equipped to use a 10″ sanding disc and a sanding belt $37^{13}/_{16}$″ × 4″ wide. Abrasive discs and belts are available in grit sizes ranging from fine to very coarse.

Operation. The belt section of the sander is for sanding wide boards. The disc and guards are easily removable and the belt section of the sander is used as shown in Fig. 3.

To sand concave surfaces remove belt guards and use upper portion of belt (Fig. 4).

To finish a chamfer on the sanding disc, simply tilt table to the required angle and lock in position (Fig. 5).

Fig. 4. Curved pieces may be finished on belt drums when belt guards are removed.

To surface narrow stock, place the belt in a horizontal position (Fig. 6).

To finish the ends of any work to any required angle on the sanding disc, tilt the table up or down (Fig. 7).

Fig. 5. Finishing a chamfer on the sanding disc.

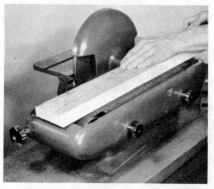

Fig. 6. Surfacing stock on the sanding belt.

To sand the surfaces of small work the belt section is usually used (Fig. 8). Note use of stop fences.

To sand and finish edges of work to any desired angle up to 45° adjust the sanding belt fence to the desired angle and lock it (Fig. 2). Note angle of tilt as shown on graduated segment.

Maintenance. To keep sander in good working condition all parts of the tool must be kept free from all dirt and accumulated sawdust. All moving parts must be lubricated as per lubrication chart furnished with each tool by the manufacturer.

Fig. 7. Finishing the end of a piece of work on the sanding disc.

Fig. 8. A stop fence is necessary in sanding small work on the belt.

CHAPTER 15

Selection and Care of Painting Tools and Equipment

—————————— • ——————————

Next to the actual paints, brushes are the most important tools used for painting and decorating. Good cheap brushes are nonexistent. Cheap brushes will ruin the best painting job. Good-quality brushes, properly taken care of, will ordinarily outlast a half dozen cheap brushes, and in the long run give a great deal more satisfaction and produce cleaner and better work. The cost of the better grade of brushes over a period of time will be considerably less. With few exceptions, all good brushes are made of hog bristles, the best of which are imported from China and Russia. The cheaper, inferior brushes are made of synthetic materials combined with a poor grade of bristle, adulterated with horsehair.

The only type of good brushes made with materials other than bristle are those that are to be used in painting structural iron or steel. Brushes for this purpose can contain a small percentage of horsehair. The paint does not have to be worked into iron or steel surfaces. Horsehair resists abrasion better than hog bristle and a small amount of horsehair will increase the life of a brush used for this purpose. Inferior brushes are cleverly camouflaged and difficult to detect; therefore do not make the mistake of selecting brushes just by appearance. When purchasing brushes select the type best suited for the job. Go to a reliable paint dealer and buy the best brush that he recommends.

All new brushes, no matter how good they are, will probably shed a few bristles. Before putting a brush into paint or varnish rub your hand back and forth across the bristles to work out loose ones.

Even good brushes will sometimes develop defects. All reputable manufacturers guarantee their brushes and will replace any defective brushes returned to them.

CHOOSING THE RIGHT BRUSH FOR THE JOB

Always choose the right type of brush for all painting and decorating work. While there are many types of brushes, you need only purchase from time to time such brushes as are needed.

Descriptions of brushes generally used are as follows:

Flat wall brush. (See Fig. 1.). Flat wall brushes are used for spreading paint on walls and must not be used for applying varnish. They are made of Chinese bristle, vulcanized in rubber, bound in metal, and available in half-inch sizes ranging from 3″ to 5″. A good all-purpose size is one 3½″ or 4″ in width.

Flat woodwork or varnish brush. (See Fig. 2.) Flat woodwork brushes can be used for both paint and varnish. They are

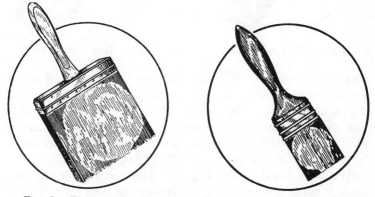

Fig. 1. Flat wall brush.   **Fig. 2.** Flat woodwork or varnish brush.

made of Chinese or Russian hog bristles and are usually metal-bound and vulcanized in rubber. They come in sizes ranging from 1″ to 3″ in width. For working around glass panes in windows and doors, the smaller sizes are preferable. For painting

and varnishing trim and other parts of the house the larger sizes
are generally used.

Flat sash brush.   (See Fig. 3.)   The flat sash brush is similar
to the flat varnish brush, but slightly thinner, and is sometimes
called a trimming brush.   Good-quality sash brushes are vulcanized in rubber and can be used for both paint and varnish.
Available in 1″, 1½″, and 2″ widths.

Oval varnish brush.   (See Fig. 4.)   The oval varnish brush is
an excellent brush made of Chinese bristles.   It is oval in shape

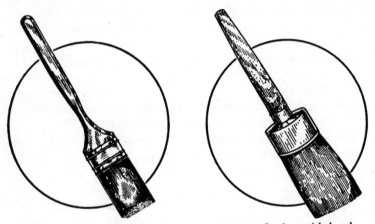

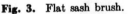

Fig. 3.   Flat sash brush.   **Fig. 4.**   Oval varnish brush.

with an open center.   It is used only for varnishing and is preferred over the modern flat varnish brush by many painters.   It
is available in many sizes, which are designated as 1/0 to 10/0.
The circumferences of these brushes vary with each manufacturer.   The 6/0, a popular size made by a well-known manufacturer, is an oval slightly under 2″ in its greatest width.

Oval sash brush.   (See Fig. 5.)   The oval sash or trimming
brush is made of Chinese bristles and can be used for both paint
and varnish.   They are available vulcanized in rubber in num-
bered sizes from 1 to 10.   The No. 6 brush of a leading manufacturer is a popular size, with a solid oval 1⅛″ in width.

Flat calcimine brush.   (See Fig. 6.)   Good calcimine brushes
should be made of stiff Russian hard bristle.   The Russian variety of bristle is heavier in texture than the Chinese and is

preferable for this particular purpose. They are used principally for painting smooth plastered walls with calcimine and should not be used for any other purpose. Flat calcimine brushes, made of either gray or yellow bristle, are available in 6″, 7″, and 8″ widths. The 7″ is the popular all-around size, with bristles 5¼″ in length.

Dutch calcimine brush. (See Fig. 7.) Calcimine brushes of

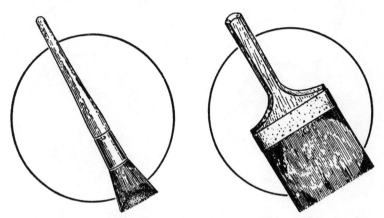

Fig. 5. Oval sash brush.   **Fig. 6.** Flat calcimine brush.

the Dutch type are used for calcimining rough plaster or stucco. They are made of gray Russian bristle, with the bristles set in knots and vulcanized in a solid rubber block, so that they will not pull out. A good general size is 6″ in width with the length of the bristle not exceeding 5″.

Whitewash brush. (See Fig. 8.) Whitewash brushes are usually made of gray and yellow Russian bristles set in cement and leather-bound. They are available in various sizes. The 9″ width is the size generally used. They are used for applying whitewash and exterior cold-water paints.

Duster brush. (See Fig. 9.) The flat type of duster brush is the one most generally used for the removal of dust before painting. The use of a dust brush is essential to clean spots and corners where a cloth will not do an efficient job. There are many types of duster brushes, but the flat variety is more practical. They are made of various kinds of bristles and horsehair and the better types are vulcanized in rubber. It is an inexpensive brush and should be used for dusting only. It is available in one size, 4½" wide.

Radiator brush. (See Fig. 10.) Radiator brushes are made with long handles and a flat, thin structure for painting between

Fig. 7. Dutch calcimine brush.   **Fig. 8.** Whitewash brush.

radiator coils and unreachable places. They are made of black Chinese bristle from 1" to 2½" in width.

Flat artist's brush. (See Fig. 11.) The flat artist's brush is made of black or white Chinese bristle, cement-set and metal-

Fig. 9. Duster brush.   **Fig. 10.** Radiator brush.

bound. It is designed for painting fine lines and for decorating. Available in widths ranging from ¼″ to 2″.

Roof-painting brush. (See Fig. 12.) The roof-painting brush shown at *A* is made of gray Russian bristle, double-nailed and leather-bound and is used for painting shingles. The brush shown

Fig. 11. Flat artist's brush.   **Fig. 12.** Roof-painting brushes.

at *C* is attached to a long handle and is used in the same manner as a broom, for painting large roof surfaces. The roof-painting brush shown at *B* is made of poorer-quality Russian bristle mixed with a percentage of horsehair. It is less expensive than the type previously described but is adequate for painting smaller metal roofs and for applying tar. It is available in two-, three-, and four-knot sizes with bristles about 3½″ in length.

Stippling brush. (See Fig. 13.) Stippling brushes are used to pound or stipple paint that has previously been applied to a smooth plaster wall, so as to give it a stipple effect. Stippling brushes are usually made of stiff gray Russian bristle.

Flat color brush. (See Fig. 14.) Flat color brushes are made of pure squirrel hair, usually called camel's hair, cement-set and bound in brass. They are usually used for the application of

Japan colors. Available in half-inch sizes ranging from 1″ to 3″ in width.

Flowing brush. (See Fig. 15.) Flowing brushes are usually made of a mixture of badger hair and French bristle with an outer layer of pure badger hair, although various other mixtures of hair and bristle are sometimes used. The type shown in Fig.

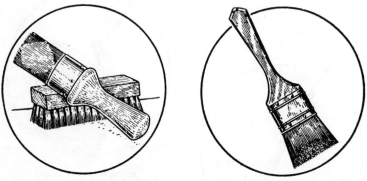

Fig. 13. Stippling brushes.   **Fig. 14.** Flat color brush.

15 is the one most generally used in applying color varnish and finishing coats on automobiles and boats.

Stencil brush. (See Fig. 16.) A stencil brush is a stiff, stubby brush used for stenciling. It is made of tampico or fiber and set in vulcanized rubber.

Waxing brush. (See Fig. 17.) Waxing brushes are used for finishing after wax has been applied to floors. They are equipped with felt protectors, to prevent scarring or marring baseboards. They are made of tampico and fiber, stapled into a solid block $7\frac{1}{4}″ \times 9\frac{1}{4}″$. Available in 15- and 25-pound sizes.

CARE OF BRUSHES

To remove short or loose bristles before using, twirl the brush by rolling the handle between the palms and against the extended fingers of the hand (Fig. 18).

Before using varnish brushes, rinse them in thinner to remove dust. To keep brushes in good condition never suspend or soak them in water. In addition to making the bristles soft and flabby, water will swell the divider or handle of the brush and will cause the brush to spread out, like a mop, and will sometimes break the ferrule.

Never let a brush rest for any length of time on the ends of the

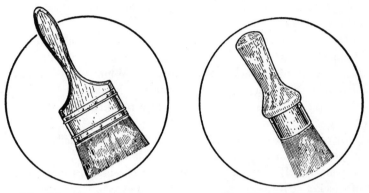

Fig. 15. Flowing brush.   Fig. 16. Stencil brush.

bristles. It will put a kink in them and will ruin the brush.

To keep brushes in good condition when in use, suspend them in the proper thinner with the bristle a short distance from the bottom of the can or paint pot. To suspend a brush properly,

Fig. 17. Waxing brush.   Fig. 18. Twirling brush to re-
                                  move loose bristles.

drill a ⅛" hole through its handle at the proper point so that a stiff wire passing through it and resting upon the upper edge of the can or paint pot will suspend it at the desired height. Several brushes can be hung on the same wire (Fig. 19).

To keep brushes overnight or for several days proceed as follows:

Work out all excess material in the brush on either a board or a newspaper.

If brushes have been used in interior or exterior oil paints they should be suspended in a mixture of two parts of raw linseed oil to one part of a good-quality thinner. While plain turpentine or thinner is often used, it is better to use the thinner specified by the manufacturer of the paint. Before re-using the brush, rinse it in clean thinner.

Brushes that have been used in varnish or enamel should be suspended in a mixture containing equal parts of varnish and turpentine. If pure turpentine is used the brushes may get full of specks. If brushes have been used in synthetic varnishes they must be washed out thoroughly immediately after use, with either the specified thinner or pure turpentine. Synthetic varnishes are labeled as such by all reputable manufacturers.

After using brushes in rubber-base paints, wash them out either in the special thinner recommended for the paint or in lacquer thinner.

Use denatured alcohol to wash out brushes that have been used in shellac. If a shellac brush becomes slightly stiff it will soften when dipped into fresh shellac. Brushes used in water paint must be washed out in warm water and hung up to dry.

Storing brushes. Brushes used in oil paint, varnish, or enamel should be thoroughly washed out in thinner. Use plenty of thinner and then pour the used thinner into a bottle. The color will settle to the bottom and the clear thinner can again be used for cleaning brushes or thinning paint. Follow this cleaning by washing the bristles with hand soap and warm water. Get the suds well into the base of the brush, and rinse. Repeat until no color comes out. Comb bristles straight, shake out all excess water, and lay brush flat. When it is thoroughly dry, wrap it in paper to keep the bristles clean and in shape (Fig. 20).

Other brushes should be treated in the same manner, using for the first cleaning the proper thinner as recommended above.

Do not attempt to clean old brushes with strong soap powders, lye or other detergents, or strong cleaners.

Never leave a brush in benzine or benzine substitutes. The

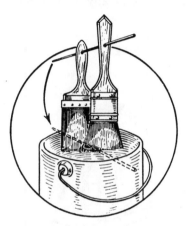

Fig. 19. Supporting brushes in thinner.

Fig. 20. Wrap brushes separately in oiled paper.

brush will become full of hardened specks of paint or varnish which can never be removed.

Never put a brush on a hot radiator to dry. It will take the life out of the bristles and ruin the brush.

OTHER TOOLS

Several ladders, extension brush holders, a putty knife, a scraping knife, and a paint spray gun are additional tools that may be required for painting and decorating work in and around the home.

Stepladders. For interior painting one or two stepladders are necessary. These should be of good, sturdy construction (Fig. 21).

If a scaffold is needed, two sturdy stepladders and a plank approximately 10″ wide, 2″ thick, and as long as required are usually used (Fig. 21).

Long ladders. Long ladders are used for exterior painting.

They are available in lengths of 8', 10', 12', 14', 16', 18', and 20'. The longer lengths are usually adequate for two-story houses. Where areas that are to be painted cannot be reached by the longest of these ladders, an extension ladder is required (Fig. 22).

Extension ladders. For some exterior jobs extension ladders are necessary. Of the several types, one generally used is shown

Fig. 21. Two stepladders and a plank used as a scaffold.
Fig. 24. (circle) Wide scraping knife.

in Fig. 22. Extension ladders consist of several long ladder units plus mechanical devices used to raise, lower, and fasten them. Two-section extension ladders will extend from 20' to 40' and each additional section extends the ladder 10' to 20'. The limited use that most people have for extension ladders does not warrant purchasing this equipment. In most localities they can be rented for any length of time for a nominal sum. Directions for raising and lowering extension ladders vary with the type and are furnished with the equipment.

Fig. 22. Long and extension ladders.

Roof ladder hooks. Roof ladder hooks are safety devices that fasten onto the rungs of the ladder and hook over the ridge of a roof to give a firmer support (Fig. 23).

Steel ladder shoes. These simple little devices should be screwed onto the bottoms of all long ladders to give them a firmer footing.

Putty knife. A putty knife, for applying putty to window sashes, is also a general-utility tool for cleaning and scraping off old paint and dirt prior to painting.

Scraping knife. Scraping knives are available in widths ranging from $2\frac{1}{2}''$ to $4''$. They are used for scraping cracked, scaled, or blistered paint from surfaces before painting (Fig. 24).

Extension brush holders. For painting places that are difficult to reach even with a ladder, an extension brush holder is used. A variety of sizes and lengths can be had (Fig. 25).

SPRAY GUNS AND COMPRESSORS

Extensive exterior painting jobs can be accomplished economically and well with spraying equipment in a fraction of the time required by the use of brushes. Contrary to general belief, even beginners with just a little practice can do a creditable job by this automatic method of paint application. Complete spray-gun equipment, including the necessary compressor, can be rented by the hour or day for a nominal fee.

Spray guns. There are many types and sizes of spray guns, each designed for a specific purpose. A typical general-utility spray gun and its parts is shown in Fig. 26. A paint spray gun is a mechanical means of bringing air and paint together, atomizing the paint stream into a spray of the required size, and ejecting

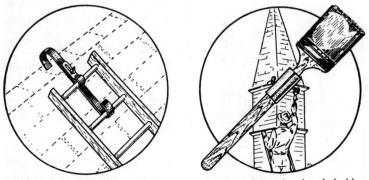

Fig. 23. Roof ladder hook   **Fig. 25.** Extension brush holder.

it by compressed air for the purpose of coating a surface. Each manufacturer furnishes specific directions for the care and the maintenance of his product. While the disassembly, reassembly, and general maintenance directions for each individual type may vary to some extent, the same general technique can be applied to practically all types of spray guns.

The type of gun shown in Fig. 26 has as one of its main features a removable spray head. The advantages of this type of head are: ease of cleaning, and inexpensive replacement in case of damage. If required, extra spray heads can be bought. The method of removing the spray head is shown in Fig. 27.

The principal parts of the spray head are the air cap, fluid tip, fluid needle, baffle, and spray-head barrel (Fig. 28).

The air cap is the part at the front of the gun that directs the compressed air into the paint stream to atomize it and form it into a suitable spray pattern (*A*, Fig. 28).

The fluid tip is another part at the front end of the gun, which meters and directs the material into the air stream. It provides a

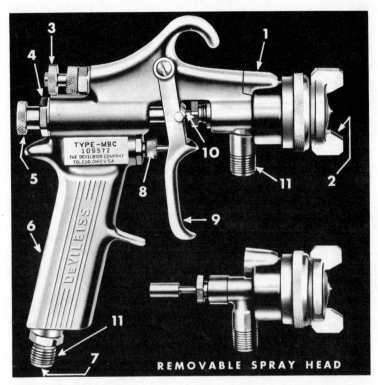

REMOVABLE SPRAY HEAD

Fig. 26. Parts and features of a well-designed, efficient spray gun.

1. Removable spray head. Saves time in changing materials and cleaning.
2. Ball-and-cone principle of nozzle parts assembly. Air-tight seating between air cap and fluid tip assures continuance of correct spray performance.
3. Graduated spray-width adjustment. Easy and instantaneous selection of desired spray width and pattern.
4. Cartridge-type fluid needle adjustment assembly. May be quickly removed and replaced as a unit.
5. Fluid adjustment. Conveniently located for quick, accurate, and easy control of fluid flow.
6. Unbreakable gun body.
7. Large air passage. Affords better atomization at lower air pressure.
8. Cartridge-type air valve. Assures perfect assembly of all parts and economical replacement.
9. Scientifically designed trigger. Gun can be held in all practical spraying positions without fatigue.
10. Stainless-steel fluid needle. Heavy, with large diameter, ground to seat perfectly, and will not rust.
11. Air and fluid connections. A choice of interchangeable thread sizes is available.

self-aligning, concentric seat for the air cap and equalizes the air
leaving the center hole of the cap (*B*, Fig. 28). The opening in the
fluid tip is called the nozzle. The comparative sizes of fluid tips and
standard nozzles are shown in Fig. 29. Standard nozzle sizes are
specified as follows: A, C, D, E, FF, FX, F, G. They are, as a

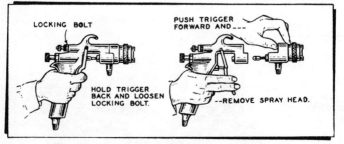

Fig. 27. Removing spray head from gun body.

rule, stamped on the collar of the needle and on the outer edge
of the fluid tip.

The sizes in general use are E, FF, FX, and F.

Air compressors. An air compressor is a mechanism designed
to supply compressed air continuously at a predetermined maximum pressure and the required minimum volume in cubic feet
per minute. There are two general types of air compressors:
single-stage and two-stage.
For all general house-painting
where a maximum pressure
not exceeding 100 pounds is
required, the single-stage type
should be used; this amount
of pressure is more than adequate. Two-stage compressor
outfits are used principally for
various industrial purposes.
These two main types of air
compressing outfits are further divided into many sub-
types. Of these, the two gen-

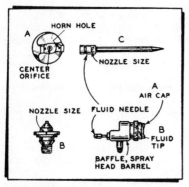

Fig. 28. Parts of spray head.

erally used are those powered by either an electric motor or a gas
engine. Single-stage compressors with suitable power equipment

are available in a self-contained, compact, portable outfit that is equipped with a handle and mounted on wheels so that the compressor can be easily moved to any required spot (Fig. 30). Operation and control of various air compressors differ in detail.

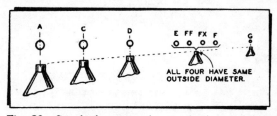

Fig. 29. Standard comparative nozzle sizes and fluid tips.

Follow all the directions for operation of any particular type.

Preparing paint for spraying. Thoroughly mix and stir the paint. If the paint contains any lumps or skins or any foreign matter whatsoever, it must be strained through a fine screen (Fig. 31). Paint that is to be used in a spray gun must be thinned to the consistency specified by the respective manufacturers.

Correct procedure for using spray gun. A spray gun must at all times be held perpendicular to the surface that is being painted; never hold the gun in any other position (Fig. 32). Hold the gun from 6″ to 8″ from the surface to obtain an even spray. A simple method of determining the proper distance is shown in Fig. 32.

Make the strokes with a free arm motion, keeping the gun the same distance from the surface at all points of the stroke (Fig. 33). The ends of all strokes are feathered out by "triggering" the gun, that is, by beginning the stroke before pulling the trigger and releasing the trigger just before ending the stroke. Arcing the gun will result in uneven application and excessive over-spray at the ends of each stroke.

At corners, spray within one or two inches of the end of each side (Fig. 34). Then, holding the gun sideways, do both unsprayed sides of the corner with one stroke. Attempting to spray corners by any other method will not only waste material, but will cause an overspray on the adjacent side (Fig. 35).

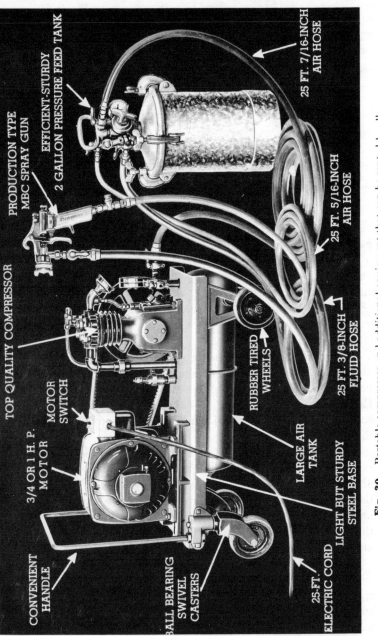

CONVENIENT HANDLE

3/4 OR 1 H. P. MOTOR

MOTOR SWITCH

BALL BEARING SWIVEL CASTERS

25-FT. ELECTRIC CORD

LIGHT BUT STURDY STEEL BASE

LARGE AIR TANK

RUBBER TIRED WHEELS

TOP QUALITY COMPRESSOR

PRODUCTION TYPE MBC SPRAY GUN

EFFICIENT-STURDY 2 GALLON PRESSURE FEED TANK

25 FT. 7/16-INCH AIR HOSE

25 FT. 5/16-INCH AIR HOSE

25 FT. 3/8-INCH FLUID HOSE

Fig. 30. Portable compressor and additional equipment that can be rented locally.

Fig. 31. Preparing paint.

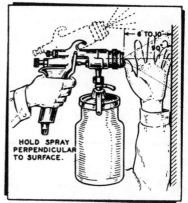

Fig. 32. Using gun, and measuring distance.

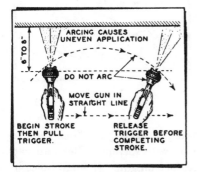

Fig. 33. Correct spray-gun strokes.

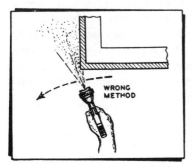

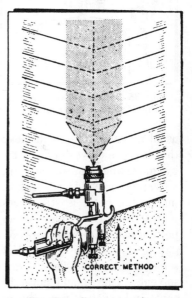

Fig. 34. Corner spraying.

Fig. 35. (left) Incorrect corner spraying causes overspray on adjoining side.

Cleaning and lubricating the gun. A spray gun is a precision instrument and should never be put away, even for a short time, without cleaning. The general procedure is as follows: Remove cup from gun. Hold a cloth over openings in air cap and pull trigger (Fig. 36). Air diverted into fluid passageways forces paint back into container. Empty the container of paint and replace with a small quantity of the type of solvent specified by the manufacturer (Fig. 37). Spray solvent through gun in the

Fig. 36. Cleaning air cap and diverting fluid into container.   **Fig. 37.**

usual manner. This will clean out passageways. Then remove the air cap and wash off the fluid tip with solvent. Clean air cap by immersing it in solvent, and replace on gun. If small holes in air cap become clogged, soak the air cap in the solvent. If reaming of the holes is still necessary after this procedure, use a matchstick, broom straw, or any other soft, thin implement. Do not dig out holes with wires or nails as cap may be permanently damaged by this practice. Note: It is a common practice among some mechanics to clean spray guns by placing the entire gun in solvent. This should never be done, as solvents remove lubricants and eventually dry out packings.

CHAPTER 16

Paints, Painting, and Finishing Procedures

Wood and wood products in a variety of species, grain patterns, texture, and colors are available for use as exterior and interior surfaces. These wood surfaces can be finished quite effectively by several different methods. Painting, which totally obscures the wood grain, is used to achieve a particular color decor. Penetrating-type preservatives and pigmented stains permit some or all of the wood grain and texture to show and provide a special color effect as well as a natural or rustic appearance. The type of finish, painted or natural, often depends on the wood to be finished.

EFFECT OF WOOD PROPERTIES

Wood surfaces that shrink and swell the least are best for painting. For this reason, vertical- or edge-grained surfaces are far better than flat-grained surfaces of any species. Also, because the swelling of wood is directly proportional to density, *low-density* species are preferred over high-density and dense wood surfaces with flat grain have been stabilized with a resin-treated paper overlay, such as overlaid exterior plywood and lumber, to make them excellent for painting.

Medium-density fiberboard products fabricated with a uniform, low-density surface for exterior use are often painted, but little is known of their long-time performance. The most widely used species for exterior siding to be painted are vertical-grained western red cedar and redwood. These species are classified in

Group I, those woods easiest to keep painted. (*See* Table **7**.) Other species in Group I are excellent for painting but are not generally available in all parts of the country.

Species that are not normally cut as vertical-grained lumber, are high in density (swelling), or have defects such as knots or pitch, are classified in Groups II through V, depending upon their general paint-holding characteristics. Many species in Groups II through IV are commonly painted, particularly the pines, Douglas fir, and spruce. These species generally require more care and attention than the species in Group I. Resinous species should be thoroughly kiln-dried at temperatures that will effectively set the pitch.

The properties of wood that detract from its paintability do not necessarily affect the finishing of such boards naturally with penetrating preservatives and stains. These finishes penetrate into wood without forming a continuous film on the surface. Therefore, they will not blister, crack, or peel even if excessive moisture penetrates into wood. One way to further improve the performance of penetrating finishes is to leave the wood surface rough-sawn. Allowing the high-density, flat-grained wood surfaces of lumber and plywood to weather several months also roughens the surface and improves it for staining. Rough-textured surfaces absorb more of the preservative and stain, insuring a more durable finish.

NATURAL FINISHES FOR EXTERIOR WOOD

The simplest of *natural finishes* for wood is natural weathering. Without paint or treatment of any kind, wood surfaces change in color and texture in a few months or years, and then may stay almost unaltered for a long time if the wood does not decay. Generally, the dark-colored woods become lighter and the light-colored woods become darker. As weathering continues, all woods become gray, accompanied by degradation of the wood cells at the surface. Unfinished wood will wear away at the rate of about ¼″ in one hundred years.

Weathered Wood

The appearance of *weathered wood* is affected by dark-colored spores and mycelia of fungi or mildew on the surface, which give the wood a dark gray blotchy and unsightly appearance. Highly colored wood extractives in such species as western red cedar and redwood also influence the color of weathered wood. The dark brown color may persist for a long time in areas not exposed to the sun and where the extractives are not removed by rain.

With *naturally weathered wood*, it is important to avoid the unsightly effect of rusting nails. Iron nails rust rapidly and produce a severe brown or black discoloration. Because of these nails rusting, *only* aluminum or stainless steel nails should be used for natural finishes.

Water-Repellent Preservatives

The *natural weathering of wood* may be modified by *treatment* with water-repellent finishes that contain a preservative (usually pentachlorophenol), a small amount of resin, and a very small amount of a water repellent which frequently is wax or waxlike in nature. The treatment, which penetrates the wood surface, retards the growth of mildew, prevents water staining of the ends of the boards, reduces warping, and protects species that have a low natural resistance to decay. A clear, golden tan color can be achieved on such popular sidings as smooth or rough-sawn western red cedar and redwood.

The preservative solution can be easily applied by dipping, brushing, or spraying. All lap and butt joints, edges, and ends of boards should be liberally treated. Rough surfaces will absorb more solution than smoothly planed surfaces and be more durable.

The initial application to smooth surfaces is usually short-lived. When the surfaces start to show a blotchy discoloration due to extractives or mildew, clean them with a detergent solution and re-treat following thorough drying. During the first two or three years, the finish may have to be applied every year or so. After weathering to uniform color, the treatments are more durable and need refinishing only when the surface becomes unevenly colored.

Pigmented colors can also be added to the water-repellent preservative solutions to provide special color effects. Two or six

TABLE 7

Characteristics of woods for painting and finishing

(Omissions in the table indicate inadequate data for classification)

Wood	Ease of keeping well-painted I—easiest V—most exacting [1]	Weathering		Appearance	
		Resistance to cupping 1—best 4—worst	Conspicuousness of checking 1—least 2—most	Color of heartwood (sapwood is always light)	Degree of figure on flat-grained surface
SOFTWOODS					
Cedar:					
Alaska	I	1	1	Yellow	Faint
California incense	I			Brown	Do.
Port-Orford	I		1	Cream	Do.
Western redcedar	I	1	1	Brown	Distinct
White	I	1		Light brown	Do.
Cypress	I	1	1	--do--	Strong
Redwood	I	1	1	Dark brown	Distinct
Pine:					
Eastern white	II	2	2	Cream	Faint
Sugar	II	2	2	--do--	Do.
Western white	II	2	2	--do--	Do.
Ponderosa	III	2	2	--do--	Distinct
Fir, commercial white	III	2	2	White	Faint
Hemlock	III	2	2	Pale brown	Do.

Wood				Color	Odor
Spruce	III	2	2	White	Do.
Douglas-fir (lumber and plywood)	IV	2	2	Pale red	Strong
Larch	IV	2	2	Brown	Do.
Pine:					
Norway	IV	2	2	Light brown	Distinct
Southern (lumber and plywood)	IV	2	2	do	Strong
Tamarack	IV	2	2	Brown	Do.
HARDWOODS					
Alder	III	2	1	Pale brown	Faint
Aspen	III	2	2	do	Do.
Basswood	III	4	2	Cream	Do.
Cottonwood	III	2	2	White	Do.
Magnolia	III	2	—	Pale brown	Do.
Poplar	III	4	1	do	Do.
Beech	IV	4	2	do	Do.
Birch	IV	4	2	Light brown	Do.
Gum	IV	4	2	Brown	Do.
Maple	IV	4	2	Light brown	Do.
Sycamore	IV	4		Pale brown	Do.
Ash	V or III	4	2	Light brown	Distinct
Butternut	V or III			do	Faint
Cherry	V or III	3		Brown	Do.
Chestnut	V or III	3	2	Light brown	Distinct
Walnut	V or IV	4	2	Dark brown	Do.
Elm	V or IV	4	2	Brown	Do.
Hickory	V or IV	4	2	Light brown	Do.
Oak, white	V or IV	4	2	Brown	Do.
Oak, red	V or IV	4	2	do	Do.

[1] Woods ranked in group V for *ease of keeping well-painted* are hardwoods with large pores that need filling with wood filler for durable painting. When so filled before painting, the second classification recorded in the table applies.

fluid ounces of colors in oil or tinting colors can be added to each gallon of treating solution. Light brown colors which match the natural color of the wood and extractives are preferred. The addition of pigment to the finish helps to stabilize the color and increases the durability of the finish. In applying pigmented systems, a complete course of siding should be finished at one time to prevent lapping.

Pigmented Penetrating Stains

The *pigmented penetrating stains* are semitransparent, permitting much of the grain pattern to show through, and penetrate into the wood without forming a continuous film on the surface. They will not blister, crack, or peel even if excessive moisture enters the wood.

Penetrating stains are suitable for both smooth and rough-textured surfaces. However, their performance is markedly improved if applied to rough-sawn, weathered, or rough-textured wood. They are especially effective on lumber and plywood that does not hold paint well, such as flat-grained surfaces of dense species. One coat of penetrating stain applied to smooth surfaces may last only two to four years, but the second application, after the surface has roughened by weathering, will last eight to ten years. A finish life of close to ten years can be achieved initially by applying two coats of stain to rough-sawn surfaces. Two-coat staining is usually best for the highly adsorptive rough-sawn or weathered surfaces to reduce lapping or uneven stain application. The second coat should always be applied the same day as the first coat and before the first coat dries.

An effective stain of this type is the Forest Products Laboratory natural finish. This finish has a linseed oil vehicle; a fungicide, pentachlorophenol, that protects the oil from mildew; and a water-repellent, paraffin wax, that protects the wood from excessive penetration of water. Durable red and brown iron oxide pigments simulate the natural colors of redwood and cedar. A variety of colors can be achieved with this finish, but the more durable ones are considered to be the red and brown iron oxide stains.

PAINTS FOR EXTERIOR WOOD

Of all the finishes, *paints* provide the most protection for wood against weathering and offer the widest selection of colors. A nonporous paint film retards penetration of moisture and reduces discoloration by wood extractives, paint peeling, and checking and warping of the wood. Paint is *not* a preservative, and it will not prevent decay if conditions are favorable for fungal growth. Original and maintenance costs are usually higher for a paint finish than for a water-repellent preservative or penetrating stain finish. The durability of paint coatings on exterior wood is affected both by variables in the wood surface and type of paint.

Application of Paint

Exterior wood surfaces can be very effectively painted by following a simple three-step procedure:

Step 1. *Water-repellent preservative treatment.* Be sure that *wood siding* and *trim* have been treated with water-repellent preservative to protect them against the entrance of rain and heavy dew at joints. If treated exterior woodwork was not installed, treat it by brushing or spraying in place. Be sure to brush well into the lap and butt joints, especially re-treating cut ends. Allow two warm, sunny days for adequate drying of the treatment before painting.

Step 2. *Primer. New wood* should be given three coats of paint. The first or prime coat is the most important and should be applied soon after the woodwork is erected; and topcoats should be applied within two days to two weeks. Use a nonporous linseed oil primer free of zinc pigments (Federal Specification TT-P-25). Apply enough primer to obscure the wood grain. Many painters tend to spread primer too thinly. For best results, be sure to follow the spreading rates recommended by the manufacturer, or approximately 400 to 450 square feet per gallon for a paint that is about 85 per cent solids by weight. A properly applied coat of a nonporous house paint primer will greatly reduce moisture blistering, peeling, and staining of paint by wood extractives.

The wood primer is *not* suitable for galvanized iron. Allow such surfaces to weather for several months and then prime with an appropriate primer, such as linseed oil or resin vehicle pigmented with metallic zinc dust (about 80 per cent) and zinc oxide (about 20 per cent).

Step 3. *Finish Coats.* When applying topcoats over the primer on new wood proceed as follows:

(1) Use two coats of a wood-quality latex, alkyd, or oil-base house paint over the nonporous primer. This is particularly important for areas that are fully exposed to the weather, such as the south side of a house.

(2) To avoid future separation between coats of paint, or intercoat peeling, apply the first topcoat within two weeks after the primer and the second within two weeks of the first.

(3) To avoid temperature blistering, *do not* apply oil-base paints on a cool surface that will be heated by the sun within a few hours. Follow the sun around the house. Temperature blistering is most common with thickly applied paints of dark colors. The blisters usually show up in the last coat of paint and occur within a few hours to one or two days after painting. They do not contain water.

(4) To avoid the wrinkling, fading, or loss of gloss of oil-base paint, and streaking of latex paints, do not paint in the evenings of cool spring and fall days when heavy dews are frequent before the surface of the paint has dried.

Repainting

(1) Repaint *only* when the old paint has worn thin and no longer protects the wood. Faded or dirty paint can often be freshened by washing. Where wood surfaces are exposed, spot prime with a zinc-free linseed oil primer before applying the finish coat. Repainting too frequently produces an excessively thick film that is more sensitive to the weather and also likely to crack abnormally across the grain of the paint. The grain of the paint is in the direction of the last brush strokes. Complete paint removal is the only cure for cross-grain cracking.

(2) Use the same brand and type of paint originally applied for the topcoat. A change is advisable only if a paint has given trouble. When repainting with latex paint, apply a nonporous, oil-base primer overall before applying the latex paint.

(3) To avoid intercoat peeling, which indicates a weak bond between coats of paint, clean the old painted surface well and allow no more than two weeks between coats in two-coat repainting. *Do not* repaint sheltered areas, such as eaves and porch ceilings, every time the weathered body of the house is painted. In repainting sheltered areas, wash the old paint surface with trisodium phosphate or with a detergent solution to remove surface contaminants that will interfere with adhesion of the new coat of paint. Following washing, rinse sheltered areas with large amounts of water and let areas dry thoroughly before repainting. When intercoat peeling does occur, complete paint removal is the only satisfactory procedure.

Blistering and Peeling

When too much water gets into paint or wood, the paint may blister and peel. The moisture blisters normally appear first and the peeling follows. But sometimes the paint peels without blistering. At other times the blisters go unnoticed. Moisture blisters usually contain water when they form, or soon afterward, and eventually dry out. Small blisters may disappear completely on drying. However, fairly large blisters may leave a rough spot on the surface. If the blistering is severe, the paint may peel.

New, thin coatings are more likely to blister because of too much moisture under them than old, thick coatings. The older and thicker coatings are too rigid to stretch, as they must do to blister, and so are more prone to cracking and peeling.

House construction features that will *minimize* water damage of outside paint are: (a) wide roof overhang, (b) wide flashing under shingles at roof edges, (c) effective vapor barriers, (d) adequate eave troughs and properly hung downspouts, and (e) adequate ventilation of the house. If these features are lacking in a new house, persistent blistering and peeling may occur.

Discoloration by Extractives

Water-soluble color extractives occur naturally in western red cedar and redwood. It is to these substances that the heartwood of these two species owes its attractive color, good stability, and natural decay resistance. *Discoloration* occurs when the *extractives* are dissolved and leached from the wood by water. When the solution of extractives reaches the painted surface, the water evaporates, leaving the extractives as a reddish-brown stain. The water that gets behind the paint and causes moisture blisters also causes migration of extractives. The discoloration produced by water wetting the siding from the back side frequently forms a rundown or streaked pattern.

The *emulsion paints* and the so-called *breather* or *low-luster oil paints* are more porous than conventional oil paints. If these paints are used on new wood without a good oil primer, or if any paint is applied too thinly on new wood (*for example,* a skimpy two-coat paint job), rain or even heavy dew can penetrate the coating and reach the wood. When the water dries from the wood, the extractives are brought to the surface of the paint. Discoloration of paint by this process forms a diffused pattern.

On rough surfaces, such as shingles, machine-grooved shakes, and rough-sawn lumber sidings, it is difficult to obtain an adequately thick coating on the high points. Therefore, extractive staining is more likely to occur on such surfaces by water penetrating through the coating. But the reddish-brown extractives will be less conspicuous if dark-colored paints are used.

Effect of Impregnated Preservatives on Painting

Wood treated with the water-soluble preservatives in common use can be painted satisfactorily after it is redried. The coating may not last quite as long as it would have on untreated wood, but there is no vast difference. A slight loss in durability is not enough to offer any practical objection to using treated wood where preservation against decay is necessary, protection against weathering desired, and appearance of painted wood important. When such treated wood is used indoors in textile or pulpmills, or other places where the relative humidity may be above 90 per cent for long periods, paint may discolor or preservative solution exude. Coal-tar creosote or other dark oily preservatives tend to stain through paint unless the treated wood has been exposed to the weather for many months before it is painted.

Wood treated with oilborne, chlorinated phenols can be painted only when the solvent oils have evaporated completely from the treated wood. If volatile solvents that evaporate rapidly are

used for the treating solution, such as in water-repellent preservatives, painting can be done only after the treated wood
has dried.

INTERIOR PAINTING

For an attractive, long-lasting paint job, you need to use a
good-quality paint; properly prepare the surface for painting;
and apply the paint correctly. Preparation of the surface—cleaning and patching—may take the most time in painting, but it
is the most important part of the job. Even the best paint will
not adhere well to an excessively dirty or greasy surface or hide
large cracks or other mars.

Paint Selection

Many different kinds and formulations of paints and other finishes are available for interior use. And new ones frequently
appear on the market.

Before making your selection use Table 8 as a guide for selecting paint. For a more specific selection consult your local paint
dealer. Reputable paint dealers keep abreast of the newest developments in the paint industry and stock the newest formulations.

Dripless paint is an example of a fairly recent development.
It has a jelled consistency in the can, but it loses that form when
picked up on a brush or roller and spreads evenly and smoothly.
It is particularly convenient when painting a ceiling.

The usual interior paint job consists of painting wallboard or
plaster walls and ceilings, woodwork, and wood windows and
doors. For these surfaces you need to choose first between
solvent-thinned paint (commonly called oil-based paint) and
water-thinned paint (commonly called latex paint, but not necessarily latex), and then between a gloss, semigloss, or flat finish.
(Enamels, which are made with a varnish, or resin, base instead
of the usual linseed-oil vehicle, are included under the broad oil-
paint grouping.)

Oil-based paints are very durable, are highly resistant to staining and damage, can withstand frequent scrubbings, and give
good one-coat coverage. Many latex paints are advertised as
having similar properties.

TABLE 8

Guide for selecting paint

	Aluminum paint	Casein	Cement base paint	Emulsion paint (including latex)	Enamel	Flat paint	Floor paint or enamel	Floor varnish	Interior varnish	Metal primer	Rubber base paint (not latex)	Sealer or undercoater	Semigloss paint	Shellac	Stain	Wax (emulsion)	Wax (liquid or paste)
Floors:																	
Asphalt tile																	X•
Concrete																X•	X•
Linoleum							X							X		X	X
Vinyl and rubber							X	X								X	X
Wood							X•	X•									X
Masonry:																	
Old	X	X	X	X	X•	X•					X	X	X•				
New			X	X	X•	X•					X	X	X•				
Metal:																	
Heating ducts	X				X•	X•				X	X		X•				
Radiators	X				X•	X•				X	X		X•				
Stairs:																	
Treads							X	X						X	X		
Risers					X•	X•			X		X		X•	X	X		
Walls and ceilings:																	
Kitchen and bathroom				X	X•						X	X	X•				
Plaster		X		X		X•					X	X	X•				
Wallboard		X		X		X•					X	X	X•				
Wood paneling				X•		X•			X								
Wood trim				X•	X•	X•			X		X	X	X•	X	X		X
Windows:																	
Aluminum	X				X•	X•				X	X		X•				
Steel	X				X•	X•				X	X		X•				
Wood sill					X•				X			X		**X**			

Black dot (X•) indicates that a primer or sealer may be necessary before the finishing coat (unless the surface has been previously finished).

The main advantages of latex paint are easier application, faster drying, and simpler tool cleanup. The brushes, rollers, and other equipment can be easily cleaned with water.

Both oil-based paint and latex paint are now available in gloss, semigloss, and flat finishes. Glossy finishes look shiny and clean easily. Flat finishes show dirt more readily but absorb light and, therefore, reduce glare. Semigloss finishes have properties of both glossy and flat finishes.

Because enamel is durable and easy to clean, semigloss or full-gloss enamel is recommended for woodwork and for the walls of kitchens, bathrooms, and laundry rooms. For the walls of nurseries and other playrooms, either oil-based or latex semigloss enamel paint is suggested. Flat paint is generally used for the walls of living rooms, dining rooms, and other nonwork or non-play rooms.

COLOR

Paints are available in a wide range of colors and shades. Dealers usually carry color charts showing the different possibilities. Some of the colors are ready mixed; others the dealer has to mix by adding or combining different colors.

Color selection is mostly a matter of personal preference. Here are some points to keep in mind in selecting your colors:

1. Light colors make a small room seem larger. Conversely, dark colors make an overly large room appear smaller.

2. Bright walls in a large room detract from otherwise decorative furnishings.

3. Ceilings appear lower when darker than the walls and higher when lighter than the walls.

4. Paint generally dries to a slightly different color or shade. For a fast preview of the final color, brush a sample swatch of the paint on a piece of clean, white blotting paper. The blotting paper will immediately absorb the wet gloss, and the color on the paper will be about the color of the paint when it dries on the wall.

5. Colors often change under artificial lighting. Look at color swatches both in daylight and under artificial lighting.

QUANTITY

For large jobs, paint is usually bought by the gallon. The label usually indicates the number of square feet a gallon will cover when applied as directed. To determine the number of gallons you need:

1. Find the area of the walls in square feet by multiplying the distance around the room by the height of the walls. (This figure will include door and window space.)

2. From this figure, subtract *one-half* of the total area, in square feet, taken up by doors and windows. To find this area, multiply the height of each unit by its width; then add the results.

3. Divide the figure obtained in step 2 by the number of square feet a gallon will cover. Then multiply by the number of coats to be applied. The result is the number of gallons needed.

Ceilings are frequently painted a different color or shade (usually white) than the walls and need to be figured separately. To find the square-foot area of the ceiling, multiply the length by the width.

Keep in mind that unpainted plaster and wallboard soak up more paint than previously painted walls and, therefore, require more paint or primer.

Some paints are guaranteed to give one-coat coverage over all or most colors if applied as directed at a rate not exceeding the number of square feet specified on the label of the paint container.

Woodwork

Woodwork (windows, doors, and baseboards) usually has a glossy finish. First, wash the surface to remove dirt and grease, and then sand it lightly to *cut* the finish so that the new paint can get a good hold. After sanding, wipe the surface to remove the dust.

You can buy liquid preparations that will soften hard, glossy finishes to provide good adhesion for the new paint.

If there are any bare spots in the wood, touch them up with an undercoater or with pigmented shellac before you paint.

Application

Read the label on the paint can before you start painting. It will contain general application instructions and may contain special instructions.

EQUIPMENT

Interior painting is usually done with brushes or with brushes and rollers (Fig. 1). Indoor spray painting is not generally done by the homeowner, except for small jobs using pressurized cans of paint. (*See* Chap. 15.)

For speed and convenience, use a roller on the walls, ceilings, and other large surfaces, and then use a brush at corners, along

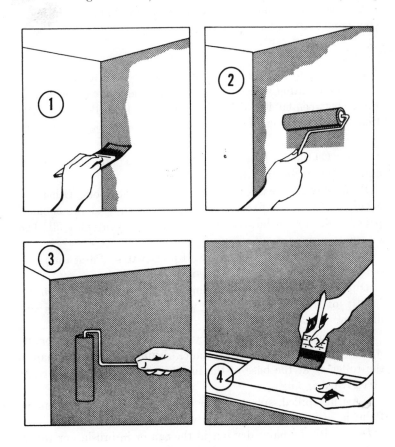

Fig. 1.

edges, and in other places that you cannot reach with a roller. Woodwork is usually painted with a brush.

Special-shaped rollers and other applicators are available for painting woodwork, corners, edges, and other close places. Some may work fine; others, not so well. You may find that a small brush is still best for such work.

Different kinds of brushes and rollers are recommended for use with different kinds of paint. *For example,* short-nap rollers are best for applying gloss enamel on smooth surfaces. Check with your paint dealer on what kind of brush or roller to buy.

You will need some other equipment for indoor painting: a step-ladder, drop cloths, and wiping rags.

PAINTING TIPS

For an easier and better paint job proceed as follows:

Do the painting when the room temperature is comfortable for work (between 60°F and 70°F). And provide good cross ventilation both to shorten the drying time and to remove fumes and odors.

Note: Check the label on the paint can for any special application and drying instructions.

Preferably, remove all furnishings from the room. Otherwise, cover the furniture, fixtures, and floor with drop cloths or newspapers. No matter how careful you may be, you will spill, drip, or splatter some paint.

Remove all light-switch and wall-plug plates. Paint the plates before you replace them after painting the room.

Dip your brush into the paint no more than one-third the length of the bristles. This will minimize splattering and dripping.

When using latex paint, wash your brush or roller occasionally with water. A buildup of the quick-drying paint in the nap of the roller or at the base of the bristles of the brush could cause excessive dripping.

Wipe up spilled, splattered, or dripped paint as you go along. Paint is easier to clean up when wet.

Do not let the paint dry out in the can or in brushes or rollers between jobs or during long interruptions in a job. After each job, replace the can lid, making sure that it is on tightly and clean brushes or rollers. During long interruptions in a job, also replace the can lid and either clean brushes or rollers or suspend them in water.

SAFETY TIPS

For a safer paint job proceed as follows:

Never paint in a completely closed room, and use caution when painting in a room where there is an open flame or fire. Some paints give off fumes that are flammable or dangerous to breathe or both. *(Avoid prolonged exposure to paint fumes for a day or two after painting. Such fumes can be especially harmful to canaries or other pet birds.)*

Use a sturdy stepladder or other support when painting high places. *Be sure* that the ladder is positioned firmly, with the legs fully opened and locked in position.

Face the ladder when climbing up or down it, holding on with at least one hand. Lean toward the ladder when painting.

Do not overreach when painting. Move the ladder frequently rather than risk a fall. And, to avoid spilling the paint, take the few seconds required to remove the paint can from the ladder before you move it.

When you finish painting, dispose of the used rags by putting them in a covered metal can. If left lying around, the oily rags could catch fire by spontaneous combustion.

Store paint in a safe, but well-ventilated, place where children and pets cannot get to it. A locked cabinet is ideal if well ventilated. Unless needed for retouching, small quantities of paint may not be worth saving.

PROCEDURE

Paint the ceiling first. *Do not* try to paint too wide a strip at a time. The next strip should be started and lapped into the previous one before the previous one dries.

If you are putting two coats on the ceiling, apply the second coat, and *cut in* at the junction with the walls, before you paint the walls.

When painting walls with a roller proceed as follows: (1) Start painting a wall at the upper left-hand corner, brush a strip just below the ceiling line for a width of 2'. (Left-handed persons may find it more convenient to start at the upper right-hand corner.) Also paint a strip along the left edge from the ceiling to the floor. (2) Starting in an unpainted area, roll upward toward the painted area. (3) Complete an area about 2′ wide and 3′ deep at a time. (4) At the bottom of the wall, *cut in* with the brush where you could not reach with the roller. Use a cardboard guard to protect the woodwork. (*See* Fig. 1.)

Paint the woodwork (windows, doors, and baseboards) last, preferably after the walls are completely dry.

Flush doors can be painted with a roller. On paneled doors, some parts can be painted with a roller, other sections will require a brush. (You may prefer your doors and other trim in natural color.)

Paint the parts of a window in the order shown in Fig. 2: (1) mullions, (2) horizontal of sash, (3) verticals of sash, (4) verticals of frame, (5) horizontal frame and sill. Windows are easier to paint and to clean afterward if the glass is masked.

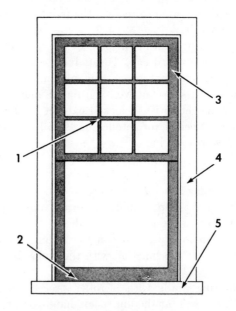

Fig. 2.

Both masking tape and liquid masking are available at local hardware and paint stores.

A simple way to protect the glass is to cover it with a piece of wet newspaper. The moisture will paste the newspaper to the glass and also prevent paint from soaking into the absorbent paper. When you strip the paper from the glass after painting, the paint will come with it.

CLEANUP

Brushes, rollers, and other equipment should be cleaned as soon as possible after use.

Equipment used to apply latex paint can be easily cleaned with soap and water. Rinse thoroughly.

Equipment used to apply oil-base paint may be a little harder to clean. Soak brushes in turpentine or thinner long enough to loosen the paint. Then work the bristles against the bottom of the container to release the paint. To release the paint in the center of the brush, squeeze or work the bristles between the thumb and forefinger. Rinse the brush in the turpentine or thinner again, and, if necessary, wash it in mild soapsuds and rinse in clear water.

PAINTING PLYWOOD

Fir plywood has a tendency to show grain pattern and to "check" after being painted, but with proper priming or sealing this versatile material can be painted, enameled or varnished as attractively as any other wood surface.

Procedures. The first step, of course, is to prepare the surface which must be smooth, clean and without any traces of oil, grease or laminating glue. Nail holes and wood blemishes should be filled and sanded, and the sandings removed with a cloth dampened with turpentine or odorless solvent.

Paints. For an *opaque finish* which hides the grain completely, the best results are obtained in the following manner:

Brush on a coat of flat oil or alkyd paint, enamel undercoat or penetrating resin sealer. *Do not* use a water-thinned latex paint for this coat, because the water may raise the grain. The flat paint may be thinned slightly as directed on the label to make it more brushable. Sand lightly and dust clean as described.

Then apply a second coat. If the finish coat is to be a gloss enamel, make this second coat a 50-50 mixture of enamel undercoat and the finish coat. When dry, sand lightly. Lastly, apply the top coat as it comes from the can.

If the top coat is to be a latex paint, then the prime coat should be either a clear resin sealer or a flat white oil paint. Finish according to the latex maker's directions for a sealed surface.

For a *clear* or *natural finish* which permits the wood grain to show through, first select plywood with an attractive grain pattern, free of blemishes and insert "plugs." Sand smooth and clean before applying any finish. To retain the completely natural appearance of the wood, first apply a coat of the clear resin sealer. After it has dried, sand to remove gloss and follow with one or two coats of flat varnish or brushing lacquer.

For *blond effects,* brush on a coat of white pigmented resin sealer thinned according to label instruction or use a white interior undercoat thinned 50-50 with turpentine or odorless solvent. After 10 to 15 minutes, dry-brush with the grain or wipe with a dry cloth. This lets the grain show through. After this coat has dried, sand lightly. Then seal with a coat of clear resin sealer, and sand lightly with fine sandpaper when dry.

At this point it is also possible to impart any desired color to the wood. Use tinted interior undercoat, thinned enamel, pigmented resin sealer (or clear sealer tinted with colors in oil) or colors in oil. Light stains may also be used. Sand lightly when dry.

If a *colored grain effect* is desired, some craftsmen do not whiten the wood as a first step. Instead, they tint clear or white resin sealer with the colors in oil to the desired shade, reduced 25 per cent with proper solvent. This is brushed on and allowed to set a few minutes, then rubbed into the pores of the wood and finally wiped off with the grain. After the surface is completely dry, it is sanded smooth and followed with the desired topcoat of varnish or brushing lacquer.

PAINTING CONTRACTORS

You may prefer to have all or part of your painting done by

a professional painter. Painting contractors usually offer three grades of paint jobs, such as *premium, standard,* and *minimum.* The difference is in the quality and cost of the work.

When you hire a contractor, it is a good idea to get a signed agreement specifying the following:

The specific price for the job.

Exactly what areas or surfaces are to be painted.

The types, brands, and quality of paints to be used and the number of coats, including primer coats, to be applied.

The measures to be taken to protect the floors, furnishings, and other parts of the house.

A completion date (allowing for possible delays, *for example,* because of bad weather).

Check the contractor's work with friends or neighbors who may have hired him in the past. *Be sure* that he is fully insured (Workmen's Compensation and Employer's Liability Insurance, Public Liability, and Property Damage Insurance). Otherwise, you could be held liable for accidents that occurred on your property.

FINISHES FOR INTERIOR WOODWORK

Interior finishing differs from exterior chiefly in that interior woodwork usually requires much less protection against moisture, more exacting standards of appearance, and a greater variety of effects. Good interior finishes used indoors should last much longer than paint coatings on exterior surfaces. Veneered panels and plywood present special finishing problems because of the tendency of these wood constructions to surface check.

Opaque Finishes

Interior surfaces may be painted with the materials and by the procedures recommended for exterior surfaces. As a rule, smoother surfaces, better color, and a more lasting sheen are demanded for interior woodwork, especially the wood trim. Therefore, enamels or semigloss enamels rather than paints are used.

Before *enameling*, the wood surface should be extremely smooth. Imperfections, such as planer marks, hammer marks, and raised grain, are accentuated by enamel finish. Raised grain is especially troublesome on flat-grained surfaces of the heavier softwoods because the hard bands of summerwood are sometimes crushed into the soft springwood in planing and later are pushed up again when the wood changes in moisture content. It is helpful to sponge softwoods with water, allow them to dry thoroughly, and then sandpaper them lightly with sharp sandpaper before enameling. In *new buildings,* woodwork should be allowed adequate time to come to its equilibrium moisture content before finishing.

For hardwoods with large pores, such as oak and ash, the pores must be filled with wood filler before the priming coat is applied. The priming coat for all woods may be the same as for exterior woodwork, or special priming paints may be used. Knots in the white pines, ponderosa pine, or southern yellow pine should be shellacked or sealed with a special knot sealer after the priming coat is dry. A coat of knot sealer is also sometimes necessary over wood of white pines and ponderosa pine to prevent pitch exudation and discoloration of light colored enamels by colored matter apparently present in the resin of the heartwood of these species.

One or two coats of enamel undercoat are next applied. This procedure should completely hide the wood and also present a surface that can easily be sandpapered smooth. For best results, the surface should be sandpapered before applying the finishing enamel, but this operation is sometimes omitted. After the finishing enamel has been applied, it may be left with its natural gloss or rubbed to a dull finish. When wood trim and paneling are finished with a flat paint, the surface preparation is not nearly as exacting.

Transparent Finishes

Transparent finishes are used on most hardwood and some softwood trim and paneling, according to personal preference. Most finishing consists of some combination of the fundamental operations of staining, filling, sealing, surface coating, or waxing. Before finishing, planer marks and other blemishes of the wood surface that would be accentuated by the finish must be removed.

Both softwoods and hardwoods are often finished without staining, especially if the wood is one with a pleasing and characteristic color. When used, however, stain often provides much more than color alone because it is absorbed unequally by different parts of the wood, and it accentuates the natural variations in the grain. With hardwoods such emphasis of the grain is usually desirable. The best stains for this purpose are dyes dissolved either in water or in oil. The water stains give the most pleasing results but raise the grain of the wood and require an extra sanding operation after the stain is dry.

The most commonly used stains are the nongrain raising ones which dry quickly and often approach the water stains in clearness and uniformity of color. Stains on softwoods color the springwood more strongly than the summerwood, reversing the natural gradation in color in a manner that is often garish. Pigment oil stains, which are essentially thin paints, are less subject to this objection and are, therefore, more suitable for *softwoods*. Alternatively, the softwood may be coated with clear sealer before applying the pigment oil stain to give more nearly uniform coloring.

In *hardwoods with large pores*, the pores must be filled before varnish or lacquer is applied if a smooth coating is desired. The filler may be transparent and without effect on the color of the finish or it may be colored to contrast with the surrounding wood.

Sealer (thinned-out varnish or lacquer) is used to prevent absorption of subsequent surface coatings and prevent the bleeding of some stains and fillers into surface coatings, especially lacquer coatings. Lacquer sealers have the advantage of being very fast-drying.

Transparent surface coatings over the sealer may be of gloss varnish, semigloss varnish, nitrocellulose lacquer, or wax. *Wax* provides a characteristic sheen without forming a thick coating and without greatly enhancing the natural luster of the wood. Coatings of a more resinous nature, especially lacquer and varnish, accentuate the natural luster of some hardwoods and seem to permit the observer to look down in the wood. *Shellac* applied by the laborious process of *French polishing* probably achieves this impression of depth most fully, but the coating is expensive and easily marred by water. Rubbing varnishes made with resins of high refractive index for light are nearly as effective as shellac. *Lacquers* have the advantages of drying rapidly and forming a hard surface but require more applications than varnish to build up a lustrous coating.

Varnish and *lacquer* usually dry with a highly glossy surface. To reduce the gloss, the surfaces may be rubbed with pumice stone and water or polishing oil. Waterproof sandpaper and water may be used instead of pumice stone. The final sheen varies with the fineness of the powdered pumice stone, coarse powders making a dull surface and fine powders a bright sheen. For very smooth surfaces with high polish, the final rubbing is done with rotten stone and oil. Varnish and lacquer made to dry to semigloss are also available.

Flat oil finishes are currently very popular. This type of finish penetrates the wood and forms no noticeable film on the surface. Two coats of oil are usually applied, which may be followed with a paste wax. Such finishes are easily applied and maintained but are more subject to soiling than a film-forming type of finish.

Filling Porous Hardwoods Before Painting

For finishing purposes, the *hardwoods* may be classified as follows:

Hardwoods with large pores	*Hardwoods with small pores*
Ash	Alder, red
Butternut	Aspen
Chestnut	Basswood
Elm	Beech
Hackberry	Cherry
Hickory	Cottonwood
Khaya (African mahogany)	Gum
Mahogany	Magnolia
Oak	Maple
Sugarberry	Poplar
Walnut	Sycamore

Birch has pores large enough to take wood filler effectively when desired but small enough, as a rule, to be finished satisfactorily without filling.

Hardwoods with small pores may be finished with paints, enamels, and varnishes in exactly the same manner as softwoods. *Hardwoods with large pores* require wood filler before they can be covered smoothly with a film-forming finish. Without filler, the pores not only appear as depressions in the coating, but also become centers of surface imperfections and early failure.

FINISHES FOR FLOORS

Wood possesses a variety of properties that make it a highly desirable flooring material for your home. A variety of wood flooring products permit a wide selection of attractive and serviceable wood floors. Selection is available not only from a variety of different wood species and grain characteristics, but also from a considerable number of distinctive flooring types and patterns.

Interior Floors

The natural color and grain of wood floors make them inherently attractive and beautiful. It is the function of floor finishes to enhance the natural beauty of wood, protect it from excessive wear and abrasion, and make the floors easier to clean. A complete finishing process may consist of the following steps: sanding the surface, applying a filler for certain woods, applying a stain to achieve a desired color effect, and applying a finish. Detailed procedures and specified materials depend largely on the species of wood used and individual preference in type of finish.

Careful *sanding* to provide a smooth surface is essential for a good finish because any irregularities or roughness in the base surface will be magnified by the finish. The production of a satisfactory surface requires sanding in several steps with progressively finer sandpaper, usually with a machine, unless the area is small. The final sanding is usually done with a 2/0 grade paper. When sanding is complete, all dust must be removed by using a vacuum cleaner or tack rag. Steel wool should not be used on floors unprotected by finish because minute steel particles left in the wood may later cause staining or discoloration.

A *filler* is required for wood with large pores, such as oak and walnut, if a smooth, glossy, varnish finish is desired. A filler may be paste or liquid, natural or colored. It is applied by brushing first across the grain and then by brushing with the grain. The surplus filler must be removed immediately after the glossy wet appearance disappears. Wipe first across the grain to pack the filler into the pores, and then complete the wiping with a few light strokes with the grain. The filler should be allowed to dry thoroughly before the finish coats are applied.

Stains are sometimes used to obtain a more nearly uniform color when individual boards vary too much in their natural color. Stains may also be used to accent the grain pattern. If the natural color of the wood is acceptable, staining is omitted. The stain should be an oil-base or a nongrain-raising stain. Stains penetrate wood only slightly. Therefore, the finish should be carefully maintained to prevent wearing through the stained layer. It is difficult to renew the stain at worn spots in a way that will match the color of the surrounding area.

Finishes commonly used for wood floors are classified either as sealers or varnishes. *Sealers,* which are usually thinned-out varnishes, are widely used in residential flooring. They penetrate the wood just enough to avoid formation of a surface coating of appreciable thickness. Wax is usually applied over the sealer. If greater gloss is desired, the sealed floor makes an excellent base for varnish. The thin surface coat of sealer and wax needs more frequent attention than varnished surfaces. Rewaxing or resealing and waxing of high-traffic areas is a relatively simple maintenance procedure.

Varnish may be based on *phenolic, alkyd, epoxy,* or *polyurethane resins.* They form a distinct coating over the wood and give a lustrous finish. The kind of service expected usually determines the type of varnish. Varnishes especially designed for homes are available. Information on types of floor finishes can be obtained from flooring manufacturers.

Durability of floor finishes can be improved by keeping them waxed. *Paste waxes* generally give the best appearance and durability. Two coats are recommended and, if a *liquid wax* is

TABLE 9

Some typical values of moisture excluding effectiveness of coatings after two weeks' exposure of wood initially from 80°F and 65 per cent relative humidity to 80°F and 97 per cent relative humidity

Coatings		Effec-
Type	Number of coats	tive- ness
		Pct.
INTERIOR COATINGS		
Uncoated wood		0
Latex paint	2	0
Floor seal	2	0
Floor seal plus wax	2	10
Linseed oil	1	1
Do	2	5
Do	3	21
Furniture wax	3	8
Phenolic varnish	1	5
Do	2	49
Do	3	73
Semigloss enamel	2	52
Cellulose lacquer	3	73
Lacquer enamel	3	76
Shellac	3	87
EXTERIOR COATINGS		
Water-repellent preservative	1	0
FPL natural finish (stain)	1	0
Exterior latex paint	2	3
House paint primer:	1	20
Plus latex paint	2	22
Plus titanium-zinc linseed oil paint (low-luster oil base) (30 pct. PVC) [1]	1	65
Titanium-alkyd oil:		
30 pct. PVC [1]	1	45
40 pct. PVC [1]	1	3
50 pct. PVC [1]	1	0
Aluminum powder in long oil phenolic varnish	1	39
Do	2	88
Do	3	95

[1] PVC (pigment volume concentration) is the volume of pigment, in percent, in the nonvolatile portion of the paint.

used, additional coats may be necessary to get an adequate film for good performance.

Porches and Decks

Exposed flooring on porches and decks is commonly painted. The recommended procedure of treating with water-repellent preservative and primer is the same as for wood siding. (*See* Chap. 24.) After the primer is applied, an undercoat and matching coat of porch and deck enamel should be applied.

Many fully exposed rustic-type decks are effectively finished with only water-repellent preservative or a penetrating-type pigmented stain. Because these finishes penetrate and form no film on the surface, they do not crack and peel. They may need more frequent refinishing than painted surfaces, but this is easily done because there is no need for laborious surface preparation as when painted surfaces start to peel.

MOISTURE-EXCLUDING EFFECTIVENESS OF COATINGS

The protection afforded by *coatings* in excluding moisture vapor from wood depends on a number of variables. Among them are film thickness, absence of defects and voids in the film, type of pigment, type of vehicle, volume ratio of pigment to vehicle, vapor-pressure gradient across the film, and length of exposure period.

The relative effectiveness of several typical treating and finishing systems for wood in retarding adsorption of water vapor at 97 per cent relative humidity is shown in Table 9. Perfect protection, or no adsorption of water, would be represented by 100 per cent effectiveness. Complete lack of protection (as with unfinished wood) by 0 per cent.

Paints which are porous, such as the latex paints and low-luster or breather-type oil-base paints formulated at a pigment volume concentration above 40 per cent, afford little protection against moisture vapor. These porous paints also permit rapid entry of water and so provide little protection against dew and rain unless applied over a nonporous primer.

CHAPTER 17

Woodworking Repairs

————————— **:** —————————

FLOORS

A familiarity with the general construction of a house floor is essential if you want to make floor repairs in a proper and efficient way. In a well-constructed house the *joists*, or beams which support the flooring, are placed no more than 16″ apart. If the joists exceed a length of 8′, they should be *bridged*, or braced, with strips of wood or nonrusting metal. Bridging prevents joist sway and helps to distribute the stress of additional weight or shock, which would otherwise concentrate on the joists immediately underneath.

There are two kinds of house floors: single and double. The *double* floor is made in two layers. The bottom layer, secured directly to the joists, is called *subflooring* and is made of rough tongue-and-groove lumber laid diagonally, or at right angles to the joists. A layer of building paper separates the subfloor from the finish floor. The *finish* floor, usually of tongue-and-groove hardwood, is laid parallel to one of the walls of the room and is secured to the subfloor with finishing nails. These nails have small heads and must be driven at an angle through the tongue edge of each board so as to conceal them beneath the adjacent board (**Figs. 1 and 2**).

In old houses, floors may sag because the joists and girders have been weakened by rot or by termites or other insects. In new houses, sagging may result from the use of green lumber or from improper construction.

Repairing a sagging floor. Sagging indicates structural weakness in the floor, serious warping of the joists, or, in severe cases,

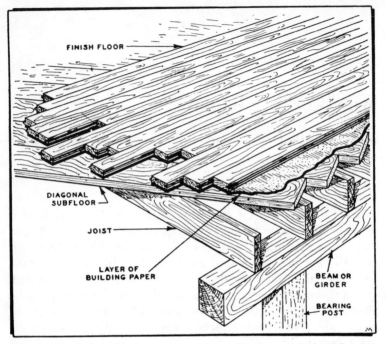

FINISH FLOOR

DIAGONAL
SUBFLOOR

JOIST

LAYER OF
BUILDING PAPER

BEAM OR
GIRDER

BEARING
POST

Fig. 1. Typical double-floor construction, with diagonal laid subflooring.

sinking of the foundation. If there is a basement beneath the sagging floor, the sag can be eliminated by using a screw jack of the type shown in Fig. 3 and several lengths of 4″ × 4″ timber.

First, cut one of the timbers 3′ to 5′ in length and lay it on the basement floor, centered beneath the sagging area. (The purpose of this timber is to distribute the strain placed on the basement floor when the sagging area above it is raised.) Next, place the screw jack on top of the timber. Nail another 4″ × 4″ along the sagging joists and measure the distance from it to the top of the jack. Cut a piece of 4″ × 4″ to that length; place it in position as shown in Fig. 3 and raise the jack slightly. Do not attempt complete leveling in one operation. Instead reraise the jack a fraction of an inch each day or so. Check the position of the floor with a level before reraising the jack.

When the floor has been leveled, measure accurately the distance from the horiontal 4″ × 4″ (nailed to the joists) and the

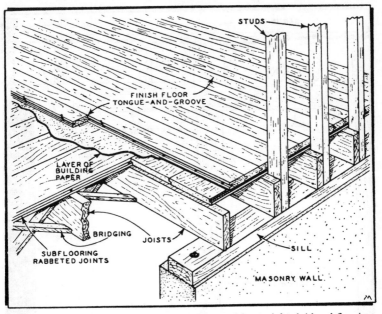

Fig. 2. Typical double-floor construction, with straight laid subflooring.

basement floor. Cut a piece of 4″ × 4″ to that length and raise the jack enough to permit this timber to stand on end under the horizontal 4″ × 4″. After checking to see that the timber is resting firmly and is in vertical alignment, remove the jack and the 4″ × 4″ placed beneath it. When an entire floor sags, it is necessary to use more than one vertical support.

Sagging or weak floors can also be raised or reinforced by using *Teleposts*, which contain built-in screw jacks (Fig. 4). Teleposts are supplied with two plates, one to rest on the basement floor and the other to fit between the top of the post and the bottom of the joist. The jack can adjust the post to any required height. When Teleposts are used, the jack should be reraised only a fraction of an inch every day or so. These posts have two advantages: they become a permanent installation and they eliminate the work required in the use of a screw jack and timbers.

When sagging occurs in an upper floor, where the joists are not exposed, the simplest method for leveling is to take up the finish flooring carefully, following directions given below for repairing

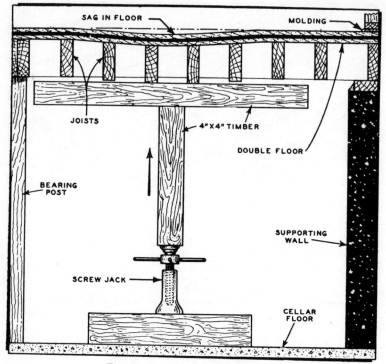

Fig. 3.   Repairing a sagging floor.

damaged floors, and then to level the low places in the subfloor with either a filler compound or filler strips.

Filler compound, a commercial product, is a semiplastic material. When using the compound, level it into place on the subflooring with a putty knife and allow it to set for several days before relaying the finish flooring. Then check the floor with a spirit level and, if the floor still sags, apply an additional layer of the compound. *Filler strips* are thin strips of wood cut to compensate for the sag in the floor.

After the floor has been leveled by one of these methods, both of which are shown in Fig. 5, the flooring may be relaid with the use of finishing nails.

Repairing a damaged or worn floor.   When floor boards are badly damaged or worn, they should be removed. A brace and bit is used to bore a hole in one of the damaged boards, as near to the joist as possible. If the floor is a single floor, no extra precautions are necessary when boring the hole. A keyhole or compass saw can be used to cut across the first board, thus facilitating its removal. After the first board has been removed, it is a comparatively easy matter to remove the remaining defective boards. If the floor is a double one, bore the hole only to the depth of the top flooring and pry up the board.

When replacing defective boards with new flooring, measure and cut the new boards to the required sizes. Square both ends with a chisel or block plane. Figure 6 shows the method of spacing, or breaking, the joints so that a board which extends over a given joist is next to one that ends on the joist. When

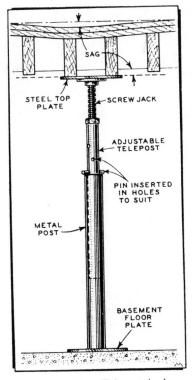

Fig. 4. Using Telepost in basement for permanent repair of sagging floors.

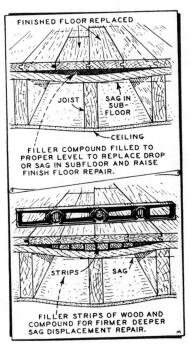

Fig. 5. Using filler compound and strips on upper floor.

the joints are broken in this manner, a strong line of joints running along the same joist is obtained. New boards can also be given additional support by nailing or screwing a small cleat to the side of the joist on which the board is secured (Fig. 6).

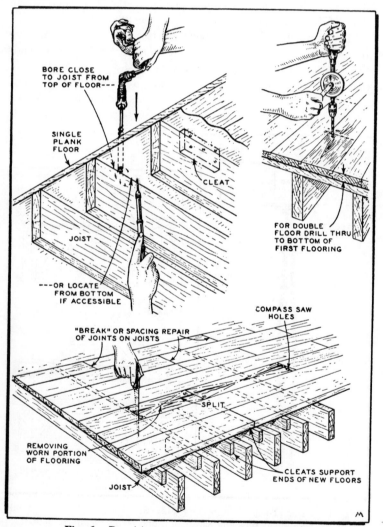

Fig. 6. Repairing worn or damaged floor boards.

Filling cracks in floors. Many older houses have planked floors containing cracks between the boards. There are several commercial plastic fillers that are used to fill cracks, but some are flexible and have a tendency to shrink and crack. Sawdust and wood glue mixed into a paste makes an excellent filler for cracks and is preferable to some commercial fillers.

Do not attempt to fill cracks before cleaning them out thoroughly. Grease or dirt in cracks will keep the filler from adhering to the wood. Use a blunt knife to pack the filler into each crack until it protrudes above the surface of the floor. Allow it to dry and set for several days, then level off with a chisel, and finally sand it down to floor level. When a crack is very wide, glue a thin strip of wood into it and plane or sand it down to floor level. Finish to match the rest of the floor.

Opening the flooring for repairs. When it is necessary to get at heating or plumbing pipes or electrical connections in order to make replacements or repairs, an opening must sometimes be made in the flooring. The procedure for opening up a planked floor is the same as that for repairing damaged or worn boards.

When tongue-and-grooved flooring has been used, the procedure is quite different. In this type of flooring, the *tongue* of one board is fitted into the *groove* of the next. To attempt prying up a board of this type would damage either the tongue or the groove or both. The method for lifting one or more boards without damaging the floor is to cut off the tongue of one board and take crosscuts along the joists. This operation can be accomplished by either a compass or keyhole saw. The three necessary cuts are shown in Fig. 6.

First, bore through the flooring at the tongue side near a joist so that a compass or keyhole saw can be inserted. After boring the hole, saw the tongue along the entire length of the board. Then saw the board at each end, as close to the joist as possible. Remove the first board by sliding a chisel into the lengthwise cut and lifting the board. After removing the first board, remove other boards by sawing each one along the joists.

Before relaying the boards, nail wood cleats to the side of each joist, flush with the underside of the floor. The cleats will support the ends of the boards and will serve as a base on which to nail them. Use finishing nails for this phase of the job and countersink the nailheads below the wood section. Use a commercial filler or a sawdust-glue paste to fill up the holes. Finish to match the rest of the floor.

COVERING FLOORS AND OTHER SURFACES

Two types of linoleum for covering floors and other surfaces are in general use: inlaid and printed. In the better grades of *inlaid* linoleum, both color and pattern go through to the backing, which is usually a specially prepared material. In the cheaper grades of so-called inlaid linoleum, the color and pattern do not go all the way through. In *printed* linoleum, sometimes called "oilcloth," the color and pattern are printed on the surface only. With proper care, a good grade of inlaid linoleum should last a lifetime.

Cleaning linoleum. Linoleum is made of gummed linseed oil mixed with finely ground cork and other materials. Because of the composition of linoleum, harsh caustic soaps and scouring powders eventually destroy the gum that constitutes the major portion of the ingredients. Cleaning should therefore be done with a mop or cloth dampened with pure soap suds. White floating soap or a special linseed-oil soap that can be procured at any paint shop is best for this purpose. The linoleum should then be mopped again with clear water to remove all dirt. Never under any circumstances flood the linoleum with water, because water will work through the joints and eventually soften and loosen the cement. When linoleum is properly treated, it should retain its brightness for a considerable length of time.

Waxing and painting linoleum. To retain its brilliance of color and smooth surface, linoleum should be given, at least once a month, a coat of paste wax or of one of the water-wax emulsions now on the market. The water-wax emulsions dry with a medium glossy finish and do not require rubbing or polishing. They are not so slippery as the paste waxes and are easier to apply. The directions for application furnished by the manufacturer should be followed closely.

If the color or finish of linoleum has worn off, the surface can be painted or lacquered satisfactorily. Neither paint nor lacquer should be applied on waxed linoleum unless all traces of wax have been removed. You may remove the wax by softening the wax coating with benzine, naphtha, or clear gasoline and wiping dry with plenty of clean rags. This job is dangerous and should never be done near a flame; to prevent fire or explosion, make certain that adequate ventilation is provided. After the linoleum has been cleaned thoroughly, allow it to dry overnight. Then apply either lacquer or paint.

Varnish is not recommended as a satisfactory finishing material for linoleum. When it is necessary to remove old and discolored varnish from linoleum before lacquering or painting, use a lukewarm solution of trisodium phosphate, about three pounds to a gallon of water. Allow the solution to remain on the linoleum only long enough to soften the varnish. Work on a small section at a time and do not use too much liquid. After the varnish has been softened, remove it with fine steel wool, thoroughly rinse with clear water, and rub the area dry before proceeding to the next section. This treatment softens the linoleum, which should be allowed to dry for 18 to 24 hours until hard, before wax, lacquer, or paint is applied.

Eliminating bulges. Bulges occur in linoleum if not enough cement was used originally or if the linoleum was not laid properly and was not forced down on the cement. If a bulge appears along a seam, lift the edge of the linoleum and apply linoleum cement to that part of the floor surface directly beneath the bulge. Use a spatula or thin, flat stick to apply the cement, which may be procured at a paint shop. Lay weights on the area to hold the linoleum firmly in place until the cement has hardened and set.

If the bulge is in the center of a strip of linoleum, make a cut with a razor blade or other sharp instrument along the pattern outline of the linoleum where the cut will not show. Press some cement into the opening and spread it with a spatula or flat, thin stick. Press the bulge down and place a weight upon it until the cement has set and hardened.

Patching linoleum. To insert a patch in damaged linoleum, use a piece of linoleum that is large enough to more than cover the damaged area. Lay the new piece on top of the damaged area and with a sharp knife, razor blade, or special linoleum knife cut through both the new and the old linoleum (Fig. 7). Remove the old linoleum and secure the new piece in place with linoleum

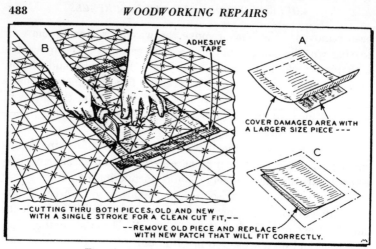

Fig. 7. Patching and matching linoleum.

cement. If you use a matching piece of linoleum, a skilfully applied patch will not be conspicuous. Although it is not always possible to use a matching piece, any piece of linoleum, even one of contrasting color, can be used effectively to form a medallion or design.

Filling holes in linoleum. To fill small holes in linoleum, smooth the edges of the holes with fine steel wool. Crush a small piece of linoleum of the right color into a fine powder. Mix the pulverized linoleum with a sufficient quantity of spar varnish to form a fairly thick paste. Force this paste into the hole as a filler. After the paste has dried, smooth it with No. 000 sandpaper and wax the surface.

Laying linoleum. It is advisable to remove old linoleum before laying new linoleum. Cut any good sections out of the old linoleum and save them for future use. If the floor boards are rough or irregular, plane them smooth. Replace any defective boards. Then wash the entire floor and allow it to dry thoroughly. When a floor is in bad condition and a good quality of inlaid linoleum is to be used, the old floor should be covered with sheets of plywood to insure a smooth, firm base.

Before laying the new linoleum, remove the quarter rounds from the foot of the baseboard (Fig. 8).

The better grades of linoleum are felt-backed and are laid

directly on the floor. If the linoleum to be used is not felt-backed, a felt base must be fitted and cemented to the floor with a special cement made by linoleum manufacturers and available at any paint or hardware store. The felt base should be rolled down so that it adheres firmly to the entire floor. Take care to see that no overlapping or bunching occurs.

Linoleum should never be laid in a cold room. You can elimi-nate the possibility of its cracking or tearing by unrolling it and

SLIT

1/4 ROUND REMOVED

WOODEN BLOCKS

KNIFE POINTS TOWARDS FLOOR AND NOT THE BASEBOARDS WHEN TRIMMING.

18"

6'-0"   3'-0"

BUTT JOINTS

6'-0"   3'-0"

LINING FELT

TOP FLOOR

SUBFLOOR

RAISE RADIATORS ABOUT 1/2" WITH WOODEN BLOCKS TO SLIP LINOLEUM UNDER THE LEGS.

Fig. 8. Laying linoleum on a typical floor.

allowing it to lie flat overnight in a room having a temperature of about 65 degrees.

A linoleum knife should be used to cut linoleum. The inner curved edge, the cutting edge, is sharp enough to cut through the linoleum as the knife is pulled along a line (Fig. 9).

Cutting linoleum to fit along the straight edges of a room presents no problem. Cutting it to fit around doorjambs and so on requires care. The best method is to make an accurate pattern of the irregularity and attach it to the linoleum with a spot of glue, then to mark out the pattern with a piece of chalk or pencil and cut along the marked line.

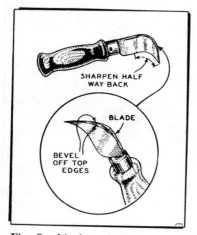

Fig. 9. Linoleum knife and correct sharpening bevel.

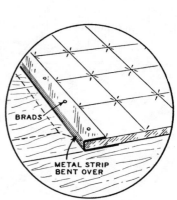

Fig. 10. Use of binding at doorways.

After the linoleum has been cut as directed, lay it with linoleum cement. With a cement spreader or putty knife, apply the cement evenly on the floor or on the previously-laid felt base. After spreading the cement over a few square feet (never more), press the linoleum down firmly on the cemented surface. Before proceeding to a new area, make certain that the surface just completed has been covered well with the cement and that the linoleum has adhered firmly to the surface. This is important, since any air bubbles that may be under the linoleum are extremely difficult to remove later. When all the linoleum has been cemented in place, it should be rolled with a heavy roller. A garden roller is satisfactory. Place bricks or other weights on all the seams to prevent them from loosening before the cement is set. Replace the quarter rounds at the foot of the baseboard. Nail them to the baseboard, not to the floor; the linoleum should be free to contract or expand when the room temperature changes.

If the linoleum ends in a doorway, it should be protected by a metal strip (Fig. 10). First nail this strip into place; then lay the linoleum on top of it and trim it to fit under the curved metal edge of the strip. Finally, bend the curved edge over to form a permanent protection for the linoleum edge. Procedures for using other types of metal edgings and bindings are shown in Figs. 11 and 12.

Applying linoleum to sink counters and walls. The methods just described may also be used in laying linoleum on sink

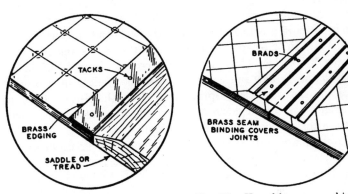

Fig. 11. Use of angle-type metal edging at doorways with treads.

Fig. 12. Use of brass seam binding at doorways without treads.

counters and plaster walls. Do not, however, lay linoleum over wallpaper. The metal strip described previously can be used on sink counters and walls as well as on floors to protect linoleum edges.

Laying linoleum blocks. Linoleum can be obtained in square blocks as well as in the conventional roll. The floor should be prepared in the same manner as for roll linoleum. It is important, when laying the blocks, to be sure that they are square with the walls and that each block is rolled firmly into place after the cement is applied.

Laying asphalt or cork floor tiles. Asphalt floor tiles can be laid on a wood floor and also on a dry concrete floor. When laying them on a wood floor, first cement down a preliminary felt base. When laying them directly on a concrete floor, coat the concrete first with a special concrete-floor primer. Then spread asphalt tile cement and lay the tiles in the same way as linoleum blocks. Cork tiles are applied in the same manner.

STAIR AND DOOR REPAIRS

Eliminating stair creaking. Stair steps consist of a horizontal board, called a *tread,* and a vertical board at the back, called a *riser* (Fig. 13). Each tread rests on the top edge of the riser of the step below and, as a rule, overhangs it, with the joint between the two covered by a molding strip. When stairs run along a wall, the inner ends of both the treads and the risers are set into grooves in a board attached to the wall and supported by it (Fig. 14). In this type of construction, the treads and risers are secured by wedges glued into the grooves. Because of faulty construction or age and continued use, the wedges may become loose and the treads may spring away from the risers. Then, as the treads are forced down on the risers, the ends of the treads move in the grooves and creaking results.

To eliminate stair creaking, have someone bear down on the tread, forcing it against the riser. Then drive a series of 2"

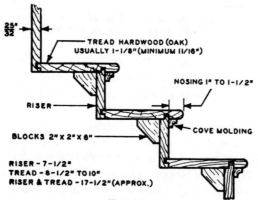

Fig. 13.

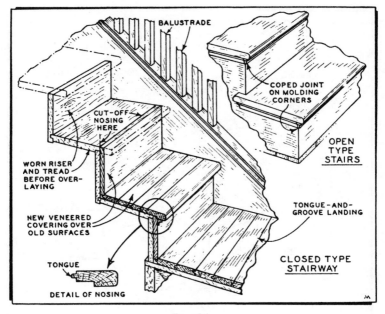

Fig. 14.

finishing nails in pairs—each of the pairs at opposite angles to each other—through the tread and into the riser. Make certain that the nails are driven at opposite angles (Fig. 15). If they are driven straight down, they will eventually work loose. Also be sure that the nails are placed far enough away from the edge of the tread so that they will enter the riser and not pass in front of or behind it. The nailheads should be countersunk with a nail set and the holes filled with plastic wood or other suitable filler. When the filler is set, sand it smooth with the surface.

In the newer type of stair construction, a tongue on the top edge of the riser fits into a groove that is cut in the under edge of the tread. In this type of construction, creaking can be eliminated by driving the thin edge of an ordinary shingle, a wooden wedge, into the joint, in order to wedge the tread firmly against the riser. To do this, first remove the molding under the overhanging front edge of the tread to expose the joint. After cutting the shingle flush with the front surface of the riser, replace the molding.

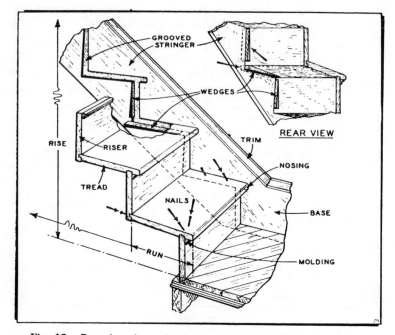

Fig. 15. Procedure for making stair repairs and eliminating creaks.

Replacing worn treads and risers. To replace worn treads or risers proceed as follows: When only the tread is to be replaced, remove it from the stairs. When a riser is to be replaced, riser and tread must be removed. Cut all nails flush with the stringers or side supports of the stairs. Old treads and risers can be used as patterns for cutting the new treads and risers to required size.

When only a tread is to be replaced, place the new tread on top of the stringers and riser. Secure tread onto stringer with finishing nails driven at an angle. Then drive several nails through the top of tread into the lower or supporting riser. When both riser and tread are to be replaced, first secure new riser to stringers; then proceed as previously described for the replacement of stair treads. Be sure to countersink all nails, fill nail holes with filler or plastic wood, and sandpaper flush with the surface.

Eliminating door sticking. Door sticking is usually caused by loose hinge screws. The top hinges loosen under continual strain, the door sags and, as a result, the corners stick. This condition can be avoided by keeping hinge screws tight. Periodic inspection and tightening of hinges should do the job.

Doors will also stick because of swelling and distortion of the doorframe. To eliminate sticking in this case is not so easy, since the door must be removed. To remove a door, open it and support the outer corner with wooden wedges to relieve the hinges of weight. Door hinges are usually made with a pin connecting the two parts of the hinge. Withdraw the pin by pulling it upward. If the pin sticks, drive it by hammering a prying bar at an upward angle against the top knob of the hinge. When removing a door, free the bottom hinge first. When replacing the door, attach the top hinge first.

If door sticking occurs because the front edge of the door is striking the doorframe, and examination shows a space between the rear edge and the frame, set the hinges deeper in the frame by cutting away the wood behind them with an ordinary wood chisel. If there is no space between the front and back edges and the frame, plane the back edge down to a perfect fit. This requires resetting the hinges, a simpler operation than resetting the lock, which would be required if the front edge were planed to fit.

If the latch on a door does not catch, insert a piece of thin plywood or hard cardboard between the hinge leaves on the door and the frame. To do this, the hinges must be unscrewed. When replacing the hinges, use longer screws to make up for the added thickness (Fig. 16).

If the outer bottom corner of a door strikes the sill, a thin wooden wedge placed behind the bottom hinge will tilt the door slightly upward, allowing it to clear the sill. If the outer top corner strikes the frame, the wedge must be placed behind the top hinge. This operation is easier than the alternative one of setting one hinge deeper into the doorframe.

Eliminating door sagging. Heavy garage doors tend to sag if their hinges are not checked and tightened periodically. Usually the bottom strikes the ground so that considerable effort is required to open or close the door.

To fix a sagging garage door, block it up with a wooden wedge. Drive the wedge in at the outer corner, along the bottom edge,

Fig. 16. Repairs to sagging and sticking doors.

so that the door hangs properly and clears without sticking (Fig. 17). Inspect the hinge screws; in nine cases out of ten it will be found that sagging has been caused by a loose hinge. Do not remove the wedge, but proceed to tighten the loose screws with a heavy-duty screwdriver. If the tightened screws appear to be holding the door in place, remove the wedge and the door will clear without sticking.

When the screws can be tightened too easily, they should be replaced with longer screws. In severe cases, the hinges must be removed and reset so that the screws will be held in solid wood. If the door continues to sag and stick, a brace may be used, as shown in Fig. 17. To attach a brace, jack up the door with a wedge until it is hanging straight. Then screw the diagonal brace, or rod, and turnbuckle as shown in Fig. 17.

Correcting door warpage. Outer door and doors between kitchens and passageways are usually subject to warpage, being exposed to dampness on one side and heat on the other. When

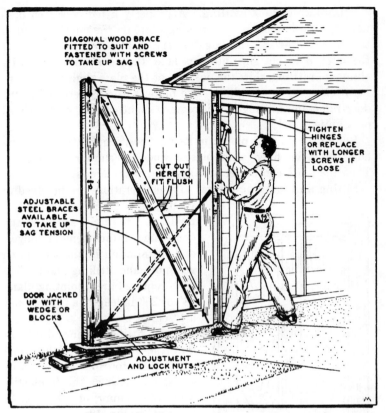

Fig. 17. Repairing a sagging garage door.

warpage occurs, the door must be taken off and laid flat on blocks of wood with the dry or concave side up. If you place heavy weights or bricks on the high end of the warped portions, the door will warp slightly in the opposite direction and, after a few days, will become straight. Before rehanging, paint and varnish the edges to check further absorption of moisture.

Eliminating door creaking. Door creaking is usually caused by rusted hinges. To eliminate this annoyance, first remove the hinge pins; the outer edge of the door should be held securely by an assistant while the pins are being removed. Then with a wad of cotton secured to a stiff wire and dipped in machine oil, swab the length of each pin opening. Then replace the pins.

Eliminating door rattling. A properly fitted doorlatch does not slip into its hole in the striking plate on the doorframe until the door is pressed firmly against the molding in the frame. If the latch does not slip into this hole, the door will rattle. To eliminate rattling, shift the position of the plate slightly by moving it closer to the molding. The plate is usually recessed in the doorframe and moving it will require slight cutting with a chisel or a knife.

Before the plate is placed in its new position, all the old screw holes must be filled with plastic wood or similar wood filler. Then the plate can be set and fastened with screws.

Fitting and hanging doors. Three operations are involved in the fitting and hanging of a door: reducing it to proper size to fit the doorframe, attachment of hinges, and installation of the lock latch assembly and striking plate. The tools required are a jointing plane 18″ or 20″ in length, a ripsaw, and a 1″ chisel.

When fitting a panel door, see that the back stile is the same width from top to bottom and of the same width as the front stile when the planing of the edges is completed (Fig. 18).

Bring the door into position with the back stile resting lightly against the edge of the doorframe to which it will be hinged. Hold the door in this position and mark a line down the other stile, using the edge of the jamb as a guide, in order to show the amount of material that will have to be removed before the door will fit between the jambs. Plane the back or hinge edge and square with the face of the door.

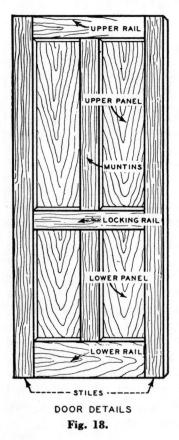

DOOR DETAILS

Fig. 18.

To find out the amount of material that must be removed from the rail, hold the door in place between the jambs. Then mark the bottom rail with a line parallel to the threshold or floor. Do not take off all the material from the bottom rail to secure the final fit. Some material must also be removed from the top rail to true up the door. After ascertaining the amount of material to be removed from both the bottom and the top rails, remove the excess material with a saw or plane. Do not plane directly from edge to edge. To avoid splitting, plane halfway in one direction, then plane the remaining half in the opposite direction. Allow $\frac{3}{16}''$ all around the door to afford easy hanging and swinging. If this precaution is taken and the door is properly hinged, it will never bind.

Attaching door hinges. The butt hinge shown in Fig. 19 is the most commonly used hinge. To attach this type of hinge, make undercuts in both the door edge and the door jamb so that the leaves of the hinges are recessed and set flush with the wood of both members.

It is good practice to locate all door hinges throughout the

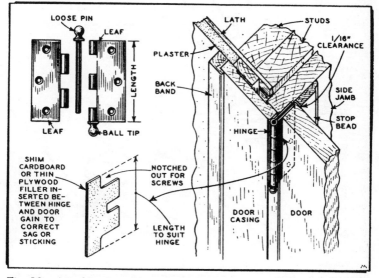

Fig. 19. Attaching butt hinge to eliminate door sag. Parts of hinge are shown (upper left).

house in the same positions. Locate the lower hinge about a foot from the floor, so that the lower edge of the hinge leaf lines up with the upper edge of the lower door rail. Locate the upper hinge about 10″ to 12″ from the top of the door.

Remove the pin from one of the hinges and place the leaf of the hinge on the door edge. Mark around the hinge leaf with a pencil or the point of a knife. On the back edge of the door, mark a line to indicate the width and the thickness or depth of the hinge leaf. Make the necessary undercut on the door edge to fit the leaf of the hinge. With a chisel and hammer, cut along the marked lines on the door edge, as shown in Fig. 20. Continue by making several cuts to approximately the depth of the undercut, as shown in the same illustration. With a chisel, pare out

Fig. 20.

the material to be removed, exercising extreme care not to make the undercut too deep. Take light paring cuts with the chisel and from time to time test the depth of the undercut with the hinge leaf. If the undercut is too deep, the door will bind against the jamb and will strain the hinge screws when it is closed. If the undercut is not deep enough, the door will not close properly.

Mark the screw holes in the proper position, drill the holes, and with screws of correct size attach the hinge leaf to the door. Attach the second hinge in the same manner.

Now assemble the leaves of the hinges and insert the pins. Hold the door in position in the doorway and mark the hinge positions on the jamb to correspond with the positions of the hinges on the door. Remove the door and separate the leaves of the hinges by removal of the pins. Place the leaves in position on the jamb, as indicated by the markings just made. Then, with a pencil or the point of a knife, mark around the outline of the hinge leaf. Make the necessary undercut as previously outlined. Drill the screw holes and secure the hinge leaves with screws of the proper size. Place the door in position and fasten the leaves together with the pins.

Installation of door locks. Locks are installed or attached to doors in different ways. The method of installation is determined by the kind or type of lock used. There are four main classifications of locks: mortise, bore-in, rim, and half-mortise. As a general rule, mortise locks, so called because they are mortised or set into the door edge, are used for all outside doors (Fig. 21). To mark the positions of the knob spindle hole, keyhole and lock edge, lay the lock against the side of the door. After making the necessary markings remove the lock and make new markings which must be the width of the thickness of the lock cover plate that is to be placed in the door edge. Drill the necessary holes of adequate size for both the keyhole and the knob spindle as shown in Fig. 21. Extend the lock edge markings around to the door edge. Using a brace and bit, cut out the mortise to the size required to receive the lock (Fig. 22). For directions on cutting out mortises, see Mortise and Tenon Joints, Chap. 3.

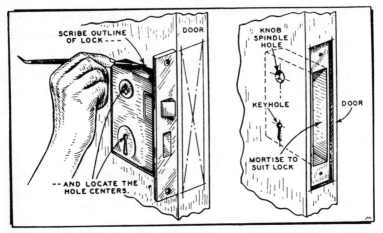

Fig. 21. Locating and installing mortise door lock.

Place the lock into the mortise and, with the point of a knife or pencil, accurately mark around the cover plate. Make the necessary undercut, following the directions just given for the undercuts of hinge leaves. This undercut must be just deep enough to permit the cover plate to fit flush with the door edge (Fig. 22). Install the lock, securing it in place with screws of the proper size and then also attach with screws the keyhole, knobs, and spindle plate.

To determine the position of the striking plate, close the door and operate both the lock and latch so that the jamb can be marked for installation of the plate. Open the door, but hold the plate in place and make a pencil mark around the plate. Make an undercut in the jamb into which the plate will fit. Hold the plate in position in the undercut and mark the jamb for mortising. With a ¼″ chisel, make the necessary mortises into the jamb to a depth sufficient for both lock bolt and latch action. Test for proper mortise depth by working the latch and lock, before attaching the striking plate to the jamb with screws of the correct size.

Bore-in locks are generally used for interior doors and are comparatively easy to install. They are installed in two holes, that are bored in the edge and in the stile of the door (Fig. 23). The procedure for cutting the mortise for the lock front is identical to that previously described (Fig. 22). Install the lock in the cut-out mortise, and complete installation in the same manner as described for mortise locks.

Tubular lock sets are a type of bore-in locks, easily installed. Using the template provided with the lock, bore two holes at right angles and cut out recess for front of lock (Fig. 24). This small cross-bore also conserves strength of the door. Adjustment for

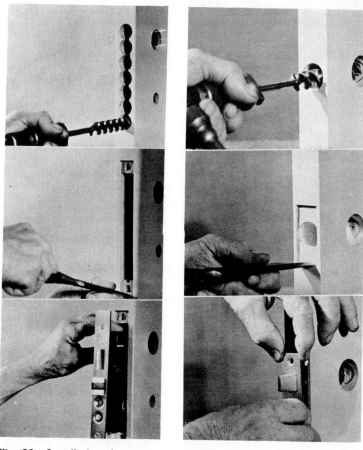

Fig. 22. Installation of a mortise lock: Top, bore holes in edge and stile; center, cut and complete with chisel; bottom, install lock.

Fig. 23. Installation of bore-in lock: Top, bore holes in edge and stile; center, cut mortise for lock front; bottom, install lock.

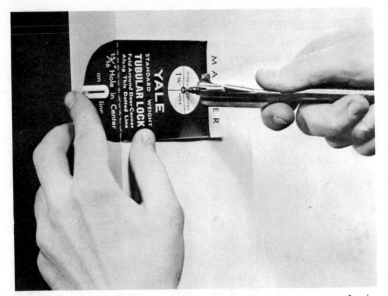

Fig. 24. Using template for locating and boring holes necessary for installation of a tubular lock.

door thickness is made by screwing outside rose to align center of lock with recess in edge of door. The inside springclamp of the locknut compensates for any dimensional changes in the wood. The latchbolt unit is inserted and interlocked with outside knob unit by merely turning the knob. Tighten inside locknut with spanner wrench or screwdriver, snap rose onto springclamp, then snap on inner knob, and the new lockset is durably and securely installed. Fig. 25 shows the four basic steps for the installation of a tubular lock.

Rim locks (copies of colonial box locks) are sometimes chosen for appearances. Night latches are the only rim locks widely used on full-size doors. These locks are placed on the surface of the door and are easily installed by simply boring a hole for the cylinder.

Half-mortise locks are generally used on cabinet doors and drawers. These are installed by cutting a recess on the inside surface of the drawer and boring a hole for the cylinder or tube of the lock.

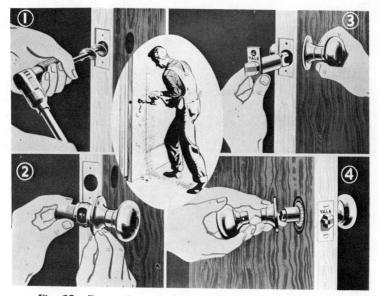

Fig. 25. Progressive steps for the installation of a tubular lock.

WINDOWS

Two kinds of windows are in general use: The casement and the double-hung. The *casement* window consists of one sash, usually metal, which is attached to each side of the window frame with hinges. When this type of window requires adjustment, it is necessary only to tighten or replace the hinge screws.

The *double-hung* window is most commonly used. It consists of two movable sashes, both assembled in the window frame, which is mounted in the wall (Fig. 26). Cords to which weights are attached run over pulleys and down both sides of each sash (Fig. 26). The weights move up and down in pockets on each side of the frame when either or both of the sashes are raised and lowered. A discussion follows of the various adjustments and repairs required by this type of window.

Fixing tight double-hung window sashes. Tight window sashes are caused by hardened paint in one or more of the grooves of the window frame in which the sashes slide, or by shrinkage or

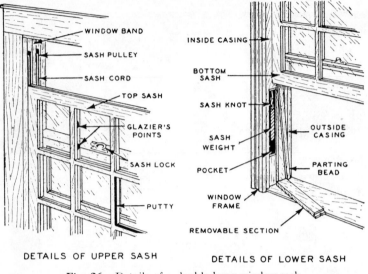

Fig. 26. Details of a double-hung window sash.

swelling of the sashes or frame, or by the settling of the walls or foundation of the house.

When paint has worked in and hardened between the edges of a sash and its groove, the molding that forms the front edge of the groove must be removed before the paint can be scraped or sanded off. If the molding is secured by screws, remove the screws, then the molding. If it is nailed, carefully work a putty knife or other thin blade under the molding to pry the nails loose. Pull out the nails with the claw of a tack hammer, using a block of wood under the hammer to prevent marring the surface of the molding. With the putty knife, scrape off the paint and smooth the surface with No. 000 sandpaper. Clean the surface with turpentine and then rub a small quantity of paraffin or wax on the groove. Replace the molding.

Tight window sashes are also caused by a swollen sash or a swollen bead molding, which forms the channel in which the sash slides. To remedy this condition, sand the beading until enough material has been removed to facilitate the sliding of the sash. However, when the condition is too severe, pare the beading with a chisel, taking light, even cuts and removing just enough material so that the sash slides easily.

If both the beading and the sash are swollen, it is necessary to remove the sash from the frame. This procedure is described below; see Replacing sash cords. Plane the sides of the sash with a jointer plane, taking light, even cuts and making careful tests between each cut to avoid removing too much material from the sash. Before replacing the sash, put a thin coat of linseed oil on the edges of the sash and in the grooves of the frame.

The binding or sticking of lower window sashes sometimes can be relieved by pulling on the sash cords and letting them snap back quickly. A few drops of linseed oil poured down the grooves also helps considerably.

Replacing sash cords. The initial step in replacing a broken sash cord is to remove the sash from the window frame. First, detach the molding that is screwed or nailed to the frame. Do this carefully, as described above, to avoid splitting or damaging the finish of the molding. Turn the lower sash partly sideways and remove it from the frame.

If the broken cord is attached to the lower sash, slip the knot on the end of the cord out of the hole in the sash. When doing this, use extreme care to prevent the knot on the good cord from slipping out of the hole, since this would permit the sash weight to drop and possibly snap the good cord when the knot hits the pulley. To remove the upper sash, it is necessary to remove the lower sash first. Then take out the beading strip that separates the two sashes and turn the upper sash partly sideways for removal.

The strip of wood that forms the sash-weight pocket cover in the side of the window frame must be taken out. It usually is found at the lower end of the groove in which the lower sash moves and is held in place by one or more screws. Unscrew and remove this cover to gain access to the sash weights.

Tie a knot in one end of the new cord and, making the necessary allowance for the knot at the other end, measure the correct length for the new sash cord. Thread the unknotted end over the pulley and down into the sash-weight pocket, drawing the cord out through the opening and tying it to the sash weight with a square or bowline knot.

Then bring the sash into position, set the knot into the hole in the sash, and replace the sash in the window frame. Replace the sash-weight pocket cover, beading, and molding in their original positions.

When sash chains are used instead of cord, a link of the chain is opened with a pair of pliers and is secured to the sash weight, then reclosed with the pliers.

Replacing broken windowpanes. Windowpanes are usually held in place with small, three-pointed metal fasteners called *glazier's points* and a triangular beading of putty. These triangular points are available in several sizes, ranging from No. 00, the largest, to No. 3. As a rule, Nos. 1 and 2 are the sizes used. Glazier's putty is available in cans of various sizes.

To replace a broken windowpane, carefully remove all the broken pieces and scrape off the old putty and glazier's points with a scraper. Spread a thin layer of putty on the back of the *rabbet*, or groove (Fig. 27). The thin layer of putty provides a seal between the glass and the inner part of the sash.

With a glass cutter, cut the glass to the required size. (For specific directions on the use of a glass cutter see Chap. 2, page **93**.) Press the new pane of glass firmly into place

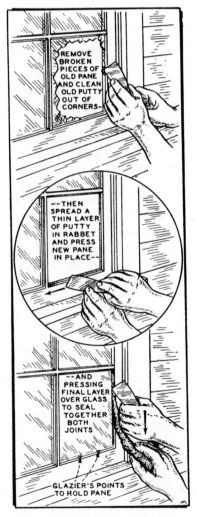

Fig. 27. Replacing a windowpane.

against the layer of putty and keep pressing it around the edges until the putty has been spread evenly between the glass and the edge of the rabbet.

Lay the glazier's points against the pane, about 3″ apart, so that the points are toward the wooden sash. With a light tack hammer drive them carefully into the sash to about half their length. Repeat this all around the pane.

Since putty does not adhere to bare wood, apply as preliminary priming a thin coating of linseed oil. Roll some putty between your hands to form a rope approximately ¼″ in diameter. Lay the rope of putty around the edge of the pane. Press it firmly into place with a putty knife to form a neat triangular beading that adheres to both the wood and the pane.

Allow at least a week for the putty to set and dry before painting. When painting putty, allow the paint to overlap about ⅛″ onto the glass pane. Overlapping seals the joint between the glass and the putty and retards the entrance of moisture, which would harden the putty and loosen the seal.

Applying weather stripping. Weather strips are used to close the joints around window sashes and doorframes; efficient weather stripping retains indoor temperature, checks the entrance of air and moisture, and results in a fuel saving of 15 to 25 per cent.

Many kinds of weather stripping are available. Some are flexible; others are rigid. The type commonly used by the home craftsman is a commercial product available at all hardware dealers. Made of a specially treated, flexible felt that is nominal in cost, easily installed, and efficient in operation, it is the most practical kind of stripping to use and, though not permanent, will last for several seasons. It may be attached to window sashes and doorframes with small tacks or brads.

To apply flexible weather stripping on double-hung windows, first close the windows. Fasten to the outside of the window frame, as close as possible to the sash, the weather stripping for the upper, or outer, sash. Then fasten the stripping for the inside of the upper sash on the inside stop-bead molding of the window frame. For the lower, or inner, sash, fasten a piece of stripping to each side and also to the bottom, so that the stripping will fit snugly against the sill of the window. Fasten a final piece of stripping to the top of the lower sash, in order to cover the crack between the upper and the lower sash. The same procedure is followed when using rigid weather stripping.

Rigid weather stripping makes for a more permanent job. It is made of light-gauge metal with a felt interior that projects just far enough to form a tight seal between the sash and the window frame. The manufacturers of rigid weather stripping provide a small cardboard gauge to aid in locating the stripping correctly along the frame and sash before it is nailed in place. The use of this gauge insures a weathertight stripping job and eliminates binding of the sash and damage to the stripping caused by its improper placement.

When applying rigid stripping, miter the corners of the stripping to make effective weathertight joints. All measurements must be absolutely correct before the strips are cut. Miters are cut with a hacksaw and miter box (see Jointing in Chap. 3 for a discussion of this).

Either flexible or rigid weather stripping can be used on steel casement windows. The felt weather stripping must be secured with a special adhesive and the rigid stripping with special clamps available for that purpose. Before using the adhesive, which may be a type of thick shellac, amberoid, or metallic cement called *liquid solder*, make certain that the metal window frames have been thoroughly scraped and cleaned of paint, rust, or corrosion and wiped with benzine. Do not apply the adhesive before the window is completely dry.

A special type of weather stripping is available for metal-framed casement windows. It is made to snap into the grooves along the edges of the sash and is held in position by the springiness of the metal itself. In fitting and securing this type of weather stripping, check all measurements carefully before cutting the material.

Eliminating window-frame leaks. Window frames are tightly fitted to the walls; in houses of good construction, the joints between both the frames and the walls are closed with sheet-metal flashings and building paper along the sides and bottoms. Even with sheet-metal flashings, the shrinkage of the wood sometimes opens the joints between the window frames and the walls, creating cracks that admit air and rain. Leaks of this type result in smudges on the inside wall areas adjacent to the window frames. It is important that such cracks be closed.

In some types of construction, the joints between the window frames and the walls are covered with either moldings or flat strips. To get at window-frame leaks, remove the strips by prying them loose with a prying bar to expose the joints. Then use a flat-ended dowel stick to force tow into the open joints to within approximately ¾" of the surface. *Tow* is a material made of the coarse part of flax or hemp and can be secured at a marine supply house.

Fill the remaining space with a *calking compound*, which can be secured at a hardware or paint store. It has the consistency of soft putty and never becomes quite hard. While a hard skin forms on the surface, the underpart remains pliable enough to take up any subsequent expansion or contraction of wood or other material and thus prevents further leakage. Force the calking compound into the cracks with a putty knife or similar tool, and allow it to set for several days. Then replace the moldings or strips that were removed.

CHAPTER 18

Interior Woodworking Projects

PLANNING THE WORKSHOP

In planning the home workshop consideration must not only be given to present equipment and requirements, but also to proper provision for accommodating any additional tools and equipment that may be added later on.

Generally, space that cannot be utilized for any other purpose in the basement, attic, or garage can be used for the-home workshop. This space need not be large. An efficient workshop accommodating a work bench and as many as four power tools (that may be acquired at some future time) will not require a space larger than 4′ × 12′ (Fig. 1).

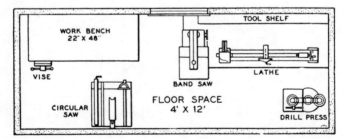

Fig. 1. Floor plan showing arrangement of a small workshop using power tools.

Where a larger space is available and a more elaborate workshop is desired the floor plans shown in Figs. 2 and 3 can be adapted to any particular requirement.

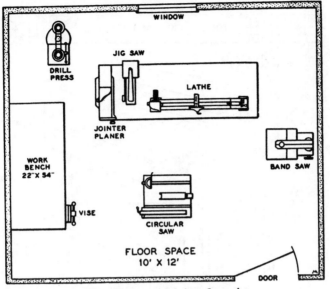

Fig. 2. Efficient workshop floor plan.

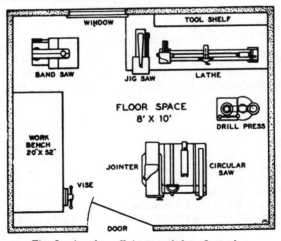

Fig. 3. Another efficient workshop floor plan.

CONSTRUCTING A WORKBENCH AND TOOL RACK

The construction of the woodworking bench and tool rack shown in Fig. 4 is a simple project that requires a minimum

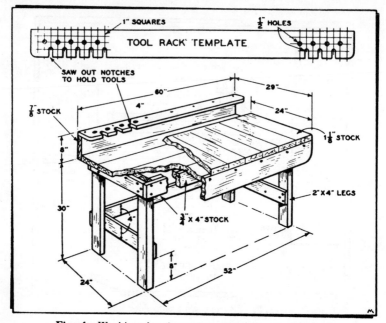

Fig. 4. Working drawings of workbench and tool rack.

amount of tools and material. Workbenches are subjected to hard usage; therefore it is good practice to secure straight, high-grade, kiln-dried birch or pine for the body of the bench, and maple for the working top. Lumber required is as follows:

BILL OF MATERIALS

Pieces	Part	Size		
4	Legs, each	$2''$	$\times 4'$	$\times 30''$
2	Top (inner) leg stretchers	$2''$	$\times 2''$	$\times 16''$
2	Top (inner) leg stretchers	$2''$	$\times 2''$	$\times 48''$
4	Top and bottom (outer) leg stretchers	$\frac{3}{4}''$	$\times 4''$	$\times 24''$
3	Top and back (outer) leg stretchers	$\frac{3}{4}''$	$\times 4''$	$\times 53\frac{1}{2}''$
6	Bottom section of top (dressed and matched) each	$\frac{3}{4}''$	$\times 5''$	$\times 60''$
1	Front apron	$\frac{3}{4}''$	$\times 6''$	$\times 60''$
1	Back (for tool rack)	$\frac{3}{4}''$	$\times 7\frac{1}{4}''$	$\times 60''$
1	Tool rack	$\frac{3}{4}''$	$\times 4''$	$\times 60''$
12	Working top (maple or other hardwood)	$1\frac{1}{8}''$	$\times 5''$	$\times 24''$

If the lumber has been cut to size, the tools required to construct this bench and tool rack are: a compass or keyhole saw, a brace and bit, and a screwdriver. If the lumber has not been cut to size, the following additional tools will be required: a marking gauge, a try square, a rule, and a saw. In the latter case, the lumber must be cut to size and prepared for use as described in Chap. 3.

To assemble the cut pieces of lumber, proceed as follows (refer to Fig. 4 throughout):

Measure 8″ from bottom of each of the four pieces (2″ × 4″ × 30″) forming the legs and fasten the four bottom outer leg stretchers with screws and glue.

Fasten the four top outer leg stretchers with screws and glue.

Fasten the four top inner leg stretchers with screws and glue to the top outer leg stretchers. Space these screws approximately 4″ apart.

Screw the six pieces of dressed and matched lumber forming bottom section of top of bench onto the frame.

With a chisel round off the bottom corners of the 6′ board forming the front apron. Fasten this front apron to the bottom section of the top. For instructions covering rounding of corners with chisel, see Chap. 2.

With a ⅜″ bit and brace and a ½″ countersink, drill and countersink three holes, 6″ apart, through each of the 12 pieces of maple or hardwood forming the working top of the bench. For directions on drilling and countersinking, see Chap. 2.

With a chisel, cut a bevel on one end of each of these 12 pieces. Screw the 12 pieces forming the working top onto the bottom section of top.

Fill countersunk screw holes with plastic wood.

Secure the piece forming the back for the tool rack with screws and glue.

Make a template of cardboard to use in marking the holes to be drilled and the notches to be cut out of the tool rack. These notches and holes, spaced at intervals of 4″ to 5″, are used to hold chisels, files and similar tools.

With a ½″ bit and brace drill holes for small tools and cut out notches with a keyhole or compass saw. For directions on the use of compass and keyhole saws see Chap. 2.

Round off two outer corners of the tool rack and fasten it to the back with screws.

Sandpaper entire job.

Suggestions for finishing.   The top of the woodworking bench should be finished with linseed oil.   Other parts of the bench, including the tool rack, should be oil-stained and varnished.

BOOK AND MAGAZINE TABLE

Low lines, an interesting surfboard shape and a slight tilt to the end panel give this useful book and magazine table character and grace .

The sturdy, unusual legs can be fabricated easily from aluminum tubing. The plan shown in Fig. 5 gives all the information required. To take care of minor variations in angle and dimensions, you probably will save yourself extra work by having the legs bent before beveling and drilling the bottom shelf, and cutting partition (C) to proper height.

Paint the legs with flat black enamel or in a color to contrast with the shelves.

Cut, rabbet, dado and drill all parts as required. Sand and

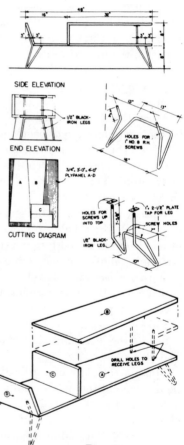

SIDE ELEVATION

END ELEVATION

1/2" BLACK-IRON LEGS

CUTTING DIAGRAM

3/4", 5-0', 4-0'
PLYPANEL A-D

HOLES FOR
"NO. 8 R.H.
SCREWS

HOLES FOR
SCREWS UP
INTO TOP

1", 2-1/2" PLATE
TAP FOR LEG

SCREW HOLES

1/2" BLACK-
IRON LEG

DRILL HOLES TO
RECEIVE LEGS

PLAN OF TOP

LEG PLATES SCREWED TO
UNDERSIDE OF TOP

Fig. 5.

PARTS REQUIRED

CODE	NO. REQ'D	SIZE	PART IDENTIFICATION
A	1	16"x44¾"	Bottom Shelf
B	1	16"x32"	Top Shelf
C	1	7¼"x14"	Divider
D	1	8½"x16"	End
	2 Sets	½" Diameter	Wrought Iron Legs
	2 Ea.	1"x2½"x⅛"	Leg Plates

Miscellaneous—6d Finish Nails and Glue
1" No. 8 R. H. Screws as required

fill exposed edges, and fit mating parts together. Glue and nail all the joints.

Fasten end (D) to bottom shelf (A). Nail partition (C) in slot, then support shelf (B) on a block while attaching to (C). Some adjustment for length of legs can be obtained by drilling blind holes underneath top shelf. Plates can be threaded up or down a few turns for positive location.

Install legs after finishing as recommended, making sure the threaded ends of the legs at open end of rack are exactly vertical.

TELEPHONE BENCH

A massive, expensive-looking effect is achieved at little cost in this design of telephone bench, through applying beveled wood molding to the edges of inexpensive fir plywood.

Take the plan shown in Fig. 6 to any welding or metal work shop to have the steel

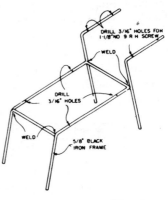

Fig. 6.

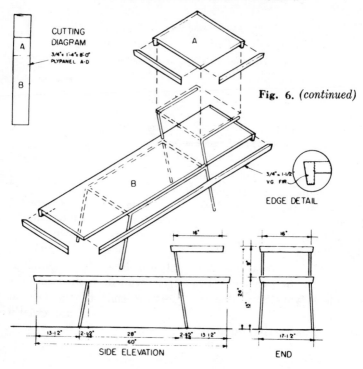

Fig. 6. *(continued)*

frame and legs fabricated, or, if you can, do it yourself. Aluminum tubing can be used for the steel frame and legs, if desired, which is easily formed. Finish in flat black enamel or in a color that contrasts with bench and shelf or in natural aluminum.

Tilt the bench panel and notched edges will fit around frame. Nail and glue molding mitred to fit around plywood panels screwed to frame. Protect the frame with masking tape while finishing as recommended.

PARTS REQUIRED

CODE	NO. REQ'D	SIZE	PART IDENTIFICATION
A	1	16"x16"	Top Shelf
B	1	16"x60"	Seat
	16 Lin. Ft.	¾"x1½"	Edging
	1 Only	⅝" Diameter	Wrought Iron Frame

MISCELLANEOUS—6d Finish Nails and Glue
1⅛'' No. 9 R. H. Screws as required
Finishing Materials

BUILT-IN MAGAZINE AND BOOK RACK

Complete flexibility to fit nearly any circumstance features this built-in magazine and book rack (Fig. 7). Contract, lengthen or expand it vertically by changing its dimensions.

Assemble the wall cabinet before hanging on stringers. All joints should be glued and nailed. Cut parts according to the diagrams shown in Fig. 7 and parts list, rabbet ends, dado top and bottom panels for

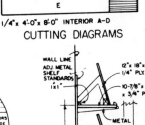

B		C
B		C
A		D
A		

3/4" x 4'-0" x 8'-0" INTERIOR A-D

				H
G				H
F	F	F	F	
E				

1/4" x 4'-0" x 8'-0" INTERIOR A-D

CUTTING DIAGRAMS

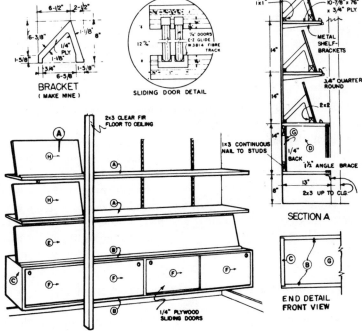

BRACKET (MAKE NINE)

SLIDING DOOR DETAIL

SECTION A

END DETAIL FRONT VIEW

Fig. 7.

PARTS REQUIRED

CODE	NO. REQ'D	SIZE	PART IDENTIFICATION
A	2	10⅞ x 76''	Shelf
B	2	13'' x 76''	Top and Bottom
C	2	13'' x 13¼''	End
D	1	11¾'' x 12½''	Standard
E	1	12'' x 76''	Shelf Back
F	4	12-13/16''x18-13/16''	Sliding Doors
G	1	12½'' x 74½''	Back of Unit
H	2	12'' x 18''	Shelf Back
	9	See Drawing	Bracket
	10½ Lin. Ft.	2'' x 2''	Back Stop
	10½ Lin. Ft.	1'' x 1''	Blocking for Bracket
	13 Lin. Ft.	1'' x 3''	Cabinet Support
	20 Lin. Ft.	¾'' Quarter Round	Magazine Support
	1 Pc.	2'' x 3''—8'-0'' Long	Wood Stanchion
	16 Lin. Ft.	Adjustable	Metal Shelf Standard
	8 Ea.	As Req'd.	Metal Shelf Brackets
	1 Ea.	1½''	Angle Brace

MISCELLANEOUS—4d and 6d finish nails & brads
glue and finishing materials.

doors, sand edges and check fit of all mating parts.

Nail ends and divider to top and bottom and check to be sure cabinet is square.

Nail 1″ x 3″ stringers to wall studs, level with floor. When you apply back (G), heads of large nails will be covered. Leave space for cabinet end, if installing at a corner.

Hang cabinet by nailing through top panel into stringer.

Bandsaw magazine rack brackets to shape, sand edges and nail into ends of 1″ x 1″ and beveled 2″ x 2″ blocking nailed to shelves. Glue and nail sloping racks to blocks and brackets, and install quarter-round along shelf edges.

Use 1½″ angle brace to attach cabinet to post, which should be a snug fit between floor and ceiling.

Finish completely as desired, slip sliding doors in place and install shelves on adjustable brackets at wall stud locations.

ROOM DIVIDER WITH STORAGE SPACE

By using various multiples of individual units as shown in Fig. 8, this room divider fills any space attractively and usefully. Cabinets may be either drawer or door sections, depending on your need and use.

Cutting diagrams (Fig. 8) and the parts list provide four sections as illustrated.

Butt joints in cabinets, which should be glued and nailed, simplify construction.

When parts are cut and fitted for the sections you select, nail sides (E) or (L) to bottoms (B) or (I). Then install backs and tops. Square up each assembly perfectly before driving nails flush.

Drawer guides can be positioned most easily before assembly.

Nail drawer sides and back to bottom, then install front panel after fitting drawer in place in the cabinet.

Paint cabinets as desired before hanging on partition posts and installing hardware.

Nail 1 x 4 strip to ceiling and nail first dadoed post to wall (at a stud, if possible).

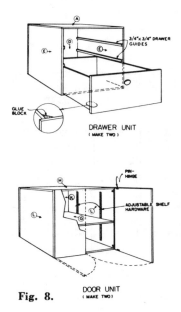

DRAWER UNIT
(MAKE TWO)

Fig. 8.

DOOR UNIT
(MAKE TWO)

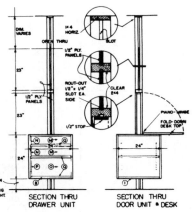

SECTION THRU
DRAWER UNIT

SECTION THRU
DOOR UNIT ● DESK

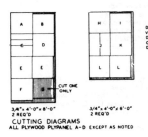

3/4"x 4'-0" x 8'-0"
2 REQ'D

3/4"x 4'-0"x 6'-0"
2 REQ'D

CUTTING DIAGRAMS
ALL PLYWOOD PLYPANEL A-D EXCEPT AS NOTED

Support cabinet at desired height on blocks and drive screws through side into that post. Slip lower square panel (completely finished) into dadoed slot, with bottom edge resting on cabinet, then toe-nail cross-member to post. Insert top partition panel in slots, fit and position each post, and attach cabinet with screws. Repeat procedure for each section.

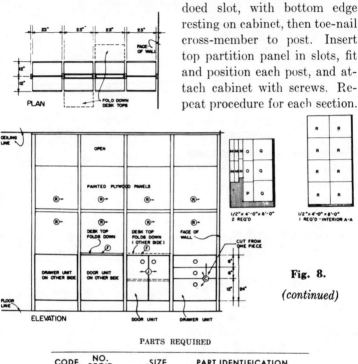

Fig. 8.

(continued)

PARTS REQUIRED

CODE	NO. REQ'D	SIZE	PART IDENTIFICATION
A	2	22½'' x 23''	Top of Drawer Unit
B	2	21'' x 23''	Bottom of Drawer Unit
C	2	23'' x 24''	Drawer Fronts
D	2	23'' x 24''	Back of Drawer Unit
E	4	22½'' x 23¼''	Side of Drawer Unit
F	2	23'' x 23''	Desk Top
G	2	21¼'' x 22½''	Adjustable Shelf
H	2	22½'' x 23''	Top of Door Unit
I	2	21'' x 23''	Bottom of Door Unit
J	2	23 ' x 24''	Door
K	2	23'' x 24''	Back of Door Unit
L	4	22½'' x 23¼''	Side of Door Unit
M	8	4¾'' x 22½''	Drawer Side
N	4	4¾'' x 20⅜''	Drawer Back
O	4	10¾'' x 22½''	Drawer Side
P	2	10¾'' x 20⅜''	Drawer Back
Q	6	20⅝'' x 22''	Drawer Bottom
R	8	23¼'' x 23½''	Plywood Panels
	48 L. F.	2'' x 4'' Clear	Partition Framing
	9 L. F.	1'' x 4'' Clear	Nailing Strip
	2 L. F.	2'' x 2'' Cut Diagonally	Glue Block—Drawer
	8 L. F.	¾'' x ¾''	Drawer Guides
	12 Ea.		Door, Drwr. & Desk Top Pulls
	4 Pr.		Pin Hinges
	6 L. F.		Adjustable Shelf Hardware
	6 Ea.		Door & Desk Top Catches
	4 L. F.		Piano Hinge

MISCELLANEOUS—6d and 8d finish nails and glue finishing materials

RECORD PLAYER AND RADIO CABINET

Figure 9 shows an attractive record player and radio cabinet that can be constructed with simple hand tools.

This plan (Fig. 9) does not give exact dimensions for certain parts because components which may be installed vary greatly. Determine space your equipment requires before laying out plywood.

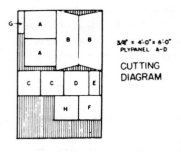

3/4" x 4'-0" x 8'-0"
PLYPANEL A-D

CUTTING
DIAGRAM

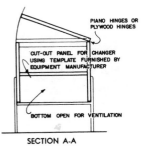

PIANO HINGES OR
PLYWOOD HINGES

CUT-OUT PANEL FOR CHANGER
USING TEMPLATE FURNISHED BY
EQUIPMENT MANUFACTURER

BOTTOM OPEN FOR VENTILATION

SECTION A-A

Cut all similar dimensions on mating or related parts without changing saw setting. All joints should be nailed and glued. Drill panels (F) and (H) for equipment before assembly.

First nail two sides (B) to ends (C), (E) to (H), and (D) to (G). Then install the shelves

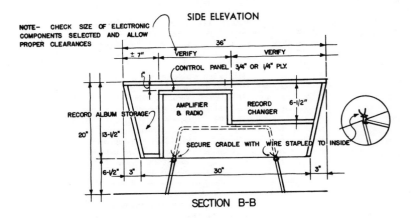

SIDE ELEVATION

NOTE— CHECK SIZE OF ELECTRONIC
COMPONENTS SELECTED AND ALLOW
PROPER CLEARANCES

36"

± 7"   VERIFY   VERIFY

CONTROL PANEL 3/4" OR 1/4" PLY.

RECORD ALBUM STORAGE

AMPLIFIER
& RADIO

RECORD
CHANGER

6-1/2"

20" 13-1/2"

SECURE CRADLE WITH WIRE STAPLED TO INSIDE

6-1/2" 3"   30"   3"

SECTION B-B

Fig. 9.

and vertical dividers according to bracing required. Amplifier and radio hang from control panel (F). If this is not practical for the chassis you have, install a half-shelf between the sides, which still will provide ventilation.

Finish completely as desired, attach to welded cradle and install hardware and components. Connect a remote speaker.

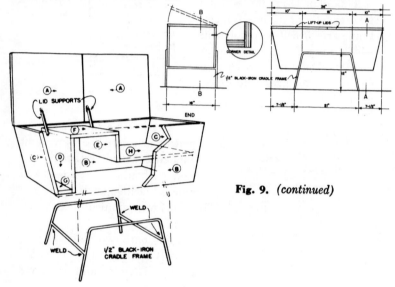

Fig. 9. *(continued)*

PARTS REQUIRED

CODE	NO. REQ'D	SIZE	PART IDENTIFICATION
A	2	16" x 18"	Lid
B	2	12¾" x 36"	Side
C	2	13¾" x 14½"	End
D	1	11" x 14½"	Vertical Divider
E	1	5½" x 14½"	Vertical Divider
F	1	* x 14½"	Control Panel
G	1	± 3¼" x 14½"	Bottom – Record Storage
H	1	* x 14½"	Record Changer Support
	1 Only	½" Diameter	Wrought Iron Cradle Frame
	2		Metal Lid Supports
	4		Cabinet Hinges

Miscellaneous: 6d finish nails and glue
　　　　　　　Screws, wire and staples as required
　　　　　　　Finishing materials
　　　　　　　* Dimensions vary – see drawings

This handsome music center (Figs. 9 *A*, and *B*, and 10)demonstrates rather dramatically that solutions to requirements of a particular situation or a combination of circumstances create the most successful designs.

In this case, (1) room acoustics dictated a change in speak-

er location from midpoint on the long living room wall; (2) it was hoped that the TV set could be seen either from the kitchen in one direction or the living room in the other; (3) storage space should be provided for a large number of long play record albums; (4) a room divider was needed between

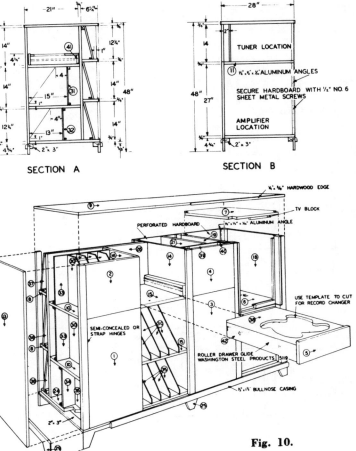

SECTION A

SECTION B

Fig. 10.

dining and living areas; and (5) an orderly, easily accessible arrangement for a large assortment of monthly magazines was most desirable.

When all those factors combined, this very satisfying arrangement of elements just naturally developed.

Study the plan Fig. 10 and you will see that all space behind the left hand door is devoted to three record album compartments only. If that exceeds your needs greatly, or if your room is not big enough for a cabinet seven feet long, eliminate that section.

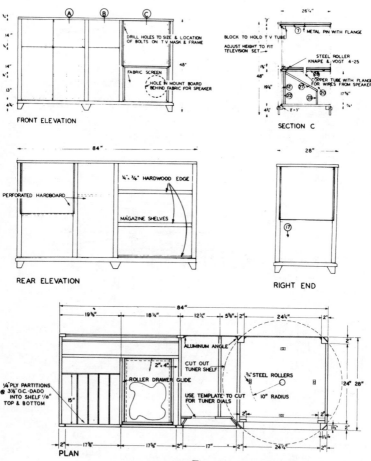

Fig. 10. *(continued)*

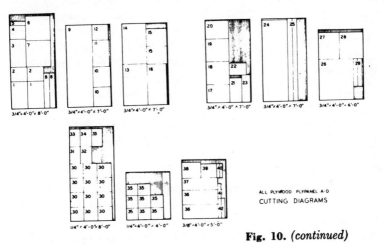

Fig. 10. *(continued)*

Dimensions given make it possible to cut all parts before assembly, but minor variations that generally crop out in a project this large make it advisable to cut and fit as you go. Identical dimensions on mating or matching parts still should be cut at the same time without changing saw setting for perfect fit.

Glue and nail all the joints. Start at the base. Nail the mitred plywood legs to the rabbeted 2″ x 3″ frame. Dado bottom panel 24 for record album partitions and notch edges for 2″ x 2″ posts, 1″ x 2″ stiles and speaker mounting board before nailing to base.

Nail all posts and stiles, divider panels 14 and 20, and ends 13 and 17 in place next.

Notice that a diagonal section is removed from the four posts about 18″ above the base. Exact length of these segments depends on the height of the TV chassis your turntable must accommodate, as they are used later for corner posts in the sub-assembly for the TV turntable.

Before installing shelves, construct the air-tight speaker enclosure shown in Section C. Dimensions and form shown were specified for the 10″ speaker used in this installation. To modify for a 12″, 15″ or co-axial speaker, consult your high-fidelity supplier. Line all surfaces of the enclosure completely with 1″ glass fiber sound absorbing blanket, to control resonance.

You now are ready to install fixed dadoed shelves with panels 16 and 26. *Note* that an arc is cut out of tuner shelf 11, to let the TV turntable swing.

Nail through 26 into back edge of magazine rack shelves 8. Bevel cleats, magazine rack panels, hardwood edge and ¼-round stop can be installed any time.

Leave space open behind panels 33 and 34, to run wiring. Cut, fit and drill your tuner control panel and install with diagonal masks 40 and partition 21.

Assemble record changer carriage after checking model you are installing to be sure you allow ample clearance for its enclosed mechanism and to pass center stile, with sliding hardware in place.

Cut, fit, drill and attach fixed shelf 28 below TV turntable. Face the upper surface with a disc of stiff plastic laminate to provide a smooth, hard track for rollers.

As a sub-assembly, join turntable top, bottom and end panels with segments from 2″ x 2″ corner posts, after checking fit

in place and notching, drilling, mortising and installing rollers and pivots as shown. Attach strips shown on either side of the picture tube opening and blocks shown above and below. Lift sub-assembly over posts into socket for pivot tube.

Drill socket in underside of top panel 9 for upper turntable pivot and attach top to posts, dividers and end 13. Nail front panel 3 in place; the amplifier can be installed through back before you install corresponding perforated panel.

Using 4d finish nails and glue, attach mitred hardwood edge around top and bullnose casing around base. These do not extend around left end in front elevation, since cabinet was built to project from wall.

Finish unit completely as desired. Slip partitions in place and hinge doors. Move into position and slide TV set into turntable compartment through back. Install and connect speaker, amplifier, tuners and changer. Apply grill cloth with prefinished molding. Attach back panels to aluminum angles for ventilation.

PARTS REQUIRED

CODE	NO. REQ'D	SIZE	PART IDENTIFICATION
1	2	17⅜″x28⅛″	Doors
2	2	17⅜″x14⅜″	Doors

PARTS REQUIRED *(continued)*

CODE	NO. REQ'D	SIZE	PART IDENTIFICATION
3	1	17"x28⅛"	Doors
4	1	17"x14⅜"	Doors
5	1	4¼"x16¼"	Changer Face
6	1	25⅛"x26¾"	Revolving Shelf
7	1	26¼"x26¾"	Revolving Top
8	2	6"x36¾"	Magazine Shelves
9	1	28"x84"	Top
10	2	18¾"x20¼"	Shelves
11	1	17½"x27"	Tuner Shelf
12	1	17"x17⅝"	Mount Board
13	1	26½"x42½"	End
14	1	26½"x41¾"	Standard
15	2	18⅛"x20¼"	Shelves
16	1	20¼"x41¾"	Standard
17	1	18⅜"x24"	End
18	1	23⅛"x24"	TV End
19	1	23⅛"x24"	TV Standard
20	1	18⅜"x24"	Standard
21	1	14"x24⅝"	Standard
22	1	11¾"x17⅝"	Speaker Frame
23	1	7½"x26¾"	Speaker Back
24	1	27"x82½"	Bottom
25	2	4⅜"x84"	Legs
26	1	36¾"x41¾"	Magazine Back
27	1	22"x26¾"	Speaker Top Enclosure
28	1	25⅞"x26¾"	TV Stationary Shelf
29	1	4⅜"x28"	Legs
30	12	14¼"x15"	Record Partitions
31	1	14"x17¾"	Record Backs
32	1	12¼"x17¾"	Record Backs
33	2	14"x18¼"	Record Backs
34	1	12¼"x18¼"	Record Backs
35	8	12½"x13"	Record Partitions
36	2	14⅝"x36¾"	Magazine Rack
37	1	12½"x36¾"	Magazine Rack
38	1	16"x19¼"	Changer Mount Bd.
39	1	14"x17¼"	Dial Panel
40	2	2½"x14"	Dial Panel Sides
41	1	3⅜"x15"	Changer Back
42	2	3⅜"x19¼"	Changer Sides
	28 Lin. Ft.	¼"x¾"	Hardwood Edging
	17 Lin. Ft.	½"x1½"	Bullnose Casing
	20 Lin. Ft.	2"x3"	Framing
	10 Lin. Ft.	½" Quarter Round	Stops for Magazines
	8 Lin. Ft.	⅝"x¾" net Moulding	For Fabric Screen

PARTS REQUIRED *(continued)*

CODE	NO. REQ'D	SIZE	PART IDENTIFICATION
	2 Lin. Ft.	¾"x1⅝" net	Bottom Edge Facing—TV Cabinet
	2 Lin. Ft.	½"x1⅛" net	Bot. Edge Support—TV Set
	14 Lin. Ft.	1"x1" Nailer	Back of Record Partitions
	10 Lin. Ft.	¾"x¾" net	Stops and Facing
	1 Pc.	1⅝"x1¾"x6"	Block to Hold TV Tube
	20 Lin. Ft.	¾"x2⅛" net	Stiles
	16 Lin. Ft.	2"x2" net	Vertical Framing
	12 Lin. Ft.	1"x2"	Cleat and Ledger
	2 Lin. Ft.	2"x4"	Blocking for Record Player
	1 Pc.	3/16"x4'-0"x4'-0"	Perforated Hardboard
	1 Ea.	1⅝" Diam.—3" Long	Copper Tube and Flange
	1 Ea.	¼" Dia.	Metal Pin with Flange
	4 Ea.	¾" Diam.	Steel Rollers
	1 Pr.	—	Drawer Guides for Changer
	5 Pr.	H-Type	Wrought-Iron Hinges
	5 Ea.	—	Wrought-Iron Door Pulls
	16 Lin. Ft.	½"x½"	Aluminum Angle

Miscellaneous—4d, 6d and 8d Finish Nails and Glue
F. H. and Sheet Metal Screws as required

PHOTOGRAPHY EQUIPMENT AND PROJECTOR CABINET

Protection for films, slides and equipment replaces possible damage and loss when this projector cabinet is put into use (Fig. 11). Also, it turns disorder and confusion, that so often handicap home film showings, into convenience and a smooth performance.

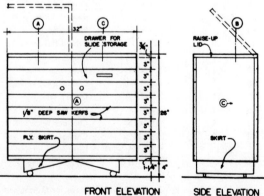

FRONT ELEVATION   SIDE ELEVATION

Fig. 11.

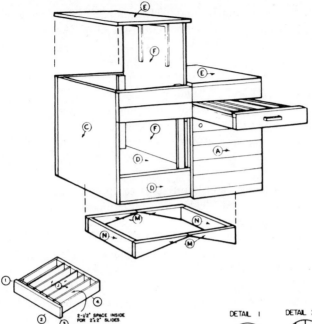

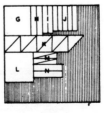

2-1/2" SPACE INSIDE
FOR 2"x 2" SLIDES

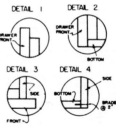

DETAIL 1

DRAWER
FRONT

DETAIL 2

DRAWER
FRONT

BOTTOM

DETAIL 3

SIDE

FRONT

DETAIL 4

SIDE

BOTTOM

BRADS
@ 2"

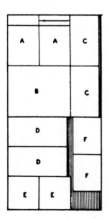

3/4"x 4'-0"x 8'-0"

1/2"x 4'-0"x 4'-0"

Fig. 11. *(continued)*

Saw framing members and structural plywood parts to exact size, sand edges and check mating parts for fit.

Use the same saw settings to groove panels (A) and (B) and to cut out doors, drawer front and facing strip as diagrammed from (A), to obtain uniform grain pattern (Fig. 12).

Glue and nail all joints.

Since you will not be able to nail through bottom panel (D) into skirt pieces after shelf (D) is in place, first attach skirt to bottom. For the same reason, nail shelf (D) to fixed divider (F) before assembly. Stand this sub-assembly on end to attach back; then fasten sides, storage compartment bottom

(L) and 32″ long facing strip cut from panel (A). It is necessary to nail through shelf into the end of 1″ x 2″ slide track, so that member should be installed before adding the bottom and skirt sub-assembly.

Now hang the doors. All door sliding panel and lid edges should be primed thoroughly after sanding, and it is important to apply equal finish coats to both inner and outer faces.

Install drawer guides, film can partitions and lid. Drawer construction is clearly shown in detail in Fig. 12. Assemble sliding panel (F) and cabinet top. Finish as desired. Attach casters and hardware fittings. (See Fig. 12).

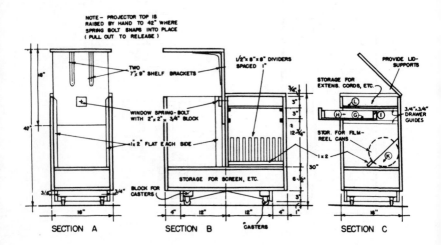

Fig. 12.

PARTS REQUIRED

CODE	NO. REQ'D	SIZE	PART IDENTIFICATION
A	1	25¼"x32"	Front of Unit
B	1	25¼"x32"	Back of Unit
C	2	14½"x25¼"	Side of Unit
D	2	14½"x30½"	Bottom and Shelf
E	2	16"x16"	Projector Top and Lid
F	2	14½"x18"	Fixed and Sliding Standard
G	1	13⅜"x14½"	Drawer Bottom
H	2	3"x14½"	Drawer Side
I	2	2½"x13⅜"	Drawer Front and Back
J	5	2½"x12½"	Drawer Dividers
K	9	8"x8"	Reel Dividers
L	1	14½"x14½"	Bottom of Compartment
M	4	3"x12"	Skirt Board
N	2	3"x14½"	Skirt Board
	5 Lin. Ft.	¾"x¾"	Drawer Guides
	2½ Lin. Ft.	2"x3"	Caster Blocks
	1 Ea.	2"x2"x¾"	Spring Bolt Block
	4½ Lin. Ft.	1"x2"	Slide Track
	2 Ea.	7"x9"	Metal Shelf Brackets
	1 Only	No. 1697	Window Spring Bolt
	4 Ea.	—	Rubber Wheel Casters
	2 Ea.	—	Door Pulls
	1 Ea.	—	Drawer Pull
	2 Pr.	—	Pin Hinges

Miscellaneous—4d and 6d Finish Nails and Glue

BUILT-IN BAR CABINET

This built-in bar cabinet (Fig. 13) offers one of the best examples of how plywood simplifies and speeds construction. Rigid panels eliminate any need for the framing normally used

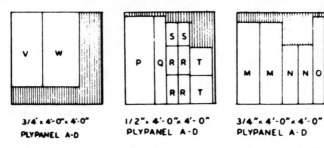

3/4" x 4'-0" x 4'-0"
PLYPANEL A-D

1/2" x 4'-0" x 4'-0"
PLYPANEL A-D

3/4" x 4'-0" x 4'-0"
PLYPANEL A-D

Fig. 12. *(continued)*

for the framing normally used in cabinets this large.

Cut parts to size, rabbet sides (A) ⅜″ deep for back panel and fit matching pieces together. To sides, join bottom shelf (B), facing strip (O), divider (Q), bottom (P) of light trough and partition (C), being careful to keep entire structure exactly square (Fig. 14). Glue and nail all the joints.

Next, fit and nail the brushed plywood back in place. Nail and glue brushed plywood to back of door material and cut

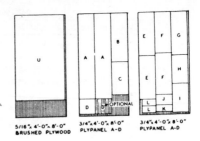

5/16″ x 4′-0″ x 8′-0″
BRUSHED PLYWOOD

3/4″ x 4′-0″ x 8′-0″
PLYPANEL A-D

3/4″ x 4′-0″ x 8′-0″
PLYPANEL A-D

Fig. 13. *(continued)*

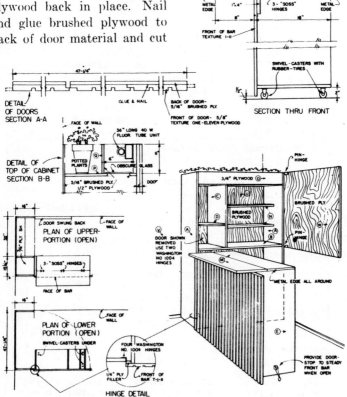

Fig. 14.

to size. Intermediate shelves may be nailed in position, or installed with adjustable shelf supports after finishing.

Before assembling the hinged front bar, notch partitions (F) and (K) for the 1″ x 4″ nailing strip across the top. Because working space is limited, assemble these partitions with fixed top (M), shelves (H), (I), (J), bottom (G) and hinged side (E) before exposed side (E) is installed. Apply texture one-eleven front, hinged top and casters last.

Move cabinet into place against wall and attach doors and hinged front bar after finishing as desired.

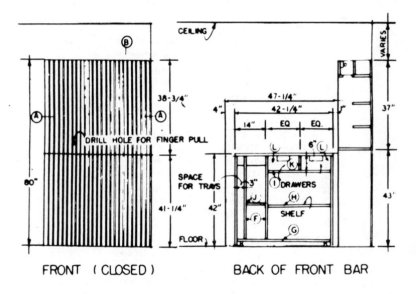

FRONT (CLOSED)   BACK OF FRONT BAR

Fig. 14. *(continued)*

PARTS REQUIRED

CODE	NO. REQ'D	SIZE	PART IDENTIFICATION
A	2	16"x80"	Side—Back Bar
B	1	15⅝"x45¾"	Lower Shelf—Back Bar
C	1	15⅝"x30½"	Standard—Back Bar
D	1	14⅛"x15⅝"	Shelf—Back Bar
E	2	15½"x40¾"	Side—Front Bar
F	2	15½"x38½"	Standard—Front Bar
G	1	15½"x40¾"	Bottom Shelf—Front Bar
H	1	15½"x26¾"	Shelf—Front Bar
I	1	15½"x26¾"	Drawer Shelf—Front Bar
J	1	9½"x15½"	Shelf—Front Bar
K	1	6"x15½"	Divider Between Drawers
L	2	6"x13"	Drawer Front
M	2	12"x42¼"	Bar Top
N	2	8"x30⅞"	Shelf—Back Bar
O	1	6"x45¾"	Face of Light Trough
P	1	15⅝"x45¾"	Bottom of Plant Box
Q	1	6"x45¾"	Divider between Plant Box and Light Trough
R	4	5⅞"x14⅜"	Drawer Side *
S	2	5⅞"x12"	Drawer Back *
T	2	12"x13⅞"	Drawer Bottom *
U	1	46½"x80"	Back of Back Bar
V	1	16"x38¾"	Door and Door Backing
W	1	31¼"x38¾"	Door and Door Backing
	3 Pcs.	16"x79½"	2" T 1-11 Doors and Bar Front**
	3½ Lin. Ft.	¼"x1"	Filler
	3½ Lin. Ft.	1"x4"	Bracing
	1 Pc.	5½"x45⅜"	Obscure Glass
	1 Only	40-Watt-36" Long	Fluorescent Tube
	2 Pcs.	12"x42¼"	Plastic Laminate Top
	11½ Lin. Ft.	For ¾" Edge	Metal Edging
	3 Ea.	"Soss"	Bar Top Hinges
	6 Ea.	For ¾" Plywood	Hinges
	2 Ea.	—	Pin Hinges
	3 Ea.	As Required	Rubber-Tired Casters
	1 Ea.	—	Door Stop for Bar

Miscellaneous—4d and 6d Finish Nails and Glue

* Parts not identified on drawings by letters

** Cut from 3—1'-4"x8'-0" Panels of 2" Texture, One-Eleven

DARK-ROOM CABINET

When time for a hobby is limited, organization of working space, equipment and materials is most important. Any photographer will be well repaid for building this dark-room cabinet (Fig. 15), in added convenience and efficiency.

If necessary, adjust any dimensions to your space, then cut parts specified in the diagrams and material list. Nail and glue all joints.

' Cut toe space, rabbet ends, and dado frame and bottom for doors. Nail ends to bottom and base strip (F), fit and nail back into rabbet, and install 1″ x 2″ framing for drawers.

Construction of drawers according to detail given in Fig. 15, and fitting guides (M) to frame and underside of drawers will be done most easily before nailing top (E) to sides.

Cut and fit sliding doors, sealing all edges carefully and painting inner and outer faces alike.

Apply plastic top, metal edging, and finish completely as required.

When building the paper cabinet shown in Fig. 15, fit all pieces carefully to insure light-

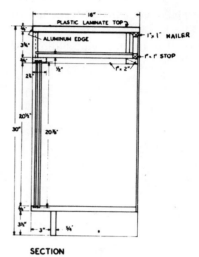

SECTION

3/4″x4′-0″x 8′-0″
PLYPANEL A-D
CUTTING DIAGRAM

1/2″x 4′-0″ x 2′-6″ PLYPANEL A-D

1/4″x 4′-0″x 5′-0″
PLYPANEL A-D

Fig. 15.

tight joints. *Note* that side (R) projects ½″ past front edge of side (J), for hinging. Dado sides for shelves, nail to back and top, and install by nailing up through middle shelf (C). Fit shelves (O), hang door, finish completely and apply felt strips and quarter-round to keep out light. Hang shelves on adjustable standards or fixed brackets, as desired.

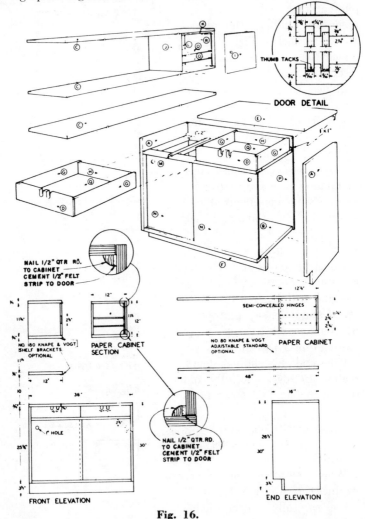

Fig. 16.

PARTS REQUIRED

CODE	NO. REQ'D	SIZE	PART IDENTIFICATION
A	2	16"x29¼"	Ends
B	1	15¾"x34½"	Bottom
C	3	12"x48"	Shelf
D	2	3¾"x17-3/16"	Drawer Front
E	1	16"x36"	Top
F	1	3½"x36"	Base
G	4	3¾"x14⅝"	Drawer Sides
H	2	3"x16"	Drawer Back
I	1	11¼"x12½"	Door—Paper Cabinet
J	1	11¼"x11½"	Side—Paper Cabinet
K	1	11½"x11½"	Top—Paper Cabinet
L	1	10¾"x11½"	Back—Paper Cabinet
M	6	¾"x15¼"	Drawer Guides
N	2	17⅝"x20⅞"	Door
O	2	11"x12"	Shelf—Paper Cabinet
P	1	25¾"x35¼"	Back
Q	2	14⅝"x16"	Drawer Bottom
R	1	11¼"x12"	Side—Paper Cabinet
	14 Lin. Ft.	1"x2"	Framing
	1 Pr.	For ½" Plywood	Semi-Concealed Hinges
	4 Lin. Ft.	—	Felt Strip and Qtr. Round
*	6 Lin. Ft.	—	Adjustable Shelf Standard
	6 Ea.	—	Shelf Brackets—12"
	6 Lin. Ft.	1"x1"	Drawer Stop and Nailer

Miscellaneous—4d and 6d Finish Nails
Waterproof Glue
* Optional—Use fixed brackets if desired

MIXING CENTER CABINET

Accurate measurements are most important before constructing this mixing center cabinet. Any or all of the several parts of the unit may be built, as desired. This flexibility of choice—with the several variable elements shown in Fig. 17—make it possible to fit practically any space available.

Cut structural parts to size after detailed dimensions have been determined, sand edges and fit together. Attach bottom to base and ledger strips first. Fasten ends and back in place, then tip forward and install intermediate standards.

Tip back onto base to install fixed shelves, frames for top

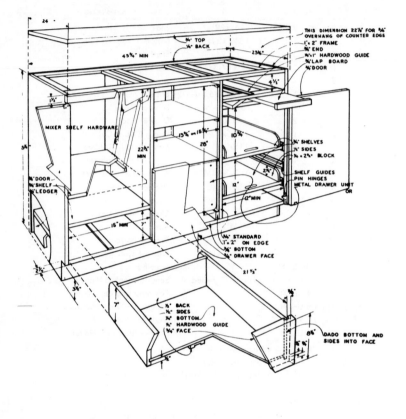

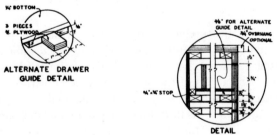

Fig. 17.

and lap board and drawer guides.

Use glue and 6d or 8d finish nails at all joints.

Move into position, level up if floor is uneven and nail to floor or wall.

Install facing strip and top, apply surfacing material, band edges and finish plywood as desired. Attach hardware and hang doors, being careful to seal edges thoroughly. Finish doors inside and out equally.

Dimensions for drawers and sliding shelves will be determined by the cabinet sizes you select. Cut all parts to size, dado the joints, sand and assemble with glue and 4d finish nails. Finish as desired.

SLIDING SPICE RACK

This unique sliding spice rack and tuckaway shelf put space to maximum use and provide for tall bottles as well as small cans and boxes (Fig. 18). This unit can easily be added to the shelves in an existing cabinet or built into a new overhead cabinet as shown in Fig. 18.

If you are building the complete overhead cabinet, measure the over-all dimensions of your space which fix the size of various parts.

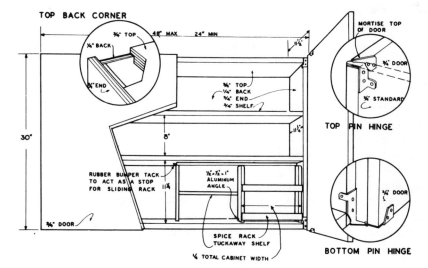

Fig. 18.

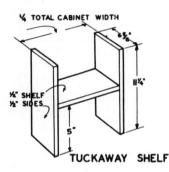

TUCKAWAY SHELF

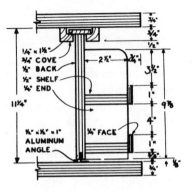

SPICE RACK SECTION

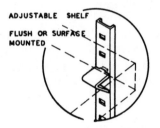

OPTIONAL ADJUSTABLE
SHELF DETAIL

Fig. 18.
(continued)

When building the sliding rack and tuckaway shelf for an existing cabinet, its size determines the variable width shown.

Cut all parts to size, sand edges and check for proper fit. All joints should be glued and nailed.

Use 6d or 8d finish nails in assembling the cabinet. Fasten the tuckaway shelf to shelves and back with 4d finish nails. Hang cabinet on wall by driving screws through back into wall studs.

Also use 4d finish nails and glue to assemble the sliding spice rack. Install track and hang doors on cabinet. Finish as desired. Be very careful to prime edges of doors and finish both faces alike.

SINK CABINET

Convenience at the sink work center saves hours of time daily, because so much housekeeping revolves around that area. A plywood sink cabinet (Fig. 19) lets you choose any color you want, to match other cabinets and provide relief from the stark monotony of an all-white kitchen.

Adjust any variable dimensions to fit your space and the size of the sink you are installing.

Cut all structural panels and frame parts to size (Fig. 19).

Use only plywood made with 100% waterproof glue (EXT-DFPA) around locations exposed to moisture or dampness. Sand edges and fit together.

Assemble with waterproof glue and 6d or 8d finish nails at all joints. Fasten bottom panel to base and ledger strips first. Then install ends, back and frame.

Tip cabinet forward so you can nail through bottom when installing the intermediate standard. After face, top and shelf are fastened, move cabi-

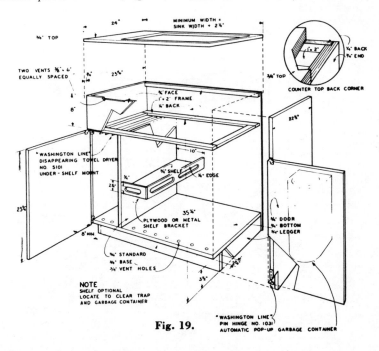

Fig. 19.

net into position and level up to correct any unevenness in the floor.

Fit and hang doors, which should be cut from the same panel as the face to insure matching grain patterns. It is very important to prime edges of doors well and to finish inner and outer faces alike.

Finish the entire cabinet as required, apply surfacing material to counter and install fixtures and accessories desired.

FRUIT-VEGETABLE STORAGE

Fruit and vegetable storage space that is easy to clean and does not collect grime is provided by convenient metal bins as shown in **Fig. 20**. The entire unit is neatly concealed by a single door beneath the cutting board, so you still have complete freedom in choice of colors for your kitchen.

To facilitate cleaning vegetables, these bins should be situated near the sink. They can be built as a separate unit (Fig. 20), or combined with other base cabinets.

Cut all structural panels and

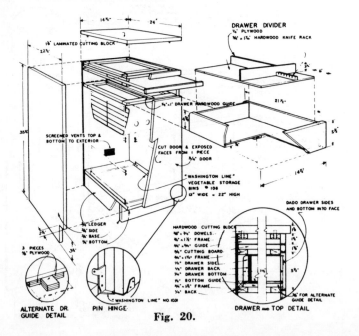

Fig. 20.

frame parts to size, sand edges and fit together.

All joints should be glued and nailed. Fasten bottom to base and ledger strips first, using 6d or 8d finish nails. Then install ends, back and frames. Move cabinet into position and level base if floor is uneven.

Cut door drawer front and face strips from one piece of plywood so grain pattern will match, sand edges and install. Be sure to prime all edges of the door and apply equal finishing coats inside and out.

Cut drawer parts, check in place for fit, sand edges and assemble with 4d or 6d finish nails.

Finish entire cabinet as desired and install cutting block and baskets.

CHAPTER 19

Exterior Woodworking Projects

————— **:** ———————————————————

CONSTRUCTION OF WINDOW, DOOR, AND PORCH SCREENS

While ready-made screens are available in a variety of sizes and shapes to meet almost all requirements, considerably better screens can be constructed at a fraction of the cost.

The screening material used, known as "screen cloth," is available in 14, 16, and 18 mesh openings per inch and in widths ranging from 18″ to 48″. It is made of finely drawn wire so that it will not exclude air and light. Since screens are exposed to all kinds of weather these fine strands of wire will rust if the metal is not corrosion-resistant. A single break in the mesh renders the entire screen useless. Bronze or copper insect-screen cloth have proved to be highly resistant to rust and other forms of corrosion that destroy ordinary screens, and will provide lasting protection.

For the handy man who would like to make his own screens, only a few simple hand tools are necessary. Materials can be readily procured at lumber and hardware dealers. Secure well-seasoned wood that is free from knots. All nails, tacks, and staples used should be of copper, while hinges, screws, handles, and corner pieces should be of brass or bronze. This will assure a rustproof screen that will give satisfactory service over a period of years.

With these materials and a cross-cut saw, a hammer, a square, and a miter box, proceed as follows. Measure each window frame carefully, as they may vary as much as ¼″. Select the type of joint preferred, mark the lumber carefully and cut exactly on the marks to insure a close fit for the finished job.

The *step joint* is the simplest and strongest joint. The upright pieces should be the full height of the frame while the cross members should be cut the width of one side member shorter than the measured width of the frame. Cut square notches, half the width of the side members (*A*, Fig. 1). Stagger the nails and drive them on a slight slant toward the inside so they won't meet and either split the wood, bend, or come out at the side. If the screen is over four feet high, strengthen it with a crosspiece (*B*, Fig. 1). Drawing *C* illustrates another simple joint that may be employed at the corners.

The *mitered joint*, strengthened with a cross-corner brace, is another easily made type (*A*, Fig. 2). Cut the lumber the full size of the openings both ways, then with a miter box saw the ends at a 45° angle. The point of the angle should be exactly on the corner of the piece. Then miter the cross-corner members, also with a 45° angle. Employ plenty of nails and check the alignment with a square as the fastening proceeds. Countersink the nails for a neat appearance. Instead of a cross-corner brace, there are many fastening appliances available at any hardware dealer that may be used in building screens. Shown in Fig. 3 are an angle (*A*), corner brace (*B*), and corrugated fasteners (*C*), all of which will add to the strength of a screen frame.

The *doweled joint* is a mitered joint fastened with two diagonal dowels instead of the corner brace (*B*, Fig. 4). After the lumber has been cut and mitered, fasten with a small nail to keep the joints from slipping; then bore two holes through the corners, insert the dowels, and glue the joint. After it has set, trim the dowels flush with the frame. The square-end doweled joint, similar to the doweled mitered joint, is shown at *C*, Fig. 4.

After sandpapering, give the frames two coats of good paint, permitting each to dry thoroughly. The first step in applying the insert of screen cloth is to lay the frame on a flat surface and place a section of lumber under each end. Then bend the frame down in the center and fasten lightly with a nail or clamp. Trim the screen cloth and tack with 4-oz. copper tacks on both ends. Release the frame and the screen cloth will be stretched tightly. Tack the sides and then cover all edges of the screen cloth with a half-round molding of appropriate size. Put identifying numbers on each screen and the corresponding window frame. When brass or bronze hangers, hinges, and handles are affixed, the screen

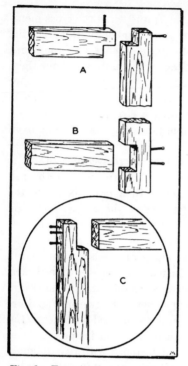

Fig. 1. Two simple types of joints used in the construction of screens.

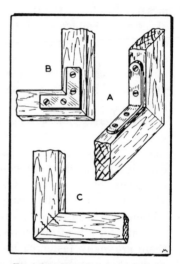

Fig. 3. Metal corner fasteners used in the construction of screens.

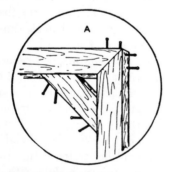

Fig. 2. Method of fastening a mitered joint with a corner brace in constructing all types of screens.

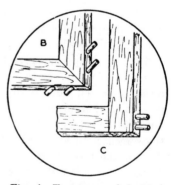

Fig. 4. Two types of doweled joints used in the construction of screens.

is ready for service. Screens should be hung on hinges and secured with hooks and eyes.

Exercise care in storing screens when they are not in use. Each spring, scrub the screens thoroughly with soap and hot water and coat with thinned clear lacquer, as copper screens may otherwise stain a house with white walls.

CONSTRUCTING AND FITTING STORM SASHES

When planning and constructing storm sashes always consider standard glass sizes. As a general rule, glass that is available in standard sizes, such as 8″ × 10″, 12″ × 14″, 16″ × 18″, and other sizes will not have to be cut if the widths of the stiles and rails of the sash are planned in accordance. In other cases, the widths of stiles and rails can be altered slightly by planing. The ideal lumber to use for storm sashes is either straight-grain kiln-dried pine or cypress, usually from 13/16″ to 1⅛″ thick.

The procedures for construction are comparatively simple. Measure each window carefully before cutting any of the lumber. Cut rabbets in the stock for the glass panes (Fig. 5; Chap. 3). While miter joints are sometimes used in making storm sashes they are not particularly recommended for this purpose. A stub tenon joint set in a mortise and secured with two nails in addition to the usual gluing is preferable (Fig. 5). For making mortise and tenon joints, see Chap. 3. Hardware dealers stock special storm-sash hinges and fasteners. The procedure for fitting and attaching hinges is similar to that described for doors in Chap. **17**. The procedure for attaching the fastener depends on the type used. Directions are usually furnished by the manufacturer. After assembling the frame of the sash and attaching hinges to the frame, proceed to set in place and putty the glass as directed in Chap. **17**. Storm sash should be painted to conform with the color scheme of the exterior of the house.

GARDEN FENCES, GATES, TRELLISES, AND PERGOLAS

The construction of these various garden accessories has been simplified to a tremendous degree by the availability of ready-cut lumber for this specific purpose. Since these garden accessories

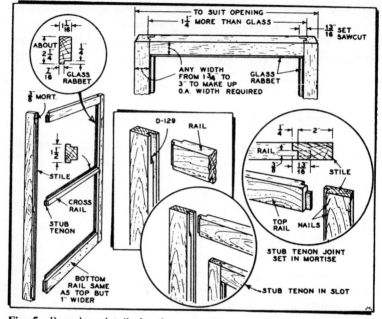

Fig. 5. Procedure details for the construction and fitting of storm sashes.

will be exposed to different weather conditions, an excellent quality of lumber should be used. While pine and cypress are used to some extent, California redwood is really the ideal type for this purpose. Redwood is comparatively inexpensive, is an easy material to either paint or stain, and if left unpainted will acquire a natural weathered effect.

In the construction of any of these projects, preferably set all posts in concrete. Coat the ends of the posts with tar where they will come in contact with the concrete; secure some roofing tar, melt it in a large galvanized pail and dip each post into the melted tar. This acts as a sealer and forms a bond between the wood and the concrete, decreasing any likelihood of moisture collecting there. Use an ordinary concrete mixture, set all posts square, and tamp the concrete well.

Building garden fences. All of the materials required for the construction of the various fences shown are available in ready-

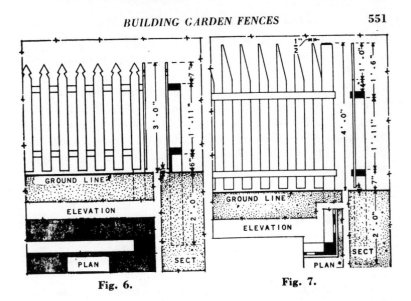

Fig. 6.   Fig. 7.

cut form. Variations of stock picket designs can be made by the ingenious man who desires to have a garden fence individual in design. An angular cut, a design of drilled holes or a silhouette cut out in each of the pickets can be used effectively to produce distinctive patterns. Secure the horizontal rails to the posts with a simple rabbet joint and countersunk screws in all of these designs. Nail the pickets or boards to the rails with galvanized nails. Fig. 6 illustrates a simplified dart motif used for the top of the pickets; a fence of this type is strictly in character with the modern derivatives of English cottage architecture. The decoration at the top of the pickets is made entirely with straight saw cuts, and can be done either at the planing mill before delivery or by the builder on the job. Place posts ten feet apart and space pickets their own width. Each ten feet of this fence will require the following materials:

2 horizontal rails	$2'' \times 4'' \times 10' 0''$
1 post	$4'' \times 4'' \times 6' 0''$
1 board	$1'' \times 8'' \times 10' 0''$
16 pickets	$1'' \times 4'' \times 35''$

Fig. 6 shows the fence three feet high. This dimension may be changed to suit the requirements of the site.

By cutting the tops of pickets symmetrically (Fig. 7), it is possible to introduce a feeling of movement into the design of a fence. Be sure to make the angle of the picket face toward the house for the aesthetic purpose of making the house itself the most important part of the landscape design. Notice the extra strips placed outside the row of pickets parallel to the rails. Place posts at ten foot intervals and carry corner posts to the full height of the fence; intermediate posts only as high as upper rail. For each ten feet of fence, the following materials are needed:

2 horizontal rails	$2'' \times 4'' \times 10' 0''$
2 strips	$1'' \times 2'' \times 10' 0''$
1 post	$4'' \times 4'' \times 7' 0''$
20 pickets	$1'' \times 4'' \times 47''$

Board fences. By so simple an expedient as notching the sides of the board, it is possible to relieve the monotony usually inherent in a board fence, and give it a very pleasant decorative effect. Rough boards may be used if the paint is to be sprayed on or if the boards are to be dipped before applying. If painted by hand, it will be far easier to use surfaced stock.

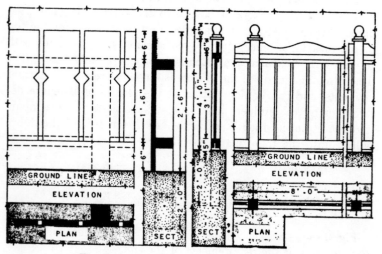

Fig. 8.   Fig. 9.

Such a fence may be of various heights. That shown in Fig. 8 is 2½′ high. Its proportions might be improved by increasing the height somewhat. Note the baseboard which is placed directly against the posts and upon which the vertical boards are set. For each ten feet of fence, the following materials are needed:

2 horizontal rails	2″ × 4″ × 10′ 0″
1 vertical post	4″ × 4″ × 6′ 0″
14 vertical boards (notched as shown)	1″ × 8″ × 2′ 0″
1 baseboard	1″ × 6″ × 10′ 0″

Though somewhat more elaborate in structure than other board fences, the design shown in Fig. 9 has the advantage of presenting exactly the same appearance from both sides. There is no "inside" or "outside." Depending upon its height, it may be used to insure privacy from passers-by. It will also serve to keep children and pets from wandering out into the street. The finial shown may, if desired, be eliminated. For each ten feet of fence, the following materials will be needed:

2 horizontal rails	2″ × 4″ × 10′ 0″
1 horizontal bottom rail	1″ × 4″ × 10′ 0″
1 horizontal top board (cut scalloped top as indicated)	1″ × 5″ × 10′ 0″
1 post	4″ × 4″ × 7′ 0″
1 square molding	1″ × 2″ × 10′ 0″
17 vertical boarding	1″ × 6″ × 3′ 0″
1 redi-cut turned finial	4″ × 4″ × 1′ 0″
1 redi-cut square finial base	1″ × 6″ × 0′ 6″

Lattice fencing. Lattice fencing of the type shown in Fig. 10 has become particularly popular because of its double usefulness in the garden: it affords a good-looking windbreak for the plants behind it and can also give support for climbers or espaliers. It is simply constructed of redwood materials obtainable at any lumber yard. Lattice strips need be nailed only to the rails and posts and at their ends. Materials needed for each ten-foot unit of fence are:

2 horizontal rails	2″ × 4″ × 10′ 0″
1 post	4″ × 4″ × 7′ 0″
35 lattice	5⁄16″ × 1⅜″ × 10′ 0″

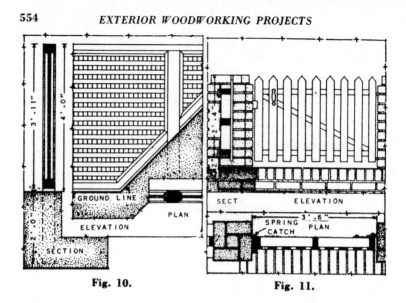

Fig. 10.   Fig. 11.

Gates. One of the simplest gates to build is the straight picket gate shown in Fig. 11. The procedures for the construction for this and other gates are similar to that described for fences. The pickets themselves are available in pre-cut redwood. The first step in its construction is to build a simple rectangular frame with a single cross brace of 2 × 4's. The pickets are placed against this, spaced at approximately their own width to fit the opening. Though illustrated as built between brick piers, it is also suitable for use with picket fences.

Note the small stopping block sunk into the brick at the left. This will not be needed if double-swing hinges are used. The materials needed are:

2 horizontal rails	....	2″ × 3″ × 3′ 6″
1 cross brace	....	2″ × 3″ × 3′ 6″
9 pickets	....	1″ × 3″ × 2′ 6″ net 2½″ wide, 35″ long in Picket Pack
1 block gate stop	....	2″ × 6″ × 3″ cut to form stop as indicated

A slightly more elaborate gate that presents the same appearance from both sides is shown in Fig. 12. The ends of the two side framing members and the top rail may be cut with a bandsaw. In building the gate, place the vertical pickets first, then cut diagonal pieces to fit. Besides their decorative value, they serve as bracing members for the gate to prevent sagging. For each such gate, materials needed are:

2 horizontal rails.................	2″ × 6″ × 3′ 6″ tongue-and-grove and glued to vertical rails
2 vertical rails....................	2″ × 4″ × 2′ 6″ ends cut as shown, grooved to receive tongue of horizontal rails
1 square	1 11/16″ × 1 11/16″ × 12′ 0″ straight molding No. 1622
1 block gate stop	2″ × 6″ × 3″ cut to form stop as indicated

Pergolas. Pergolas add beauty and utility to a garden and are inexpensive to build. In order to use standard lengths of material and to prevent waste this pergola has been laid out on a two-foot module or unit plant (Figs. 13 and 13A). All dimensions are taken from center line to center line. A dimension less than one module would be one-half module or one foot. Any dimension less than one foot should be used only to space lattice uniformly. One complete unit can be built and another unit added later. The sizes of individual members, such as posts, beams, rafters, and lattice, may be whatever standard size preferred that is procurable.

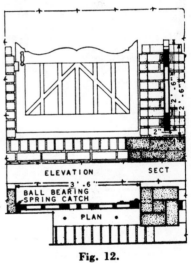

Fig. 12.

Posts should be constructed of an all-heart grade of lumber.

The brackets, beam, and rafter end designs can run from the straight line effects to the scroll type. Scroll ends can be cut and shaped by hand tools, if necessary. However, if power equipment is available it can be used to advantage. Materials required are as follows:

Fig. 13. Construction details and completed pergola.

MATERIAL LISTS

Posts Set One Module on Center

4 Posts	....	4″ × 4″ × 10′ 0″
2 Beams	....	4″ × 4″ × 8′ 0″
4 Rafters	....	2″ × 6″ × 10′ 0″
4 Brackets	....	3″ × 6″ × 2′ 0″
2 Bottom rails	....	2″ × 4″ × 2′ 0″
14 Roof lattice	....	5/16″ × 1 5/8″ × 8′ 0″
4 Side panels	....	5/16″ × 1 5/8″ × 7′ 0″
16 Side panels	....	5/16″ × 1 5/8″ × 2′ 0″

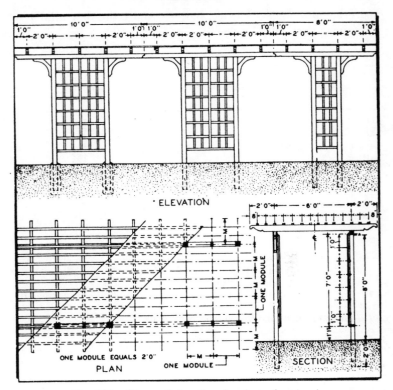

Fig. 13A. Plan and elevation drawings of a pergola.

Posts Set Two Modules on Center

4 Posts	....	$4'' \times 4'' \times 10' \, 0''$
2 Beams	....	$4'' \times 4'' \times 10' \, 0''$
5 Rafters	....	$2'' \times 6'' \times 10' \, 0''$
4 Brackets	....	$3'' \times 6'' \times 2' \, 0''$
2 Bottom rails	....	$2'' \times 4'' \times 4' \, 0''$
2 Middle rails	....	$2'' \times 4'' \times 7' \, 0''$
14 Roof lattice	....	$\frac{5}{16}'' \times 1\frac{5}{8}'' \times 10' \, 0''$
8 Side panels	....	$\frac{5}{16}'' \times 1\frac{5}{8}'' \times 7' \, 0''$
16 Side panels	....	$\frac{5}{16}'' \times 1\frac{5}{8}'' \times 4' \, 0''$

Trellises. A number of suggested trellis designs are shown in Fig. 14. As can be seen, their construction is extremely simple. With a little originality trellises can be built in many pleasing and original designs. Lattice, battens, and lath are available in the following standard sizes:

LATTICE, BATTENS, OR LATH FOR TRELLISES

Type	Thickness in Inches	Width in Inches
Lattice	$\frac{5}{16}$	$1\frac{1}{16}$
Lattice	$\frac{5}{16}$	$1\frac{1}{8}$
Lattice	$\frac{5}{16}$	$1\frac{3}{8}$
Lattice	$\frac{5}{16}$	$1\frac{5}{8}$
Lattice	$\frac{5}{16}$	$1\frac{3}{4}$
Batten	$\frac{3}{8}$	$2\frac{1}{8}$
Batten	$\frac{3}{8}$	$2\frac{1}{4}$
Batten	$\frac{5}{16}$	$2\frac{1}{2}$
Batten	$\frac{3}{8}$	$2\frac{1}{2}$
Batten	$\frac{3}{8}$	$2\frac{3}{4}$
Lath	$\frac{3}{8}$	$1\frac{1}{2}$

Lattice lengths—Standard lengths are 6′ and longer in multiples of 1′ up to and including 10′, and in multiples of 2′ from 10′ to 20′.

Batten lengths—3′ to 10′ in 1′ multiples, and in multiples of 2′ from 10′ to 20′.

Lath lengths—4′, 6′, and 8′. 50 laths per bundle.

The number of lineal feet of lattice required for each design is shown in Fig. 14.

GARDEN FURNITURE

The construction of attractive and serviceable garden furniture presents no special difficulties. The suggested designs shown in Figs. 15 to 21 are simple in construction. If power equipment is not available they can all be constructed with the hand tools generally found in a home tool kit.

Lawn chair. The chair shown in Fig. 15 is a variation of the conventional Adirondack-type chair, featuring folding arm extensions and supports. Cut all parts to sizes and shapes (Fig. 15) from $\frac{7}{8}''$ clear kiln-dried lumber. The curved members forming the arm rests, the supports, and the chair seat can be cut out on a bandsaw. If a bandsaw is not available, proceed as described in Chap. 2 for cutting convex and concave cuts with a saw and chisel. After cutting all members to size and shaping, assemble with countersunk screws and nails in the following order.

Secure apron to the two front uprights, then attach the side pieces to the uprights. Next, with hinges secure the hinged part of each of the arms. Assemble and secure the back supports to the bottom side members (Fig. 15). Secure the crosspiece forming

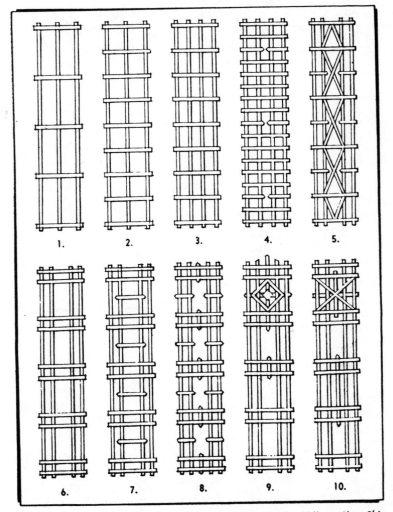

Fig. 14. Suggested trellis designs and material required. (All are 1′ × 6′.) 1. 24 lineal feet; 2. 30 lineal feet; 3. 36 lineal feet; 4. 48 lineal feet; 5. 48 lineal feet; 6. 36 lineal feet; 7. to 10. 42 lineal feet.

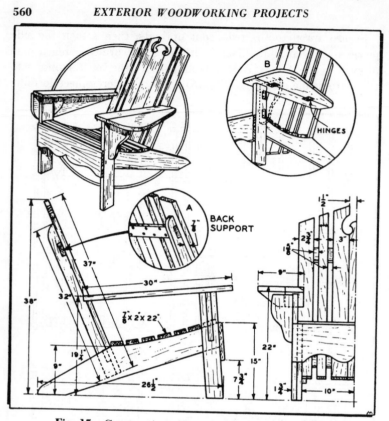

Fig. 15. Construction of lawn chair with folding arms.

the back support (*A*, Fig. 15). Nail pieces forming seat and back members and proceed by securing the arms to the back and the front uprights. Finally, fit and secure the folding arm supports in place with hinges (*B*, Fig. 15). Sand and finish the completely assembled chair.

Roll-away lounge. The comfortable roll-away lounge shown in Fig. 16 is a unique piece of garden furniture that can easily be constructed of 1⅛″ kiln-dried clear pine or cypress. While the dimensions given in the drawing will accommodate a **24″ × 60″** plastic-covered pad of foamite rubber, dimensions can be altered as desired.

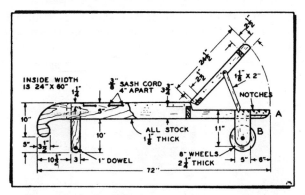

Fig. 16. Constructing a roll-away lounge.

As can be seen in the working drawing (Fig. 16), all of the joints are butted together and secured with countersunk screws. A series of $\frac{7}{16}''$ holes are drilled in the main frame and the hinge section of the lounge, through which is threaded a $\frac{3}{8}''$ sash cord. This cord is laced and forms the necessary support for the padding. Make the entire pad of two thicknesses of 1″ rubber foam, cement together and cover with one of the many types of waterproof and washable plastic materials now available at local upholstery or hardware stores. The hinged section can be adjusted to several heights by means of the notch supports fastened to the main frame (*A*, Fig. 16). Bandsaw the 8″ wheels from $2\frac{1}{4}''$ stock or from two thicknesses of $1\frac{1}{8}''$ stock glued together. For a discussion of procedures on gluing and clamping see Chap. 3. Mount the 8″ wheels on a 1″ hardwood dowel with $1\frac{1}{4}''$ dowels on the end of the axle to hold them in place (*B*, Fig. 16). Assemble and finish as desired.

Roll-away lawn seat. This lawn seat is a companion piece to the roll-away lounge previously described. The novel feature of this piece of garden furniture is the two removable chairs which can be placed in almost any desired position (Figs. 17 and 18). The seats are perfectly square and are identical with the exception of the arms. One of the seats has the arm on the left, while the other has it on the right. Construction details are shown in Fig. 19. The completeness of this working drawing, combined with the simplicity of construction, makes any detailed instructions unnecessary. When assembled, the lawn seat should be finished.

Lawn tables. The designer of the lawn table shown in Fig. 20 conceived the clever idea of making the tops of these tables from

Fig. 17. Roll-away lawn seat.

Fig. 18. Roll-away lawn seat.

discarded barrel tops. Where barrel tops are not available, cut the table tops from $1\frac{1}{8}''$ stock either to the size shown or to any size desired and bevel off the edges on the shaper. Use $\frac{3}{4}''$ stock for the legs and stretchers of the table and bandsaw them to the required shape. Half-lapped joints are used throughout with the exception of the necessary dado cuts for setting in the legs at the required angle (*A*, Fig. 20). See Chap. 3 for the making of dado joints. Assemble the table with countersunk flathead wood screws. Sand the top smooth and finish natural by

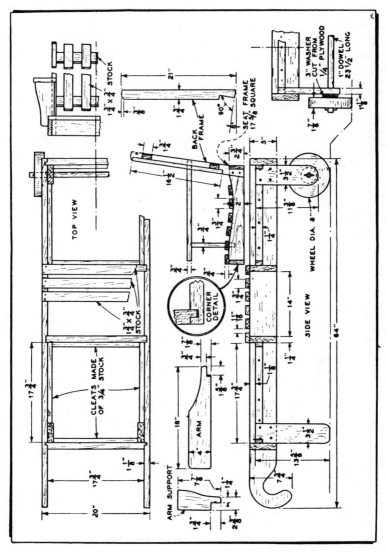

Fig. 19. Construction and details of a roll-away lawn seat.

applying several coats of clear Valspar or similar waterproof varnish. The balance of the table should be either painted or lacquered.

Outdoor gymnasium for the children. The working plans for an outdoor gymnasium of simple yet sturdy construction that can be fitted into a comparatively small space are shown in Fig. 21. This outdoor gym can be assembled with carriage and log bolts to make it easy to take apart and set up in the basement for use during the winter months.

Clear $2'' \times 4''$ pine or cypress is used for most of the parts. The bottom frame, which comes in contact with the ground, should be given a coat of creosote to prevent the wood from rotting. Assemble the framework of the gym with carriage and log bolts. Make the ladder rungs and the teeter-totter handles from either old broom handles or $1\frac{1}{4}''$ maple dowels. The teeter-totter is mounted on a piece of $\frac{3}{4}''$ or $1''$ pipe cut to size shown with regular pipe straps for fittings (A, Fig. 21). To add rigidity to the entire structure, put metal reinforcement plates on all corners and bracing members (Chap. 3).

Round or break all edges and sharp corners before proceeding with the finishing and painting.

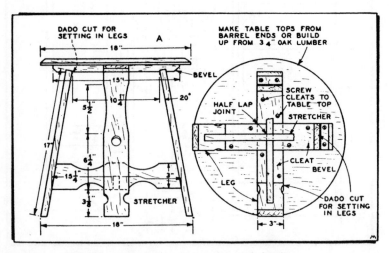

Fig. 20. Lawn table construction and details.

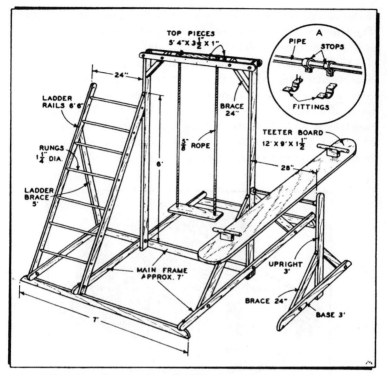

Fig. 21. Construction of children's outdoor gymnasium.

TOOL SHED AND LATH HOUSE

For anyone seriously interested in gardening, a small lath house or greenhouse is almost an essential. Almost any space in the garden will do for such a structure. It can be screened by shrubbery or, if neatly painted, can be exposed to view as a functional part of the garden itself (Fig. 22). The combination lath house and tool shed detailed in the working drawings, Figs. 23 and 24, occupies a space of 12′ × 24′, but may be scaled either up or down, according to requirements. Notice, for instance, that the lath portion is planned in 6′ units or modules so that the rear wall could be placed at various distances back from the tool shed. If it is necessary to make a narrow building, an 8′ width would prove economical because lumber dealers stock this length of material and consequently there would be little waste in cutting. The whole structure may be erected easily without special tools.

Note that the complete bill of materials for the construction of the tool and lath house includes those required for the workbenches and tables (Fig. 25). A notation, such as ⅞′ listed in the column headed "Pieces Required," indicates that seven pieces will be needed, each 8′ long. Because the wood will be exposed to weathering and alternate wetting and drying, a durable species of lumber such as California redwood should be used. All items on the material list are usually carried in stock by lumber dealers.

Fig. 22. Completed tool shed and lath house.

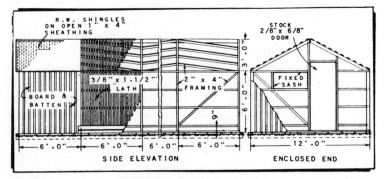

Fig. 23. Elevation details.

Structural details. Notice that roof bracing in the lath house portion of the structure is designed to carry off rainwater. Braces are slanted toward alternate rafters. (Only nailing strips are necessary under the shingled portion of the roof.)

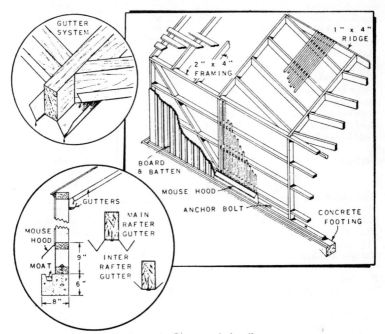

Fig. 24. Structural details.

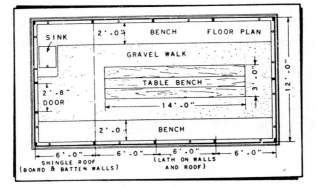

Fig. 25. Floor plan.

LATH HOUSE—MATERIAL LIST

Item	Pieces	Net Length	Pieces Required
Sills			2/10′ 2/12′ 2/14′
Studs	13	5′ 8″	1/6′ 6/12′
Horizontal braces	36	6′ 0″	18/12′
Diagonal braces	21	2′ 4″	7/8′
Plates			6/12′
Rafters	14	6′ 7″	7/14′
Nailing joist	24	6′ 0″	12/12′
Ridge boards	2	12′ 0″	2/12′
Door header	1	2′ 8″ ⎫	1/6′
Window frame	1	1′ 8″ ⎭	
Boards—sides	24	6′ 0″	12/12′
Boards—ends	48		2/6′ 8/8′ 3/14′ 4/18′
Battens			4/18′ 3/6′ 8/8′ 3/14′ 12/12′
Roof sheathing	20	6′ 6″	10/14′
Shingles			1 Square
Side lath			3 Bundles 6′
End lath			1 Bundle 6′
Top lath			3 Bundles 8′
Cornice molding	4	12′ 0″	4/12′
Benches:			
Horizontal supports	13	2′ 0″ ⎫	3/12′
	3	3′ 0″ ⎭	
Legs	18	3′ 0″	9/6′
Top (sides)			8/12′ 1/6′
Top (center)			3/14′

Nail gutters of galvanized metal or copper to the underside of roof members. These may be obtained from a local sheet metal worker.

The necessary concrete foundation can be poured per standard procedures. Other constructional details are shown in Figs. 23 and 24.

The moat in the concrete foundation receives water from the gutter system, so that it may be drained off at a convenient point.

CHAPTER *20*

Construction of Stairs

———————— • ————————

Stairways in houses should be designed and constructed to afford safety and adequate headroom for the occupants as well as space for the passage of furniture. The two types of stairs commonly used in houses are (a) the finished main stairs leading to the second floor or split-level floors and (b) the basement or service stairs leading to the basement or to the garage area. The main stairs are designed to provide ascent and descent and may be made a feature of the interior design. The service stairs to the basement areas are usually somewhat steeper and are constructed of less-expensive materials, although safety and convenience should be the prime factors in their design.

Most *finish* and *service stairs* are constructed in place. The *main stairs* are assembled with prefabricated parts, which include housed stringers, treads, and risers. *Basement stairs* may be made simply of 2″ by 12″ carriages and plank treads. In split-level design or a midfloor outside entry, stairways are often completely finished with plastered walls, handrails, and appropriate moldings.

Wood species appropriate for main stairway components include oak, birch, maple, and similar hardwoods. Treads and risers for the basement or service stairways may be of Douglas fir, southern pine, and similar species. A hardwood tread with a softwood or lower-grade hardwood riser may be combined to provide greater resistance to wear.

TYPES OF STAIRWAYS

Three general types of stairway runs commonly used in house construction are the *straight run* (*A*, Fig. 1), the *long L* (*B*, Fig. 1), and the *narrow U* (*A*, Fig. 2). Another type is similar to the *long L* except that *winders* or *pie shaped* treads (*B*, Fig. 2) are substituted for the landing. This type of stairs is *not* desirable and should be avoided whenever possible because it is obviously not as convenient or as safe as the *long L*. It is used where the stair run is not sufficient for the more conventional stairway containing a landing. In such instances, the winders should be adjusted to replace the landings so that the width of the tread, 18″ from the narrow end, will not be less than the tread width on the straight run (*A*, Fig. 3). Therefore, if the standard tread is 10″ wide, the winder tread should be at least 10″ wide at the 18″ line.

Another basic rule in stair layout concerns the landing at the top of the stairs when the door opens into the stairway, such as on a stair to the basement. This landing, as well as middle landings, should not be less than 2′ 6″ long (*B*, Fig. 3).

Sufficient headroom in a stairway is a primary requisite. For main stairways, clear vertical distance should not be less than 6′ 8″ (*A*, Fig. 4). Basement or service stairs should provide not less than a 6′ 4″ clearance.

The minimum tread width and riser height must also be considered. For *closed stairs*, a 1″ tread width and an 8¼″ riser height should be considered a minimum even for basement stairways (*B*, Fig. 4). Risers with less height are always more desirable. The nosing projection should be at least 1⅛″, but if the projection is too much greater, the stairs will be awkward and difficult to climb.

RATIO OF RISER TO TREAD

There is a definite relation between the height of a riser and the width of a tread, and all stairs should be laid out to conform to well-established rules governing these relations. If the combination of run and rise is too great, there is undue strain on the leg muscles and on the heart of the climber. If the combination

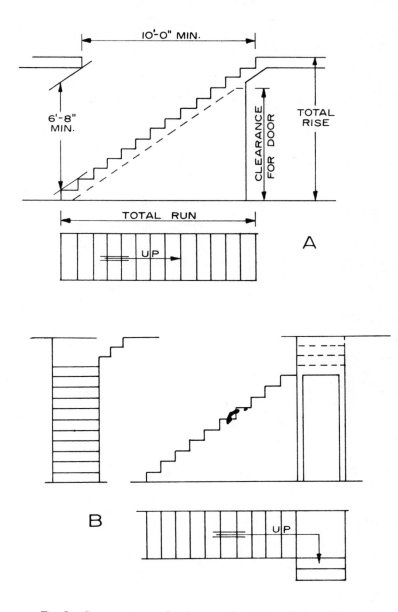

Fig. 1. Common types of stair runs. *A*, straight. *B*, long "L".

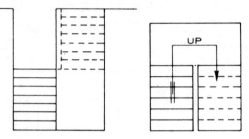

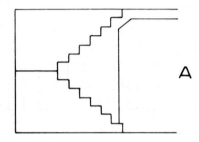

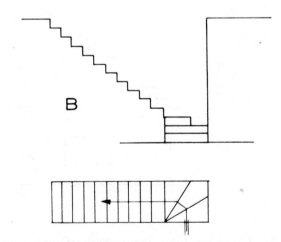

Fig. 2. Space-saving stairs. *A*, narrow "U". *B*, winder.

of run and rise is too small, his or her foot may kick the riser at each step and an attempt to shorten stride may be tiring. Experience has proved that a riser 7½″ to 7¾″ high with appropriate tread width combines both safety and comfort.

A rule of thumb which sets forth a good relation between the height of the riser and the width of the tread is as follows.

The tread width multiplied by the riser height in inches should equal to 72 to 75. The stairs shown in *B*, Fig. 4 would conform to this rule (9 times 8¼″ = 74¼″). If the tread is 10″, the riser should be 7½″, which is more desirable for common stairways. Another rule sometimes used: the tread width plus twice the riser height should equal about 25.

These desirable riser heights should be used to determine the number of steps between floors. *For example,* fourteen risers are commonly used for main stairs between the first and second floors. The 8′ ceiling height of the first floor plus the upper story floor joists, subfloor, and finish floor result in a floor-to-floor

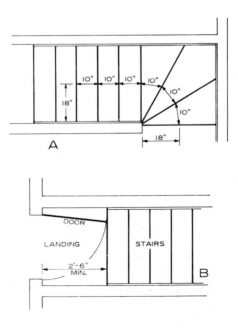

Fig. 3. Stair layout. *A*, winder treads. *B*, landings.

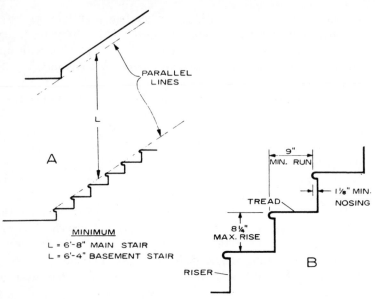

Fig. 4. Stairway dimensions. *A,* minimum headroom.
B, closed stair dimensions.

height of about 105″. Therefore, 14 divided into 105 is exactly
7½″, the height of each riser. Fifteen risers used for this height
would result in a 7″ riser height.

STAIR WIDTHS AND HANDRAILS

The width of main stairs should not be less than 2′ 8″ clear
of the handrail. However, many main stairs are designed with a
distance of 3′ 6″ between the centerline of the enclosing sidewalls. This will result in a stairway with a width of about 3′.
Split-level entrance stairs are even wider; for basement stairs,
the minimum clear width is 2′ 6″.

A continuous handrail should be used on at least one side of
the stairway when there are more than three risers. When stairs
are open on two sides, there should be protective railings on each
side.

FRAMING FOR STAIRS

Openings in the floor for stairways, fireplaces, and chimneys are framed out during construction of the floor. (*See* Chap. 21, Figs. 9 and 11.) The long dimension of stairway openings may be either parallel or at right angles to the joists. However, it is much easier to frame a stairway opening when its length is parallel to the joists. For *basement stairways*, the rough openings may be about 9′ 6″ long by 32″ wide (two joist spaces). Openings in the second floor for the *main stair* are usually a minimum of 10′ long. Widths may be 3′ or more. Depending on the short header required for one or both ends, the opening is usually framed as shown in *A*, Fig. 5 when joists parallel the length of the opening. Nailing should conform to that shown in Chap. 21, Figs. 9 and 11.

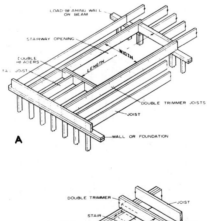

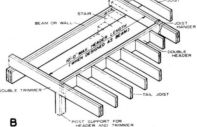

Fig. 5. Framing for stairs. *A*, length of opening parallel to joists. *B*, length of opening perpendicular to joists.

When the length of the stair opening is perpendicular to the length of the joists, a long doubled header is required (*B*, Fig. 5). A header under these conditions without a supporting wall beneath is usually limited to a 10′ length. A load-bearing wall under all or part of this opening simplifies the framing immensely, as the joists will then bear on the top plate of the wall rather than be supported at the header by joist hangers or other means. Nailing should conform to that shown in Chap. 21, Figs. 9 and 11.

The framing for an L-shaped stairway is usually supported in the basement by a post at the corner of the opening or by a load-bearing wall beneath. When a similar stair leads from the first to the second floor, the landing can be framed out (Fig. 6). The platform frame is nailed into the enclosing stud walls and provides a nailing area for the subfloor as well as a support for the stair carriages.

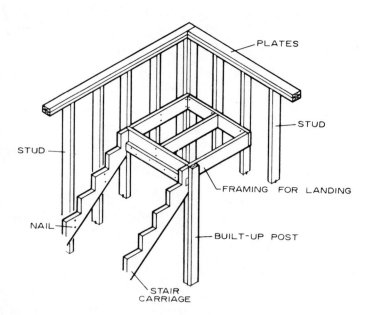

Fig. 6. Framing for stair landing.

STAIRWAY DETAILS

BASEMENT STAIRS

Stair carriages which carry the treads and support the loads on the stair are made in two ways. Rough stair carriages commonly used for basement stairs are made from 2″ by 12″ planks. The effective depth below the tread and riser notches must be at least 3½″ (*A*, Fig. 7). Such carriages are usually placed only at each side of the stairs. However, an intermediate carriage is required at the center of the stairs when the treads are $1\frac{1}{16}''$ thick and the stairs wider than 2′ 6″. Three carriages are also required when treads are $1\frac{5}{8}''$ thick and stairs are wider than 3′. The carriages are fastened to the joist header at the top of the stairway or rest on a supporting ledger nailed to the header (*B*, Fig. 7).

Firestops should be used at the top and bottom of all stairs as shown at *A*, Fig. 7.

Perhaps the simplest system is one in which carriages are not cut out for the treads and risers. Rather, cleats are nailed to the side of the unnotched carriage and the treads nailed to them. This design may not be as desirable as the notched carriage system when walls are present. Carriages may also be supported by walls located below them.

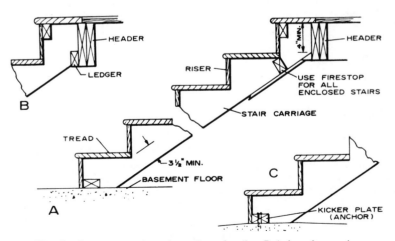

Fig. 7. Basement stairs. *A*, carriage details. *B*, ledger for carriage. *C*, kicker plate.

The bottom of the stair carriages may rest and be anchored to the basement floor. A better method is to use an anchored 2″ by 4″ or 2″ by 6″ treated *kicker plate* (*C*, Fig. 7).

Basement stair treads can consist of simple 1½″ thick plank treads without risers. From the standpoint of appearance and maintenance, the use of 1⅛″ finished tread material and nominal 1″ boards for risers is usually justified. Use finishing nails to fasten them to the plank carriages.

A *fully enclosed stairway* might be used from the main floor to the attic. It combines the rough notched carriage with a finish stringer along each side (*A*, Fig. 8). The finish stringer is fastened to the wall, before carriages are fastened. Treads and risers are cut to fit snugly between the stringers and are fastened to the rough carriage with finishing nails (*A*, Fig. 8). This may be varied by nailing the rough carriage directly to the wall and by notching the finished stringer to fit (*B*, Fig. 8). The treads and risers are installed as previously described.

MAIN STAIRWAY

An *open* main stairway with its railing and balusters ending in a *newel* post can be very decorative and pleasing in the traditional house interior. It can also be translated to a contemporary stairway design and again result in a pleasing feature.

The main stairway differs from the other types previously described because of (a) the housed stringers which replace the

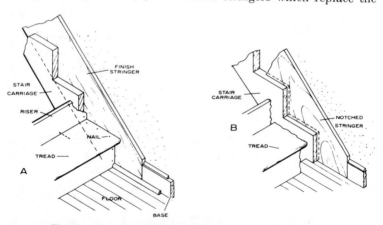

Fig. 8. Enclosed stairway details. *A*, with full stringer. *B*, with notched stringer.

rough plank carriage; (b) the routed and grooved treads and risers; (c) the decorative railing and balusters in open stairways; and (d) the wood species, most of which can be given a natural finish.

The supporting member of the finished main stairway is the housed stringer (*A*, Fig. 9). One is used on each side of the stairway and fastened to the plastered or finished walls. They are routed to fit both the tread and the riser. The stair is assembled by means of hardwood wedges which are spread with glue and driven under the ends of the treads and in back of the risers. Assembly is usually done from under and the rear side of the stairway. In addition, nails are used to fasten the riser to the tread between the ends of the step (*B*, Fig. 9). When treads and risers are wedged and glued into housed stringers, the maxi-

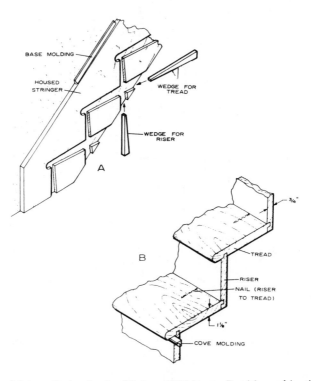

Fig. 9. Main stair detail. *A*, with housed stringer. *B*, with combination of treads and risers.

mum allowable width is usually 3′ 6″. For wider stairs, a notched carriage is used between the housed stringers.

When stairs are open on one side, a railing and balusters should be used. The balusters may be fastened to the end of the treads which have a finished return (Fig. 10). The balusters are also fastened to a railing which is terminated at a newel post. Balusters may be turned to form doweled ends, which fit into drilled holes in the treads and the railing. A stringer and appropriate moldings are used to complete the stairway trim.

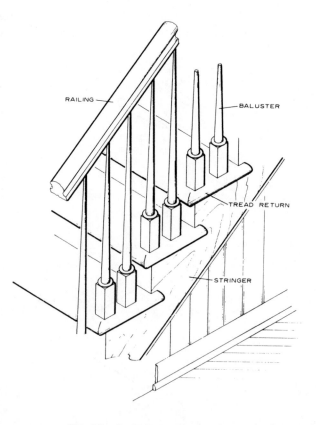

Fig. 10. Details of open main stairway.

ATTIC FOLDING STAIRS

Where attics are used primarily for storage and where space for a fixed stairway is not available, *hinged* or *folding* stairs are often used and may be purchased ready to install. They operate through an opening in the ceiling of a hall and swing up into the attic space, out of the way when not in use. Where such stairs are to be installed, the attic floor joists should be designed for limited floor loading. One common size of folding stairs requires only a 26″ by 54″ rough opening. These openings should be framed out as described for normal stair openings.

EXTERIOR STAIRS

Proportioning of risers and treads in laying out *porch steps* or *approaches to terraces* should be as carefully considered as the design of interior stairways. Similar riser-to-tread ratios can be used. The riser used in principal exterior steps should be between 6″ and 7″ in height. The need for a good support or foundation for outside steps is often overlooked. Where wood steps are used, the bottom step should be concrete or supported by treated wood members. Where the steps are located over backfill or disturbed ground, the foundation should be carried down to undisturbed ground.

CHAPTER 21

Floor Framing

The *floor framing* in a wood frame house consists specifically of the posts, beams, sill plates, joists, and subfloor. (*See* Chap. 1, sections on Framing.) When these are assembled on a foundation, they form a level, anchored platform for the rest of the house. The posts and center beams of wood or steel, which support the inside ends of the joists, are sometimes replaced with a wood frame or masonry wall when the basement area is divided into rooms. Wood frame houses may also be constructed upon a concrete floor slab or over a crawl-space area with floor framing similar to that used for a full basement.

DESIGN

One of the important factors in the design of wood floor systems is to equalize shrinkage and expansion of the wood framing at the outside walls and at the center beam. This is usually accomplished by using approximately the same total depth of wood at the center beam as the outside framing. Therefore, as beams and joists approach moisture equilibrium or the moisture content they reach in service, there are only small differences in the amount of shrinkage. This will minimize plaster cracks and prevent sticking doors and other inconveniences caused by uneven shrinkage. If there is a total of 12″ of wood at the foundation wall (including joists and sill plate), this should be balanced with about 12″ of wood at the center beam.

Moisture content of beams and joists used in floor framing should not exceed 19 per cent. However, a moisture content of about 15 per cent is much more desirable. Dimension material can be obtained at these moisture contents when so specified. When moisture contents are in the higher ranges, it is good practice to allow joists and beams to approach their moisture equilibrium before applying inside finish and trim, such as baseboard, base shoe, door jambs, and casings.

Grades of dimension lumber vary considerably by species. For specific uses in this book, a sequence of first-, second-, third-, fourth-, and sometimes fifth-grade material is used. In general, the first grade is for a high or special use, the second for better than average, the third for average, and the fourth and fifth for more economical construction. Joists and girders are usually second-grade material of a species, while sills and posts are usually of third or fourth grade. (*See* Chap. 3, section on Lumber Grades.)

NAILING PRACTICES

Of primary consideration in the construction of a house is the method used to fasten the various wood members together. These connections are most commonly made with nails, but on occasion metal straps, lag screws, bolts, and adhesives may be used. (*See* Chap. 3, section on Nail Holding.)

Proper fastening of frame members and covering materials provides the rigidity and strength to resist severe windstorms and other hazards. Good nailing is also important from the standpoint of normal performance of wood parts. *For example,* proper fastening of intersection walls usually reduces plaster cracking at the inside corners. (*See* Chap. 3, Fig. 5 for sizes of common and finishing nails.)

Nailing practices for the framing and sheathing of a well-constructed wood frame house is shown in Table 10.

POSTS AND GIRDERS

Wood or *steel posts* are generally used in the basement to support wood girders or steel beams. Masonry piers may also be used for this purpose and are commonly employed in crawl-space houses.

The round steel post can be used to support both wood girders and steel beams and is normally supplied with a steel bearing

TABLE 10

Recommended schedule for nailing the framing and sheathing of a well-constructed wood-frame house

Joining	Nailing method	Nails		
		Number	Size	Placement
Header to joist	End-nail	3	16d	
Joist to sill or girder	Toenail	2 3	10d or 8d	
Header and stringer joist to sill	Toenail	3	10d	16 in. on center
Bridging to joist	Toenail each end	2	8d	
Ledger strip to beam, 2 in. thick		3	16d	At each joist
Subfloor, boards:				
1 by 6 in. and smaller		2	8d	To each joist
1 by 8 in.		3	8d	To each joist
Subfloor, plywood:				
At edges			8d	6 in. on center
At intermediate joists			8d	8 in. on center
Subfloor (2 by 6 in., T&G) to joist or girder	Blind-nail (casing) and face-nail	2	16d	
Soleplate to stud, horizontal assembly	End-nail	2	16d	At each stud
Top plate to stud	End-nail	2	16d	
Stud to soleplate	Toenail	4	8d	
Soleplate to joist or blocking	Face-nail	2	16d	16 in. on center
Doubled studs	Face-nail, stagger	2	10d	16 in. on center
End stud of intersecting wall to exterior wall stud	Face-nail	2	16d	16 in. on center
Upper top plate to lower top plate	Face-nail	2	16d	16 in. on center
Upper top plate, laps and intersections				

Joining	Nailing method	Number of nails	Size	Placement
Ceiling joist to top wall plates	Toenail	3	8d	
Ceiling joist laps at partition	Face-nail	4	16d	
Rafter to top plate	Toenail	2	8d	
Rafter to ceiling joist	Face-nail	5	10d	
Rafter to valley or hip rafter	Toenail	3	10d	
Ridge board to rafter	End-nail	3	10d	
Rafter to rafter through ridge board	Toenail	4	8d	
	Edge-nail	1	10d	
Collar beam to rafter:				
2 in. member	Face-nail	2	12d	
1 in. member	Face-nail	3	8d	
1-in. diagonal let-in brace to each stud and plate (4 nails at top)		2	8d	
Built-up corner studs:				
Studs to blocking	Face-nail	2	10d	Each side
Intersecting stud to corner studs	Face-nail		16d	12 in. on center
Built-up girders and beams, three or more members	Face-nail		20d	32 in. on center, each side
Wall sheathing:				
1 by 8 in. or less, horizontal	Face-nail	2	8d	At each stud
1 by 6 in. or greater, diagonal	Face-nail	3	8d	At each stud
Wall sheathing, vertically applied plywood:				
3/8 in. and less thick	Face-nail		6d	6 in. edge
1/2 in. and over thick	Face-nail		8d	12 in. intermediate
Wall sheathing, vertically applied fiberboard:				
1/2 in. thick	Face-nail			1½ in. roofing nail } 3 in. edge and
25/32 in. thick	Face-nail			1¾ in. roofing nail } 6 in. intermediate
Roof sheathing, boards, 4-, 6-, 8-in. width	Face-nail	2	8d	At each rafter
Roof sheathing, plywood:				
3/8 in. and less thick	Face-nail		6d }	6 in. edge and 12 in. intermediate
1/2 in. and over thick	Face-nail		8d }	

plate at each end. Be sure to secure anchoring to the girder or beam (Fig. 1).

Wood posts should be solid and not less than 6″ by 6″ in size for freestanding use in a basement. When combined with a framed wall, they may be 4″ by 6″ to conform to the depth of the studs. Wood posts should be squared at both ends and securely fastened to the girder (Fig. 2). The bottom of the post should rest on and be pinned to a masonry pedestal 2″ to 3″ above the finish floor. In moist or wet conditions it is good practice to treat the bottom end of the post or use a moisture-proof covering over the pedestal. (*See* Chap. 3, section on Posts.)

Both wood girders and steel beams are used in present-day house construction. The standard *I-beam* and wide *flange beam* are the most commonly used steel beam shapes. Wood girders are of two types—*solid* and *built up*. The built-up beam is preferred because it can be made up from drier dimension material and is more stable. Commercially available glue-laminated beams may be desirable where exposed in finished basement rooms.

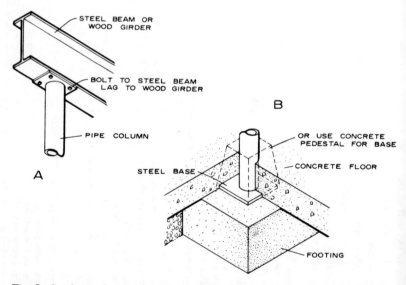

Fig. 1. Steel post for wood or steel girder. *A,* connection to beam. *B,* base plate also may be mounted on and anchored to a concrete pedestal.

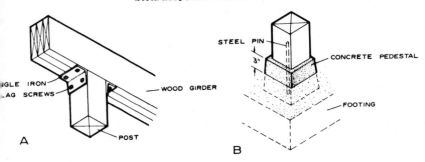

Fig. 2. Wood post for wood girder. *A,* connection to girder. *B,* base.

The built-up girder (Fig. 3) is usually made up of two or more pieces of 2″ dimension lumber spiked together, the ends of the pieces joining over a supporting post. A two-piece girder may be nailed from one side with tenpenny nails, two at the end of each piece and others driven stagger-fashion 16″ apart. A three-piece girder is nailed from each side with twentypenny nails, two near each end of each piece and others driven stagger-fashion 32″ apart.

Ends of wood girders should bear at least 4″ on the masonry walls or pilasters. When wood is untreated, a ½″ air space should be provided at each end and at each side of wood girders framing into masonry (Fig. 3). In termite-infested areas, these pockets should be lined with metal. The top of the girder should be level with the top of the sill plates on the foundation walls, unless *ledger strips* are used. If steel plates are used under ends of girders, they should be of full bearing size.

GIRDER-JOIST INSTALLATION

The simplest method of floor joist framing is one where the joists bear directly on the wood girder or steel beam, in which case the top of the beam coincides with the top of the anchored sill (Fig. 3). This method is used when basement heights provide adequate headroom below the girder. When wood girders are used in this manner, the main disadvantage is that shrinkage is usually greater at the girder than at the foundation.

For more uniform shrinkage at the inner beam and the outer

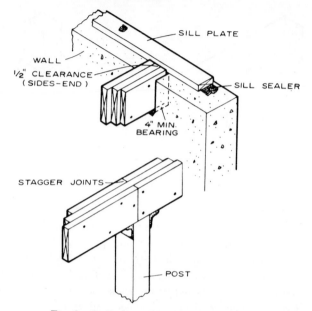

Fig. 3. Built-up wood girder.

wall and to provide greater headroom, joist hangers or a supporting ledger strip are commonly used. Depending on sizes of joists and wood girders, joists may be supported on the ledger strip in several ways (Fig. 4). Each provides about the same depth of wood subject to shrinkage at the outer wall and at the center wood girder. A continuous horizontal tie between exterior walls is obtained by nailing notched joists together (*A*, Fig. 4). Joists must always bear on the ledgers. In *B*, Fig. 4, the connecting scab at each pair of joists provides this tie and also a nailing area for the subfloor. A steel strap is used to tie the joists together when the tops of the beam and the joists are level (*C*, Fig. 4). It is important that a small space be allowed above the beam to provide for shrinkage of the joists.

When a space is required for heat ducts in a partition supported on the girder, a *spaced wood girder* is sometimes necessary (Fig. 5). Solid blocking is used at intervals between the two members. A single post support for a spaced girder usually requires a bolster, preferably metal, with sufficient span to support the two members.

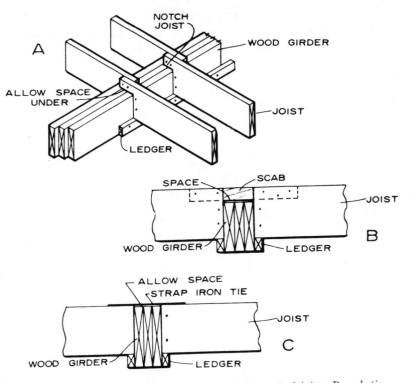

Fig. 4. Ledger on center wood girder. *A,* notched joist. *B,* scab tie between joist. *C,* flush joist.

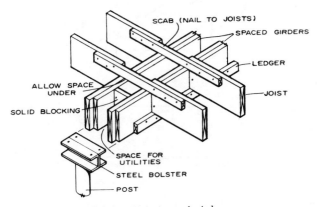

Fig. 5. Spaced wood girder.

Joists may be arranged with a steel beam generally the same way as illustrated for a wood beam. Perhaps the most common methods used, depending on joist sizes, are as follows:

1. The joists rest directly on the top of the beam.

2. Joists rest on a wood ledger or steel angle iron, which is bolted to the web (*A*, Fig. 6).

3. Joists bear directly on the flange of the beam (*B*, Fig. 6). In the third method, wood blocking is required between the joists near the beam flange to prevent overturning.

WOOD SILL CONSTRUCTION

The two general types of wood sill construction used over the foundation wall conform either to platform or balloon framing. The *box sill* is commonly used in platform construction. It consists of a 2″ or thicker plate anchored to the foundation wall over a sill sealer which provides support and fastening for the joists and header at the ends of the joists (Fig. 7). Some houses are constructed without benefit of an anchored sill plate although

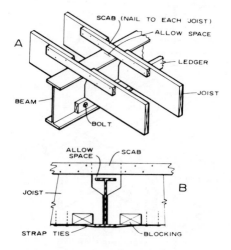

Fig. 6. Steel beam and joists. *A*, bearing on ledger. *B*, bearing on flange.

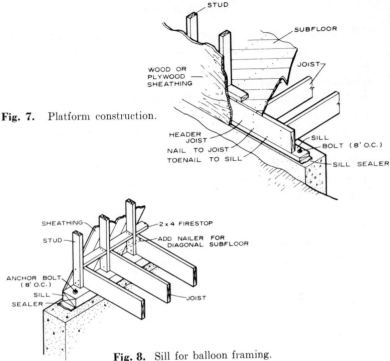

Fig. 7. Platform construction.

Fig. 8. Sill for balloon framing.

this is not entirely desirable. (*See* Chap. 1, section on Woods and Wood-Based Products for Various House Uses, Foundations —Sills and Beams.) The floor framing should then be anchored with metal strapping installed during pouring operations.

Balloon frame construction uses a nominal 2″ or thicker wood sill upon which the joists rest. The studs also bear on this member and are nailed both to the floor joists and the sill. The subfloor is laid diagonally or at right angles to the joists and a firestop added between the studs at the floorline (Fig. 8). When diagonal subfloor is used, a nailing member is normally required between joists and studs at the wall lines.

Because there is less potential shrinkage in exterior walls with balloon framing than in the platform type, balloon framing is usually preferred over the platform type in full two-story brick or stone-veneer houses.

FLOOR JOISTS

Floor joists are selected primarily to meet strength and stiffness requirements. Strength requirements depend upon the loads to be carried. Stiffness requirements place an arbitrary control on deflection under load. Stiffness is also important in limiting vibrations from moving loads that are often a cause of annoyance to occupants. Other desirable qualities for floor joists are good nail-holding ability and freedom from warp. (*See* Chap. 1, section on Framing—Joists, Rafters, and Headers.)

Wood-floor joists are generally of 2″ (nominal) thickness and of 8″, 10″, or 12″ (nominal) depth. The size depends upon the loading, length of span, spacing between joists, and the species and grade of lumber used. As previously mentioned, grades in species vary a great deal. *For example,* the grades generally used for joists are *Standard* for Douglas fir, *No. 2* or *No. 2KD* for southern pine, and comparable grades for other species.

Joist Installation

After the sill plates have been anchored to the foundation walls or piers, the joists are located according to the house design. (Sixteen-inch center-to-center spacing is commonly used.)

Any joists having a slight bow edgewise should be so placed that the crown is on top. A crowned joist will tend to straighten out when subfloor and normal floor loads are applied. Since knots on the upper side of a joist are on the compression side of the member and will have less effect on strength, the largest edge knots should be placed on top.

The header joist is fastened by nailing into the end of each joist with three sixteenpenny nails. In addition, the header joist and the stringer joists parallel to the exterior walls in platform construction (Fig. 9) are toenailed to the sill with tenpenny nails spaced 16″ on center. Each joist should be toenailed to the sill and center beam with two tenpenny or three eightpenny nails. Then the joists should be nailed to each other with three or four sixteenpenny nails when they lap over the center beam. If a nominal 2″ scab is used across the butt ended joists, it should be nailed to each joist with at least three sixteenpenny nails at each side of the joint. These and other nailing patterns and

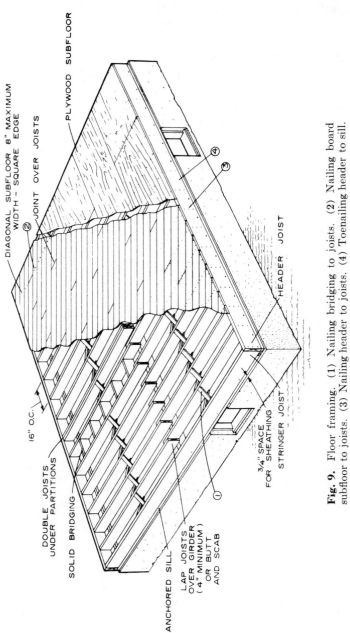

PLYWOOD SUBFLOOR

DIAGONAL SUBFLOOR 8" MAXIMUM WIDTH – SQUARE EDGE

② JOINT OVER JOISTS

16" O.C.

④

③

HEADER JOIST

DOUBLE JOISTS UNDER PARTITIONS

SOLID BRIDGING

ANCHORED SILL

LAP JOISTS OVER GIRDER (4" MINIMUM) OR BUTT AND SCAB

①

¾" SPACE FOR SHEATHING

STRINGER JOIST

Fig. 9. Floor framing. (1) Nailing bridging to joists. (2) Nailing board subfloor to joists. (3) Nailing header to joists. (4) Toenailing header to sill.

practices are shown in Table 10.

The *in-line* joist splice is sometimes used in framing the floor and ceiling joists. This system normally allows the use of one smaller joist size when center supports are present. It consists of uneven length joists; the long overhanging joist is cantilevered over the center support, then spliced to the supported joist (Fig. 10). Overhang joists are alternated. Depending on the span, species, and joist size, the overhang varies between 1' 10" and 2' 10". Plywood splice plates are used on each side of the end joints.

It is good practice to double joists under all parallel-bearing partition walls. If spacing is required for heat ducts, solid blocking is used between the joists (Fig. 9).

Framing for Floor Openings

When framing for large openings such as stairwells, fireplaces, and chimneys, the opening should be doubled. A method of framing and nailing for floor openings is shown in Fig. 11.

Joist hangers and short sections of angle iron are often used to support headers and tail beams for large openings. (*See* Chap. 23, Construction of Stairs.)

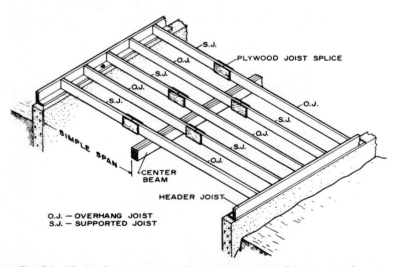

Fig. 10. "In-line" joist system. Alternate extension of joists over the center support with plywood gusset joint allows the use of a smaller joist size.

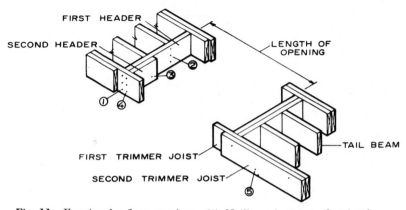

Fig. 11. Framing for floor openings. (1) Nailing trimmer to first header. (2) Nailing header to tail beams. (3) Nailing header together. (4) Nailing trimmer to second header. (5) Nailing trimmers together.

BRIDGING

Cross bridging between wood joists has often been used in house construction, but research by several laboratories has questioned the benefits of bridging in relation to its cost, especially in normal house construction. Even with tight-fitting, well-installed bridging, there is no significant ability to transfer loads after subfloor and finish floor are installed. Some building codes require the use of *cross bridging* or *solid bridging*. (*See* Table 10.)

Solid bridging is often used between joists to provide a more rigid base for partitions located above joist spaces. Well-fitted solid bridging securely nailed to the joists will aid in supporting partitions above them (Fig. 9). Load-bearing partitions should be supported by doubled joists.

SUBFLOOR

Subflooring is used over the floor joists to form a working platform and base for finish flooring. It usually consists of (a) square-edge or tongued-and-grooved boards no wider than 8″ and not less than ¾″ thick or (b) plywood ½″ to ¾″ thick, depending on species, type of finish floor, and spacing of joists (Fig. 9). (*See* Chap. 1, section on Subfloors.)

Boards

Subflooring may be applied either *diagonally* (common) or at *right angles* to the joists. When subflooring is placed at right angles to the joists, the finish floor should be laid at right angles to the subflooring. Diagonal subflooring permits finish flooring to be laid either parallel or at right angles (common) to the joists. End joints of the boards should always be made directly over the joists. Subfloor is nailed to each joist with two eight-penny nails for 8″ widths.

The joist spacing should not exceed 16″ on center when finish flooring is laid parallel to the joists or where parquet finish flooring is used. The spacing should not exceed 24″ on center when finish flooring at least $25\!\!/\!_{32}''$ thick is at right angles to the joists.

Where balloon framing is used, blocking should be installed between ends of joists at the wall of nailing the ends of diagonal subfloor boards (Fig. 8).

Plywood

Plywood can be obtained in a number of grades designed to meet a broad range of end-use requirements. All interior-type grades are also available with waterproof adhesive identical with those used in exterior plywood. This type is useful where a hazard of prolonged moisture exists, such as in underlayments or subfloors adjacent to plumbing fixtures and for roof sheathing which may be exposed for long periods during construction. Under normal conditions and for sheathing used on walls, standard sheathing grades are satisfactory.

Plywood suitable for subfloor, such as standard sheathing, Structural I and II, and C-C Exterior grades, has a panel identification index marking on each sheet. These markings indicate the allowable spacing of rafters and floor joists for the various thicknesses when the plywood is used as roof sheathing or subfloor. *For example*, an index mark of $32\!\!/\!_{16}$ indicates that the plywood panel is suitable for a maximum spacing of 32″ for rafters and 16″ for floor joists. Therefore, no problem of strength differences between species is involved since the correct identification is shown for each panel.

Normally, when some type of underlayment is used over the

plywood subfloor, the minimum thickness of the subfloor for species such as Douglas fir and southern pine is $\frac{1}{2}''$ when joists are spaced 16″ on center and $\frac{5}{8}''$ for such plywood as western hemlock, western white pine, ponderosa pine, and similar species. These thicknesses of plywood might be used for 24″ spacing of joists when a finish $\frac{25}{32}''$ strip flooring is installed at right angles to the joists. It is very important to have a solid and safe platform for the workmen during construction of the remainder of the house. For this reason, it is necessary to have a slightly thicker plywood subfloor, especially when joist spacing is greater than 16″ on center.

Plywood can also serve as combined plywood subfloor and underlayment, eliminating separate underlayment because the plywood functions as both a structural subfloor and as a good substrate. This is applied to thin resilient floorings, carpeting, and other nonstructural finish flooring. The plywood used in this manner must be tongued-and-grooved or blocked with 2″ lumber along the unsupported edges. Following are recommendations for its use:

Grade: Underlayment, underlayment with exterior glue, C-C plugged.

Spacing and *thickness:*

(a) For species such as Douglas fir (coast type) and southern pine: $\frac{1}{2}''$ minimum thickness for 16″ joist spacing, $\frac{5}{8}''$ for 20″ joist spacing, and $\frac{3}{4}''$ for 24″ joist spacing.

(b) For species such as western hemlock, western white pine, and ponderosa pine: $\frac{5}{8}''$ minimum thickness for 16″ joist spacing, $\frac{3}{4}''$ for 20″ joist spacing, and $\frac{7}{8}''$ for 24″ joist spacing.

Plywood should be installed with the grain direction of the outer plies at right angles to the joists and be staggered so that end joints in adjacent panels break over different joists. Plywood should be nailed to the joist at each bearing with eightpenny common or sevenpenny threaded nails for plywood $\frac{1}{2}''$ to $\frac{3}{4}''$ thick. Space nails 6″ apart along all edges and 10″ along intermediate members. When plywood serves as both subfloor and underlayment, nails may be spaced 6″ to 7″ apart at all joists and blocking. Use eightpenny or ninepenny common nails or sevenpenny or eightpenny threaded nails.

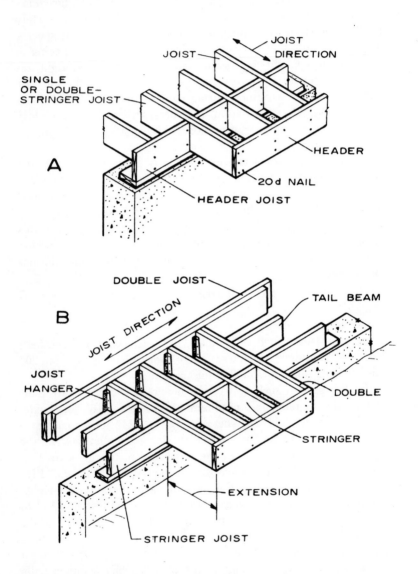

Fig. 12. Floor framing at wall projections. *A*, projection of joists for bay window extensions. *B*, projection at right angles to joists.

For the best performance, plywood should *not* be laid up with tight joints, whether used on the interior or exterior. The following spaces are recommendations by the American Plywood Association:

Plywood Location and Use	*Spacing* Edges (Inches)	Ends (Inches)
Underlayment or interior wall lining	$\frac{1}{32}$	$\frac{1}{32}$
Panel siding and combination subfloor underlayment	$\frac{1}{16}$	$\frac{1}{16}$
Roof sheathing, subflooring, and wall sheathing. (Under wet or humid conditions, spacing should be doubled.)	$\frac{1}{8}$	$\frac{1}{16}$

FLOOR FRAMING AT WALL PROJECTIONS

The framing for wall projections—such as a *bay window* or first- or second-floor extensions beyond the lower wall—should generally consist of projection of the floor joists (Fig. 12). This extension normally should not exceed 24″ unless designed specifically for great projections, which may require special anchorage at the opposite ends of the joists. The joists forming each side of the bay should be doubled. Nailing, in general, should conform to that for stair openings. The subflooring is carried to and sawed flush with the outer framing member. Rafters are often carried by a header constructed in the main wall over the bay area, which supports the roofload. Therefore, the wall of the bay has less load to support.

Projections at right angles to the length of the floor joists should generally be limited to small areas and extensions of not more than 24″. In this construction, the stringer should be carried by doubled joists (*B*, Fig. 12). Joist hangers or a ledger will provide good connections for the ends of members.

CHAPTER 22

Basement Rooms

——————————•——————————
•
•

Many houses are now designed so that one or more of the rooms in lower floors are constructed on a concrete slab. In multilevel houses, this area may include a family room, a spare bedroom, or a study. Furthermore, it is sometimes necessary to provide a room in the basement of an existing house. Therefore, in a new house or in remodeling the basement of an existing one, several factors should be considered, including insulation, waterproofing, and vapor resistance.

FLOORS

In the construction of a new building having basement rooms, provision should be made for reduction of heat loss and for prevention of ground moisture movement. Perimeter insulation reduces heat loss and a vapor barrier under a concrete slab will prevent problems caused by a concrete floor damp from ground moisture (Fig. 1). Providing these essential details is somewhat more difficult in existing construction than in new construction.

The installation of a vapor barrier over an existing unprotected concrete slab is normally required when the floor is at or below the outside ground level and some type of finish floor is used. Flooring manufacturers recommend that preparation of the slab for wood-strip flooring consist of the following steps:

1. Mop or spread a coating of tar or asphalt mastic followed by an asphalt felt paper.

2. Lay short lengths of 2″ by 4″ screeds in a coating of tar or

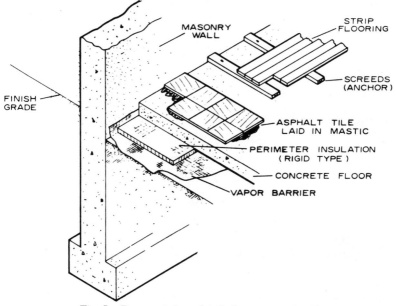

Fig. 1. Basement floor details for new construction.

asphalt, spacing the rows about 12″ apart, starting at one wall and ending at the opposite wall.

3. Place insulation around the perimeter, between screeds, where the outside ground level is near the basement floor elevation.

4. Install wood-strip flooring across the wood screeds.

This procedure can be varied somewhat by placing a conventional vapor barrier of good quality directly over the slab. Two-by four-inch furring strips spaced 12″ to 16″ apart are then anchored to the slab with concrete nails or with other types of commercial anchors. Some leveling of the 2 by 4's might be required. Strip flooring is then nailed to the furring strips after perimeter insulation is placed (Fig. 2). If a wood-block flooring is desired under these conditions, a plywood subfloor may be used over the furring strips. Plywood, ½″ or ⅝″ thick, is normally used if the edges are unblocked and furring strips are spaced 16″ or more apart.

When insulation is not required around the perimeter because of the height of the outside grade above the basement floor, a

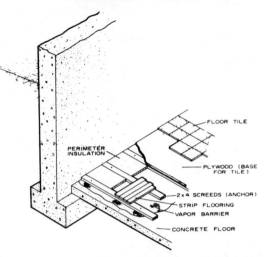

Fig. 2. Basement floor details for existing construction.

much simpler method can be used for wood-block or other type of tile finish. An asphalt mastic coating, followed by a good vapor barrier, serves as a base for the tile. An adhesive recommended by the flooring manufacturer is then used over the vapor barrier, after which the wood tile is applied. It is important that a smooth, vapor-tight base be provided for the tile.

It is likely that such floor construction should be used only under favorable conditions where drain tile is placed at the outside footings and soil conditions are favorable. When the slab or walls of an existing house are inclined to be damp, it is often difficult to insure a dry basement. Under such conditions, it is often advisable to use resilient tile or a similar finish over some type of stable base such as plywood. This construction is to be preceded by installation of vapor barriers and protective coatings.

WALLS

The use of an *interior finish* over masonry basement walls is usually desirable for habitable rooms. Furthermore, if the outside wall is partially exposed, it is advisable to use *insulation* between the wall and the inside finish. *Waterproofing* the wall is important if there is any possibility of moisture entry. It can be done by applying one of the many waterproof coatings available to the inner surface of the masonry.

After the wall has been waterproofed, furring strips are commonly used to prepare the wall for interior finish. A 2″ by 2″ bottom plate is anchored to the floor at the junction of the wall and the floor. A 2″ by 2″ or larger top plate is fastened to the bottom of the joists, to the joist blocks, or anchored to the wall (Fig. 3). Studs or furring strips, 2″ by 2″ or larger in size, are then placed between the top and the bottom plates, anchoring them at the center when necessary with concrete nails or similar fasteners (Fig. 3). Electrical outlets and conduit should be installed and insulation with vapor barrier placed between the furring strips. The interior finish of gypsum board, fiberboard, plywood, or other material is then installed. *Furring strips* are commonly spaced 16″ on center, but this depends on the type and thickness of the interior finish.

Foamed plastic insulation is sometimes used on masonry walls without furring. It is important that the inner face of the wall be smooth and level without protrusions when this method is used. After the wall has been waterproofed, ribbons of adhesive are applied to the wall and sheets of foam insulation installed (Fig.

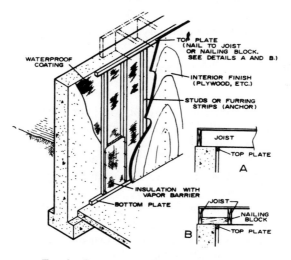

Fig. 3. Basement wall finish with furring strips.

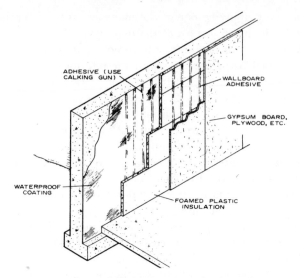

Fig. 4. Basement wall finish without furring strips.

4). Dry wall adhesive is then applied and the gypsum board, plywood, or other finish pressed into place. Manufacturers' recommendations on adhesives and methods of installation should be followed. Most foam plastic insulations have some vapor resistance in themselves, so the need for a separate vapor barrier is not as great as when blanket-type insulation is used.

CEILINGS

Some type of finish is usually desirable for the ceiling of the basement room. Gypsum board, plywood, or fiberboard sheets may be used and nailed directly to the joists. Acoustic ceiling tile and similar materials normally require additional nailing areas. This may be supplied by 1" by 2" or 1" by 3" strips nailed across the joists and spaced to conform to the size of the ceiling tile (Fig. 5).

A *suspended ceiling,* consisting of light metal angles hung from the ceiling joists, may also be desirable. Tiles are then dropped into place. This will decrease sound transfer from the rooms above. *Be sure* to install ceiling lights, heat supply and return ducts, or other utilities before the finish is applied.

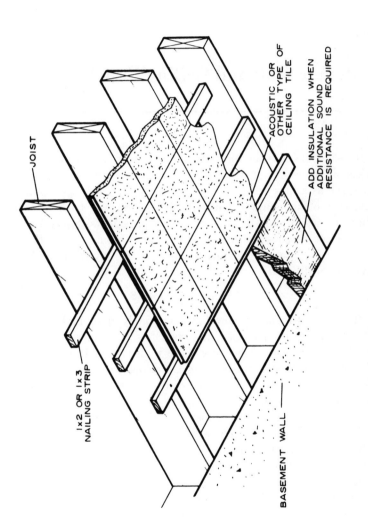

JOIST

1x2 OR 1x3 NAILING STRIP

ACOUSTIC OR OTHER TYPE OF CEILING TILE

ADD INSULATION WHEN ADDITIONAL SOUND RESISTANCE IS REQUIRED

BASEMENT WALL

Fig. 5. Installation of ceiling tile.

CHAPTER 23

Interior Wall and Ceiling Finish

—————————— **:** ——————————

Interior finish is the material used to cover the interior framed areas or structures of walls and ceilings. It should be prefinished or serve as a base for paint or other finishes including wallpaper. Because of moisture conditions, finishes in the bath and the kitchen areas should have more rigid requirements. Several types of interior finishes are used in the modern home: (a) lath and plaster, (b) wood paneling, fiberboard, or plywood, and (c) gypsum wallboard.

TYPES OF FINISHES

Though lath and plaster finish is widely used in home construction, use of dry wall materials has been increasing. Dry wall is often selected because there is usually a time saving in the work. A plaster finish, being a wet material, requires drying time before other interior work can be started; dry wall finish does not. A gypsum dry wall demands a moderately low moisture content of the framing members in order to prevent *nail pops.* This happens when frame members dry out to moisture equilibrium, causing the nailhead to form small *humps* on the surface of the board. Furthermore, stud alignment is more important for single-layer gypsum finish in order to prevent a wavy, uneven appearance. Therefore, there are advantages to both plaster and gypsum dry wall finishes, and each should be considered along with the initial cost and future maintenance involved.

A plaster finish requires some type of base upon which to be applied. *Rock lath* is the most common such base. *Fiberboard lath* is also used; and *wood lath,* common many years ago, is permitted in some areas. *Metal lath* or similar mesh forms are normally used only in bathrooms and as reinforcement. They provide a rigid base for plaster finish but usually cost more than other materials. Some of the rigid foam insulations cemented to masonry walls also serve as plaster bases.

There are many types of dry wall finishes. One of the most widely used is gypsum board in 4' by 8' sheets and in lengths up to 16', used for horizontal application. Plywood, hardboard, fiberboard, particle board, wood paneling, and similar types, many in prefinished form, are also used.

LATH AND PLASTER

Plaster Base

A plaster finish requires some type of base upon which to be applied. The base must have bonding qualities so that plaster adheres to, or is keyed to, the base which has been fastened to the framing members.

One of the most common types of plaster base that may be used on sidewalls or ceilings is *gypsum lath* which is 16" by 48" and is applied horizontally across the framing members. It has paper faces with a gypsum filler. For stud or joist spacing of 16" on center, 3/8" thickness is used. For 24" on-center spacing, 1/2" thickness is required. This material can be obtained with a foil back that serves as a vapor barrier. If the foil faces an air space, it also has reflective insulating value. Gypsum lath may be obtained with perforations, which, by improving the bond, would lengthen the time the plaster would remain intact when exposed to fire. Some city building codes require such perforation.

Insulating fiberboard lath, 1/2" in thickness and 16" by 48" in size, is also used as a plaster base. It has greater insulating value than the gypsum lath, but horizontal joints must usually be reinforced with metal clips.

Metal lath in various forms such as diamond mesh, flat rib, and wire lath is another type of plaster base. It is 27" by 96" in size and is galvanized or painted to resist rusting.

Installation of Plaster Base

Gypsum lath should be applied horizontally with joints broken

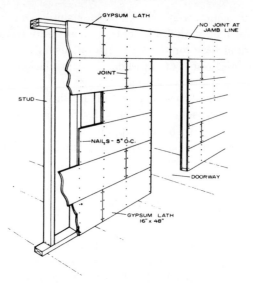

Fig. 1. Application of gypsum lath.

(Fig. 1). Vertical joints should be made over the center of studs or joists and nailed with 12-gage or 13-gage gypsum lathing nails 1½" long and with a ⅜" flat head. Nails should be spaced 5" on center, or four nails for the 16" height, and used at each stud or joist crossing. Some manufacturers specify the ring-shank nails with a slightly greater spacing. Lath joints over heads of openings should not occur at the jamb lines (Fig. 1).

Insulating lath should be installed in much the same manner as gypsum lath, except that slightly longer blued nails should be used. A special waterproof facing is provided on one type of gypsum board for use as a ceramic tile base when the tile is applied with an adhesive.

Metal lath is often used as a plaster base around tub recesses and other bath and kitchen areas (Fig. 2). It is also used when a ceramic tile is applied over a plastic base. It must be backed with water-resistant sheathing paper over the framing. The metal lath is applied horizontally over the waterproof backing with side and end joints lapped. It is nailed with No. 11 and No. 12 roofing nails. These are long enough to provide about 1½" penetration into the framing member or blocking.

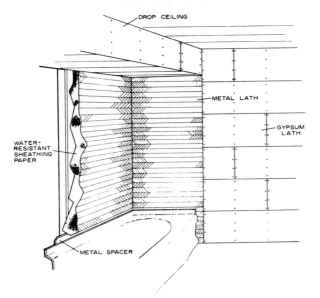

Fig. 2. Application of metal lath.

Plaster Reinforcing

Because some drying usually takes place in wood framing members after a house is completed, some shrinkage can be expected. This may cause plaster cracks to develop around openings and in corners. To minimize, if not eliminate, this cracking, use expanded metal lath in key positions over the plaster-base material as reinforcement. Strips of expanded metal lath may be used over window and door openings (*A*, Fig. 3). A strip about 10″ by 20″ is placed diagonally across each upper corner of the opening and tacked into place.

Metal lath should also be used under flush ceiling beams to prevent plaster cracks (*B*, Fig. 3). On wood drop beams extending below the ceiling line, the metal lath is applied with self-furring nails to provide space for keying of the plaster.

Corner beads of expanded metal lath or of perforated metal should be installed on all exterior corners (Fig. 4). They should be applied plumb and level. The bead acts as a leveling edge when walls are plastered and reinforces the corner against me-

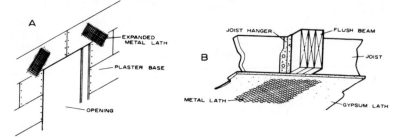

Fig. 3. Metal lath used to minimize cracking. *A,* at door and window openings. *B,* under flush beams.

chanical damage. To minimize plaster cracks, inside corners at the juncture of walls and of ceilings should also be reinforced. Metal lath or wire fabric *(cornerites)* are tacked lightly into place in these areas. Cornerites provide a key width of **2″** to **2½″** at each side for plaster.

Plaster Grounds

Plaster grounds are strips of wood used as guides or strike-off edges when plastering and are located around window and door openings and at the base of the walls. Grounds around interior door openings are often full-width pieces nailed to the sides over the studs and to the underside of the header (*A,* Fig. 5). They are 5¼″ in width, which coincides with standard jamb widths for interior walls with a plaster finish, and they are removed after plaster has dried. Narrow-strip grounds might also be used around these interior openings (*B,* Fig. 5).

In window and exterior door openings, the frames are normally in place before plaster is applied. Therefore, the inside edges of the side and head jamb can serve as grounds. The edge of the window sill might also be used as a ground, or a narrow ⅞″ thick ground strip is nailed to the edge of the 2″ by 4″ sill. Narrow ⅞″ by 1″ grounds might also be used around window and door openings (*C,* Fig. 5). These are normally left in place and are covered by casing.

A similar narrow ground or screed is used at the bottom of the wall in controlling thickness of the gypsum plaster and providing an even surface for the baseboard and molding (*A,* Fig.

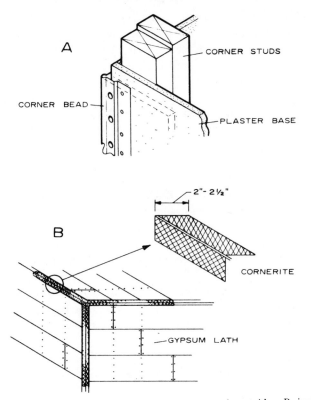

Fig. 4. Reinforcing of plaster at corners. *A*, outside. *B*, inside.

5). These strips are also left in place after plaster has been applied.

Plaster Materials

Plaster for interior finishing is made from combinations of sand, lime, or prepared plaster and water. Waterproof-finish wall materials are available and should be used in bathrooms, especially in showers or tub recesses when tile is not used, and sometimes in the kitchen wainscot.

Method of Application

Plaster should be applied in three-coat or two-coat double-up work. The minimum thickness over $\frac{3}{8}''$ gypsum lath should be about ½". The first plaster coat over metal lath is called the scratch coat and is scratched, after a slight set has occurred, to insure a good bond for the second coat. The second coat is called the brown or leveling coat, and leveling is done during the application of this coat.

The *double-up work*, combining the scratch and brown coat, is used on gypsum or insulating lath, and leveling and plumbing of walls and ceilings are done during application.

The *final* or *finish coat* consists of two general types: the *sand float* finish and the *putty* finish. In the sand float finish, lime is mixed with sand and results in a textured finish, the texture depending on the coarseness of the sand used. Putty finish is used without sand and has a smooth finish. This is common in kitchens and bathrooms where a gloss paint or enamel finish is used and in other rooms where a smooth finish is desired. "Keene's" cement is often used as a finish plaster in bathrooms because of its durability.

The plastering operation should not be done in freezing weather without constant heat for protection from freezing. In normal construction, the heating unit is in place before plastering is started.

Insulating plaster, consisting of a vermiculite, perlite, or other aggregate with the plaster mix, may also be used for wall and ceiling finishes.

DRY WALL FINISH

Dry wall finish is a material that requires little, if any, water for application. Dry wall finish includes gypsum board, plywood, fiberboard, or similar sheet material, as well as wood paneling in various thicknesses and forms.

The use of thin sheet materials such as gypsum board or plywood requires that studs and ceiling joists have good alignment to provide a smooth, even surface. Wood sheathing will often correct misaligned studs on exterior walls. A *strong back* provides for aligning of ceiling joists of unfinished attics (*A*, Fig. 6) and can be used at the center of the span when ceiling joists are uneven.

See Table 11 for thicknesses of wood materials commonly used for interior covering.

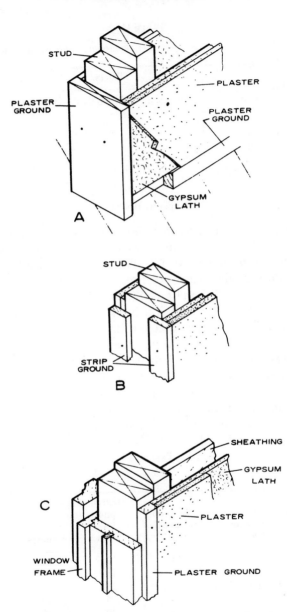

Fig. 5. Plaster grounds. *A*, at doorway and floor. *B*, strip ground at doorway. *C*, ground at window.

TABLE 11

Maximum thicknesses for plywood, fiberboard, and wood paneling

Framing spaced (inches)	Thickness		
	Plywood	Fiberboard	Paneling
	In.	*In.*	*In.*
16	¼	½	⅜
20	⅜	¾	½
24	⅜	¾	⅚

Gypsum Board

Gypsum board is a sheet material composed of a gypsum filler faced with paper. Sheets are 4′ wide and 8′ in length but can be obtained in lengths up to 16′. The edges along the length are usually tapered, although some types are tapered on all edges. This allows for a filled and taped joint. This material may also be obtained with a foil back which serves as a vapor barrier on exterior walls. It is also available with vinyl or other prefinished surfaces. In new construction, ½″ thickness is recommended for single-layer application. In laminated two-ply applications, two ⅜″ thick sheets are used. The ⅜″ thickness, while considered minimum for 16″ stud spacing in single-layer applications, is specified for repair and remodeling work.

Table 12 lists maximum member spacing for the various thicknesses of gypsum board.

TABLE 12

Gypsum board thickness (single layer)

Installed long direction of sheet	Minimum thickness	Maximum spacing of supports (on center)	
		Walls	Ceilings
	In.	*In.*	*In.*
Parallel to framing members	⅜	16	
	½	24	16
	⅝	24	16
Right angles to framing members	⅜	16	16
	½	24	24
	⅝	24	24

When the single-layer procedure is used, the 4' wide gypsum sheets are applied vertically or horizontally on the walls after the ceiling has been covered. Vertical application covers three stud spaces when studs are spaced 16" on center and two when spacing is 24". Edges should be centered on studs, and only moderate contact should be made between edges of the sheet.

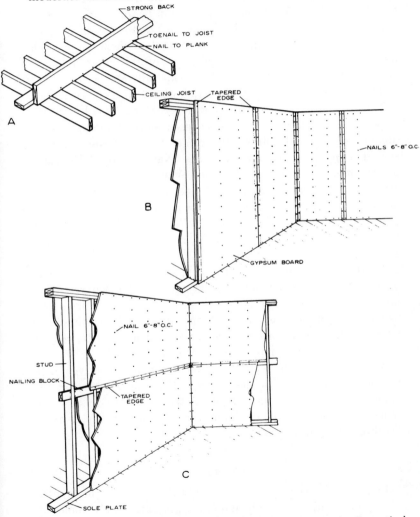

Fig. 6. Application of gypsum board finish. *A*, strong back. *B*, vertical application. *C*, horizontal application.

Fivepenny cooler-type nails ($1\frac{5}{8}''$ long) should be used with $\frac{1}{2}''$ gypsum, and fourpenny ($1\frac{3}{8}''$ long) with the $\frac{3}{8}''$ thick material. Ring-shanked nails, about $\frac{1}{8}''$ shorter, can also be used. Some manufacturers recommend the use of special screws to reduce *bulging* of the surface (*nail pops* caused by drying out of the frame members). If moisture content of the framing members is less than 15 percent when gypsum board is applied, *nail pops* will be greatly reduced. It is good practice, when framing members have a high moisture content to allow them to approach moisture equilibrium before application of the gypsum board. Nails should be spaced $6''$ to $8''$ for sidewalls and $5''$ to $7''$ for ceiling application (*B*, Fig. 6). Minimum edge distance is $\frac{3}{8}''$.

The *horizontal* method of application is best adapted to rooms in which full-length sheets can be used since it minimizes the number of vertical joints. Where joints are necessary, they should be made at windows or doors. Nail spacing is the same as that used in vertical application. When studs are spaced $16''$ on center, horizontal nailing blocks between studs are normally not required when stud spacing is not greater than $16''$ on center and gypsum board is $\frac{3}{8}''$ or thicker. When spacing is greater, or an impact-resistant joint is required, nailing blocks may be used (*C*, Fig. 6).

Another method of gypsum board application (laminated two-ply) includes an undercourse of $\frac{3}{8}''$ material applied vertically and nailed in place. The finish $\frac{3}{8}''$ sheet is applied horizontally, usually in room-size lengths, with an adhesive. This adhesive is either applied in ribbons or is spread with a notched trowel. *Be sure* to follow the manufacturer's recommendations.

Nails in the finish gypsum wallboard should be driven with the heads slightly below the surface. The crowned head of the hammer will form a small dimple in the wallboard (*A*, Fig. 7). A nail set should *not* be used, and care should be taken to avoid breaking the paper face.

Taping

Joint cement *spackle* is used to apply the tape over the tapered edge joints and to smooth and level the surface. It comes in powder form and is mixed with water to a soft putty consistency so that it can be easily spread with a trowel or putty knife. It can also be obtained in premixed form.

The procedure for taping (*B*, Fig. 7) is as follows:

1. Use a wide spackling knife (5″) and spread the cement in the tapered edges, starting at the top of the wall.

2. Press the tape into the recess with the putty knife until the joint cement is forced through the perforations.

3. Cover the tape with additional cement, feathering the outer edges.

4. Allow to dry, sand the joint light, and then apply the second coat, feathering the edges. A steel trowel is sometimes used in applying the second coat. For good results, a third coat may be

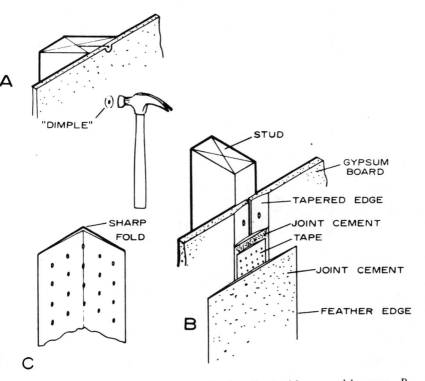

Fig. 7. Finishing gypsum dry wall. *A*, nail set with crowned hammer. *B*, cementing and taping joint. *C*, taping at inside corners.

applied, feathering beyond the second coat.

5. After the joint cement is dry, sand smooth with an electric hand vibrating sander. (*See* Chap. 6, sections on Sanders.)

6. For hiding hammer indentations, fill with joint cement and sand smooth when dry. Repeat with the second coat when necessary.

Interior corners may be treated with tape. Fold the tape down the center to a right angle (*C*, Fig. 7) and (1) apply cement at the corner, (2) press the tape in place, and (3) finish the corner with joint cement. Sand smooth when dry and apply a second coat.

The interior corners between walls and ceilings may also be concealed with some type of molding (*D*, Fig. 7). When moldings are used, taping this joint is not necessary. Wallboard corner beads at exterior corners will prevent damage to the gypsum board. They are fastened in place and covered with the joint cement.

Plywood

Prefinished plywood is available in a number of species, and its use should not be overlooked for accent walls or to cover entire room wall areas. Plywood for interior covering may be used in 4' by 8' and longer sheets. They may be applied ver-

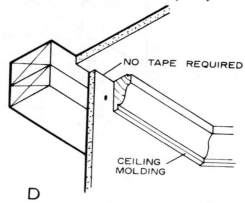

NO TAPE REQUIRED

CEILING MOLDING

Fig. 7.   **D**

(continued)   *D*, alternate finish at ceiling.

tically or horizontally, but with solid backing at all edges. For 16″ frame member spacing, ¼″ thickness is considered minimum. For 20″ or 24″ spacing, ⅜″ plywood is the minimum thickness. Casing or finishing nails 1¼″ to 1½″ long are used. Space them 8″ apart on the walls and 6″ apart on the ceilings. Edge nailing distance should be not less than ⅜″. Allow ⅟₃₂″ end and edge distance between sheets when installing. Most wood or wood-base panel materials should be exposed to the conditions of the room before installation. Place them around the heated room for at least 24 hours.

Adhesives may also be used to fasten prefinished plywood and other sheet materials to wall studs. These panel adhesives usually eliminate the need for more than two guide nails for each sheet. Application usually conforms to the following procedure: (a) position the sheet and fasten it with two nails for guides at the top or side, (b) remove plywood and spread contact or similar adhesive on the framing members, (c) press the plywood in place for full contact using the nails for positioning, (d) pull the plywood away from the studs and allow adhesive to set, and (e) press plywood against the framing members and tap lightly with a rubber mallet for full contact. Manufacturers of adhesives supply full instructions for application of sheet materials.

Hardboard and Fiberboard

Hardboard and *fiberboard* are applied the same way as plywood. *Hardboard* must be at least ¼″ when used over open framing spaced 16″ on center. Rigid backing of some type is required for ⅛″ hardboard.

Fiberboard in tongued-and-grooved plank or sheet form must be ½″ thick when frame members are spaced 16″ on center and ¾″ when 24″ spacing is used as previously described. The casing or finishing nails must be slightly longer than those used for plywood or hardboard, and spacing is about the same. Fiberboard is also used in the ceiling as acoustic tile and may be nailed to strips fastened to ceiling joists. It is also installed in 12″ by 12″ or larger tile forms on wood or metal hangers which are hung from the ceiling joists. This is called a *suspended ceiling*.

Wood Paneling

Various types and patterns of woods are available for application on walls to obtain desired decorative effects. For informal treatment, knotty pine, white-pocket Douglas fir, sound wormy chestnut, and pecky cypress, finished natural or stained and varnished, may be used to cover one or more sides of a room. *Wood paneling* should be thoroughly seasoned to a moisture content near the average it reaches in service. In most areas it is about 8 percent. Allow the material to reach this condition by placing it around the wall of the heated room. Boards may be applied horizontally or vertically, but the same general methods of application should pertain to each. The following may be used as a guide in the application of matched wood paneling:

1. Apply over a vapor barrier and insulation when application

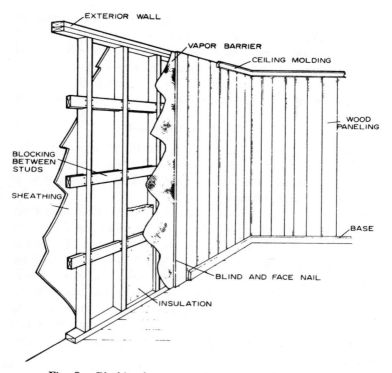

Fig. 8.   Blocking between studs for vertical wood paneling.

is on the exterior wall framing or blocking (Fig. 8).

2. Boards should not be wider than 8″ except when a long tongue or matched edges are used.

3. Thickness should be at least ⅜″ for 16″ spacing of frame members, ½″ for 20″ spacing, and ⅝″ for 24″ spacing.

4. Maximum spacing of supports for nailing should be 24″ on center (blocking for vertical applications).

5. Nails should be fivepenny or sixpenny casing or finishing nails.

Use two nails for boards 6″ or less wide and three nails for 8″ and wider boards. One nail can be blind-nailed in matched paneling.

Wood paneling in the form of *small plywood squares* can also be used for an interior wall covering (Fig. 9). When these squares are used over framing and a vapor barrier, blocking should be so located that each edge has full bearing. Each edge should be fastened with casing or finish nails. When two sides are tongued-and-grooved, one edge (tongued side) may be blind-nailed. When paneling (16″ by 48″ or larger) crosses studs, it should also be nailed at each intermediate bearing. Matched (tongued-and-grooved) sides should be used when no horizontal blocking is provided or paneling is not used over a solid backing.

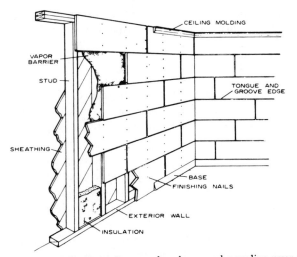

Fig. 9. Application of tongued-and-grooved paneling over studs.

CHAPTER 24

Exterior Wood Coverings

———————— $\vdots$ ————————————————————

Because siding and other types of coverings used for exterior walls have an important influence on the appearance as well as on the maintenance of the house, a careful selection of the pattern should be made. The homeowner now has a choice of many wood and wood-base materials which may be used to cover exterior walls. Masonry, veneers, metal or plastic siding, and other nonwood materials are additional choices. *Wood siding* can be obtained in many different patterns and can be finished naturally, stained, or painted. Wood shingles, plywood, wood siding, or paneling, fiberboard, and hardboard are some of the types used as exterior coverings. Many prefinished sidings are available, and the coatings and films applied to several types of base materials presumably eliminate the need of refinishing for many years.

WOOD SIDING

One of the materials most characteristic of the exteriors of American houses is *wood siding*. The essential properties required for siding are good painting characteristics, easy working qualities, and freedom from warp. Such properties are present to a *high degree* in the cedars, eastern white pine, sugar pine, western white pine, cypress, and redwood; to a *good degree* in western hemlock, ponderosa pine, the spruces, and yellow poplar; and to a *fair degree* in Douglas fir, western larch, and southern pine.

Material used for exterior siding which is to be painted should preferably be of a high grade and free from knots, pitch pockets, and waney edges. Vertical grain and mixed grain (both vertical and flat) are available in some species such as redwood and western red cedar.

The moisture content at the time of application should be that which it would attain in service. This would be approximately 10 to 12 percent except in the dry southwestern states where the moisture content should average about 8 to 9 per cent. To minimize seasonal movement due to changes in moisture content, vertical-grain (edge-grain) siding is preferred. While this is not as important for a stained finish, the use of edge-grain siding for a paint finish will result in longer paint life. A three-minute dip in a water-repellent preservative before siding is installed will not only result in longer paint life but also will resist moisture entry and decay. Some manufacturers supply siding with this treatment. Freshly cut ends should be brush-treated on the job.

HORIZONTAL SIDINGS

Some wood-siding patterns are used only horizontally and others only vertically. Some may be used in either manner if adequate nailing areas are provided. Following are descriptions of each of the general types.

Bevel Siding

Plain bevel siding can be obtained in sizes from $\frac{1}{2}''$ by 4" to $\frac{1}{2}''$ by 8" and also in sizes of $\frac{3}{4}''$ by 8" and $\frac{3}{4}''$ by 10" (Fig. 1). "Anzac" siding (Fig. 1) is $\frac{3}{4}''$ by 12" in size. Usually the finished width of bevel siding is about $\frac{1}{2}''$ less than the size listed. One side of bevel siding has a smooth planed surface, while the other has a rough resawn surface. For a stained finish, the rough or sawn side is exposed because wood stain is most successful and longer lasting on rough wood surfaces.

Dolly Varden Siding

Dolly Varden siding is similar to true bevel siding except that shiplap edges are used, resulting in a constant exposure distance (Fig. 1). Because it lies flat against the studs, it is sometimes used for garages and similar buildings without sheathing. Diagonal bracing is then needed to provide racking resistance to the wall.

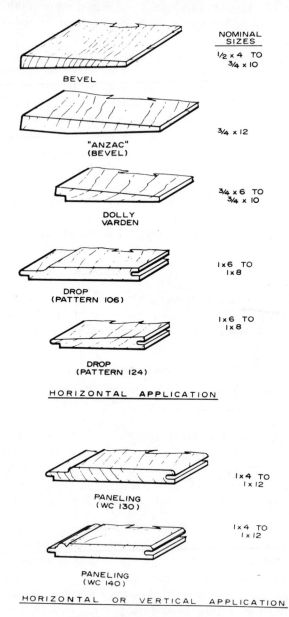

NOMINAL
SIZES

1/2 x 4 TO
3/4 x 10

BEVEL

3/4 x 12

"ANZAC"
(BEVEL)

3/4 x 6 TO
3/4 x 10

DOLLY
VARDEN

1 x 6 TO
1 x 8

DROP
(PATTERN 106)

1 x 6 TO
1 x 8

DROP
(PATTERN 124)

HORIZONTAL   APPLICATION

1 x 4 TO
1 x 12

PANELING
(WC 130)

1 x 4 TO
1 x 12

PANELING
(WC 140)

HORIZONTAL   OR   VERTICAL   APPLICATION

Fig. 1. Wood siding types.

Other Horizontal Sidings

Regular *drop sidings* can be obtained in several patterns, two of which are shown in Fig. 1. This siding, with matched or ship-lap edges, can be obtained in 1″ and 6″ and 1″ by 8″ sizes. This type is commonly used for lower-cost dwellings and for garages, usually without benefit of sheathing. Tests conducted have shown that the tongued-and-grooved (matched) patterns have greater resistance to the penetration of wind-driven rain than the shiplap patterns when both are treated with a water-repellent preservative.

Fiberboard and hardboard sidings are also available in various forms. Some have a backing to provide rigidity and strength while others are used directly over sheathing. Plywood horizontal lap siding, with medium density overlaid surface, is also available as an exterior covering material. It is usually ⅜″ thick and 12″ and 16″ wide. It is applied in much the same manner as wood siding, except that a shingle wedge is used behind each vertical joint.

SIDINGS FOR HORIZONTAL OR VERTICAL APPLICATIONS

A number of siding or paneling patterns can be used horizontally or vertically (Fig. 1). These are manufactured in nominal 1″ thicknesses and in widths from 4″ to 12″. Both dressed and matched and shiplapped edges are available. The narrow- and medium-width patterns will likely be more satisfactory when there are moderate moisture-content changes. Wide patterns are more successful if they are vertical grain to keep shrinkage to a minimum. The correct moisture content is also important to prevent shrinkage to a point where the tongue is exposed when tongue-and-grooved siding is wide.

Treating the edges of both drop and the matched and ship-lapped sidings with water-repellent preservative usually prevents wind-driven rain from penetrating the joints if exposed to weather. In areas under wide overhangs, or in porches and other protected sections, this treatment is not as important. Some manufacturers provide siding with this treatment applied at the factory.

Sidings for Vertical Application

A method of siding application, popular for some architectural styles, utilizes rough sawn boards and battens applied vertically. These boards can be arranged in various ways: (a) board and batten, (b) batten and board, (c) board and board (Fig. 2). As in the vertical application of most siding materials, nominal 1″ sheathing boards or plywood sheathing ⅝″ or ¾″ thick should

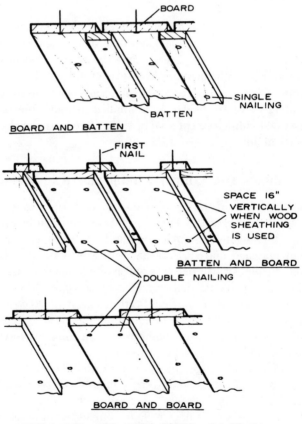

BOARD

SINGLE
NAILING

BATTEN

BOARD AND BATTEN

FIRST
NAIL

SPACE 16"
VERTICALLY
WHEN WOOD
SHEATHING
IS USED

BATTEN AND BOARD

DOUBLE NAILING

BOARD AND BOARD

NOTE : NAIL FOR FIRST BOARD - 8 d OR 9 d
NAIL FOR SECOND BOARD - 12 d

Fig. 2. Vertical board siding.

be used for nailing surfaces. When other types of sheathing materials or thinner plywood are used, nailing blocks between studs commonly provide the nailing areas. Nailers of 1" by 4", laid horizontally and spaced from 16" to 24" apart vertically, can be used over nonwood sheathing. Special or thicker casing is sometimes required around doors and window frames when this procedure is used. It is good practice to use a building paper over the sheathing before applying the vertical siding.

SIDING WITH SHEET MATERIALS

A number of sheet materials are now available for use as siding. These include plywood in a variety of face treatments and species, paper-overlaid plywood, and hardboard. Plywood or paper-overlaid plywood is sometimes used without sheathing and is known as panel siding, with ⅜" often considered the minimum thickness for such use for 16" stud spacing. However, from the standpoint of stiffness and strength, better performance is usually obtained by using ½" or ⅝" thickness.

These 4' by 8' and longer sheets must be applied vertically with intermediate and perimeter nailing to provide the desired rigidity. Most other methods of applying sheet materials require some type of sheathing beneath. When horizontal joints are necessary, they should be protected by a simple flashing.

An exterior-grade plywood should always be used for siding and can be obtained in such surfaces as grooved, brushed, and saw-textured. These surfaces are usually finished with some type of stain. If shiplap or matched edges are not provided, some method of providing a waterproof joint should be used. This often consists of caulking and a batten at each joint and a batten at each stud if closer spacing is desired for appearance. An edge treatment of water-repellent preservative will also aid in reducing moisture penetration. Allow ¹⁄₁₆" edge and end spacing when installing plywood in sheet form.

Exterior grade particle board might also be considered for panel siding. Normally ⅝" thickness is required for 16" stud spacing and ¾" for 24" stud spacing.

Paper-overlaid plywood has many of the advantages of plywood with the addition of providing a very satisfactory base for paint. A medium-density, overlaid plywood is most commonly used.

Hardboard sheets used for siding are applied the same way as plywood—by using battens at vertical points and at intermediate studs. Medium-density fiberboards might also be used in some areas as exterior coverings over certain types of sheathing.

Many of these sheet materials resist the passage of water vapor. When they are used, it is important that a good vapor barrier, well installed, be employed on the warm side of the insulated walls. (*See* Chap. 15, Thermal Insulation, Vapor Barriers, and Sound Insulation.)

WOOD SHINGLES AND SHAKES

Wood shingles and *shakes* are desirable for sidewalls in many styles of houses. In Cape Cod or Colonial houses, shingles may be painted or stained. For ranch or contemporary designs, wide exposures of shingles or shakes often add a desired effect. They are easily stained and, therefore, provide a finish which is long lasting on those species commonly used for shingles.

Grades and Species

Western red cedar is perhaps the most available species, although northern white cedar, bald cypress, and redwood are also satisfactory. The heartwood of these species has a natural decay resistance which is desirable if shingles are to remain unpainted or unstained.

Western red cedar shingles can be obtained in three grades. The first grade (No. 1) is all heartwood, edge grain, and knot free. It is primarily intended for roofs but is desirable in double-course sidewall application where much of the face is exposed.

Second-grade shingles (No. 2) are often used in single-course application for sidewalls, since only three-fourths of the shingle length is blemish free. A 1″ width of sapwood and mixed vertical and flat grain are permissible.

The third-grade shingle (No. 3) is clear for 6″ from the butt. Flat grain is acceptable, as are greater widths of sapwood. Third-grade shingles are likely to be somewhat thinner than the first and second grades. They are used for secondary buildings and sometimes as the undercourse in double-course application.

A lower grade than the third grade, known as under-coursing shingle, is used only as the under and completely covered course in double-course sidewall application.

Shingle Sizes

Wood shingles are available in three standard lengths—16″, 18″, and 24″. The 16″ length is perhaps the most popular, having five butt thicknesses per 2″ when green (designated as ⅝). These shingles are packed in bundles with 20 courses on each side. Four bundles will cover 100 square feet of wall or roof with an exposure of 5″. The 18″ and the 24″ length shingles have thicker butts, five in 2¼″ for the 18″ shingles and four in 2″ for the 24″ lengths.

Shakes are usually available in several types, the most popular being the split and resawn. The sawed face is used as the back face. The butt thickness of each shake ranges between ¾″ and 1½″. They are usually packed in bundles (20 sq. ft.), five bundles to the square.

OTHER EXTERIOR FINISH

Nonwood materials, such as asbestos cement siding and shingles, metal sidings, and the like are available and are used in some types of architectural design. Stucco or a cement plaster finish, preferably over a wire mesh base, is most often seen in the southwest and the west coast areas. Masonry veneers may be used effectively with wood siding in various finishes to enhance the beauty of both materials.

Some homeowners favor an exterior covering which requires a minimum of maintenance. While some of the nonwood materials are chosen for this reason, developments by the paint industry are providing comparable long-life coatings for wood-base materials. Plastic films on wood siding or plywood are also promising, so that little or no refinishing is indicated for the life of the house.

INSTALLATION OF SIDING

One of the important factors in successful performance of

various siding materials is the type of fasteners used. Nails are the most common of these, and it is poor economy to use them sparingly. Corrosion-resistant nails, galvanized or made of aluminum, stainless steel, or similar metals may cost more, but their use will insure spot-free siding under adverse conditions.

Two types of nails are commonly used with siding, the finishing nail having a small head and the siding nail having a moderate size flathead. The *small head finishing nail* is set (driven with a nail set) about $\frac{1}{16}''$ below the face of the siding, and the hole is filled with putty after the prime coat of paint is applied. The *flathead siding nail* is commonly used and driven flush with the face of the siding. The head is later covered with paint. (*See* Chap. 3, Fig. 5 and Table 4.)

Ordinary steel wire nails tend to rust in a short time and cause a disfiguring stain on the face of the siding. In some cases, the small-head nails will show rust spots through the putty and the paint. Noncorrosive nails that will not cause rust are available.

Siding to be *natural finished* with a water-repellent preservative or stain should be fastened with stainless steel or aluminum nails. In some types of prefinished sidings, nails with color-matched heads are supplied.

In recent years, nails with modified shanks have become quite popular. These nails include the *annularly* threaded shank nail and the *helically* threaded shank nail. Both have greater withdrawal resistance than the smooth shank nail and, for this reason, a shorter nail is often used.

Exposed nails in siding should be driven just flush with the surface of the wood. Overdriving may not only show the hammer mark but may also cause objectionable splitting and crushing of the wood. In sidings with prefinished surfaces or overlays, the nails should be driven so as not to damage the finished surface.

Bevel Siding

The minimum lap for *bevel siding* should not be less than 1″. The average exposure distance is usually determined by the distance from the underside of the window sill to the top of the drip cap (Fig. 3). From the standpoint of weather resistance

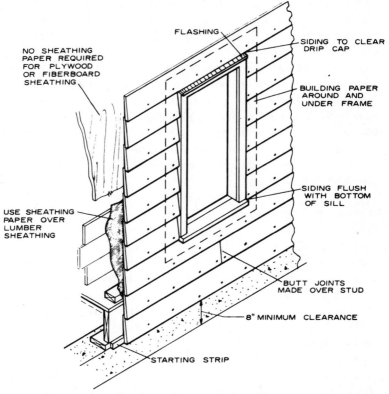

Fig. 3. Installation of bevel siding.

and appearance, the butt edge of the first course of siding above the window should coincide with the top of the window drip cap. In many one-story houses with an overhang, this course of siding is often replaced with a frieze board. It is also desirable that the bottom of a siding course be flush with the underside of the window sill. This may not always be possible because of varying window heights and the types of windows that might be used in a house.

One procedure used to determine the siding exposure width so that it is about equal both above and below the window sill is as follows:

Divide the overall height of the window frame by the approximate recommended exposure distance for the siding used (4 for

6″ wide siding, 6 for 8″ siding, 8 for 10″ siding, and 10 for 12″ siding). This will result in the number of courses between the top and bottom of the window. *For example*, the overall height of the window from top of the drip cap to the bottom of the sill is 61″. If 12″ siding is used, the number of courses would be $61/10 = 6.1$ or six courses. To obtain the exact exposure distance, divide 61 by 6 and the result would be $10\frac{1}{6}″$. The next step is to determine the exposure distance from the bottom of the sill to just below the top of the foundation wall. If this is 31″, three courses at $10\frac{1}{3}″$ each should be used. Therefore, the exposure distance above and below the window would be almost the same (Fig. 3).

When this procedure is not satisfactory because of big differences in the two areas, it is preferable to use an equal exposure distance for the entire wall height and notch the siding at the window sill. The fit should be tight to prevent moisture entry.

Siding may be installed starting with the bottom course. It is normally blocked out with a starting strip the same thickness as the top of the siding board (Fig. 3). Each succeeding course overlaps the upper edge of the lower course. Siding should be nailed to each stud or on 16″ centers. When plywood or wood sheathing or spaced wood nailing strips are used over nonwood sheathing, sevenpenny or eightpenny nails ($2\frac{1}{4}″$ and $2\frac{1}{2}″$ long) may be used for $\frac{3}{4}″$ thick siding. If gypsum or fiberboard sheathing is used, the tenpenny nail is used to penetrate into the stud. For $\frac{1}{2}″$ thick siding, nails may be $\frac{1}{4}″$ shorter than those used for $\frac{3}{4}″$ siding.

The nails should be located far enough up from the butt to miss the top of the lower siding course (Fig. 4). This clearance distance is usually $\frac{1}{8}″$. This allows for slight movement of the siding due to moisture changes without causing splitting. Such an allowance is especially required for the wider sidings of 8″ to 12″ wide.

It is good practice to avoid butt joints whenever possible. Use the longer sections of siding under windows and other long stretches and utilize the shorter lengths for areas between windows and doors. If unavoidable, butt joints should be made over a stud and staggered between courses as much as practical (Fig. 3).

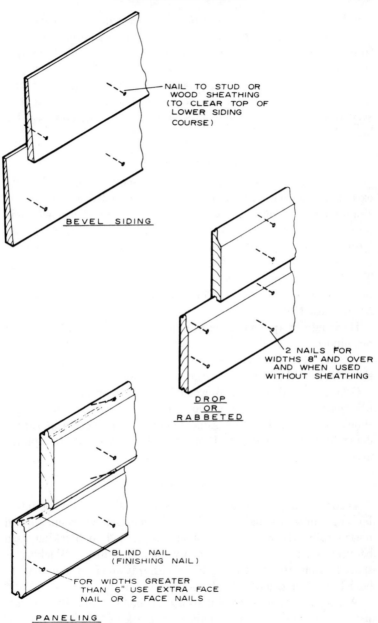

NAIL TO STUD OR
WOOD SHEATHING
(TO CLEAR TOP OF
LOWER SIDING
COURSE)

BEVEL SIDING

2 NAILS FOR
WIDTHS 8" AND OVER
AND WHEN USED
WITHOUT SHEATHING

DROP
OR
RABBETED

BLIND NAIL
(FINISHING NAIL)

FOR WIDTHS GREATER
THAN 6" USE EXTRA FACE
NAIL OR 2 FACE NAILS

PANELING

Fig. 4. Nailing of siding.

Siding should be *square cut* to provide a good joint at window and door casings and at butt joints. Open joints permit moisture to enter, often leading to paint deterioration. It is good practice to brush or dip the freshly cut ends of the siding in a water-repellent preservative before boards are nailed in place. Using a small finger-actuated oil can to apply the water-repellent preservative at end and butt joints after siding is in place is also helpful.

Drop and Similar Sidings

Drop siding is installed much the same way as lap siding except for spacing and nailing. Drop, Dolly Varden, and similar sidings have a constant exposure distance. This face width is normally $5\frac{1}{4}''$ for $1''$ by $6''$ siding and $7\frac{1}{4}''$ for $1''$ by $8''$ siding. Normally, one or two eightpenny nails or ninepenny nails should be used at each stud crossing depending on the width (Fig. 4). The length of the nail depends on the type of sheathing used, but penetration into the stud or through the wood backing should be at least $1\frac{1}{2}''$.

Horizontally applied matched paneling in narrow widths should be blind nailed at the tongue with a corrosion-resistant finishing nail (Fig. 4). For widths greater than $6''$, an additional nail should be used as shown in the illustration.

Other materials such as plywood, hardboard, or medium-density fiberboard, which are used horizontally in widths up to $12''$, should be applied in the same manner as lap or drop siding, depending on the pattern. Prepackaged siding should be applied according to the manufacturers' directions.

Vertical Sidings

Vertically applied matched and similar sidings having inter-lapping joints are nailed in the same manner as when applied horizontally. However, they should be nailed to blocking used between studs or to wood or plywood sheathing. Blocking is spaced from $16''$ to $24''$ apart. With plywood or nominal $1''$ board sheathing, nails should be spaced on $16''$ centers.

When the various combinations of boards and battens are used, they should also be nailed to blocking spaced from $16''$ to $24''$ apart between studs, or closer for wood sheathing. The first boards or battens should be fastened with one eightpenny nail or ninepenny nail at each blocking, to provide at least 1½″ penetration. For wide underboards, two nails spaced about 2″ apart may be used rather than the single row along the center (Fig. 2). The second or top boards or battens should be nailed with twelvepenny nails. Nails of the top board or batten should always miss the underboards and not be nailed through them (Fig. 2). In such applications, double nails should be spaced closely to prevent splitting if the board shrinks. It is also good practice to use a sheathing paper, such as 15-pound asphalt felt, under vertical siding.

Plywood and Other Sheet Siding

Exterior-grade plywood, paper-overlaid plywood, and similar sheet materials used for siding are usually applied vertically. When used over sheathing, plywood should be at least ¼″ thick, although ⁵⁄₁₆″ and ⅜″ will normally provide a more even surface. Hardboard should be ¼″ thick and materials such as medium-density fiberboard should be ½″.

All nailing should be over studs and total effective penetration into wood should be at least 1½″. *For example,* ⅜″ plywood siding over ¾″ wood sheathing would require about a sevenpenny nail, which is 2¼″ long. This would result in a 1⅛″ penetration into the stud, but a total effective penetration of 1⅞″ into the wood.

Plywood should be nailed at 6″ intervals around the perimeter and 12″ at intermediate members. Hardboard siding should be nailed at 4″ and 8″ intervals. All types of sheet material should have a joint caulked with mastic unless the joints are of the interlapping or matched type or battens are installed. A strip of 15-pound asphalt felt under uncalked joints is good practice.

Corner Treatment

The method of finishing wood siding or other materials at exterior corners is often influenced by the overall design of the house. A mitered corner effect on horizontal siding or the using of corner boards are perhaps the most common methods of treatment.

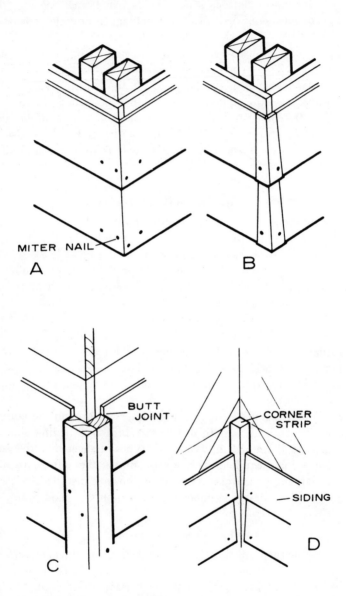

Fig. 5. Siding details. *A*, miter corner. *B*, metal corners. *C*, corner boards. *D*, siding return at roof.

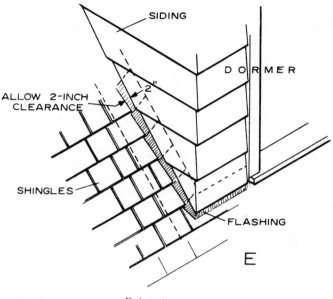

Fig. 5.
(continued)

E, interior corner.

Mitering corners (*A*, Fig. 5) of bevel and similar sidings, unless carefully done to prevent openings, is not always satisfactory. To maintain a good joint, it is necessary that the joint fit tightly the full depth of the miter. It is also good practice to treat the ends with a water-repellent preservative prior to nailing.

Metal corners (*B*, Fig. 5) are perhaps more commonly used than the mitered corner and they give a mitered effect. They are easily placed over each corner as the siding is installed. The metal corners should fit tightly without openings and should be nailed on each side to the sheathing or corner stud beneath. If made of galvanized iron, they should be cleaned with a mild acid wash and primed with a metal primer before the house is painted to prevent early peeling of the paint. Weathering of the metal will also prepare it for the prime paint coat.

Corner boards of various types and sizes may be used for horizontal siding of all types (*C*, Fig. 5). They also provide a satisfactory termination for plywood and similar sheet materials. Vertical applications of matched paneling or of boards and battens are terminated by lapping one side and nailing into the edge of this member, as well as to the nailing members beneath. Corner boards are usually 1⅛″ or 1⅜″ material and for a distinctive appearance may be quite narrow. Plain outside casing commonly used for window and door frames can be adapted for corner boards.

Prefinished shingle or shake exteriors sometimes are used with color-matched metal corners. They can also be lapped over the adjacent corner shingle, alternating each course. This is called *lacing*. This type of corner treatment usually requires that some kind of flashing be used beneath.

Interior corners (*E*, Fig. 5) are butted against a square corner board of nominal 1¼″ or 1⅜″ size, depending on the thickness of the siding.

When siding returns against a roof surface, such as at a dormer, there should be a clearance of about 2″ (*D*, Fig. 5). Siding cut tight against the shingles retains moisture after rains and usually results in paint peeling. Shingle flashing extending well up on the dormer wall will provide the necessary resistance to entry of wind-driven rain. Be sure to use a water-repellent preservative on the ends of the siding at the roof line.

Material Transition

At times, the materials used in the gable ends and in the walls below differ in form and application. The details of construction used at the juncture of the two materials should be such that good drainage is assured. *For example,* if vertical boards and battens are used at the gable end and horizontal siding below, a drip cap or similar molding might be used (Fig. 6). Flashing should be used over and above the drip cap so that moisture will clear the gable material.

Another method of material transition might also be used. By extending the plate and studs of the gable end out from the wall a short distance, or by the use of furring strips, the gable siding will project beyond the wall siding and provide good drainage (Fig. 7).

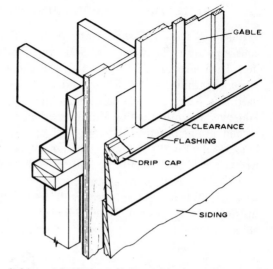

Fig. 6. Gable-end finish (material transition).

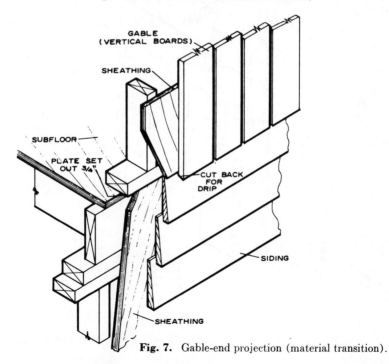

Fig. 7. Gable-end projection (material transition).

INSTALLATION OF WOOD SHINGLES AND SHAKES

Wood shingles and *shakes* are applied in a single- or double-course pattern. They may be used over wood or plywood sheathing. If sheathing is $\frac{3}{8}''$ plywood, use threaded nails. For non-wood sheathing, $1''$ by $3''$ or $1''$ by $4''$ wood nailing strips are used as a base. In the single-course method, one course is simply laid over the other as lap siding is applied. The shingles can be second grade because only one-half or less of the butt portion is exposed (Fig. 8). Shingles should not be soaked before application but should usually be laid up with about $\frac{1}{8}''$ to $\frac{1}{4}''$ space between adjacent shingles to allow for expansion during rainy weather. When a *siding effect* is desired, shingles should be laid up so that they are only lightly in contact. Prestained or treated shingles provide the best results for this method.

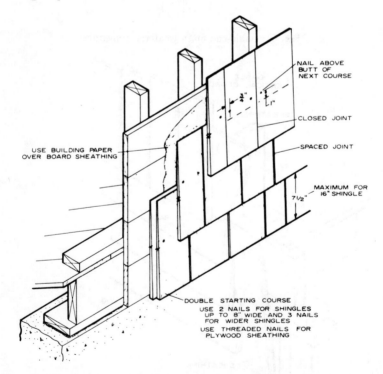

Fig. 8. Single coursing of sidewalls (wood shingles-shakes).

In a double-course method, the undercourse is applied over the wall and the top course nailed directly over a $\frac{1}{4}''$ to $\frac{1}{2}''$ projection of the butt (Fig. 9). The first course should be nailed only enough to hold it in place while the outer course is being applied. The first shingles can be of a lower quality, such as third grade or the undercourse grade. The top course, because much of the shingle length is exposed, should be first-grade shingles.

Exposure distance for various-length shingles and shakes can be guided by those shown in Table 13.

As in roof shingles, joints should be *broken* so that the butt joints of the upper shingles are at least $1\frac{1}{2}''$ from the under shingle joints.

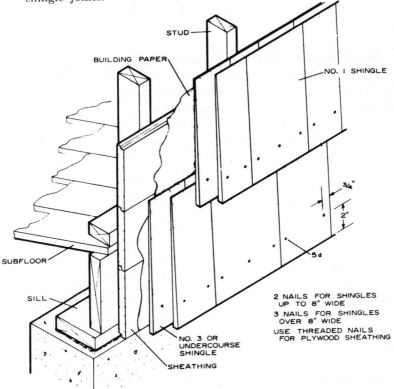

Fig. 9. Double coursing of sidewalls (wood shingles-shakes).

TABLE 13

Exposure distances for wood shingles and shakes on sidewalls

Material	Length	Maximum exposure		
		Single coursing	Double coursing	
			No. 1 grade	No. 2 grade
	In.	*In.*	*In.*	*In.*
Shingles	16	7½	12	10
	18	8½	14	11
	24	11½	16	14
Shakes (hand split	18	8½	14	-------
and resawn)	24	11½	20	-------
	32	15	-------	

Closed or open joints may be used in the application of shingles to sidewalls at the discretion of the worker (Fig. 8). Spacing of ¼″ to ⅜″ produces an individual effect, while close spacing produces a shadow line similar to bevel siding.

Shingles and shakes should be applied with rust-resistant nails long enough to penetrate into the wood backing strips or sheathing. In single coursing, a threepenny or fourpenny zinc-coated *shingle* nail is commonly used. In double coursing, where nails are exposed, a fivepenny zinc-coated nail with a small flat head is used for the top course and threepenny or fourpenny size for the undercourse. Be sure to use building paper over lumber sheathing.

Nails should be placed in from the edge of the shingle a distance of ¾″ (Fig. 8). Use two nails for each shingle up to 8″ wide and three nails for shingles over 8″. In single-course applications, nails should be placed 1″ above the butt line of the next higher course. In double coursing, the use of a piece of shiplap sheathing as a guide allows the outer course to extend ½″ below the undercourse, producing a shadow line (Fig. 9). Nails should be placed 2″ above the bottom of the shingle or shake. Rived or fluted processed shakes, usually factory stained, are available and have a distinct effect when laid with closely fitted edges in a double-course pattern.

CHAPTER 25

Floor Coverings

The term *finish flooring* refers to the material used as the final wearing surface that is applied to a floor. Perhaps in its simplest form it might be paint over a concrete floor slab. Any one of the many resilient tile floorings applied directly to the concrete slab would likely be an improvement from the standpoint of maintenance but not necessarily from the standpoint of comfort.

FLOORING MATERIALS

Numerous flooring materials are available and may be used over a variety of floors. Each has a property that adapts it to a particular usage. Of the practical properties, durability and maintenance ease are the most important. The initial cost, comfort, and beauty or appearance must also be considered.

There is a wide selection of wood materials that are used for flooring. Hardwoods and softwoods are available as *strip flooring* in a variety of widths and thicknesses and as random-width planks and block flooring. Other materials include linoleum, asphalt, rubber, cork, vinyl, and other materials in tile or sheet forms. Tile flooring is also available in a particle board which is manufactured with small wood particles combined with resin and fabricated under high pressure. Ceramic tile and carpeting are used in many areas nowadays. Plastic floor coverings used over concrete or stable wood subfloors are another variation in the types of finishes available.

WOOD-STRIP FLOORING

Softwood finish flooring costs less than most hardwood species and is often used to good advantage in bedroom and closet areas where traffic is light. It might also be selected to fit the interior decor. It is less dense than the hardwoods, less wear resistant, and shows surface abrasions more readily. Softwoods most commonly used for flooring are southern pine, Douglas fir, redwood, and western hemlock.

Softwood flooring has tongued-and-grooved edges and may be hollow-backed or grooved. Some types are also end-matched. Vertical-grain flooring generally has better wearing qualities than flat-grain flooring under hard usage. Table 14 lists the grades and description of softwood strip.

The *hardwoods* commonly used for flooring are red oak, white oak, beech, birch, maple, and pecan. (*See* Table 14.) Manufacturers supply both prefinished and unfinished flooring.

The most widely used pattern is a $25/32''$ by $2\frac{1}{4}''$ strip flooring. These strips are laid lengthwise in a room and normally at right angles to the floor joists. Some type of subfloor of diagonal boards or plywood is normally used under the finish floor. This type of strip flooring is *tongued-and-grooved* and *end-matched* (Fig. 1). Strips are of random length and vary from 2' to 16" or more. End-matched strip flooring in $25/32''$ thickness is generally hollow-backed (A, Fig. 1). The face is slightly wider than the bottom so that tight joints result when flooring is laid. The tongue fits tightly into the groove to prevent movement and floor *squeaks*. These details are designed to provide beautiful finished floors that require a minimum of maintenance.

Another matched pattern is available in $3/8''$ by $2''$ size (B, Fig. 1). This is used for remodeling work or when subfloor is edge-blocked or thick enough to provide very little deflection under loads.

Square-edged strip flooring (C, Fig. 1) is used occasionally. It is $3/8''$ by $2''$ in size and is laid up over a substantial subfloor; face nailing is required.

Wood-block flooring (Fig. 2) is made in a number of patterns. Blocks may vary in size from 4" by 4" to 9" by 9" and larger. Its thickness varies by type from $25/32''$ for laminated blocking

TABLE 14

Grade and description of strip flooring of several species and grain orientation

Species	Grain orientation	Size		First grade	Second grade	Third grade
		Thickness	Width			
		In.	*In.*			
			SOFTWOODS			
Douglas-fir and hemlock	Edge grain	$^{25}/_{32}$	$2^3/_8$–$5^3/_{16}$	B and Better	C	
	Flat grain	$^{25}/_{32}$	$2^3/_8$–$5^3/_{16}$	C and Better	D	D
			HARDWOODS			
Southern pine	Edge grain and Flat grain	$^5/_{16}$–$1^5/_{16}$	$1^3/_4$–$5^3/_{16}$	B and Better	C and Better	D (and No. 2)
Oak	Edge grain	$^{25}/_{32}$	$1^1/_2$–$3^1/_4$	Clear	Select	
	Flat grain	$^3/_8$	$1^1/_2$, 2	Clear	Select	No. 1 Common
		$^1/_2$	$1^1/_2$, 2			
Beech, birch, maple, and pecan[1]		$^{25}/_{32}$	$1^1/_2$–$3^1/_4$	First grade	Second grade	
		$^3/_8$	$1^1/_2$, 2			
		$^1/_2$	$1^1/_2$, 2			

[1] Special grades are available in which uniformity of color is a requirement.

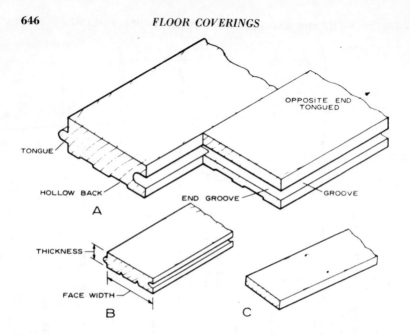

Fig. 1. Types of strip flooring. *A,* side- and end-matched ($25\frac{}{32}''$). *B,* thin flooring strips (matched). *C,* thin flooring strips (square-edged).

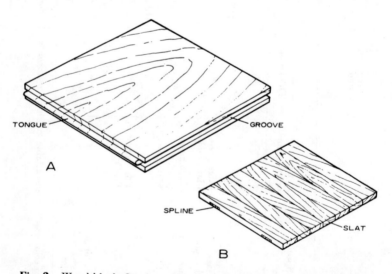

Fig. 2. Wood-block flooring. *A,* tongued-and-grooved. *B,* square-edged (splined).

or plywood block tile (*A*, Fig. 2) to ⅛″ stabilized veneer. Solid wood tile is often made up of narrow strips of wood splined or keyed together in a number of ways. Edges of the thicker tile are tongued-and-grooved, but thinner sections of wood are usually square-edged (*B*, Fig. 2). Plywood blocks may be ⅜″ and thicker and are usually tongued-and-grooved. Many block floors are factory finished and require only waxing after installation. While stabilized veneer squares are still in the development stage, it is likely that research will produce a low-cost wood tile which can even compete with some of the cheaper nonwood resilient tile now available.

Installation of Wood-Strip Flooring

Flooring should be laid after plastering or other interior wall and ceiling finish is completed and dried out, when windows and exterior doors are in place, and when most of the interior trim, except base, casing, and jambs, are applied so that it may not be damaged by wetting or by construction activity.

Board subfloors should be clean, level, and covered with a deadening felt or heavy building paper. This felt or paper will stop a certain amount of dust, will deaden sound, and where a crawl space is used will increase the warmth of the floor by preventing air infiltration. To provide nailing into the joists wherever possible, location of the joists should be chalklined on the paper as a guide. *Plywood subfloor* does not normally require building paper.

Strip flooring should normally be laid crosswise to the floor joists (*A*, Fig. 3). In conventionally designed houses, the floor joists span the width of the building over a center-supporting beam or wall. Hence, the finish flooring of the entire floor area of a rectangular house will be laid in the same direction. Flooring with *L*- or *T*-shaped plans will usually have a direction change at the wings, depending on joist direction. As joists usually span the short way in a living room, the flooring will be laid lengthwise to the room. This is desirable for the sake of appearance and will also reduce shrinkage and swelling effects on the flooring during seasonal changes.

Flooring should be delivered only during dry weather and stored in the warmest and driest place available in the house.

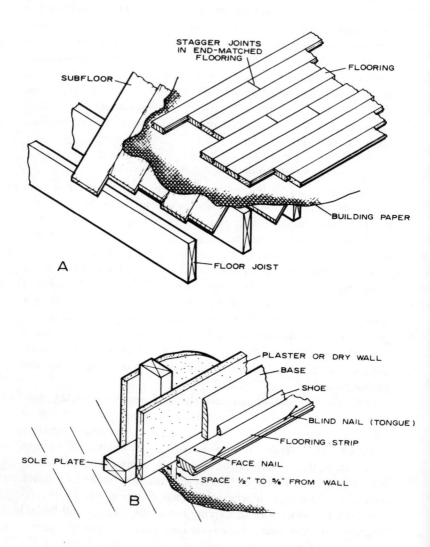

Fig. 3. Application of strip flooring. *A*, general application.
B, starting strip.

The recommended average moisture content for flooring at the time of installation varies somewhat in different sections of the United States. Moisture absorbed after delivery to the site of the house will cause open joints between flooring strips to appear after several months of the heating season.

Floor squeaks are usually caused by the movement of one board against another. Such movement may occur because (a) floor joists are too light, causing excessive deflection, (b) sleepers over concrete slabs are not held down tightly, (c) tongues are loose fitting, or (d) nailing is poor. Adequate nailing is an important means of minimizing squeaks; another is to apply the finish floors only after the joists have dried to 12 per cent moisture content or less. A much better job results when it is possible to nail the finish floor through the subfloor into the joists than if the finish floor is nailed *only* to the subfloor.

Various types of nails are used in nailing different thicknesses of flooring. For $^{25}\!/_{32}$" flooring, use eightpenny flooring nails; for $\frac{1}{2}$" use sixpenny; and for $\frac{3}{8}$" use fourpenny casing nails. These types of flooring are blind-nailed. For thinner square-edged flooring, use a $1\frac{1}{2}$" flooring brad and face nail every seven inches with two nails, one near each edge of the strip, into the subfloor.

The ring shank and screw shank type of nails have been developed in recent years for nailing of flooring. When using these nails, be sure to check with the floor manufacturer's recommendations as to size and diameter for specific uses. Flooring brads are also available with blunted points to prevent splitting of the tongue.

Figure *B*, 3 shows the method of nailing the first strip of flooring placed $\frac{1}{2}$" to $^5\!/_8$" away from the wall. The space is to allow for expansion of the flooring when moisture content increases. The nail is driven straight down through the board at the groove edge. The nails should be driven into the joist and near enough to the edge so that they will be covered by the base or shoe molding. The first strip of flooring can also be nailed through the tongue. Figure *A*, 4 shows in detail how nails should be driven into the tongue of the flooring at an angle of 45° to 50°. The nail should not be driven quite flush in order to prevent damaging the edge by the hammerhead (*B*, Fig. 4). The nail

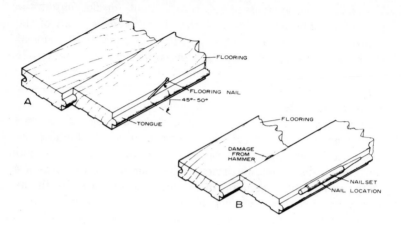

Fig. 4. Nailing of flooring. *A,* nail angle. *B,* setting of nail.

can be set with the end of a large-size nail set or by laying the nail set flatwise against the flooring (*B,* Fig. 4). Nailing devices using standard flooring or special nails are often used by flooring contractors. One blow of the hammer on the plunger drives and sets the nail.

To prevent splitting the flooring, it is sometimes desirable to predrill through the tongue, especially at the ends of the strip. For the second course of flooring from the wall, select pieces so that the butt joints will be well separated from those in the first course. Under normal conditions each board should be driven up tightly. Crooked pieces may require wedging to force them into alinement or may be cut and used at the ends of the course or in closets. In completing the flooring, a ½″ to ⅝″ space is provided between the wall and the last flooring strip. Because of the closeness of the wall, this strip is usually face-nailed so that the base or shoe covers the set nailheads.

Installation of Wood Flooring Over Concrete Slabs

The most desirable properties in a vapor barrier to be used under a concrete slab are: (a) good vapor transmission rating (less than 0.5 perimeter); (b) resistance to damage by moisture and rot; and (c) ability to withstand normal usage during pouring operations.

The vapor barrier is placed under a slab during construction. An alternate method must be used when the concrete is already in place. (*See* Chap. 22, Fig. 2.)

Another method of preparing a base for wood flooring when there is no vapor barrier under the slab is shown in Fig. 5. To resist decay, treated 1″ by 4″ furring strips are anchored to the existing slab, shimming when necessary to provide a level base. Strips should be spaced no more than 16″ on center. A good waterproof or water-vapor-resistant coating on the concrete before the treated strips are applied is usually recommended to aid in reducing moisture movement. A vapor barrier, such as a 4-mil polyethylene or similar membrane, is then laid over the anchored 1″ by 4″ wood strips and a second set of 1 by 4's nailed to the first. Use 1½″ long nails spaced 12″ to 16″ apart in a staggered pattern. The moisture content of these second members should be about the same as that of the strip flooring to be applied (6 to 11 per cent). Strip flooring can then be installed as previously described in this chapter.

When other types of finish floor, such as a resilient tile, are used, plywood is placed over the 1 by 4's as a base.

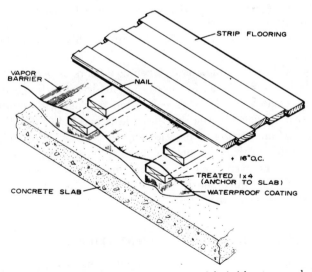

Fig. 5. Base for wood flooring on concrete slab (without an underlying vapor barrier).

WOOD AND PARTICLE BOARD TILE FLOORING

Wood and *particle board tile* are applied with adhesive on a plywood or similar base. The exception is $25\!\!/\!_{32}''$ wood-block floor, which has tongues on two edges and grooves on the other two edges. If the base is wood, these tiles are commonly nailed through the tongue into the subfloor. However, wood block may be applied on concrete slabs with an adhesive. *Wood-block flooring* is installed by changing the grain direction of alternate blocks. This minimizes the effects of shrinking and swelling of the wood.

One type of wood-floor tile is made up of a number of narrow slats to form 4″ by 4″ and larger squares. Four or more of these squares with alternating grain direction form a block. Slats, squares, and blocks are held together with an easily removed membrane. Adhesive is spread on the concrete slab or underlayment with a notched trowel and the blocks installed immediately. The membrane is then removed and the blocks tamped in place for full adhesive contact. Be sure to follow the manufacturer's recommendations for the adhesive and method of application.

Plywood squares with tongued-and-grooved edges are another form of wood tile. Installation is much the same as for the wood tile previously described. Usually tile of this type is factory finished.

A wood-base product used for finish floors is *particle board tile*. It is commonly 9″ by 9″ by ⅜″ in size with tongued-and-grooved edges. The back face is often marked with small saw kerfs to stabilize the tile and provide a better key for the adhesive. Manufacturer's directions as to the type of adhesive and method of installation are usually very complete. Some manufacturers even include instructions on the preparation of the base upon which the tile is to be laid. This tile should not be used over concrete.

BASE FOR RESILIENT FLOORS

Resilient floors should *not* be installed directly over a board or plank subfloor. Underlayment grade of wood-based panels

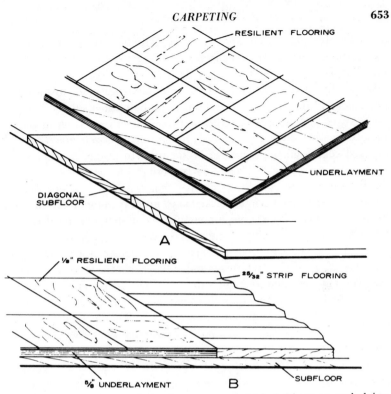

Fig. 6. Base for wood flooring on concrete slab (without an underlying vapor barrier).

such as plywood, particle board, and hardboard is widely used for suspended floor applications (*A*, Fig. 6).

Plywood or particle board panels 4′ by 8′ and in a range of thicknesses from ⅜″ to ¾″ are generally selected for use in new construction. Sheets of untempered hardboard, plywood, or particle board 4′ by 4′ or larger and ¼″ or ⅜″ in thickness are used in remodeling work because of the floor thicknesses involved. The underlayment grade of particle board is a standard product and is available from many producers. Manufacturer's instructions should be followed in the care and use of the product. Plywood underlayment is also a standard product and is available in interior types, exterior types, and interior types with an exterior glueline. The underlayment grade provides for a sanded panel with a C-plugged or better face play and a C-ply or better immediately under the face. This construction resists damage to the floor surface from concentrated loads such as chair legs and the like.

Generally, underlayment panels are separate and installed over structurally adequate subfloors. Combination subfloor underlayment panels of plywood construction find increasing usage. Panels for this dual use generally have tongued-and-grooved or blocked edges and C-plugged or better faces to provide a smooth, even surface for the resilient floor covering.

The method of installing plywood combination subfloor and underlayment has been covered in Chap. 21, section on Subfloor—Plywood. Underlayment should be laid up as described with $\frac{1}{32}''$ edge and end spacing. Sand smooth to provide a level base for the resilient flooring. To prevent nails from showing on the surface of the tile, joists and subfloor should have a moisture content near the average value they reach in service.

The thickness of the underlayment will vary somewhat depending on the floors in adjoining rooms. The installation of tile in a kitchen area, *for example*, is usually made over a $\frac{5}{8}''$ underlayment when finish floors in the adjoining living or dining areas are $\frac{25}{32}''$ strip flooring (*B*, Fig. 6). When thinner wood floors are used in adjoining rooms, adjustments are made in the thickness of the underlayment.

Concrete for resilient floors should be prepared with a good vapor barrier installed somewhere between the soil and the finish floor, preferably just under the slab. Concrete should be leveled carefully when a resilient floor is to be used directly on the slab; this will minimize dips and waves.

Tile should not be laid on a concrete slab until the slab has completely dried. One method which may be used to determine if the slab is dry is to place a small square of polyethylene or other low-perm material on the slab overnight. If the underside is dry in the morning, the slab is usually considered dry enough for the installation of the tile.

CARPETING

Carpeting of a home from living room to kitchen and bath is becoming more popular as new carpeting materials are developed. The cost, however, may be considerably higher than a finished wood floor, and the life of the carpeting before replacement would be much less than that of the wood floor. Many wise homeowners or builders will specify *oak floors* even though they expect to carpet some areas. The resale value of the home is then retained even if the carpeting is removed. However, the advantage of carpeting in sound-absorption and impact-resistant materials should be considered. This is particularly important in multifloor apartments where impact noise reduction is an extremely important phase of construction. If carpeting is to be used, subfloor can consist of ⅝″ (minimum) tongued-and-grooved plywood (over 16″ joist spacing). Top face of the plywood should be C-plugged grade or better. Mastic adhesives are also being used to advantage in applying plywood to floor joists. Plywood, particle board, or other underlayments are also used for a carpet base when installed over subfloor.

CHAPTER 26

Interior Doors, Frames, Trim, Cabinets, and Other Millwork

Interior trim, door frames, and doors are normally installed after the finish floor is in place. Cabinets, built-in bookcases and fireplace mantels, and other millwork units are also placed and secured at this time. (*See also* Chap. 27, Exterior Frames, Windows, and Doors.)

DECORATIVE TREATMENT

The *decorative treatment* for interior doors, trim, and other millwork may be paint or a natural finish with stain, varnish, or other nonpigmented material. The paint or natural finish desired for the woodwork in various rooms often determines the type of species of wood to be used. Interior finish that is to be painted should be smooth, close grained, and free from pitch streaks. Some species having these requirements in a high degree include ponderosa pine, northern white pine, redwood, and spruce. When hardness and resistance to hard usage are additional requirements, species such as birch, gum, and yellow poplar are desirable.

For natural-finish treatment, a pleasing figure, hardness, and uniform color are usually desirable. Species with these requirements include ash, birch, cherry, maple, oak, and walnut. Some require staining for best appearance.

The recommended moisture content for interior finish varies from 6 per cent to 11 per cent, depending on the climatic condition.

TRIM PARTS FOR DOORS AND FRAMES

Door Frames

Rough openings in the stud walls for interior doors are usually framed out to be 3″ more than the door height and 2½″ more than the door width. This provides for the frame and its plumbing and leveling in the opening. Interior door frames are made up of two side *jambs* and a head jamb and include stop moldings upon which the door closes. The most common of these jambs is the one-piece type (*A*, Fig. 1). Jambs may be obtained in standard 5¼″ widths for plaster walls and 4⅝″ widths for walls with ½″ dry wall finish. The two-piece and three-piece adjustable jambs are also standard types (*B* and *C*, Fig. 1). Their principal advantage is in being adaptable to a variety of wall thicknesses.

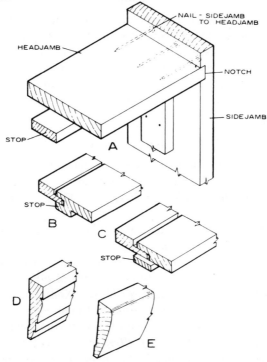

Fig. 1. Interior door parts. *A*, door jambs and stops. *B*, two-piece jamb. *C*, three-piece jamb. *D*, Colonial casing. *E*, ranch casing.

Some manufacturers produce interior door frames with the door fitted and prehung, ready for installing. Application of the casing completes the job. When used with two-piece or three-piece jambs, casings can even be installed at the factory.

Common minimum widths for single interior doors are: (a) bedroom and other habitable rooms, 2′ 6″; (b) bathrooms, 2′ 4″; (c) small closet and linen closets, 2′. These sizes vary a great deal, and sliding doors, folding-door units, and similar types are often used for wardrobes and may be 6′ or more in width. In most cases, the jamb, stop, and casing parts are used in some manner to frame and finish the opening.

Standard interior and exterior door heights are 6′ 8″ for first floors, but 6′ 6″ doors are sometimes used on the upper floors.

Casings

Casing is the edge trim around interior door openings and is also used to finish the room side of windows and exterior door frames. Casing usually varies in width from 2¼″ to 3½″, depending on the style. Casing may be obtained in thicknesses from ½″ to ¾″, although 11⁄16″ is standard in many of the narrow-line patterns. Two common patterns are shown in *D* and *E*, Fig. 1.

Interior Doors

As in exterior door styles, the two general interior types are the flush and the panel door. Novelty doors, such as the folding-door unit, might be flush or louvered. Most standard interior doors are 1⅜″ thick.

The *flush interior door* is usually made up with a hollow core of light framework of some type with thin plywood or hardboard (*A*, Fig. 2). Plywood-faced flush doors may be obtained in gum, birch, oak, mahogany, and woods of other species, most of which are suitable for natural finish. Nonselected grades are usually painted as are hardboard-faced doors.

The *panel door* consists of solid *stiles* (vertical side members), *rails* (cross pieces), and *panel filters* of various types. The five-cross panel and the colonial-type panel doors are perhaps the most common of this style (*B* and *C*, Fig. 2). The *louvered door* (*D*, Fig. 2) is also popular and is commonly used for closets

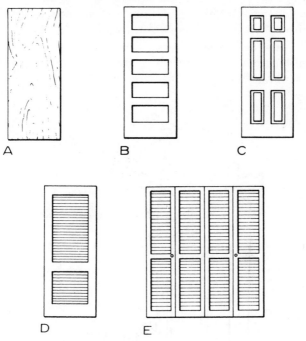

Fig. 2. Interior doors. *A*, flush. *B*, panel (five-cross). *C*, panel (Colonial). *D*, louvered. *E*, folding (louvered).

because it provides some ventilation. Large openings for wardrobes are finished with sliding or folding doors or with flush or louvered doors (*E*, Fig. 2). Such doors are usually 1⅛″ thick.

Hinged doors should open or swing in the direction of natural entry—against a blank wall whenever possible—and should not be obstructed by other swinging doors. Doors should *never* be hinged to swing into a hallway.

Door Frame and Trim Installation

When the frame and doors are not assembled and prefitted, the side jambs should be fabricated by nailing through the notch into the head jamb with three sevenpenny or eightpenny coated nails (*A*, Fig. 1). The assembled frames are then fastened in the rough openings by shingle wedges used between the side jamb and the stud (*A*, Fig. 3). One jamb is plumbed and leveled using four or five sets of shingle wedges for the height of the frame.

Two eightpenny finishing nails are used at each wedged area, one driven so that the doorstop will cover it (*A*, Fig. 3). The opposite side jamb is now fastened in place with shingle wedges and finishing nails, using the first jamb as a guide in keeping a uniform width.

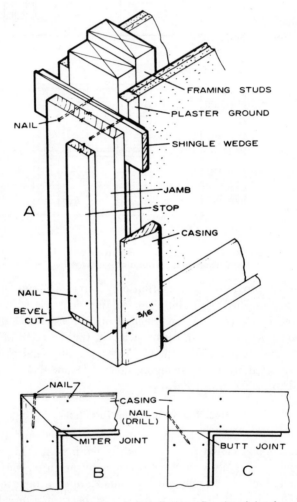

Fig. 3. Doorframe and trim. *A*, installation. *B*, miter joint for casing. *C*, butt joint for casing.

Casings are nailed to both the jamb and the framing studs or header, allowing about a $\frac{3}{16}''$ edge distance from the face of the jamb (*A*, Fig. 3). Finish or casing nails in sixpenny or seven-penny sizes, depending on the thickness of the casing, are used to nail into the stud. Fourpenny or fivepenny finishing nails or $1\frac{1}{2}''$ brads are used to fasten the thinner edge of the casing to the jamb. In hardwood, it is advisable to predrill to prevent splitting. Nails in the casing are located in pairs (*A*, Fig. 3) and spaced about 16″ apart along the full height of the opening and at the head jamb.

Casing with any form of molded shape must have a *mitered joint* at the corners (*B*, Fig. 3). When casing is square edged, a *butt joint* may be made at the junction of the side and head casing (*C*, Fig. 3). If the moisture content of the casing is well above that recommended, a mitered joint may open slightly at the outer edge as the material dries. This can be minimized by using a small glued spline at the corner of the mitered joint. Actually, use of a spline joint under any moisture condition is considered good practice, and some prefitted jamb, door, and casing units are provided with splined joints. Nailing into the joint after drilling will aid in retaining a close fit (*B* and *C*, Fig. 3).

The door opening is now complete except for fitting and secur-ing the hardware and nailing the stops in proper position. In-terior doors are normally hung with two $3\frac{1}{2}''$ by $3\frac{1}{2}''$ loose-pin butt hinges. The door is fitted into the opening with the *clear-ances* shown in Fig. 4. The clearance and location of hinges, lock set, and doorknob may vary somewhat, but they are gen-erally accepted by craftsmen and conform to most millwork standards. The edge of the lock stile should be beveled slightly to permit the door to clear the jamb when swung open. If the door is to swing across heavy carpeting, the bottom clearance may be slightly more.

Thresholds are used under exterior doors to close the space allowed for clearance. *Weather strips* around exterior door open-ings are very effective in reducing air infiltration.

In fitting doors, the stops are usually temporarily nailed in place until the door has been hung. Stops for doors in single-

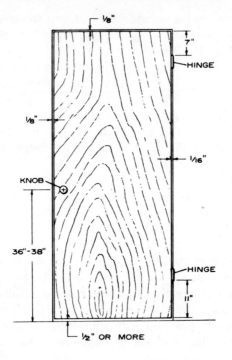

Fig. 4. Door clearances.

piece jambs are generally $\frac{7}{16}''$ thick and may be $\frac{3}{4}''$ to $2\frac{1}{4}''$ wide. They are installed with a mitered joint at the junction of the side and head jambs. A 45° bevel cut at the bottom of the stop, about 1″ to $1\frac{1}{2}''$ above the finish floor, will eliminate a dirt pocket and make cleaning or refinishing of the floor easier (*A*, Fig. 3).

Some manufacturers supply prefitted door jambs and doors with the hinge slots routed and ready for installation. A similar door buck of sheet metal with formed stops and casing is also available.

INSTALLATION OF DOOR HARDWARE

Hardware for doors may be obtained in a number of finishes; brass, bronze, and nickel are perhaps the most common. Door sets are usually classed as: (a) entry lock for exterior doors,

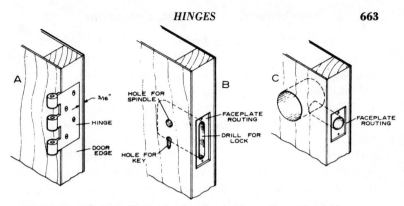

Fig. 5. Installation of door hardware. *A,* hinge. *B,* mortise lock. *C,* bored lock set.

(b) bathroom set (inside lock control with safety slot for opening from the outside), (c) bedroom lock (keyed lock), and (d) passage set (without lock).

Hinges

Using three hinges for hanging 1¾″ exterior doors and two hinges for the lighter interior doors is common practice. There is some tendency for exterior doors to warp during the winter because of the difference in exposure on the opposite sides. The three hinges reduce this tendency. Three hinges are also useful on doors that lead to unheated attics and for wider and heavier doors that may be used within the house.

Loose-pin butt hinges should be used and must be of the proper size for the door they support. For 1¾″ thick doors, use 4″ by 4″ butts; for 1⅜″ doors, 3½″ by 3½″ butts. After the door is fitted to the framed opening, with the proper clearances, hinge halves are fitted to the door. They are routed into the door edge with about a 3⁄16″ back distance (*A,* Fig. 5). One hinge half should be set flush with the surface and must be fastened square with the edge of the door. Screws are included with each pair of hinges.

The door is now placed in the opening and blocked up at the bottom for proper clearance. The jamb is marked at the hinge locations, and the remaining hinge half is routed and fastened in place. The door is then positioned in the opening and the pins slipped in place. If hinges have been installed correctly and the jambs are plumb, the door will swing freely.

Locks

Different types of door locks differ in their installation, in cost and in the amount of labor required to set them. Lock sets are supplied with instructions that should be followed for installation. Some types require drilling of the edge and face of the door and routing of the edge to accommodate the lock set and faceplate (*B*, Fig. 5). A more common bored type (*C*, Fig. 5) is much easier to install since it requires only one hole drilled in the edge and one in the face of the door. Boring jigs and faceplate markers are available to provide accurate installation. The lock should be installed so that the doorknob is 36″ to 38″ above the floorline. Most sets come with paper templates marking the location of the lock and size of the holes to be drilled.

Strike Plate

The *strike plate* which is routed into the door jamb holds the door in place by contact with the latch. To install the plate, mark the location of the latch on the door jamb and locate the strike plate in this way. Rout out the marked outline with a chisel and also rout for the latch (*A*, Fig. 6). The strike plate should be flush with or slightly below the face of the door jamb. When the door is latched, its face should be flush with the edge of the jamb.

Doorstop

The stop which has been set temporarily during fitting of the door and installation of the hardware may now be nailed in place permanently. Finish nails or brads, 1½″ long, should be used. The stop at the lock side should be nailed first, setting it tight against the door face when the door is latched. Space the nails 16″ apart in pairs (*A*, Fig. 6).

The stop behind the hinge side is nailed next, and a $\frac{1}{32}$″ clearance from the door face should be allowed (*B*, Fig. 3) to prevent scraping as the door is opened. The head jamb stop is then nailed in place. Remember that when door and trim are painted, some of the clearances will be taken up.

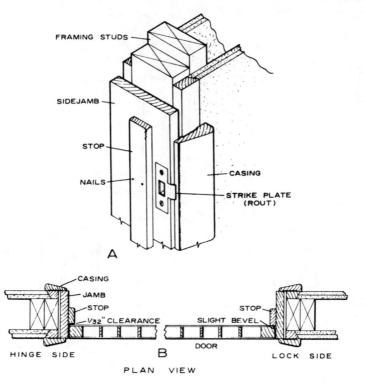

Fig. 6. Door details. *A*, installation of strike plate. *B*, location of stops.

WOOD TRIM INSTALLATION

The casing around the window frames on the interior of the house should be the same pattern as that used around the interior door frames. Other trim which is used for a double-hung window frame includes the sash stops, stool, and apron (*A*, Fig. 7). Another method of using trim around windows has the entire opening enclosed with casing (*B*, Fig. 7). The stool is then a filler member between the bottom sash rail and the bottom casing.

The *stool* is the horizontal trim member that laps the window sill and extends beyond the casing at the sides, with each end notched against the plastered wall. The *apron* serves as a finish

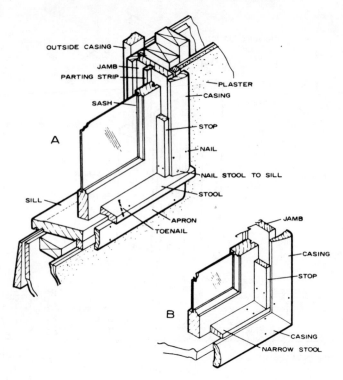

Fig. 7. Installation of window trim. *A*, with stool and apron. *B*, enclosed with casing.

member below the stool. The window stool is the first piece of window trim to be installed and is notched and fitted against the edge of the jamb and the plaster line, with the outside edge being flush against the bottom rail of the window sash (*A*, Fig. 7). The stool is blind nailed at the ends that the casing and the stop will cover the nailheads. Predrilling is usually necessary to prevent splitting. The stool should also be nailed at midpoint to the sill and to the apron with finishing nails. Face nailing to the sill is sometimes substituted or supplemented with toe-nailing of the outer edge to the sill (*A*, Fig. 7).

The casing is applied and nailed as described for door frames (*A*, Fig. 3), except that the inner edge is flush with the inner face of the jambs so that the stop will cover the joint between the jamb and casing. The window stops are then nailed to the jambs so that the window sash slides smoothly. Channel-type weather stripping often includes full-width metal subjambs into which the upper and lower sash slides replacing the parting strip. Stops are located against these instead of the sash to provide a small amount of pressure. The apron is cut to a length equal to the outer width of the casing line (*A*, Fig. 7). It is nailed to the window sill and to the 2″ by 4″ framing sill below.

When casing is used to finish the bottom of the window frame as well as the sides and top, the narrow stool butts against the side window jamb. Casing is then mitered at the bottom corners (*B*, Fig. 7) and nailed as previously described.

BASE AND CEILING MOLDINGS

Base Moldings

Base molding serves as a finish between the finished wall and floor. It is available in several widths and forms. Two-piece base consists of a baseboard topped with a small base cap (*A*, Fig. 8). When plaster is not straight and true, the small base molding will conform more closely to the variations than will

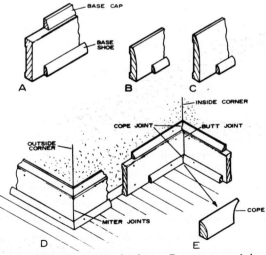

Fig. 8. Base molding. *A*, square-edge base. *B*, narrow ranch base. *C*, wide ranch base. *D*, installation. *E*, cope.

the wider base alone. A common size for this type of baseboard
is ⅝″ by 3¼″ or wider. One-piece base varies in size from ⁷⁄₁₆″
by 2¼″ to ½″ by ¾″ and wider (*B* and *C*, Fig. **8**). Although a
wood member is desirable at the junction of the wall and carpeting to serve as a protective *bumper*, wood trim is sometimes
eliminated entirely.

Most baseboards are finished with a base shoe, ½″ by ¾″ in
size (*A*, *B*, *C*, Fig. **8**). A single-base molding without the shoe
is sometimes placed at the wall floor junction, especially where
carpeting might be used.

Installation of Base Molding

Square-edged baseboard should be installed with a butt joint at
inside corners and a mitered joint at outside corners (*D*, Fig. **8**).
It should be nailed to each stud with two eightpenny finishing
nails. Molded single-piece base, base moldings, and base shoe
should have a coped joint at inside corners and a mitered joint
at outside corners. A *coped joint* is one in which the first piece
is square-cut against the plaster or base and the second, molding
coped. This is accomplished by sawing a 45° miter cut and trimming the molding along the inner line of the miter with a coping
saw (*E*, Fig. **8**). The *base shoe* should be nailed into the subfloor with long slender nails and not into the baseboard itself.
Therefore, if there is a small amount of shrinkage of the joists,
no opening will occur under the shoe.

Ceiling Moldings

Ceiling moldings are sometimes used at the junction of wall
and ceiling for an architectural effect or to terminate dry wall
paneling of gypsum board or wood (*A*, Fig. **9**). As in the base
moldings, inside corners should also be *cope-jointed*. This insures
a tight joint and retains a good fit if there are minor moisture
changes.

A *cutback edge* at the outside of the molding will partially
conceal any unevenness of the plaster and make painting easier
where there are color changes (*B*, Fig. **9**). For gypsum dry wall
construction, a small *crown molding* might be desirable (*C*, Fig.
9). Finish nails should be driven into the upper wallplates and
also into the ceiling joists for large moldings when possible.

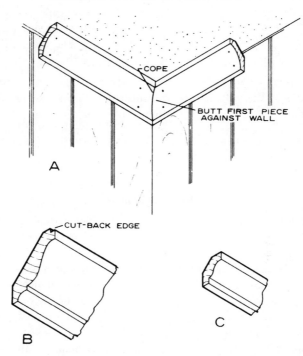

Fig. 9. Ceiling moldings. *A,* installation (inside corner). *B,* crown molding. *C,* small crown molding.

CABINETS AND OTHER MILLWORK

Millwork as a general term usually includes most of those wood materials and house components which require manufacturing. This not only covers the interior trim, doors, and other items previously described, but also such items as kitchen cabinets, fireplace mantels, china cabinets, and similar units. Most of these units are produced in a millwork manufacturing plant and are ready to install in the house. They differ from some other items because they usually require only fastening to the wall or to the floor.

While many units are custom made, others can be ordered directly from stock. *For example,* kitchen cabinets are often stock items which may be obtained in 3″ width increments, usually beginning at widths of 12″ or 15″ and on up to 48″ widths.

As in the case of interior trim, the cabinets, shelving, and similar items can be made of various wood species. If the millwork is to be painted, ponderosa pine, southern pine, Douglas fir, gum, and similar species may be used. Birch, oak, redwood, and knotty pine, or other species with attractive surface variations are some of the woods that are finished with varnish or sealers.

Recommended moisture content for bookcases and other interior millwork may vary from 6 to 11 per cent in different parts of the country.

Kitchen Cabinets

The kitchen usually contains more millwork than the rest of the rooms in the house combined. This is in the form of wall and base cabinets, broom closets, and other items. An efficient plan with properly arranged cabinets will not only reduce work and save steps for the housewife; it will often reduce costs because of the need for a smaller area. Location of the refrigerator, sink, dishwasher, and range, together with the cabinets, is also important from the standpoint of plumbing and electrical connections. Good light, both natural and artificial, is also important in designing a pleasant kitchen.

Kitchen cabinets, both base and wall units, should be constructed to a standard of height and depth. Figure 10 shows common base cabinet counter heights and depths as well as clearances for wall cabinets. While the counter height limits range from 30″ to 38″, the standard height is usually 36″. Wall cabinets vary in height depending on the type of installation at the counter. The tops of wall cabinets are located at the same height, either free or under a 12″ to 14″ drop ceiling or storage cabinet. Wall cabinets can also be obtained in 12″, 15″, 18″, and 24″ heights. The shorter wall cabinets are usually placed over refrigerators.

Narrow wall cabinets are furnished with single doors; the wider ones, with double doors (*A*, Fig. 11). Base cabinets may be obtained in full-door or full-drawer units or with both drawers and doors (*B*, Fig. 11). Sink fronts or sink base cabinets, corner cabinets, broom closets, and desks are some of the special units

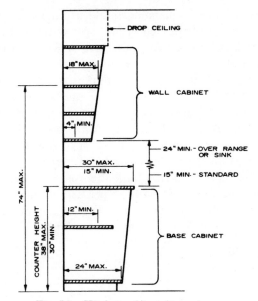

DROP CEILING

18" MAX.

WALL CABINET

4" MIN.

24" MIN. - OVER RANGE OR SINK

30" MAX.
15" MIN.

15" MIN. - STANDARD

74" MAX.

COUNTER HEIGHT
38" MAX.
30" MIN.

12" MIN.

BASE CABINET

24" MAX.

Fig. 10. Kitchen cabinet dimensions.

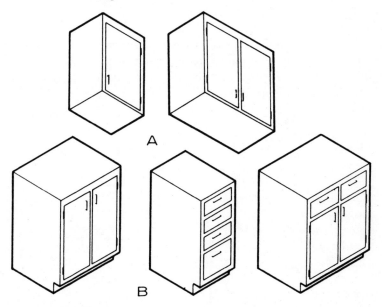

A

B

Fig. 11. Kitchen cabinets. *A*, wall cabinets. *B*, base cabinets.

which may be used in planning the ideal kitchen. Cabinets are fastened to the wall through cleats located at the back of each cabinet. It is good practice to use long screws to penetrate into each wall stud.

Four basic layouts are commonly used in the design of a kitchen. The *U-type* with the sink at the bottom of the U and the range and refrigerator on opposite sides is very efficient (*A*, Fig. 12). The *L-type* (*B*, Fig. 12), with the sink and range on one leg and the refrigerator on the other, is sometimes used with a dining space in the opposite corner. The *parallel wall* or *pullman kitchen plan* (*C*, Fig. 12) is often used in narrow kitchens and can be quite efficient with proper arrangement of the sink, range, and refrigerator. The *sidewall type* (*D*, Fig. 12) usually is preferred for small apartments. All cabinets, the sink, range, and refrigerator are located along one wall. It must be kept in mind that counter space is usually somewhat limited in small kitchens.

Closets and Wardrobes

The simple *clothes closet* is normally furnished with a shelf and a rod. Others may have small low cabinets for the storage of shoes and similar items. Larger *wardrobes* with *sliding* or *folding doors,* in addition to space for hanging clothes, may contain a dresser complete with drawers and mirror. Many *built-in combinations* are possible, all of which reduce the amount of bedroom furniture needed. *Linen closets* may be simply a series

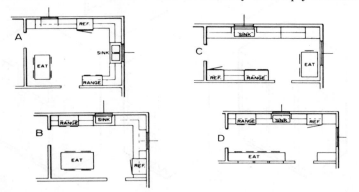

Fig. 12. Kitchen layouts. *A*, U-type. *B*, L-type. *C*, "parallel wall" type. *D*, sidewall type.

of shelves behind a flush or panel door. Others may consist of an open cabinet with doors and drawers built directly into a notch or corner of the wall located near the bedrooms and bath.

Mantels

The type of *mantel* used for a fireplace depends on the style and design of the house and its interior finish. The contemporary fireplace may have no mantel at all, or at best a simple wood molding used as a transition between the masonry and the wall finish. However, the colonial or formal interior usually has a well-designed mantel enclosing the fireplace opening. This may vary from a simple mantel (Fig. 13) to a more elaborate unit combining paneling and built-in cabinets along the entire wall. In each design, however, it is important that no wood or other combustible material be placed within 3½″ of the edges of the fireplace opening. Furthermore, any projection more than 1½″ in front of the fireplace, such as the mantel shelf, should be at least 12½″ above the opening. Mantels are fastened to the header and framing studs above and on each side of the fireplace.

Fig. 13. Fireplace mantel.

China Cases

Another millwork item often incorporated in the dining room of a formal or traditional design is the *china case*. It is usually designed to fit into one or two corners of the room. This corner cabinet often has glazed doors above and single-panel doors or double-panel doors below (Fig. 14). It may be 7' or more high with a drop ceiling above with a face width of about 3'. Shelves are supplied in both the upper and lower cabinets.

China cases or storage shelves in dining rooms of contemporary houses may be built in place. A row of cabinets or shelves may act as a separator between dining room and kitchen and serve as a storage area for both rooms.

Fig. 14. Corner china case.

CHAPTER 27

Exterior Frames, Windows, and Doors

Windows, doors, and their frames are millwork items that are usually fully assembled at the factory. Window units, *for example*, often have the sash fitted and weatherstripped, frame assembled, and exterior casing in place. Standard combination storms and screens or separate units can also be included. Door frames are normally assembled ready for use in the building. All such wood components are treated with a water-repellent preservative at the factory to provide protection before and after they are placed in the walls. (*See also* Chap. 26, Interior Doors, Frames, Trim, Cabinets and Other Millwork.)

Windows exist mainly to allow entry of light and air, but they may also be an important part of the architectural design. Some variation may occur, but normally in habitable rooms the glass area should be not less than 10 per cent of the floor area. Natural ventilation should be not less than 4 per cent of the floor area in a habitable room unless a complete air-conditioning system is used.

TYPES OF WINDOWS

Windows are available in many types, each having advantages. The principal types are double-hung, casement, stationary, awning, and horizontal sliding. They may be made of wood or metal. Heat loss through metal frames and sash is much greater than through similar wood units. Glass blocks are sometimes used for admitting light in places where transparency or ventilation is not required.

Insulated glass, used both for stationary and movable sash,

consists of two or more sheets of spaced glass with hermetically sealed edges. This type has more resistance to heat loss than a single thickness and is often used without a storm sash.

Wood sash and door and window frames should be made from a clear grade of all-heartwood stock of a decay-resistant wood species or from wood which is given a preservative treatment. Species commonly used include ponderosa and other pines, the cedars, cypress, redwood, and the spruces.

Tables showing glass size, sash size, and rough opening size are available at lumber dealers, so that the wall openings can be framed accordingly.

DOUBLE-HUNG WINDOWS

The *double-hung window* is perhaps the most familiar window type. It consists of an upper and lower sash that slide vertically in separate grooves in the side jambs or in full-width metal weatherstripping (Fig. 1). This type of window provides a maximum face opening for ventilation of one-half the total window area. Each sash is provided with springs, balances, or *compression weatherstripping* to hold it in place in any location. *For example*, compression weatherstripping prevents air infiltration, provides tension, and acts as a counterbalance. Several types allow the sash to be removed for easy painting or repair.

The *jambs* (sides and top of the frames) are made of nominal 1″ lumber; the width provides for use with dry wall or plastered interior finish. Sills are made from nominal 2″ lumber and sloped at about 3 in 12 for good drainage (*D*, Fig. 1). Sash are normally 1⅜″ thick and wood combination storm and screen windows are usually 1⅛″ thick.

Sash may be divided into a number of lights by small wood members called *muntins*. A ranch-type house may provide the best appearance with top and bottom sash divided into two horizontal lights. A colonial or Cape Cod house usually has each sash divided into six or eight lights. Some manufacturers provide preassembled dividers which snap in place over a single light, dividing it into six or eight lights. This simplifies painting and other maintenance.

Assembled frames are placed in the rough opening over strips

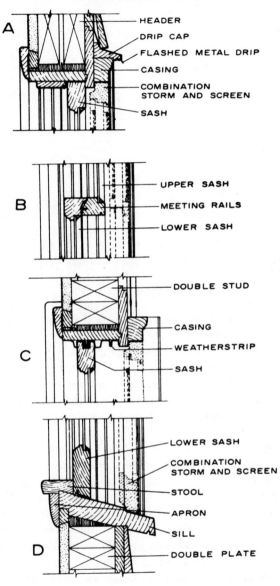

Fig. 1. Double-hung windows. Cross sections: *A*, head jamb. *B*, meeting rails. *C*, side jambs. *D*, sill.

of building paper put around the perimeter to minimize air infiltration. The frame is plumbed and nailed to side studs and header through the casings or the blind stops at the sides. Where nails are exposed, such as on the casing, use the corrosion-resistant type.

Hardware for double-hung windows includes the sash lifts that are fastened to the bottom rail, although they are sometimes eliminated by providing a finger groove in the rail. Other hardware consists of sash locks or fasteners located at the meeting rail. They not only lock the window, but also draw the sash together to provide a *windtight* fit.

Double-hung windows can be arranged as a single unit, doubled (or mullion) type, or in groups of three or more. One or two double-hung windows on each side of a large stationary insulated window are often used to effect a window wall. Such large openings must be framed with headers large enough to carry roofloads.

CASEMENT WINDOWS

Casement windows consist of side-hinged sash, usually designed to swing outward (Fig. 2) because they can be made more weathertight than the in-swinging style. Screens are located inside these out-swinging windows, and winter protection is obtained with a storm sash or by using insulated glass in the sash. One advantage of the casement window over the double-hung type is that the entire window area can be opened for ventilation.

Weatherstripping is provided for the casement window, and units are usually received from the factory entirely assembled with hardware in place. Closing hardware consists of a rotary operator and sash lock. As in the double-hung units, the casement sash can be used in many ways—as a pair or in combinations of two or more pairs. Style variations are achieved by divided lights. Snap-in muntins provide a small, multiple-pane appearance for traditional styling.

Metal sash are sometimes used, but, because of low insulating value, should be installed carefully to prevent condensation and frosting on the interior surfaces during cold weather. A full storm window unit may be used to eliminate this problem in cold climates.

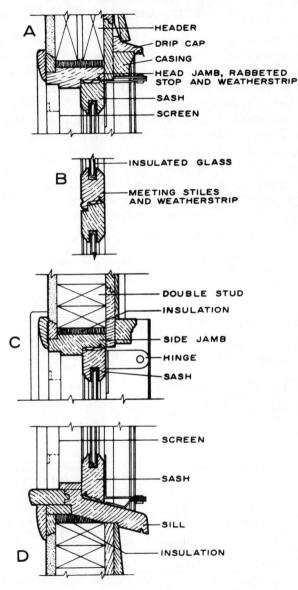

Fig. 2. Out-swinging casement sash. Cross sections: *A*, head jamb. *B*, meeting stiles. *C*, side jambs. *D*, sill.

STATIONARY WINDOWS

Stationary windows used alone or in combination with double-hung or casement windows usually consist of a wood sash with a large single light of insulated glass. They are designed to provide light, as well as for attractive appearance, and are fastened permanently into the frame (Fig. 3). Because of their size (sometimes 6' to 8' wide) 1¾″ thick sash is used to provide strength. The thickness is usually required because of the thickness of the insulating glass.

Other types of stationary windows may be used without a sash. The glass is set directly into rabbeted frame members and held in place with stops. As with all window sash units, back puttying and face puttying of the glass (with or without a stop) will assure moisture resistance.

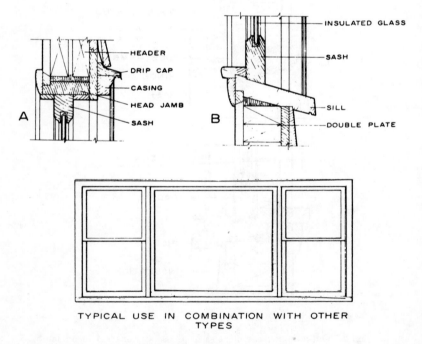

TYPICAL USE IN COMBINATION WITH OTHER TYPES

Fig. 3. Stationary window. Cross sections: *A*, head jamb. *B*, sill.

AWNING WINDOWS

An *awning window unit* consists of a frame in which one or more operative sash are installed (Fig. 4). These units often are made up for a large window wall and consist of three or more units in width and height.

Sash of the awning type are made to swing outward at the bottom. A similar unit, called the *hopper type,* is one in which the top of the sash swings inward. Both types provide protection from rain when open.

Jambs are usually $1\frac{1}{16}''$ or more thick because they are rabbeted, while the sill is at least $1\frac{5}{16}''$ thick when two or more sash are used in a complete frame. Each sash may also be provided with an individual frame, so that any combination in width and height can be used. Awning or hopper window units may consist of a combination of one or more fixed sash with the remainder being the operable type. Operable sash are provided with hinges, pivots, and sash-supporting arms.

Weatherstripping and storm sash and screens are usually provided. The storm sash is eliminated when the windows are glazed with insulated glass.

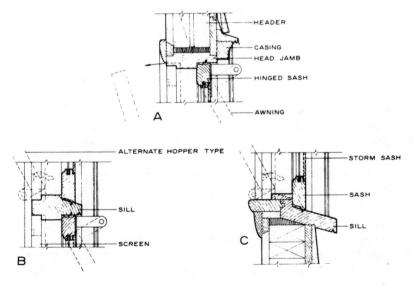

Fig. 4. Awning window. Cross sections: *A,* head jamb. *B,* horizontal mullion. *C,* sill.

HORIZONTAL SLIDING WINDOW UNITS

Horizontal sliding windows appear similar to casement sash. However, the sash (in pairs) slide horizontally in separate tracks or guides located on the sill and head jamb. Multiple window openings consist of two or more single units and may be used when a window wall effect is desired. As in most modern window units of all types, weatherstripping, water-repellent preservative treatments, and sometimes hardware are included in these fully factory-assembled units.

EXTERIOR DOORS AND FRAMES

Exterior doors are 1¾″ thick and not less than 6′ 8″ high. The main entrance door is 3′ wide and the side or rear service door 2′ 8″ wide.

The frames for these doors are made of 1⅛″ or thicker material, so that rabbeting of side and head jambs provides stops for the main door (Fig. 5). The wood sill is often oak for wear resistance, but when softer species are used, a metal nosing and weatherstrips are included. As in many of the window units, the outside casings provide space for the 1⅛″ combination or screen door.

The frame is nailed to studs and headers of the rough opening through the outside casing. The sill must rest firmly on the header or stringer joist of the floor framing, which commonly must be trimmed with a saw and hand ax or other means. After finish flooring is in place, a hardwood or metal threshold with a plastic weatherstop covers the joints between the floor and sill.

The exterior trim around the main entrance door can vary from a simple casing to a molded or plain pilaster with a decorative head casing. Decorative designs should always be in keeping with the architecture of the house. Many combinations of door and entry designs are used with contemporary houses, and manufacturers have millwork which is adaptable to most styles. If there an entry hall, it is usually desirable to have glass included in the main door if no other light is provided.

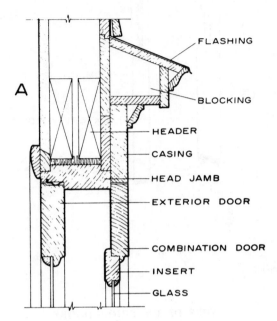

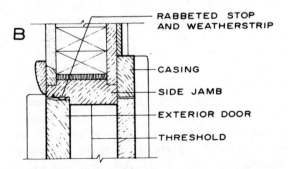

Fig. 5. Exterior door and frame. Exterior door and combination door (screen and storm). Cross sections: *A*, head jamb. *B*, side jamb.

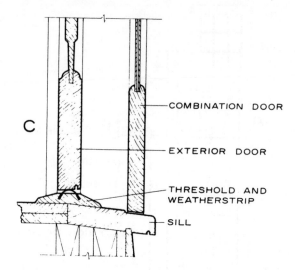

Fig. 5. *C*, sill.

(continued)

TYPES OF EXTERIOR DOORS

Exterior doors and outside combination and storm doors can be obtained in a number of designs to fit the style of almost any house. Doors in the traditional pattern are usually the *panel type* (*A*, Fig. 6). They consist of *stiles* (solid vertical members), *rails* (solid cross members), and *filler panels* in a number of designs. Glazed upper panels are combined with raised wood or plywood lower panels.

Exterior flush doors should be of the solid-core type rather than hollow-core to minimize warping during the heating season. (Warping is caused by a difference in moisture content on the exposed and unexposed faces.) Flush doors consist of thin plywood faces over a framework of wood with a wood-block or particle-board core. Many combinations of designs can be obtained, ranging from plain flush doors to others with a variety of panels and glazed openings (*B*, Fig. 6).

Wood combination doors (storm and screen) are available in

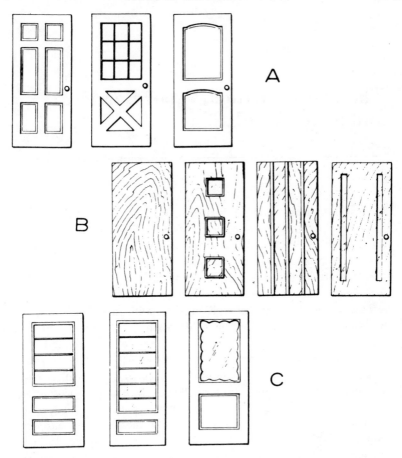

Fig. 6. Exterior doors. *A*, traditional panel. *B*, flush. *C*, combination.

several styles (*C*, Fig. 6). Panels which include screen and storm inserts are normally located in the upper portion of the door. Some types can be obtained with self-storing features, similar to window combination units. Heat loss through metal combination doors is greater than through similar-type wood doors.

Weatherstripping of the 1¾″ thick exterior door will reduce both air infiltration and frosting of the glass on the storm door during cold weather.

CHAPTER 28

Thermal Insulation, Vapor Barriers, and Sound Insulation

Most materials used in houses have some insulating value. Even air spaces between studs resist the passage of heat. When these stud spaces are filled or partially filled with a material high in resistance to heat transmission, namely thermal insulation, the stud space has many times the insulating value of the air alone.

The inflow of heat through outside walls and roofs in hot weather or its outflow during cold weather have important effects upon (a) the comfort of the occupants of a house and (b) the cost of providing either heating or cooling to maintain temperatures at acceptable limits for occupancy. During cold weather, high resistance to heat flow also means a saving in fuel. While the wood in the walls provides good insulation, commercial insulating materials are usually incorporated into exposed walls, ceilings, and floors to increase the resistance to heat passage. The use of insulation in warmer climates is justified with air conditioning, not only because of reduced operating costs but also because units of smaller capacity are required. Therefore, whether from the standpoint of thermal insulation alone in cold climates or whether for the benefit of reducing cooling costs, the use of 2″ or more of insulation in the walls can certainly be justified.

CLASSES OF INSULATING MATERIALS

Commercial insulation is manufactured in a variety of forms and types, each with advantages for specific uses. Materials commonly used for insulation may be grouped in the following classes: (1) flexible insulation (blanket and batt); (2) loose fill insulation; (3) reflective insulation; (4) rigid insulation (structural and nonstructural); and (5) miscellaneous types.

The thermal properties of most building materials are known, and the rate of heat flow or coefficient of transmission for most combinations of construction can be calculated. This coefficient, or *U-value*, is a measure of heat transmission between air on the warm side and air on the cold side of the construction unit. The insulating value of the wall will vary with different types of construction, with materials used in construction, and with different types and thickness of insulation. Comparisons of U-values may be made and used to evaluate different combinations of materials and insulation based on overall heat loss, potential fuel savings, influence on comfort, and installation costs.

Air spaces add to the total resistance of a wall section to heat transmission; but an empty air space is not as effective as one filled with an insulating material. Great importance is frequently given to dead air spaces in speaking of a wall section. Actually, the air is never dead in cells where there are differences in temperature on opposite sides of the space since the difference causes convection currents.

FLEXIBLE INSULATING MATERIALS

Flexible insulation is manufactured in two types, *blanket* and *batt*. *Blanket insulation* (*A*, Fig. 1) is furnished in rolls or packages in widths suited to 16″ and 24″ stud and joist spacing. Usual thicknesses are 1½″, 2″, and 3″. The body of the blanket is made of felted mats of mineral or vegetable fibers, such as rock or glass wool, wood fiber, and cotton. Organic insulations are treated to make them resistant to fire, decay, insects, and vermin. Most blanket insulation is covered with paper or other sheet material with tabs on the sides for fastening to studs or joists. One covering sheet serves as a vapor barrier to resist movement of water vapor and should always face the warm side of the wall. Aluminum foil or asphalt or plastic laminated paper are commonly used as barrier materials. *Batt insulation* (*B*,

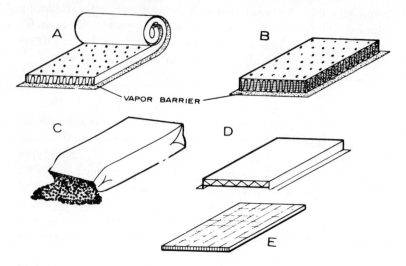

Fig. 1.   Types of insulation.

Fig. 1) is also made of fibrous material preformed to thicknesses of 4″ and 6″ for 16″ and 24″ joist spacing. It is supplied with or without a vapor barrier. (*See* section on Vapor Barriers, in this chapter.) One friction type of fibrous glass batt is supplied without a covering and is designed to remain in place without the normal fastening methods.

LOOSE FILL INSULATION

Loose fill insulation (*C*, Fig. 1) is usually composed of materials used in bulk form, supplied in bags or bales, and placed by pouring, blowing, or packing by hand. This includes rock or glass wool, wood fibers, shredded redwood bark, cork, wood-pulp products, vermiculite, sawdust, and shavings. *Fill insulation* is suited for use between first-floor ceiling joists in unheated attics. It is also used in sidewalls of existing houses that were not insulated during construction. Where no vapor barrier was installed during construction, suitable paint coatings, as described later in this chapter, should be used for vapor barriers when blown insulation is added to an existing house.

REFLECTIVE INSULATION

Most materials reflect some radiant heat, and some materials have this property to a very high degree. Materials high in reflective properties include aluminum foil, sheet metal with tin coating, and paper products coated with a reflective oxide composition. Such materials can be used in enclosed stud spaces, in attics, and in similar locations to retard heat transfer by radiation. These *reflective insulations* are effective *only* when used where the reflective surface faces an air space at least ¾″ or more deep. Where a reflective surface contacts another material, the reflective properties are lost and the material has little or no insulating value.

Reflective insulations are equally effective regardless of whether the reflective surface faces the warm or cold side. There is a decided difference in the equivalent conductance and the resistance to heat flow. The difference depends on (a) the orientation of the reflecting material and the dead air space, (b) the direction of heat flow (horizontal, up, or down), and (c) the mean summer or winter temperatures. Each possibility requires separate consideration. Reflective insulation is perhaps more effective in preventing summer heat flow through ceilings and walls. It should likely be considered more for use in the southern United States than in the northern.

Reflective insulation of the foil type is sometimes applied to blankets and to the stud surface side of gypsum lath. Metal foil suitably mounted on some supporting base makes an excellent vapor barrier. The type of reflective insulation shown in *D*, Fig. 1, includes reflective surfaces and air spaces between the outer sheets.

RIGID INSULATION

Rigid insulation is usually a *fiberboard material* manufactured in sheet and other forms (*E*, Fig. 1). The most common types are made from processed wood, sugarcane, or other vegetable products. Structural insulating boards, in densities ranging from 15 pounds to 31 pounds per cubic foot, are fabricated in such forms as building boards, roof decking, sheathing, and wallboard. While they have moderately good insulating properties, their primary purpose is structural.

Roof insulation is nonstructural and serves mainly to provide thermal resistance to heat flow in roofs. It is called *slab* or *block* insulation and is manufactured in rigid units ½″ to 3″ thick and usually 2′ by 4′ in size.

In house construction, perhaps the most common forms of rigid insulation are sheathing and decorative coverings in sheets or in tile squares. *Sheathing board* is made in thicknesses of ½″ and $^{25}/_{32}$″. It is coated or impregnated with an asphalt compound to provide water resistance. *Sheets* are made in 2′ by 8′ size for horizontal application and 4′ by 8′ or longer for vertical application.

MISCELLANEOUS INSULATION

Some insulations do not fit in the classifications previously described, such as insulation blankets made up of multiple layers of corrugated paper. Other types, such as lightweight vermiculite and perlite aggregates, are sometimes used in plaster as a means of reducing heat transmission.

Other materials are foamed-in-place insulations, which include sprayed and plastic foam types. Sprayed insulation is usually inorganic fibrous material blown against a clean surface which has been primed with an adhesive coating. It is often left exposed for acoustical as well as insulating properties.

Expanded *polystyrene* and *urethane* plastic foams may be molded or foamed-in-place. Urethane insulation may also be applied by spraying. Polystyrene and urethane in board form can be obtained in thicknesses from ½″ to 2″.

See Table 15 for thermal conductivity values of some insulating materials. These are expressed as "k" values or heat conductivity and are defined as the amount of heat, in British thermal units, that will pass in one hour through one square foot of material one inch thick per 1°F temperature difference between faces of the material. *For example,* "k" represents heat loss; the lower this numerical value, the better the insulating qualities.

Insulation is also rated on its resistance or "R" value, which is merely another expression of the insulating value. The "R" value is usually expressed as the total resistance of the wall or of a thick insulating blanket or batt, whereas "k" is the rating per inch of thickness. *For example,* a "k" value of one inch of insulation is 0.25. Then the resistance, "R" is $\frac{1}{0.25}$ or 4.0. For 3 inches of this insulation, the total "R" is three times 4.0, or 12.0.

TABLE 15

Thermal conductivity values of some insulating materials

Insulation group		"k" range (conductivity)
General	Specific type	
Flexible		0.25 — 0.27
Fill	Standard materials	.28 — .30
	Vermiculite	.45 — .48
Reflective (2 sides)		(¹)
Rigid	Insulating fiberboard	.35 — .36
	Sheathing fiberboard	.42 — .55
Foam	Polystyrene	.25 — .29
	Urethane	.15 — .17
Wood	Low density	.60 — .65

¹ Insulating value is equal to slightly more than 1 inch of flexible insulation. (Resistance, "R" = 4.3)

The "U" value is the overall heat loss value of all materials in the wall. The lower this value, the better the insulating value. Specific insulating values for various materials are also available. For comparison with Table 15, the "U" value of the window glass is:

Glass	*U value*
Single	1.13
Double	
Insulated, with ¼" air space	.61
Storm sash over single glazed window	.53

WHERE TO INSULATE

To reduce heat loss from the house during the cold weather in most climates, all walls, ceilings, roofs, and floors that separate the heated spaces from the unheated spaces should be insulated. Insulation should be placed on all outside walls and in the ceiling (*A*, Fig. 2). In houses involving unheated crawl spaces, it should be placed between the floor joists or around the wall perimeter. If a flexible type of insulation (blanket or batt) is used, it should be well supported between joists by slats and a galvanized wire mesh or by a rigid board with the vapor barrier installed toward the subflooring. Press-fit or friction insulations fit tightly between joists and require only a small amount of support to hold them in place. Reflective insulation is often used for crawl spaces, but only one dead air space should be assumed in calculating heat loss when the crawl space is ventilated. A ground cover of roll roofing or plastic film such as polyethylene should be placed on the soil of crawl spaces to decrease the moisture content of the space as well as of the wood members.

In one and one-half story houses, insulation should be placed along all walls, floors, and ceilings that are adjacent to unheated areas (*B*, Fig. 2). These include stairways, dwarf (knee) walls, and dormers. Provisions should be made for ventilation of the unheated areas.

Where attic space is unheated and a stairway is included, insulation should be used around the stairway as well as in the first-floor ceiling (*C*, Fig. 2). The door leading to the attic should be weatherstripped to prevent heat loss. Walls adjoining an unheated garage or porch should also be insulated.

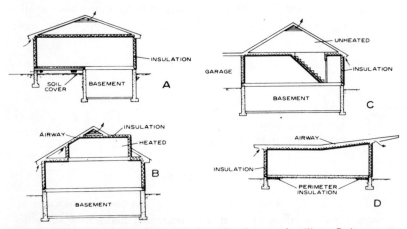

Fig. 2. Placement of insulation. *A*, in walls, floor, and ceiling. *B*, in one and one-half story house. *C*, at attic door. *D*, in flat roof.

In houses with flat or low-pitched roofs (*D*, Fig. 2), insulation should be used in the ceiling area with sufficient space allowed above for clear unobstructed ventilation between the joists. Insulation should be used along the perimeter of houses built on slabs. A vapor barrier should be included under the slab.

In the summer, outside surfaces exposed to the direct rays of the sun may attain temperatures of 50°F or more above shade temperatures and will tend to transfer this heat toward the inside of the house. Insulation in the walls and in attic areas retards the flow of heat and consequently less heat is transferred through such areas resulting in improved summer comfort conditions.

Where air-conditioning systems are used, insulation should be placed in all exposed ceilings and walls in the same manner as insulating against cold weather heat loss. Shading of glass against direct rays of the sun and the use of insulated glass will aid in reducing the air-conditioning load.

Ventilation of attic and roof spaces is an important adjunct to insulation. Without ventilation, an attic space may become very hot and hold the heat for many hours. (*See* Chap. **31**, Ventilation.) More heat will be transmitted through the ceiling when the attic temperature is 150°F than when it is 100° to 120°F. Ventilation methods suggested for protection against cold weather condensation apply equally well to protection against excessive hot weather roof temperatures.

The use of storm windows or insulated glass will greatly reduce heat loss. Almost twice as much heat loss occurs through a single glass as through a window glazed with insulated glass or protected by a storm sash. Furthermore, double glass will normally prevent surface condensation and frost forming on inner glass surfaces in winter. When excessive condensation persists, paint failures or even decay of the sash rail or other parts can occur.

HOW TO INSTALL INSULATION

Blanket insulation or batt insulation with a vapor barrier should be placed between framing members so that the tabs of the barrier lap the edge of the studs as well as the top and bottom plates. This method assures a minimum amount of vapor loss as compared to the loss occurring when tabs are stapled to the sides of the studs. To protect the head and soleplate as well as the headers over openings, it is good practice to use narrow strips of vapor-barrier material along the top and bottom of the wall (*A*, Fig. 3). Ordinarily, these areas are not covered too well by the barrier on the blanket or batt. A hand stapler is commonly used to fasten the insulation and the barriers in place.

For insulation without a barrier (press-fit or friction-type), a plastic film vapor barrier such as 4-mil polyethylene is commonly used to envelop the entire exposed wall and ceiling (*B*, Fig. 3). It covers the openings as well as window and door headers and edge studs. This system is one of the best from

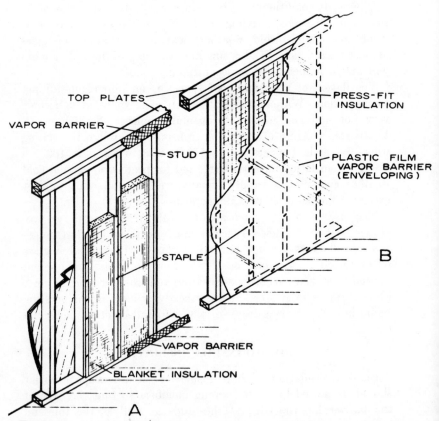

Fig. 3. Application of insulation. *A*, wall section with blanket type. *B*, wall section with "press-fit" insulation.

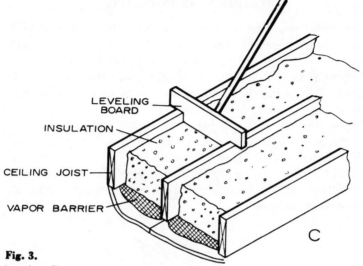

Fig. 3.
(continued) C, ceiling with full insulation.

the standpoint of resistance to vapor movement. Furthermore, it does not have the installation inconveniences encountered when tabs of the insulation are stapled over the edges of the studs. After the dry wall is installed or plastering is completed, the film is trimmed around the window and door openings.

Reflective insulation, in a single sheet form with two reflective surfaces, should be placed to divide the space formed by the framing members into two approximately equal spaces. Some reflective insulations include air spaces and are furnished with nailing tabs. This type is fastened to the studs to provide at least a ¾″ space on each side of the reflective surfaces.

Fill insulation is commonly used in ceiling areas and is poured or blown into place (*C,* Fig. 3). A vapor barrier should be used on the warm side (the bottom, in case of ceiling joists) before insulation is placed. A leveling board, as shown in the illustration, will give a constant insulation thickness. Thick *batt insulation* is also used in ceiling areas. Batt and fill insulation might also be combined to obtain the desired thickness with the vapor barrier against the back face of the ceiling finish. Ceiling insulation six or more inches thick greatly reduces heat loss in the winter and also provides summertime protection.

PRECAUTIONS IN INSULATING

Areas over door and window frames and along side and head jambs also require insulation. Because these areas are filled with small sections of insulation, a vapor barrier must be used around the opening as well as over the header above the openings (*A*, Fig. 4). Enveloping the entire wall eliminates the need for this type of vapor-barrier installation.

In one and one-half and two-story houses and in basements, the area at the joist header at outside walls should be insulated and protected with a vapor barrier (*B*, Fig. 4).

Insulation should be placed behind electrical outlet boxes and other utility connections in exposed walls to minimize condensation on cold surfaces.

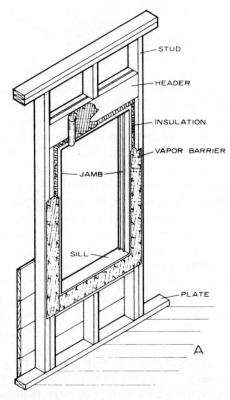

Fig. 4. Precautions in insulating. *A*, around openings.

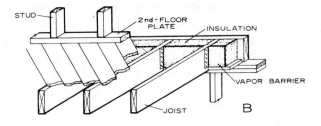

STUD

2nd-FLOOR PLATE

INSULATION

VAPOR BARRIER

JOIST

B

Fig. 4.
(continued)　　　　　*B,* joist space in outside walls.

VAPOR BARRIERS

Some discussion of vapor barriers has been included in previous sections of this chapter because vapor barriers are usually a part of flexible insulation. *A,* Figure 5 illustrates water vapor from inside the house moved out through the wall. When the vapor met outside cold air, moisture condensed and froze. As the outside temperatures rose in the spring and summer, ice melted, and the moisture was free to move through the siding and destroy the paint coating. *B,* Figure 5, shows that the vapor barrier (on the warm side of the wall) has prevented moisture from getting into the walls.

Most building materials are permeable to water vapor. This presents problems because considerable water vapor is generated in a house from cooking, dishwashing, laundering, bathing, humidifiers, and other sources. In cold climates during cold

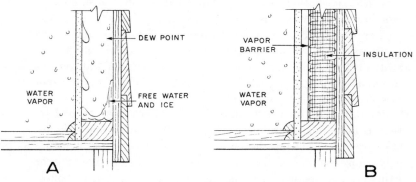

DEW POINT

WATER VAPOR

FREE WATER AND ICE

A

VAPOR BARRIER

INSULATION

WATER VAPOR

B

Fig. 5.

weather, this vapor may pass through wall and ceiling materials and condense in the wall or attic space; therefore, in severe cases it may damage the exterior paint and interior finish or even result in decay in structural members. For protection, a material highly resistive to vapor transmission, called a *vapor barrier*, should be used on the warm side of a wall or below the insulation in an attic space.

Among the effective vapor-barrier materials are asphalt laminated papers, aluminum foil, and plastic films. Most blanket and batt insulations are provided with a vapor barrier on one side, some of them with paper-backed aluminum foil. Foil-backed gypsum lath or gypsum boards are also available and serve as excellent vapor barriers.

The perm (a measure of water-vapor movement through a material) values of vapor barriers vary, but ordinarily it is good practice to use those which have values less than $\frac{1}{4}$ (0.25) perm. Although a value of $\frac{1}{2}$ perm is considered adequate, aging reduces the effectiveness of some materials.

Some types of flexible blanket and batt insulation have a barrier material on one side. Such flexible insulations should be attached with the tabs at their sides fastened on the inside (narrow) edges of the studs, and the blanket should be cut long enough so that the cover sheet can lap over the face of the sole-plate at the bottom and over the plate at the top of the stud space. When a positive seal is desired, wall-height rolls of plastic film vapor barriers should be applied over studs, plates, and window and door headers. This system (called enveloping) is used over insulation having no vapor barrier or to insure excellent protection when used over any type of insulation. The barrier should be fitted tightly around outlet boxes and sealed if necessary. A ribbon of sealing compound around an outlet or switch box will minimize vapor loss at this area. Cold air returns in outside walls should consist of metal ducts to prevent vapor loss and subsequent paint problems.

Paint coatings on plaster may be very effective as vapor barriers if materials are properly chosen and applied. They *do not* offer protection during the period of construction, and moisture may cause paint blisters on exterior paint before the interior paint can be applied. This is most likely to happen in houses that are constructed during periods when outdoor temperatures are 25°F or more below inside temperatures. Paint coatings cannot be considered a substitute for the membrane types of vapor barriers, but they do provide some protection for houses where other types of vapor barriers were not installed during construction.

Of the various types of paint, one coat of *aluminum primer* followed by two decorative coats of *flat wall* or *lead* and *oil* paint is quite effective. For rough plaster or for houses in very cold climates, two coats of aluminum primer may be necessary. A primer and sealer of the pigmented type, followed by decorative finish coats or two coats of rubber-base paint, are also effective in retarding vapor transmission.

Because no type of vapor barrier can be considered 100 per cent resistive and some vapor leakage into the wall may be expected, the flow of vapor to the outside should not be impeded by materials of relatively high vapor resistance on the cold side of the vapor barrier. *For example,* sheathing paper should be of a type that is waterproof but not highly vapor resistant. This also applies to *permanent* outer coverings or siding. In such cases, the vapor barrier should have an equally low perm value. This will reduce the danger of condensation on cold surfaces within the wall.

SOUND INSULATION

Development of the *quiet* home or the need for incorporating sound insulation in a new house is becoming more and more important. In the past, the reduction of sound transfer between rooms was more important in apartments, hotels, and motels than in private homes. House designs now often incorporate a family room or *active* living room as well as *quiet* living room. It is usually desirable in such designs to isolate these rooms from the remainder of the house. *Sound insulation* between the bedroom area and the living area is usually desirable, as is isolation of the bathrooms. Isolation from outdoor sounds is also often advisable. Therefore, sound control has become a vital part of house design and construction and will be even more important in the coming years.

HOW SOUND TRAVELS

How does sound travel? How is it transferred through a wall or floor? Airborne noises inside a house, such as loud conversation or a barking dog, create sound waves which radiate outward from the source through the air until they strike a wall, floor, or ceiling. These surfaces are set in vibration by the fluctuating pressure of the sound wave in the air. Because the wall vibrates, it conducts sound to the other side in varying degrees, depending on the wall construction.

The resistance of a building element, such as a wall, to the passage of airborne sound is rated by its *Sound Transmission Class* (STC). Therefore, the higher the number, the better the sound barrier. The approximate effectiveness of walls with varying STC numbers is shown in the following table.

STC No.	*Effectiveness*
25	Normal speech can be understood quite easily
35	Loud speech audible but not intelligible
45	Must strain to hear loud speech
48	Some loud speech barely audible
50	Loud speech not audible

Sound travels readily through the air and also through some materials. When airborne sound strikes a conventional wall, the studs act as sound conductors unless they are separated in some way from the covering material. Electrical switches or convenience outlets placed back-to-back in a wall readily pass sound. Faulty construction, such as poorly fitted doors, often allows sound to travel through. Therefore, good construction practices are important in providing sound-resistant walls.

Thick walls of dense materials such as masonry can stop sound. But in the wood frame house, an interior masonry wall results in increased costs and structural problems created by heavy walls. To provide a satisfactory sound-resistant wall economically has been a problem. At one time, sound-resistant frame construction for the home involved significant additional costs because it usually meant double walls or suspended ceilings. A relatively simple system has been developed using sound-deadening insulating board in conjunction with a gypsum board outer covering. This provides good sound transmission resistance suitable for use in the home with only slight additional cost. A number of combinations are possible with this system, providing different STC ratings.

WALL CONSTRUCTION

As the STC table shows, a wall providing sufficient resistance to airborne sound transfer more than likely has an STC rating of 45 or greater. Therefore, in construction of such a wall between the rooms of a house, its cost as related to the STC rating should be considered. As shown in Fig. 6, details *A*, with gypsum wallboard, and *B*, with plastered wall, are commonly used for partition walls. However, the hypothetical rating of 45 cannot be obtained in this construction. An 8″ concrete block wall (*C*, Fig. 6) has the minimum rating, but this construction is not always practical in a wood frame house.

Good STC ratings can be obtained in a wood frame wall by using a combination of materials for *D* and *E*, Fig. 6. One-half-inch sound-deadening board nailed to the studs, followed by a lamination of ½″ gypsum wallboard, will provide an STC value

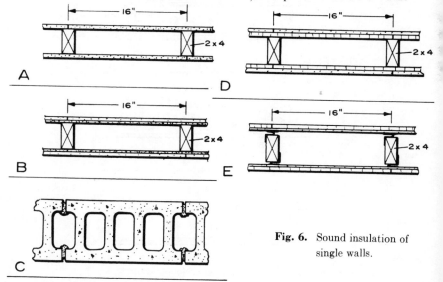

Fig. 6. Sound insulation of single walls.

of 46 at a relatively low cost. A slightly better rating can be obtained by using ⅝″ gypsum wallboard rather than ½″. A very satisfactory STC rating of 52 can be obtained by using resilient clips to fasten gypsum backed boards to the studs, followed by adhesive laminated ½″ fiberboard (*E*, Fig. 6). This method further isolates the wall covering from the framing.

A similar isolation system consists of resilient channels nailed horizontally to 2″ by 4″ studs spaced 16″ on center. Channels are spaced 24″ apart vertically and ⅝″ gypsum wallboard is screwed to the channels. An STC rating of 47 is therefore obtained at a moderately low cost.

The use of a double wall, which may consist of a 2 by 6 or wider plate and staggered 2″ by 4″ studs, is sometimes desirable. One-half-inch gypsum wallboard on each side of this wall (*A*, Fig. 7) results in an STC value of 45. However, two layers

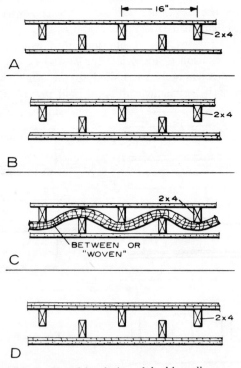

Fig. 7. Sound insulation of double walls.

of $\frac{5}{8}''$ gypsum wallboard add little, if any, additional sound-transfer resistance (*B*, Fig. 7). When $1\frac{1}{2}''$ blanket insulation is added to this construction (*C*, Fig. 7), the STC rating increases to **49**. This insulation may be installed as shown in the illustration or placed between studs on one wall. A single wall with $3\frac{1}{2}''$ of insulation will show a marked improvement over an open stud space and is low in cost.

The use of $\frac{1}{2}''$ sound-deadening board and a lamination of gypsum wallboard in the double wall will result in an STC rating of 50 (*D*, Fig. 7). The addition of blanket insulation to this combination will likely provide an even higher value, perhaps 53 or 54.

FLOOR-CEILING CONSTRUCTION

Sound insulation between an upper floor and the ceiling of a lower floor not only involves resistance of airborne sounds but also that of impact noises. Therefore, impact noise control must be considered as well as the STC value. Impact noise is caused by an object striking or sliding along a wall or floor surface, such as dropped objects, footsteps, or moving furniture. It may also be caused by the vibration of a dishwasher, bathtub, food-disposal apparatus, or other equipment. In all instances, the floor is set into vibration by the impact or contact and sound is radiated from both sides of the floor.

A method of measuring impact noise has been developed and is commonly expressed as *Impact Noise Ratings* (INR). (INR ratings, however, are being abandoned in favor of *Impact Insulation Class* (IIC) ratings. IIC is a new system utilized in the Federal Housing Administration recommended criteria for impact sound insulation.) The greater the positive value of the INR, the more resistant is the floor to impact-noise transfer. *For example*, an INR of −2 is better than one of −17, and one of +5 INR is a further improvement in resistance to impact-noise transfer.

Figure 8 shows STC and approximate INR (db) values for several types of floor constructions. *A*, Figure 8, perhaps a minimum floor assembly with tongued-and-grooved floor and $\frac{3}{8}''$ gypsum board ceiling, has an STC value of 30 and an approx-

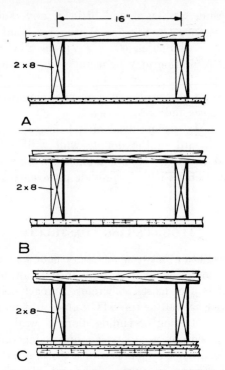

Fig. 8. Relative impact and sound transfer in floor-ceiling combinations (2″ by 8″ joists).

imate INR value of −18. This is improved somewhat by construction shown in *B*, Fig. 8, and still further by the combination of materials in *C*, Fig. 8.

The value of isolating the ceiling joists from a gypsum lath and plaster ceiling by means of spring clips is illustrated in *A*, Fig. 9. An STC value of 52 and an approximate INR value of −2 result.

Foam rubber padding and carpeting improve both the STC and the INR values. The STC value increases from 31 to 45 and the approximate INR from −17 to −5 (*B* and *C*, Fig. 9). This can likely be further improved by using an isolated ceiling finish with spring clips. The use of sound-deadening board and a lamination of gypsum board for the ceiling would also improve resistance to sound transfer.

An economical construction similar to (but an improvement

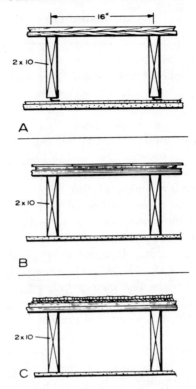

Fig. 9. Relative impact and sound transfer in floor-ceiling combinations
(2″ by 10″ joists).

over) *C*, Fig. 9, with an STC value of **48** and an approximate
INR of +18, consists of the following: (a) a pad and carpet
over ⅝″ tongued-and-grooved plywood underlayment, (b) 3″
fiberglass insulating batts between joists, (c) resilient channels
spaced 24″ apart, across the bottom of the joists, and (d) ⅝″
gypsum board screwed to the bottom of the channels and finished
with taped joints.

The use of separate floor joists with staggered ceiling joists
below provides reasonable values but adds a good deal to construction costs. Separate joists with insulation between and a
soundboard between subfloor and finish provide an STC rating
of 53 and an approximate INR value of −3.

SOUND ABSORPTION

Design of the *quiet* house can incorporate another system of sound insulation, namely, *sound absorption*. Sound-absorbing materials can minimize the amount of noise by stopping the reflection of sound back into a room. Sound-absorbing materials do not necessarily have resistance to airborne sounds. Perhaps the most commonly used sound-absorbing material is *acoustic tile*. Wood fiber or similar materials are used in the manufacture of the tile, which is usually processed to provide some fire resistance and designed with numerous tiny sound traps on the tile surfaces. These may consist of tiny drilled or punched holes, fissured surfaces, or a combination of both.

Acoustic tile is most often used in the ceiling and areas where it is not· subjected to excessive· mechanical damage, such as above a wall wainscoting. It is normally manufactured in sizes from 12″ by 12″ to 12″ by 48″. Thicknesses vary from ½″ to ¾″, and the tile is usually factory finished ready for application. Paint or other finishes which fill or cover the tiny holes or fissures for trapping sound will greatly reduce its efficiency.

Acoustic tile may be applied to existing ceilings or any smooth surface with a mastic adhesive designed specifically for this purpose or to furring strips nailed to the underside of the ceiling joists. Nailing or stapling tile is the normal application method in this system. It is also used with a mechanical suspension system involving small "H," "Z," or "T" members. Manufacturers' recommendations should be followed in application and finishing.

CHAPTER 29

Porches and Garages

An attached porch or garage which is in keeping with the house design usually adds to its overall pleasing appearance. Therefore, any similar attachments to the house after it has been built should also be in keeping structurally and architecturally with the basic design. In such additions, the connections of the porch or garage to the main house should be by means of the framing members and roof sheathing. Rafters, ceiling joists, and studs should be securely attached by nailing to the house framing.

When *additions* are made to an existing house, the siding or other finish is removed so that framing members can be easily and correctly fastened to the house. In many instances, the siding can be cut with a skill saw to the outline of the addition and removed only where necessary. When concrete foundations, piers, or slabs are added, they should also be structurally correct. Footings should be of sufficient size, the bottoms located below the frostline, and the foundation wall anchored to the house foundation when possible.

PORCHES

There are many types and designs of porches, some with roof slopes continuous with the roof of the house itself. Other porch roofs may have just enough pitch to provide drainage. The fundamental construction principles are somewhat alike no matter what type is built. Therefore, a general description—together with several construction details—can apply to several types.

Figure 1 shows the construction details of a typical flat-roofed porch with a concrete slab floor. An attached porch can be open or fully enclosed, or it can be constructed with a concrete slab floor (insulated or uninsulated). A porch can also be constructed using wood floor framing over a crawl space (Fig. 2). Most details of such a unit should comply with those previously outlined for various parts of the house itself.

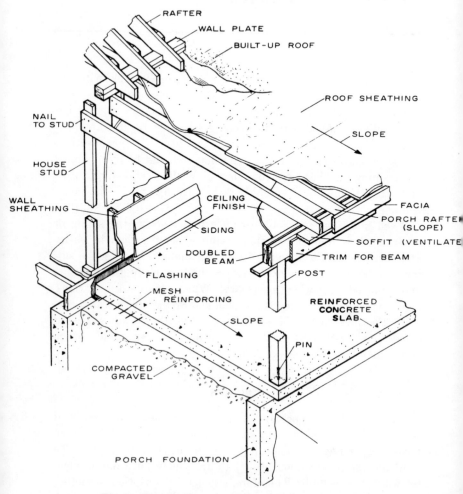

Fig. 1. Details of porch construction for concrete slab.

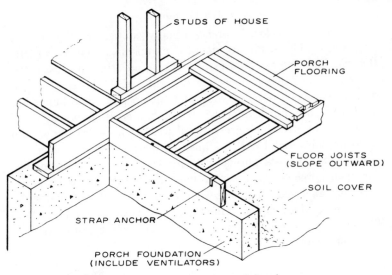

Fig. 2. Porch floor with wood framing.

Porch Framing and Floors

Porch floors, whether wood or concrete, should have sufficient slope away from the house to provide good drainage. Weep holes or drains should be provided in any solid or fully sheathed perimeter wall. Open wood balusters with top and bottom railings should be constructed so that the bottom rail is free of the floor surface.

Floor framing for wood floor construction should be at least 18″ above the soil. The use of a soil cover of polyethylene or similar material under a partially open or a closed porch is good practice. (*See* Chap. 21, Floor Framing.)

Slats or grillwork used around an open crawl space should be made with a removable section for entry in areas where termites may be present. A fully enclosed crawl-space foundation should be vented or have an opening to the basement.

Wood species used for finish porch floor should have good decay and wear resistance, be nonsplintering, and be free from warping. Species commonly used are cypress, Douglas fir, western larch, southern pine, and redwood. Only treated material should be used where moisture conditions are severe.

Porch Columns

Supports for enclosed porches usually consist of fully framed stud walls. The studs are doubled at openings and at corners. Because both interior and exterior finish coverings are used, the walls are constructed much like the walls of the house. In open or partially open porches, solid or built-up posts or columns are used. A more finished or cased column is often made up of doubled 2 by 4's which are covered with 1" by 4" casing on two opposite sides and 1" by 6" finish casing on the other sides (*A*, Fig. 3). Solid posts normally 4" by 4" in size are used mainly for open porches. An open railing may be used between posts.

A formal design of a large house entrance often includes the use of round built-up columns topped by *Doric* or *Ionic* capitals. These columns are factory made and ready for installation at the house site.

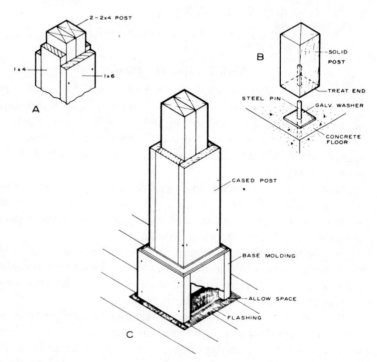

Fig. 3. Post details. *A*, cased post. *B*, pin anchor and spacer. *C*, flashing at base.

The base of posts or columns in open porches should be designed so that no pockets are formed to retain moisture and encourage decay. In single posts, a steel pin may be used to locate the post and a large galvanized washer or similar spacer used to keep the bottom of the post above the concrete or wood floor (*B*, Fig. 3). The bottom of the post should be treated to minimize moisture penetration. Often single posts of this type are made from a decay-resistant wood species. A cased post can be flashed under the base molding (*C*, Fig. 3). Post anchors which provide connections to the floor and to the post are available commercially, as are post caps.

Balustrade

A porch *balustrade* usually consists of one or two railings with *balusters* between them. They are designed for an open porch in order to provide protection and to improve the appearance. There are innumerable combinations and arrangements of them. A closed balustrade may be used with screens or combination windows above (*A*, Fig. 4). A balustrade with decorative railings may be used for an open porch (*B*, Fig. 4). This type can also be used with full-height removable screens.

All balustrade members that are exposed to water and snow should be designed to shed water. The top of the railing should be tapered and connections with balusters protected as much as possible (*A*, Fig. 5). Railings should not contact a concrete floor but should be blocked to provide a small space beneath. When wood must be in contact with the concrete, it should be treated to resist decay.

Connection of the railing with a post should be made in a way that prevents moisture from being trapped. One method provides a small space between the post and the end of the railing (*B*, Fig. 5). When the railing is treated with paint or water-repellent preservative, this type of connection should provide good service. Exposed members, such as posts, balusters, and railings, should be all-heartwood stock of decay-resistant or treated wood to minimize decay.

GARAGES

Garages can be classified as attached, detached, basement, or

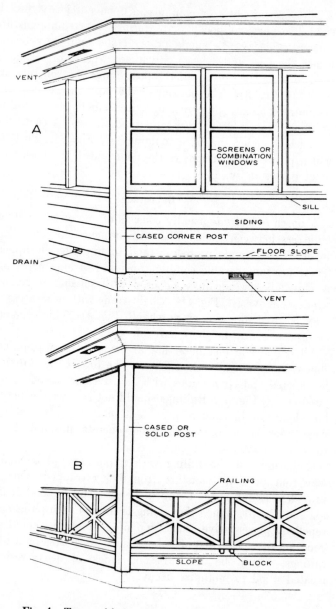

Fig. 4. Types of balustrades. *A*, closed. *B*, open.

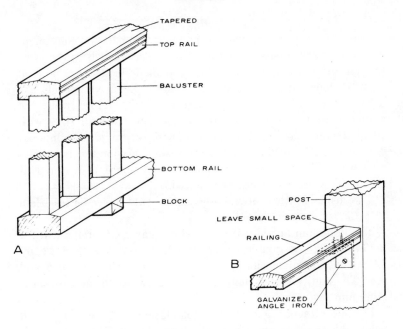

Fig. 5. Railing details. *A*, balustrade assembly. *B*, rail-to-post connection.

carport. The selection of a garage type is often determined by the limitations of the site and the size of the lot. Where space is not a limitation, the attached garage has much in its favor. It may give better architectural lines to the house, it is warmer during cold weather, and it provides covered protection to passengers, convenient space for storage, and a short, direct entrance to the house.

Building regulations often require that detached garages be located away from the house toward the rear of the lot. Where there is considerable slope to a lot, basement garages may be desirable, and generally such garages will cost less than those above grade.

Carports are car-storage spaces, generally attached to the house, that have roofs but often have no sidewalls. To improve the appearance and utility of this type of structure, storage cabinets are often used on a side and at the end of the carport.

Size

It is a mistake to design the garage too small for convenient use. Cars vary in size from the small import models to the large foreign and domestic sedans. Many popular models are now up to 215″ long, and the larger and more expensive models are usually over 230″ (almost 20′ in length). Therefore, while the garage need not necessarily be designed to take all sizes with adequate room around the car, it is wise to provide a minimum distance of 21′ to 22′ between the inside face of the front and rear walls. If additional storage or work space is required at the back, a greater depth is required.

The inside width of a single garage should never be less than 11′; 13′ is much more satisfactory.

The minimum outside size for a single garage, therefore, would be 14′ by 22′. A double garage should be not less than 22′ by 22′ in outside dimensions to provide reasonable clearance and use. The addition of a shop or storage area would increase these minimum sizes.

For an attached garage, the foundation wall should extend below the frostline and about 8″ above the finish floor level. It should be not less than 6″ thick, but it is usually more because of the difficulty of trenching this width. The sill plate should be anchored to the foundation wall with anchor bolts spaced about 8′ apart, at least two bolts in each sill piece. Extra anchors may be required at the side of the main door. The framing of the sidewalls and roof and the application of the exterior covering material of an attached garage should be similar to that of the house.

The interior finish of the garage is often a matter of choice. The studs may be left exposed or covered with some type of sheet material or they may be plastered. Some building codes require that the wall between the house and the attached garage be made of fire-resistant material. Local building regulations and fire codes should be consulted before construction is begun.

If fill is required below the floor, it should preferably be sand or gravel well-compacted and tamped. If other types of soil fill are used, it should be wet down so that it will be well-compacted and can then be well-tamped. Time must be allowed before pouring. Unless these precautions are taken, the concrete floor will likely settle and crack.

The floor should be of concrete not less than 4″ thick and laid with a pitch of about 2″ from the back to the front of the garage. The use of wire reinforcing mesh is often advisable. The garage floor should be set about one inch above the drive or apron level. It is desirable at this point to have an expansion joint between the garage floor and the driveway or apron.

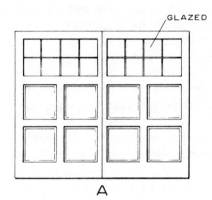

GLAZED

A

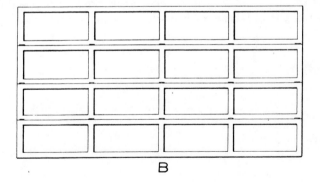

B

Fig. 6. Garage doors. *A*, one-section swing. *B*, sectional.

Garage Doors

The two overhead garage doors most commonly used are the sectional and the single-section swing types. The *swing door* (*A*, Fig. 6) is hung with side and overhead brackets and an overhead track and must be moved outward slightly at the bottom as it is opened. The *sectional-type door* (*B*, Fig. 6), in four or five horizontal hinged sections, has a similar track extending along the sides and under the ceiling framing, with a roller for the side of each section. It is opened by lifting and is adaptable to automatic electric opening with remote-control devices. The standard desirable size for a single door is 9' in width by 6½' or 7' in height. Double doors are usually 16' by 6½' or 17' in size.

Doors vary in design, but those most often used are the panel type with solid stiles and rails and panel fillers. A glazed panel section is often included. Clearance above the top of the door required for overhead doors is usually about 12". However, low headroom brackets are available when such clearance is not possible.

The header beam over garage doors should be designed for the snow load which might be imposed on the roof above. In wide openings, this may be a steel I-beam or a built-up wood section. For spans of 8' or 9', two doubled 2 by 10's of high-grade Douglas fir or similar species are commonly used when only snow loads must be considered. If floor loads are also imposed on the header, a steel I-beam or wide-flange beam is usually selected.

CHAPTER 30

Roof Coverings

Roof coverings should provide a long-lived waterproof finish that will protect the building and its contents from rain, snow, and wind. Many materials have withstood the test of time and have proved satisfactory under given service conditions.

MATERIALS

Materials used for pitched roofs are wood, asphalt, and asbestos shingles, and also tile and slate. *Sheet* materials such as roll roofing, galvanized iron, aluminum, copper, and tin are also used. Perhaps the most common covering for flat or low-pitched roofs is the built-up roof with a gravel topping or cap sheet. *Plastic films*, often backed with an asbestos sheet, are also being applied on low-slope roofs. While these materials are relatively new, it is likely that their use will increase, especially for roofs with unusual shapes. The choice of roofing materials is usually influenced by cost, local code requirements, house design, or preferences based on past experience.

In *shingle application*, the exposure distance is important and the amount of exposure generally depends on the roof slope and the type of material used. This may vary from a 5″ exposure for standard-size asphalt and wood shingles on a moderately steep slope to about 3½″ for flatter slopes. However, even flatter slopes can be used for asphalt shingles with double underlay and triple shingle coverage. Built-up construction is used mainly for flat or low-pitched roofs but can be adapted to steeper slopes by the use of special materials and methods.

Roof underlay material usually consists of 15-pound or 30-pound asphalt-saturated felt and should be used in moderate- and lower-slope roofs covered with asphalt, asbestos, or slate shingles, or tile roofing. It is not commonly used for wood shingles or shakes. In areas where moderate to severe snowfalls occur, cornices without proper protection will often be plagued with ice dams (*A*, Fig. 1). These are formed when snow melts, runs down the roof, and freezes at the colder cornice area. Gradually, the ice forms a dam that backs up water under the shingles. Under these conditions, it is good practice to use an under-course (**36″** width) of 45-pound or heavier smooth-surface roll roofing along the eave line as a flashing (*B*, Fig. 1). This will minimize the chance of water backing up and entering the wall. However, good attic ventilation and sufficient ceiling insulation are of primary importance in eliminating this harmful nuisance. These details are described in Chap. 31, Ventilation.

Metal roofs (tin, copper, galvanized iron, or aluminum) are sometimes used on flat decks of dormers, porches, or entryways. Joints should be watertight and the deck properly flashed at the juncture with the house. Nails should be of the same metal as that used on the roof, except that with tin roofs, steel nails may be used. All exposed nailheads in tin roofs should be soldered with a rosin-core solder.

WOOD SHINGLES

Wood shingles of the types commonly used for house roofs are

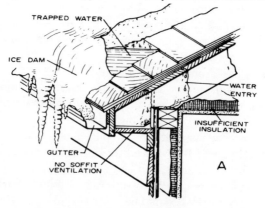

Fig. 1. Snow and ice dams.

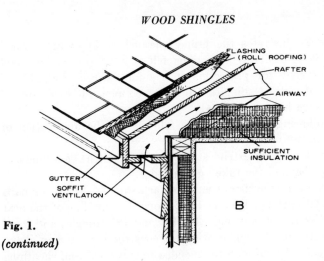

Fig. 1.
(continued)

No. 1 grade. Such shingles are all-heartwood, all-edge-grain, and tapered. Second-grade shingles make good roofs for secondary buildings as well as excellent sidewalls for primary buildings. Western red cedar and redwood are the principal commercial shingle woods since their heartwood has high-decay resistance and low shrinkage.

Four bundles of 16″ shingles laid 5″ *to the weather* will cover 100 square feet. Shingles are of random widths, the narrower shingles being in the lower grades. Recommended exposures for the standard shingle sizes are shown in Table 16.

TABLE 16

Recommended exposure for wood shingles[1]

| Shingle length | Shingle thickness (Green) | Maximum exposure | |
		Slope less [2] than 4 in 12	Slope 5 in 12 and over
In.		*In.*	*In.*
16	5 butts in 2 in.	3¾	5
18	5 butts in 2¼ in.	4¼	5½
24	4 butts in 2 in.	5¾	7½

[1] As recommended by the Red Cedar Shingle and Handsplit Shake Bureau.
[2] Minimum slope for main roofs—4 in 12.
 Minimum slope for porch roofs—3 in 12.

Figure 2 illustrates the proper method of applying a wood shingle roof. Underlay or roofing felt is not required for wood shingles except for protection in ice-dam areas. Spaced roof boards under wood shingles are most common, although spaced or solid sheathing is optional.

The following rules should be followed in the application of wood shingles:

1. Shingles should extend about 1½" beyond the eave line and about ¾" beyond the rake (gable) edge.

2. Use two rust-resistant nails in each shingle. Space the nails about ¾" from the edge and 1½" above the butt line of the next course. Use threepenny nails for 16" and 18" shingles and fourpenny nails for 24" shingles in new construction. A *ring shank* nail (threaded) is often recommended for plywood roof sheathing less than ½" thick.

3. The first course of shingles should be doubled. In all courses, allow ⅛" to ¼" space between each shingle for expansion when wet. The joints between shingles should be offset at least 1½" from the joints between shingles in the course below. The joints in succeeding courses should be spaced so that they do not directly line up with joints in the second course below.

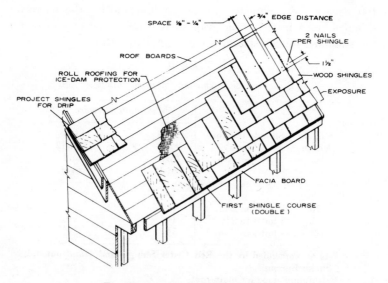

Fig. 2. Installation of wood shingles.

4. When valleys are present, shingle away from the valleys, selecting and precutting wide valley shingles.

5. A metal edging along the gable end will aid in guiding the water away from the sidewalls.

6. In laying No. 1 all-heartwood edge-grain shingles no splitting of wide shingles is necessary.

Wood shakes are applied much the same as wood shingles. Because shakes are much thicker (longer shakes have the thicker butts), long galvanized nails are used. To create a rustic appearance, the butts are often laid unevenly. Shakes are longer than shingles and, therefore, have a greater exposure. Exposure distance is usually $7\frac{1}{2}''$ for $18''$ shakes, $10''$ for $24''$ shakes, and $13''$ for $32''$ shakes. Shakes are *not* smooth on both faces; and since wind-driven snow might enter, it is essential to use an underlay between each course. An $18''$ wide layer of 30-pound asphalt felt should be used between each course with the bottom edge positioned above the butt edge of the shakes a distance equal to double the weather exposure. A $36''$ wide starting strip of the asphalt felt is used at the eave line. *Solid sheathing* should be used when wood shakes are used for roofs in areas where wind-driven snow is expected.

ASPHALT SHINGLES

The usual minimum recommended weight for *asphalt shingles* is 235 pounds for square butt strip shingles. This may change in later years since 210 pounds (weight per square) was considered a minimum several years ago. *Strip shingles* with a 300-pound weight per square are available, as are lock-type and other shingles weighing 250 pounds and more. Asphalt shingles are also available with *seal-type tabs* for wind resistance. Many workers apply a small spot of asphalt roof cement under each tab after installation of regular asphalt shingles to provide similar protection.

The *square butt strip shingle* is $12''$ by $36''$ and has three tabs. It is usually laid with $5''$ exposed to the weather. There are 27 strips in a bundle; three bundles will cover 100 square feet. Bundles should be piled flat for storage so that strips will not curl when the bundles are opened for use. The method of laying an asphalt shingle roof is shown in *A*, Fig. 3. A metal edging is often used at the gable end to provide additional protection (*B*, Fig. 3).

See Table 17 to determine the need for and the method of applying *underlayment* for asphalt shingles on roofs of various slopes. Underlayment is commonly 15-pound saturated felt. (Headlap for single coverage of underlayment should be 2″ and for double coverage, 19″.)

TABLE 17

Underlayment requirements for asphalt shingles

Underlayment	Minimum roof slope	
	Double coverage [1] shingles	Triple coverage [1] shingles
Not required	7 in 12	[2] 4 in 12
Single	[2] 4 in 12	[3] 3 in 12
Double	2 in 12	2 in 12

[1] Double coverage for a 12- by 36-in. shingle is usually an exposure of about 5 in. and about 4 in. for triple coverage.
[2] May be 3 in 12 for porch roofs.
[3] May be 2 in 12 for porch roofs.

An asphalt shingle roof can also be protected from ice dams by adding an initial layer of 45-pound or heavier roll roofing, 36″ wide. This will also insure good ventilation and insulation within the attic space (*B*, Fig. 1).

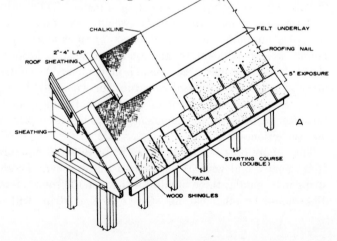

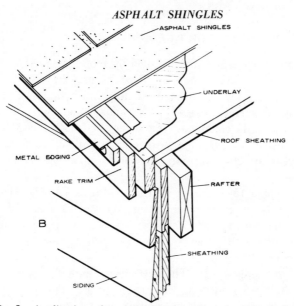

Fig. 3. Application of asphalt shingles. *A*, normal method with strip shingles. *B*, metal edging at gable end.

A course of wood shingles or a metal edging should be used along the eave line before application of the asphalt shingles. The first course of asphalt shingles is doubled; or a starter course may be used under the first asphalt shingle course. This first course should extend downward beyond the wood shingles (or edging) about ½″ to prevent the water from backing up under the shingles. A ½″ projection should also be used at the rake.

Several chalklines on the underlay will help aline the shingles so that tab notches will be in a straight line for good appearance. Each shingle strip should be fastened securely according to the manufacturer's directions. The use of six 1″ galvanized roofing nails for each 12″ by 36″ strip is considered good practice in areas of high winds. A sealed tab or the use of asphalt sealer will also aid in preventing wind damage during storms. Some workers use four nails for each strip when tabs are sealed. When a nail penetrates a crack or knothole, it should be removed, the hole sealed, and the nail replaced in sound wood; otherwise it will gradually work out and cause a hump in the shingle above it.

BUILT-UP ROOFS

Built-up roof coverings are installed by roofing companies that specialize in this work. Roofs of this type may have 3, 4, or 5 layers of roofer's felt, each mopped down with tar or asphalt, with the final surface coated with asphalt and covered with gravel embedded in asphalt or tar, or covered with a cap sheet. For convenience it is customary to refer to built-up roofs as 10-year, 15-year, or 20-year roofs, depending upon the method of application.

For example, a 15-year roof over a wood deck (*A*, Fig. 4) may have a base layer of 30-pound saturated roofer's felt laid dry, with edges lapped and held down with roofing nails. All nailing should be done with either (a) roofing nails having $\frac{3}{8}''$ heads driven through 1″ diameter tin caps or (b) special roofing nails having 1″ diameter heads. The dry sheet is intended to prevent tar or asphalt from entering the rafter spaces. Three layers of 15-pound saturated felt follow, each of which is mopped on with hot tar—not nailed. The final coat of tar or asphalt may be covered with roofing gravel or a cap sheet of roll roofing.

The cornice or eave line of projecting roofs is usually finished with metal edging or flashing, which acts as a drip. A metal gravel strip is used in conjunction with the flashing at the eaves when the roof is covered with gravel (*B*, Fig. 4). Where built-up roofing is finished against another wall, the roofing is turned up on the wall sheathing over a cant strip and is often also flashed with metal (*C*, Fig. 4). This flashing is generally extended up about 4″ above the bottom of the siding.

OTHER ROOF COVERINGS

Other roof coverings, including asbestos, slate, tile, metal, and others, many of which require specialized applicators, are perhaps less commonly used than wood or asphalt shingles and built-up roofs. Several new materials, such as plastic films and coatings, are showing promise for future moderate-cost roof coverings. However, most of them are more expensive than the materials now commonly being used for houses. These newer

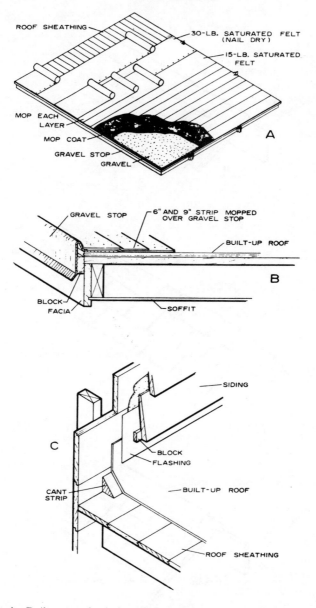

Fig. 4. Built-up roof. *A*, installation of roof. *B*, gravel stop. *C*, flashing at building line.

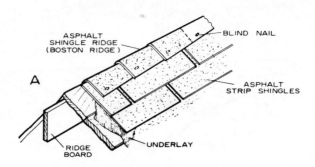

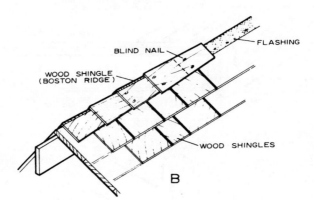

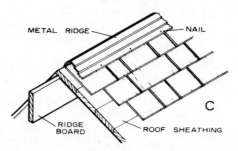

Fig. 5. Finish at ridge. *A*, Boston ridge with asphalt shingles. *B*, Boston ridge with wood shingles. *C*, metal ridge.

materials, as well as other new products, are likely to come into more general use during the next decade.

FINISH AT RIDGE AND HIP

The most common type of ridge and hip finish for wood and asphalt shingles is known as the *Boston ridge*. Asphalt shingle squares (one-third of a 12″ by 36″ strip) are used over the ridge and blind nailed (*A*, Fig. 5). Each shingle is lapped 5″ to 6″ to give double coverage. In areas where driving rains occur, it is well to use metal flashing under the shingle ridge. The use of a ribbon of asphalt roofing cement under each lap will also greatly reduce the chance of water penetration.

A wood shingle roof (*B*, Fig. 5) also should be finished in a Boston ridge. Shingles 6″ wide are alternately lapped, fitted, and blind nailed. As shown in the illustration, the shingles are nailed in place so that exposed trimmed edges are alternately lapped. *Preassembled hip* and *ridge units* are available and save both time and money.

A *metal ridge roll* can also be used on asphalt shingle or wood shingle roofs (*C*, Fig. 5). This ridge is formed to the roof slope and should be copper, galvanized iron, or aluminum. Some metal ridges are formed so that they provide an outlet ventilating area. However, the design should be such that it prevents rain or snow from blowing in.

CHAPTER 31

Ventilation

————— **⁞** —————————————————————

Condensation of moisture vapor may occur in attic spaces and under flat roofs during cold weather. Even where vapor barriers are used, some vapor will probably work into these spaces around pipes and other inadequately protected areas and some through the vapor barrier itself. Although the amount might be unimportant if equally distributed, it may be sufficiently concentrated in some cold spot to cause damage. While wood shingle and wood shake roofs do not resist vapor movement, such roofings as asphalt shingles and built-up roofs are highly resistant. The most practical method of removing the moisture is by adequately ventilating the roof spaces.

A warm attic that is inadequately ventilated and insulated may cause formation of *ice dams* at the cornice. During cold weather after a heavy snowfall, heat causes the snow next to the roof to melt. (*See* Fig. 1, Chap. 30.) Water running down the roof freezes on the colder surface of the cornice, often forming an ice dam at the gutter which may cause water to back up at the eaves and into the wall and ceiling. Similar dams often form in roof valleys. Ventilation, therefore, provides part of the answer to the problems. With a well-insulated ceiling and adequate ventilation, attic temperatures are low and melting of snow over the attic space will be greatly reduced.

In hot weather, ventilation of attic and roof spaces offers an effective means of removing hot air, thereby lowering the temperature in these spaces. Insulation should be used between ceiling joists below the attic or roof space to further retard heat flow into the rooms below and materially improve comfort conditions.

It is common practice to install louvered openings in the end walls of gable roofs for ventilation. Air movement through such openings depends primarily on wind direction and velocity. No appreciable movement can be expected when there is no wind or unless one or more openings face the wind. More positive air movement can be obtained by providing openings in the soffit areas of the roof overhang in addition to openings at the gable ends or ridge. Hip roof houses are best ventilated by inlet ventilators in the soffit area and by outlet ventilators along the ridge. The differences in temperature between the attic and the outside will then create an air movement independent of the wind, also a more positive movement when there is wind.

Where there is a crawl space under the house or the porch, ventilation is necessary to remove moisture vapor rising from the soil. Such vapor may otherwise condense on the wood below the floor and facilitate decay. A permanent vapor barrier on the soil of the crawl space greatly reduces the amount of ventilating area required.

Tight construction (including storm windows and storm doors) and the use of humidifiers have created potential moisture problems which must be resolved through planning of adequate ventilation as well as through the proper use of vapor barriers. Blocking of ventilating areas, *for example,* must be avoided since such practices will prevent ventilation of attic spaces. Inadequate ventilation will often lead to moisture problems which, to correct, can result in unnecessary costs.

AREA OF VENTILATORS

Types of ventilators and minimum recommended sizes have been generally established for various types of roofs. The minimum net area for attic- or roof-space ventilators is based on the projected ceiling area of the rooms below (Fig. 1). The ratio of ventilator openings as shown in Fig. 1 are net areas, and the actual area must be increased to allow for any restrictions such as louvers and wire cloth or screen. The screen area should be double the specified net area as shown in Figs. 1, 2, and 3.

To obtain extra area of screen without adding to the area of

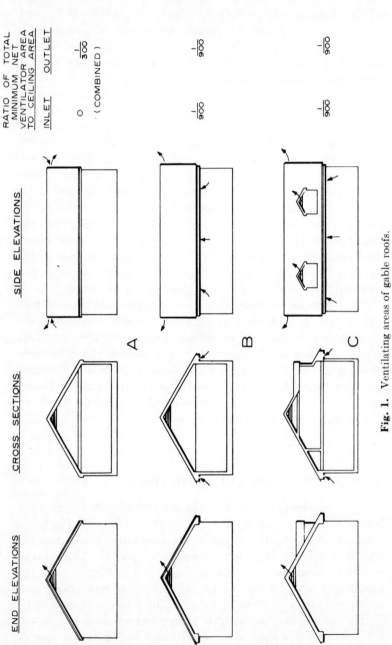

Fig. 1. Ventilating areas of gable roofs.

the vent, use a frame of required size to hold the screen away from the ventilator opening. Use as coarse a screen as conditions permit, not smaller than No. 16, since lint and dirt tend to clog fine mesh screens. Screens should be installed in such a way that paint brushes will not easily contact the screen and close the mesh with paint.

GABLE ROOFS

Louvered openings are generally provided in the end walls of *gable roofs* and should be as close to the ridge as possible (*A*, Fig. 1). The net area for the openings should be 1/300 of the ceiling area (*A*, Fig. 1). *For example,* where the ceiling area equals 1,200 square feet, the minimum total net area of the ventilators should be 4 square feet.

As previously explained, more positive air movement can be obtained if additional openings are provided in the soffit area. The minimum ventilation areas for this method are shown in *B*, Fig. 1.

Where there are rooms in the attic with sloping ceilings under the roof, the insulation should follow the roof slope and be so placed that there is a free opening of at least 1½" between the roof boards and insulation for air movement (*C*, Fig. 1).

HIP ROOFS

Hip roofs should have air-inlet openings in the soffit area of the eaves and outlet openings at or near the peak. For minimum net areas of openings see *A*, Fig. 2. The most efficient type of inlet opening is the continuous slot, which should provide a free opening of not less than ¾". The air-outlet opening near the peak can be a globe-type metal ventilator or several smaller roof ventilators located near the ridge. They can be located below the peak on the rear slope of the roof so that they will not be visible from the front of the house. Gabled extensions of a hip-roof house are sometimes used to provide efficient outlet ventilators (*B*, Fig. 2).

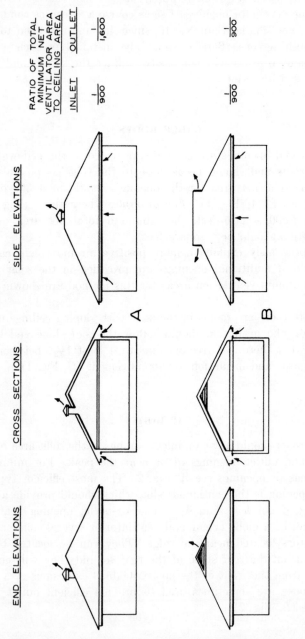

Fig. 2. Ventilating areas of hip roofs.

FLAT ROOFS

A greater ratio of ventilating area is required in some types of *flat roofs* than in pitched roofs because the air movement is less positive and is dependent upon wind. It is important that there be a clear open space above the ceiling insulation and below the roof sheathing for free air movement from inlet to outlet openings. Solid blocking should *not* be used for bridging or for bracing over bearing partitions if its use prevents the air circulation.

Perhaps the most common type of flat or low-pitched roof is one in which the rafters extend beyond the wall, forming an overhang (*A*, Fig. 3). When soffits are used, this area can contain the combined inlet-outlet ventilators, preferably a continuous slot. When single ventilators are used, they should be distributed evenly along the overhang.

A parapet-type wall and flat roof combination may be constructed with the ceiling joists separate from the roof joists or combined. When members are separate the space between can be used for an airway (*B*, Fig. 3). Inlet and outlet vents are then located as shown in the illustration, or a series of outlet stack vents can be used along the center line of the roof in combination with the inlet vents. When ceiling joists and flat rafters are served by one member in parapet construction, vents may be located as shown in *C*, Fig. 3. Wall-inlet ventilators combined with center stack outlet vents might also be used in this type of roof.

TYPES AND LOCATION OF OUTLET VENTILATORS

Various styles of gable-end ventilators are available ready for installation. Many are made with metal louvers and frames, while others may be made of wood to fit the house design more closely. However, the most important factors are to have sufficient net ventilating area and to locate ventilators as close to the ridge as possible without affecting house appearance.

One of the types commonly used fits the slope of the roof and is located near the ridge (*A*, Fig. 4). It can be made of wood or metal; in metal it is often adjustable to conform to the roof slope. A wood ventilator of this type is enclosed in a frame and

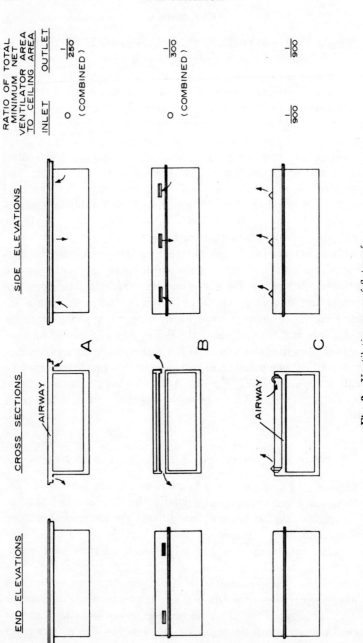

Fig. 3. Ventilating area of flat roofs.

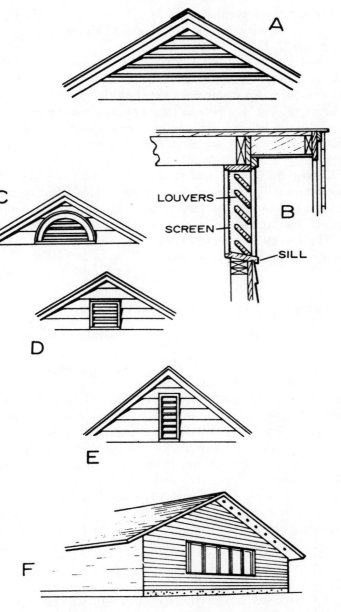

Fig. 4. Outlet ventilators. *A*, triangular. *B*, typical cross section. *C*, half-circle. *D*, square. *E*, vertical. *F*, soffit.

placed in the rough opening much as a window frame (*B*, Fig. 4). Other forms of gable-end ventilators which might be used are shown in *C*, *D*, and *E*, Fig. 4.

A system of attic ventilation which can be used on houses with a wide roof overhang at the gable end consists of a series of small vents or a continuous slot located on the underside of the soffit areas (*F*, Fig. 4). Several large openings located near the ridge might also be used. This system is especially desirable on low-pitched roofs where standard wall ventilators may not be suitable.

It is important that the roof framing at the wall line does not block off ventilation areas to the attic area. This might be accomplished by the use of a *ladder* frame extension. A flat nailing block used at the wall line will provide airways into the attic. This can also be adapted to narrower rake sections by providing ventilating areas to the attic.

TYPES AND LOCATION OF INLET VENTILATORS

Small, well-distributed ventilators or a continuous slot in the soffit provide inlet ventilation. These small louvered and screened vents can be obtained in most local lumberyards or hardware stores and are simple to install.

Only small sections need to be cut out of the soffit and can be sawed out before the soffit is applied. It is more desirable to use a number of smaller well-distributed ventilators than several large ones (*A*, Fig. 5). Any blocking which might be required between rafters at the wall line should be installed in order to provide an airway into the attic area.

A continuous screened slot, which is often desirable, should be located near the outer edge of the soffit near the facia (*B*, Fig. 5). Locating the slot in this area will minimize the chance of snow entering. This type may also be used on the extension of flat roofs.

CRAWL-SPACE VENTILATION AND SOIL COVER

The crawl space below the floor of a basementless house and

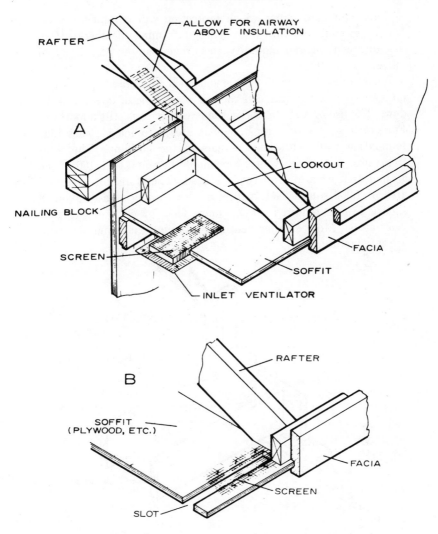

Fig. 5. Inlet ventilators. *A,* small insert ventilator. *B,* slot ventilator.

under porches should be ventilated and protected from ground moisture by the use of a *soil cover* (Fig. 6). The soil cover should be a vapor barrier with a perm value of less than 1.0. This includes such barrier materials as plastic films, roll roofing, and asphalt laminated paper. Such protection will minimize the effect of ground moisture on the wood framing members. High moisture content and humidity encourage staining and decay of untreated members.

Where there is a partial basement open to a crawl-space area, no wall vents are required if there is some type of operable window. The use of a soil cover in the crawl space is still important. For crawl spaces with no basement area, provide at least four foundation wall vents near corners of the building. The total free (net) area of the ventilators should be equal to 1/160 of the ground area when no soil cover is used. Therefore, for a ground area of 1,200 square feet, a total net ventilating area of about 8 square feet is required, or 2 square feet for each of the four ventilators. More smaller ventilators having the same net ratio are satisfactory.

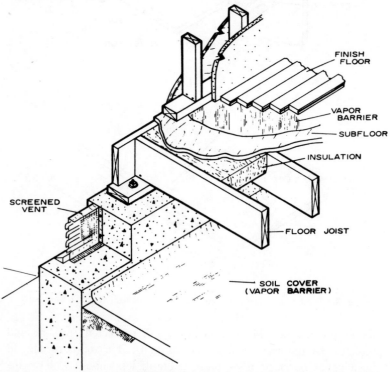

FINISH FLOOR

VAPOR BARRIER

SUBFLOOR

INSULATION

SCREENED VENT

FLOOR JOIST

SOIL COVER (VAPOR BARRIER)

Fig. 6. Crawl-space ventilator and soil cover.

When a vapor-barrier ground cover is used, the required ventilating area is greatly reduced. The net ventilating area required with a ground cover is 1/1600 of the ground area, or for the 1,200-square-foot house, an area of 0.75 square foot. This should be divided between two small ventilators located on opposite sides of the crawl space. Vents should be covered (Fig. 6) with a corrosion-resistant screen of No. 8 mesh.

The use of a ground cover is normally recommended under all conditions. It not only protects wood framing members from ground moisture but also allows the use of small, inconspicuous ventilators.

Index